THE
MIDWEST

THE
MIDWEST

The Greenwood Encyclopedia of
American Regional Cultures

Edited by
Joseph W. Slade
and Judith Yaross Lee

Foreword by William Ferris, Consulting Editor

Paul S. Piper, Librarian Advisor

GREENWOOD PRESS
Westport, Connecticut • London

Library of Congress Cataloging-in-Publication Data

The Midwest : the Greenwood encyclopedia of American regional cultures / edited by Joseph W.
  Slade and Judith Yaross Lee; foreword by William Ferris, consulting editor.
    p. cm.
    Includes bibliographical references and index.
    ISBN 0–313–33266–5 (set: alk. paper)—ISBN 0–313–32493–X (alk. paper)
    1. Middle West—Civilization—Encyclopedias. 2. Middle West—History—Encyclopedias.
  3. Middle West—Social life and customs—Encyclopedias. 4. Popular culture—Middle West—
  Encyclopedias. 5. Regionalism—Middle West—Encyclopedias. I. Slade, Joseph W. II. Lee,
  Judith Yaross, 1949– III. Series.
  F351.M59 2004
  977'.003—dc22   2004056060

British Library Cataloguing in Publication Data is available.

Library of Congress Catalog Card Number: 2004056060
ISBN: 0–313–33266–5 (set)
        0–313–32733–5 (The Great Plains Region)
        0–313–32954–0 (The Mid-Atlantic Region)
        0–313–32493–X (The Midwest)
        0–313–32753–X (New England)
        0–313–33043–3 (The Pacific Region)
        0–313–32817–X (The Rocky Mountain Region)
        0–313–32734–3 (The South)
        0–313–32805–6 (The Southwest)

First published in 2004

Greenwood Press, 88 Post Road West, Westport, CT 06881
An imprint of Greenwood Publishing Group, Inc.
www.greenwood.com

Printed in the United States of America

The paper used in this book complies with the
Permanent Paper Standard issued by the National
Information Standards Organization (Z39.48–1984).

10 9 8 7 6 5 4 3 2 1

A volume this large indebts its editors to a great many people. Our thanks go first to our contributors, who understood even before we did the magnitude of this project and agreed to work on it anyway. A number of students, research associates, and volunteers in the Central Region Humanities Center provided much-needed editorial assistance: Jennifer Scott, Kathy Keltner, Sayonada Thomas, Yih-Shan Shih, Whitney Fromholtz, and Jean Andrews. Diana Glaizer, the CRHC's Administrative Associate extraordinaire, kept up with whatever needed doing: formatting manuscripts, checking fugitive details, managing correspondence, and keeping the editors on task. We need to thank as well Karen Riggs, Director of Ohio University's School of Telecommunications, and Greg Shepherd, Director of the School of Communication Studies, for their support.

The Central Region Humanities Center where this volume took shape owes its existence to the National Endowment for the Humanities, the Ohio Humanities Council, the Ohio University Foundation, Ohio University's Dean of the College of Communication Kathy Krendl and Vice-President for Research Jack Bantle, our 30 faculty colleagues on the Ohio University American Studies Steering Committee, and the 500 scholars and humanities professionals across the states of Indiana, Kentucky, Michigan, Ohio, and West Virginia—the area that the NEH designated the Central Region—who have collaborated with us over the years. To them we express our deep appreciation for the opportunity to lead the CRHC, to foster new knowledge about American regional culture, and to promote appreciation of the Midwest.

This book is for Marya Slade, a midwesterner like her mother.

CONTENTS

Contents

# FOREWORD

Region inspires and grounds the American experience. Whether we are drawn to them or flee from them, the places in which we live etch themselves into our memory in powerful, enduring ways. For over three centuries Americans have crafted a collective memory of places that constitute our nation's distinctive regions. These regions are embedded in every aspect of American history and culture.

American places have inspired poets and writers from Walt Whitman and Henry David Thoreau to Mark Twain and William Faulkner. These writers grounded their work in the places where they lived. When asked why he never traveled, Thoreau replied, "I have traveled widely in Concord."

William Faulkner remarked that early in his career as a writer he realized that he could devote a lifetime to writing and never fully exhaust his "little postage stamp of native soil."

In each region American writers have framed their work with what Eudora Welty calls "sense of place." Through their writing we encounter the diverse, richly detailed regions of our nation.

In his ballads Woody Guthrie chronicles American places that stretch from "the great Atlantic Ocean to the wide Pacific shore," while Muddy Waters anchors his blues in the Mississippi Delta and his home on Stovall's Plantation.

American corporate worlds like the Bell system neatly organize their divisions by region. And government commissions like the Appalachian Regional Commission, the Mississippi River Commission, and the Delta Development Commission define their mission in terms of geographic places.

When we consider that artists and writers are inspired by place and that government and corporate worlds are similarly grounded in place, it is hardly surprising that we also identify political leaders in terms of their regional culture. We think of John Kennedy as a New Englander, of Ann Richards as a Texan, and of Jimmy Carter as a Georgian.

Because Americans are so deeply immersed in their sense of place, we use region like a compass to provide direction as we negotiate our lives. Through sense of place we find our bearings, our true north. When we meet people for the first time, we ask that familiar American question, "Where are you from?" By identifying others through a region, a city, a community, we frame them with a place and find the bearings with which we can engage them.

Sense of place operates at all levels of our society—from personal to corporate and government worlds. While the power of place has long been understood and integrated in meaningful ways with our institutions, Americans have been slow to seriously study their regions in a focused, thoughtful way. As a young nation, we have been reluctant to confront the places we are "from." As we mature as a nation, Americans are more engaged with the places in which they live and increasingly seek to understand the history and culture of their regions.

The growing importance of regional studies within the academy is an understandable and appropriate response to the need Americans feel to understand the places in which they live. Such study empowers the individual, their community, and their region through a deeper engagement with the American experience. Americans resent that their regions are considered "overfly zones" in America, and through regional studies they ground themselves in their community's history and culture.

The Greenwood Encyclopedia of American Regional Cultures provides an exciting, comprehensive view of our nation's regions. The set devotes volumes to New England, the Mid-Atlantic, the South, the Midwest, the Southwest, the Great Plains, the Rocky Mountains, and the Pacific. Together these volumes offer a refreshing new view of America's regions as they stretch from the Atlantic to the Pacific.

The sheer size of our nation makes it difficult to imagine its diverse worlds as a single country with a shared culture. Our landscapes, our speech patterns, and our foodways all change sharply from region to region. The synergy of different regional worlds bound together within a single nation is what defines the American character. These diverse worlds coexist with the knowledge that America will always be defined by its distinctly different places.

American Regional Cultures explores in exciting ways the history and culture of each American region. Its volumes allow us to savor individual regional traditions and to compare these traditions with those of other regions. Each volume features chapters on architecture, art, ecology and environment, ethnicity, fashion, film and theater, folklore, food, language, literature, music, religion, and sports and recreation. Together these chapters offer a rich portrait of each region. The series is an important teaching resource that will significantly enrich learning at secondary, college, and university levels.

Over the past forty years a growing number of colleges and universities have launched regional studies programs that today offer exciting courses and degrees for both American and international students. During this time the National Endowment for the Humanities (NEH) has funded regional studies initiatives that range from new curricula to the creation of museum exhibits, films, and encyclopedias that focus on American regions. Throughout the nation, universities with regional studies programs recently received NEH support to assist with the programs that they are building.

The National Endowment for the Arts (NEA) has similarly encouraged regional initiatives within the art world. NEA's state arts councils work together within regional organizations to fund arts projects that impact their region.

The growing study of region helps Americans see themselves and the places they come from in insightful ways. As we understand the places that nurture us, we build a stronger foundation for our life. When speaking of how she raised her children, my mother often uses the phrase "Give them their roots, and they will find their wings." Thanks to *American Regional Cultures*, these roots are now far more accessible for all Americans. This impressive set significantly advances our understanding of American regions and the mythic power these places hold for our nation.

William Ferris
University of North Carolina
at Chapel Hill

PREFACE

We are pleased to present *The Greenwood Encyclopedia of American Regional Cultures*, the first book project of any kind, reference or otherwise, to examine cultural regionalism throughout the United States.

The sense of place has an intrinsic role in American consciousness. Across its vast expanses, the United States varies dramatically in its geography and its people. Americans seem especially cognizant of the regions from which they hail. Whether one considers the indigenous American Indian tribes and their relationships to the land, the many waves of immigrants who settled in particular regions of the nation, or the subsequent generations who came to identify themselves as New Englanders or Southerners or Midwesterners, and so forth, the connection of American culture to the sense of regionalism has been a consistent pattern throughout the nation's history.

It can be said that behind every travelogue on television, behind every road novel, behind every cross-country journey, is the desire to grasp the identity of other regions. This project was conceived to fill a surprising gap in publishing on American regionalism and on the many vernacular expressions of culture that one finds throughout the country.

This reference set is designed so that it will be useful to high school and college researchers alike, as well as to the general reader and scholar. Toward this goal, we consulted several members of Greenwood's Library Advisory Board as we determined both the content and the format of this encyclopedia project. Furthermore, we used the *National Standards: United States History* and also the *Curriculum Standards for Social Studies* as guides in choosing a wealth of content that would help researchers gain historical comprehension of how people in, and from, all regions have helped shape American cultures.

American Regional Cultures is divided geographically into eight volumes: *The Great Plains Region, The Mid-Atlantic Region, The Midwest, New England, The Pacific Region, The Rocky Mountain Region, The South,* and *The Southwest*. To ensure that cultural elements from each state would be discussed, we assigned each state to a particular region as follows:

The Great Plains Region: Kansas, Nebraska, North Dakota, Oklahoma, South Dakota

The Mid-Atlantic Region: Delaware, District of Columbia, Maryland, New Jersey, New York, Pennsylvania, West Virginia

The Midwest: Illinois, Indiana, Iowa, Michigan, Minnesota, Missouri, Ohio, Wisconsin

New England: Connecticut, Maine, Massachusetts, New Hampshire, Rhode Island, Vermont

The Pacific Region: Alaska, California, Hawai'i, Oregon, Washington

The Rocky Mountain Region: Colorado, Idaho, Montana, Utah, Wyoming

The South: Alabama, Arkansas, Florida, Georgia, Kentucky, Louisiana, Mississippi, North Carolina, South Carolina, Tennessee, Virginia

The Southwest: Arizona, Nevada, New Mexico, Texas

Each regional volume consists of rigorous, detailed overviews on all elements of culture, with chapters on the following topics: architecture, art, ecology and environment, ethnicity, fashion, film and theater, folklore, food, language, literature, music, religion, and sports and recreation. These chapters examine the many significant elements of those particular aspects of regional culture as they have evolved over time, through the beginning of the twenty-first century. Each chapter seeks not to impose a homogenized identity upon each region but, rather, to develop a synthesis or thematically arranged discussion of the diverse elements of each region. For example, in turning to the chapter on music in *The Pacific Region*, a reader will discover information on Pacific regional music as it has manifested itself in such wide-ranging genres as American Indian tribal performances, Hawaiian stylings, Hispanic and Asian traditions, West Coast jazz, surf rock, folk scenes, San Francisco psychedelia, country rock, the L.A. hard-rock scene, Northwest "grunge" rock, West Coast hip-hop, and Northern California ska-punk. Multiply this by thirteen chapters and again by eight volumes, and you get a sense of the enormous wealth of information covered in this landmark set.

In addition, each chapter concludes with helpful references to further resources, including, in most cases, printed resources, Web sites, films or videos, recordings, festivals or events, organizations, and special collections. Photos, drawings, and maps illustrate each volume. A timeline of major events for the region provides context for understanding the cultural development of the region. A bibliography, primarily of general sources about the region, precedes the index.

We would not have been able to publish such an enormous reference set without the work of our volume editors and the more than one hundred contributors that they recruited for this project. It is their efforts that have made *American Regional Cultures* come to life. We also would like to single out two people for their help: William Ferris, former chairman of the National Endowment for the Humanities and currently Distinguished Professor of History and senior associate director for the Center for the Study of the American South, University of North Carolina at Chapel Hill, who served as consulting editor for and was instrumental in the planning of this set and in the recruitment of its volume editors; and Paul S. Piper, Reference Librarian at Western Washington University, who in his role as librarian advisor, helped shape both content and format, with a particular focus on helping improve reader interface.

With their help, we present *The Greenwood Encyclopedia of American Regional Cultures*.

Rob Kirkpatrick, Senior Acquisitions Editor
Anne Thompson, Senior Development Editor
Greenwood Publishing Group

INTRODUCTION

Two contrary conceptions of the Midwest dominate the American imagination. One, recently popularized in Jonathan Franzen's novel *The Corrections* (2001), sees the region as the Hinterland. This backwater, populated by rubes and suburbanites, is so inhospitable to artists and intellectuals that its most talented sons and daughters revolt from the village for the vitality of the coasts. The other Midwest, symbolized by sturdy families at county fairs and their urban cousins in factories, is the Heartland: breadbasket and hog-butcher to the world, the engine of America's wealth and its indomitable spirit, the actual and metaphorical Middletown. Turning their back on the Eden of Mark Twain's childhood Missouri, snobs contrast Hinterland prairie and Heartland malls with the splendors of other regions: Allegheny and Rocky Mountains, New England culture, southern decadence, and western wildness all look down on midwestern flatness of land, lifestyle, and twang. Where Carl Sandburg (1878–1967) appraised Chicago as "City of the Big Shoulders," Sinclair Lewis (1885–1951) sneered at Babbitt and his friends on Main Street. More recently, Garrison Keillor has turned critique into comically faint praise, defining the region more simply, but also more ambivalently, as home. For thirty years, Keillor has recounted the weekly "news" of an imaginary midwestern town, Lake Wobegon, Minnesota, where "all the women are strong, all the men are good looking, and all the children are above average." Whereas Lake Wobegon's mythic founders looked around for the mouth of the Mississippi and concluded, "It doesn't start here," their descendants have discovered that escape is also exile.[1] Keillor's ambivalence suits the contemporary mood as midwestern pride is increasingly tested.

Regions are, of course, imaginative constructions. But the American imagination has proved especially fickle toward the Midwest. As James R. Shortridge concluded after analyzing hundreds of representations, Americans associate the pastoralism of farm life with cultural wholesomeness and thereby identify the Midwest as "genuine America," "the keeper of the nation's values."[2] Nonetheless, the

Midwest's quintessential Americanness has also been perceived as nebulousness, and midwestern representativeness has led, paradoxically, to the region's invisibility. Our most famous writers and political figures—Mark Twain and Abraham Lincoln, for instance—have been claimed as national heroes by a process that erased such regional qualities as their blend of conservative social values and progressive reform politics. Similarly, aggressive commercial development of and along the Ohio and Mississippi rivers has been deemed a national rather than regional story—except, of course, when crass midwestern commercialism has provided invidious contrast to clean eastern capital. As a result, midwestern moderation and thoughtfulness become blandness and timidity; their persistence, pig-headedness; their modesty, banality.

The understanding of *Midwest* that drives this volume spins regional modesty and moderation to reflect the experience of people who dwell at the center of the American landscape and whose history exemplifies American dreams and nightmares. For us, Hinterland and Heartland remain salient—the Midwest is still a crossroads of migration and commerce, still represents the nation in microcosm *and* in flux—but they also merge to suggest the ambiguities of the Borderland. As defined by Gloria Anzaldúa, "Borderlands are physically present wherever two or more cultures edge each other, where people of different races occupy the same territory, where under, lower, middle and upper classes touch, where the space between two individuals shrinks with intimacy."[3] In this postmodern space coexist not only factories and farms, but also farms that are factories and factories that export jobs as well as goods. As Hinterland and Heartland, the Midwest created modern America. Contemporary America, in turn, is recreating the Midwest as the Borderland.

THE HINTERLAND

Accusations of the Midwest's social inferiority date back to the eighteenth century, when the British, French, and Spanish empires contended for power in a series of European and colonial wars. In 1700 France claimed all the land drained by the Great Lakes and the Ohio and Mississippi rivers—a region designated *Louisiana*—as a result of explorations by Jacques Marquette (1637–1675), Louis Jolliet (1645–1700), and René-Robert Cavelier, Lord de La Salle (1643–1687). French claims to so much of North America exacerbated ongoing hostilities with England over European dominance by limiting British settlement to the area east of the Appalachians. With only about 85,000 settlers even in 1760, the French did not challenge Indian rights to the land or its bounty and thus enjoyed largely hospitable relations with native people, with whom they traded, married, and collaborated against the British, who pursued agricultural and communal control of land at the Indians' expense.[4] This effort ended in eastern Louisiana in 1763 with the British victory in the Seven Years' War (French and Indian War, 1755–1763); French lands east of the Mississippi, annexed into British America, became colonies of the new United States.

As Brian Beltman describes in the chapter on Ethnicity, at the time of European contact in the seventeenth century, several dozen indigenous nations lived in what is now the Midwest. Three language groups predominated: the Iroquoian, Algonquian, and Souian. Iroquoian nations included the Erie and Hurons, who lived between their namesake Great Lakes. East of the Mississippi River in contemporary Wisconsin, Illinois, Indiana, Ohio, and Michigan lived a great variety of Algonquins: Menominee, Sauk, Meskwaki (Fox), Peoria, Potawatomi, Miami, Kickapoo, Illinois, Ojibwe (Chippewa), and Shawnee. The Souian group included the Winnebago of central Wisconsin in addition to prairie peoples west of the Mississippi, including the Iowa, Missouria, Omaha, and Dakota. The ancestors of these Mississippian cultures created the Woodlands civilization (Adena, 1000–100 B.C.E., and Hopewell, 100 B.C.E.–500 C.E.) whose earthen monuments, described by John E. Hancock in the chapter on architecture, awed European explorers, fed eighteenth-century interest in archaeology (then a new science), and command respect to this day.

Indeed, the Midwest did not see the orderly progression of land from virgin territory to state that is often chronicled in state histories: Ohio, 1803; Indiana, 1816; Illinois, 1818; Missouri, 1821; Michigan, 1837; Iowa, 1846; Wisconsin, 1848; Minnesota, 1858. Quite the contrary. West of the Mississippi, the struggle among European powers continued by proxy for fifteen more years: present-day Iowa bounced between France (1682–1762 and 1800–1803) and Spain (1762–1800) until it was sold to the United States as part of the Louisiana Purchase in 1803. Midwestern Indians fought hard to retain their lands, relying on both arms and diplomacy, for a century after Britain acquired the Northwest Territory in 1763, until the 1862 Dakota Conflict ("Sioux Uprising") of southern Minnesota.

Three problems fed the hostilities. First, parties to a treaty often lacked (or were perceived to lack) the power to execute it. For example, Indians rejected the French right to concede their native homelands to the British in the 1763 Treaty of Paris; fifty years later, on the heels of the Removal Act (1830), the U.S. Army engaged in fifteen weeks of fighting across western Illinois and southern Wisconsin (the Black Hawk War of 1832) when Black Hawk (1767–1838) claimed that Sauk land had been ceded illegally to the United States and led 1,500 members of three tribes to resettle it. Similarly, even after Congress provided penalties of $1,000 for unsanctioned settlement (the Indian Intercourse Act of 1790 required native lands to be ceded through treaty to the United States before purchase by any individual or state), American authorities could not prevent white settlers from crossing boundaries and claiming land. Second, the Native Americans viewed a treaty as a conclusion to the question of territorial sovereignty, whereas the Americans conceptualized it as a temporary measure, open to later renegotiation in response to population or other pressures. The Northwest Ordinance of 1787 required Indian consent for U.S. acquisition of native territory, setting the stage for forced consent in the new American nation's first expression of manifest destiny.

Bloody battles erupted across Ohio, Michigan, and Indiana from the 1790s to the 1840s, many fought by a confederation of Miamis, Shawnees, Delawares, and Ottawas under the leadership of Blue Jacket (Shawnee, also known as *Weyapiersenwah* [c. 1743–1808?]) and Little Turtle (Miami, 1752–1812), who rejected what Blue Jacket called the Americans' "premeditated design to root us out of our land." Finally, British and French forces continued to vie with each other for Indian alliances against the United States. The Midwestern Indians exploited international conflicts to their advantage in the War of 1812, especially the Great Lakes battles, and suffered domestically when they failed.[5] The century-long string of skirmishes punctuated by major battles and treaties kept the Midwest a frontier, a subordinate zone where groups competed for power and control on the margins of settled space, for eighty years after the American Revolution supposedly ended North American colonization.

Over the period from the Revolution to the Civil War these clashes reinforced easterners' views of the Midwest as a hinterland inferior to the civilized centers of the Atlantic coast. Indeed, inequity between the Midwest and the seats of influence in Boston, New York, and Washington, D.C., reinforced the contrast between them and portrayed the Midwest as, in Edward Watts's phrase, "an American Colony," subordinate to the East. So did the former British colonies' claim to that land: Connecticut and other states established claims to particular lands in the Northwest Territory, with the Northwest Ordinance serving as the equivalent of a colonial charter.[6]

Colonial relations between the Midwest and East have continued in many fields, midwestern excellence (even superiority) notwithstanding. The revolt from the village that signaled the advent of urban modernity a century ago led to the Chicago Renaissance and thence to literary modernism, as Joseph Csicsila describes in his discussion of post–Civil War midwestern literature. Great midwestern universities still compare themselves to Harvard, especially the University of Chicago, which claims more Nobel Prize winners among faculty and alumni than any other institution in the world. Library holdings of the midwestern universities in the Big Ten Conference, which emerged from the efforts of Northwestern, Chicago, Wisconsin, Michigan, Minnesota, Illinois, and Purdue universities to regulate intercollegiate atheletics in 1895, exceeded 54 million volumes in 2001–2002.[7] Midwestern fashion and mass media especially feel the dominance of the coasts. The Rock and Roll Hall of Fame is located in Cleveland, but holds its annual induction ceremonies in New York. The satiric newsmagazine *The Onion* recently moved from Wisconsin to New York.

The Midwest's economy also sustained eastern snobbery. Before the development of heavy industry, midwestern trade with the East reinforced colonial relations by providing raw goods such as furs and clay for manufacture elsewhere. The Yankees, midland southerners, and Europeans who arrived in the nineteenth century were economic migrants seeking in the Midwest a success that had eluded them at home. Their achievements defied stereotypes about the abilities of the uncouth but reinforced eastern prejudices against merchants and small farmers. Compared to old eastern capital earned from textile mills, trans-Atlantic trade (in goods and slaves), and Wall Street, midwestern money is newer and lower-class.

Economic subordination to the Atlantic seaboard also gave rise to the erroneous depiction of the Midwest as landlocked, though water asserts itself everywhere as a means of transport and linkage. Our region's boundaries are marked by the continent's most important inland waters—the five Great Lakes and the river roads of the Ohio, Mississippi, and Missouri. Dozens of other waterways cross the interior. The North American equivalent of the Tigris and Euphrates, the Ohio and Mississippi nurtured the complex ancient civilizations such as Cahokia in southern Illinois. Throughout the eighteenth century native peoples in the Upper Midwest migrated by river to hunting grounds further south. When white settlers deemed the old portages inhospitable to large-scale shipping along natural waterways, they created the Erie, St. Lawrence, and other canals as highways to the sea. The jet age has reduced this vast floodplain to "fly-over America," which Saul Steinberg ridiculed as the undistinguished flat green space between the Hudson River and the Pacific Ocean in his famous cover for the *New Yorker* magazine.[8]

The region's identity crisis also owes something to disagreement over exactly what areas constitute it. In fact, the region lacked an agreed-upon name until after the Civil War, perhaps in a rejection of the conflict's north-south orientation as westward expansion reached the Pacific coast. The term *Midwest* dates from 1894, as a shortening of "Middle West." In 1942 the Census Bureau defined four regions—Northeast, South, West, and Midwest—for purposes of presenting census data, but these categories have not been universally accepted. So conflicting are conceptions of the region that a 1960 symposium at Notre Dame University asked, "Midwest: Myth or Reality?" and nearly thirty years later geographer James R. Shortridge wrote an entire book, *The Middle West: Its Meaning in American Culture* (1989), exploring its definition.

The ambiguity arises because Americans typically divide the nation into political areas, that is, states, which do not cohere with cultural and geographical regions. In terms of settlement patterns and political history, the eastern border of the Midwest belongs in western Pennsylvania, where the frontier met New England, because Fort Duquesne, Pittsburgh, at the confluence of the Ohio and Monongahela rivers, belonged to the French until 1758. The same logic suggests incorporating Kentucky and West Virginia into the Midwest. Both allied with the Union during the Civil War, although their heritage of slavery (prohibited in the Northwest Territory) linked them with the South. By contrast, as Chris Mayda, Artimus Keiffer, and Joseph W. Slade point out in their chapter on Ecology and Environment, the topography and other geographical patterns of southeastern Ohio, southwestern Missouri, and northwestern Minnesota belong to Appalachia, the Ozarks, and the Great Plains, respectively.

Whatever its source, regional insecurity manifests itself in midwesterners' (in)famous modesty. In describing the Midwest as "the anti-region," Andrew Cayton speculates that a regional heritage of profound diversity, economic struggle, and social compromise has led midwesterners "to render themselves inconspicuous" by making a fetish of "niceness."[9] But despite the tendency to accept the Midwest as the Hinterland, the region has so nearly encapsulated the American experience that it seemed not unique but representative.

THE MIDWEST AS HEARTLAND

If the United States were an experiment in nation-building, the Midwest has been its laboratory. The Northwest Ordinance of 1787—which prohibited slavery, encouraged education, and established steps for statehood—encouraged Frederick Jackson Turner to conflate regional history with national ideology in his 1893 thesis that American democracy advanced as the frontier receded.[10] For generations, our politics—driven by the tension between urban and rural—matched those of the nation; eight presidents have come from Ohio, and another four from Illinois, Missouri, and Iowa. Corporations choose midwestern malls to test products on consumers they consider quintessentially American. Pioneering sociologists Robert and Helen Lynd found their statistical "Middletown" in Muncie, Indiana; historian Walter Havighurst designated the region "Heartland."

Of many factors that transformed the Midwest into the Heartland, three stand out as cultural forces. Foremost is the flat, well-irrigated terrain, a farmer's and builder's dream, land that inspired migration and transportation systems for it. Second is the mixture of people who displaced the Native Americans in the nineteenth century and blended diverse values into a regional ethos. New Englanders brought their penchant for communal and self-improvement, southerners provided their individualism and social conservatism, and Europeans shared with American migrants a relentless economic drive. Third is the moderate ratio of people to space. Through most of the twentieth century, the region's many small cities and rural villages tempered rural rootedness with urban mobility, energy, and resources. Ideas bigger than the local population required outreach to the region and the nation—which, by virtue of its location at the heart of North America, were close at hand.

Whereas the label *Midwest* plays into the insecurity of being neither here nor there, *Heartland* celebrates the region's centrality. A spate of recent books with *heartland* in their titles invoke the region's wholesomeness, representativeness, and pastoralism, and challenge implications of homogeneity and sentimentality. *Heartland* is more than a metaphor, however. The U.S. Census has pinpointed the statistical center of American population in the Midwest since 1860, although its influence is waning as the midpoint drifts toward the Southwest (the 2000 median is in Indiana, the mean in Missouri).[11]

With the exception of intentional communities such as the free black settlement of Roberts, Indiana, and the Dutch enclave in Holland, Michigan, even small midwestern communities had ethnically diverse populations. Ethnic and geographical origin differentiates English speakers from southern Missouri to northern Minnesota, as Beverly Flanigan makes clear in the chapter on Language. Arriving specifically to make a living, midwesterners were united by a shared economic ambition and common commercial culture. The regional obsession with making money eventually led to the development of the cash register in Dayton (James Ritty, 1879) and the adding machine in St. Louis (William S. Burroughs, 1888). African Americans found themselves less welcome. Although Black Laws restricted settlement, economic opportunity, and the franchise, the 1860 census documented that 72 percent of the 63,699 blacks in the former Northwest Territory were scattered among small towns and villages, not concentrated in cities. By 1880, two-thirds of all foreign-born farmers lived in the Midwest.[12]

The population assured that the Midwest was never monolithic, and the Civil War offers a case in point. Citizens of the region fought on both Union and Confederate sides, and the midwestern states provided entry and exit points for the Underground Railway. Significantly, the Midwest also was the center of turning points for both sides in the sectional crisis: the 1820 Missouri Compromise, which enabled the slave state to enter the Union if balanced by the free state of Maine; the 1857 Dred Scott decision, which defined a slave as property by upholding his status in free Illinois; and even the 1860 election for president, which determined the future of the Union, when both Republican candidate Abraham Lincoln and Democratic candidate Stephen Douglas were from Illinois. The Midwest's representativeness, like the myth that it lacks a distinct culture, owes much to this amalgamation. Brian Wilson's chapter on Religion joins Beltman's chapter on Ethnicity in surveying the diverse people of the Midwest.

Flat midwestern land nurtured farms and factories. John Deere (1804–1886) inaugurated modern farming in Moline, Illinois, in 1837 with a steel plow to break up prairie sod. Cyrus McCormick (1809–1884) had invented the mechanical reaper in 1831, but it caught on only in the 1840s, after he identified its ideal application—large-scale agriculture on the midwestern plains. Other technical innovations also spurred industrial growth: machine tools in Cincinnati, turbines in Kokomo, the assembly line in Detroit, microwave ovens in Amana (Iowa). John D. Rockefeller (1839–1937) invented modern corporate capitalism in 1882 in Cleveland when he established the first commercial trust company to consolidate the wealth and power of his oil refining business. In the course of twenty years, his business had bought out so many competitors that it controlled all but 5 to 10 percent of the oil produced in the United States.

Midwestern geography promoted modern transportation systems. Distance from the coasts demanded continual improvement of travel by land, water, and air. Flat terrain made building easy. The National Road delivered migrants to the midwestern states and territories; the Santa Fe and Oregon Trails began at St. Louis. Regular steamboat service began in 1812 on the Mississippi River, which still brings corn to market. Railroads easily traversed the prairie, making railroads hubs of Chicago, St. Louis, and Kansas City, accelerating access to markets and providing new destinations for internal and international migrations. This influx gave rise to the region's diverse folklife, as Ruth Olson's chapter on Folklore describes.

Nineteenth-century transportation industries also positioned the region for twentieth-century leadership in automotive engineering and aviation. John Fisher's carriage works in Sandusky, Ohio; B. F. Goodrich's rubber factory in Akron; U.S. Steel's Gary works; Carl B. Fisher's Indianapolis testing tracks—all adapted to automobile production after Henry Ford began mass production of the Model T in 1908. Ford's River Rouge (Michigan) factory, designed for continuous production in flowing streams, revolutionized industrial architecture. Improvements in auto engineering, in turn, made Cleveland—already a hub for rail cargo—a center for investigations of flight. The city began hosting national air races with the Pulitzer Trophy race of 1920, a tradition that continues today with the annual Cleveland Air Show.

Cultural byproducts of the automobile also originated in the Midwest. Malls began with the 1922 Country Club Plaza of Kansas City, Missouri (where in 1909 Ford had built a plant to reassemble cars shipped knocked-down for cheap transport), and reached their apotheosis seventy years later when the Mall of America opened in Bloomington, Minnesota. The quintessential burger and milkshake drive-in franchise was born when Ray Kroc opened his first McDonald's in Des Plaines, Illinois, in 1955. As Lucy Long details in the chapter on Food, other fast-food chains also began in the Midwest.

With excellent transportation, low population densities, and a commercial ethos, the region pioneered large-scale marketing. Milwaukee became a center of beer manufacture because the city's population was too small to drink all the beer produced, and its rail and water shipping systems enabled prompt, cheap export. Aaron Montgomery Ward (1844–1913) devised the idea of catalog sales in 1872. Ward's catalog offered rural and small-town customers superior selection at cheaper prices; his innovations included the now-familiar money-back guarantee to win approval from customers skeptical of buying goods unexamined. His business model inspired competition in 1891 from Richard Sears (1864–1914), a former Minnesota railroad employee who partnered with Alva Curtis Roebuck to compete with Ward. A century after Ward's innovations, Gary Comer reinvented Chicago's ailing catalog business: now located in Wisconsin (and owned by Sears), Lands' End markets upscale products with a midwestern concern for high quality, honest talk, and moderate cost. The same values pervade the still-successful catalogs of J. C. Penney and Spiegel, which also have regional roots.

Midwesterners marketed ideas as well as goods: national movements that defined progressive society began or gathered steam here. Peter Onuf and Andrew Cayton were only slightly joking when they suggested that the Civil War might be conceptualized as a typical midwestern reform movement.[13] Abolitionism thrived. Across the river from Kentucky, Cincinnati gave Harriet Beecher Stowe (1811–1896) the details for America's central abolitionist tract, *Uncle Tom's Cabin* (1852). Strong midwestern women also guided temperance and other American movements. Their dress reforms reflected the region's ethos of practicality, as Joseph W. Slade, Jennifer A. Scott, and Schuyler Cone observe in the chapter on Fashion. At the 1851 women's rights convention in Akron, Ohio, former slave Sojourner Truth (1797–1883) of Michigan asked, "and ar'nt' I a woman?" and in the process challenged racial and gender stereotypes. Oberlin College, which introduced coeducation the year after its 1833 founding, led the nation in developing women leaders, including women rights activist Lucy Stone (1818–1893). Indeed, as early as 1912 a writer in *Century Magazine* attributed midwestern women's strength of character and purpose to their advanced education, proclaiming, "No people in the world offer so many of their daughters a college education or discriminate less against daughters in providing opportunities."[14] When education failed to produce opportunity, Betty Friedan (b. 1921) of Peoria, Illinois, launched America's second wave of feminism with *The Feminine Mystique* (1963).

The region's industrial economy sparked the modern labor movement. Workers lost the early confrontations. Chicago's Haymarket Square was the center for the May 1, 1886, nationwide strike for the eight-hour workday at McCormick's Harvester Works; the ensuing gun-battle between police and unionists led to the arrest of eight leaders, four of whom were hanged the next year. During the 1893 depression, members of the American Railway Union workers walked off the job when the Pullman Car Works cut wages by 25 percent; although the strike spread to twenty-seven states and the Labor Department upheld the workers' grievances, the federal government established a key antilabor precedent when it broke the strike for interfering with U.S. mail delivery. The young United Automobile Workers (UAW) had its first major success in the Flint, Michigan, "Sit-Down Strike" of 1936–1937 against General Motors, then the world's largest manufacturer. The strike, which had begun in the Cleveland Fisher Body plant, spread quickly to more 100,000 GM workers nationwide.

These battles drew national attention to local labor leaders. Chicago-based Mary Harris "Mother" Jones (1830–1930) energized striking workers in strikes from California to New York during a sixty-year career. Bessie Abramowitz Hillman (1889–1970) led the 1910 strike against Chicago's Hart, Schaffner and Marx factory that eventually led to the founding of the Amalgamated Clothing Workers of America. From his early years as an Iowa miner John L. Lewis (1880–1969) advocated for midwestern workers—first through the United Mine Workers of

America and after 1935 through the American Federation of Labor (AFL) and the Committee for Industrial Organization (CIO). Regional labor strife gradually converted Indiana-born Eugene V. Debs (1855–1926) to activism. Debs founded the American Railway Union (ARU), and eventually became the presidential candidate of the Socialist Party of America in every election from 1900 to 1920.

Among the most widely admired midwestern reforms were those of Hull House, America's preeminent settlement house, established in 1889 Chicago by two Illinois women, Jane Addams (1860–1935) and Ellen Gates Starr (1859–1940). Hull House blended education and social services for the poor with political advocacy on their behalf. Causes included laws governing factory labor, tenement housing, and sanitation in addition to day care, kindergartens, and municipal playgrounds. Innovations at Hull House reached far beyond the neighborhood. Addams grounded social activism with philosophical ideals of democracy and liberalism, working with John Dewey (1859–1952) and other faculty at the University of Chicago to found its School of Social Work and develop a research tradition of social science to support political initiatives. Dewey's commitment to empiricism and democratic social relevance, so evident in his collaboration with Addams, advanced the movement known as pragmatism, America's chief contribution to philosophy. By putting social science in the service of democracy, Dewey and Addams also shaped the Chicago approach to sociology (in the world's first sociology department), and established research methods for the field as a whole.[15]

As the progressive midwestern spirit endures, most obviously in the activist entertainment of Michigan's Michael Moore and Minnesota's Al Franken, so does its conservative counterpart remain potent. In 1924, when Wisconsin senator Robert La Follette (1908–1957) ran for president on the Progressive Party ticket against Calvin Coolidge, the Ku Klux Klan was so active that it held the mayoralty in ten Ohio cities, including Toledo, Akron, and Columbus, the state capital.[16] The Klan's success was no anomaly. Lynchings occurred in Marion, Indiana (1930), Duluth, Minnesota (1920), and Springfield, Illinois (1908)—the last-named an impetus for the founding of the National Association for the Advancement of Colored People (NAACP). Father Charles E. Coughlin (1891–1975) of Detroit won America's first mass radio audience when he began his anti-Semitic reactionary rants in 1930. The red scares of the 1950s, led by Senator Joseph R. McCarthy (1908–1957) of Wisconsin, were also home-grown. In the late 1970s, American Nazis sought to march through Jewish neighborhoods in Skokie, Illiniois. The king of conservative talk-shows, Rush Limbaugh (b. 1951), born in Cape Girardeau, Missouri, and educated at Southern Missouri State University, speaks from—and to—the Heartland.

Perhaps because the Midwest lacks the glamor of New York and Hollywood, it feels the pulse of American popular culture. Both Oprah Winfrey and Jerry Springer broadcast from Chicago. Popular American music has a distinctly midwestern beat, as Richard Wetzel's chapter on Music points out. Less well known is that comics also reflect a midwestern sensibility. The modern comic book was born in 1933 from the innovations of two Cleveland high schoolers, Jerry Siegel and Joe Shuster, creators of Superman. Superman also enacts the ultimate midwestern fantasy: the mild-mannered youth from the Hinterland takes Heartland values to the big city, where he emerges to everyone's astonishment as the strongest and best of men. Midwestern niceness joined with capitalism to spark the greeting card industry: its giants flank the region, Hallmark in Kansas City and American Greetings in Cleveland. Hugh Hefner likewise traded on the wholesomeness of the midwestern girl next door when he invented *Playboy* in 1953. Not surprisingly, in this context, the Midwest also pioneered the scholarly study of American popular culture and hosts its premier academic centers: the Kinsey and Folklore Institutes at Indiana University, the Popular Library and Department of Popular Culture at Bowling Green State University, and the Cartoon Library at The Ohio State University.

Midwestern contributions to American culture extend from the ridiculous to the sublime. As detailed in Robert Stearns's chapter on Art, the region's democratic ethos not only inspired artists to paint ordinary people's daily lives, most famously in *American Gothic* (1930) by Grant Wood (1891–1942) of Iowa, but also sustained a tradition of public art. The skyscraper was born in Chicago not only because the growing manufacturing center and transportation hub needed to build upward, as Joseph Frey points out in the chapter on Architecture, but also because the Midwest brought together the required material resources such as steel, human resources such as Louis Sullivan, and institutional resources such as Daniel Burnham's city plan. The atomic age began here as well, when Enrico Fermi and other scientists at the University of Chicago's Manhattan Project generated the world's first self-sustained nuclear reaction, unleashing atomic energy for war and peace from a lab beneath the football stadium, Stagg Field, on December 2, 1942, at 3:36 P.M. Out of irreverence and energy, the Heartland gave birth to the modern world. A sculpture by Henry Moore marks the spot.

A CONTEMPORARY BORDERLAND

For all their power, both the Heartland myth of national representativeness and the Hinterland tale of regional subordination omit important subplots: the role and experience of minorities, migrations from Asia and Latin America (and to the Sunbelt), deindustrialization and globalization of the economy, pollution of land, air, and water. Conceptualizing the Midwest as a Borderland, however, integrates the disparate strands of the regional narrative, recognizing that the Heartland was born of the Hinterland. Midwestern writers could experiment freely, Marilyn J. Atlas has observed, because they had less to lose than did canonical New Englanders.[17] The same could be said for midwestern innovators from industry to higher education.

As Gloria Anzaldúa defines it, the Borderland is both a literal and metaphorical place. "A borderland is a vague and undetermined place created by the emotional residue of an unnatural boundary," she points out in *Borderlands/LaFrontera*, which introduced the term. "It is in a constant state of transition. The prohibited and forbidden are its inhabitants." The midwestern Borderland incorporates the paradox of relations between this region and the nation: central but peripheral, heartland and hinterland, the postindustrial manufacturer and industrial farmer, among America's whitest regions (83.8 percent overall, 94.9 percent in Iowa), yet also increasingly, as Richard Rodriguez would characterize it, *brown*.[18]

The Great Migration that brought African Americans from the South to the Midwest expanded a black presence that has received little attention in Heartland narratives. Haitian-born Jean Baptiste Point du Sable (1745?–1818), whose mother

The Quad Cities as the Quintessential Midwest

Straddling the Mississippi River, the Quad Cities of Moline and Rock Island, Illinois, and Davenport and Bettendorf, Iowa, encapsulate the complicated history of the Midwest. Inhabited since 10,000 B.C.E., Rock Island became home in about 1730 C.E. to Sauk and Meskwaki (Fox) Indians. The area's population of some 7,000 made it among North America's largest Native American centers at the time. The Sauk at their most powerful controlled most of Iowa along with adjacent portions of Missouri, Illinois, and Wisconsin from their capital of Saukenuk on Rock Island. European exploration, trading, and settlement set neighboring nations in motion. The eviction of the Sauk following the 1832 Black Hawk War marked the determination of white Americans to dominate the continent for economic gain. Not surprisingly, when the treaty ending the war was signed at Rock Island's Fort Armstrong, its colonel George Davenport (1783–1845), a fur trader who gave his name to the city across the river, was among the first to buy ceded land.

The four towns that emerged united French and British colonial pasts and attracted a typical midwestern population of settlers from Atlantic states and German, Swedish, Belgian, and Irish backgrounds. Midwestern agriculture was enhanced in 1837 when John Deere developed the first successful sod-busting steel plow. Deere used the water from the Mississippi to generate power for the factory he later built in Moline. Quad Cities mills thrived on river traffic that brought more than 2,000 steamboats annually to their docks. The name *Moline* derives from the French *moulin*, that is, mill.

Although the area belonged to the Union, proximity to slaveholding Missouri put the Quad Cities at the center of sectional strife. Named for a Rock Islander's slave, the 1857 Dred Scott decision of the Supreme Court upheld the principle that slaves were property, not persons, whose status did not change upon removal from slave Missouri to free Illinois. The decision inflamed tensions leading to the Civil War, during which some twelve thousand Confederate soldiers were imprisoned on Rock Island. Most died in the midwestern winter.

Hinterland, Heartland, and Borderland all manifest themselves in the Quad Cities today. Davenport's Putnam Museum of History and Natural Science features North American prehistory and the colonization of the frontier. Nearby, buffalo graze at the childhood home of Wild West showman "Buffalo" Bill Cody. Deere's administrative center, a landmark building designed by Eero Saarinen, symbolizes links between the planting of the prairie and industrialization of America. The Black Hawk State Historic Site recalls the economic struggles of the twentieth century as well as the nineteenth: during the Great Depression, some two hundred World War I veterans working in the Civilian Conservation Corps (CCC) created a park here. The Mississippi Valley Blues Festival, held annually July 2–4 in Davenport, honors the river's role in bringing musicians north. The uncertain future of deindustrialized America stares us in the face in "Mother and Daughter, Davenport, Iowa," a photograph by Minneapolis photographer Alec Soth announcing his New York show in the *New Yorker*. The East reserves the right to validate artistic achievement, and Soth's photograph respects eastern prejudice. The portrait of two generations, their sensual outfits coordinating with each other but clashing with homey surroundings and sultry looks, recalls the unfashionable Hinterland and ironically evokes the fecund Heartland; emphasis on legs over faces and the daughter's sexuality over the mother's signals the unsettled terrain of the Borderland.

was a Negro slave and whose father was from a wealthy fur-trading family, has not always received credit for establishing Chicago as a center of Great Lakes trade. In the 2000 census 24.9 percent of Illinois residents (16.2 percent of midwesterners overall) identified themselves as persons of color. Chicago's Latin population ranks in size second only to that of Los Angeles.

If Harlem was the site of the African American literary renaissance, its nascence was here, in the Midwest. It was in the Midwest that Paul Laurence Dunbar (1872–1906) of Dayton, influenced by the Hoosier dialect writing of James Whitcomb Riley (1849–1916), wrote poetry and prose drawing on his parents' experience as former slaves and his own experience of opportunity and frustration. Here also Charles Waddell Chesnutt (1858–1932) of Cleveland, trained as a lawyer but, able to work only as a court stenographer, wrote the novels and short stories that won him recognition as America's first major black novelist. Still, the tensions of the Borderland meant that the 1893 World's Columbian Exposition in Chicago was, despite the efforts of Frederick Douglass and others, a white city racially as well as architecturally. Yet sixty years later, the grieving mother of fourteen-year-old Chicagoan Emmett Till (1941–1955) felt sufficiently secure to challenge the Mississippi men who killed him, and her outrage fueled the civil rights movement. Today, hip-hop performers on both coasts buy background music from Mark Williams and Joe Kent, the Trackboyz of St. Louis, America's hottest hip-hop scene.

The midwestern Borderland also exposes contradictions in the story of Native Americans. Only a few Indian tribes remained on the edges of the Midwest in Missouri, Wisconsin, Minnesota, and Michigan until the 1950s, when yet another national land grab—this time for oil—returned Native Americans from western reservations to establish new communities in Detroit, Dayton, and other cities. Today the Shki Bmaadzi Singers of the Urban Natives of Chicago Youth Council are renewing old traditions and establishing new ones. Lac Courte Orielles Chippewa run public radio station WOJB 88.9 FM in Hayward, Wisconsin. The American Indian Studies Institute at Indiana University documents endangered languages. Students study Ojibwe at the University of Minnesota (Minneapolis) and Nishinaabe at Bay Mills Community College (Brimley, Michigan). "We've always been adapting to different people—the French, English, Americans," observes Johnathan Buffalo of the Meskwaki people, who returned to Iowa in 1857 from exile in Kansas, eventually buying 7,000 acres on which to maintain their traditional lives and religion. "And we're still here."[19]

Irony rules the day. As Mayda, Keiffer, and Slade point out in the chapter on Ecology and Environment, the Midwest's industrial development and agribusiness threaten the natural and human resources on which they rely. Yet Ford's historic River Rouge plant in Dearborn, Michigan, where both modern assembly lines and environmental pollution were born, now boasts a new plant. Designed by architect William McDonough, the new facility combines such "green" technologies as a soil- and plant-covered roof that insulates the structure and filters rainwater and energy cells fueled by fumes from paint solvents. More troubling are charges that the great midwestern agricultural machine, whose corn, wheat, and beef fed the nation—and whose technologies fed the world—has caused evils ranging from epidemic obesity to the 2003 invasion of Iraq. In this view, abundant, cheap midwestern corn makes the cheap, supersized soft-drinks and hamburgers that have expanded waistlines wherever the American diet prevails, including places as far away as Okinawa, Japan. Chemical fertilizers get triply blamed: in addition to polluting waterways, they contribute to global warming and energy dependence, through their reliance on oil. But residents of the "Rust Belt" worry less about the environment than about life in an economic Borderland where neither farm nor factory offers work. Nor do local merchants. In a process that Ron Powers calls "the reengineering of heartland society," the mercantile class—the backbone of midwestern communities—has disappeared, displaced by Wal-Mart. The title of Powers's book sums up his dismay over the impact on Hannibal, Missouri, "America's hometown," where he, like Mark Twain, grew up: *Tom and Huck Don't Live Here Anymore*.[20]

But of course they never did. Tom and Huck were imaginative constructions, as were the Heartland and Hinterland myths. More to the point, Twain's visions of midwestern childhood include Injun Joe, Pap Finn, the feuding Shepherdsons, and free but re-enslaved Jim. Midwestern films embrace similar extremes, as Rodney Hill explains in the chapter on Film and Theater. Never the Heartland nor the Hinterland, the Midwest was always both at once—that is, the Borderland, which promoted progressivism *and* reproduced racism. In the Borderland life imitates art: real tourists seek communion and self-fulfillment on the Field of Dreams built in Dyersville, Iowa, for the 1989 film based on W. P. Kinsella's novel *Shoeless Joe* (1982). In the Borderland a postindustrial economy dominated by semiskilled service jobs and highly specialized information work is replacing the industrial economy based on high-wage skilled factory jobs. But once again immigrants are also forging the region's future.

Denison, Iowa, provides a case in point. Like factories throughout the Midwest, meat-packing plants in Denison supported a middle-class lifestyle for workers with high school diplomas throughout the postwar years. Then in 1981, Denison's plants automated the meat-cutting process, replaced skilled workers with machine attendants, and cut wages by 40 percent. Children avoided following in their parents' footsteps. The workforce aged, and (assisted by the farm crisis) rural communities hemorrhaged talent. Iowa has great state universities and private colleges, but 40 percent of their graduates leave the state. But even downscaled factory jobs offered Mexican immigrants more than farm labor: twice the pay, half the living costs, and accelerated access to the American dream of homeownership and better lives for their families. In 2002, Denison's population of 7,300 officially included 1,240 Latinos; unofficial estimates put the number as high as 2,500 (35 percent). And the town's schools, retailers, and industies grew in the 1990s after a decade of decline.[21]

Never simply the pastoral dream or the industrial engine, the Midwest remains as it has been: a Borderland where identity is in flux. In the Borderland, superhero comics for kids have given way to Harvey Pekar's adult tales of a Cleveland antihero, the ironically titled *American Splendor* (1976–1986). Each installment details Pekar's daily experiences of friendship, disappointment, and rumination—the antithesis of an action plot. But Pekar is also Everyman, finding meaning and satisfaction where he can and making art from it.

The Midwest also needs to transform its postindustrial experiences into a compelling new story: How the region will develop an information economy while automation expands, government revenues fall, education funding shrinks, and even the most local of mass media, radio and newspapers, succumb to national and regional feeds. Innovations in computing, such as Compuserve's introduction of computer time-sharing (1969), consumer e-mail service (1979), and real-time chat (1980) have not sparked a high-tech corridor in Columbus, Ohio, to compete with those in Silicon Valley and Boston; on the contrary, the 1998 purchase of Compuserve by America Online reaffirmed old colonial practices. On the other hand, new technologies tantalize with promises of regional economic renewal. Agricultural engineers led by Yuanhui Zhang of the University of Illinois have converted swine manure into oil using a new thermochemical conversion (TCC) process. Thus, a farm raising 10,000 market hogs annually could also produce 5,000 barrels of crude oil per year—raising farmers' incomes 10 percent, reducing oil imports 21 barrels per pig, and diminishing the environmental impact of hog farming and oil refining. The process can also recycle human waste. This postmodern alchemy underscores how, amid contemporary contradictions, midwesterners can develop what Anzaldúa calls "a new *mestiza* consciousness . . . a consciousness of the Borderlands."[22] Public investment in such new thinking will be central to success. The future of the Midwest seems shaky as Heartland triumph and Hinterland reticence yield to Borderland ambiguity. It has been so for 200 years, however, and the Borderland still beckons midwesterners with hope.

Judith Yaross Lee

ARCHITECTURE

Joseph Frey
and John E. Hancock

The open vistas of the midwestern terrain inspired the imaginations of builders both pre-historic and modern. Wandering bands of hunters entered the Midwest as long as 13,000 years ago, gradually following and settling within the improved postglacial ecologies of the region. By the first millennium B.C.E., monumental architecture appeared in the form of large burial mounds reflecting settled social patterns, advanced surveying technologies, and sophisticated ceremonial activities. By about 100 B.C.E. new architectural inspirations included vast earthen-walled enclosures through the Ohio Valley region—surrounding hilltops and forming elaborate geometric figures on the alluvial valley terraces. Among these, and throughout the Midwest as a whole, mound building continued, as did construction of monumental timber-framed structures for everyday and ceremonial use. By 1000 C.E., new architectural traditions had emerged. Especially to the north, in Wisconsin and Iowa, animal effigy mounds were common. Along the central Mississippi Valley, large towns and cities were forming around a highly successful corn agriculture economy. Chief among these was Cahokia, the grand "City of the Sun," located near the modern city of St. Louis. By the time of European contact, all these monumental architectural traditions were but distant memories and ruins, already reclaimed by the forests. Scholars around the world continue to be awed by their historical importance.

The modern Midwest has its monumental buildings, too, constructed from steel, concrete, and synthetics. They shape the skylines of the region's major cities, most notably that of Chicago, which gave its name to a school of architecture. Well before skyscrapers arose, however, early European settlers created vernacular structures from the trees, sod, clay, and rock of their new home. The environment and the economy pressed midwesterners to think in terms of form and function even as industrialization transformed the landscape and technologies such as elevators fed aspirations to soar. It is no exaggeration to say that the Midwest remains an architectural laboratory. The designs of its great innovators have been replicated around the world.

THE PREHISTORIC PERIOD

When European American settlers began arriving in what is now the Midwest, it was not empty land. Besides many tribes of Indians, they also found immense works of monumental architecture, technically and compositionally sophisticated earthen structures whose original purposes were obscured by time, just as their shapes were obscured by centuries of forest growth.

The first Euro-American settlement in "The Northwest" was planned respectfully among such ancient remains. The street grid and buildings of Marietta, Ohio, are still oriented around wide embankment walls, precise earthen platforms, and a beautiful, large mound. The generals of George Washington's army, the "Society of the Cincinnati," laid out this place, optimistic that such respect for a distinguished antiquity would characterize the new society they hoped to create, in what historian Roger Kennedy has called "The Great Valley of the Ohio."

But it was not to be. In 200 years, we have destroyed the vast majority of such monuments throughout the Midwest. Farming, looting, industry, and urban sprawl have all taken their toll. Only the exquisite drawings by nineteenth-century surveyors now reflect these vanished places. Indeed, American archaeology was born out of the mid-nineteenth-century public enthusiasm for the "mound builders," but like the earthworks themselves, this enthusiasm has been declining ever since.

Monumental earthen architecture was ubiquitous across the entire region, from the Marietta Earthworks to the Grand Mound of International Falls, Minnesota. Although burial mounds were the most common, other shapes proliferated. Many of them memorialized, or supported, elaborate timber structures. Overall, the buildings of our Native predecessors revealed great skill, extreme precision, and often a scale beyond our comprehension. They mastered with great care and artistry the abundant tectonic resources at hand: earth, water, and the trees of the forest.

Like any regionally identifiable architecture, the mounds and earthworks, and the timber structures that were among them, partake of qualitative features rooted in the climate, topography, and ecology of their environment. It is this rootedness in the qualities of a place and landscape, more than the superficial features of any "style," that gives truth and life to architectural traditions, and reveals their resonance with the ways that life is lived there.

Most of the Midwest was covered in mixed hardwood forests, over alternating swaths of hilly and flat landscape, laced by many rivers and streams. The forests were dense and enclosing, edging off in the north to pine and birch, and in the west to open prairie. Abundant game and water, edible plants, and timber of all sizes supported patterns of seasonal migration. People set up small, short- and medium-term settlements, and had intimate knowledge of the ways of the Earth (soils, drainage, plants, stone, and timber) and of the heavens (sun, moon, order, and the seasons).

The earliest monumental architecture coincided here, as elsewhere, with an increasingly place-specific existence and a desire to mark territory, to remember the deceased, and to embody the cosmic and social orders. In the woodlands of the Midwest, monumentality was usually created with earth, ensuring duration and memory, and a seamless merging with the eternal landscape. Many of these monumental civic and ceremonial centers preceded the development of large towns and cities by many centuries.

Ancient Earthen Architecture

The ancient earthen architecture of the Midwest takes five basic forms: circular mounds, usually but not always associated with burials; earth-walled hilltop enclosures; earth-walled geometric enclosures generally on flat ground; animal effigies; and rectilinear platform mounds. Each tends to be associated with particular cultural periods and traditions. In simplest terms, these are "Early Woodland" from about 1000 to 100 B.C.E. including "Adena" cultural traits (notably a marked development of ceremonial burial practices); "Middle Woodland" extending to about 500 C.E. and corresponding more or less to "Hopewell" lifeways (a great flowering that influenced most of the eastern United States through wide interaction networks); and "Mississippian," the most general term for those maize-growing and city-building cultures that flourished nearly up to European contact.

The general features of these traditions overlap and merge considerably, and continue to be present in the many tribes associated with this region, as well as the American South, since contact. So although specific tribal, ancestral links to the Ancient Ones are not always known, it is important to emphasize that ancestors of modern Native peoples created these magnificent works; their descendants continue to find them deeply meaningful.

The design of more ephemeral buildings (like houses, ceremonial buildings, shelters, or storage facilities) was probably more continuous across these epochs and even into early twentieth-century Native settlements. There is also increasing evidence that the forms of timber structures are reflected in some of the earthworks. Apparently, the wooden architecture was often burned, or carefully dismantled, and permanently marked by an earthen shape.

Mounds

Conical or dome-shaped mounds are found all across the region, dating back to 2500 B.C.E. Excavations have generally revealed a primary, central burial, often in a log-lined chamber. Other tombs were sometimes added within expanding layers of earth, explaining why some mounds, like the one overlooking Miamisburg, Ohio, grew so large. The multiple burials probably belonged to a related clan group, though in later times unrelated local groups also created so-called intrusive burials, making ad hoc use of the preexisting monuments to remember their own dead.

Conical mound building was a dominant architectural practice of the Early Woodland or Adena culture, associated with their elaborate burial rituals. The more monumental of these, such as the Conus at Marietta, were often surrounded by a shallow, circular ring and ditch, with a single gateway crossing over into the mound precinct. Adena builders also created ring-and-ditch constructions with level interiors, likely forerunners of the geometric enclosures built by their Hopewell successors.

Hopewell and Mississippian societies continued to build mounds as burial markers but, unlike the Adena, devised their most monumental constructions of other forms and uses entirely. The Hopewell created a few complex mounds, multilobed accretions of rounded shapes almost resembling animal effigies, like the so-called Eagle at Newark, Ohio, or the Tremper mound near Portsmouth, Ohio. Post-mold patterns have shown that there were elaborate buildings under each of these, corresponding to the complex shapes.

Earth-Walled Hilltop Enclosures

Hopewell people also created massive earthen embankments surrounding level hilltops. Early settlers and archaeologists named them "forts" since a protective function seemed self-evident. "Fort Ancient" near Cincinnati, Ohio, is the largest and best preserved of these: About a hundred acres are ringed, and the walls grow to over 20 feet tall. The design also included elaborate water ponds and sixty-seven gateways defined by complex patterns of walkovers, limestone pavements, retaining walls, and auxiliary mounds.

More recent studies have refuted the military intentions: The local populations were far too small to guard such a huge perimeter; the water ponds were on the inside and so were useless as a moat; and there is little evidence that the many openings were ever closed off. Yet at the nearby Pollock Earthworks (where the earthen walls close only the small end of a plateau otherwise ringed by sheer cliffs) a huge stockade of timber poles and mud-plaster was erected, just for a short time, and then quickly burned and buried. This, with evidence of charred earth and timbers from other sites, suggests that any period of fear or hostility was brief, or sporadic; no evidence has been found of Hopewell military conflict.

Geometric Enclosures

The most architecturally spectacular, if ineffable, Native constructions in the Midwest are the huge geometric enclosures along the tributaries of the Ohio River. Although earlier "Adena" people had created small earthen rings, the full grandeur, scale, and precision of earthen geometry was the achievement of their "Hopewell" successors. It may have been at one of their two richest sites, "Mound City" at Chillicothe, Ohio, where this idea first took hold. There, a collection of many mounds, mostly memorials to ceremonial funerary buildings, were enclosed by a low earthen embankment. The shape is a square with rounded corners, significantly resembling the individual buildings found under the mounds.

Soon thereafter, this idea of marking huge geometric shapes across the river terraces developed into many variations: circles, squares, octagons, rhomboids, and distinctive tripartite combinations. Sometimes these enclosed significant communal burial complexes that were memorialized under great mounds, such as at Seip or the Hopewell Mound Group, both in Ross County, Ohio.

South-central Ohio, along the Scioto drainage, is clearly the heartland of Hopewell cultural practices, yet the most spectacular of the Natives' monumental creations is sixty miles to the northeast, at Newark. There, over four square miles, the ancients built a vast complex, including, most notably, a perfect circle-octagon formation that marks, along its central axis, the northernmost extreme rise-point of the moon. This alignment reveals their knowledge of the 18.6-year cycle of the moon's movement on the horizon. Indeed, all eight of the cycle's critical points are marked by this geometric figure (with margins of error smaller than those at Stonehenge). The walls of this monument are perfectly formed, flat, and at eye level: an ideal instrument for directing the vision of the gathered community to the distant horizons for these generation-defining celestial events.

The Hopewell lived in dispersed, possibly temporary settlements no larger than an extended family; so the huge earthwork complexes probably saw periodic gatherings and celebrations of the civic, religious, festive, commercial, and funerary activities that were unified into the fabric of ancient life. The exact geometric shapes, the perfect construction, the astronomical encoding, and the massive dimensions all reflect the "cosmological plan" (the unity of sky with earth, of sacred with everyday, and of human groups with their neighbors) basic to all religious and cultural experience. Periodic activities at the earthworks helped keep dispersed families and clans organized, and in touch with their common beliefs.

Another clue to this connectivity is visible on the nineteenth-century plans of Newark: One of several pairs of parallel walls, about 200 feet apart, heads off to the southwest on a perfectly straight course which, as Dr. Bradley Lepper has shown using modern maps and photos, could have led all the way to Chillicothe. Such a practice of connecting ceremonial centers over long distances, with perfectly straight highways, was used centuries later in the Chaco region of New Mexico.

The geometric patterns found in the earthworks, linked squares and circles and circles within circles, are reflected abstractly in the exquisite shapes these same people cut from mica and copper, and deposited with their loved ones. And although these carefully crafted artifacts, made from exotic materials from far away, were also shaped into animal figures, the idea of shaping the earth into animal forms would have to wait another several hundred years and would reach its most prolific development far to the north along the upper Mississippi River.

Houses

Houses and other structures of similar scale were built on a wooden framework. Thin saplings were set in the ground and bent over and tied into a dome-shaped roof, and then covered with bark sheets or woven-cattail mats, possibly anchored with another, external grid of saplings. Or thicker vertical poles were erected and interwoven with twigs and covered with mud plaster and angular, thatched, overhanging roofs. Although early settlements have proven difficult to find, and controversies ensue about their density and permanence, the houses we do know of were spacious, sturdy, and comfortable, often outfitted with built-in benches, central fires, vestibules, and other features still discernible in traditional Native American house building.

Most ceremonial buildings, such as the "charnel houses" found under several mounds at Mound City, resembled dwellings in scale and construction, but were outfitted with clay-lined pits and other features useful in the dismemberment and cremation of the dead. Some Hopewell sites had very large ritual buildings: beneath the Liberty-Harness Mound, just south of Chillicothe, was a vast, monumental floor plan with three chambers supported by a precise grid of timber columns, on exact axes of symmetry.

The techniques of building in timber across the Midwest, in response to the resources of the woodland ecology and the constraints of the continental climate, did not vary much across distance or time. Indeed, the ancient ways likely resemble very closely those that were recorded by the first European explorers, the more or less continuous traditions among eastern woodland tribes from the Iroquois Longhouses of the Northeast to the mound-top Temple-Houses of the lower Mississippi.

Effigies

Although the Hopewell worked mostly in geometric shapes, their successors a few centuries later favored animal effigies. The Great Serpent Mound near Peebles, Ohio, is probably the most famous in the world. Undulating across a gently rising ridge, it stretches exquisitely from a coiled tail to a head, or open mouth, which seems to grasp at an orb, perhaps an egg, an eye, or the sun. This head feature is aligned toward the summer solstice sunset, also hanging precariously atop a distinctive natural cliff which, from below, itself resembles a serpent's head jutting from the undulating hillside. Recent carbon-dating situates this creature at about 1070 C.E., contemporary with the great Mississippian cultures to the west and, intriguingly, with the bright appearance of Halley's Comet in 1066, perhaps suggesting an entirely different meaning for this orb with tail formation.

It is the upper Mississippi Valley that boasts the greatest proliferation of such animal figures. Like the geometric earthworks, the numerous effigies enabled their builders to imagine and visualize the cosmological order, their own relations with the earth, sky, order and time. Most likely, they embodied the animal spirits through which the people identified themselves on a continuum with the natural world and within particular social clan structures.

Across southeastern Minnesota, northeastern Iowa, and southern Wisconsin, a culture sometimes called the Effigy Mound People flourished from about 400 to 1300 C.E., with lifeways resembling the earlier Hopewell. Among their small settlements and cultivated gardens, they created often great clusters of effigies such as the "Great Marching Bear Group" at Effigy Mounds National Monument near Marquette, Iowa. There, ten bears make a procession across the landscape, accompanied by three birds and two linear mounds. Nearby a monumental "Great Bear" slumbers, with a 70-foot shoulder span and a complete length of 130 feet. A total of 200 mounds, built over a time span of 2,500 years, occupy this preserve. No burials are associated with these effigies; there seems to have been little burial ceremonialism at all among the effigy-builders of the upper Mississippi. Not far away near West Bend, Wisconsin, in Lizard Mound County Park about thirty mounds are especially well preserved, the largest in the form of a reptilian creature. Another impressive cluster of thirty-three effigies of panther and deer are still intact at Sheboygan Mound Park at Sheboygan, Wisconsin.

By about 1400 C.E., these ways of life had been replaced throughout the region by intensive corn agriculture and the new social and economic arrangements required to produce, store, guard, trade, and divide this concentrated wealth. Large villages grew under an elite ruler class, with vividly hierarchical and defensive architecture to match. These were the great walled, pyramid-centered cities of the Mississippi Valley, most prominently Cahokia ("The City of the Sun"), near East Saint Louis, Illinois.

The rectangular platform mounds were the grandest features of these Mississippian cities. Often two- or three-tiered masses of earth were used to elevate the house of the political or spritual leader, where he could command, visually and literally, the wide, flat Mississippi River plain. At its peak from about 1100 to 1300 C.E., Cahokia covered almost six square miles, and had at least 20,000 inhabitants, more than any European city at the time. The plan was rectilinear, with houses arranged around open plazas. There were at least 120 flat-topped mounds of various sizes, many of them platforms for important buildings, temples, or houses.

Dominating the city, above the huge open central plaza, was "Monk's Mound": with four levels and more than 14 acres at its base, it is the largest earthen structure in all of North America, perhaps the world. To the west was the Woodhenge, a circle of about sixty long poles, probably tied to the Cahokians' sun-centered worship practices and a calendrical marker for their all-important agricultural cycles. Vast fields of maize were arrayed outside the city walls, along the wide, fertile valley floor, and under the strict gaze of the priestly elite who surveyed it all from a grand, thatched-roofed Temple-House atop the highest mound.

Outlying towns along the central Mississippi and its tributaries followed a similar pattern. Far up the Illinois watershed, Aztalan State Park near Lake Mills, Wisconsin (named after its presumed resemblance to an Aztec site), contains a far-northern example of pyramidal platform building, in the midst of what was a large, stockaded town. Aztalan is clearly related to the cultural, economic, and town-planning patterns seen at Cahokia, as is Towosahgy, in southeastern Missouri, a fortified village of 1100 to 1400 C.E., also centered on a large platform mound. Angel Mounds near Evansville, Indiana, are also the remains of a large town, with a population of at least 3,000 at about the same period. Its complex of massive platform mounds is similar also to Cahokia, and its economy was supported by hunting and farming the rich valley of the Ohio River. At least 200 dwellings—likely of wattle and daub, with thick, steep thatched roofs like most Mississippian buildings—stood among grand plazas and were surrounded by a stockade with bastions, now partially reconstructed. The largest of the platform mounds stood 44 feet high. These Mississippian temple mounds, and the corn-based rituals and life ways that built them, continue to hold meaning for the modern Chickasaw, Choctaw, and Creek tribes in the southeastern United States.

Early settlers of Marietta, Ohio, planned the town around preexisting earthen structures. Courtesy of John Hancock.

Smaller in size but meticulous in research is the contemporaneous settlement, now partially reconstructed, at "Sun Watch Village" in Dayton, Ohio. An open plaza nearly 200 feet across contains a huge cedar pole, placed to cast its shadow toward specific buildings (some reconstructed), to mark events on the annual calendar such as the equinox, and planting and harvesting dates. Clearly, sun markers were important in an agricultural society where sustenance depended on the orderly, controlled procession of the sky and the earth.

The Midwest is home to some of the most significant ancient architectural and urban traditions in the world, including probably the largest earthen mound, and the largest concentrations of geometric earthworks and of animal effigies. They reflect a wide spectrum of social development and lifeways, from hunter–gatherers to complex urban civilizations. The fact that these remains have been so obscured by time, by forests, by racism, and by their own deterioration should not deter efforts to make them better known, bringing them and our Native American predecessors in this gracious landscape more vividly into the public imagination.

THE EUROPEAN SETTLEMENT PERIOD

The more recent architecture of the Midwest, like that of any region, cannot be considered in a vacuum. Many of the forces that influenced how buildings were designed and built were felt all across the country. Architects from more established eastern cities followed the western expansion, so much of the story of midwestern architecture continues a story that began elsewhere. Yet unique influences came into play, resulting in work by architects and laypersons alike that broke new ground—both literally and metaphorically. Some of the results have become internationally recognized landmarks. However, the scope of midwestern architecture encompasses more than just those structures and architects who had impact on architecture outside the region. Regional vernacular architecture is notable for its own sake.

Stretching from the wooded hills along the Ohio River to the broad, open prairies of Iowa, from the dense forests of Minnesota's lake country to the cypress swamps that covered much of Missouri's "boot heel," a region as broad east to west and long north to south as the Midwest was bound to engender a variety of vernacular styles that directly addressed local climates and exploited readily available building materials. Plentiful supplies of wood throughout much of the region meant that timber buildings dominated, with log construction more popular in the lower Midwest and a mix of styles to the north. In the western reaches of the Midwest, where wood became scarcer as the landscape made the transition into the Great Plains, the crude masonry construction of that region was often utilized. The Euro-American settlers to all of these areas also brought with them building styles and techniques that were familiar to them from the places they left, whether other parts of the United States or the countries from where they emigrated. Still, the realities of living in the frontier imposed a necessarily utilitarian sensibility, and most of the construction during the early times of midwestern settlement reflected such practicality.

The pace of western expansion by Euro-American settlers into the interior Midwest was rapid, relative to the development of seaboard regions, which began much earlier. And as towns and cities became more established, resources (labor,

Italianate Honolulu House, 1860, Marshall, Michigan. Photo by Robert J. Smith/Travel Michigan.

financing, and materials) became more available to construct more extravagant buildings, especially after the railroads were developed, creating a nationwide network for trade. Demand rose as the region became more and more settled, and building continued on an ever-grander scale. Perhaps in an effort to shed the stigma of being provincial, midwesterners tended to follow the architectural fashions set by the establishment in "cosmopolitan" eastern cities like New York and Boston. Fine examples of such romantic styles as federal or adam (Lincoln Home, 1841, Springfield, Illinois), Greek revival (Stonehall, c. 1838, Marshall, Michigan), Italianate (Honolulu House, 1860, Marshall, Michigan), and Victorian (Kilgore House, c.1865, Peru, Indiana) can still be found throughout the region, especially in the residential architecture of smaller cities and towns. Even modest workmen's cottages often contained elements of these styles. Commercial development often centered around public squares or along main streets, with closely placed storefronts on the ground floor with a couple of stories above for nonretail businesses or housing. Cedarburg, Wisconsin, and Galena, Illinois, have especially well-preserved central business districts, and the buildings there reflect vernacular interpretations of popular styles.

As competition between developing cities heated up, advances in building technologies and shifts in styles became necessary to their growth and prosperity. Thus it is in large cities, like Detroit, Cleveland, Minneapolis, Milwaukee, and St. Louis, where the development of architecture movements in the Midwest can best be traced. Yet it is at this point in a discussion of midwestern architecture that it can be helpful to at once narrow the view somewhat and broaden the scope beyond the region and to look at the impact of one midwestern city: Chicago, rail hub not just of the region but of the entire nation.

In the decades following the Great Fire in 1871, Chicago experienced unprecedented growth and became a hotbed of architectural innovation. The city and its immediate environs saw some of the most important developments in modern architecture, the impact of which were felt throughout the region, the country, and even the world. Such domination can sometimes overshadow achievements made elsewhere in the Midwest. Yet other cities and towns also contributed to the region's architectural legacy and to the ever more global art and science of architecture today.

Of the more original eastern architects who influenced post–Chicago Fire architecture in the Midwest, Frank Furness (1839–1912) and Henry Hobson Richardson (1838–1886) played especially important roles, setting in motion the progression of major architectural movements of the region. Though based in Philadelphia, Furness influenced the Midwest through Louis Sullivan (1856–1924), who worked for Furness and continued his eccentric ornamentation after coming to Chicago in 1873. This chain of influence was extended even further when Sullivan hired Wisconsinite Frank Lloyd Wright (1867–1959) to help design the Auditorium Building (1889; Chicago, Illinois; Adler and Sullivan). Richardson's impact from Boston was more direct. His sparse, muscular design for the Marshall Field Wholesale Store (1887; Chicago, Illinois; demolished) was a great influence, especially on Sullivan, and can easily be seen in the Auditorium Building, a prime example of the Chicago school.

Not an institution of learning, the "Chicago school" identifies an approach to architecture first developed by architects in that city. Applying the latest technological advancements, Chicago architects not only pioneered the best way to build "skyscrapers" but also defined the artistic parameters for how they should look, relying heavily on the structural elements for inspiration. "Form follows function," said Sullivan, by which he meant that a building's purpose should determine its looks. Early champions and prime practitioners of the style included Sullivan and his partner Dankmar Adler (1844–1900; Chicago Stock Exchange; 1894; Chicago, Illinois; demolished), William Holabird (1854–1923) and Martin Roche (1855–1927; Marquette Building; 1895; Chicago, Illinois), Daniel Burham (1846–1912) and John Wellborn Root (1850–1891; Western Reserve Building; 1891; Cleveland, Ohio), and William Le Baron Jenney (1832–1907; Second Leiter Building; 1891; Chicago, Illinois). These architects led the early development of the skyscraper, the definitive achievement of American architecture in the late nineteenth century.

Adaptable to most uses, the Chicago school prevailed until the last decade of the nineteenth century and survived well into the twentieth century. But in the mid-1890s the brawny elements of the Chicago school gave way to a more "refined" and more "civilized" style, the classically inspired beaux-arts. It was named after the Ècole des Beaux-Arts, an actual school in Paris that stressed the order and ornamentation of classicism, the architecture of ancient Greece and Rome. Many American architects studied there, including Richardson and Sullivan. Although their sensibilities about ornament broke from classicism, their sense of order could be directly traced to it. But they were anomalies. Architects trained in beaux-arts tended to ornament their buildings in ways that were also consistent with classicism. Beaux-arts was popular in eastern cities before coming to the Midwest, and the turning point in the region was the "White City" built for the 1893 World's Columbian Exposition, held in what is today Chicago's Jackson Park.

As a result of the popularity of the exposition, beaux-arts became the prevailing style throughout the Midwest for the rest of the nineteenth century and the early part of the twentieth. This can be seen in the designs of many civic buildings, such as the Allen County Courthouse (1902; Ft. Wayne, Indiana; Brentwood Tolan [1855–1923]) and the Minnesota State Capitol (1905; St. Paul, Cass Gilbert [1859–1934]), constructed in the region during this era.

Although classicism dominated large-scale building, residential building was undergoing a transformation. This was largely driven by Sullivan's former chief draftsman, Frank Lloyd Wright. The predominant domestic style of architecture at the time was Victorian, characterized by ornate ornamentation and by well-delineated rooms whose purposes were as tightly defined as their inhabitants' social roles. Wright broke down the walls inside the house, creating interiors with rooms that flowed into, rather than abutted against, each other. His exterior designs were no less revolutionary, shunning accepted ornamentation for new designs inspired by the local landscape. Rather than sit *upon* the land, Wright sought to integrate his houses *with* the land, and the style was named after much of the midwestern landscape: the prairie school. Although prairie designs for civic, religious, commercial, and even industrial buildings were executed, it was largely a residential style.

Minnesota State Capitol, 1905, St. Paul, Minnesota, Cass Gilbert (1859–1934). Courtesy Minnesota Tourism.

Eventually, the formality of classicism was loosened as the first glimpses of a more modern style emerged after World War I. Like the rest of the country, the Midwest embraced art deco, a style named after *L'Exposition des Arts Decoratifs et Industrials Modernes,* an exhibition for decorative and industrial design held in Paris in 1925. Merged with the flowing forms of art deco, classicism was "stripped" and "streamlined" to its basic elements, creating art moderne and streamline moderne. These exuberant styles were in many ways a return to the romantic historical styles that dominated in the nineteenth century. Though decidedly more "modern," art deco, like the earlier revival styles, also reflected the extravagance of the era—until the party ended and most large-scale building with it, in the Great Depression. Further architectural advancement was retarded by World War II. Not until well after that conflict ended did large-scale construction begin again. And when it did, what went up looked nothing like what had been built before.

At about the same time that art deco and its variations were sweeping the United States, another movement was emerging in Europe, one that would ultimately have an even greater impact on midwestern architecture: the international style, or modernism. International stylists sought to redefine all aesthetic and artistic parameters, architectural included. Among these new thinkers was Ludwig Mies van der Rohe (1886–1969), a German émigré who came to the Midwest. International stylists like him greatly respected and admired the practical designs of the Chicago school, but they reduced it to the barest structural essentials. The result was the seemingly simple "glass box." This style became popular in the 1950s and predominated for the next twenty years.

Modernism was founded upon a strict set of design rules that permitted little variation. "Less is more," Mies said, explaining his sparse designs. Though not without its merits, this unadorned design ethic did wear thin with the public, and in its wake came postmodernism. It was everything the international style was not. The decoration long shunned by modernists was applied liberally by postmodernists, often in overscaled and eclectic interpretations that further taunted strict adherents to the international style.

By this time, however, local midwestern movements such as the Chicago and prairie schools and, to a lesser degree, modernism had long since given way to styles that swapped and borrowed from elsewhere. Although local architecture has always felt outside influences, rapid global transportation and communications accelerate their impact. And like just about any other service, industry, or art, architecture is no longer strictly local, but more and more reliant on and influenced by national and global trends.

PREVALENT STYLES OF ARCHITECTURE

Midwestern Vernacular Architecture

Unfortunately, little midwestern architecture remains from the colonial days or even the days of western expansion. Most of the area was considered wilderness frontier, even into the nineteenth century, when a series of conflicts and treaties with the Native American nations led to permanent settlement by Euro-Americans once and for all. As a result, much of what was built was constructed more out of practicality than out of style, and that practicality often meant security as well. The timber garrisons of Fort Mackinaw, built by the British during the American Revolutionary War to guard the straits between Lakes Huron and Michigan, provide some idea of such early frontier log construction.

Farther south, along the banks of the Mississippi in Ste. Genevieve, Missouri, the strong influence France once had on the New World is still evident. First settled in the 1720s as a river port in what was then the Louisiana Territory, Ste. Genevieve boasted buildings, such as the Jean Baptiste Bequette House (c. 1780s) built in a French Creole vernacular style more associated with—and better suited to the climate in—the regions around New Orleans. Although France extensively explored the Midwest, often laying the first European claims to areas in it, French influence in the region was effectively eliminated by the French and Indian War (1755–1763) and finally by the Louisiana Purchase (1803).

Various religious colonies in the Midwest also left unique legacies. The Mormon Temple (c. 1835) in Kirkland, Ohio, is an eclectic mix of federal and gothic elements. In Bishop Hill, Illinois, Swedish settlers used a similarly understated, dignified style in the Steeple Building (1854), Bjorkland Hotel (c. 1855), and communal housing (1854). The simple wooden structures of the Iowa Amana colonies of the mid-eighteenth century perhaps reflect the order of the settlers' religious beliefs.

With much of the region suitable for agriculture, farm structures, especially barns and corn cribs, create an entire subgroup of vernacular architecture. Such buildings were often built in styles that incorporated elements from both the Old World and the New, mixing lumber, stone, and brick construction, depending on what materials were available. Though based on the practical demands of farming, barn designs did not lack decoration. Practical elements such as wind vanes and lightning rods often received aesthetic consideration. Farm houses were typically simple structures as well, most often of wood and usually with a broad porch to serve as an outside room in the harsh summer heat. The tallest structures for miles around, grain elevators built to store and transfer harvested grains to rail cars are a fine example of functional design for a specific, regionalized purpose. Their tall, long walls also made perfect billboards.

The desire for more creature comforts and luxury—including aesthetically pleasing designs that catered to the tastes of the day—soon compelled settlers to construct less rustic buildings. Stylistic influences often had roots in immigrants' homelands. Milwaukee's City Hall (1895; H. C. Koch, 1840–1910) was designed in a Flemish Renaissance style that evokes the architecture of Northern Europe, from where many nineteenth-century settlers to the city originated. The Romanesque style also called Europe to mind. H. Richardson is probably the most well-known architect designing in this vein, and his influence can be seen in the Mabel Tainter Memorial Building (1889; Menomonee, Wisconsin; Harvey Ellis).

Designs for religious buildings especially looked across the Atlantic for inspiration. The Church of St. Stanislaus (1894; Winnona, Minnesota; Charles G. Maybury & Son) exhibits a Central European influence. Byzantine elements were incorporated in Holy Trinity Russian Orthodox Cathedral (1899; Chicago, Illinois; Louis Sullivan) to create a church that resembled the parishioners' church in provincial Russia. Onion domes were a common feature in churches of other Orthodox sects. With its twin minarets, the Isaac M. Wise Temple in Cincinnati, Ohio (1866; James K. Wilson), borrows heavily from the motifs of the Holy Land.

By contrast, residential vernacular architecture increasingly became homegrown, though such eclectic historical styles never disappeared, waxing and waning in popularity. By the turn of the twentieth century, however romantic revival styles were giving way to more native styles such as prairie, bungalow, and American four square. The last two often adapted elements from historical styles and were also strongly influenced by the designs of the prairie school. From its offices in Chicago, mail-order giant Sears, Roebuck and Company sold houses in kits from 1908 until the Great Depression halted production in 1933. These homes came in the popular styles of the era, and many still stand throughout the Midwest.

In an attempt to fill the housing shortage following World War II, the Lustron Corporation built all of the components for its steel houses, including appliances, in a former aircraft factory in Columbus, Ohio. The ranch-style houses were then assembled on site in the Midwest and elsewhere. Influences on residential architecture since the mid-twentieth century, however, have had more to do with lifestyle than with architectural style, with the popularity of television eventually transforming the living room into the great room and more cars creating the need for larger and often more prominent garages. The grid layout common to towns and cities in the nineteenth century gave way to the curving streets of suburban housing tracts.

The Lustron Corporation built all of the components for its steel houses in a former aircraft factory in Columbus, Ohio. The ranch-style houses were then assembled on site. Lustron House, Chesterton, Indiana. Courtesy Library of Congress.

The automobile also sparked vernacular architecture; the need for business to attract the attention of customers traveling at mile-a-minute speeds turned buildings into icons of advertising. McDonald's first franchise restaurant in Des Plaines, Illinois (1955), is a prime postwar example. But the impact of the automobile began well before that, resulting in colorful roadside architecture, such as the tourist cabins and motels built along early major highways like Route 66. Vernacular architecture in this idiom survives to this day, in the form of such literal translations as the Longaberger Home Office (1997; Newark, Ohio) designed to look like one of the baskets the company manufactures.

THE CHICAGO SCHOOL, BEAUX-ARTS, AND THE CITY BEAUTIFUL

As noted earlier, architects in Chicago, like none before them anywhere else in the world, applied what were then the latest technological advancements to the problem of designing and constructing taller buildings. The results were groundbreaking.

Foremost among these advances was skeletal metal frame construction, which replaced thick, load-bearing masonry walls as the structural support elements holding up the building. It was revolutionary because load-bearing construction required thicker walls for taller structures. The members of a skeletal frame could be much thinner. And the matrix of columns, beams, and girders of iron (eventually replaced by lighter, stronger steel) bore the load, or weight, of the building, turning the walls into nothing but "curtains" of brick and glass hung from the frame to keep out the elements.

A skyscraper's skeletal frame is like the support poles of a tepee; and like a tepee's animal hides, the walls of skeletal frame skyscrapers can be nothing but thin barriers to separate the inside from the outside. But without both components, there is no building.

The main innovator in the development of skeletal frame construction was William Le Baron Jenney, an engineer by training but, according to his one-time

Buildings or Balloons: Of Branches, Boulders, and Bricks

For centuries wooden buildings had been built pretty much in the same way, with a frame of heavy timber beams. They were fastened together by trimming the end of a beam into a "tenon," or tongue, which was then inserted into a "mortise," or hole, in another beam. It was then held in place with a wooden peg—early nails being too expensive—driven through another hole bored through the mortise into the tenon. The rest of the building was then attached to this strong frame. Skilled craftsmen could construct a sturdy building in this way given enough time, but rapidly growing midwestern communities lacked sufficient craftsmen and time. How then to keep a town growing without a large pool of skilled labor or the time to construct buildings quickly enough to keep up with the growth?

Like the skeletal frame that came afterward—and that was probably the greatest factor in making skyscrapers possible—the solution to this problem resulted from emerging technology. But instead of advances in the manufacture of structural iron and steel beams for construction, a big part of this solution came in a different shape: round. That was the shape of new circular saws, driven by steam, that could quickly cut lumber into standard sizes.

The main building component was the two-by-four. It could be quickly sawn to length, then hammered together with cheap machine-made nails—another recent advancement—to fashion a frame that looked light enough to blow away in the wind and so was called a "balloon" frame. When first developed in the early 1830s in Chicago, a building built with a balloon frame could be constructed in half the time and at half the cost of a conventionally constructed building. Soon balloon framing became the standard method of building throughout the frontier West. But in Chicago, much of the city did indeed disappear when wooden balloon-frame buildings became fuel for the Great Fire of 1871.

In their place, however, rose the first skyscrapers, built with a frame not of wood but of metal—a frame quite similar in function to wooden balloon framing, which remains important to American architecture. To this day, most wooden buildings constructed in the United States are built with a variation of the balloon frame.

Although wood was not the only building material used in the Midwest, timber was indeed plentiful, and standardized lumber made it an even more attractive material for construction. The region's geology enhanced wood's desirability. Much of the Midwest sits on ancient seabed, and the resulting sedimentary rocks can be soft, making them poor architectural and construction materials. Some of these softer stones, such as the honey-hued Joliet-Lemont limestone, were used in building. More durable stones were also found in the region, however: Saint Cloud (Minnesota) red granite and Indiana limestone.

The uniform composition, texture, and neutral color of limestone have made it a desirable building material ever since it was first quarried in Indiana in 1827. The state has used it widely, especially in civic buildings. But just as the railroads brought outside influences into the Midwest, the railroads also sparked demand for Indiana limestone throughout the region and beyond. Indiana limestone was used extensively to clad skyscrapers in cities like Chicago and Detroit. Outside the region, the Empire State Building (1931; New York, New York; Shreve, Lamb & Harmon Associates), the National Cathedral in Washington, D.C. (1907–1990; various architects), and the Biltmore House (1895; Asheville, North Carolina; Richard Morris Hunt) all made use of this stone.

The main drawback of wood is of course that it burns easily. But where satisfactory stone could not be easily quarried, the only other fireproof choice was brick. Although brick also depends on geology, the clay to make it is more plentiful than stone. And while brick making is also labor intensive, the small size and uniformity of bricks make them easier to transport and work with. For these reasons, bricks were a popular construction material in the Midwest. Areas such as the Hocking River Valley, known for what's called "Athens Block" brick, also became centers of manufacture. Bricks were versatile in the hands of skilled masons, who could fashion elaborate patterns and designs with them. With stone accents, brick buildings could easily take on the dignity of an all-stone structure.

employee Sullivan, "not an architect except by the courtesy of terms." Jenney designed the Home Insurance Building (1885; Chicago, Illinois; demolished), which historian Carl Condit considered "the decisive step" in the evolution of iron and steel framing, if not the first true skyscraper.

The impact of the skeletal frame construction was dramatic: the supporting elements are narrower than in load-bearing wall construction, freeing up more space within the building and creating much larger openings for windows, a consideration that was especially important at the time. The incandescent bulbs of the day were not nearly as bright and efficient as today's fluorescent lights. Neither was there any air conditioning, so larger windows also meant better ventilation.

Other advances in technology important to the development of the skyscraper were the perfection of the safety elevator by, among others, Elisha Graves Otis; effective fireproofing; more stable foundation systems; and advancements in plate-glass making. At first, however, these developments could not allay the public's fear of riding small moving rooms to the tops of buildings hundreds of feet above the ground. The first subways were also being developed at this time, and people were afraid to venture underground to ride them as well. To help instill confidence in the new-fangled "birdcages," as skyscrapers were derisively called, the architects often took offices on the top floor. Ultimately, however, market forces largely drove the public's acceptance of skyscrapers.

Coincidentally, the practical solutions for making tall buildings structurally possible were being developed just as the real estate business and geographical limitations in Chicago, and later other cities, were making them economically feasible as well. Landlocked within Lake Michigan, the Main and South branches of the Chicago River, and encroaching railroad yards, the central business core had only one way to go, and that was up.

Sullivan was the first to lay out the design problem of the tall office building, and he defined it in practical terms. Every building contained these following elements: below-grade levels for mechanicals; a ground floor occupied by merchants; an easily accessed second floor for other such tenants; above that, a series of identical floors containing offices; and, at the top, another mechanical floor. In many ways, this basic organization is still valid today.

Translating those basic parts into a design, Sullivan used a classical column as a model. In this tripartite, or three-part, configuration, each element of the building roughly corresponds to a section of the column. The lower merchant floors correspond to a column's base; the stacked identical floors of offices comprise the shaft; and above the top mechanical floor is a cornice, a kind of projecting decorative ledge that corresponds with a column's capital. Sullivan envisioned "a proud, soaring thing," and the Wainwright Building (1891; St. Louis, Missouri; Adler and Sullivan) is a prime example of the clarity of his simple yet elegant plan for tall commercial buildings.

Although he could express the skyscraper façade in classical terms and proportions, Sullivan's ornament did not look to Europe for inspiration. Rather than just reproduce the ornamental elements he studied at the École des Beaux-Arts, he turned to nature to devise a system of ornamentation based on organic and geometric patterns and shapes. Getting more and more elaborate as his career progressed, Sullivan's ornament style fell out of favor early in the twentieth century, viewed by many critics as excessive. He received fewer and fewer large commissions and eventually died destitute in 1924. His late career, however, is notable for a series of small midwestern banks, the National Farmers Bank (1908; Owatonna, Minnesota) being perhaps the most prominent among them.

Sullivan was the first to apply an artistic or aesthetic solution to the skyscraper, but the collective approach of the Chicago school was driven primarily by practical solutions to the problems inherent in a tall office

Wainwright Building, Seventh and Chestnut Streets, St. Louis County, Missouri. Courtesy Library of Congress.

building: structure and foundation, light, and ventilation. To provide the last two, various floor plans were developed to make sure that each office had its own window, either looking out onto a street or alley or looking into an inward-facing light court and airshaft. Although we take such conveniences for granted with today's fluorescent lighting and air conditioning, solutions to the Midwest's extremes of climate had to be devised. To further aid in providing light and ventilation, the so-called Chicago window was developed, comprised of double-hung sashes on each side of a large fixed center pane.

Making Tall Buildings Profitable

Ultimately, such practicality was born of financial necessity. Bankrolled by speculators, tall office buildings could be successful if they were profitable. Hence, the solutions the Chicago school arrived at were, above all, economically driven. And almost by default, an aesthetic ethic resulted from technological answers to the economic questions raised by the tall office block. The Chicago school is defined by this aesthetic of practicality as much as it is by the technological solutions it engendered. Walls that no longer supported any loads allowed architects a freer hand in treating those walls' aesthetic elements. Buildings of the Chicago school tended to be more subdued in their ornamentation. Even the choice of material to cover the skeletal frame was often modest. Terra cotta, a fired clay similar to that of flower pots, was used extensively because of its low cost and light weight, and because it could be molded into any shape and glazed in any color.

Cass Gilbert, the architect of the neo-gothic Woolworth Building (1907; New York City) defined a skyscraper as "a machine that makes land pay." So developers undertook the building of tall office buildings for one reason: to make money. The way to make money was to attract and keep tenants, and the more cheaply a developer and his architect could do that, the more money the developer made. Consequently, the impact of developers cannot be underestimated. Men like easterner Peter Brooks and his Chicago agent Owen Aldis, who together financed the Rookery (1888; Chicago, Illinois; Burnham & Root), among other buildings, may have had as much impact as the architects who designed them on the ultimate shape of those buildings, and thus on the built environment of the Midwest. In fact, Sullivan named Aldis one of the two people responsible for the modern office building. (The other was William Hale, an innovator of elevator technology.)

But what visually characterizes a building of the Chicago school, in addition to Sullivan's basic vertical layout, is the articulation of structure. The underlying skeletal elements supporting the building are expressed on the outside. The vertical components of the frame are often thrust out from the windows to exaggerate them. Ornamentation, though perhaps sometimes exuberant in comparison to the glass boxes of the later international style, is still restrained by the standards of the day.

The World's Fair

Where the Chicago school might have led if the beaux-arts style for the 1893 World's Columbian Exposition had not had such an impact, no one can say. What Sullivan did say, however, was that the fair set American architecture back fifty years. (He also stated that since bankers worked in post-fair buildings that looked like Roman temples, they should wear togas!) Still, it doesn't take much imagination to see how the glass boxes of the international style that came more than half a century later expressed the basic lessons of the Chicago school, stripped to their barest essentials. But the fair and its beaux-arts design did indeed have an undeniable impact.

Chicago had lobbied hard to be the site for the World's Fair celebrating the four hundredth anniversary of Columbus's landing in the New World—in fact, the "Windy City" was named not for Chicago's weather but for the boasting of its civic boosters at the time. Daniel Burnham's business and political acumen, combined with his firm's ability to design durable, attractive, and profitable buildings, was enough to persuade the fair's organizing committee to hire as supervising architects Burnham and Root, whose pre-fair designs such as that of Cleveland's Society for Saving Building (1889) reflected the more muscular Chicago school. They were determined to make good on all the promises to impress the world.

Root, considered an original though undisciplined talent, died before the plans were executed; what impact his death had on the final design of the fair is impossible to determine. But in his absence Burnham turned to a cadre of eastern architects who favored the classically influenced beaux-arts style, relying heavily on the advice of New Yorkers Charles McKim (1847–1909) and Richard Morris Hunt (1827–1895). With a pool of local talent, the obvious question is: Why? And perhaps the answer is that Burnham the politician was trying to purchase some respectability for the fair and for the city of Chicago—and the rest of the Midwest, for that matter—still considered by many as part of the wild, wild West.

Popular opinion at the time held that Burnham had overseen a smashing success. The final design of the fair was a monument to beaux-arts planning and architecture and excluded the Chicago school. The fair's White City, as it was popularly called, was not, however, without its detractors; European critics expected something fresh from the New World, not a reproduction of the ruins found in their own countries. The only remaining building in the Jackson Park fair site, the Palace of Fine Arts, now the Museum of Science and Industry (1893; D. H. Burnham and Co.), provides a glimpse of what they saw.

But the impact of the White City—on architecture, urban planning, and even society as a whole—is undeniable. At a time when cities were considered almost hopelessly dismal places, the fair provided a vision of what they could be. It instilled some sense of social responsibility in municipal governments and local business communities, putting in motion the City Beautiful Movement, which looked to solve typical plights of cities, such as substandard housing and sanitation. The City Beautiful Movement was embraced by cities across the Midwest, sparking architectural planning—along with cultural interest and social activism—to become a driving force in politics and development during the late nineteenth and early twentieth centuries. In architecture, the beaux-arts style became the preferred choice of business and political leaders. In the classically influenced designs, they saw integrity, stability, and other virtues they wished to promote.

On the merits of his plan for the Columbian Exposition and then those of subsequent designs, Burnham became the premier city planner of the era. He was engaged to create municipal plans for Cleveland, San Francisco, Washington, D.C., and even Manila in the Philip-

Skyscrapers without Steel

There is some debate about what building deserves the title of "World's First Skyscraper," but buildings deserving other titles are known for certain.

Tall buildings can be constructed in ways other than skeletal metal frame construction. One is the old-fashioned way, with load-bearing masonry walls thick enough to carry the weight of story upon story. That's how architects Burnham & Root designed the Monadnock Building (1891; Chicago, Illinois). To support its sixteen floors, the walls are $8\frac{1}{2}$ feet thick in the basement, 6 feet thick at the ground level, and then taper to $1\frac{1}{2}$ feet at the top. The result was the tallest office building in the world at the time, and it is still the tallest with load-bearing walls.

Even if it didn't employ the modern construction techniques of the Chicago school, the Monadnock's form was designed in the tripartite configuration of base-shaft-capital. A pure form with no applied decoration, the building is "honest" in that it expresses its underlying masonry structure. This is a characteristic of modernist design, and although the Monadnock is not a building of the international style, modernists respect its adherence to modernist principles.

Another popular structural system for tall buildings is reinforced concrete construction. Rather than a matrix of metal columns, beams, and girders bolted or riveted together, reinforced concrete construction consists of thin steel bars that are bound together inside a form, then covered in concrete and left to cure. Slab floors are then formed the same way, supported by the concrete columns. The process is then repeated, story by story, up and across the building. Although use of concrete as a building material dates back to Roman times, it was not adapted for skyscrapers until more than ten years after the widespread use of skeletal metal frame construction in them. But the application of reinforced concrete construction in skyscrapers was also pioneered in the Midwest.

At fifteen stories tall, the building holding the title as the first reinforced-concrete high-rise office building is the Ingalls Building (1903; Cincinnati, Ohio; Alfred O. Elzner [1862–1933] and George M. Anderson [1869–1916]). Yet despite its ground-breaking feat of engineering, the building features a façade executed in the still-popular beaux-arts style, effectively hiding any signs of technical innovation. However, left exposed, concrete can often be seen in the construction of other structures, such as silos.

pines. Yet Burnham's impact went well beyond that. He is credited with creating the modern architecture firm, transforming his business to pay as much attention to relationships with clients as his partner Root once paid to designs.

If anything reflects Burnham's oft-quoted saw ("Make no little plans; they have no magic to stir men's blood"), it's The Plan of Chicago (1909), a master plan for his firm's hometown, commissioned not by city government but by the Commercial Club of Chicago and co-authored with Edward Bennett (1874–1954). Double-decked Wacker Drive, the beaux-arts design of Grant Park, and the Michigan Avenue Bridge are realized elements of his elaborate plan, which came nowhere near full realization. Yet he was convinced that such improvements, such broad shifts in perspective, would make for a better city—both for business and for the citizenry.

Ultimately, then, The Plan of Chicago—indeed, the entire City Beautiful Movement—posited this: An attractive, livable city is good for commerce; public and private monies invested in improvements to the urban environment will thus be returned through increased business. And it is this reciprocal, symbiotic spirit of civic betterment that is perhaps the greatest legacy of the 1893 World's Columbian Exposition, the City Beautiful Movement, The Plan of Chicago, and perhaps even of Burnham himself. It is a progressive legacy from the Midwest to the world.

THE PRAIRIE SCHOOL

Frank Lloyd Wright was born in rural Wisconsin in 1867. The impact of nature and the prairie landscape had a profound influence on his designs; the five years he spent working in the office of Adler and Sullivan refined that influence. There he executed ornamental designs for such Adler and Sullivan commissions as the Garrick Theater (1892; Chicago, Illinois; demolished) and, many believe, the complete design for the Charnley house (1891; Chicago, Illinois). Although Wright called Sullivan his "Lieber Meister" and was considered "a good pencil in the Master's hand," Sullivan fired Wright for "bootlegged" houses that Wright designed while "moonlighting."

Wright then set up his own practice and soon established himself as a sought-after architect of cutting-edge homes for wealthy clients looking for something new. Wright was often uncompromising in his demands of his clients, pushing for free rein in the design of their homes. Such tenacity paid off. In the next twenty years, Wright fully developed a uniquely American architectural style, the prairie school, that did not look to Europe for influence as the beaux-arts style did. In this way, Wright continued the quest for a national style that had obsessed his mentor. But while Sullivan had first defined the elements of a skyscraper, Wright's most famous architectural contributions were anything but vertical.

Prairie school houses were often characterized by ground-hugging, horizontal designs with flat or slightly pitched roofs and broad overhanging eaves. Although Wright was commissioned to design houses for clients all across the country in this period, some of the best examples of the prairie school were built in the Midwest, where, despite their urban sites, they reflected the native landscape. In the Winslow House (1893; River Forest, Illinois), Bradley House (1900; Kankakee, Illinois), Clooney House (1908; Riverside, Illinois), and Robie House (1909; Chicago, Illinois), the development and variety of the prairie school can be traced.

Personal tragedy visited Wright in the prime of his career. An employee set fire to Taliesin and murdered Wright's lover and six other occupants, and his ground-breaking style fell out of favor after World War I. But ever the self-promoter, he continued to secure clients willing to look beyond the established styles of the day. In the interwar and post–World War II periods, he designed some of his most famous buildings, such as the Johnson Wax Administration Building and Research Tower (1939 and 1951, respectively; Racine, Wisconsin), and Annunciation Greek Orthodox Church (completed posthumously in 1961; Wauwatosa, Wisconsin). These buildings, like the rest of his designs in this phase of his career, were dramatic departures from his prairie school houses.

Like his mentor, Wright was also an architectural theorist, and expressed his grandest vision in Broadacre City, a utopian community that was realized only as a model. In the 1930s, he foresaw a bucolic, automobile-based community that in some ways resembles today's suburbs. To train aspiring architects, Wright established the Taliesin Fellowship, a kind of school, near Spring Green, Wisconsin (1925–1959). Like his Home and Studio (1889–1911) in Oak Park, Illinois, before it, Taliesin was a laboratory for Wright's ideas. There "apprentices" studied other arts and disciplines, in addition to architecture, as they worked at the facility, both maintaining and building it while helping with the commissions that came to Wright's office.

Despite his many other achievements, Wright will probably always be best known as the founder of the prairie school, a movement that included other important architects including Dwight Perkins (1867–1941), noted for Carl Schurz High School (1909; Chicago, Illinois); Hugh Garden (1873–1961) and Richard Schmidt (1865–1958), for the Chapin and Gore Building (1904; Chicago, Illinois); Walter Burley Griffin (1876–1937), for the Stinson Memorial Library (1914; Anna, Illinois); William Gary Purcell (1880–1965); and George Grant Elmslie (1869–1952), for the Woodbury Country Courthouse (1917; Sioux City, Iowa).

ART DECO

Just as the dominance of the distinctive Chicago and prairie schools faded, so did that of the beaux-arts style, though not completely until the 1920s. The transition to art moderne and art deco was partially made by stripping away the more elaborate elements of classicism to "streamline" it or by applying sometimes classically inspired decorative elements in exuberant, modern forms. Art deco was considered a style of the future and was used extensively in the Century of Progress, the 1933 World's Fair in Chicago. It was also a versatile style, and architects applied it to just about every building type, such as factories (Campana Building; 1937; Batavia, Illinois; Frank D. Chase and William James Smith) and railway stations (Cincinnati Union Terminal; 1933; Cincinnati, Ohio; Fellheimer and Wagner). Although the style is most often associated with skyscrapers, epitomized by New York City's Empire State Building and Chrysler Building (1930, William van Alen [1883–1954]), it was also very popular in smaller midwestern cities looking to present a modern face. Detroit, Michigan (Fischer Building; 1928; Albert Kahn [1869–1942]) and Kansas City, Missouri (City Hall; 1937, Wight & Wight) have large concentrations of art deco towers.

Art deco and art moderne skyscrapers are characterized by elements that together accentuate the height and verticality of the structures. Closely spaced and uninterrupted "piers" project forward from recessed rows of windows, often separated by dark "spandrels" between the tops and bottoms of the stacked windows, and rise to the apex of the building. The result, in effect, is vertical stripes. Another important design element of the style was the "setback." Rather than being sheer facades on one plane, like Chicago school skyscrapers, the facades of art deco and art moderne skyscrapers often step back, like a set of stairs or boxes of decreasing size stacked atop each other. While dramatically emphasizing the building's height, setbacks also responded to new urban zoning codes that sought to keep streets from becoming deep, dark canyons.

An early influential design for this style of skyscrapers was one of the 264 entries into the 1922 competition to design a new building for the *Chicago Tribune* newspaper. Publisher Colonel Robert R. McCormick wanted "the most beautiful office building in the world," and the winning entry, a neo-gothic design by New York architects Howells & Hood (completed in 1925), was widely hailed as a success. However, it was the second-place entry, by the Finnish-born Eliel Saarinen (1873–1950), that probably had the greatest impact on architects, especially on designers of art deco setback skyscrapers. Saarinen's entry was dramatically vertical, using the closely spaced piers and setbacks that would become the hallmarks of art deco and art moderne skyscrapers. However, despite his influence on the style, Saarinen's buildings are more idiosyncratic and cannot strictly be called art deco. His designs for Cranbrook Academy (1928–1942; Bloomfield Hills, Michigan), where he also taught, are perfect examples of his more personal style.

The Stock Market Crash of 1929 and the Great Depression that ensued put an end to most privately financed construction, yet building on a smaller scale continued through government "make-work" programs like the Works Progress Administration and the Civilian Conservation Corps. Mostly civic structures, such as post offices (Oak Park, Illinois, Station; 1933; White & Weber) and recreational facilities (Gooseberry Falls State Park; 1935–1940; Two Harbors, Minnesota; Edward W. Barber and others) were built, with many post offices in the art deco and art moderne styles, the recreational facilities often in the rustic style. As the country slowly recovered from the Great Depression, large construction projects were delayed further by the onset of World War II, but even before the war started, a new architectural movement had begun to make inroads in the region.

THE INTERNATIONAL STYLE

The international style, as its name implies, was not confined to just one region. Its roots reach all the way to Europe. Understanding development of the international style—or modernism—and how it became so prevalent in the Midwest from the 1950s to the 1970s, requires following its roots to the beginning.

The international style was a direct response to the social disorder and construction after World War I. Many of the old monarchical powers were defeated and destroyed, and with them their fundamental artistic and architectural values. New governing systems, artists said, demanded new artistic beliefs, and into the architectural void came the international style. The Bauhaus, an avant-garde school for industrial and fine arts in Germany, was an important source for these new ideas. It was founded by Walter Gropius (1883–1969) shortly after World War I but was closed by the Nazis in 1933, when Ludwig Mies van der Rohe was the director. Both fled Germany before the start of World War II, emigrating to the United

States and bringing their design philosophy with them. Gropius headed for Boston to become a professor at the Harvard School of Design; in 1938, Mies went to Chicago where he had been appointed director of Architecture at the Armour Institute, which two years later became the Illinois Institute of Technology (IIT). Mies would subsequently design almost twenty buildings, all in the international style, for the new IIT campus, the most famous of them being Crown Hall (1956).

Although the pioneers of the movement came from Europe, the name *international style* was itself coined in the United States after an exhibition at New York City's Museum of Modern Art in 1932. Co-curators Henry-Russell Hitchcock (1903–1987) and Philip Johnson (b. 1906), who would himself become an architect, surveyed architecture from 1922 to the time of the exhibition, mostly from Europe, and saw in all the buildings three similar characteristics. First, the buildings emphasized their volume rather than their mass. In other words, they defined the space that the buildings enclosed, not the area that the buildings occupied. Second, the designs relied on regularity rather than axial symmetry. Put another way, instead of dividing a building down the middle to create two mirror images of half of the façade, the designs repeated design elements along a plane. Finally, and most drastically, all applied ornament, elements that served no purpose except to be decorative, was gone. Ornamentation that made reference to historical styles like classicism was especially shunned. Instead, the beauty of the buildings was expressed in the proportions of their designs, the grace of the materials, and the quality of the craftsmanship.

Taught by modernists like Mies, an entire generation of architects learned these principles. They produced buildings that began to reshape cities, not only in the Midwest but around the world, thirty years after the international style had been defined.

The world got an early look at what the future would bring in 1922, when Gropius submitted his entry to the Tribune Competition. Adhering to the characteristics of the international style long before they had been codified, his building looked nothing like the other entries. Though never built, it exerted profound influence on later modernists, as can be seen in Mies's design for 860–880 N. Lake Shore Drive (1951; Chicago, Illinois). Just how different this pair of glass boxes looked when constructed can be seen by comparing them to the last skyscraper completed in the Chicago, only fifteen years before. Though "modern" by the standards of the day, the limestone-clad, art moderne Field Building (1934; Graham, Anderson, Probst & White) seems almost old-fashioned by comparison.

Although modernism would soon dominate design, it had its detractors. To Frank Lloyd Wright, who practiced architecture until his death in 1959, the international style was yet another European influence that had no place in the uniquely American style he was still pursuing. Yet to many, modernism was not so much a complete rethinking of earlier architecture as a return to the basic tenets of the Chicago school. With its strong structural expression and minimalist—for the day—approach to ornamentation, the Chicago school influenced modernists in Europe. Just as the Rolling Stones and other British rock bands borrowed heavily from American blues, so the international style had its roots in the Midwest as well. And both were also reintroduced to the country as if entirely new.

Yet while there are similarities between the Chicago school and modernism, just as there are between early American blues and the music of early English rock bands, many elements were altered as if through mistranslation. For instance, Sullivan's "form follows function" maxim seemed to have become "form follows structure," with many modernist designs dictated by the engineering systems employed to support them.

The skeletal frame of the Chicago school, stripped to the bone, was the precedent-shattering 860–880 N. Lake Shore Drive, which became the prototype for international-style "glass-box" skyscrapers that were built in most American cities, such as Mies's own Lafayette Park (1963; Detroit, Michigan). All these skyscrapers contained a glass-enclosed lobby recessed behind "pilotis" (stilt-like columns) and identical floors stacked under a flat roof. Though much shorter at just three stories, Mies's Home Federal Building (1962; Des Moines, Iowa) displays the same basic elements. There are, however, other ways to support a tall building.

The Ninth District Federal Reserve Bank Building (1973; Minneapolis, Minnesota; Gunnar Birkerts Architects Inc., architects; Leslie E. Robertson Associates, structural engineers) was the first building to employ a catenary support—a chain or cable anchored at two points as in a suspension bridge. To withstand wind forces, structural engineer Fazlur Kahn (1929–1982) employed a system of external cross braces on the tapering sides of the John Hancock Center (1969; Skidmore, Owings & Merrill; Chicago, Illinois). To brace the then world's tallest building, Sears Tower (1974; Skidmore, Owings & Merrill; Chicago, Illinois), Kahn engineered a "bundled tube" system. Nine square steel "tubes," each ending at a different height, were secured to each other, providing greater strength to the entire structure, much as twigs lashed together are stronger than the individual sticks.

Because the design of modernist buildings depended more on the structure than on the use of the structure, however, they varied little in appearance from one type of building to another. All black-framed glass boxes, 860–880 N. Lake Shore Drive and the Everett McKinley Dirksen and John C. Klusynski Buildings (1964 and 1974, respectively; Chicago, Illinois; Ludwig Mies van der Rohe) look strikingly similar, although their uses are entirely different: 860–880 are apartment buildings, and the Dirksen Building is a courthouse, whereas the Klusynski Building, adjoining the Dirksen, is composed of offices. Such consistency of design—or lack of variation, as critics would contend—is a large part of what ultimately caused the international style to fall out of favor.

Yet there can be great variety within the limitations dictated by the international style, as can easily be seen in Columbus, Indiana. Since the 1940s, this small midwestern city has brought to it some of the world's most prominent architects to design its buildings, creating a veritable living museum of mid- to late-twentieth-century architecture. The simple glass box of The Republic (1971; Skidmore, Owings & Merrill) encloses printing presses, which seem to be incorporated as part of the design. Sheer brick walls, punctuated by stark window and door apertures, characterize the Cleo Rogers Memorial Library (1969; I. M. Pei).

Cars Design Buildings

The centuries-old division between cities and the countryside was first blurred with the arrival of the railroads, which created fast and convenient transportation links between urban centers and outlying areas. The outlying areas could then be settled by people who worked in the city and who could afford to build homes in these new suburbs. Riverside, Illinois, ten miles outside of Chicago, was one of the first of these new suburbs, and many still consider it to be the finest.

Financed by eastern investors and planned by Frederick Law Olmsted (1822–1903) and Calvert Vaux (1824–1895), who also designed Central Park (1858–1878; New York City), Riverside's 1868 plan was laid out along the banks of the Des Plaines River, not in a grid of streets as in a city, but in meandering, tree-lined lanes. Along them were constructed homes and a village center for Chicago's business elite. Although Riverside was served by a railroad, Olmsted and Vaux had originally planned for a grand boulevard to Chicago to carry carriage traffic. It was never built, but their vision eventually came true, albeit with less landscaping, when automobiles traveling on multilane, limited-access highways became the prime form of transportation.

The impact of automobiles on architecture cannot be denied, though it is rarely cited in the discussions of individual buildings. Instead, their effect is measured in larger ways, such as how cities are planned to accommodate cars. For residential design, houses in middle-class suburbs were built farther apart and on larger lots than in cities. Alleys gave way to driveways that opened onto the street and led to garages placed at the front of the house. This was not, however, the design standard for more aristocratic communities.

Commercially, the urban department store gave way to the suburban shopping center, a collection of stores built around a parking lot. Sited in an upscale suburb, incorporating offices, apartments, and other elements in addition to stores—all built around a landscaped parking lot—Market Square (1916; Lake Forest, Illinois; Howard Van Doren Shaw [1869–1926]) was perhaps the first of such automobile-friendly developments. Tiny by today's standards, the trend it started nonetheless led to the shopping malls we know today, ultimately culminating in the largest in the country, Mall of America (1992; Bloomington, Minnesota; Melvin Simon and Associates, developers). Yet while Market Square faced the street with a welcoming Old World-inspired façade, today's large malls instead turn in on themselves, creating interior environments that do little to address the vista from the parking lot surrounding it.

Mall of America (1992), Bloomington, Minnesota. Courtesy Minnesota Tourism.

Suburbs were first established as residential havens from the city, but business soon followed. Yet, rather than relocating to suburban skyscrapers—which would eventually be built in the clusters near highway interchanges in outlying suburbs—businesses first developed corporate campuses. Clusters of low-rise buildings were arranged in park settings as in a university. Eero Saarinen (1910–1961), Eliel's son, designed the General Motors Technical Center (1948–1656; Warren, Michigan), in many ways transplanting Mies's master plan for the campus of the Illinois Institute of Technology (1940; Chicago, Illinois) to a remote site, but keeping the purity of the international style intact. For the John

Gateway Arch (1965), Jefferson National Expansion Memorial Park, St. Louis, Missouri. Getty Images/PhotoDisc.

Deere & Company Headquarters (1964; Moline, Illinois), Saarinen altered the formula somewhat, using steel that weathered, lending to the lakeside buildings an almost rustic look.

Probably Eero Saarinen's most famous building in the Midwest, if not the world, is the Gateway Arch (1965). Part of the Jefferson National Expansion Memorial in St. Louis, the Arch is sited near another engineering marvel, Eads Bridge (1874). The first bridge over the Mississippi at St. Louis, Eads's three steel arch spans were the first constructed with cantilever methods, eliminating the need for falsework—temporary supports that would have obstructed river traffic.

The migration of residents and business to the suburbs engendered by the automobile placed a strain on midwestern cities. One solution, also imported from Europe, was the large housing project. Between World War I and II, Swiss architect Le Corbusier (Charles-Edouard Jeanneret, 1887–1965) formed an entire theory of how people could live in tall apartment buildings arranged in a parklike setting. "Machines for living," he called them.

Such developments were adopted as an alternative to the crowded, blighted slums and ghettos of inner cities, and many were constructed from the 1920s into the 1960s. One of the largest developments of its kind at the time, Marshall Field Garden Apartments (1929; Chicago, Illinois; Andrew L. Thomas) was privately funded. Other efforts were publicly funded through state, local and federal governments. But despite noble intentions, high-rise apartment blocks often proved to be no housing solution for the underclasses. Projects such as Pruitt-Igoe (1956; St. Louis, Missouri; Minoru Yamasaki [1912–1986]; demolished) proved to be abject failures. Its destruction signaled the end to large-scale urban housing solutions and, it has been said, the end of modernism's ideals as well.

Also contributing to the hardship of midwestern cities was the social unrest of the late 1950s and 1960s. Civil rights, political, and anti-Vietnam War demonstrations helped instill fear of the cities, and its impact can be seen in the era's architecture. Unlike the buildings built before them, buildings of the international style often stood apart, placed in plazas. And often the ground floor was nothing but an empty lobby. Although this created an orderly setting, it did not translate into a lively streetscape, and often such places became barren and foreboding. One solution was to turn the building inside out, to look in on itself rather than out onto the street.

Though in a suburban setting, Atlanta-based architect John Portman's (1924–) Hyatt Regency O'Hare (1971; Rosemont, Illinois) is built around an interior atrium that all but denies its setting. Comprised of a center seventy-three-story building surrounded by six other towers of twenty-one and thirty-nine stories, the Renaissance Center (1977; Detroit, Michigan; John Portman & Associates) is probably the largest of these "cities within a city."

With the declining influence of the international style, and with a greater stress on contextualism—the integration of new structures with the existing built environment—such insular and isolationist influences also waned. The unregulated spread of car-based suburbs is also being rethought, as environmental and social consequences are reassessed. This too will have an effect on how midwestern buildings of the future will be planned, designed, and built.

POSTMODERNISM AND BEYOND

As its name makes plain, postmodernism came after modernism, but it also relates to styles that preceded it. Modernist architecture was not only very precise, but it was also, some critics contended, predictable, because in place of historically referenced ornament it relied on a set of strict rules. Parodying Mies's dictum, "Less is more," Philadelphia architect Robert Venturi (b. 1925) quipped, "Less is a bore," reflecting a willingness to look to the past, beyond modernism's formality, to historical influence for design and ornament.

There is a big difference, however, between the way postmodernists treated styles from the past and the way beaux-arts architects applied the design elements of classicism. The Allen Art Museum Addition (1976; Oberlin, Ohio; Robert Venturi) neither faithfully reproduces the renaissance revival style of the original structure next to it (1907; Cass Gilbert) nor strictly obeys the rules of the international style. Instead, the addition takes cues from the historic style of the original building and combines them with modernist elements, resulting in a design that is neither international style nor purely historical.

Once the modernist style's taboo against historically referenced and applied ornament was broken, architects took a wide open approach. Even international style prophet Philip Johnson hopped on the postmodern bandwagon. The 190 S. LaSalle St. Building (1987; Chicago, Illinois; Burgee Architects with Philip Johnson) incorporated gothic and renaissance elements, at once eschewing the international style and yet referencing it in the design's glass curtain wall. One of the most exuberant postmodernist designs was the result of another celebrated architecture competition—that for a new public library in Chicago. The winning entry for the Harold Washington Library Center (1991; Hammond, Beeby & Babka; Chicago, Illinois) borrows from the Chicago school, beaux-arts, and the international style to create a three-dimensional textbook of the major architectural movements of the region. Reflecting a sense of humor that postmodernists often incorporated into their designs, owls perch on the cornice, playfully evoking the wisdom to be gained within the library's walls. The drastic difference between modernism and postmodernism can be seen by comparing this library design to that of the stark, quiet dignity of the Cleo Rogers Memorial Library in Columbus, Indiana (1969; I. M. Pei and Partners).

At the other end of the spectrum, architects have also looked to free themselves from all historical references, including those of the now decades-old international style. Recent examples include the Quadracci Pavilion at the Milwaukee Art Museum (2001; Milwaukee, Wisconsin; Santiago Calatrava [b. 1951]), Case Western University's Peter B. Lewis Building (2002; Cleveland, Ohio; Frank O. Gehry [b. 1929]), and the Lois & Richard Rosenthal Center for Contemporary Art (2003; Cincinnati, Ohio; Zaha Hadid [b. 1950]). But while the last-named has been called the most important building completed in the nation since the Cold War, none of the designs can be considered products of the Midwest. Calatrava is based in Switzerland, Gehry in California, and Hadid in England, and they all came to these projects because of their international fame and reputation for buildings that they designed for other places. This reflects a trend of engaging well-known architects from outside the region to give new projects instant renown.

Architecture, like any other art or business—and architecture is both—is more and more subject to global influence. Yet the flow of that influence goes both ways. While midwestern architecture will never again be influenced solely by the people who live there, if indeed it ever was, midwestern architects still influence the architecture of the world, as they have for almost a century and a half. Considered within the region itself, the architectural legacy of the Midwest is rich indeed. Taken in the greater contexts of the nation and of the world, that legacy only becomes richer.

RESOURCE GUIDE

Printed Sources

Prehistoric Period

Birmingham, Robert A., and Leslie E. Eisenberg. *Indian Mounds of Wisconsin.* Madison: University of Wisconsin Press, 2000.

Chappell, Sally A. *Cahokia: Mirror of the Cosmos.* Chicago: University of Chicago Press, 2002.

Emerson, Thomas E., and R. Barry Lewis. *Cahokia and the Hinterlands: Middle Mississippian Cultures of the Midwest.* Urbana: University of Illinois Press, 1991.

Fowler, Melvin L. *The Cahokia Atlas: A Historical Atlas of Cahokia Archaeology.* Rev. ed. Urbana: University of Illinois Press, 1997.

Hall, Robert L. *An Archaeology of the Soul: North American Indian Belief and Ritual.* Urbana: University of Illinois Press, 1997.

Hively, Ray, and Robert Horn. "Geometry and Astronomy in Prehistoric Ohio." *Archaeoastronomy* 4 (1982): 1–20.

Kennedy, Roger G. *Hidden Cities: The Discovery and Loss of Ancient North American Civilization.* New York: The Free Press, 1994.

Kopper, Philip. *The Smithsonian Book of North American Indians: Before the Coming of Europeans.* Washington, D.C.: Smithsonian Institution Press, 1986.

Lapham, Increase A. *The Antiquities of Wisconsin: As Surveyed and Described.* Washington, DC: Smithsonian Institution, 1855. Electronic ed. www.library.wisc.edu/etext/Antiquities/.

Lepper, Bradley. "The Great Serpent," *Timeline (Journal of the Ohio Historical Society)* 15, no. 5 (1998): 30–45.

McDonald, Jerry, and Susan Woodward. *Indian Mounds of the Middle Ohio Valley.* 2nd ed. Blacksburg, VA: McDonald and Woodward, 2002.

Mink, Claudia Gellman. *Cahokia, City of the Sun: Prehistoric Urban Center in the American Bottom.* Collinsville, IL: Cahokia Mounds Museum Society, 1992.

Morgan, William N. *Prehistoric Architecture of the Eastern United States.* Cambridge, MA: MIT Press, 1980.

Nabokov, Peter, and Robert Easton. *Native American Architecture.* New York: Oxford University Press, 1989.

Squier, Ephriam, and Edwin J. Davis. *Ancient Monuments of the Mississippi Valley.* 1848. Reprint, Washington, DC: Smithsonian Institution, 1998.

Thomas, David Hurst. *Exploring Ancient Native America.* New York: Routledge, 1999.

Eighteenth Century to the Present (The Historic Period)

Andrews, Wayne. *Architecture in Chicago and Mid-America: A Photographic History.* New York: Harper & Row, 1973.

Condit, Carl W. *The Chicago School of Architecture: A History of Commercial and Public Buildings in the Chicago Area 1875–1925.* Chicago: The University of Chicago Press, 1964.

Gill, Brendan. *Many Masks: A Life of Frank Lloyd Wright.* New York: G. P. Putnam's Sons, 1987.

Hammett, Ralph W. *Architecture in the United States: A Survey of Architectural Styles Since 1776.* New York: John Wiley & Sons, 1976.

McAlester, Virginia, and Lee McAlester. *A Field Guide to American Houses.* New York: Alfred A. Knopf, 1993.

Roth, Leland M. *A Concise History of American Architecture.* New York: Harper & Row, 1979.

Smith, G. E. Kidder, and Marshall B. Davidson. *A Pictorial History of Architecture in America.* New York: American Heritage, 1976.

Upton, Dell, and John Michael Vlach, eds. *Common Places: Readings in American Vernacular Architecture.* Athens: University of Georgia Press, 1986.

Web Sites

Cahokia Mounds State Historic Site
www.medicine.wustl.edu/~mckinney/cahokia/cahokia.html

The best overall site on Cahokia, its layout, architecture, history, and exhibits.

CERHAS (Center for the Electronic Reconstruction of Historical and Archaeological Sites)
www.earthworks.uc.edu

CERHAS, at the University of Cincinnati, illustrates architectural and landscape reconstructions of the giant earthwork complexes throughout the greater Ohio River valley region.

Effigy Mounds National Monument
www.nps.gov/efmo/

Describes the extensive Effigy Mound National Monument, near Marquette, Iowa.

The Great Buildings Collection
www.greatbuildings.com

An online architecture reference, containing 3D models, photographic images and architectural drawings, commentaries and bibliographies for structures and architects. Linked to Architecture Week online magazine.

Indian Mounds of the United States
www.greatdreams.com/mounds.htm

Provides an interactive, state-by-state listing of links to mound and earthwork sites throughout the country.

Mound and Effigy Building Cultures of North America
http://freepages.genealogy.rootsweb.com/~sewis/mound_index.htm

Another list of links to mound and effigy sites, organized by state.

National Register of Historic Places
National Park Service
1201 Eye Street, NW
8th Floor (MS 2280)

Washington, DC 20005
Phone: (202) 354-2213 or 354-2210
Email: nr_info@nps.gov
www.cr.nps.gov/nr

Administered by the National Park Service, the National Register is the nation's official list of historically important sites, including the nation's more than 2,300 National Historic Landmarks. The Web site includes state-by-state search functions.

National Trust for Historic Preservation
1785 Massachusetts Avenue, NW
Washington, DC 20036-2117
Phone: (202) 588-6000
www.nationaltrust.org

Founded in 1949, the Trust is an advocacy group for the protection of places important to the history of the country, including architecturally significant buildings.

Ohio Historical Society
www.ohiohistory.org/places/topic.html

Provides descriptive links and access information for the many pre-historic and historic Native American sites in Ohio.

Skyscrapers.com
www.skyscrapers.com

The largest database of information on high-rise building, the site is searchable by building, city and companies.

Unified Vision: The Architecture and Design of the Prairie School.
www.artsmia.org/unified-vision/collection

A comprehensive online guide to The Architecture and Design of the Prairie School collection at the Minneapolis Institute of Arts, it includes virtual tours of buildings by a variety of prairie school architects, in addition to information about the material in the collection, considered one of the top three prairie school collections in the country.

Videos/Multimedia Resources

Hancock, John E., Project Director. *EarthWorks: Virtual Explorations of the Ancient Ohio Valley* (Little Miami River). CD-ROM. Cincinnati: University of Cincinnati/CERHAS, 2004.

Law, Thomas, Producer. *Searching for the Great Hopewell Road*. Videorecording, 60 mins. Cincinnati: Pangea Productions, 1989.

Museum and Site Resources

Angel Mounds, Evansville, Indiana: A new museum, well-preserved platform mounds, and a reconstructed "temple-house" and stockade illustrate effectively the architectural practices of the Mississippian culture.

Aztalan State Park, near Lake Mills, Wisconsin: Contains a pyramidal platform building, in the midst of what was a large, stockaded town of the Mississippian period.

Cahokia Mounds, near East Saint Louis, Illinois: A spectacular museum exhibit, the well-preserved remains of the Monk's Mound and a number of others enable visitors to understand both the monumental and domestic architectural traditions at the greatest of the Mississippian cities.

Dickson Mounds and Museum, near Havana, Illinois: A branch of the Illinois State Museum and a National Historic Site, this is one of the major on-site archaeological museums in the country, portraying 12,000 years of human habitation in the Illinois River Valley.

Effigy Mounds National Monument, near Marquette, Iowa: The site contains 195 mounds of which 31 are effigies. Others are conical, linear, and compound. The mounds date from about 500 B.C.E. until the early European contact period.

Fort Ancient: A computer model courtesy of CERHAS/University of Cincinnati is available at www.earthworks.uc.edu. Although preserved as an Ohio State Memorial, with a museum and walking trails that enable visitors to explore the Hopewell culture's largest and best-preserved hilltop enclosure, the site of Fort Ancient in Warren County, near Lebanon, Ohio is difficult to perceive from the ground due to its size and forest cover.

Grand Mound and Visitors' Center, International Falls, Minnesota: The largest mound in Minnesota, attributed to the Laurel Indians of the upper Great Lakes region, contemporary with the Hopewell.

The Great Serpent Mound, near Peebles, Ohio: Preserved as a state memorial, the world-famous serpent can be visited, viewed from an observation tower, and also contextualized on its "snakelike" rocky bluff overlooking Brush Creek and (in season) against the summer solstice sunset.

Hopewell Culture National Historical Park, Chillicothe, Ohio: Headquartered at the restored "Mound City" site, the park offers an interactive interpretive program including descriptions of the several large outlying geometric earthworks that it is in the process of acquiring.

Indian Mounds Park, St. Paul, Minnesota: Six surviving burial mounds atop a bluff and attributed to the Hopewell era about 2,000 years ago.

Lizard Mound County Park, West Bend, Wisconsin: About thirty well-preserved mounds, the largest of which is in the form of a reptilian creature.

Marietta Earthworks, Marietta, Ohio: Most of the ancient features drawn on Squier and Davis's plan of 1848 are preserved (except the low enclosing embankment walls) among the parks, streets, and monuments of this small, historic city.

Mounds State Park, Anderson, Indiana: A new museum and an exceptional collection of well-preserved, small earthworks illustrate variations on Adena and Hopewell earthen architecture.

Octagon and Great Circle Earthworks, Newark, Ohio: Two of the most spectacular remnants of the Hopewell culture's greatest ceremonial center are preserved here, including the precise circle-octagon lunar observatory and the monumental Great Circle with its interior ditch.

Ohio Historical Society Museum, Columbus, Ohio: Probably the premiere collection of Hopewell artifacts, presented along with descriptions of the earthwork and mound sites where they were discovered.

Rockwell Mound, Havana, Illinois: Within the town is one of the largest and best-preserved mounds in the Midwest, attributed to Hopewell times; it was also the site of Lincoln-Douglas debates.

Sheboygan Mound Park, Sheboygan, Wisconsin: An impressive cluster of thirty-three effigies of panther and deer.

Sun Watch Village, Dayton, Ohio: A museum and several beautifully reconstructed houses portray life in the eastern Midwest in Mississippian times.

Towasaghy, in southeastern Missouri: Remains of fortified village and important ceremonial center of the Mississippian era, centered on a large platform mound. A kiosk presents related exhibits.

Organizations, Museums, Special Collections

Chicago Architecture Foundation (C.A.F.)
224 S. Michigan Avenue
Chicago, IL 60604
Phone: (312) 922-3432
www.architecture.org/

Dedicated to advancing public interest and education in architecture and related design, C.A.F. conducts tours, holds lectures, displays exhibits, and provides other programs.

Columbus, Indiana, Visitors Center
506 Fifth Street
Columbus, IN 47201
Phone: (800) 468-6564 or (812) 378-2622
Email: visitcol@kiva.net
columbus.in.us/index.asp

Bus tours of the city's architecture are conducted year-round, and walking tours are offered June through October. Both leave from the visitors' center.

Cranbrook Educational Community
39221 Woodward Avenue
P.O. Box 801
Bloomfield Hills, MI 48303-0801
Phone: (877) 462-7262
www.cranbrook.edu

Founded by Detroit philanthropists George and Ellen Booth, Cranbrook encompasses art and science museums, house and gardens, K-12 schools and the graduate academy of art, some housed in buildings designed by Eliel Saarinen and Albert Kahn.

Frank Lloyd Wright Home and Studio Foundation
951 Chicago Avenue
Oak Park, IL 60302
Phone: (708) 848-1976
Email: flwpr@wrightplus.org
www.wrightplus.org

Wright's Oak Park home was a laboratory for his prairie school ideas and is open to the public for tours.

Taliesin Preservation, Inc.
P.O. Box 399
5607 City Highway C
Spring Green, WI 53588-0399
Phone: (608) 588-7900
Email: visitctr@mhtc.net
www.taliesinpreservation.org

Begun later than his Oak Park Home, Wright's Spring Green, Wisconsin estate includes buildings from every phase of his career, and is also open for public tours.

ART

Robert Stearns

The arts, in the broadest sense of the word, have traditions in the Midwest that date back to the useful and spiritual creations of Native Americans as early as 5000 B.C.E. The creators of these objects and sites did not consider them to be "art" in the Western sense of the word, yet they function as an indelible backdrop for their makers' descendants and the millions of immigrants to this region. Every indigenous and immigrant group that has lived in the Midwest has contributed unique visions that draw from ethnic and national heritages. They have created a full spectrum of artistic expressions that reflect the physical landscape and social environments that comprise the American Midwest, a region of the country that historian Frederick Jackson Turner called "the most American of American regions."[1]

Study of the arts of the Midwest Region reveals a recurring American trait: the separation of the "high" arts from that of the "grassroots." After documenting the history of westward expansion in the nineteenth century, art and artists took different paths in the twentieth. One path emulated European traditions and emerging trends in modern art, while the other celebrated everyday life through handcrafted objects and images of the common man. The first takes us on a journey from the founding of the Midwest's art museums to its centers for "advanced" contemporary art. The second begins with simple Shaker and Amish designs and the influence of the Arts and Crafts Movement and continues with the American Scene painters and post office murals of the 1930s. By the 1940s, when modern art prevailed over Regionalism, these roads could not have been farther apart. These paths found points of intersection in the 1960s when contemporary artists gained inspiration from folk art and "outsider" artists. By the end of the twentieth century, many leading artists now expressed their sense of self and place through a reexamination of personal histories, ethnic and cultural backgrounds, and their relationship to their immediate communities. These paths simultaneously affirm and challenge the notion of a "self-contained" Midwest as expressed by cultural historian Karal Ann Marling:

Whatever else it was or will be as hard geographic fact, the American heartland is a place that exists in the heart. It is a dream, like Lake Wobegon or Oz. A wish. A vision of perfection that belongs inside a glass snowglobe, safe and whole and self-contained.[2]

NATIVE AMERICAN ART

In talking about the art of Native Americans, it is important to remember that none of the hundreds of distinct languages spoken by Native American tribes have a word for the concept of art as we know it. For the Native American the creation of images and objects was integral to the nature of life, death, and the spiritual world and was not a separate elitist discipline.

The present-day Midwest occupies portions of two separate Native American regions: the western Woodlands to the east of the Mississippi and the eastern Plains to the west. The Woodland region is home to the Ojibwa, Winnebago, Kickapoo, Illinois, Peoria, Miami, Adena, and Potawatomi tribes, among others. The eastern Plains region is home to tribes including the Iowa, Missouri, Omaha, and Santee and Yankton Dakota.

Some of the earliest images known are pictographs (paint or other material applied to a rock surface) and petroglyphs (images carved into stone). These may be the oldest human-made visual images that remain of cultures that inhabited many areas of the country. In the Midwest, some of the most intriguing and numerous images, known as the Jeffers Petroglyphs, are found in southwest Minnesota. The Jeffers Petroglyphs site, located about 120 miles southwest of Minneapolis, is one of the most abundant collections of images, containing over 2,000 carvings of humans, animals, tools, and unidentifiable shapes by ancient Native Americans, appearing to reflect periodic use of the site over as much as 5,000 years. The petroglyphs are carved in a bedrock outcrop surrounded by vast prairie lands. The images do not appear to have been created by any one culture since their iconography can be traced to Cheyenne, Dakota, Hidatsa, and other tribes.

Another valuable collection of petroglyphs is found at the Sanilac Historic site near New Greenleaf, Michigan, about 80 miles north of Detroit. First uncovered after massive forest fires swept the Lower Peninsula of Michigan in 1881, the images may have been created 300 to 1,000 years ago. Some of the markings include relatively modern images revealing contact with Europeans.

Native American burial and effigy mounds are found throughout the Ohio and Mississippi River valleys, with the highest concentration found in southern Ohio. Indians of the Middle Woodland period constructed burial mounds to usher the dead into the afterlife. They offer a glimpse into the Hopewell culture that thrived in the area from

Raven effigy platform pipe, 200 B.C.E.–400 C.E. Courtesy Illinois State Museum of Natural History and Art.

about 200 B.C.E. to 400 C.E. Delicately carved stone pipes, cut copper figures, and wafer-thin mica shapes were placed beside and on top of the dead. The materials used—marine shells and beads from the Atlantic coast, mica from the southeastern Appalachians, and obsidian from the Yellowstone area—indicate that extensive trading networks linked tribes in distant parts of the region.

Perhaps best known of the burial mounds is the Serpent Mound, located about 70 miles east of Cincinnati, Ohio. It may be better described as an effigy mound constructed in the form of an uncoiling snake or dragon, and it is believed to have been built by the Fort Ancient Indians around 1000 C.E. Similarly shaped serpent effigy mounds are to be found in Scotland and in Ontario, Canada. The earthen mound measures a quarter mile in length and rises about 4 to 5 feet above the surrounding landscape on a bluff above the Brush Creek. Numerous burial mounds from the Middle Woodlands era are located in the immediate vicinity, suggesting that the site was considered sacred for thousands of years. Many interpretations have been offered to explain the meaning of the Serpent Mound's form. The oval shape at the serpent's mouth, for example, has been variously described as the serpent's head, an egg, an enlarged eye, or even the sun about to be swallowed.

The Serpent Mound, located about 70 miles east of Cincinnati, Ohio, was constructed in the form of an uncoiling snake or dragon. Courtesy National Park Service, Midwest Archeological Center, Lincoln, Nebraska, National Historic Landmark File.

Another significant site is Cahokia, near present-day St. Louis. The massive earthen mound is almost 100 feet high with a base measuring 1,000 by 800 feet. Cahokia is a key site of the widespread Mississippian culture that was ruled by a lineage of powerful chieftains who dominated a highly organized agricultural society for several centuries beginning in about 500 C.E. It was believed that the chieftains maintained their powers long after death through effigy images created in stone, shell, copper, and other materials. Some of these images bear strong resemblance to the iconography of the Aztec cultures of central Mexico.

Whereas painting and sculpture were male domains, women were responsible for producing clothing, textiles, and regalia. Vestments for formal events were considered the highest form of artistic expression in the eastern Woodlands and Plains. Because of their fragile nature, few of these items remain, but collections of them were assembled in the last half of the nineteenth century and can be found at the National Museum of the American Indian in New York City, the Detroit Institute

Cahokia is a key site of the widespread Mississippian culture.
Courtesy National Park Service, Midwest Archeological
Center, Lincoln, Nebraska, National Historic Landmark File.

of Arts, the Field Museum of Natural History in Chicago, and the Eiteljorg Museum of American Indians and Western Art in Indianapolis.

EUROPEAN ARRIVALS

Much of the Midwest is dominated by the Great Lakes whose huge bodies of freshwater are relatively recent geographic features created by recurrent Ice Ages. The Lakes provided easy access to the interior of the continent for the first European explorers who arrived in the 1600s. The virgin hardwood forests that covered most of the region were more difficult to penetrate. Early explorations were aimed at finding the "Northwest Passage," a water route that would permit trade between Europe and China. Abundant wildlife yielded valuable furs and a lucrative trade between Native Americans, British and Scottish traders, and the French Canadian canoemen. Early mapmakers charted the region, naming many of the geographic features for words in the local languages. As long as the lands west and north of the Ohio River remained open yet isolated from the growing colonies on the East Coast, a cooperative relationship existed between the indigenous peoples and the trappers and traders. In 1787, less than a dozen years after the nation's founding, however, the United States Congress passed the Northwest Ordinance, annexing the lands then known as the Northwest Territories that now form the states of Ohio, Michigan, Indiana, Illinois, Wisconsin, and eastern Minnesota. One of the most significant acts of the young Congress, the Northwest Ordinance did far more than add a huge piece of real estate to the country. Its articles proscribed how and by whom the land was to be settled. It forged the character of the entire region and offers clues to understanding the region's present-day culture.

The Northwest Ordinance called for the sale of land to people who would establish farms, businesses, and institutions of public education. It outlawed slavery, ordained religious freedom, and described how new states would be formed and governed. The Ordinance, conceived by Thomas Jefferson, came close to manifesting Jefferson's vision of a "yeoman" democracy: an elective, self-governing society founded on the values of self-reliance, land ownership, industriousness, and public spirit. Although the Northwest Ordinance contained specific provisions to protect Native American rights, property, and liberties, the provisions were soon forgotten as settlements were established and grew.

The first wave of settlers came from the increasingly crowded cities of the East Coast, and they brought with them the crafts and artifacts of New England and the Atlantic seaboard. Although some individual families set out on their own, many people moved into the Territories in groups often affiliated by religious beliefs. From the mid-eighteenth to the mid-nineteenth century, many sects of the

Christian Church, including the Shakers, Quakers, Mennonites, and Amish, found refuge from religious persecution and the self-imposed isolation they sought in the new states carved out of the Northwest Territories. The Amish, for example, were rooted in the religiously conservative Anabaptist movement that rejected all forms of ornamentation prevalent in the Roman Catholic Church. It wasn't until the late nineteenth century that Amish women began to create the subtle but beautifully crafted bed quilts for which they have become famous. The Shakers are well known for their stoic surroundings and for the design of their buildings, furniture, quilts, and utilitarian objects. They were unusual among the religious sects that founded communities in the region because they integrated visual elements into their lifestyle.

Other groups were bound together by national and ethnic origins. The earliest immigrants arriving from Western Europe were English, Scottish, and French, followed by Germans, Scandinavians, and others from Central and Eastern Europe, driven from their homelands by wars, famine and the possibility of a better life. Each group brought with it a distinct cultural signature based on ethnic and folk traditions. The present-day southwestern Indiana town of New Harmony was founded as a religious community in 1814 by German immigrants. It quickly became a successful farming center but was sold to Robert Owen, a wealthy Welsh businessman and social reformer. With visions of a progressive, intellectual utopia, Owen and his followers established America's first public infant school, kindergarten, trade school, women's club, free library, and dramatic club. In 1828, after only four years, Owen's experiment failed for lack of funds. New Harmony thrives today, however, reflecting a unique blend of the past and present. It is home to important modern structures designed by architects Philip Johnson and Richard Meier and the New Harmony Gallery of Contemporary Art.

Following the Northwest Ordinance of 1787, the two most significant events in the formation of the region and the country were the Louisiana Purchase of 1803 and the Homestead Act of 1862. The Louisiana Purchase added 800,000 square miles of territory west of the Mississippi River—including present-day western Minnesota, Iowa, and Missouri. The Homestead Act turned over those public lands and more to private ownership.

Although there was considerable settlement of the region before 1860, and the major cities of Chicago, Detroit, Cincinnati, and St. Louis were well established, the massive wave of settlers and the growth of the cities did not come until after the signing of the Homestead Act and the end of the Civil War. Throughout this century of growth, artists of a wide variety of talents recorded the enormous changes taking place.

ART IN THE EARLY NINETEENTH CENTURY

In the early nineteenth century, before the advent of photography, painting and the graphic arts were the critical means of recording history. Portraits, landscapes, and genre scenes were the most frequent formats. Subjects included political and military leaders, Indian gatherings, and scenes picturing settlers in everyday activities. Because few of the cities were large enough to support professional artistic careers, many of the artists moved from place to place. Two of the earliest itinerant painters were Samuel Seymour and James Otto Lewis, who recorded the signing of several Indian treaties in the 1820s and visited sites in Minnesota, Wisconsin, Indiana, and Illinois. Of the many itinerant painters, George Catlin (1796–1872) was among the most prolific. He was best known for his depictions of Indian communities, which he painted at Fort Snelling (now Minneapolis), Fort Dearborn (now Chicago), and other western outposts. Catlin lived in St. Louis from 1830 to 1836, using the city as a base for his wide-flung travels.

From the late 1700s to the mid-1800s, more artists were active east of the Mississippi, partly because of the earlier settlement of Cincinnati, Indianapolis, and Detroit. These cities were more closely associated with the culture of the Northeast. The outpost of St. Louis, far to the west, was another significant center for artists because of its location as the "Gateway to the West," at the confluence of the Mississippi and Missouri rivers.

Cincinnati was the earliest to develop as an artistic center and was considered the art capital of the Ohio River Valley region. With the steamboat allowing two-way traffic on the Ohio River, Cincinnati developed into a major port with the resources to support a community of artists. Fledgling museums and art academies were established in Cincinnati in the 1820s that helped attract and train artists from smaller towns and East Coast cities. Important support for the long-term development of art and artists in Cincinnati came from retired lawyer Nicholas Longworth. Longworth encouraged local sculptors and painters to travel to the East and to Europe to gain additional training and experience. He and subsequent generations of Longworths purchased art works, amassing a sizable collection that was displayed in the downtown Longworth home that today is known as the Taft Museum.

Among the best known of Cincinnati's early portraitists was Aaron H. Corwine (1802–1830) who painted portraits of Andrew Jackson and the Marquis de Lafayette in 1825. Robert S. Duncanson (1821/22–1872) was active in Cincinnati in the mid-1800s and is considered one of the finest artists of the period. Duncanson was born in New York State of Canadian, Scottish, and African heritage. He moved to Cincinnati in the early 1840s and established his career there. His dramatic landscapes were widely acclaimed. He began visiting Detroit in 1845, which for several years he considered his second home.

Sculptor Hiram Powers (1805–1873) arrived in Cincinnati with his family in about 1818. He received mechanical training and showed considerable artistic skill. He was encouraged to give up a post he held at a small museum and, with support from Nicholas Longworth, traveled to Washington, D.C., New York, and Boston, finally settling in Florence, Italy. Powers earned acclaim as one of the nineteenth century's most gifted sculptors. Like many of his fellow American sculptors, Powers had little choice but to learn his craft and establish a career in Europe. Powers' marble *Persephone*, first carved in 1839–1840, was so popular that nearly a hundred copies of it were produced and sold in Europe and America.

Detroit was the commercial and political center of life in the region between Lake Erie and Lake Michigan in the first half of the nineteenth century, serving as the territorial capital until Michigan achieved statehood in 1837 and as state capital for ten more years until the government center was moved to Lansing. As in other parts of the region, artistic activity in Detroit was largely limited to itinerant portraitists visiting from other cities. One of the earliest genre painters was

Thomas Mickell Burnham (1818–1866), who lived in Detroit in the 1830s. He departed for Boston in 1840, but not before painting *First State Election in Detroit, Michigan, 1837*. In his painting, the Detroit City Hall to the right forms an imposing backdrop to the motley crowd and the more frontierlike chaos in the background.

By the 1820s and 1830s, St. Louis became the leading artistic center of the western part of the region. After the historic transcontinental Lewis and Clark expedition of 1803–1805, William Clark settled in St. Louis and became superintendent of Indian affairs. Clark collected Indian artifacts and paintings of Indian leaders and villages. His contacts with Indian leaders were important sources of subject matter for itinerant painters who traveled through the region, including George Catlin. Many artists visited St. Louis in the mid-1800s to find portrait commissions and create panoramic views of the city on the Mississippi, which were exhibited throughout the region and on the East Coast.

The most famous Missouri artist of the period was George Caleb Bingham (1811–1879). Bingham initially worked as an itinerant portraitist and was largely self-taught, with brief apprenticeships and visits to East Coast academies and museums. His strong compositions, characteristic shading, and palette combined with innovative subject matter made his genre paintings very popular. His work was avidly sought by collectors in East Coast cities and sold through the American Art-Union lottery program in New York City.

Lottery programs were prevalent in the nineteenth century as a means for artists to sell works and for collectors of modest means to buy them. Subscribers to the Art-Unions bought "chances" to acquire works listed in a circular, and the proceeds were used to purchase the paintings and prints from the artists. The Western Art-Union was formed in Cincinnati in 1847—other Art-Unions were formed in other cities—and was, for a while, the most successful such scheme in the country next to the American Art-Union in New York. At one point, as many as 5,000 subscribers participated in the program before it was closed down owing to internal bickering and legal proceedings brought against it.

From the Civil War to the Turn of the Century

With increasing settlement and the growth of the region's cities after the Civil War, artistic activity expanded. Statehood for Iowa, Wisconsin, and Minnesota in the 1840s and 1850s brought economic stability and opportunities for artists to work and teach there.

The wave of German immigration that followed the revolutions in Germany in 1848 strongly influenced the makeup of Wisconsin's artistic community. Many of Milwaukee's artists of the latter nineteenth century studied in Berlin and Munich. Among Milwaukee's most influential painters and teachers were Henry Vianden (1814–1899), who emigrated from Germany in 1849 and remained in Milwaukee for fifty years, and Richard Lorenz (1858–1915), who first arrived in Milwaukee in 1886. Vianden and Lorenz's influence can be seen in their many students, who themselves became teachers and important portrait, landscape, and panorama artists, and established a number of art associations, schools, and galleries, some of which developed into the Milwaukee Art Museum.

Just as Wisconsin's artistic community was impacted by German immigration,

The Cleveland Museum of Art

The Cleveland Museum of Art opened in 1916 with a structure that combined utility and beauty with a design that set professional standards for museums well into the next decade. Arriving at that point was not an easy or quick task. Sarah M. Kimball was one of the first to propose that a museum should be built. In 1882, Mrs. Kimball briefly opened her large Euclid Avenue home to the public with a display of her art collection acquired during trips to Europe. She called her home the temporary gallery of the Cleveland Museum of Art.

Three people's bequests were critical to amassing the means to create the museum Mrs. Kimball envisioned. Hinman B. Hurlbut, Horace A. Kelley, and John Huntington left wills committing money and works of art for the purpose. J. H. Wade, grandson of the founder of the Western Union Company, gave land in the area now known as University Circle. Henry Clay Ranney, a lawyer, played the critical role of executor to all three estates and facilitated the Wade gift of land.

Without a professional museum administrator at the helm of the project, plans for the museum were in the hands of estate trustees and the benefactors' families. It was not until 1905 that the three estates agreed to join forces, each contributing money to build three connected but separately administered museums.

A decade more would pass before the Museum would finally open in 1916. Indeed, it took thirty-five years from the first bequest from Hinman Hurlbut to attain the vision of a museum. During the design process, the Hurlbut estate was discovered to be insufficient to build its part of the project, which forced significant reductions in the building's program. The revelation led to the formation of an entity to be known as the Cleveland Museum of Art, allowing for the construction and administration of a single institution.

Frederic Allen Whiting was hired as the first director of the museum in 1913. Whiting focused his attention on the task of developing important collections. In 1920, he promoted the then unorthodox idea of presenting the art of "primitive" Americans, such as Peruvian, Mexican, and North American Indians. He articulated the need for the museum to distinguish itself from other American museums by assembling unique collections beyond those of Classical antiquities and European masters. Whiting first pursued the arts of India, which later led to the museum's world leadership role in Asian art collections and scholarship. See www.clevelandart.org.

Minnesota's was colored by immigration from Scandinavia. The Dane Peter Gui Clausen painted theater sets, portraits, and panoramas of St. Anthony Falls. The Norwegian Herbjörn Gausta (1854–1924) first settled on a farm near Harmony, Minnesota, and later moved to Minneapolis. The Norska Konstförenigen, the first Scandinavian art society in the United States, sponsored exhibitions by Scandinavian artists from 1887 to 1893. The Minneapolis Society of Fine Arts was established in 1883 and the Minneapolis School of Fine Arts in 1886, directed by Stephen Arnold Douglas Volk (1856–1935), son of the influential Chicago sculptor Leonard Volk. Volk created murals for the State Capitol building in St. Paul, designed by New York architect Cass Gilbert.

Cincinnati reached a high point as an art center in the late nineteenth century with the presence of Frank Duveneck (1848–1919) and John Twachtman (1853–1902) and their followers. Both traveled and studied at the Royal Academy in Munich and were influenced by teachers who advocated the aggressive realism of French painter Gustave Courbet. Twachtman returned to Cincinnati for extended periods but also lived in Venice and New York City. Duveneck received little support in Cincinnati for his realist paintings, but he returned there frequently and began teaching in 1874. His instruction was important in the development of the next generation of artists in the Midwest.

Columbus and Cleveland, Ohio, both produced important artists in the later nineteenth and early twentieth centuries. Alice Schille (1869–1965) is among Columbus's most widely known artists of the period. She gained early training at the Columbus Art School (now known as the Columbus College of Art and Design) from 1891 to 1893 and further instruction under William Merritt Chase in New York. She returned to Columbus in 1904 and taught at the Columbus Art School until 1948. Schille is best known for her impressionistic watercolors and brilliant palette.

Archibald Willard (1836–1918) was one of the leading nineteenth-century painters in Cleveland. One of the founders and first president of the Cleveland Art Club, Willard created humorous popular genre scenes distributed as colored lithographs. He is best known for his painting *The Spirit of '76* (c. 1895), the depiction of a Revolutionary War fife-and-drum trio. For a city of its size and industrial wealth in the late nineteenth century, however, Cleveland offered few ongoing exhibition opportunities for its artists until the Cleveland Museum was dedicated in 1916.

Detroit's artistic and intellectual community came alive after the Civil War. After a thirty-year absence, the figure painter John Mix Stanley (1814–1872) in 1863 returned to Detroit where he lived until his death. Shortly after his return he began *The Trial of Red Jacket* (1863–1868). The picture recreates an early nineteenth-century meeting of Seneca Indians debating the topic of assimilating into white society. The picture was shown in Detroit, Buffalo, Chicago, and New York. Typical for the times, one- and two-painting exhibitions were taken from city to city, with small admission fees charged to cover expenses and provide income for the artist. *The Trial of Red Jacket* earned Stanley $8,000.

During the last quarter of the century, numerous art societies and associations were formed by artists and interested citizens in Detroit, including the long-lived Water Color Society, founded in 1883. The Detroit Art Loan Exhibition held in 1883 displayed almost three thousand paintings from Europe and the United States, including many by Detroit artists. The Art-Loan Exhibi-

The Detroit Institute of Arts

The Detroit Institute of Arts was founded as the Detroit Museum of Art in 1885 and dedicated its first building on September 1, 1888. It was created by forty civic-minded residents with an initial gift of $10,000 from Senator Thomas W. Palmer to purchase works for a civic art collection. William Brearley, advertising manager of the *Detroit Evening News*, raised an additional $90,000 in a few months to ensure construction of a museum building and initial operating costs.

The museum's collections began early with a gift from James E. Scripps, principal stockholder of the *Evening News*. The gift included seventy European Old Masters paintings, which became the core of the museum's collection of Dutch and Flemish masters.

Artist John Ward Dunsmore served briefly as the museum's first director but resigned to oversee its art school, which remained part of its program for a decade until 1899. Amand H. Griffith, director from 1890 to 1913, oversaw significant expansions of the museum's facilities. When these expansions taxed the original location, a new building was planned for a much larger site on Woodward Avenue. The site was purchased in 1910, but construction did not begin until 1922 due to a long legal battle over financial contributions to the private museum from the city of Detroit. A solution was reached in 1919 when the museum corporation gave its original building and all its collections to the city of Detroit and was reestablished as the Detroit Institute of Art (DIA), a municipally owned museum. The DIA remains a department of city government and is overseen by the Detroit Arts Commission, whose members include mayoral appointees and members of the Institute's staff. A separate, private, nonprofit organization, the Founders Society is a continuation of the original private corporation and provides support for purchasing works of art and funding major exhibitions and special museum services.

Construction of the Institute's new building on Woodward Avenue took five years and was dedicated on October 7, 1927, just two years before the Stock Market Crash of 1929. The ensuing Depression decimated city finances as well as the automobile-manufacturing fortunes of many of the Institute's benefactors. The museum was forced to operate with greatly reduced staff through the 1930s and into the 1940s, regaining strength after World War II. See www.dia.org.

tion inspired citizens to establish the Detroit Museum of Art, later known as the Detroit Institute of Arts.

Indianapolis became the center of art activity in Indiana in the later 1800s when a succession of art schools and artists' associations were formed to promote the work of local artists, particularly the Art Association of Indianapolis, which held regular exhibitions from 1883 to 1896. A number of artists were drawn to the city from smaller towns. With exposure to professional training, many of these artists, like others of the time, were influenced by the European styles prevailing in Munich and Paris. Artists Theodore Clement Steele (1847–1926), Samuel Richards (1853–1893), John Ottis Adams (1851–1927), William Forsyth (1854–1935), and Richard Gruelle (1851–1914) gained regional fame as the Five Hoosier Painters. By 1893, Indianapolis had earned such a widespread reputation as an outpost of modern artistic thinking that Steele and Forsyth were invited to show pictures at the 1893 Columbian Exposition in Chicago. The country's most avant-garde publication, *Modern Art*, was published for two years in Indianapolis.

To the south of Indianapolis, Brown County became the region's most active summer art colony in the first decades of the twentieth century when Steele purchased land, built a house, and invited colleagues from around the Midwest to join him to paint the primitive locale. Brown County remains a popular tourist destination.

Although challenged for supremacy by the rapidly growing cultural community in Chicago, St. Louis remained an important center for art in the later nineteenth century. William Merritt Chase, the American Impressionist, lived and worked in St. Louis in late 1870, and the city gained its most important asset in 1879 with the establishment of the St. Louis School of Fine Arts and the appointment of Halsey Cooley Ives (1846–1911) as its director. The school was associated with Washington University, and its collection would eventually become the St. Louis Museum of Art following the Louisiana Purchase Exposition of 1904. Ives was the region's leading arts scholar and educator and advocated the integration of the fine arts and crafts. Ives was appointed commissioner of the mammoth art exhibitions for both the Chicago World's Fair in 1893 and the St. Louis World's Fair in 1904.

Chicago so dominated the cultural life of Illinois that little activity elsewhere in the state is well documented. Chicago's artistic hegemony in the region began to take hold in the 1830s but was augmented by the 1855 arrival of George Peter Alexander Healy (1813–1894), one of the most famous portrait painters of the nineteenth century.

The 1859 Chicago Exhibition of the Fine Arts was a major creative event for the city, followed the next year by the formation of the Chicago Art Union, which operated an art lottery and an exhibition program. The Civil War slowed most cultural activities, but in 1866 the Academy of Fine Arts was organized to offer a school for training and galleries for exhibitions. The Great Fire of 1871 was a disaster for the city as well as its artistic community. The Academy building and many artists' studios were destroyed, and many artists left the city.

As in Detroit, many art associations were formed in the later 1800s, and one of the most important in Chicago was the Central Art Association, formed by patrons, artists, and writers. The Central Art Association promoted Chicago and midwestern artists through exhibitions, lectures, and publications. The Association published *Arts* (later *Arts for America*), which covered national news on the arts, but focused on the Midwest. The Association's mission was inspired by strong feelings that surfaced during the Columbian Exposition that "an art at once modern and American ought rightly to be centered in the Midwest, the American heartland, with Chicago as its headquarters."[3]

Sculpture in the Midwest experienced its first, explosive blossoming with the opening of the Columbian Exposition. American artists Daniel Chester French, Augustus Saint-Gaudens, and Frederick MacMonnies, among many others, presented a dazzling array of works in what Saint-Gaudens extravagantly called "the greatest gathering of artists since the Italian Renaissance."[4] MacMonnies created the elaborate *Barge of State* or *Triumph of Columbia* (1893) for the fountain in the grand lagoon. Most important for the region, however, was the placement of several works by Chicago sculptor Lorado Taft (1860–1936). Taft was both an artist and historian, compiling one of the first surveys of American sculpture, *The History of American Sculpture*, in 1903.[5] The dedication of Taft's *Fountain of the Great Lakes* in 1913 at the south wall of the Art Institute of Chicago marked a new era in the city's—and the country's—approach to art in the public realm. Taft received the commission as the first endeavor of a million-dollar fund established by Benjamin Franklin Ferguson for the creation of *publicly* owned sculpture. The effort was part of the larger concept of civic improvement born at the time of the Columbian Exposition, the City Beautiful program. Civic leaders across

The Art Institute of Chicago

The origins of the Art Institute of Chicago are rooted in the artist-managed Chicago Academy of Design, founded in 1866 and headed by sculptor Leonard Volk. The Academy provided classes in the fine arts and held periodic exhibitions in its galleries. The Academy building and all its contents were destroyed by the Great Chicago Fire of 1871. It managed to reopen in 1873 but was plagued by financial mismanagement that was exacerbated by an economic depression in 1877.

Recognizing the imperative of an institution devoted to the fine arts, a group of citizens founded the Chicago Academy of Fine Arts in 1879 and appointed William M. R. French as its professional director. The new Academy functioned in space rented at the corner of State and Monroe streets. In 1882, the new Academy changed its name to the Art Institute of Chicago and constructed a building at the corner of Michigan Avenue and Van Buren Street. In 1887, a new facility was built on the property, which by 1892 was also considered to be insufficient for the Institute's fast-growing needs. The trustees sold the property to the Chicago Club and looked to the managers of the forthcoming 1893 World's Columbian Exposition for a cooperative solution.

The solution was found in the construction of a hall for the World's Congresses for the 1893 World's Fair, designed by the firm Shepley, Rutan and Coolidge. Located off the main grounds of the fair, on the east side of Michigan Avenue at Adams Street, the building reverted to the permanent use of the Art Institute at the close of the exposition in the fall of 1893. That building remains at the core of the Institute's complex.

William French served as director of the Institute for thirty-five years until 1914, during which the Institute achieved its general architectural configuration. French oversaw the foundation of the museum's collections based on major private donations and the establishment of the School of the Art Institute, which has been the Midwest's most influential training ground for artists in the region. See www.artic.edu.

the country came to believe that art and well-designed buildings could improve the physical environment and moral climate of their communities. While the Beaux Arts and Neoclassical fashion of that era waned, the broad concept remains an influential force in city planning today.

Meet Me at the Fairs

By the end of the nineteenth century, with the U.S. territory stretching from the Atlantic to the Pacific oceans, historian Frederick Jackson Turner declared the American frontier closed. What had been the "West" at the beginning of the century was now bordered by the "Far West." People living in between began to see themselves as "in the middle," as *mid*western. Turner delivered his comments at a conference at the 1893 World's Fair—the Columbian Exposition, held in Chicago at the time of the quadricentennial of Columbus's arrival in the "New World." That Chicago hosted the *nation's* celebration of the event says a lot about how far Chicago and the region had come in little more than a quarter century.

Millions of acres of hardwood forests had been felled for farmland, and thousands of small towns grew to serve the farm families' needs with stores and banks and schools. In addition to the fertile farmland nearly everywhere, oil and mineral resources were discovered, and industry flourished. Mass production and assembly-line manufacturing created new steel, rubber, and auto industries. The Midwest was not only the nation's breadbasket; it had become its factory as well. The growth of the cities and industries had brought wealth, and wealth brought the ability to show off to the world.

The Midwest has hosted three major World's Fairs: Chicago's Columbian Exposition of 1893, St. Louis's Louisiana Purchase Exposition of 1904, and, again, Chicago's Century of Progress Exposition of 1933–1934. All three presented trade and technological innovations from around the world, but the first two made the most significant contributions to the arts at the time.

The Chicago Fair of 1893 was immense, with acres of white pavilions and palaces that dazzled the more than 27 million visitors. Walter Besant, commentator for *Cosmopolitan*, described it as "the greatest and most poetical dream that we have ever seen . . . it is Dreamland."[6] Among the many state, national, and international pavilions, the 1893 fair hosted large exhibitions of painting and sculpture in the Women's Building and the Palace of Fine Arts, a permanent structure that has been used since by the Chicago Museum of Science and Industry. Over 10,000 works of art were on view, including neo-Classical sculptures placed throughout the grounds. Halsey Ives, the director of St. Louis's Museum of Fine Arts, oversaw the exhibitions. In addition to works by American artists, the exhibition featured works from Canada, Western and Eastern Europe, Southeast Asia, Japan, Brazil, and Mexico.

Reviewer Ernest Knaufft noted with a hint of East Coast prejudice:

> Beyond the fact that the American exhibit shows that we take no second place in the art of the world, there is no great surprise in store for us. Most of our best art comes from New York or Boston. . . . The West has sent us no prodigies. . . . Thomas Moran [a founder of the Hudson River School] has no youthful follower.[7]

Most of the fair's architecture was neo-Classical in style. A notable exception was that of the Idaho pavilion whose exterior design resembled a Swiss chalet. Inside was one of the country's first significant displays of objects, furnishings, and decorations inspired by the Arts and Crafts Movement. Records show that nearly

18 million people visited the Idaho pavilion, making it one of the most popular at the fair.

The Columbian Exposition was an awe-inspiring sight to many, especially those who came to visit from small midwestern towns. Chicago window-display designer L. Frank Baum used it as an inspiration for his "Emerald City" that beckoned Dorothy and her crew from the Kansas farmland in his book, *The Wizard of Oz*.

If the Chicago fair was vast, St. Louis' Louisiana Purchase Exposition in 1904 was twice the size, covering over 1200 acres. The St. Louis fair also featured a large exhibition of domestic and international arts, again directed by Halsey Ives. The art exhibition was held in the Palace of Fine Arts, built specifically for the purpose of exhibiting fine art and the only permanent building on the exposition grounds. After the fair the Palace became the new home of the St. Louis Art Museum.

For the St. Louis exhibition, Ives approached the selection and presentation of the arts in a unique way. In his own words, Ives describes its organization as "a broader classification than has prevailed at previous international expositions. It has effaced the line that heretofore has separated 'fine art,' so called, from 'industrial art.'"[10] At the time of the Chicago Exposition, the Arts and Crafts Movement had not become visible enough to exert great influence on the world of art. Within ten years, however, its influence was so strongly felt that it succeeded in elevating the "crafts" to the level of the fine arts.

These two spectacular World's Fairs garnered international attention as they intended, but state fairs have been annual rituals of local life in the Midwest. While nearly every state in the union holds an annual fair in its capital city, midwestern states have defined the

St. Louis Art Museum

The St. Louis Art Museum was first known as the St. Louis School and Museum of Fine Arts, initiated within Washington University. It emerged from the university's patronage of artists to create works of art as early as its founding in 1853. Wayman Crow, a founding board member, and William Eliot, founding chancellor, led the efforts to create the museum as a department of the university. In dedication remarks on May 10, 1881, Crow announced that the museum's mission was "to educate the public taste, instil [sic] sound principles of aesthetic culture and foster a distinctly American type of art."[8] Washington University viewed the museum not as a storehouse of historical objects but as a catalyst for the creation of new art.

A young designer and educator, Halsey C. Ives, was selected to head the new school and museum. Ives's innovative approach to art education underscored the interrelationship of fine arts, design, and crafts through rigorous technical training and through examples of great art and design. His ideas were formed during his studies at what is now the Victoria and Albert Museum in London, and they echoed the philosophy of William Morris and the founders of the Arts and Crafts Movement. For his first exhibition in the new museum, Ives assembled the most ambitious collection of art to date in the region, including 143 paintings, of which nearly three-quarters were by living artists. He maintained the museum's emphasis on modern art and came to be considered the major cultural authority in the region, leading to his appointment as director of the art exhibitions of both the Chicago and St. Louis World's Fairs.

By the 1890s, both the university and its museum had outgrown their original downtown facilities. In 1894, the university purchased land on the edge of the city adjacent to Forest Park and created a plan for future expansion. At the same time, the St. Louis City Council began to pursue the possibility of a World's Fair to commemorate the centennial of the 1803 Louisiana Purchase. Similar to the strategic planning for Chicago's World's Fair that resulted in a new building for the Art Institute, the city of St. Louis and Washington University envisioned a permanent structure for the 1904 fair that would host the fine arts exhibition and, later, the relocated museum.

Officially opened on August 13, 1906, the new St. Louis Museum of Fine Arts was a popular success. Inspired by its mission to offer "an American art message for the world,"[9] the citizens of St. Louis passed a tax proposal the following year to help finance the museum, establishing the first municipally supported art museum in the United States.

quintessential statewide gathering of city and farm folks. State fairs serve to bring the far-flung farm and town populations together once a year to share in the harvest of fruits and vegetables, hogs and horses, tractors and bailers, but also quilts, crafts and paintings. The Ohio and Michigan state fairs served as important venues for the display of local and professional artists' works in the nineteenth century. Today nearly every midwestern state fair continues to provide an alternative to the established museums and commercial galleries for local and regional artists to exhibit their work.

Arts and Crafts

The movement known as Arts and Crafts began in England in the 1850s with the work of William Morris, John Ruskin, and others who sought escape from the overdecorated and mass-produced excesses of the Victorian style. The movement soon emerged in the United States, where its influences affected the most significant design reforms of the century. Its goals included "the revival of handcraftsmanship . . . the cultivation of the aesthetic of simplicity, and the elevation of decorative arts to the status of fine arts through design unity."[11] Aside from style alone, Arts and Crafts advocates had a more progressive social agenda. They sought to change society. They believed that "handmade objects were morally superior to ones made by machine and that these objects had the power to improve people's lives."[12]

The influence of the Arts and Crafts Movement in the Midwest is clearly seen in the designs of Chicago architect Frank Lloyd Wright, whose work is more fully explored in the chapter on architecture. Wright was drawn to the clean, unadorned sense of design and saw in the movement's philosophy an aesthetic that was eminently suitable to the open, earthy landscape of the Midwest. Wright's contributions to the movement can be seen in his designs for furniture, lighting fixtures, and windows.

The Arts and Crafts style and its progressive philosophy have had a long-lasting impact in the Midwest that continues today. An art pottery industry was already established in the clay-rich regions of the Ohio River Valley. The introduction of the Arts and Crafts style and philosophy immediately influenced the designs of Rookwood Pottery of Cincinnati. Founded in 1880 by Marie Longworth Nichols, a descendant of Nicholas Longworth, Rookwood in its early designs reflected Asian and European influences. Following the 1893 fair, Arts and Crafts predominated. Other art pottery studios including Roseville, Zanesville, Hull, and Weller Pottery operated in the Ohio Valley area. In Indiana, Overbeck Pottery, owned and operated by the four Overbeck sisters, was active in Cambridge City from 1911 to 1955.

Grand Rapids, Michigan, an important center for the production of furniture, held annual trade fairs in the 1890s. The Grand Rapids Furniture Fair of 1900 introduced the region to Gustav Stickley's "New Furniture," and the Charles P. Limbert Company of Grand Rapids (and later, Holland, Michigan) quickly adopted high-quality, handcrafted production standards for the creation of furniture and lighting under the name Holland Dutch Arts and Crafts. Grand Rapids was also the home of the Stickley Brothers Company, founded in 1891 by brothers of Gustav Stickley, who, like the Limbert Company, adopted the Arts and Crafts style around 1900.

An art pottery industry was established in the clay-rich regions of the Ohio River Valley. The introduction of the Arts and Crafts style and philosophy immediately influenced the designs of Rookwood Pottery of Cincinnati. Courtesy Cincinnati Museum Center, Cincinnati Historical Society.

Metals ranging from cast iron to copper and silver were important materials for Arts and Crafts designers. Chicago architect Louis Sullivan (1856–1924), Frank Lloyd Wright's mentor, designed ornate ironwork inspired by lush vegetation to adorn the façades and balusters of his buildings. John Pontus Petterson (1884–1949) from Norway and Julius Olaf Randahl (1880–1972) both settled in Chicago in the early 1900s and produced elegant works in silver.

The Arts and Crafts Movement influenced the field of graphic design, and midwesterner William Joseph "Dard" Hunter (1883–1966) was one of its leading exponents. Hunter worked as a graphic artist in the early 1900s at Roycroft, the preeminent Arts and Crafts studio in East Aurora, New York. Hunter expanded on the crafts of type design and handmade paper, creating a unique and recognizable style. In 1919, he relocated to his hometown of Chillicothe, Ohio.

The Arts and Crafts Movement fostered the establishment of training centers, schools, and colleges that promoted the aesthetic in the late nineteenth and early twentieth centuries. Because it advocated the equality of crafts and the fine arts, it benefited women who were encouraged to gain expertise in production techniques, providing a source of income outside the home. Still, men dominated the fields of design and studio management. Although the movement achieved many of its goals, its emphasis on handcrafted production could not survive the economic pressures of a growing market for furnishings, housewares, and other domestic goods in the 1920s, and the demand for inexpensive goods in the 1930s. Its legacy, however, is still with us. The easily recognizable Arts and Crafts style regained popularity at the end of the twentieth century, and today many artisan studios throughout the Midwest produce handmade goods still influenced by its aesthetics. The movement was largely responsible for the widespread interest in handmade crafts of all kinds and styles and the establishment in the 1960s and 1970s of arts and crafts associations in large and smaller cities that present annual and semiannual crafts fairs.

PICTURING THE SURROUNDING WORLD: THE AMERICAN SCENE AND REGIONALIST PAINTERS

World War I was a shattering experience for all Americans. Although the country was not attacked directly, thousands of American soldiers lost their lives and a sense of quiet isolation from the rest of the world was obliterated. People began to feel the need to understand what America was and who they were within it. Painters, writers, and composers explored the meaning of life around them by observing the characteristics of their particular region. The Ashcan School, so called because its artists depicted common people and places, was founded by Robert Henri, John Sloan, and others in New York in the early 1900s. After World War I, the Ashcan School provided inspiration to artists around the country to view everyday events as well. Capturing the "American Scene," its practitioners were primarily painters and graphic artists. American Scene painters were active from the late 1910s through the mid-1940s. The American Scene has been characterized as a primarily urban movement, while the Regionalists have been characterized as rural. Even so, the American Scene can also be understood as a larger, more encompassing movement including the Regionalists, Urban Realists, and Social Realists.

The American Scene was strong in the Midwest where the sense of being a "midwesterner" was relatively new and the need to define what that meant was especially strong. These artists sought to embody American identity through images of everyday life and work on farms, in small towns and big cities, and in shops and factories. For most of the second half of the twentieth century, modern art critics dismissed these works as provincial and unimportant. In recent years, however, a new generation of critics and curators has delved into these artists' works and has begun to reassess them and their place in history. They are now seen to have created a significant body of work that chronicled important transitions in the culture of the country. Their works convey more than the idyllic escapism of which they have been accused: a rich array of messages about the challenges of farm and city life, the effects of industry on society, and the abuses of political power.

Among many talented artists of the American Scene in the Midwest, four were particularly engaged by their surrounding worlds, and their images respond with visual power: Archibald Motley, Bernece Berkman, Clarence Holbrook Carter, and Joe Jones.

American Scene: Motley, Berkman, Carter, and Jones

City life was the principal subject of Archibald J. Motley, Jr. (1891–1981). Motley was born in New Orleans and raised in Chicago from the age of two. Motley took an interest in his African American heritage, maintaining contact with his family in the South. He studied at the School of the Art Institute of Chicago beginning in 1914, and through his training and the contacts he made in New York, he was prepared to participate in the renaissance of black culture that took place in Chicago and Harlem in the 1920s. Yet, he felt that the Afrocentric interests of many of Harlem's intellectuals did not give attention to a uniquely urban, African American culture that was developing. He chose to remain in Chicago; his stylized, vividly colored images teem with the life of Chicago's Southside Bronzeville neighborhood.

Bernece Berkman (1911–1979) was inspired by urban life and wove her sympathies for American workers into her paintings. Berkman was born in 1911 in Chicago and, like so many of her midwestern colleagues, studied at the School of the Art Institute of Chicago. She studied with two of Chicago's important early modernists, Todros Geller and Rudolph Weiseborn. They introduced her to Cubism and Expressionism and instilled the idea that art could serve as a tool for social reform. Berkman's energetic compositions verge on the abstract, yet exhibit her sympathies for the plight of workers and the poor.

Clarence Holbrook Carter (1904–2000) was born in Portsmouth in southern Ohio and attended the Cleveland School of Art from 1923 to 1927. He studied briefly in Italy and Paris, returning to Cleveland in 1928 where he taught at the Cleveland Museum of Art for ten years and served as the north-

Bernece Berkman, *Laundry Workers*, 1938. Oil on canvas, 40 x 30 inches. Courtesy Collection of the Flint Institute of Arts, on permanent loan from the Isable Foundation, L200337.

eastern Ohio supervisor of the Federal Works Project in 1937. In 1938 he completed a series of murals for the walls of the Portsmouth, Ohio, post office. From 1938 to 1944, Carter lived in Pittsburgh and later moved to Bucks County, Pennsylvania. Two distinct periods mark his works: an almost surreal Magic Realism that captured locales of his Ohio boyhood and, later, completely abstract studies in form and color.

Joe Jones (1909–1963) was born in St. Louis, Missouri. He was largely self-taught and yet garnered national respect for his paintings that reflected the spirit of the American Scene and conveyed his strong political and social convictions. After his social activism drew intense criticism in his native St. Louis, he chose to move to New York in 1935. He was awarded a Guggenheim Fellowship in 1937 and was commissioned to create five large murals by the Works Progress Administration (WPA) for post offices in Kansas, Arkansas, and Missouri. His works are marked by their strong composition and graphic presentation of their messages.

There were many other artists active in the Midwest at the time associated with a variety of approaches ranging from forms of Magic Realism, Social Realism, and American Expressionism. The often ethereal images of Charles Burchfield, the

Clarence Holbrook Carter, *Outside the Limits*, 1938–1946. Oil on canvas. Courtesy Allentown Art Museum.

precisionist modernism of Edmund Lewandowski, and the earth-toned, expressionist paintings of Zoltan Sepeshy attest to the diversity of manifestations of the American Scene. Although these and others were widely exhibited, their names and works were less visible to the general public than the Midwest's most celebrated trio of artists, Thomas Hart Benton of Missouri, John Steuart Curry of Kansas, and Grant Wood of Iowa.

Benton, Curry, and Wood

By the mid-1930s, Grant Wood (1891–1842), Thomas Hart Benton (1889–1975), and John Steuart Curry (1897–1946) were known collectively as the Regionalists. Their predominantly rural and farm-life images were exhibited widely and reproduced frequently in nationally circulated magazines such as *Time* and *Life*. This national visibility brought public attention to their images. For many people in the country, their pictures epitomized the quintessential Midwest.

Wood, Benton, and Curry were established as artists long before the Regionalist label was coined. Conservative critic Thomas Craven promoted the style and praised it for its accessibility to the general public. The three artists barely knew one another before 1934. In the 1910s and 1920s, each studied art in the Midwest, traveled to New York and Europe, and immersed himself in techniques of "advanced modern art." However, they all eventually returned to the Midwest to explore what they felt was a new kind of modernism, a style that eschewed abstraction in favor of a narrative realism and that conveyed pictures of the people and places around them. By examining the specific details of the lives of everyday people, they strove to uncover the universality of humankind. Both Wood and Curry died in the 1940s at the early ages of fifty-one and forty-nine, respectively. Thomas Hart Benton would live into the mid-1970s and witness the demise of Regionalism and the rise of Abstract Expressionism, led by Jackson Pollock, one of Benton's own students.

Benton was born in 1889 in Neosho, Missouri, to a family of prominent politicians. Early in life he resolved to become an artist, enrolling at the School of the Art Institute of Chicago at the age of seventeen and continuing his studies in Paris at the Academie Julian for three more years. He returned to New York City in 1911 and experimented with many styles of modern art. Dissatisfied with all of them, he returned to an inventively composed, figurative style that would become his signature. While in New York, Benton created a series of murals titled *America Today* for the New School of Social Research. These dynamic images reflected Benton's view of American life with energetic compositions and an unusual use of space that intertwined the overlapping narratives.

Benton became familiar with the techniques of filmmaking and the social power of the medium of cinema while designing soundstage sets in Hollywood, which had a significant effect on his large mural projects. The Whitney Museum of American Art commissioned his next set of murals, *The Arts of Life in America* (1932). By focusing on popular culture and leisure, Benton proposed that "Americans could discover regenerative spiritual and communal values by embracing indigenous folk culture."[13] His last mural project of the decade was carried out in his home state of Missouri for the Missouri Statehouse in Jefferson. *A Social History of the State of Missouri* (1935–1936) celebrated the people and cultures of the state. With its completion, Benton returned permanently to Missouri to teach at the Kansas City Art Institute but not before delivering a diatribe against the New York art world. Benton's combative manners and the rising tide of abstract modern art led to his dismissal from his teaching job in 1941. He continued to paint until his death in Kansas City in 1975.

Grant Wood was born on a farm near Anamosa, Iowa, in 1891. He lived in near isolation from the larger world until his father died in 1901 when the family moved to Cedar Rapids, Iowa. Wood's artistic talents were recognized early. He contributed drawings to the school yearbook and designed theater sets with his friend and future artistic colleague, Marvin Cone. Upon graduation in 1910, Wood went to Minneapolis to enroll in a summer course at the Minneapolis School of Design and Handicraft to study with Ernest Batchelder, a nationally known architect and designer in the Arts and Crafts style. In 1913, Wood moved to Chicago and took night courses at the School of the Art Institute of Chicago, returning to Cedar Rapids in 1919 where he taught in public schools until 1925.

The 1930 exhibition of *American Gothic* at the Art Institute of Chicago made Wood's name a household word in America. His opportunities expanded in all directions, but rather than leave Iowa, he chose to further root his career there. He established the Stone City Colony and Art School in 1932. John Steuart Curry joined Wood there as a guest teacher in 1933. In 1934, Wood took a teaching appointment at the University of Iowa and moved to Iowa City. It was not until this time that he met Thomas Hart Benton.

At the height of the Great Depression, Wood, like others at the time, faced deprivation by embracing visions of a better time. The quirky geometry of *Spring*

Turning (1936), for example, shows Wood at his most minimal and sensual. Historian Wanda Corn observed, "Mingling eroticism with ecstasy, Wood made the relationship between the farmer and the landscape into a Wagnerian love duet."[14]

John Steuart Curry was born in 1897 on a farm near Dunavant, Kansas. Like Wood, he showed artistic talent at a young age, and both his mother and father accepted and supported his desire to become an artist. He left high school early, briefly attended the Kansas City Art Institute, and studied for two years at the School of the Art Institute of Chicago. Curry spent the next decade and a half in and around New York City and did not return to the Midwest until 1936. Initially, he set about to be an illustrator and by the age of twenty-four was illustrating stories in *Boy's Life* and *The Saturday Evening Post*. Within a few years, however, his editors complained that his work was too much like painting, and he received fewer and fewer commissions. With help from friends, he studied for eight months in Paris, returning to the United States in 1927. His first major painting, *Baptism in Kansas* (1928), gained the attention of critics and of Gertrude Vanderbilt, who granted Curry a $200-a-month stipend to allow him to concentrate on painting. Subsequent works focused on midwestern subjects and themes, even though he continued to work in New York. He was a guest instructor at the Cooper Union and the Art Students League in New York City and, in 1935, was commissioned by the Federal Arts Project to create a mural for the Department of Justice Building in Washington, D.C. In 1936 he returned to the Midwest when he was appointed artist-in-residence at the University of Wisconsin, Madison, where he would remain until his death ten years later. His association was not with the Art Department but with the Department of Agriculture, a unique appointment in American universities, and one that recognized his penchant for canvases of farm life. Curry did not press for innovation but reflected more about art and what its role should be. During these years he achieved one of his life's goals of making art that was relevant to the daily lives of rural men and women.

Far from a cultural backwater, Madison and its university were at the forefront of midwestern progressive thinking, and it was progressive to portray farm life as a hallowed calling. In Madison, Curry produced two of his most masterful works: *Wisconsin Landscape* (1937–1939) and a study for an uncompleted mural for the Statehouse in Topeka, Kansas, *John Brown* (1939). *Wisconsin Landscape* is a sylvan tableau, yet also a dynamic composition of horizontal bands of color flecked with sunlight and shadows created by the scudding clouds. A careful reading also reveals it as a study of the advanced farming techniques of crop rotation and soil conservation that would have saved many midwestern farms from devastation during the Dust Bowl years.

MODERN ART COMES TO THE MIDWEST

As the 1930s came to a close and war broke out in Europe, the psychological landscape of America began to shift again. While those changes were occurring everywhere, Iowa City was the site of a tempest that illustrates the situation. Grant Wood had been associated with the University of Iowa since 1934. For the next few years he was the university's brightest celebrity. At first he was greeted with acclaim because he brought a liberal point of view to the previously conservative

The WPA's Treasury Section of Fine Arts and Federal Arts Project

Shortly after his inauguration in 1933, President Roosevelt and his administration moved quickly to create the New Deal to address the massive levels of unemployment that had spread in the years following the Stock Market Crash in 1929. The midwestern drought and crop failures of 1935 and 1936 added thousands of dispossessed farm families to the burdens of the federal government. The Works Progress Administration (WPA) was formed in May 1935 to create jobs. Within the WPA, two programs addressed the needs of artists. The Treasury Relief Art Project or the Treasury Section of Fine Arts, run by the Treasury Department, employed artists to create works for existing federal buildings. The Federal Project Number One (Federal One) was an agency under the WPA that employed writers, performing artists, and visual artists for all kinds of activities. It was made up of four divisions, one of which was the Federal Art Project (FAP). The FAP was allocated the largest amount of money. Its director, Holger Cahill, was convinced that his mission was greater than just employing artists: that it was to foster a renaissance of American art, a democratic American art that would become a part of everyone's daily lives.

Occurring at the zenith of the reputations of Benton, Wood, and Curry, much—but not all—of the output of artists employed by the New Deal programs emulated the realist format and local subject matter that made the Regionalists' works popular and accessible to the general public. The Treasury Section of Fine Arts was responsible for the creation of hundreds of murals that decorated the lobbies of post offices in rural communities throughout the country.[15] The Federal Arts Project also commissioned murals as well as a number of other relief programs.

The Farm Security Administration

The New Deal's efforts to aid dispossessed midwestern and southern farm families included low-cost loans, housing assistance, and land renewal projects through the Resettlement Administration, which in 1937 would become known as the Farm Security Administration (FSA). To promote and justify its massive and expensive efforts, the FSA created its Historical Section to document the plight of families and gain popular support for its work. Roy Stryker headed the effort to "introduce America to Americans."[16] Stryker hired some of the country's best photographers to carry out his plan: Walker Evans, Dorothea Lange, Arthur Rothstein, and Russell Lee in the beginning. Although Lee remained throughout, the others left and new artists joined the staff, including Marion Post Wolcott, John Vachon, and Gordon Parks. The program achieved many of its goals, not the least of which was to document a society in transition. It was not focused exclusively on the Midwest, but through the newly founded mass-media magazines, *Life* (established in 1936) and *Look* (established in 1937), images of life in the Midwest entered millions of American homes. Thousands of negatives produced during the project's lifetime are now housed at the National Archives in Washington, D.C., and are available to everyone for the cost of printing.

academic environment. Six years later, however, with younger faculty members arriving, Wood's focus on local subjects and themes was seen as reactionary, even dangerously nationalistic. Academic squabbles between Wood and his department chairman were nasty enough, but the arrival of the then young Horst W. Janson, the eminent art historian and future author of the ubiquitous text, *The History of*

In 1937 the Farm Security Administration (FSA) created its Historical Section to document the plight of farm families and gain popular support for its work. The program achieved many of its goals, not the least of which was to document a rural society in transition. Photograph by Marion Post Wolcott, Minneapolis, Minnesota, 1941. Courtesy Library of Congress.

Art, was more significant on a national scale. Janson, a champion of European modern art, published several articles that condemned Wood and the other Regionalists, citing the parallel between their style and the Social Realism that was acceptable to the German Nazis. By associating Realism with Fascism, Janson destroyed Wood and Regionalist painting, consigning it to the dustbin of American art history for decades.

Janson's arrival in Iowa City in 1939 coincided with a wave of interest in modern art in the Midwest and around the country. Hungarian-born artist László Moholy-Nagy arrived in Chicago in 1937 seeking refuge from impending war in Europe. There he had established what has been referred to as the New Bauhaus and the Institute of Design and claimed, with others, that the principles of modern art and the new technologies aligned with it were the true conveyors of "democratic" values. His use of kinetic technologies, sometimes called constructivism, powerfully influenced artists working in media as diverse as film and sculpture.

New York's Museum of Modern Art had been established in 1929 to provide an institutional endorsement for what had been an exclusively European artistic expression. The museum's director, Alfred Barr, approached the subject in a broad and inclusive manner, presenting painting and sculpture, of course, but also photography as well as graphic, architectural, and industrial design. This broad view of art appealed to the midwestern pragmatic way of thinking, and groups interested in learning more about modern art began to assemble in large and midsized cities.

One of the first of these associations was founded in 1939 in Cincinnati, Ohio, as the Modern Art Society, spearheaded by three of the city's prominent women: Rita Rentschler, Betty Pollak, and Peggy Frank Crawford, wife of the American painter Ralston Crawford. The Modern Art Society was originally housed in the basement of the Cincinnati Art Museum where it presented exhibitions and lectures through the 1940s and 1950s. Its activities and the scale of the art it presented grew. Inspired by the Museum of Modern Art, the Modern Art Society featured displays of modern domestic, industrial, and graphic design in addition to exhibitions of painting and sculpture.

Minneapolis's Walker Art Center was at the forefront of these midwestern modern art outposts, with a building of its own and an important collection of modern art developing as early as the mid-1940s. Many others, like Cincinnati's Modern Art Society, were special interest groups that were initially housed within their city's established art museum, later to reestablish themselves as separate entities with their own buildings. In Chicago, collectors of modern art whose interests were not sufficiently addressed by the Art Institute of Chicago created the Museum of Contemporary Art. Cleveland's Museum of Contemporary Art began as the New Gallery, a commercial space catering to local collectors. Later reestablished as a nonprofit institution, it operated as the Cleveland Center for Contemporary Art before becoming the Museum of Contemporary Art Cleveland. Rather than forming a conventional art center, the city of Columbus, Indiana, and members of the families of the founder of Cummins Engine Company, have created a unique community by commissioning architects from around the country and the world to design nearly every major structure in the town. Here major works of art can be found, including an amusing kinetic "clock" by French sculptor Jean Tinguely and a large bronze by English sculptor Henry Moore.

After the War: Contemporary Art in the Midwest

Before World War II, Paris had reigned as the art capital of the world. Following the war, the spotlight shifted to New York with the emergence of Ab-

Walker Art Center

The Walker Art Center began with the vision of Thomas Barlow Walker, who made his fortune in the lumber industry and real estate speculation. In 1874, Walker began to collect paintings and prints for his Minneapolis home which he opened to the public in 1879. By the 1920s, the Walker Art Galleries had expanded so greatly that a private foundation was established and a new building constructed on Lyndale Avenue, the site of the present museum. The newly named Walker Art Gallery opened in May 1927, a few months before Walker's death.

During the Depression, the Walker Art Gallery, like many other museums in the country, operated with a minimal staff. But unlike other museums, the Walker Art Gallery would undergo a fundamental transformation during the period. Without T. B. Walker's personal passion and with its fortunes drastically reduced, the T. B. Walker Foundation had few resources to support the Gallery's activities. By 1938, the museum was "practically defunct."[17] Alternatives for the building's use had to be explored. The newly formed Minnesota Arts Council was seeking exhibition opportunities for Minnesota artists, and Walker family members agreed to let the Council use the Gallery but provided no financial assistance. Assistance was found through the New Deal's Federal Art Project, which was promoting a program to support community-based art centers around the country. Discussions among all involved led to a dramatic change in the purpose and function of the Walker Art Gallery.

The new operation would reinstall the T. B. Walker collections, add present exhibitions of Minnesota artists, and provide free workshops in the arts and a variety of other services to area artists and community organizations. The aim of the new art center was to encourage the "average man to participate in the experience of art . . . actual participation rather than passive appreciation."[18] Daniel Defenbacher, director of the WPA's community art center program, was persuaded to relocate to Minneapolis to become the first director of the "new" Walker Art Center, which opened in 1940.

Federal support did not last more than a few years, but its leverage instilled a new multidisciplinary focus quite different from Mr. Walker's original concept. The Walker Art Center's collections and programs would now focus exclusively on contemporary art and later embrace the media of film and performing arts. See www.walkerart.org.

Midwest but Not Midwest

Throughout the twentieth century, many significant artists who were born and raised in the region chose to pursue their careers elsewhere. Many relocated in the nation's cultural capital, New York City. Among notable examples are urban realist painter George Bellows (1882–1925), a leading figure of the Ashcan School, and Pop artist Roy Lichtenstein (1923–1997), both of whom were raised in Columbus, Ohio. Bellows frequently visited his hometown but maintained his residence in New York. Similarly, Midwest-born designer Russel Wright (1904–1976) had early aspirations to become a farmer but followed a successful career in New York as one of the country's best-known designers of furniture, ceramics, and other household items. Contemporary artists Leon Golub (1922–), Nancy Spero (1926–), Jim Dine (1935–), and artist/architect Maya Lin (1959–), among many others, have strong ties to the Midwest, but like Bellows, Lichtenstein, and Wright have found New York to be a productive location for their work.

Conversely, some artists are well known for their depictions of the Midwest, yet never lived in the region. Charles Sheeler (1883–1965), for example, who was fascinated with the industrial age and its machines, created many paintings and photographs of midwestern factories, particularly the Ford Company's River Rouge plant near Detroit. Sheeler, however, was born and raised in Philadelphia and remained on the East Coast most of his life.

stract Expressionism and the energetic paintings of Jackson Pollock and Willem de Kooning and the sculptures of David Smith, among others. William Burroughs was leading the beatnik poets, and Jack Kerouac was "on the road." More mobile than ever before, American artists gravitated to New York, many leaving their midwestern homes to seek communal inspiration in Manhattan's Greenwich Village.

Midwestern museums and modern art centers introduced their visitors to the new ideas coming from New York. Increasingly, the new art was referred to as "contemporary art," distinguishing it from "modern art" as both postwar and American-based. The modern art associations and societies gradually changed their names to reflect the new perspective, becoming museums and centers of contemporary art. With an expanding economy, the mid-1960s through the 1980s was an era of growth and vitality for these centers, a period spanning the height of the popularity of Andy Warhol and Roy Lichtenstein's Pop Art, through the white-hot investment art market of the 1980s that introduced the work of New York artists Keith Haring, David Salle, Julian Schnabel, and others. There was an eager and growing audience for special exhibitions that were ushered in with wild parties, at which guests arrived in "dress-as-the-art" fashions. It was "in" to be Pop and hip to be minimal. The art of the 1960s embodied the broader culture's sense of daring and rebellion, as was reflected in many of the exhibitions.

Many large and medium-sized cities in the Midwest developed a cadre of artists who forged unique visual vocabularies in the 1950s and 1960s. Among those to become most visible nationally were Charles Biederman, Richard Anuszkiewicz, and Julian Stanczak in Chicago and Cleveland. While their styles could not have been more different outwardly, they shared a respect for craftsmanship in the production of their works.

Curator Patricia McDonnell has described Charles Biederman (1906–) as the "sage of Red Wing, Minnesota."[19] Born in Cleveland and trained in Chicago, New York, and Paris, Biederman has lived since 1942 in Red Wing, a small town on the Mississippi River about forty miles southeast of Minneapolis. Although he has worked in near isolation from cosmopolitan art worlds for more than sixty years, his vibrantly colored, intricately crafted, geometric reliefs can be found in the most important museum collections around the world. Biederman's compositions are derived from his observation of nature. His works are not pictorial renditions of that nature, however. Rather, they are sensory responses to the light, shade, color, and space of the Minnesota forests and fields. Furthermore, their dimensional quality reveals unique perspectives from different angles, encouraging a viewer's direct engagement with the works.

Born in Cleveland in 1906 of Czechoslovakian parents, Biederman grew up in Cleveland and enrolled at the School of the Art Institute of Chicago in 1926. He was attracted to the Art Institute's collections of European modern art and moved to New York in 1934 to make contact with the cutting edge of modernism. After a year in Paris in 1936 and a few more years in New York, Biederman returned to Chicago disenchanted with what he felt to be Paris and New York's trendy environments. Increasingly drawn to nature as a primary source of inspiration, Biederman moved further away from the metropolis in 1942 to Red Wing where he has created hundreds of works and self-published thirteen volumes of observations on modern art.

Richard Anuszkiewicz (1930–   ) and Julian Stanczak (1928–   ) both graduated from the Cleveland Institute of Art, and both studied under color theorist Josef Albers at Yale University. Stanczak was born in Poland and Anuszkiewicz in Erie, Pennsylvania, of Polish immigrant parents. Their work rose to prominence in New York art circles in the late 1950s and 1960s with exhibitions in private galleries. Stanczak's exhibition at the Martha Jackson Gallery in New York was titled "Optical Art," which was shortened in an article in *Time* magazine to "Op Art" for its rigorous geometry and optical play of color and line. The term came to define a significant movement of the time and was the subject of a major exhibition, *The Responsive Eye*, held at the Museum of Modern Art in 1965. With its subject matter of pure perception, Stanczak's art would appear to convey little of the region from which it emerged. Yet, he has insisted that his work is deeply rooted in the natural world, recalling his fascination with the constant movement and changing effects of light reflecting off the waters of the Ohio River, which he could see from his house where he lived in Cincinnati as a young faculty member from 1957 to 1964.[20]

A little earlier in Chicago, an ex–World War II sailor was exploring quite a different approach. Horace Clifford (H. C.) Westermann (1922–1981) was born and raised in Los Angeles. He arrived in Chicago in 1947 to study at the School of the Art Institute of Chicago under the GI bill and left in 1961 to live the rest of his life in Connecticut, but he has always been closely associated with Chicago. Unconcerned with art theories and trends of the day, Westermann created objects to please himself, yet his sensitive responses to issues of the world around him earned the admiration of local collectors and the respect of a younger generation of artists who appreciated his personal vision and his attention to craftsmanship exhibited in works like *Angry Young Machine* (1959).

Westermann's independent vision was appreciated by a younger group of artists who came to be broadly identified as the Chicago Imagists but exhibited under a number of fanciful names such as the Nonplussed Some, False Image, and most often as the Hairy Who. Feeling the need to stake an identity distanced from New York, these artists drew inspiration from comic strips and mass media as well as "outsider" artists to create a quirky, ironic, surreal style. Their work was introduced to the public through exhibitions organized by curator Donald Baum held at the Hyde Park Art Center in Chicago beginning in the mid-1960s. The first exhibitions included the work of Jim Nutt, Karl Wirsum, Gladys Nilsson, and others and later included works by Roger Brown and Ed Paschke. Of these, Nutt, Brown, and Paschke are the most notable.

Jim Nutt (1938–) received training at the School of the Art Institute of Chicago and graduated in 1965. Nutt's paintings and drawings contain fantastic characters in often-unexplainable situations made the more opaque by oddly placed captions. Ed Paschke (1939–) was born in Chicago; a childhood interest in animation and cartoons led him to a career in art. He received his BFA degree in 1961 and his MFA degree in 1970, both from the School of the Art Institute of Chicago. His early work contained themes of violence and aggression and later came to be recognized for brilliant color and a busy but carefully worked surface.

Roger Brown (1941–) was born and raised in Alabama. With early plans to become a preacher, he decided instead to attend art school and moved to Chicago in 1962 to pursue studies at the American Academy of Art and the School of the Art Institute of Chicago. Brown's glowing canvases often rely on the repeated use of simplified, cartooned images of power poles, apartment houses, and city dwellers. Brown's paintings also place his urban subjects in the context of the not-so-distant farmscapes of the Midwest, as in *The Entry of Christ into Chicago, 1976* (1976).

The Chicago Imagists are not alone in their interest in folk and outsider artists and in embrace of locale as subject matter. Aminah Brenda Lynn Robinson (1940–) of Columbus, Ohio, has combined her studies in art history and philosophy at the Ohio State University with her neighborhood roots and her friendship with folk artist and woodcarver Elijah Pierce to create thousands of works since the 1960s. Robinson adopted the name Aminah after a visit to Egypt in 1979. Using scraps of fabric, buttons, leather, glass, and all media of painting and drawing, she fabricates works like *One Day in 1307 A.D.: King Abubakari II* (1985–1992). The large fabric assemblage evokes the possible voyage of the African king Abubakari to the Americas long before the European arrival and draws parallels to the slave trade of the Middle Passage and to life in her neighborhood of Columbus.

Folk Art and the "Outsider"

Until the publication of Jean Lipman's 1948 book, *American Folk Art in Wood, Metal and Stone*, folk art was relegated to the margins of American art history. Previously, inspiration for the academically trained artist came mostly from Europe. Even "primitive" art collectors in the United States took their cue from European collections of African and New Guinea artifacts, which valued clear tribal traditions. Unique and personal expressions by people with no training and even people suffering from mental disorders began to pique the interest of artists in the 1950s. These untrained artists, free to express themselves using any form and any material at hand, created wholly unique things.

As trained artists in the twentieth century broke away from European models and sought to distance themselves from the New York art world, they found inspiration in these new forms. The Chicago Imagists, including Roger Brown, Karl Wirsum, and Jim Nutt—all studying at the School of the Art Institute of Chicago in the late 1960s—were among those to "discover" local outsider artists Lee Godie (1908–1994) and Joseph Yoakum (1886–1972), for example, and the Kentucky woodcarver Edgar Tolson (1904–1984).[21]

Inspired by a dream while living alone in a Chicago housing project at the age of seventy-six, Yoakum began to render views of the world as he remembered them, claiming to have visited every site when he was young. He used maps and globes as aids in the creation of thousands of landscapes, using colored pencil and ballpoint pen on paper to portray scenes such as *Lake Ferth of Fourth. Eastern Ireland. WE.*

Lee Godie is famous for standing on the steps of the Art Institute of Chicago and selling her paintings, claiming to be a French Impressionist "better than Cezanne." Frequently homeless later in life, Godie populated her idealized portraits with elegant vamps and flappers, and dashing young men sporting sideburns and crisp uniforms. A few months before she died, Godie made a triumphant, if feeble, entry to the retrospective exhibition of her work at the Chicago Cultural Center in 1994.

Woodcarving and sign painting are frequent outlets for folk artists. Woodcarver Elijah Pierce (1892–1984) was born on a Mississippi farm, and painter William Hawkins (1895–1990) was born in rural Kentucky. They both relocated to Columbus, Ohio, but neither received formal training.

Pierce began carving wooden farm animals at an early age but took up barbering as a trade. He was religious and served as a lay preacher in his church. His Long Street barbershop became the social center of the African American community in Columbus. Pierce continued to carve throughout his life, creating hundreds of sculptures and assemblages that conveyed a spiritual and humorous view of the world.

Hawkins held a number of unskilled jobs in Columbus and began drawing and painting as early as the 1930s. He did not adopt the style for which he is known until he was nearly eighty years old. His subjects range from prehistoric animals to local scenes of Columbus derived from photographs in newspapers and magazines. Nearly every painting is inscribed proudly and largely, "William Hawkins Born July 27, 1895."

High Art at the Grassroots: Visibility for Local Artists

The region's established museums and contemporary art centers provided important venues for presenting a broad spectrum of art but often did not satisfy the needs of artists in their own communities. Some of the large museums offered annual exhibitions of local talent, often juried by visiting curators. The Cleveland Museum of Art, for example, presented the "May Show," which for years was a popular outlet for both artists and collectors interested in purchasing affordable works that had received the museum's imprimatur. The Art Institute of Chicago also provided exhibition opportunities for Chicago artists, many of whom had studied at its school.

By the 1970s, the first baby-boom generation of students was graduating from art schools that had developed increasingly sophisticated curricula. Cranbrook Academy of Art near Detroit, Kansas City Art Institute, Minneapolis College of

Art and Design, and Wright State University in Dayton, Ohio, among others, were sending professionally trained artists out into the world. Many wanted to show their work but received scant attention from the established museums and contemporary art centers.

In response, they created their own modest places to gather and exhibit. Using abandoned warehouses and storefronts with money shared from what they earned from day jobs, they created supportive communities of their own. The National Endowment for the Arts recognized these efforts and began to provide financial assistance in the mid-1970s. These "alternative spaces" were vital to a generation of artists living in the Midwest in the 1970s. The names of these exhibition spaces were often enigmatic, self-referential, or simply acronyms such as N.A.M.E. Gallery in Chicago, SPACES in Cleveland, and C.A.G.E.—Cincinnati Artists Group Effort. These scrappy, energetic places filled a niche that museums, contemporary art centers, and private galleries could not: exhibiting art that had no historical pedigree and no commercial value. With increasing support from the NEA, the Alternative Space Movement was a national phenomenon in the 1970s and 1980s.

Noncommercial artists' spaces can be found in smaller towns as well as large cities. The New Harmony Gallery of Contemporary Art is located in New Harmony, Indiana, the state's earliest religious and utopian community. Legion Arts CSPS is located in Cedar Rapids, Iowa, home of Iowa favorite-son Grant Wood. Originally an Iowa City-based artists' collective known as the Drawing Legion, Legion Arts relocated to Cedar Rapids and operates in a building that originally served as a Czech and Slovak community hall, the derivation of the acronym (Czech and Slovak Prudential Society) CSPS. Legion Arts maintains a community-based program that imports experimental artists from New York and Los Angeles, blending them into a month's program that might include Blue Grass music one night and the opening of a show of paintings by a recent immigrant to Cedar Rapids' Czech and Slovak community the next.

Blurring the Boundaries: Mingling the Media

These artist-run spaces often erased boundaries between art forms. They were seldom devoted solely to the visual arts, variously presenting informal screenings of film and video, dance events, and the newly emerging form of "performance art" that evolved from the 1960s phenomenon of Happenings. This evolution was not unique to the Midwest, but uniquely local groups emerged there such as the "art band," Devo, and the performance collective the Patiosville Beatniks, from Cleveland. Devo's strong visual image, and the Beatniks' funky retro, fifties-style kitsch, were charming and attracted attention from small artists' spaces around the country, to which they toured successfully for a few years in the early 1980s. Devo received recording contracts and won a cult following similar to the popular New York-based Talking Heads. At about the same time, the artist Hudson from Cincinnati also garnered attention for his outlandish, tongue-in-cheek drag performances that combined autobiographical texts with lip-synched, diva impersonations.

The Walker Art Center played a significant role in the field of interdisciplinary art in the Midwest by initiating tours of performance artists who could get additional engagements at smaller venues throughout the region. The Walker commissioned new works by nationally known crossover artists such as Laurie Anderson, Philip Glass, Robert Wilson, Spaulding Gray, and the Wooster Group. These commissions brought together visual and performance artists, resulting in hybrids of art that defied conventional definitions. Collaborations with other arts centers in the region such as Hancher Auditorium at the University of Iowa, the Goodman Theater and the Museum of Contemporary Art in Chicago, and the Wexner Center for the Arts in Columbus, Ohio, created large-scale productions that appeared at national and international venues such as the Brooklyn Academy of Music's Next Wave Festival.

The technical media of film and video can offer intimate and personal experiences as well. Diane Kitchen (1949–) in Milwaukee and Leighton Pierce in Iowa City create such encounters that resonate with the unique qualities of their locales. Kitchen, born in Akron, Ohio, works in two directions: ethnographic documentations of the indigenous people of the Amazon River Basin and a more personal genre closer to her Wisconsin home. Her *Wot the Ancient Sod* (2001, 16 mm film, silent; 17 minutes) is a purely poetic visual essay using light, shadow, and pattern to evoke natural forms. The "sod" of her title is the naturally composting earth that enriches her garden soil. Similarly, Leighton Pierce's subject matter is close to home. Born in Rochester, New York, in 1954, Pierce lives in Iowa City where he produces what have been called miniature cinematic works. *The Back Steps* (2001, digital video, color, sound; 5½ minutes) presents images of his children at play during a Halloween party. Painterly forms emerge and submerge back into darkness, revealing Pierce's studies of music composition. Works by Kitchen and Pierce were included in the 2002 Biennial Exhibition at the Whitney Museum of American Art in New York.

Photography

Iowa writer Michael Martone observed that "an aerial [photograph] of the Grand Canyon is just another spectacular picture. Some things are easy to see. The Midwest is hard to see, especially when you are in it."[22] Photography is one of the most compelling media to capture a sense of place because it collects all details of a scene, allowing the artist to inject his or her point of view through the selection, not the rendering, of subjects. From Edward Curtis's late nineteenth-century factual and fictional portraits of American Indians to the Farm Security Administration (FSA) photographers' recordings of human struggles in the Depression years, photography has documented and poetically portrayed the Midwest for a hundred and fifty years. County and state historical societies house vast collections of amateur and professional images that chronicle the changing shape of the land and the cities of the region.

Contemporary photographic artists in the Midwest continue the legacy of documenting and interpreting the region around them. Among many excellent examples, three stand out for their inventive approaches: Terry Evans of Chicago, Eric Rippert of Cleveland, and Paul Shambroom of Minneapolis.

Terry Evans (1944–) now lives in Chicago after many years in Kansas where she used to create aerial photographs of the ecologically endangered prairies. In her new urban environment, she was challenged to invent a new strategy for observing the midwestern landscape. Granted access to the vast specimen archives at

Chicago's Field Museum of Natural History, she began creating images of flora and fauna lying in their storage drawers. These strikingly composed pictures conflate time and space, as their subjects were collected from myriad locations in the nineteenth century.

Eric Rippert (1963–) lives in Cleveland, Ohio, which he uses as a frequent backdrop in his images. Using toys and dolls placed in the very near foreground, Rippert creates a fictional landscape based in reality. His series, *Midwest Tableaux*, including *Gus* (1998), is a commentary on the efforts of urban developers who erect tourist attractions—Jacobs Field, a sports arena, is in the background—only to lay waste to the land around them.

Paul Shambroom (1956–) lives in Minneapolis and has explored the nature of power in a number of series in recent years, including a group of works photographed inside nuclear weapons facilities. From quite a different perspective, he observes the power of the democratic process through a series of images of town council meetings. These large-format images, printed on canvas to emulate the look of classical painting, reveal the workings of government in small-town midwestern America.

Art for People: Different Views of Art and the Public

The long history of art in public places in the Midwest began with conventional memorial statues, plazas, and ceremonial arches. Perhaps because of its open spaces and the "democratic" culture dating back to the foundation of the Northwest Territories, the Midwest has been a crucible for unique innovations in the relationship between art and the public. As already described, New Deal programs commissioned many artists to create murals for public buildings in the 1930s, which remain as both artworks and records of how artists and communities saw themselves at the time they were created.

Perhaps the region's most distinctive public "artwork" is St. Louis's Gateway Arch, which serves both as a monolithic tribute to the city's role as the Gateway to the West and as a building housing observation points and historical collections. Created by architect Eero Saarinen, whose design was selected in a 1947 competition, the structure is 630 feet high and 630 feet across at the base. Construction was begun in 1961 and completed in 1966. Gateway Arch remains one of St. Louis's most recognizable structures and one of its most popular tourist attractions.

In the contemporary era, the National Endowment for the Arts, established at the time the Gateway Arch was completed, created a new and sometimes contentious conversation between artists and the public through its Works of Art in Public Places program. The program began in the Midwest, in Grand Rapids, Michigan, with the commission of *La Grande Vitesse* (1969) by Alexander Calder (1898–1976). Visiting from his Roxbury, Connecticut, studio, Calder studied the design of the buildings surrounding the plaza where the sculpture would be sited and created a form that he felt would be an artistic monument, yet one that responded to its physical location. The result—a 54-foot long by 43-foot high by 30-foot wide abstract red steel form weighing more than 42 tons—was dedicated on June 14, 1969, and was immediately embraced and rejected by different segments of the community. Despite being selected by a committee of art specialists and community leaders, it took several years before the broader community came to accept the unusual work. It is now considered one of Grand Rapids' most cherished landmarks and a tourist attraction whose form is seen on street signs, city vehicles, and official stationery.

Although it took many years to be fully absorbed, the lesson learned from the commission of *La Grande Vitesse*, and other works created with public funds, was the need for broad community involvement in the selection process for a public work of art to be truly "public."

Calder's international reputation aided but did not ensure public acceptance, as was also the case with Pablo Picasso's monumental Chicago sculpture, located in downtown Daley Plaza. The Chicago Picasso, *Untitled* (1967), raised the ire of Alderman John Hoellen, who wanted to have it "deported" soon after it was installed in 1967. Even ten years later, architect Jerrold Loebl urged that it be moved from the plaza to make way for a memorial to honor the late Mayor Daley.[23] That did not happen, but it demonstrates the challenges that face the placement of modern art in public places.

International reputation alone does not guarantee acceptance or permanence. Internationally renowned sculptor Michael Heizer was commissioned in 1980 by the state of Michigan to create *This Equals That*, a massive work for Lansing that was expected to attract visitors to Lansing the way that the Calder and Picasso sculptures had drawn visitors to Grand Rapids and Chicago. Unfortunately, the work resonated neither with the Lansing community nor with tourists, and the work was dismantled in 2002, recalling the earlier fate of Richard Serra's *Tilted Arc* in New York City.

By the 1980s, some artists began to recognize the difference between "art in public places"—private artistic expressions placed in public locations—and "public art"—art that expresses the values of a community. Siah Armajani (1939–) is one of those and has spent years striving for public art. Born in Iran and immigrating to the United States to attend Macalester College in Minnesota, Armajani was deeply moved by the writings of the American philosophers Ralph Waldo Emerson and Henry David Thoreau, who advocated the simple values of an uncomplicated life. Armajani has drawn upon American vernacular architectural forms such as covered bridges, farm sheds, picnic tables, and the like to create restful outdoor spaces where people can sit, read, talk, or eat lunch. People who use Armajani's "gardens" and "reading rooms" are seldom aware that they are in the midst of a work by a contemporary artist. Armajani's largest permanent sculpture is the *Irene Hickson Whitney Bridge*, a 375-foot footbridge completed in 1988, spanning sixteen lanes of traffic separating two public parks in Minneapolis.

Many other artists in the Midwest have reflected upon the image and history of communities in creating large public works. Andrew Leicester's *Flying Pigs* (1988), a series of four columns topped with whimsically adorned porcine figures, is located along Cincinnati's Riverfront Park beside the Ohio River. The sculpture refers to the city's origins as a pork-packing center in the nineteenth century. Many citizens criticized the work at first, feeling that the allusion was uncomplimentary. Most people, however, have good-naturedly come to recognize and embrace it as a monument to the city's history.

Locale, history, and technology come together in the work of Indianapolis artist Greg Hull (1960–), who has created interactive installations and sculptural works since the early 1990s. Born in Richmond, Indiana, Hull studied at the Kansas City

Art Institute and the University of Delaware. Hull's 1997 work *Amelia's Gate* was completed shortly after the "Mo-Kan" Bridge over the Missouri River was rededicated the *Amelia Earhart Memorial Bridge*, in honor of the aviator who was born a few miles away in Atchison, Kansas. The superstructure of the bridge is used to support two powerful vertical beacons of light and fiber-optic cables that trace the curve of the bridge's upper girders. The vertical beams project light 10,000 feet in the air and can be seen from 12 miles away, poetically offering Amelia a guiding light for her return home.

Public art can take the form of permanent installations or temporary projects. Inspired by a 1998 project in Zurich, Switzerland, the city of Chicago, for example, mounted an outdoor exhibition of artist-decorated sculptures in 1999, "Cows on Parade." The hapless animal that upset Mother O'Leary's lantern and ignited the Great Fire of 1871 was no doubt an inspiration for the theme. Organized by the Chicago Department of Cultural Affairs, the project provided selected artists with blank, life-sized cast figures and a stipend for materials. The resulting collection of inventive interpretations was placed along Michigan Avenue and other locations around Chicago, creating one of the city's most popular tourist attractions of the summer. Following the exhibition, the sculptures were auctioned to raise money to support city cultural organizations.[24]

Besides creating works for public spaces, artists have found ways to engage the public in the creation of works. Ann Hamilton, for example, has gathered large numbers of people to work along with her to accomplish the tasks required to complete and maintain some of her installations. Born in 1956 in Lima, Ohio, Hamilton had taught for several years at the University of California, Santa Barbara, before returning to Columbus permanently in the early 1990s. In 1989, she was commissioned to create a temporary work for a series of exhibitions inaugurating the Wexner Center for the Arts at The Ohio State University. Using the building site's agricultural history, Hamilton chose corn and moths—a pest to corn—as her primary materials in the work, *dominion* (1989). Dozens of family members, friends, and students covered the walls of the gallery in cornhusks and dusted the floor with cornmeal. Over the duration of the exhibition, many more people tended the moths and a different person every day sat in mute attendance, lending a human presence to the cycle of birth, growth, and harvest. Hamilton's strategy of engaging her community fosters a sense of communal ownership.

COMMUNICATING THE ARTS

Newsletters, bulletins, magazines, and broadsides about artistic events have been informing the midwestern public since the mid-nineteenth century. *Modern Art*, published in the 1890s in Indianapolis, was the country's most advanced journal for modern art criticism at the time, and Chicago's *Arts* and *Art Review* rivaled New York publications, while focusing on midwestern activities of the time. Addressing the mass market, *Time* and *Life* magazines in the 1930s brought the nation's attention to the work of Thomas Hart Benton and the Regionalist painters as well as images of the Dust Bowl devastation by Walker Evans, Dorothea Lange, and others. Every city's daily newspaper and weekly "arts and culture" tabloids continue to provide exposure for local artists, museums, and commercial galleries. The New York–based publication, *Art Now Gallery Guide*, publishes monthly regional editions that provide brief commentaries on selected exhibitions and extensive listings of museum and gallery exhibitions in most cities throughout the region.

Midwestern publications focusing specifically on art and the arts of the region have included the Walker Art Center's *Design Quarterly* (*DQ*), which began publication in the 1940s and addressed regional and national topics of graphic, industrial, and architectural design for decades. At its zenith, *DQ* was one of the leading journals of its kind in the country. It ceased publication after it unsuccessfully attempted to become an independent magazine in the early 1990s.

The Chicago-based *New Art Examiner* also was a long-running success, providing reportage and critical reviews of exhibitions throughout the region beginning in 1973. Publishing monthly, the *Examiner* covered topics that were not addressed in the larger East Coast art journals. Nearing its twentieth year in 2002, the *Examiner* faced financial difficulties and an uncertain future and closed its office in midyear.

Dialogue magazine began publication in the offices of the Akron Art Institute, now the Akron Art Museum, in Akron, Ohio. The museum's director at the time, John Coplans, was a founder of *Artforum* magazine, one of the country's leading avant-garde art journals. Coplans saw a need for Ohio museums, especially those with contemporary art

Supporting the Arts

In addition to earned revenues, private support through individual and corporate patronage and contributions has always been the mainstay of income for museums, community art centers, and artists themselves. Public support, too, has been critical and has been available in varying amounts through state, county, and municipal government programs. Seen from the broadest perspective, public support for the arts consists of a network of agencies at the federal, regional, state, and local levels. The federal government, through the National Endowment for the Arts (NEA), provides grants directly to arts organizations as well as to regional and state agencies that then provide support for local organizations.

State arts agencies have been established by each state legislature to provide funds to nonprofit arts organizations that best serve their state's citizens and their cultural interests. Each state's agency has different guidelines and procedures for applying for funds.

Regional arts organizations were established in the 1970s to aid the NEA and state arts agencies in encouraging cultural exchanges among the states in the regions established by the federal government. In the Midwest, Mid-America Arts Alliance and Arts Midwest work with the state arts councils of those states covered in this volume. Both have programs that advance the visual and performing arts by assisting arts organizations to bring exhibitions and concerts to audiences in the region and beyond.

County and municipal governments have established agencies that further assist activities on a community level. In addition to providing funds, they often serve as important advocates for the arts. Local arts agencies receive funds from a variety of sources, including hotel/motel taxes, city and county appropriations, and, in some cases, a small percentage of public construction funds for the creation of public art.

activities, to share information about their programs with a broader public. Initially a simple tabloid printed on newsprint, *Dialogue* later became a bound magazine publishing bimonthly in color, reporting on artists, exhibitions, and events in Ohio, Indiana, Michigan, and Illinois, with support from the Ohio Arts Council and the National Endowment for the Arts. Diminishing state and federal funds, however, put the magazine in jeopardy more than once. It reorganized as a for-profit magazine in early 2002 and continues as "the art, architecture, and design journal of the Heartland."

RESOURCE GUIDE
Printed Sources

Gerdts, William. *Art Across America: Two Centuries of Regional Painting, 1710 to 1920.* New York: Abbeville, 1990. Three-volume set providing a highly detailed, state-by-state account of painters, publications, and artistic associations.

Haskell, Barbara. *The American Century: Art & Culture, 1900–1950.* New York: Whitney Museum, 1999. First of a two-volume set providing a broad overview of American culture with parallel discussions of art, music, dance, film and popular culture.

Hurley, F. Jack. *Portrait of a Decade: Roy Stryker and the Development of Documentary Photography in the Thirties.* Baton Rouge: Louisiana State University, 1972.

Landau, Diana. *Ohio: The Spirit of America.* New York: Abrams, 2001. Small-format book that is one in a series of volumes that provides a colorful cultural overview of each state.

Lipman, Jean. *American Folk Art in Wood, Metal and Stone.* N.p.: Pantheon, 1948; reprint, New York: Dover Publications, 1972. One of the first definitive publications on American Folk Art from all regions of the country.

Penney, David W. *Native Arts of North America.* Paris: Finest SA, 1998. Well-illustrated, region-by-region survey of Native American arts, including some background on contemporary artists.

Stearns, Robert, ed. *Illusions of Eden: Visions of the American Heartland.* Minneapolis: Arts Midwest, 2000. A reinterpretation of the role of American Scene and Regionalist painting and concurrent photography, placing that work in the context of contemporary art.

Organizations, Museums, Special Collections

This is a selected list of museums not already profiled in sidebars. This list does not include university art galleries and museums.

Illinois

Art Institute of Chicago
111 South Michigan Avenue
Chicago, IL 60603-6110
Phone: (312) 443-3600
www.artic.edu

Balzekas Museum of Lithuanian Culture
6500 S. Pulaski Road
Chicago, IL 60629
Phone: (773) 582-6500
Fax: (773) 582-5133
E-mail: editor@lithuanianmuseum.org
www.lithaz.org/museums/balzekas

Chicago Cultural Center
78 E. Washington Street
Chicago, IL 60602
Phone: (312) 742-0079
www.ci.chi.il.us/Tourism/CultureCenterTour/

Chicago Historical Society
Clark Street at North Avenue

Chicago, IL 60614-6071
Phone: (312) 642-4600
Fax: (312) 266-2077
www.chicagohs.org

DuSable Museum of African-American History
740 East 56th Place
Chicago, IL 60637
Phone: (773) 947-0600
www.dusablemuseum.org

Ethnic Heritage Museum
1129 S. Main Street
Rockford, IL 61101
Phone: (815) 962-7402
www.artcom.com/Museums/nv/af/61101-14.htm

Goethe-Institut
150 North Michigan Avenue, Suite 200
Chicago, IL 60601
Phone: (312) 263-0472
Fax: (312) 263-0476
www.goethe.de/uk/chi/enindex.htm

Hellenic Museum and Cultural Center
801 W. Adams Avenue, 4th Floor
Chicago, IL 60607
Phone: (312) 655-1234
Fax: (312) 655-1221
www.hellenicmuseum.org

Hyde Part Art Center
5307 S. Hyde Park Boulevard
(Del Prado Apartment Bldg.)
Chicago, IL 60615
Phone: (773) 324-5520
Fax: (773) 324-6641
E-mail: info@hydeparkart.org
www.hydeparkart.org

Instituto Italiano di Cultura
500 N. Michigan Avenue, Suite 1450
Chicago, IL 60611
Phone: (312) 822-9545
Fax: (312) 822-9622
www.iicch.org/english.htm

Mexican Fine Arts Center Museum
1852 W. 19th Street
Chicago, IL 60608
Phone: (312) 738-1503
www.mfacmchicago.org

Museum of Contemporary Art
220 E. Chicago Avenue
Chicago, IL 60611

Phone: (312) 280-2660
Fax: (312) 397-4095
www.mcachicago.org

Oriental Institute
University of Chicago
1155 E. 58th Street
Chicago, IL 60637
Phone: (773) 702-9514
Fax: (773), 702-9853
www-oi.uchicago.edu/OI/default.html

Polish Museum of America
984 North Milwaukee Avenue
Chicago, IL 60622
Phone: (773) 384-3352
Fax: (773) 384-3799
www.pma.prcua.org

Spertus Museum (of the Spertus Institute of Jewish Studies)
618 S. Michigan Avenue
Chicago, IL 60605
Phone: (312) 322-1747
www.spertus.edu/museum.html

Swedish-American Museum Center
5211 North Clark
Chicago, IL 60640
Phone: (773) 728-8111
E-mail: Museum@samac.org
www.samac.org

Ukrainian National Museum of Chicago
721 N. Oakley
Chicago, IL 60612
Phone: (312) 421-8020
E-mail: info@ukrntlmuseum.org
www.ukrntlmuseum.org

Indiana

Eiteljorg Museum of American Indian and Western Art
500 W. Washington Street
Indianapolis, IN 46204
Phone: (317) 636-WEST (9378)
www.eiteljorg.org

Historic New Harmony, Inc.
Director: Connie Weinzapfel
P.O. Box 579
New Harmony, IN 47631
Phone: (800) 231-2168
E-mail: harmony@usi.edu
www.newharmony.org

Indianapolis Museum of Art
4000 Michigan Road
Indianapolis, IN 46208-3326
Phone: (317) 923-1331
E-mail: ima@ima-art.org
www.ima-art.org

Swope Art Museum
25 S. 7th Street
Terre Haute, IN 47807
Phone: (812) 238-1676
Fax: (812) 238-1677
Director: David Vollmer
E-mail: vollmer@swope.org
www.swope.org

Iowa

African American Historical Museum and Cultural Center of Iowa
55 12th Avenue, SE
P.O. Box 1626
Cedar Rapids, IA 52406-1626
Phone: (319) 862-2101
Fax: (319) 862-2105
www.blackiowa.org

Cedar Rapids Museum of Art
410 Third Avenue S.E.
Cedar Rapids, IA 52401
Phone: (319) 366-7503
Fax: (319) 366-4111
E-mail: info@crma.org
www.crma.org

Danish Immigrant Museum
2212 Washington Street
P.O. Box 470
Elk Horn, IA 51531-0470
Phone: (712) 764-7001 or (800) 759-9192
Fax: (712) 764-7002
Director: Dr. John Mark Nielsen
E-mail: director@danishmuseum.org
www.dkmuseum.org

Davenport Museum of Art
1737 W. 12th Street
Davenport, IA 52804
Phone: (563) 326-7804
Fax: (563) 326-7876
www.art-dma.org

Des Moines Art Center
4700 Grand Avenue
Des Moines, IA 50312-2099

Phone: (515) 277-4405
Fax: (515) 271-0357
Contact: M. Jessica Rowe, Deputy Director
E-mail: mjrowe@desmoinesartcenter.org
www.desmoinesartcenter.org

German American Heritage Center
712 W. 2nd Street
P.O. Box 243
Davenport, IA 52805
Phone: (563) 322-8844
E-mail: director@gahc.org
www.wiu.edu/users/mfbdw/gahc_web/index.html

The National Czech & Slovak Museum & Library
30–16th Avenue SW
Cedar Rapids, IA 52404-5904
Phone: (319) 362-8500
Fax: (319) 363-2209
www.ncsml.org

Pella Historical Village
507 Franklin Street
Pella, IA 50219
Phone: (641) 628-4311
Fax: (641) 628-9192
E-mail: e-mail info@pellatuliptime.com
www.pellatuliptime.com

Michigan

Charles H. Wright Museum of African-American History
315 E. Warren Avenue
Detroit, MI 48201-1443
Phone: (313) 494-5800
Fax: (313) 494-5855
www.maah-detroit.org

The Detroit Institute of Arts
5200 Woodward Avenue
Detroit, MI 48202
Phone: (313) 833-7900
www.dia.org

Grand Rapids Art Museum
155 Division North
Grand Rapids, MI 49503-3154
Phone: (616) 831-1000
www.gramonline.org

Holland Museum
31 W. 10th St.
Holland, MI 49423
Contact: Maude Jouppi
Phone: (616) 394-1362 or (888) 200-9123 (toll free)

E-mail: hollandmuseum@hollandmuseum.org
www.wowcom.net/commerce/museum/index.shtml

Michigan Historical Center
702 W. Kalamazoo Street
Lansing, MI 48909-8240
Phone: (517) 373-3559 or (800) 827-7007
www.michigan.gov/hal/0,1607,7-160-17445_19273—,00.html

Michigan State University Museum
Campus, West Circle Drive
East Lansing, MI 48824-1045
Phone: (517) 355-7474
www.museum.msu.edu

Muskegon Museum of Art
296 W. Webster Avenue
Muskegon, MI 49440
Phone: (231) 720-2570
Fax: (231) 720-2585
www.muskegonartmuseum.org

Minnesota

The American Swedish Institute
2600 Park Avenue
Minneapolis, MN 55407
Phone: (612) 871-4907
E-mail: information@americanswedishinst.org
www.americanswedishinst.org

Czech and Slovak Sokol
383 Michigan Street
Saint Paul, MN 55102
Phone: (651) 290-0542
www.sokolmn.org

Immigration History Research Center
University of Minnesota
College of Liberal Arts
311 Andersen Library
222-21st Avenue South
Minneapolis, MN 55455-0439
Phone: (612) 625-4800
Fax: (612) 626-0018
www1.umn.edu/ihrc

Minneapolis Institute of Arts
2400 Third Avenue South
Minneapolis, MN 55404
Phone: (612) 870-3131 or (888)-MIA-ARTS (642-2787)
www.artsmia.org

Minnesota Museum of American Art
505 Landmark Center
75 W. Fifth Street

St. Paul, MN 55102
Contact: Bruce Lilly, Director
Phone: (651) 292-4380
E-mail: blilly@mmaa.org
www.mmaa.org

Tweed Museum of Art
University of Minnesota Duluth
1201 Ordean Court
10 University Drive
Duluth, MN 55812-2496
Phone: (218) 726-8222
Fax: (218) 726-8503
E-mail: tma@d.umn.edu
www.d.umn.edu/tma

Walker Art Center
725 Vineland Place
Minneapolis, MN 55403
Phone: (612) 375-7622
E-mail: webmaster@walkerart.org
www.walkerart.org

Missouri

Contemporary Art Museum
3750 Washington Boulevard
St. Louis, MO 63108
Phone: (314) 535-4660
Fax: (314) 535-1226
www.contemporarystl.org

Kemper Museum of Contemporary Art
4420 Warwick Boulevard
Kansas City, MO 64111
Phone: (816) 753-5784
Fax: (816) 753-5806
www.kemperart.org

Laumeier Sculpture Park
12580 Rott Road
St. Louis, MO 63127
Phone: (314) 821-1209
Fax: (314) 821-1248
E-mail: info@laumeier.org
www.laumeier.org

Nance Museum
P.O. Box 292
Lone Jack, MO 64070
Phone: (816) 697-2526
E-mail: pjnmuseum@worldnet.att.net
home.att.net/~pjnmuseum/book.html

Negro Leagues Baseball Museum
1616 E. 18th Street
Kansas City, MO 64108-1610
Phone: (816) 221-1920
Fax: (816) 221-8424
www.nlbm.com

Nelson-Atkins Museum of Art
4525 Oak Street
Kansas City, MO 64111
Phone: (816) 561-4000
www.nelson-atkins.org

Ozarks Afro-American Heritage Museum
Fr. Moses Berry
Curator, OAAHM
P.O. Box 265
Ash Grove, MO 65604
Phone: (417) 672-3104
www.oaahm.org

St. Charles Historic District [no address listed]
Greater St. Charles Convention and Visitors Bureau
Phone: (800) 366-2427
E-mail: www.historicstcharles.com
www.cr.nps.gov/nr/travel/lewisandclark/stc.htm

St. Louis Art Museum
Forest Park
1 Fine Arts Drive
St. Louis, MO 63110
Phone: (314) 721-0072
E-mail: abenz@slam.org
www.slam.org

State Historical Society of Missouri
1020 Lowry Street
Columbia, MO 65201-7298
Phone: (573) 882-7083
Fax: (573) 884-4950
www.umsystem.edu/shs/

Ohio

African American Museum
1765 Crawford Road
Cleveland, OH 44106
Phone: (216) 791-1700
Fax: (216) 791-1774
E-mail: ourstory@aamcleveland.org
www.aamcleveland.org

Akron Art Museum
70 East Market Street

Akron, OH 44308-2084
Phone: (330) 376-9185
Fax: (330) 376-1180
E-mail: mail@akronartmuseum.org
www.akronartmuseum.org

Butler Institute of American Art, Youngstown
524 Wick Avenue
Youngstown, OH 44502
Phone: (330) 743-1711
E-mail: k_platt@butlerart.com
www.butlerart.com

Canton Art Museum
1001 Market Avenue North
Canton, OH 44702
Phone: (330) 453-7666
Fax: (330) 453-1034
Executive Director: M.J. Albacete
E-mail: al@cantonart.org
www.cantonart.org

Cincinnati Art Museum
953 Eden Park Road
Cincinnati, OH 45202
Phone: (513) 721-ARTS
www.cincinnatiartmuseum.org

The Cleveland Museum of Art
11150 East Boulevard
Cleveland, OH 44106
Phone: (216) 421-7340
E-mail: info@clevelandart.org
www.clevelandart.org

Columbus Museum of Art
480 East Broad Street
Columbus, OH 43215
Phone: (614) 221-6801
E-mail: info@columbusmuseum.org
www.columbusmuseum.org

Contemporary Art Center
44 East 6th Street
Cincinnati, OH 45202
Phone: (513) 345-8400
Fax: (513) 721-7418
www.contemporaryartscenter.org

Dayton Art Institute
456 Belmonte Park North
Dayton, OH 45405
Phone: (937) 223-5277
Fax: (937) 223-3140
E-mail: info@daytonartinstitute.org
www.daytonartinstitute.org

Museum of Contemporary Art Cleveland
8501 Carnegie Avenue
Cleveland, OH 44106
Phone: (216) 421-8671
www.MOCAcleveland.org

The National Afro-American Museum and Cultural Center
P.O. Box 578
1350 Brush Row Road
Wilberforce, OH 45384
Phone: (937) 376-4944 or (800) 752-2603
Director: Vernon Courtney
www.ohiohistory.org/places/afroam

Ohio Historical Center
1982 Velma Avenue
Columbus, OH 43211
Phone: (614) 297-2300 Museum
(614) 297-2621 Group Tours
(614) 297-2510 Archives-Library
Fax: (614) 297-2233
Contact: Sharon Antle
www.ohiohistory.org/places/ohc

Pyramid Hill Sculpture Park and Museum
222 High Street
Suite 201
Hamilton, OH 45011
Phone: (513) 868-8336
www.pyramidhill.org

The Riffe Gallery
Ohio Arts Council
727 E. Main Street
Columbus, OH 43205-1793
Phone: (614) 466-2613
Fax: (614) 466-4494
E-mail: webmaster@oac.state.oh.us
www.oac.state.oh.us

Sauder Village
22611 St. Rt. 2
Archbold, OH 43502
Phone: (800) 590-9755
www.saudervillage.com/home/default.asp

Springfield Museum of Art
107 Cliff Park Road
Springfield, OH 45501
Phone: (937) 325-4673
Director: Mark Chepp
www.spfld-museum-of-art.org

SunWatch Indian Village
2301 West River Road
Dayton, OH 45418-2815

Phone: (937) 268-8199
Fax: (937) 268-1760
www.sunwatch.org/special_events.html

Taft Museum
316 Pike Street
Cincinnati, OH 45202
Phone: (513) 241-0343
Fax: (513) 241-2266/7762
E-mail: taftmuseum@taftmuseum.org
www.taftmuseum.org

Toledo Museum of Art
Mailing address: P.O. Box 1013
Toledo, OH 43697
Location: 2445 Monroe Street at Scottwood Avenue
Toledo, OH 43620
Phone: (419) 255-8000 or 800-644-6862
E-mail: information@toledomuseum.org
www.toledomuseum.org

Underground Railroad Museum
The Underground Railroad Foundation
P.O. Box 47
Flushing, OH 43977
Phone: (740) 968-2080
E-mail: ugrrf@ugrrf.org
Curator: John S. Mattox
www.ugrrf.org

Wexner Center for the Arts
The Ohio State University
1871 North High Street
Columbus, OH 43210-1393
Phone: (614) 292-3535
Fax: (614) 292-3369
www.wexarts.org

Wisconsin

John Michael Kohler Arts Center
608 New York Avenue
P.O. Box 489
Sheboygan, WI 53082-0489
Phone: (920) 458-6144
Fax: (920) 458-4473
www.jmkac.org

Madison Museum of Contemporary Art
211 State Street
Madison, WI 53703
Phone: (608) 257-0158
www.mmoca.org

Milwaukee Art Museum
700 N. Art Museum Drive
Milwaukee, WI 53202
Phone: (414) 224-3200
Fax: (414) 271-7588
www.mam.org

Old World Wisconsin
S103 W37890 Highway 67
Eagle, WI 53119
Phone: (262) 594-6300
E-mail: oww@whs.wisc.edu
www.wisconsinhistory.org/oww

The Wisconsin Historical Museum of the Wisconsin Historical Society
Capitol Square at 30 N. Carroll Street
Madison, WI 53703
Phone: (608) 264-6555
E-mail: museum@whs.wisc.edu
www.wisconsinhistory.org/museum/visit.asp

Other Resources

Information about Folk and Outsider Artists

Intuit: The Center for Intuitive and Outsider Art
756 N. Milwaukee Avenue
Chicago, IL 60622
Phone: (312) 243-9088
Fax: (312) 243-9089
E-mail: intuit@art.org
www.outsider.art.org

General Information and Opportunities for Artists

Art in the Heartland
408 Washington Street
Columbus, IN 47201
Phone: (812) 376-3465 or (866) 372-8576
E-mail: sbreeding@artintheheartland.com or banderson@stillframes.com
www.artintheheartland.com

Selected Public Support Agencies/Regional Organizations

Arts Midwest
2908 Hennepin Avenue
Suite 200
Minneapolis, MN 55408-1954
Phone: (612) 341-0755
Fax: (612) 341-0902
E-mail: general@artsmidwest.org
www.artsmidwest.org

ExhibitsUSA
912 Baltimore
Suite 700
Kansas City, MO 64105
Phone: (816) 421-1388 or (800) 735-2966
Fax: (816) 421-3918
Contact: Mary Kennedy McCabe, Executive Director
www.eusa.org

Mid-America Arts Alliance (same contact information as above)
912 Baltimore
Suite 700
Kansas City, MO 64105
Phone: (816) 421-1388 or (800) 735-2966
Fax: (816) 421-3918
Contact: Mary Kennedy McCabe, Executive Director
E-mail: info@maaa.org
www.maaa.org

State Arts Agencies

Illinois Arts Council
James R. Thompson Center
100 West Randolph
Suite 10-500
Chicago, IL 60601
Phone: (312) 814-6750
Fax: (312) 814-1471
E-mail: info@arts.state.il.us
www.state.il.us/agency/iac/

Indiana Arts Commission
150 W. Market Street, #618
Indianapolis, IN 46204
Phone: (317) 232-1268
Fax: (317) 232-5595
Contact: Dorothy L. Ilgen, Executive Director
E-mail: arts@iac.in.state.us
www.state.in.us/iac/

Iowa Arts Council
Div. of Iowa Department of Cultural Affairs
600 E. Locust
Des Moines, IA 50319-0290
Phone: (515) 281-6412
Fax: (515) 242-6498
Contact: Anita Walker, Executive Director
E-mail: Anita.Walker@iowa.gov
www.iowaartscouncil.org

Michigan Council for Arts and Cultural Affairs
702 West Kalamazoo
P.O. Box 30705
Lansing, MI 48909-8205
Phone: (517) 241-4011

Fax: (517) 241-3979
Contact: Craig Ruff, Chairman
E-mail: artsinfo@michigan.gov
www.michigan.gov/hal/0,1607,7-160-17445_19272—,00.html

Minnesota State Arts Board
Park Square Court, Suite 200
400 Sibley Street
Saint Paul, MN 55101-1928
Phone: (615) 215-1600 or (800) 8MN-ARTS (866-2787)
Fax: (651) 215-1602
E-mail: msab@arts.state.mn.us
www.state.mn.us

Missouri Arts Council
Department of Economic Development
P.O. Box 1157
Jefferson City, MO 65102-1157
Phone: (573) 751-4962
Fax: (573) 751-7258
E-mail: moarts@ded.mo.gov
www.ded.state.mo.us

Ohio Arts Council
727 E. Main Street
Columbus OH 43205-1796
Phone: (614) 466-2613 or (888) 2GETOAC
Fax: (614) 466-4494
E-mail: webmaster@oac.state.oh.us
www.oac.state.oh.us

Wisconsin Arts Board
101 E. Wilson Street, First Floor
Madison, WI 53702
Phone: (608) 266-0190
Fax: (608) 267-0380
E-mail: artsboard@arts.state.wi.us
www.arts.state.wi.us

Arts Agencies Network

Americans for the Arts
(formerly known as National Assembly of State Arts Agencies)
Washington Office:
1000 Vermont Avenue, NW, 6th Floor
Washington, DC 20005
Phone: (202) 371-2830
Fax: (202) 371-0424

New York Office:
One East 53rd Street
New York, NY 10022
Phone: (212) 223-2787
Fax: (212) 980-4857
E-mail: webmaster@artsusa.org
www.nalaa.org

ECOLOGY AND ENVIRONMENT

Chris Mayda, Artimus Keiffer, and Joseph W. Slade

"The Middle West is flat."
—John Fraser Hart[1]

The opening sentence of a benchmark essay (1972) by one of America's most respected rural geographers, Hart's pithy characterization of terrain seemed to sum up the region's physical attributes for scholars just becoming accustomed to classifying regional differences. Most people would not dispute Hart's observation, but, as with all generalizations, there is more, and so it is with the Midwest. Sequences of rolling hills, dams of moraine tailings, escarpments of prehistoric lakes, steep slopes of glacial-melt outwash, and ravines cutting through sedimentary bedrock leave this area scored by anomalies. Included are broken land, dissected plains, and the Driftless, a relatively rough-terrain tract of land in and surrounding southwestern Wisconsin that was once surrounded but never covered by a continental glacier. There are geologic features resulting from glacial action like kames (steep-sided hills), eskers (winding steep-sided ridges of sand and gravel), and drumlins (elongated mounds). The absence of "mountains" is very real, as is the abundance of water and extreme variations of temperature. In a real sense, then, the Midwest is the flat, wet, and seasonal space between the continent's real mountain ranges: the Appalachians to the east and the Rockies to the west. The Midwest was home 2,000 years ago to the mound builders. In the thirteenth and fourteenth centuries, it supported a major Native American civilization, when Cahokia flourished near today's St. Louis on the banks of the upper Mississippi River. During the early part of the nineteenth century, it was the agrarian Eden for ethnic European Protestant farmers and entrepreneurs. It is where the national agricultural economy began in the mid-nineteenth century and where the Industrial Revolution took off.

As the nation grew westward, the midwest provided the natural resources needed for settlement of newly acquired lands. Some pioneers solidified those dreams into utopian settlements and religious communities. The Midwest became the transportation hub of the nation's industrial heartland—the "crossroads." The might of the pre–World War I Industrial Revolution and a post–World War II industrial complex was located in this conjunction of the populated East and the newly expanded

West. If East were to meet West, it was in the Middle West, the area between the great rivers that had to be conquered. On the eastern end, resources barely hid in outcroppings covered by shallow soils. On the western side, "prairie schooners" departing from Council Bluffs sailed like ships across the smooth, flat expanse of rich, glaciated soils. Ready transportation in the form of rivers draining lakes and rains (with the help of canals and bridges) linked the region to all parts of the country and brought the region's bounty to the coastlines. Appealing as a frontier, relished as a challenge, the Midwest was a giant mixer that would eventually include almost every ethnic minority. This blending of regional cultures, traditional values, and common sense came to immortalize the region as the home to all things American.

As a result, the Midwest is a repository of the assimilated. The first inhabitants left mysterious effigy mounds for later settlers to ponder. The first Anglo settlers were not displaced Europeans, but instead first- and second-generation Americans from the populated coast. Although agricultural and industrial opportunities drew some later migrants directly from abroad, still others came to the region to reside with family or find jobs like those they were used to in Europe. One result of these push and pull factors was the unique American landscape of isolated, dispersed farmsteads, a gridlike maze of endless cornfields and farms that filled the rolling hills with the sounds and smells of dairy farming and swine production. Crucial to these developments was the "Protestant work ethic" that diffused with the religions that preached hard work and the exploitation of nature for human progress.

But there is more, much more, in this snapshot of the Midwest. The work ethic that trademarked the American agrarian lifestyle has been replaced by agrotechnology. More recently, the rusted remnants of manufacturing muscle have been replaced by other sinews of the American economy. Though less than 2 percent of midwesterners are still farmers and manufacturing continues to decline, the population is still stereotyped by older images. To many, especially those on the other side of the mountains, it is a simple way to characterize the middle. It is satisfying to romanticize what once was the engine of America, what once seemed the dominant American psyche.

The Midwest is still home not simply to the Rust and Snow belts, but also to the vital Corn and Dairy belts. The industrial infrastructure has deteriorated, but its legacy of blue-collar workers is still visible. In the last half of the twentieth century, both the agricultural and industrial economies changed radically, and both have left behind a recognizable landscape of previous occupancy. Moreover, the agricultural and industrial heritage of the Midwest still serves as the nexus of its hope that opportunities may yet resurface. This chapter deals with the landscape, the settlement, and the economy of rural and urban areas, and demonstrates how the physical environment and human activities formed a region once seen as the "heartland" of America and continue to shape the present and future of the Midwest.

For our purposes, the Midwest includes the eight states of Illinois, Indiana, Iowa, Michigan, Minnesota, Missouri, Ohio, and Wisconsin, all of which contain or are contained within complex environmental and ecologic systems. For this reason, geographers often look beyond politically derived state boundaries to regions that are based on physiographic, environmental, and ecologic systems, regions that are somehow distinct from their surrounding area. Regions can be based on any number of features, but here they will be described as combinations of physiographic, ecologic, and environmental features.

LAND

The vastness of the Midwest fascinated early colonists. The land unfolded toward a distant horizon, as if a gigantic hand had leveled it. Closer acquaintance, of course, taught European settlers what the American Indians of the region had already learned, that the features of its terrain varied widely, sometimes dramatically. The prairies that seemed like seas to James Fenimore Cooper's Leatherstocking were bordered to the north by actual inland seas, and to the south by hills and uplands. All of these surfaces afforded nature canvases of opportunity.

Geological and Geographical Features

Two geological elements of the midwestern landscape are its relative flatness and its glacial drift topography. As with most regions, the Midwest's natural landscape boundaries are not obvious but rather subtle transitions from one area to another. The general boundaries stretch from west of the Appalachians to the Great Plains, and from the Gulf Coastal Plain in the south to the Laurentian Upland in the north. The obvious exception is the Ozark Uplands area in Arkansas and Missouri. Several subregions exist within this Midwest; these are usually transitional, with divisions commonly based on vegetational and glaciated history. Midwestern subregions are delineated in two major categories:

Lakes Region

Not limited to the Great Lakes states alongside Lakes Ontario, Erie, and Michigan, the region includes most of southern Ontario Province (Canada), all of Michigan's Lower Peninsula, northern Ohio, Indiana, and Illinois, and eastern Wisconsin and northern Minnesota along a line followed by U.S. Interstate 94 from St. Paul, Minnesota, to Madison, Wisconsin. This region was originally forested

The Sleeping Bear Sand Dunes were formed 3,000–4,000 years ago as Lake Michigan shrank during one of its phases. Photo by Chris Mayda.

and is the most recently glaciated, with moraines, swamps, natural lakes, lacustrine plains, and old shorelines indicating the fluctuating edges of the Great Lakes. As elevations changed over time, they left behind the famous dunes of Indiana and Michigan. Perhaps the most famous are the Sleeping Bear Sand Dunes, which were formed 3,000 to 4,000 years ago as Lake Michigan shrank during one of its phases.

Central Lowlands

The Central Lowlands extends south of the Lakes Region to the interior plateaus south of the Ohio River (Kentucky) and west of the Allegheny Plateau as well as east of the drier, short-grass region of the Great Plains of the Dakotas, Nebraska, and Kansas. Three subdivisions fall within this subregion:

- The Glaciated Till Plain—an area of deep, rich glacial deposits and few lakes located generally south of the Great Lakes and north of the Ohio River. It is considered the "heartland" of the Midwest.
- The Dissected Till Plain—the western part of the region extending from southern Minnesota through south-central Missouri into eastern Kansas. The topography here is more developed. A slight escarpment emerges and disappears between the 97th and 99th parallel. It is the usual dividing line between the Midwest and the Great Plains.
- The Driftless—located mostly in southwestern Wisconsin, with small portions extending into the surrounding states. The Driftless escaped glaciation, though glaciated areas surround it. The dissected plateau is rougher than the surrounding region topographically because glaciers never flattened and smoothed it.

The Lakes Region

Moraines, swamps, and lakes contribute to the topographic features of the Lakes Region. Small rolling ridges called drumlins or moraines provide topographic relief. Melting glaciers left terminal and recessional moraines to accent the flat basin. The most recent of the postglacial areas, the Lakes Region is patterned with poorly developed drainage systems resulting in swampy wetlands. The flattest places are the lacustrine (related to lakes) plains, which formed as the glacial ice retreated; these were extensions of the present-day Great Lakes. The Lakes Region extends as far south as the Wabash River in Indiana, where the highest elevation reaches only 1058 feet above sea level. To the west, it surrounds Lake Michigan and extends northward to the Driftless area in Wisconsin. The lakes were formed as huge boulders were torn from the surface while glaciers passed overhead. Depressions left in the ground from these boulders are called kettles. When groundwater intersects the depressions, they form kettle lakes.

The Lakes Region is divided between the Eastern Lakes and Western Lakes subregions. The Eastern Lakes Region consists of most of Michigan as well as a narrow band along Ohio, Indiana, Illinois, and Wisconsin, hugging the current Great Lakes. The Western Lakes Region constitutes much of Minnesota and Wisconsin and then extends into south-central Iowa. Across the Lakes Region, but especially in Minnesota and Michigan, is the glacial relief that the region is known for, configured and sculpted by lakes and accompanying wetlands.

The heart of the Eastern Lake Region is the Red River and its outwash valley. This 700-mile-long, 250-mile-wide relic of the Pleistocene epoch was known at one time as Lake Agassiz, named for Professor Louis Agassiz (1807–1873), the first advocate of the glacial drift theory. Reaching into Manitoba, Lake Winnipeg is the extant remains of Lake Agassiz, an ice-dammed lake reported to have been one of the largest on Earth. The Lacustrine Plain of the Red River has been fertilized by lake sediment deposits.

The flat lacustrine plains of the Eastern Lake section of Michigan and Ohio are the situations of Saginaw and Toledo, which are also located within ancient lake basins. The site of Saginaw has been periodically covered by the Great Lakes. Toledo, situated at the mouth of today's Maumee River, at the southern end of Lake Erie, was once the middle of ancient Lake Maumee. This huge prehistoric lake extended as far west as Fort Wayne, Indiana, and south to Findlay, Ohio. In Ohio the Lakes Region follows a narrow 10-mile band around Lake Erie and slowly widens west of Cleveland to fifty miles wide west of Toledo. It extends into the floodplain of the Maumee River. The Lake Erie shore counties account for 4 percent of the land and 16 percent of the population, making it the most urban part of the state. The area southwest of Toledo was called the Black Swamp, notorious for being almost impassable during early European settlement.

The Lakes Region has a preponderance of wetland features that often occur in the depressions between drumlins. Wetlands nestle against the Great Lakes, or land once covered by the Great Lakes, such as the northeastern section of Minnesota, which consists almost entirely of wetlands of one type or another. In Michigan the Upper Peninsula can roughly be divided into an eastern region of forested swamps, muskegs, and barrens, and the western edge, the Superior Uplands, a part of the Canadian Shield. The principal characteristics of wetlands are the soils, types of water, and plants called *hydrophytes*. The combination of these three characteristics distinguishes one wetland from another. Wetlands are either coastal or inland; most in the Lakes Region are inland. These fall into three categories: riverine (of river channels or floodplains), lacustrine (of lakes and deltas), and palustrine (of shallow ponds, marshes, and swamps). Riverine wetlands are usually called bottomlands, freshwater marshes, or delta marshes. Lacustrine wetlands are also freshwater marshes as well as shrub and forest wetlands. Palustrine wetlands are ephemeral ponds, peatlands, and bogs.

Wetland features attest to their different ecologies. *Marshes* are connected to large freshwater lakes, such as Lakes Michigan and Huron. The coastal plains of these lakes have many broad soggy swaths and embayments, often with marl (crumbly soil of lime, clay, and sand used for fertilizer). Dredging for marl has destroyed

Black Swamp

Another name for the Black Swamp is the Maumee Lacustrine Plain, which was formed by a succession of glacial lobes ending about 13,000 years ago. This very flat plain was part of glacial Lake Maumee, the predecessor to modern-day Lake Erie. The little relief in the landscape comes from beach ridges formed by the ancient lakeshore. The Black Swamp is poorly drained bottomland that retarded early settlement, and many eastern Native American tribes were given reservation land there. Later, when the use of clay drainage tile, manufactured in Akron, allowed the swamp to be drained, the Black Swamp became the last settled area of Michigan and a major agricultural area. With the water gone, almost 6 feet of topsoil was left. Noting the rich soils, legislators once again relocated the Indian tribes so that commercial developers could farm there.

Bogs are surfaces covered with sphagnum moss, flowers, low heath evergreens and, sometimes, trees. Courtesy Fen Wetland Field-Cedar Bog Nature Preserve.

many marshes. Marshes are often crucial habitat for waterfowl, spawning fish, muskrat, and fox. *Swamps* are forested wetlands with little or no peat, vegetated mostly by trees and shrubs, often associated with rivers, slow streams, or isolated depressions. The flat, sandy lake plain along Lake Michigan is dotted with swamps featuring mixtures of conifer and hardwood trees. *Peatlands* are areas in which plant debris decays very slowly; the organic material accumulates into dark brown or black peat. In the Lakes Region the peatlands resulted from poor drainage and cool climates, with little evaporation during the summer. Over six million areas of peatlands are in northeastern Minnesota. In Minnesota and Michigan (Upper Peninsula) spruce peatlands are called *muskegs*. *Bogs* are surfaces entirely covered with living sphagnum moss, low heath evergreens, and, sometimes, trees; conifer bogs can be extremely acid. A bog receives only precipitation and has no significant inflows or outflows. It is characterized by slowly decaying vegetation, as in the peat bogs found on the margins of lakes and ponds or in glacial outwashes such as kettle holes. Minnesota and Wisconsin have conifer bogs in Black Lake and Bois Brule public land areas. *Potholes* are small saucer-shaped depressional wetlands left by glaciers; they are significant recharge areas for groundwater. The Prairie Pothole region extends from southern Alberta into the eastern Dakotas and western Minnesota and north-central Iowa.

The Central Lowlands

The Central Lowlands is the flattest part of the somewhat larger Prairie Region. At the time of the first European influx, forests surrounded natural open spaces. The edge of the Prairie Region is marked in many places by a west-facing escarpment demarcating the Appalachian Plateau. Central Illinois and all of Iowa form the "Prairie Peninsula" of the vast and almost treeless tall-grass Prairie Region, the Grand Prairie, which sprouts grasses up to 10 feet high. As we have noted, the Central Lowlands is divided into three distinct parts: the Glaciated Till Plain, the Dissected Till Plain, and the Driftless.

The Till Plain stretches from the Appalachian Plateau in the east across central Ohio, Indiana, most of Illinois, and then into Iowa. Much of this expanse is synonymous with the Corn Belt, centered in the Dissected Till Plain of southern and eastern Iowa. The Till Plain bedrock is buried under glacial drift deposited during previous Ice Ages. Moraines are its chief topographic feature. Much of Illinois is also covered with loess, the fine silt picked up by winter winds and deposited as the glaciers retreated. The drift and loess have contributed to the flat landscape and the productive soils of the Corn Belt.

The central part of Ohio, Indiana, and Illinois is the Till Plain proper, a flat to gently rolling landscape overlain with glacial till (an unsorted mixture of sand, silt, clay, and boulders) from at least eight different glacial events. Ohio actually has several easily defined regions, depending on glaciation boundaries, in-

Disappearing Wetlands

Wetlands are still abundant in the Midwest, especially in the Great Lakes region. Previously thought of as wastelands, wetlands are saturated soils called swamps, bogs, sloughs, potholes, and marshes. All have important functions.

In 1780, the coterminous United States contained about 221 million acres of wetlands. Twenty-one states possessed over 3 million acres of wetlands each, much of it in the Midwest. By 1980, only 104 million acres remained, a loss of over 53 percent. Midwestern states have lost the most: Illinois, Indiana, Iowa, and Ohio have lost about 70 percent of their wetland acreage. Over 36 million acres (or one-third of all U.S. wetland loss) in those states have been transformed by agricultural development and population growth.

Wetlands interrelate with other ecosystems to provide protective boundaries for both land and life. Wetlands protect shorelines, but they also retain water, filter it, and recharge aquifers. They retard stormwater runoff and thereby lessen erosion and flooding; their soils remove toxins and synthetic nutrients, thereby ameliorating pollution. Wetlands also provide nesting and migration habitats for waterfowl, as well as spawning and nursery grounds for fish, frogs, and turtles. Despite these undeniable benefits, wetlands still fall prey to suburban sprawl. States have now passed environmental laws to help protect remaining wetlands. Wetland policies today require that developers who fill in wetlands must create new wetlands and then maintain them for five years. Only time will tell if these mitigated wetlands are as successful as natural wetlands in buffering water sources from pollutants such as nitrates and phosphorus.

cluding a hilly, nonglaciated strip in the southeast that is actually part of the Appalachians. In Indiana the Till Plain is called the Tipton Till Plain. Illinois's till plain is the eastern extension of the tall-grass Prairie Peninsula, the easternmost extension of the grasslands. Illinois is the tall-grass prairie because it receives a higher precipitation than the regions to the west and is therefore richer in taller grasses such as big bluestem and Indian grass. It is, however, a transition area and has more trees than the tall-grass prairie to the west, yet fewer than the deciduous tree zone to the east. Till plains were once heavily forested in beech, maple, and elm, with a sprinkling of open space and peat bogs. Westward through the plain the open grass areas became increasingly dominant. Today the forested parts of the plain have been cleared, and the fertile glacial till and loess soil are intensively farmed. Much of the till plain is *tiled* to promote drainage, especially in low-lying areas.

Much of Iowa and northern Missouri comprise the Dissected Till Plain. This area is more broken than the area to the east, largely because it was covered by

Iowa best epitomizes the Corn Belt, leading the nation in corn production (17.9 percent of U.S. total [1997]) and the amount of harvested cropland (7.5 percent of U.S. total [1997]). Courtesy Library of Congress.

the early Kansas and Iowan glacial periods, but not the more recent Wisconsin stage. As a result, the land has had more time than the Till Plains to the east to show weathering and to be "dissected" by stream erosion. When Europeans arrived, it was mostly open savannah and forests of white oak, hickory, and elm. A case could be made that the dissected till plain of Iowa is the "true prairie," with the perfect climate and soil for growing the most sought after grain in America, corn, 80 percent of which is used to feed livestock and supply the over 200 pounds of meat each American eats annually. Most of the presettlement vegetation in the state was tall grass, flourishing in the cherished chernozem soils of the wettest prairie region; black earth, rich in humus and very fertile. Fire, drought, and bison grazing historically controlled the land, but combines, hogs, and hybrid seed now shape it.

Tiling

The Midwest Region was glacially formed with many wetlands: swamps, bogs, and marshes. Although the land was fertile, it could not be used efficiently as farmland until the wetlands could be drained. Surface ditches and subsurface drainage, called tiling, provided dry land and controlled flooding.

Farmers who settled the land buried permeable drainage pipes 3 to 6 feet below the root zone of the crop. The pipes were usually made of clay, the "tiles." They removed standing or excess water on poorly drained land, rerouting it to nearby streams. After 1970, many of these "tiles" were replaced with perforated polyethylene tubing. The pattern of tiling would depend on the field: some farmers would pinpoint a particular wet spot in a field, while others might drain an entire field through a branching pattern. The tiles helped aerate land bogged by glaciers. Crops do not grow well in saturated soils. When tiles were installed, the saturated level of the fields would lie below the crop roots, thus allowing the crop to grow to its full potential. Tiling reduces wetlands, however, disturbing ecological balance.

The Missouri Anomaly

Missouri's landscape does not quite fit in our three subdivisions. Located in the unglaciated section of the lowlands, south of the Missouri River, is Missouri's transitional area of low, rolling, asymmetrical cuestas, in contrast to the plateau Ozarks to the east and the flatter glaciated plains to the north. Nor is it as flat as the High Plains to the west. Once a mix of tall-grass prairie and oak and hickory forest, today it is a tall-grass prairie with over 90 percent of the area under agricultural development, growing corn and soybeans. The soils are the fertile mollisols, as is the case in most of the lowland till plain. This region was glaciated, but not in the most recent advance, so the landscape is more dissected because it has had time to erode. Row crops have increased erosion in the glacial till soil, sending sediment into nearby streams and rivers. This region has many birds, reptiles, and butterflies and was once home to bison. The area surrounding the Missouri River was known historically as Little Dixie. As the name implies, it shared many southern traits, including slaves who raised cotton in the boot heel of Missouri, which was admitted to the Union in 1821 as a slave state.

But Missouri is the most bifurcated among the midwestern states because one-half of it lies within the Central Lowlands and the other half within the Ozark Plateau, which is divided between the rough Salem Plateau and the smoother, more productive Springfield Plateau to the west. Few features of landscape or economy are shared between the Central Lowlands region and the Ozarks. The Ozark area is more similar geologically and culturally to both the Interior Plateau (Tennessee and Kentucky) and the Appalachians. The Ozarks, often called mountains, are actually a plateau—the product of uplift and erosion that create the look of mountains. Because the area was not glaciated even to the degree of the northern half of Missouri, the southern landscape is filled with "hills and hollers." The core here is granite, though much of the surface has a limestone cap with karst features. The St. Francois Mountains in the eastern section, along the Mississippi River, were an active mining region of zinc and lead in the nineteenth century. Vegetation remains much as it was prior to European influx, a mixed forest of pine and oak.

Karst is limestone that has been subjected to rainwater and dissolves under the action of carbon dioxide in the rain into carbonate rocks (limestone). Little water accumulates on the surface of a karst landscape because most of the water is underground, flowing through cavities dissolved by rainwater. This makes for unusual terrain filled with fluctuating springs, springs spouting from rock, sinkholes, and caves, all the result of the action of water on porous limestone. Karst topography is difficult to traverse and is also not good for agriculture generally; this poor area was not as attractive to settlement as other parts of the frontier west. Today, however, tourism has blossomed in the Ozarks. The Army Corps of Engineers built dams along the White River, which created lakes for sports and habitat for some wetland-loving birds. Speculators sold lots along the lakes created by the dams to many midwesterners who were seeking a "mountain" second home. As a result, the population of the region has increased 90 percent since 1970. Tourism actually began to develop in the late nineteenth century, when Americans came for the purported health benefits of spring-fed waters. After 1950, Branson, Missouri, grew from a small town into a country-and-western family vacationland. One of the attractions is the White River itself, a major basin that cuts through the southern part of the state and into Arkansas. The prairie and forest of the Springfield Plateau, some 40 percent of Missouri, have become home to mixed farming and beef and dairy operations. The state's third largest city, Springfield, the undeniable capital of the Ozarks, is about thirty-five miles north of Branson.

The Driftless is located mostly in southwestern Wisconsin. Photo by Chris Mayda.

Returning to our three subregions of the Central Lowlands, we move to the Driftless area much farther north. Because of its unglaciated past, the hills of the Driftless are not low, rolling bumps, but significant and steep, with irregular features jutting from the landscape floor. The Driftless covers 15,000 square miles, with over 13,000 in Wisconsin and the remainder shared by Minnesota, Iowa, and Illinois. The Wisconsin portion contains few lakes. Theoretically, the highland area to the north may have blocked the ice advances, or the lobes of ice on either side may have joined to the south before the ice could completely cover the enclosed ground, and so the Driftless escaped as the ice retreated. Weathering continually since a shallow sea withdrew at the close of the Paleozoic era, it has been left with gorges such as the Mississippi flowing some 500 feet below the upland area. The result is a landscape of monuments, cliffs, and rock bridges—generally a topography seldom seen in the Central Lowlands. The present relief of the Driftless, however, is an example of what the entire region might have looked like prior to glacial activity.

In the Driftless the soils, topography, and economy differ sharply from those that surround it. The region has easily accessible minerals because ores were not scraped off by the glaciers; mining for lead began in Wisconsin in the early nineteenth century. Mining was so important here that agriculture other than small vegetable gardens was forbidden. Today the area is used for cattle but is not as agriculturally productive as the surrounding glaciated areas. Hills and valleys have often been emphasized by human interventions such as lumbering, mining, and farming.

WATER

Successive ice ages that scoured the land left behind one of the region's most important resources in the form of lakes both large and small. These appealed to early European settlers, who could hardly travel ten miles without encountering a lake beside which they could establish a farm. Numerous bodies of water dotting the terrain help to distinguish the Midwest from the mountains and deserts further west, as do the signatures of the mighty rivers that configure the center of the North American continent. All have affected the region's ecology and economy.

Aquatic Features

Water is abundant, though not equally distributed throughout the Midwest. Receiving ample precipitation, it has enjoyed abundant freshwater sources, a legacy of its Ice Age history. Not surprisingly, the Midwest is less reliant on irrigation than the West. The continental glaciers left thousands of natural inland lakes, including the largest system of surface freshwater in the world, the Great Lakes. This vast reservoir, combined with many rivers, plentiful groundwater, and seasonal snow pack, makes the Great Lakes Region home to 16 percent of the world's freshwater. The region's freshwater supports commerce, agriculture, fishing industries, and urban and recreational needs. The extraordinary population explosion in the twentieth century, however, strained freshwater supplies. Human activity and its increased pollution of freshwater have had a monumental impact.

Great Lakes

The Great Lakes are large enough to affect the climate of the region. The five lakes, Superior, Michigan, Huron, Erie, and Ontario, span 750 miles mostly along the U.S. and Canadian border. Fully one-tenth of the U.S. population and one-fourth of the Canadian population live in the narrowly confined Great Lakes Basin. Only Lake Michigan lies completely within the United States. The lakes are interconnected physically, but a series of rapids and falls historically made continuous passage through the system hazardous.

Smaller Lakes

Although Michigan, Minnesota, and Wisconsin are defined by their proximity to the Great Lakes, as are northern Ohio, Indiana, and Illinois, each state contains thousands of interior secondary lakes. Michigan and Minnesota account for around 10,000 lakes each, and Wisconsin another 3,800 lakes, all remnants of glacial action. Since Pleistocene glaciation occurred only about 8,000 years ago, the fairly young geo-

Tiffin Report

Michigan was developed much later than Ohio, largely because Ohio was easily reached by way of the Ohio River and the National Road, whereas the Black Swamp rendered the northern reaches of Michigan impassable. The swamp appalled early surveyors. In 1815, the surveyor general, Edward Tiffin, wrote that land along what is now the baseline of Michigan (the now-famous 8 Mile Road) was "with some few exceptions, low, wet land, with a very thick growth of underbrush, intermixed with very bad marshes . . . and that continuing north and eastward, the number and extent of the swamps increases." The report continues to describe the territory as "a poor, barren, sandy land . . . so bad that there would not be more than one acre out of a hundred, if there would be one out of a thousand, that would in any case admit of cultivation."[2]

Land in Michigan was originally intended as a bounty and reward to soldiers. After Tiffin issued his report, the government decided that soldiers would complain less if bounty land were in Missouri. Settlement of Michigan remained sparse until 1825, when the Erie Canal improved access.

logical area has not yet developed the drainage patterns of drier areas and is still pockmarked with wetland marshes and bogs. Michigan was so saturated, in fact, that the original Surveyor's Report (1815) discouraged settlement and farming. Drained today, many wetlands are gone. Residents seldom know the extent of human-induced change in the landscape. Agricultural production was possible only after the land was drained by ditches dug in the ground and lined with perforated pipes, or "tiled." For example, in Minnesota more than 90 percent of the prairie wetlands have been drained. Also common is the damming of small streams and rivers, which are then channeled into farming areas for irrigation.

RIVERS

Subjects of story and song, the major midwestern rivers have inspired awe, affection, and fear. Their size was an element of their beauty. They carried people to new homes and products to new markets; their confluences gave rise to glittering cities; their billions upon billions of gallons fertilized the country's breadbasket; their twisting lengths created networks that unified the region even as their boundaries delineated new states of the Union. But their power, while crucial to agricultural and industrial development, has always resisted human control. Even today, flooding remains a fact of life, to be expected from arteries that must drain the huge central mass of the continent.

Ohio River

The largest drainage basin river in the Midwest is the Ohio River, which drains portions of three states, Ohio, Indiana, and Illinois. The basin is home to 9 percent of the American population, or about 25 million people. Beginning at the junction of the Allegheny and Monongahela rivers in Pittsburgh, the early starting point for European western influx, the Ohio flows west to meet the Mississippi at Cairo, Illinois. Along the way, the Ohio receives 95 percent of its water from tributaries, the most notable being the Wabash (Illinois/Indiana), the Tennessee, and the Cumberland rivers. The flow historically was mostly free of obstacles, with the exception of minor falls and rapids at Louisville, Kentucky, and steamboats appeared on the Ohio in 1811. Later, to control the volume and quality of flow and reduce periodic flooding, the Army Corps of Engineers constructed a series of locks, dams, and power-generating facilities along its route.

It took twenty dams to provide the minimum required depth for modern navigation and flood control on the river. Here, too, the benefits of commercial navigation have to be weighed against environmental impact. Rivers become relatively stagnant when flowing into reservoirs; increased sediment and decreased oxygen encourage algae blooms, bacterial contamination, and invasive species. Hydropower facilities along the Ohio generate about 6 percent of all U.S. electricity. Hydropower energy is cleaner than either coal and oil, but has its own environmental costs. Hydropower facilities can cause high fish mortality and hamper the circulation of oxygen. Many power plants located on the Ohio River use river water for steam production to run the turbines for electrical generation. Unfortunately, this changes the temperature and chemical content of the water that is then returned to the river.

Upper Mississippi River

The Upper Mississippi flows from its source in Lake Itasca in northern Minnesota to the junction with the Ohio River at Cairo, Illinois, gathering power and volume from every tributary. Unlike the Mississippi Alluvial plain south of Cairo, the upper reaches of the river are mountainous, with high bluffs often dropping down to the river below. The upper Mississippi River watershed services about 15 million Americans. The river is also an important habitat for 25 percent of all North American fish species and a crucial flyway zone for 40 percent of North American fowl. Many hundreds of other animals and plants rely on its shorelines. The Upper Mississippi was home to early Paleo-Indian settlements, including one of the major Native American civilizations prior to European contact, the Cahokia mound builders across the river from today's St. Louis. The river created and made wealthy (and sometimes destroyed) many other settlements of those who emigrated to the interior, and it figured prominently in the art and culture that ensued. To say that midwesterners have exploited and loved the river for the past 200 years is to speak the obvious; for many Americans, the upper reaches of the fabled "Father of Waters" are as synonymous with the Midwest as the lower reaches are with the South. Its natural and commercial value for the region and for the nation is incalculable. To anyone viewing modern barge traffic against its vibrant shorelines, the Upper Mississippi seems alive in both respects.

Wabash River

Rising in Ohio, the Wabash River is the longest river in Indiana. Flowing east to west across rural Indiana, it defines the southern extent of the Lakes Region and then turns south where it divides Illinois and Indiana before emptying into the Ohio. The river is a popular canoeing destination because of its gentle gradient, calm waters, and picturesque rural setting. Like the Ohio and the Mississippi, the Wabash has been cherished in memory and song ("On the Banks of the Wabash") for its beauty and beneficence. But the river today suffers from degraded water quality and periodic flooding, which have caused damage to such urban areas as Lafayette and Terre Haute. Retaining wetland areas and creating ponds would probably help.

Cuyahoga River, Ohio

The Cuyahoga is a relatively short river, flowing a contorted path over a hundred miles, though a crow could easily fly the thirty miles from its source to Lake Erie. Its name is an Indian term meaning "crooked river." It was originally home to Native Americans who hunted and fished along the river; European settlers also profited from its resources. During the early nineteenth century the Ohio Canal connected the Ohio River with the Cuyahoga, transforming it into an important transporation route. As industry took hold along its banks, turbines at Cuyahoga Falls powered even more industrial development. So much raw sewage, oil, paints, and other pollutants were dumped directly into its waters that it became a dead river by the mid-twentieth century. The Cuyahoga's notoreity peaked in 1969, when the oil-soaked water caught fire. The incident proved a blessing, however, for it was the genesis of the environmental movement to clean waters in America, spawning the Clean Water Act and helping to create both federal and state Environmental Protection agencies. In any case, the river has made a comeback since environmental controls halted the dumping of raw sewage and eliminated industrial pollutants. No longer a dead zone, it has aquatic life; its beaches, once closed due to severe pollution, are again open for recreation.

Red River Valley, Minnesota/North Dakota

The Red River, flowing in the former bed of the ancient glacial Lake Agassiz, divides Minnesota from North Dakota in the upper reaches of the western Lake Region and is part of the Hudson Bay drainage system. Once the valley was bog, potholes, and tall-grass prairie. Drained, it is one of America's most fertile agricultural lands. Crops include wheat, sugar beets, barley, sunflowers, and canola. The change from wetland to farmland has altered the river's sediment flow. The river has responded by cutting deeper channels, leading to still more erosion. Sediment and erosion have threatened native habitats for fish, plants, and animals, and generally decreased the biodiversity in the valley. Another result has been flooding: because the river flows north, it can encounter ice jamming during spring thaw. Despite levees built to reinforce its banks, the Red River poured into Grand Forks, North Dakota, in the disastrous flood of 1997.

The Missouri River

With the Ohio and Mississippi, the Missouri River is one of the triad of titanic waterways that embrace and nurture the land mass of the Midwest. Among American rivers, it is second in length only to the Mississippi. It flows 2,315 miles from its headwaters in Montana to its mouth on the Mississippi at St. Louis, along the way forming parts of the western borders of Iowa and Missouri. Acquired along with the Mississippi in the Louisiana Purchase of 1803, the Missouri Valley fascinated Lewis and Clark in part because of its importance to Native Americans. The account of Lewis and Clark's explorations of the Missouri's features from 1804 to 1806 still fascinates us today. Soon after the arrival of the first Europeans, the river became the main conduit of the fur trade in the West; steamboats began regularly to ply significant stretches of its length in 1819. Nicknamed "the Big Muddy," today it carries large quantities of mud as well as commercial traffic. Tug-guided barges ferry wheat, corn, and soybeans from Sioux City, Iowa, to Kansas City, Missouri, and return with cement, fertilizer, and gasoline. An extensive system of more than one hundred dams on the river and its tributaries now help control its periodic flooding and routinely irrigate nearby agricultural enterprises.

WEATHER AND CLIMATE

Perhaps more than most Americans, midwesterners talk a lot about the weather. Temperate weather contributes to a favorable quality of life for the Midwest's citizens, and of course profoundly influences agricultural and rural life. But climate also governs the ecological balance of the habitats of flora and fauna.

Central Lowlands

The climate of the eastern United States from the Atlantic coast to the 100th meridian is classified as humid continental. Thus, annual temperatures in the Central Lowlands range from warm, wet summers to cold, dry winters. Unprotected by mountain barriers, the flat topography allows Arctic air masses to invade. Inhabitants chilled by winters joke that the only thing between the North Pole and the Midwest is a barbed wire fence. Flatness also allows the formation of traveling wave cyclones when cold air meets humid maritime air masses from the Gulf of Mexico. Extremes between high- and low-pressure systems form cycles of storms that track across the Midwest lowlands year round. Ample precipitation, generally over 25 inches annually, supports numerous grain crops. Corn and soybeans are grown in abundance.

Great Lakes Region

Two elements differentiate the climates of the Great Lakes region and the Central Lowlands. The first is winter icing as the consequence of a fluctuating freezing line across water and land. As a result, areas farther north have a growing season of about 90 days. By contrast, areas along the lee side of the Great Lakes enjoy a 160- to 180-day growing season, increasing in the southerly reaches near the Ohio River to almost 200 days. The second element is lake-effect snow. Leeward shorelines receive abundant snowfall. Arctic air washes over the warmer lakes, which modify the cool air by condensing it into clouds as it is forced up and over recessional lake ridges. In winter, snow can exceed 100 inches. Although lake-effect snows can reach as far south as the Ohio River, depending on wind speed and direction, the snow is usually concentrated on the southeast side of the lakes. This area has come to be known as the "Snow Belt." Seasonal variations around the Great Lakes create weather conditions amenable to the growing of fruit along the western shore of Michigan and along the western shores of Lake Erie and Lake Ontario, also known as the "Niagara Fruit Belt."

MAJOR BIOMES

The Midwestern biomes (large ecosystems of relatively uniform climate in which plants, animals, insects, and people are interdependent) are tall-grass prairies and temperate broadleaf deciduous forests. The tall-grass prairies are largely found in the till plains, while the

Lake-Effect Fruit—Michigan

The Great Lakes affect temperature and climatic conditions in the nearby shore areas. The lake effect in Michigan allows the western shore of Michigan to grow fruit that ordinarily cannot grow at these high latitudes. The moderating force of Lake Michigan delays the blossoming of the fruit trees in the spring when the lake keeps the local air cool longer than the surrounding area. Consequently, fruit trees do not blossom until the danger of frosts is gone. During the summer, the lake keeps the air around the lake cooler than the continental extremes found further inland, providing an ideal temperature (less than 85 degrees F) for fruit trees such as the cherries of the Mission Peninsula. In the fall the first frost is delayed because the early cold northern air is warmed as it passes over the lake and moderates the temperature over the land. Therefore fall begins later than in inland areas. In winter, the coastal region is warmed by the lake, which seldom freezes over. The lake moderates the air and keeps the temperatures above that required by the fruit trees (above –10 degrees F).

temperate broadleaf forests are located chiefly in the Lakes Region, which transitions in the north to the Superior Uplands conifer boreal forest. The two midwestern biomes vary in characteristics.

Temperate Deciduous Biome

The deciduous region is largely a temperate, humid-continental area with the exception of the lake-effect regions along the leeward coasts of the Great Lakes. Average rainfall is 45 to 50 inches distributed throughout the year. A temperate climate is one where the climate has both a warm and a cool season, as distinguished from the boreal or tropical forests to the north and south, which tend to be either cold or warm, respectively.

Trees in the temperate deciduous forest are commonly oak, maple, hickory, and beech. Most of the midwestern deciduous forest is second- or third-growth because, as settlement expanded westward, the original forested area was cut and used for blast furnaces, railroad ties, phone poles, and housing. The Lakes Region also contains the Superior Upland region, a boreal forest mixture of hardwood and conifer forests mixed in with wetlands, often conifer bogs. This remote region has a short growing season. The dominant species of forest is black spruce mixed with a tall shrub layer of speckled alder and winterberry. Deep in the remote northern reaches of boreal forest are also old-growth mixed conifer and oak forests. Sphagnum mosses layer the ground. The ecosystem was shaped by both wind and fire to create a mosaic pattern of white pine/oak/swamp. Conifer bog fires in this area occurred approximately every one hundred years. Given fire suppression practiced since the arrival of Europeans, the wind has had a larger impact. Trees are blown down, not burned. Attempts to control forest use have affected succession and rejuvenation. For example, in the early twentieth century the uplands were clearcut of many of their trees; later fires were devastating because of the slash that remained. Extensive logging for pine early in the twentieth century encouraged the growth of more maples, aspens, and birch.

Deciduous forest soils are alfisols (rich brown forest soil) enriched by the leaves that fall annually to the forest floor. The leaves decompose, forming humus, in the fall and winter. This humus provides necessary nutrients to make the region even more agriculturally productive.

In the deciduous areas of the Midwest, the fauna are herbivores (plant eaters) and omnivores (both meat and plant eaters). Herbivores include white-tailed deer, gray squirrel, and chipmunks. Omnivores include raccoon, opossum, skunk, and black bear. There originally were many carnivores (meat eaters) as well, such as timber wolves, mountain lions, and bobcats, but humans have largely eliminated these, and many species are extinct. The populations of some animals, like the white-tailed deer and raccoons, have increased since humans reduced their predators. Bird species include omnivores, some of which nest in tree cavities (e.g., woodpeckers), and seed-eaters (e.g., blue jays), who disperse acorns and other seeds into abandoned farmlands and pastures. Migratory birds are insectivorous (insect eaters) and include warblers, wrens, and thrushes. Hummingbirds also abound. The more remote Superior Upland teems with natural habitat animals, such as wolves, woodchucks, martens, and beavers. The shoreline wetlands of Lake Superior provide summer range for birds such as the Kirtland's Warbler, and migratory and breeding stopovers for others. Conifer bogs are home to birds such as chukar, ducks, and geese, as well as mammals such as moose, coyote, wolf, and bobcats. The shores also are important for aquatic diversity and hatcheries.

Tall-Grass Prairie Biome

The Tall-Grass Prairie is the wettest area of the Prairie Region. With about 40 inches of precipitation annually, the biome offers good conditions for growing corn. The humid continental climate allows a sufficient growing season between the last spring and the first autumn frost. Land loses its warmth more quickly than water, and without the water to moderate its temperature, continental climates are subjected to wide fluctuations in both diurnal and seasonal temperatures.

Grasses have long roots and grow from the base instead of the tip. Tall-grass varieties such as Bluestem often grow up to 10 feet tall, sending roots equally deep into the soil. Because the long roots hold the sod together, they help prevent soil erosion. They also enrich the soil when they decompose. This type of vegetation pattern allows for grazing animals. Millions of buffalo once roamed these prairies, providing a natural niche in the regional ecosystem that kept the grasses trimmed and the soil broken (from their hooves) to encourage new growth. The region was also home to many varieties of wildflowers, some now gone forever. It is generally believed that, historically, human-induced burns controlled the growth patterns in this region. According to that theory, the oak–hickory forests that have emerged in the last 150 years or so are due to the suppression of fires since the arrival of Europeans.

Grasses add the organic matter that forms the humus-rich, fertile *mollisol* soils. Mollisols are among the most fertile soils on Earth. Fertility is very evident in central Iowa where *loess* (the wind-blown silt from glacial drift) combines with the deep humus. Burrowing animals and decomposers (ground squirrels and gophers,

White-Tailed Deer

White-tailed deer are located throughout the eastern United States and Canada. They weigh about 300 pounds full grown and live in woods, though they are increasingly being found in suburban areas, where they eat almost anything. At one time threatened by hunting and land development, white-tailed deer populations have surged dramatically, principally because hunting has been restricted to the fall and because natural predators such as wolves and bobcats have disappeared. Iowa reintroduced the deer in the 1930s, because they were thought to be extinct in the state. By 1980, Iowa's white-tailed deer numbered 55,000; by 2003, they had reached 210,000. One result is an increase in deer-vehicle crashes. Iowa alone saw 13,137 crashes in 1997; nearly a third of all rural crashes involved a white-tailed deer. Crashes can be fatal to both deer and driver. Other problems are that deer harbor deer ticks, the primary vector for Lyme disease, and they are predisposed to the deer equivalent of Mad Cow disease, chronic wasting disease (CWD). After forty-four deer were found with CWD in 2002, Wisconsin established a 411-square-mile CWD eradication zone in the southwest which reduced herd size somewhat.[3]

Deer-Vehicle Crashes in Midwestern States

	Number of Deer (2003)	Number of Crashes
Illinois	700,000	23,695 (2002)
Indiana	450,000	11,371 (2000)
Iowa	500,000	7,800 (2002)
Michigan	1,800,000	66,993 (2001)
Minnesota	1,100,000	5,557 (2002)
Ohio	550,000	34,224 (2001)
Wisconsin	1,400,000	20,470 (2002)

Deer in large numbers damage crops and destroy seedlings of valuable trees such as hemlocks and oaks. They also destroy wildflowers and the bushes that sustain birds and butterflies. States have begun to alter hunting seasons to thin the herds, sometimes over vocal opposition, in order to restore some kind of balance.

and earthworms and ants) loosen, aerate, and disperse nutrients to the soil. The soil insulates them from climatic extremes, and provides a refuge from predators and fire. Early European settlers in the prairie sometimes built their homes from sod for the same reasons. Different grassland regimes (tall versus short) are defined by water availability, which in turn, influences the crops produced.

The animal types on the prairie changed radically after European settlement. Prior to that time, the region teemed with grazing animals such as buffalo, pronghorn antelope, and elk, and with the gray wolves that were their natural predators. Converting most of the land to agricultural use drove many of these animals from the landscape. Where buffalo once grazed, domesticated herbivores like cattle and sheep now eat the much-reduced grasses. Birds of prey (raptors) such as hawks and eagles are still prevalent because the region provides them with hunting grounds, but many raptors are now endangered by alterations in the prairie habitat. Some species of birds and butterflies, such as the Henslow Sparrow and the Regal Fritillary, have been reduced and threatened as their habitat has shrunk. The Henslow Sparrow, at one time the most prevalent bird in Illinois, is now found only in the few remaining fragments of the original prairie.

SETTLEMENT AND THE ENVIRONMENT

The environment beckoned benignly both to the original settlers and their European successors. Micro-ecologies determined the settlement patterns of American Indians, some of whom migrated seasonally. Early European farmers, drawn to an area that seemed empty and waiting, put down roots as they sprinkled themselves throughout the Northwest Territory. Federal surveyors drew topographical grids to apportion land for ownership, laid out villages and towns, and planned roads, highways, and railroads that would concentrate midwesterners at transportation junctions.

Spatial Patterns of the Midwest Amerindians

Original aboriginal peoples in North America are generally divided into three time periods in the Midwest: Paleo-Indian (12,000 years B.C.E.), Archaic (9000 years B.C.E.), and Woodland (3000 years B.C.E.). Although each group left behind specific artifacts, the lack of written history makes it difficult to assign definite dates or specific reasons for their spatial distribution. We do know something of the general characteristics associated with each group from traditions passed from time period to time period. Each of these groups established cultures that were "advanced" for their day: hierarchical organization, spiritual foundations, weapon and tool technologies, and what we choose to think of as respectful exploitation of environment. Because of their small numbers and relatively simple technology, their impact on the environment was low. Whatever their origins (Eurasia or South Pacific Islands), they were the original immigrants to the Midwest. Here at first their small groups lived in isolation, developing their own methods for survival and their own structures of culture. When quests for food and shelter brought them into contact with other groups, they established tribal boundaries.

Paleo-Indian Period

Although some archaeological findings suggest a pre-projectile society, this information is sketchy. Artifactual evidence establishes the presence of Paleo-Indian groups in the Late Pleistocene, beginning about 12,000 B.C.E. They lived throughout the Midwest; archaeological remnants of their lives can be found along what were glacial fronts in areas as diverse as Saginaw, Michigan, or the Upper Mississippi River Valley. Primarily nomadic hunters, they followed game that provided food, skins for clothing, and bones for tools. They stalked the wooly mammoth, giant beaver, and caribou along the swath of rich vegetation on the edges of the retreating glaciers.

Excavated kill sites indicate the hunting, skinning, and cooking of these plentiful carnivores and herbivores. The main weapon was the spear, whose point was usually flaked from flint and whose shaft may have had a cord attached to it for easy retrieval. At some point the Paleo-Indian groups learned to project the spear from a cross-bow device whose strings were made from rolled, sinewy muscle tissue. The projectile usually included a "flute" (central lengthwise groove) that allowed it to be tied to the foreshaft. Flutes whose form and design are associated with different areas can date the various groups. Since one kill could last for weeks, temporary camps could last long enough to leave traces. Usually, these camps favored higher ground locations for drainage and a vantage point for observation. Being nomadic, Paleo-Indians limited their material culture to what they could carry; sedentary camps for growing food were not necessary. Warmer climate and glacial retreat may have caused the number of Paleo-Indians to decline. As the glaciers retreated, the exposed prairie redefined hunting habits: the groups now pursued buffalo instead of mammoths. In addition, archaeological evidence indicates trade among midwestern groups: flint from southern Indiana and Illinois can be found in burial areas of Wisconsin and Minnesota.

Archaic Period

Although the late Paleo-Indian populations did not die out, their culture did. Climatic change induced cultural change apparent in the material artifacts left by the succeeding group of Amerindians in about 9000 B.C.E. During this post–Ice Age period, warmer temperatures allowed deciduous forests to encroach on the coniferous stands. It is difficult to imagine the lengthy process in which shifting environmental conditions encourage the northward expansion of both flora and fauna, but descendants of the Paleo peoples had to adapt to changes, many of them beneficial. Deciduous forests provided more variations in food products for both animals and humans. Even though Archaic people still hunted, they focused on small game. They gathered available edible materials, and they used runoff valleys to fish. Since they were not confined to one ecosystem, they developed an array of tools to find and process food. They seemed to have developed a more intimate knowledge of their environment than their predecessors. As populations increased and various groups split off, cultural variations evolved among "nations" clustered around local resources. They usually chose to live alongside lakes and streams during the warmer months and to retreat into higher elevations during the winter. Water provided aquatic sustenance and also transportation. Elevated sites provided more protection from the elements and allowed for harvest of abundant fall fruits.

Archaic peoples were seminomadic but at the same time more territorial. Their seasonal village sites centered on ceremonial structures and cemeteries with stone fixtures, indicators of a more stationary disposition. Greater rootedness permitted a wider, more dependable diet, more leisure time, and greater division of labor and occupational specialization. As a result, the very young and very old did not constitute societal burdens. Living in the wilderness required innovations reflected in changing traditions. The greater number of high-quality artifacts from the Archaic period, some of them evidence of long-distance trade, suggests a more complex social structure. Moreover, warmer climate and increased population altered still further the Archaic culture of tradition and innovation, moving Native Americans to a new stage of development.

Woodland Period

The period beginning in approximately 3000 B.C.E. represents the apogee of aboriginal peoples not only in the Midwest but also in the culture area east of the Rocky Mountains. The firing of clay and the use of salt for glazing pottery were unique innovations. Scholars divide the Woodland era into early, middle, and late subperiods according to the increasing complexity of style and decoration of pottery found at sucessive sites. The transition from Archaic to Woodland is not well defined because midwestern Native Americans continued their by-then traditional hunting and gathering. What marks the shift is the increasingly sedentary nature of the various groups (now distinguished by tribal divisions) and the widespread domestication of plants and animals. Woodland Indians more directly controlled their environment and probably lived longer; in any case, populations swelled. Although stationary settlements and domestication may not have been universal throughout the entire Amerindian culture, in the Midwest they were environmentally feasible.

Crops grew on the floodplains, where dense stands of trees did not have to be cleared, in fertile alluvial soils that were naturally fertilized by annual spring floods. The Woodland people introduced early conservation techniques by growing crops together. This maximized space and prevented soil, nutrient, and crop loss. One practice is called the "Three Sisters": maize was used as a support for beans, while broadleaf squashes were planted at the base to condense morning dew and provide shade. Where semipermanent settlements arose, however, they probably lasted only twenty to thirty years, until firewood and game became scarce. Crop yields probably would start to diminish as well. As environmental degradation took place, groups would move to other locations, perhaps dividing in the process to create new settlements. The mechanism that linked these separated communities may have been spiritual rather than social. During the Early and Middle subperiods, impressive religious structures, usually in the form of burial mounds or earthworks representing animals, were constructed. They imply the establishment of an elite group responsible for developing these large projects. It is not known if the pottery traditions, agricultural practices, and burial-cult activities evolved in the Midwest or diffused from elsewhere. The best guess is that they are a compilation of techniques used throughout the Americas. Traits that linked the midwestern tribes with other groups during the Early and Middle Woodland periods include monumental architecture, religion and government, long-distance trade, social stratification, food surpluses, and increased wealth.

Among the best known midwestern cultures were the Adena (Early Woodland and Hopewell Middle Woodland), the mound builders. Although they represented two distinct cultures, they overlapped for about 700 years. The Hopewell, who flourished until about 500 C.E., continued many of the traditions of the Adena but made them more numerous, elaborate, and sophisticated. Mounds are to be found in the Fort Hill, Chillicothe, and Newark sites in the southeastern part of Ohio and in the southwestern portions of Michigan. Some mounds took the shape of effigies of animals or birds, such as the Serpent Mound in southern Ohio. Many of these effigies were lost when European farmers cultivated their homesteads, but some still remain, though often degraded by plows and earth-movers. Effigy and linear mounds can be found in southern Wisconsin and northeastern Iowa, where they can be dated by their association with the development of the bow and arrow and the beginnings of a corn culture.

A more recent culture, the Oneonta, took up residence on the bottomland of the Mississippi River. For this reason, their Late Woodland period is sometimes called the Mississippian era. This ideal location capitalized on fertile soils for growing corn and nearby woodlands for hunting, fuel, and building materials. The best known of these sites was at Cahokia, near the confluence of the Mississippi and Missouri rivers. The agricultural peoples here established an extensive exchange network with other Native Americans, as evidenced by the spread of their artifacts throughout the northern hemisphere.

The Oneonta of Cahokia flourished in the twelfth and thirteenth centuries, but apparently dispersed during the fourteenth, perhaps because of ecological changes in soil fertility, a diminished supply of woodlands, or a decrease in wild game animals. The Oneonta moved from the Mississippi River Valley into Iowa and southern Minnesota. It was here that the first Europeans, French fur trappers, had contact with the "Ioway" people.

The period that greeted the Europeans and the one best known to us today is the Late Woodland period. Here lived the descendants of the Hopewell who had settled into sedentary villages dependent on local hunting and food production. Many archaeologists also see it as a period of cultural decline. Moats or earthen mounds surrounded many settlements, defensive measures that might have contributed to inbreeding and stasis. Artifacts found from this period were made of local materials, were of cruder construction, and were intended for daily rather than ceremonial use.

At the time of European contact, the Iroquoians were the largest tribal family (based on linguistic similarities) living in the Great Lakes region. Among the tribes in the region were the Hurons (Ontario and Michigan) and the League of Five Nations (Seneca, Cayuga, Onondaga, Oneida, and Mohawk), centered mostly in the New York area but spilling over into adjacent western grounds. Generally, the Iroquoian tribes were sedentary, living in longhouses in semipermanent villages where they practiced agriculture, raising mostly corn, beans, and squash. Southern Algonquians lived in the southern Midwest and spread into Michigan during the fifteenth century, a period of warfare between Iroquoian and Algonquian tribes. Some of the Algonquian were the Miami (Ohio), Potawatomi (parts of southern Michigan, Indiana, Illinois, and northern Ohio), Renards (Fox) (Wisconsin, Minnesota), Menominee (upper Wisconsin and Michigan), Poteoustumis (Michigan), Sakis (Illinois), Shawnee, and Kickapoos (northern Great Lakes and later Ohio Valley).

A later subset of this period, sometimes called the Fort Ancient phase after a ruin near Cincinnati, saw tribes building fortified sites around central courtyards and, later, accepting European ideas and innovations into the Amerindian culture. Many tribes settled on previously abandoned sites and interacted with European traders and surveyors as they made their way into the new territories. Soon, the Europeans pitted various tribes against each other in an effort to disorganize the various nations for conquest. The environmental, ecological, spiritual, and social traditions that had been such a major part of the Midwest for 10,000 years quickly vanished. The subsequent defeat of the Amerindians, followed by rapid transformation of the environment by the quickly approaching immigrants, is, shall we say, history. Or perhaps, as John B. Jackson has observed, the sense of time itself has changed:

> While it is obvious that neither landscape [the European American and the Native American] was exclusively loyal to one notion of time—cyclical or linear—it is no less obvious that the distinction between them is based on diametrically opposed concepts of reality: timeless eternity, manifesting itself in the yearly recurrence of the seasons; and time as gift, to be accounted for when history finally comes to an end.[4]

European Settlement

French fur trappers were the first Europeans in the Great Lakes Region. Settlement farther south began as the American Revolution ended. Between 1781 and 1785, Massachusetts, Connecticut, Virginia, and New York gave up most of their claims (Maryland had already done so) to western territories so that the newly established federal government could raise money by selling lots. Under the Ordinance of 1785, Congress authorized the sale of mile-square units at a minimum auction price of one dollar an acre. Although the original thirteen colonies employed the metes and bounds system, federal surveyors adopted a township and range survey, carving landscape into a rectangular grid regardless of topography. The first boundaries under this new system were laid in the Seven Ranges along the Ohio River in 1786. The Northwest Ordinance of 1787 provided for the eventual establishment of three to five states from a huge tract north of the Ohio River and west of Pennsylvania called the Northwest Territory. Private corporations such as the Ohio Company began landing settlers in Ohio at Marietta, at the junction of the Ohio and Muskingum rivers, and other companies soon founded Gallipolis and Cincinnati. The Northwest Territory became the states of Ohio (1803), Indiana (1816), Illinois (1818), Michigan (1837), and Wisconsin (1848). Included in the Territory was the portion of Minnesota east of the Mississippi. Boundary conflicts were common. To settle one dispute, for example, Michigan gave up Toledo to Ohio in order to claim the Upper Peninsula from Wisconsin. Missouri (1821), Iowa (1846), and the western portion of Minnesota (1858) were originally parts of the Louisiana Purchase (1803).

At the beginning of settlement, the Midwest drew its population from all parts of the Atlantic seaboard. Traces of each of the three major cultural hearths (New England, Mid-Atlantic, and Upland South) are visible on the landscape today in the styles of homes and ethnic institutions. The major groups to settle the area were the Germans, English, Scots, and Irish. Migration from the New England hearth flowed along the Erie Canal after it opened in 1825, as people chose to travel westward by barge from New York. Settlement along Lake Erie blossomed. Immigrants flowed into the Western Reserve of northern Ohio, into what would become Michigan, especially around Detroit, and then, skirting the Black Swamp, into Wisconsin and Minnesota. As any study of toponyms shows, they brought with them familiar names for their new towns; New Yorkers, for example, liked Genesee, Batavia, Ithaca, and New Buffalo. In fact, many names across the Midwest can be classified as "New England Extended." During the early nineteenth century, classical names such as Syracuse and Troy were popular. Ohio alone has 158 towns with classical places names, Illinois 131, and Michigan 103.[5] New England architectural styles sprang up in these places as well.

The majority of settlers came from the mid-Atlantic hearth. They moved down the Ohio River on barge and flatboat and, later, steamer. Most came from southern Pennsylvania, using Pittsburgh as a transit point to Cincinnati, which was itself a jumping off place for points on the way to St. Louis, the Gateway to the (real) West. Scots-Irish moved along the Ohio to the Miami Valley in southwestern Ohio. Pennsylvania Germans built their new homes in the fertile farmland of the north-central part of the state. Most of the utopian pioneers came from this hearth as well. (More utopian communities were established in the Midwest than in any other part of America; see the chapters on **Ethnicity** and **Religion**.) Rappites took up land in New Harmony, Indiana, and the German Settlement Society founded Hermann, Missouri, to mention just two. Because government policies allowed vast numbers to claim land, by 1803 settlers, speculators, and squatters swelled the Ohio population to 60,000, more than enough to qualify for statehood.[6]

Routes from the Upland South hearth were slightly more diverse. Because Virginia still retained some rights to a portion of southern Ohio, citizens of the former colony were encouraged to move west; others came through the Cumberland Gap. Seeking familiar landscape, they preferred the broken terrain and Appalachian outcroppings in southeast Ohio, and further west, in the Ozarks. Throughout the southern fringes of the Midwest, the population streams from the Mid-Atlantic and the Upland South met and mingled, setting ethnic and occupational patterns for the future. A variety of religious groups also made their way to the Northwest Territory, often settling communities based on religious ideals. According to the first census in 1790, 90 percent of landholders in the new region were farmers.

Waves of later immigration floated new settlers to the far corners of the eight states, drawn by the promise of land, work, and wealth from agriculture, mining, lumbering, and manufacturing. Or perhaps a better metaphor might be buckets of paint poured liberally on the flatness, spattering settlements here and there, some isolated, some not, until the technologies of the twentieth century concentrated industry and agribusiness and caused the spatters to flow back toward dense centers on this canvas of color and nationality.

TRANSPORTATION, AGRICULTURE, NATURAL RESOURCES, AND INDUSTRY

Although it is possible to treat these factors in a different order, transportation seems primary. Waterways fostered the great riverine midwestern cultures of Native Americans, and later carried European settlers from the original colonies deep into the Midwest. Flatboats, barges, and steamers of the nineteenth century, traveling along rivers and canals, carried seed and fertilizer to farmers and carried their wheat, corn, pigs, and cattle to markets back East, tasks performed by railroads and highways today. Those same transportation networks allowed industries to flourish, both those that extracted raw materials from the mines of midwestern states and shipped them to smelting centers, and those that processed energy and metal into finished products to be distributed around the world.

Transportation

Natural transportation networks expanded the import of the region. Native Americans and later French fur trappers passed through the Great Lakes system by portaging their canoes. As the interior developed agriculturally and industrially, a need arose for a more continuous transportation network from the highest lake (Superior), to the lowest (Ontario). In 1825, New York State opened the Erie Canal connecting Buffalo on Lake Erie with the Hudson River at Albany to corner the eastern market for midwestern resources. Grain, ore, coal, furs, hides, and lumber could then flow from Cleveland to Manhattan, where jobbers loaded ships bound for Europe. The canal was just as important to midwesterners, who now could trade freely with an Atlantic port despite the natural barriers of the Piedmont Plateau. The Niagara Escarpment, epitomized by Niagara Falls, was the largest of the trappers' portaging steps. In 1829, Canadian investors bypassed it by building the Welland Canal linking Lake Erie with Lake Ontario; in 1932, it was widened and deepened into the Welland Ship Canal that large vessels could navigate. Just as significantly, goods and immigrants could flow the other way, and both began to pour into the Midwest, where canal-building became a craze. In 1855, Michigan borrowed from the federal government to complete the Soo Canal linking Lakes Superior and Huron. In Illinois, the Illinois and Michigan Canal (1848) permitted farmers in the Mississippi and Illinois valleys to send their produce eastward by way of the Great Lakes. After 1900 the Chicago Sanitary and Ship Canal enabled ships to travel between Lake Michigan and the Mississippi River by way of the Chicago, Des Plaines, and Illinois rivers; this engineering feat made the Chicago River flow backwards. The St. Lawrence Seaway, opened in 1959, allowed large tankers of the post–World War II era to pass from one Great Lake to another and onto the Atlantic and back. By the late twentieth century, supertankers could no longer fit within the width of the Seaway locks. In 2004, studies were under way to decide whether to upgrade the Seaway.

After the Louisiana Purchase of 1803, goods could flow down the Ohio River into the Mississippi and from thence to the port of New Orleans. The Ohio, whose major branches are the Muskingum, Kanawha, Big Sandy, Scioto, Licking, Great Miami, Kentucky, Green, Wabash, Cumberland, and Tennessee rivers, served as a major artery of trade and migration for the eastern Midwest, as did the Red and

Missouri rivers on the western edge of Minnesota and Iowa. Although never as monumental as the canal systems for Great Lakes traffic, other canal networks were important connectors of rivers. Whereas unruly rivers flood in spring and freeze in winter, canals south of the Lake Region could be controlled through locks and pumps. Ohio's Ohio and Erie Canal joined Cleveland and Portsmouth in 1832; the Miami and Erie, constructed in 1845, connected Toledo and Cincinnati. These networks made it possible for small towns such as Nelsonville, Ohio, to boom; it quickly became famous for the "Star" bricks that could now be delivered to builders in the East but also to overland transshipment routes to Iowa and points west. Although many canals from the pre–Civil War period are no longer used for commerce, more modern dam–canal systems built by the Army Corps of Engineers now control flooding of the Ohio and Missouri rivers.

Transportation canals were superseded in the early half of the nineteenth century by railroads, some of which used filled-in canals as foundations. In 1856, the Illinois Central Railroad, with 700 miles of track originating at Cairo, was the world's longest single railroad. Other midwestern states followed suit. Iowa's experience, though late, was typical. The first railroad to traverse Iowa, from the Mississippi River to Council Bluffs, was completed in 1867. By 1870, four railroads crisscrossed the state to tie into rapidly expanding grids joining other states. The Midwest became the transportation hub of the country with Chicago at its core, gathering goods from the hinterlands and setting the stage for the American industrial machine.

In the twentieth century, the railroad grid was supplemented and then surpassed by the interstate highway system, propelled by the Federal Aid Road Act (1916). Significant arteries had, of course, appeared earlier. The first major road to cross the Midwest from east to west was the Cumberland Road, or the National Road (now U.S. Highway 40), built in the early 1800s, which ran from Maryland to Indianapolis (1830) and beyond to Vandalia, Illinois (1840). After the Civil War, midwestern states began building more roads, but it was the automobile that spurred truly intensive construction in the early twentieth century. Construction of a major north-south road, the Dixie Highway, began in 1915. Eventually, it ran from Michigan's Straits of Mackinac to Florida's Miami. Its eastern fork passes through Detroit and Cincinnati; its western leg connects South Bend, Indiana, with Louisville, Kentucky, and Atlanta, Georgia. Wisconsin's tradition of numbering highways became standard in the nation. Hundreds of thousands of miles of highways now blanket the Midwest; trucks carrying the nation's goods traverse them. Air traffic also knits the midwestern states with each other and with every place else. Chicago remains the hub, but airports at Cincinnati, St. Louis, Minneapolis–St. Paul, and Detroit are among the nation's busiest.

Agriculture and Food Production

The Midwest is known as the "Breadbasket of America" because it perfectly combines flat land, long growing season, and well-watered fertile soils. Although other regions now compete in production of midwestern crops, they lack the same combination of natural resources. Humans cultivating the vast fields of the region required mechanical assistance from midwestern blacksmiths. One of these, John Deere (1804–1886), mass-produced the steel plow. By 1857, his factory at Moline,

Illinois, turned out 10,000 plows annually. Within a few more years, the farm implements forged by Deere had broken the sod of the prairies and grasslands. Cyrus McCormick (1809–1884), with his father the inventor of the wheat reaper, opened a Chicago factory in 1847 and from there exported this mechanical marvel around the world. His company became International Harvester. The many fertilizer and insecticide companies eventually superseded by Monsanto, the St. Louis, Missouri, supplier of many other agricultural products, added still more power to the midwestern farmer.

Flour mills sprang up in Chicago, St. Louis, Cleveland, and Indianapolis to process wheat and other grains. By 1900, flour industries had moved further north. Pillsbury, founded in 1869 in Minneapolis, eventually became a subsidiary of General Mills, owner of Green Giant vegetables (1925), and fast-food franchiser Burger King (1967). Battle Creek, Michigan, became home to cereal companies such as Post and Kellogg. Quaker Oats, started in 1882 in Cedar Rapids, Iowa, soon absorbed rival companies in Ravenna and Akron, Ohio, to create an automated, vertically integrated company that dominanted the market for oats. In 1900, Illinois led the nation in the production of distilled liquors, especially those made from corn. The Ball Company of Muncie, Indiana, and Owens-Illinois of Toledo, Ohio, automated glass making to provide packaging for the heartland's fruits and vegetables and for the beer made by Milwaukee and St. Louis.

Early in the nineteenth century, farmers in the Midwest drove their herds of livestock to markets south and east, but as water transportation evolved they began slaughtering it first, using Cincinnati (called "Porkopolis" in 1840) as the first meat-packing center. As the frontier moved westward, and as railroads serviced new territory, stockyards sprang up in all the region's cities. Increasingly, however, as ranchers in the further West supplied more and more beef to the nation, cattle flowed through Chicago. Numerous large companies such as Armour and Swift sprang up to convert cattle, sheep, hogs, and horses into meat, fertilizer, skins, glue, hair, and soap. The introduction of refrigerated railroad cars in 1882 made it possible for Chicago butchers to dress meat for consumers in Washington and Philadelphia. Chicago was also a major manufacturer of cans by 1878; factories there cooked and canned the region's agricultural bounty for the rest of the nation. Nineteenth-century development of auctions, jobbing, and distribution centers, especially a network of grain elevators and warehouses, and greater specialization in farm products, accelerated productivity.

Wheat grew abundantly. According to the 1860 census, the total American wheat production of 1859 was 173 million bushels, of which 46 percent came from the five midwestern states bordering on the Great Lakes. As banks loaned capital for farmers to invest, they farmed more acreage; midwestern insurance companies guaranteed their survival against bad weather and disasters. State and county farm agents helped to improve and diversify crops. Iowa farmers in 1928, for example, began experimenting with a hybrid corn that dramatically increased yields.

Today the Midwest has three main agricultural regions: the Corn/Soy Belt, the Dairy Belt, and the Fruit Belt. The Corn/Soy Belt spreads across the central glaciated till plain of Ohio, encompasses the landscapes of Indiana, Illinois, and Iowa, and reaches further west into central Nebraska. The soils of Ohio, the eastern extension of the Corn Belt, are up to 400 feet deep, glacial drift with some loess mantle in the south. Forty-five percent of Ohio's land is still given over to agricul-

The city of Chicago, Illinois, on the shore of Lake Michigan, 1997. Of all the Great Lakes, only Lake Michigan is completely within the United States. Photo by Richard B. Mieremet. Courtesy NOAA.

ture, but Iowa best epitomizes the Corn Belt, leading the nation in corn production (17.9 percent of the U.S. total [1997]) and the amount of harvested cropland (7.5 percent of the U.S. total [1997]). Traditionally, the corn was a perfect value-added commodity, first as whisky, a form in which it was easier to ship, and then as feed for livestock; Iowa produces almost one-quarter of the U.S. total of hogs annually. Soybeans, introduced as a substitute for other protein foods and as a source of oil during World War II, now cover hundreds of thousands of acres, as do feed grains and hay, sugar beets, and canola; tobacco is still grown in some areas of Ohio.

The historic home to the Dairy Belt has been Wisconsin. The shorter growing season made it difficult to make a profit growing grains, but roughage for dairy cows was abundant. By 1900, Green Bay, Wisconsin, was packaging cheese in huge quantities. The number of individual dairy farms has been declining for some decades, however. The average Wisconsin dairy farmer is now over sixty years of age and milks, on average, about fifty cows. Wisconsin dairy farms are much smaller than the new Concentrated Animal Feeding Operation (CAFO) dairies in California, which average 400 cows, making California America's top dairy state in the late twentieth century. A new dairy region has emerged in New Mexico as well. The Fruit Belt, as noted earlier, is along the leeward side of Lakes Michigan, Erie, and Ontario. Growers ship tons of apples, peaches, blueberries, pears, plums, strawberries, cantaloupes, and grapes annually.

Natural Resources

Minerals and extractable resources have been almost as important to the Midwest as its crops. Although New England launched America's Industrial Revolution, it could not surge until the enormous coal and iron reserves of the Midwest were discovered and exploited. Other minerals were almost as important. Galena, Illinois, grew wealthy from a boom in lead that began in 1807. Miners in that city shipped 800 million tons of lead over the Galena River to the nearby Mississippi during the first half of the nineteenth century. The Territory of Wisconsin was proclaimed from the state's "birthplace," at Mineral Point, in 1836, where Cornish immigrants flocked to work the newly discovered lead mines. As indicated earlier, lead mining and copper also shaped the early economy of Missouri. Copper mining began in earnest in the 1840s, however, in Michigan's Upper Peninsula, when the Keweenaw Range yielded quantities greater at the time than any in the world. Ohio settlers mined iron in Jackson, Scioto, and Lawrence counties as early as 1800. Michigan discovered iron ore near Negaunee in 1845. Where the Canadian Shield joins the midwestern prairies lay vast reserves. Later in the century, prospecting uncovered huge veins of iron in the Mesabi and Vermillion Ranges of Minnesota's Superior Uplands, whence miners shipped tens of millions of tons of ore.

In 1900, the Midwest furnished a third of the nation's bituminous coal, though it was generally of a lower grade than that found eastward, toward Pennsylvania. Coal from Ohio, Indiana, Illinois, and Missouri fueled the furnaces of the steel mills that spread across the southern edges of Lake Erie. Indiana, Illinois, Michigan, and Ohio exploit petroleum deposits for oil and natural gas. Limestone mining remains common in Missouri, Illinois, Indiana, Minnesota, and Iowa, and gravel, clay, gypsum, and chalk are still important throughout the region. A combination of economic and environmental factors has led to the abandonment of many coal mines, especially in Ohio, some of which have become heritage tourist sites. "The Little Cities of the Black Diamond," for example, is a citizens' organization that promotes the history of southeastern Ohio mining towns near New Straitsville. The fabled lumberjacks of the region cut and processed the pine forests of Michigan, Minnesota, and Wisconsin, often selling the lumber to citizens in treeless areas of Illinois, Iowa, and points further west. Between 1860 and 1910, lumber companies exercised almost as much political and economic power as the railroads. In 1900, the Midwest furnished almost half of the nation's commercial lumber, though annual output has declined steadily ever since. By that year, however, Grand Rapids, Michigan, had become one of the first furniture capitals of the nation.

Industry

Transportation and natural resources propelled the booming heavy industries of the region and built great cities in the process. By the late nineteenth century, ships on the Great Lakes carried iron ore from the Laurentian Uplands, principally the Keweenaw Peninsula of Michigan and the Mesabi Range of Minnesota, and coal from the Appalachian Plateau (with outcroppings in Ohio, Indiana, Illinois, and Missouri), both raw materials for steel. Chicago, Gary, Duluth, Detroit, Toledo, and Cleveland in the United States, and Toronto and Hamilton in Canada, were the result. The Bessemer steel process, by producing strong steel cheap enough to compete with the price of iron, was the catalyst for the amazing rail networks and the skyscrapers of cities. Innumerable steel plants sprang up throughout the region, with U.S. Steel, owned by J. P. Morgan, setting the pace. Indiana produced more steel than any other state. Its production facilities were centered in the Calumet Region in the northeast, in Burns Harbor, East Chicago, and Gary. The steel industry, however, was only one of the foundational industries for the midwestern industrial hub. Perhaps the most important was the auto industry.

Chrysler Plant, Hamtramck, Wayne County, Michigan, 1936. Courtesy Library of Congress.

Midwesterners began building vehicles in the mid-nineteenth century. The Studebaker brothers opened their wagon works in South Bend, Indiana, in 1852; they were the largest supplier of wagons in the United States, a factor that eased the company's transition to self-propulsion later. Elwood G. Haynes (1857–1925) tested a successful gasoline-powered vehicle in 1894 in Kokomo, Indiana. Ransom E. Olds (1864–1950) built Michigan's first automobile factory in Detroit in 1899, but Henry Ford (1863–1947) put Motown on the map by opening his plant in 1903, just after Barney Oldfield (1877–1946), the Ohio speed demon, won his first race (1902) in a Ford-built car in that city. Detroit soon established horizontal linkages with Indianapolis for engines, Sandusky for auto bodies, Toledo for windshields, and Akron for tires. In all those cities, smokestacks belched black smoke, furnaces spat sparks of hot metal, and refineries filled the air with chemical stench. This string of cities, collectively called the "Foundry," formed the backbone of America's economy. Here capital, labor, and production all came together. Below the level of the smokestacks were the steeples of the ethnic churches, the long silhouettes of rolling mills, the tin roofs of warehouses, the irregular outlines of unimaginative corporate offices, hastily constructed blocks of worker homes, ramshackle stores stocked with cheap food, clothing, and equipment, and the occasional public school. It was as if the Industrial Revolution had signed its name on the landscape—human engineering made vernacular. Seen from the air, the industrial belt still looks like a cliché of history.

Drawn by the promise of jobs, housing, and services—lives better than the ones they left behind—millions migrated to the cities for employment, many from the South. Chicago, Detroit, Cleveland, Toledo, Akron, Flint, and many other midwestern cities swelled under the influx of middle-class and blue-collar job-seekers. The United Automobile Workers Union, begun in Detroit in 1935, improved wages and working conditions. Today, many of those jobs are gone, some to Sunbelt climes, some to other countries, and the trend continues as automation and competition from abroad reduce the need for skilled labor. Michigan alone has lost 170,000 manufacturing jobs since 2000.[7] As a result, for many, that episode of the American industrial saga is over. The cities that accommodated dreams are diminished, their infrastructures in shambles. The labor pool leaves; the poor and aged remain. Rusting factories, collapsed smokestacks, brownfields, high crime, unemployment, and gang activity are the visual reminders of once booming cities unprepared for the transition to postindustrialism.

Yet the Midwest is still a major manufacturer of the products that made the region legendary. These range from automobiles and motorcycles, tires and rubber, aircraft and farm implements, earth-movers, machine tools, and appliances to glass, paper, detergents, pesticides, paints, plastics, metals, chemicals, and pharmaceuticals. Its rivers and coal mines are still a major source of the nation's energy; its cornfields produce the ethanol that compensates for declining petroleum reserves. The Midwest is moving slowly but solidly into the information age, following the imperatives of an economy that emphasizes research laboratories, data processing (CDW Computer Centers in Illinois), control technologies (Johnson Controls in Wisconsin), office machines (NCR in Ohio), and telephones (Sprint in Ohio, and Telephone and Data Systems in Illinois), not to mention banking and insurance and education, the crucial components of the service sector. In a vote of confidence in the region's future, a consortium of the nation's universities chose Indianapolis as the headquarters of Internet II. The eight states of the Midwest remain home to 136 of the nation's Fortune 500 corporations; Illinois alone has 32.

URBAN AREAS

Midwestern cities have suffered downturns because of industrial declines, population loss, and a shrinking economic base. Workers who could afford it have departed for the warmer climate and greater job opportunities of the Sunbelt. The less affluent populations who remain in the city cores suffer from high unemployment rates and more limited access to social services that the cities struggle to provide. As investment in local growth has fallen off and revenues from business and property taxes have eroded, urban schools are deteriorating. If we look only at the cores of such cities as Dayton, Ohio, we see the ruin of the once affluent and stable. Matters are often different, however, amid the ubiquitous suburban sprawl outside their central business districts (CBD). In the past twenty years, midwestern suburban areas grew at a quicker rate than every midwestern CBD. When suburban areas grow in population, they also grow in income, as workers take jobs in sectors that enable them to escape the poorer quality of life in inner cities.

Many forces drove this shift to expansion outside cities, but two are important. First, the housing stock and the mass transit systems in many central cities have deteriorated. Thus, the inner core of cities like Detroit is home mostly to those who need to stay close to low-paying jobs. After World War II, when government loans spurred new housing outside of the city limits, the indirect effect was to encourage community tracts that were racially discriminatory, at least until the 1960s. Wealthier whites fled inner cities for the spacious homes and superior schools of the suburbs, a landscape shaped principally by the automobile. Second, tax incentives, shortsighted planning, and lax environmental regulations fostered the development of farmland for residential use rather than the re-development of existing urban sites. It is estimated that every minute two acres of prime farmland are lost to development in the Midwest, a process almost literally visible along highway corridors outside such cities as Indianapolis, Columbus, and St. Louis.

Here manufacturing satellites, office complexes, branch banks, groceries, corporate headquarters, car dealerships, fast-food restaurants, video rental outlets, hardware and sports shops, storage lots, and medical centers catering to an aging population mingle with tracts of housing. Midwestern mercantile traditions, exemplified in the great department stores like Marshall Field's that drew shoppers to the cities, and in the region-based mail-order houses such as Sears Roebuck that flooded rural communities with consumer goods, have resurfaced in the malls of suburbia. The shopping center, predecessor of the mall, was a post–World War II midwestern response to the automobile. It has reached an apotheosis in the largest mall in the world, the Mall of America, located in Bloomington, Minnesota, at the junction of Interstate 494 and Highway 77, just outside the downtown density of Minneapolis-St. Paul. As much a tourist destination as a shopping opportunity, the Mall of America houses 520 stores, the nation's largest indoor theme park, a gigantic walkthrough aquarium, fourteen movie theaters, fifty restaurants, and numerous other commercial attractions; its parking lot is larger than many midwestern villages. The mall opened in 1992; by 2004, according to its Web site, its more than 11,000 employees had generated $1.7 billion in revenues.

Beyond suburbia and its malls lies what is now being called the Midwest's exurbia, or "edge cities," the gated communities and golf courses of an even wealthier population, who drive very large sports utility vehicles (SUVs) to and from houses of 10,000 square feet. In some ways, then, the Midwest is still surging—at least for some of its citizens and entrepreneurs—horizontally across its landscape instead of vertically in its older metropolises. Such changes are obviously altering the character of the region.

Major Midwestern Cities

Deterioration and recharacterization notwithstanding, the Midwest is still celebrated for its cities. Many of these cities are fighting their way back to greater degrees of health, introducing zoning reform, designating areas for mixed use, cleaning up pollution, razing unused smokestacks and derelict factories, building sports arenas in inner cores, fostering inner-city cultural life through subsidized museum and theater districts, offering tax abatements to information businesses and dotcom companies (especially around colleges and universities), funding retraining programs for their labor forces, and creating economic task forces to globalize industries. The success of such strategies varies, of course. The major cities, ranked by size, are Chicago, Illinois; Detroit, Michigan; Cleveland, Ohio; Minneapolis/St. Paul, the Twin Cities of Minnesota; and St. Louis, Missouri. All grew as they adapted to their geography.

Chicago is the third largest city in America, with more than 8.3 million residents in a metropolitan area that extends across 16 counties and three states (Illinois, Wisconsin, and Indiana). It spreads over the plains of ancient Lake Chicago (now Lake Michigan) at the mouth of the Chicago River. Although that river itself was not great, its nearness to the Mississippi System and the Great Lake System initiated its growth from a settlement at the military outpost of Fort Dearborn to a modern metropolis. Chicago actually sits on a subtle continental divide, with water to the west flowing into the Mississippi Basin and to the east into the Great Lakes. Chicago's natural drainage is poor because of the flatness of the lacustrine plain and the low gradient of its streams, so that the city's sewage once flowed into Lake Michigan. But its situation enabled it to capitalize first on agricultural and then on industrial distribution, initially as a hub of water routes, then as the center of the nation's nineteenth-century railroad and twentieth-century trucking networks and airline corridors. Built originally of lumber from the northern Midwest, Chicago was nearly destroyed by the Great Fire of 1871. It reinvented itself in concrete and steel skyscrapers crafted by great architects, and it continues to do so today, renovating pockets of blight and creating others, empowering and enriching new ranks of professionals, losing some industries and building others. Host to two World's Fairs, proud of energy levels it compares to New York City's, it still calls itself America's "Second City" and draws strength from great universities, unparalleled museums, celebrated sports teams, a rich polyglot cultural heritage, and, some would say, sheer chutzpah.

The population of Michigan largely lives in the southeastern corridor from Detroit west to Lansing. Detroit remains the largest city. French fur traders originally gravitated here to take advantage of the location along the straits of the Detroit River, and gave their settlement the name Ville d'etroit—Village of the Strait. Access to water routes, the capitalization of heavy industry, and the influx of workers drove its development. Until 1950, Detroit was an economic powerhouse of two million people, employed mostly in the automobile industry. It now has less than half its 1950 population and remains one of the most segregated cities in America. Detroit itself is over 90 percent black, and the surrounding areas are over 90 percent white. Not surprisingly, disparities abound: Bloomfield Hills, one of its suburbs, is one of the most affluent zip codes in the nation, in sharp contrast to blighted neighborhoods in the inner core. Both the general density of population and its socioeconomic segregation have had a devastating effect on the ecology and environment of the southeastern portion of the state, especially its fragile, wetland landscape, which requires massive cleanup. The city's success in revitalizing its downtown with huge projects such as the Renaissance Center has been mixed. Despite the city's enormous population loss in the past half-century, the surrounding areas, which extend into Canada via a tunnel, have grown substantially, making the metropolitan area the eighth largest in the United Satess.

Ohio's large urban areas developed during the industrial growth of America into urban corridors (Cleveland–Akron–Youngstown, Columbus–Dayton–Cincinnati). Seventy-four percent of Ohio's population is urban. The Cleveland metropolitan area is the nation's fifteenth largest at 2.9 million, though it has been losing population, as have many midwestern cities. Cleveland sits on the western edge of the Appalachian Plateau and the lacustrine plain formed by Lake Erie, at the junction of the lake with the Cuyahoga River. Its site, originally purchased from the state of Connecticut as part of the Western Reserve, began growing in the early nineteenth century when the Ohio Canal connected it to the Ohio River. Proximity to shipping lanes and nearby coal and iron deposits swiftly made it both a transportation and manufacturing center. Despite the decline of its industry, Clevelanders still operate more than 4,000 factories. Slums dot the metropolitan area, and segregation is still a serious problem for African Americans (who comprise 45 percent of the inner city's population), but suburban areas such as Shaker Heights are prosperous.

The major urban area in Minnesota is the Twin Cities of Minneapolis/St. Paul, the nation's sixteenth largest metropolis, with 2.8 million residents. The cities were built on either side of the junction of the Minnesota and Mississippi rivers, on the edge of the grassland region to the south and the forests to the north. Minneapolis took its name from the Sioux word for water, *minne*, because of the twenty-two lakes that lay within the settlement. Finance, transportation, trade, and industry built it and its neighbor, St. Paul, named after a church devoted to the saint, now the state's capital. Excellent water and rail connections and proximity to agricultural output led to the area's becoming a flour-milling and meat-packing center. After World War II, the cities began producing computers and electronic equipment. Minneapolis is headquarters to the Ninth Federal Reserve Banking District, and thus a major financial center of the Midwest, a circumstance that has led to large-scale service industries. Long dependent on coal-burning power plants, the two cities committed in December 2003 to reducing industrial pollutants, mercury emissions, and greenhouse gases by 2009.

It is instructive to discuss St. Louis, Missouri, started as a fort built by French fur traders in 1764 at the junction of the Missouri and Mississippi rivers, by contrasting it with Cairo, Illinois, located at the equally dominant junction of the Ohio and Mississippi rivers. St. Louis is a major metropolitan area of over 2 million inhabitants, whereas Cairo, Illinois, is a shrinking community of just over 3600. The reasons for the difference have to do with geography. Cairo could never become a major city because of its poorly drained, often flooded location. By contrast, St. Louis stands on a bluff, a position that secured its future. During the early 1800s, St. Louis was the gateway to the West (a role now symbolized by its great arch) for wagon trains and one of the main ports for Mississippi steamboat traffic. After the Civil War, it became a railway hub as well. Having spread along the river for almost twenty miles, it now covers an area of more than sixty square miles. Redevelopment projects have renovated many neighborhoods abandoned by those who left during the precipitous population decline (27 percent) of the 1970s. Downtown malls, sports arenas, and refurbished parks have restored some life to some blighted sectors. Like Minneapolis, St. Louis is the headquarters of one of the banks of the Federal Reserve, a factor that has assisted in the slow transformation of its economy to service and information sectors.

ENVIRONMENTAL ISSUES

Often well-intentioned exploitation of midwestern bounty has left a dismal ecological legacy. Human population surges erased some animals and many more plants from the landscape. Rapacious logging altered environmental balance. The plow literally destroyed the prairies. The wind and water erosion that followed stripped away centuries of topsoil. Fertilizers and mining byproducts and industrial waste polluted waterways and poisoned the land. Dams and powerplants diminished the quality of water and air. Today midwestern states battle against histories of offense and neglect.

Water

Many waterways in the Midwest are polluted. Rampant violations of laws aimed at stopping industrial water pollution have left the Great Lakes vulnerable. From

1998 to 2004, industrial toxins in the Great Lakes increased by 25 percent. Of the top 183 polluters, 125 were in Michigan, but budget shortfalls have prevented the state's Department of Environmental Quality from prosecuting all but the most egregious cases; the water supply of the entire state is now at serious risk. Other lake states likewise lack funds to monitor and address the dumping of waste. To the north, paper mill owners flushed acids and iron miners dumped taconite (a chert that contains the iron ore) tailings directly into Lake Superior, a practice halted only in 1978. Other nonpoint source pollution includes urban waste from the 40 million people within the Great Lakes drainage area, soil erosion, and chemicals used to increase agricultural yields. Shipping through the waterways has also had polluting effects, with invasive species entering the water system by way of bilge water, upsetting the ecosystem balance. The outflow from the Great Lakes is only about 1 percent annually (Lake Superior retains its water for up to 191 years); therefore, pollutants that enter the lakes are retained and become concentrated over time.

In 2002, a report issued by Indiana's Department of Environmental Management said that most of the state's waterways, including the Ohio, did not meet state water standards. Pollution of the Ohio River, the most important transportation corridor for the historical expansion into the trans-Appalachian frontier, reflects its role in the economic activities of people settled in close proximity. Only the Mississippi River and the Pacific Ocean receive more pollutants. The Ohio's beauty belies how its central location during early industrial development subjected the river to pollution on a grand scale during a time when few Americans considered the consequences of dumping waste into waterways. Active mining (and abandoned coal mines) remains the dominant form of nonpoint pollution upriver, while agricultural runoff generates the most pollution in the lower section.

The absolute damage to the environment is difficult to determine. Although agriculture and industry are the largest generators of water pollution, others have been identified by monitoring effluents generated into the atmosphere. Still others include byproducts of urban development. When wetlands are drained and streams rechanneled, sediment loads destroy fish spawning sites and foster hypoxia (oxygen deficiency) that hinders other aquatic life. Nitrogen and phosphorus in runoff from dairy farms and associated feedlots augment the growth of algae in ponds and boost nitrate levels in drinking water. Such runoff poses health risks to local populations. In Milwaukee in 1993, drinking water contaminated with cryptosporidium from livestock manure killed sixty-nine people and more than 400,000 had to be treated for various symptoms.

The stress placed on outdated water and sewage treatment plants by increased populations can quickly become uncontrollable. Another toxic threat is mercury. Although mercury is found naturally in the atmosphere, human activities in the Midwest, such as coal combustion, industrial operations, and waste incineration, are responsible for over 75 percent of elevated mercury levels in water, sediment, and biota. Most worrisome is the accumulation of mercury in fish, especially in the Great Lakes and Lake Region, where commercial fishing, once significant, has declined owing to pollution. It is unsafe to eat bottom-feeding fish from the Great Lakes (though Lake Superior whitefish are still prized), and many native species such as pike, lake salmon, and lake trout have been displaced by the nonnative alewife. Fish and the rest of the aquatic food web are susceptible to mercury levels in sediment; heavy metals accumulate in the food chain through a process called *biological magnification*. In 2003, Ohio state fish advisories were tightened for women of childbearing age and for children in northeastern and northwestern Ohio because of the high levels of mercury and PCBs found in larger, edible species. Consumers were warned not to eat more than one meal per month that included fish from Lake Erie.[8] A national program assessing environmental issues is the U.S. Geological Survey's National Water Quality Assessment program (NAWQA), which is investigating point and nonpoint sources in the lake states. Results currently show a high concentration of nitrogen and phosphorus in urban and cropland runoff, as well as dangerously high accumulations of chemicals in fish and stream sediment.

Beyond these specifics, pollutants upset the entire equilibrium of aquatic ecosytems. Prior to heavy human impact, the intertwined plant and animal ecosystems changed with the seasons on the river. During periods of flooding,

Sediment Settling and Mussel Beds

Mussels seem innocuous lying on the bottom of rivers, but they are useful to the ecosystem—and to humans—because they both filter water and monitor its quality. They have been most abundant in the Midwest, though over half of the 122 species identified are now extinct or endangered because humans have built dams, farmed destructively, and introduced invasive species.

Dams provide power and assist navigation on rivers, but they also impede the migration of fish. Mussels ride on the gills of fish, without harming them, in order to be carried to suitable areas where they drop off and reproduce. Dams interfere with this process. In addition, dams impede the flow of rivers; even relatively stagnant water is hostile to mussels. Sediment from erosion caused by agricultural production smothers mussels. With the sediment comes a variety of pollutants such as polychlorinated biphenyls (PCBs), lead, and mercury, which destroy mussel beds. Invasive species can destroy the balance of ecosystems. The zebra mussel has destroyed large numbers of native mussels. Originally traced to ballast water on ships from the Caspian Sea that was emptied into Lake Erie, zebra mussels attached to almost any surface, including other mussels. They reproduce quickly and use up resources, leaving nothing for the native species. Barges and their bilge water have probably spread zebra mussels in the Ohio River.

plants and animals flourished throughout the flood basin, and during times of recession, retreated back to the river. Because aquatic species move, their proliferation depends on the natural rhythms of the river region, including side channels, backwaters, and wetlands. Birds also require river sloughs and floodplains for their migration and procreation. Ecosystem communities in this region changed radically in the twentieth century; many species are now endangered or extinct. Now largely human induced and dynamic, the Ohio River ecosystem's "new balance" has yet to be realized. Even after passage of New Clean Air and Clean Water Acts in 2003, the Midwest has a long way to go toward restoring of the environmental health of its waterways.

Land

Europeans developed cultural patterns of land use that were very different from those in place prior to their arrival. Although the Native Americans did not leave a pristine landscape, their manner of living supported a lower physiographic density. Because they used only what they needed, the environment maintained its own balance, and although many Native Americans were agrarian, they did not "own" the land, nor did they divide it into units as the Europeans would.[9] The imperialism of the various European groups was often quite similar despite their other cul-

Table 1. Tall-grass prairie extent past and present

Tall-Grass Prairie Location	Past Area (hectares)	Current Area (hectares)	Percent Decline
Illinois	8,500,000	930	99.9
Indiana	2,800,000	404	99.9
Iowa	12,000,000	12,140	99.9
Minnesota	7,300,000	45,000	99.4
Wisconsin	2,400,000	1,000	99.9

Source: "Regional Trends of Biological Resources—Grasslands, Prairie Grasses," U.S. Geological Surveys. www.npwrc.usgs.gov/resource/2000/grlands/pastpres.htm.

tural differences. For Europeans the land and its resources were to be conquered. The Prairie, for example, seemed to be there for one reason alone: to farm.

As a result, 99 percent of the Tall-Grass Prairie vegetation is gone (see Table 1). The most prevalent crops in the region, however, are also grass varieties: wheat, corn, and oats. Most of the Midwest is now under corn cultivation, whereas wheat is most common in the drier, Western Short-Grass Prairie.

We are only now learning something about the stewardship of Native Americans. Human-induced fire, for example, shaped the Prairies. Fire kept open areas grassy, cleared the understory of forested areas, encouraged fire-tolerant and sun-loving plants to thrive, and stimulated the growth of edible plants such as a variety of berries. After relocating Native Americans, Europeans stopped the burning and clearing. Only recently have Americans come to think of the burning of the prairie as a balancing force for nature rather than as destructive.

The price of agricultural largess is the loss of the many native plant and animal

Suburban sprawl. Over the past twenty years, midwestern suburban areas have continued to encroach on farmlands. Photo by Chris Mayda.

habitats of the Tall-Grass Prairie. Scientists, activists, and farmers in Iowa have worked to restore the "natural" native plant and animal habitats prior to European settlement, using strategies that include a conservation of diversity. Citizens of other states have joined the effort. At the Fermi National Accelerator Laboratory near Batavia, Illinois, for example, the high-energy accelerator operated by an academic consortium, the physicist Robert R. Wilson several decades ago enlisted historians, biologists, and botanists to recreate the historic Illinois prairie inside the mile-diameter proton accelerator ring. They searched for fragments of prairie along abandoned railroads, transplanted long grasses and many species of other native vegetation, introduced a herd of bison, and periodically burned the landscape.[10] This technique of rethinking the landscape actually began in 1935 Wisconsin with Aldo Leopold. Although the ring now supports an amazing number of historically important species of plants and animals, the experimenters have reached the conclusion that they cannot restore the natural environment, because it is not "real."

Other matters of concern have to do with the scale of modern farming. Leaving aside the transformation of the Prairie, agribusiness has created many problems. Southwestern Missouri, for example, has many concentrated animal

Land Ethic

The land ethic simply enlarges the boundaries of the community to include soils, waters, plants, and animals, or collectively: the land.

In those days we had never heard of passing up a chance to kill a wolf. In a second we were pumping lead into the pack, but with more excitement than accuracy; how to aim a steep downhill shot is always confusing. When our rifles were empty, the old wolf was down, and a pup was dragging a leg into impassable side-rocks.

We reached the old wolf in time to watch a fierce green fire dying in her eyes. I realized then, and have known ever since, that there was something known only to her and to the mountain. I was young then, and full of trigger-itch; I thought that because fewer wolves meant more deer, that no wolves would mean hunters' paradise. But after seeing the green fire die, I sensed that neither the wolf nor the mountain agreed with such a view.[11]

Wisconsin is important to the history of ecologic conservation, for the first attempts to restore prairies and pine woodlands took root here. In 1935, Aldo Leopold's *Sand County Almanac* articulated a new land ethic, one that respected the ecosystems that existed before heavy farming transformed the landscape. Leopold identified the role of fire in managing the prairies, advocated restoring species within the ecosystem to which they once belonged, and generally attacked the excessive commodification of land. Despite revision and skepticism from postmodernists who suggest that trying to restore is merely to create simulacra of reality, Leopold's land ethic still attracts followers.

feeding operations (CAFOs), especially for poultry. As profits and yields increase from agricultural conglomeration, so does pollution from animal waste and technologies of scale: pesticides, herbicides, and chemical fertilizers. Nitrogen and phosphorus in affected surface and groundwater exceed healthy levels for plant uptake. In humans, too much nitrogen can trigger "blue baby syndrome" by lowering oxygen to fatal levels. Too much phosphorus in drinking water and water catchment areas causes eutrophication (stimulation of algae blooms) and disruption of aquatic plant and animal life. Safe levels for the use of these potential pollutants are not set individually and seldom in conjunction with each other.

Not all agricultural practices are adding to the region's pollution problems. Many farmers are involved in more sustainable methods, using fewer pollutants and raising animals less intensively. These methods are easier on the land and encourage long-term production methods. At issue is whether they can be the mainstay of American agriculture techniques if the population continues to grow at its current rate and if sprawl continues to encroach on farmlands.

Other factors are less obvious. The Minnesota landscape underwent resource depletion during the 1800s as the mining and logging industries operated without environmental restrictions. Now increased tourism places pressure on the grasslands of Minnesota. This transitional zone has numerous lakes, including the largest, Bemidji and Mille Lacs. Population sprawl in the Brainerd-Baxter area may affect the headwaters of the Mississippi River. The building of second or retirement homes on lakeshores, especially that of Lake Superior, is putting heavy strains on water and land, especially from septic systems. Vacation homes in Wisconsin and in the dune areas of Indiana and Michigan also fall into this category of threat.

And, of course, much serious damage remains. Parts of northern Illinois, for example, are rife with hazardous waste from industry and military installations. Designating some areas as Superfund sites will help, but it is impossible to restore the lost wetlands and biodiversity around metropolitan Chicago. Ohio's industrial history has left behind 21,775 brownfields in the state.[12] It has lost 90 percent of its original wetlands, and suburbanization threatens the remainder. Currently, many Superfund sites have been identified but few have been restored.

Cheshire

Settled 200 years ago on the banks of the Ohio River across from West Virginia and 85 miles southeast of Columbus, Cheshire, Ohio, was abandoned in August 2003. The 221 residents received $20 million in resettlement funds provided that they vacated their dwellings near the coal-burning utility operated by American Electric Power. AEP reported that it was buying out the residents in order to expand the Cheshire facility. Those accepting the buyout were required to sign a contract forfeiting their right to sue the company for any illnesses arising from the plant's emissions. Ninety percent of the residents took the offer; the remaining citizens, all elderly, declined to leave their homes.

Cheshire's plants and coking ovens have been part of a major midwestern coal network for just thirty years. In 1971, the Cheshire area was the third largest major receiver of coal in the Midwest after Chicago and Detroit.[13] The General James M. Gavin Power Plant, one of the largest coal-fired plants in the world, came online in Cheshire in 1974. Burning 25,000 tons of coal a day, it generates 2600 megawatts of electricity, enough for two million homes. The Gavin plant, one of the dirtiest sources of electricity in the United States, spews multiple-colored soot, sulfuric acid, and coal ash on the village that sits in its shadow.

The plant emits a smog that creates nitrous oxide and contributes to global warming; it is also a source of acid rain that has plagued midwestern and northeastern cities. Acid rain sterilizes mountain lakes, eats into stone, damages forests, and fosters breathing problems. Because of the first Clean Air Act (1971), Ohio plants have switched to burning less polluting subbituminous coal rather than bituminous Great Lakes coal, which is high in acid content. The Gavin plant also reduced its pollution by 90 percent by installing scrubbers. In 1990 it released 374,920 tons of sulfuric oxide; in 2001, only 46,300 tons. Even with these changes, however, the Gavin plant could not dissipate its emissions widely enough to avoid the town. It remains among the top ten polluters of sulfuric acid, nitrogen oxide, and mercury.[14]

Air

Among the most potent greenhouse gases are carbon dioxide (CO_2) and nitrous oxide (N_2O). Six midwestern states (Minnesota, Wisconsin, Michigan, Illinois, Indiana, and Ohio) operate 140 carbon dioxide (CO_2)-producing power plants. These power plants annually release 2 percent of the planet's CO_2 and one-quarter of the CO_2 in the United States (see Table 2). Ohio leads the nation in electric utility-generated nitrous oxide emissions. Ninety-nine percent of power plant-generated CO_2 in the Midwest is from coal. Because of emissions

Cheshire, Ohio, was abandoned in August 2003. Photo by Chris Mayda.

from one of its coal-burning plants, American Electric Power (AEP) was forced to purchase an entire town and move its inhabitants; AEP itself generates 2 percent of the Midwest's CO_2.

CONCLUSION

The history of the Midwest reflects many phases of national development. Most European settlers were farmers during the early nineteenth century. The sheer success of the agricultural sector created a demand for an advanced transportation network, first by waterways, then by rail and highways. The transportation routes and the region's natural resources spurred the Midwest's industrial growth, and the nation profited from midwestern manufacturing well into the 1960s. Automation and globalization and the onset of an information economy in the late twentieth century ended the boom. The cost, in terms of degradation of the environment and reduced opportunities for the Midwest's citizens, has been enormous. The challenge for midwestern leaders is to develop effective strategies to bring redevelopment and investment through innovation and retraining, and through local,

Table 2. Electric utility CO_2 emissions in the six-state Midwest Region

	Illinois	Indiana	Michigan	Minnesota	Ohio	Wisconsin
Total CO_2	239,116,570	214,353,950	203,061,550	98,969,820	275,655,550	109,657,270
Utility CO_2 (tons)	92,596,000	137,368,000	81,041,000	36,914,000	138,782,000	51,654,000
Coal Plant CO_2 (tons)	88,698,000	135,863,000	78,289,000	36,336,000	138,406,000	50,594,000
CO_2 Utility share	38.72%	64.08%	39.91%	37.30%	50.35%	47.10%

Source: "Climate: Climate Change and Midwest Power Plants," www.ehw.org/Climate_Change/MWClimate-LR.pdf.

state, and federal subsidies. We can hope that the region will return to a more sustainable economy through agricultural wisdom, careful urban planning, and new economic creativity.

RESOURCE GUIDE

Printed Sources

Bartsch, Charles. *Brownfield Policies in the Midwest*. Chicago: Federal Reserve Bank of Chicago, 1995.

Bernard, Richard M. *Snowbelt Cities: Metropolitan Politics in the Northeast and Midwest Since World War II*. Bloomington: Indiana University Press, 1990.

Buckler, W. R. *Dune Type Inventory and Barrier Dune Classification Study of Michigan's Lake Michigan Shore*. Lansing, MI: Department of Environmental Quality, 2001.

Cain, L. P. "William Dean's Theory of Urban Growth: Chicago's Commerce and Industry, 1854–1871." *Journal of Economic History* 45 (June 1985): 241–249.

Cayton, Andrew R. L., and Susan E. Gray, eds. *The American Midwest: Essays on Regional History*. Bloomington: Indiana University Press, 2001.

Checkoway, Barry, and Carl V. Patton, eds. *The Metropolitan Midwest: Policy Problems and Prospects for Change*. Urbana: University of Illinois Press, 1985.

Clean Air Task Force. *Climate: Climate Change and Midwest Power Plants*. Boston: Clean Air Task Force, 2002. www.ehw.org/Climate_Change/MWClimate-LR.pdf/.

Cronon, William. *Nature's Metropolis: Chicago and the Great West*. New York: W.W. Norton, 1991.

Dahl, T. E. *Wetland Losses in the United States: 1780's to 1980's*. Washington, DC: U.S. Fish and Wildlife Service, 1990.

Doolittle, William E. "Agriculture in North America on the Eve of Contact: A Reassessment." *Annals of the Association of American Geographers* 82 (1992): 386–401.

Dunlop, M. H. *Sixty Miles from Contentment: Traveling the Nineteenth-Century Interior*. New York: Basic Books, 1998.

Environmental Protection Agency. "The Great Lakes: An Environmental Atlas and Resource Book." Washington, DC: U.S. Government Printing Office, 2003. http://www.epa.gov/glnpo/atlas.

Garreau, Joel. *The Nine Nations of North America*. Boston: Houghton Mifflin, 1981.

Gruenwald, Kim M. *River of Enterprise: The Commercial Origins of Regional Identity in the Ohio Valley, 1790–1850*. Bloomington: Indiana University Press, 2002.

Hart, John Fraser. "The Middle West." *Annals of the Association of American Geographers* 62 (1972): 258–282.

Hudson, John. *Across This Land*. Baltimore, MD: Johns Hopkins University Press, 2002.

Keating, William. *Narrative of an Expedition to the Source of St. Peter's River*. Minneapolis: Ross & Haines, 1959.

Kolpin, D. W., G. Hallberg, D. A. Sneck-Fahrer, and R. Libra. *Agricultural Chemicals in Iowa's Ground Water, 1982–95—What Are the Trends?* Fact Sheet FS-116-97. Washington, DC: U.S. Geological Survey, 1997.

Lass, William E. *Minnesota: A History*. New York: W.W. Norton, 1977.

Mac, M.J., P.A. Opler, C.E. Puckett-Haecker, and P.D. Doran, eds. *Status and Trends of the Nation's Biological Resources*. Jamestown, ND: Northern Prairie Wildlife Research Center, 1998. www.npwrc.usgs.gov/resource/2000/grlands/grlands.htm (Version 21JAN2000).

Madison, James, ed. *Heart Land*. Bloomington: Indiana University Press, 1990.

Martin, Lawrence. *The Physical Geography of Wisconsin*. Madison: University of Wisconsin Press. 1965.

Nelson, John C. "Presettlement Vegetation Patterns Along the 5th Principal Meridian, Missouri Territory, 1815." *American Midland Naturalist* 137 (1997): 79–94.

ORSANCO. *Assessment of Overland Runoff Nonpoint Source Pollution.* Indianapolis: Ohio River Valley Water Sanitation Commission, 2003.

Salisbury, Neal. "The Indians' Old World: Native Americans and the Coming of Europeans." *The William and Mary Quarterly* 53 (July 1996): 435–458.

Teaford, Jon C. *Cities of the Heartland: The Rise and Fall of the Industrial Midwest.* Bloomington: Indiana University Press, 1993.

Thompson, George F., ed. *Landscape in America.* Austin: University of Texas Press, 1995.

USGS. "Assessing Mercury Levels in Small Lakes in Voyageurs National Park in Northern Minnesota. Reconnaissance Data Collection, 2000." www.mn.water.usgs.gov/active_projects/00330t.html.

———. "The Quality of Our Nation's Water: Nutrients and Pesticides." Circular 1225. Reston, VA: U.S. Geologic Survey, 2003.

Walker, Kenneth R. *A History of the Midwest: From Beginning to 1970.* Little Rock, AR: Pioneer Press, 1974.

Web Sites

The American Geography; or, A View of the Present Situation of the United States of America
www.memory.loc.gov/cgi-/

American Memory: Historical Collections of the National Digital Library; see especially Jedidiah Morse's (1761–1826) early (1794) text on the Ohio River valley.

Economic Snapshot (August 3, 2001)
www.pbs.org/newshour/bb/economy/july-dec01/snapshot 8-3.html/

Despite widespread unemployment, economic diversification has helped the Midwest.

Economic Turnaround: A Regional Look at the Economy
www.pbs.org/newshour/bb/economy/july-dec03/econ 10-03.html/

The economy of the Midwest improved in late 2003.

Environmental Protection Agency
www.epa.gov/

This is a gateway to all state environmental agencies, each of which contains information on environmental issues ranging from specific toxins and damage to Superfund sites.

Flood of 1993
www.pbs.org/wgbh/nova/transcripts/2307tfloo.html/

The Mississippi River flood of 1993 was devastating to the region.

The Great Black Swamp
www.wbgutv.bgsu.edu/local/past/gbs/about.html/

Documentary on the famous swamp as a barrier to settlement and as an ecological wonder.

Great Lakes: An Environmental Atlas and Resource Book
www.epa.gov/glnpo/atlas/

Resource on ecosystems, exploitation, toxins, geology, wetlands, water levels, and so on, produced by a joint American and Canadian project.

Great Lakes Information Network (GLIN)
www.glrc.org/

Information on the environment, economy, and geography, with subjects ranging from industrial products to invasive species.

Midwest Power Plant Pollution
www.pbs.org/newshour/bb/environment/jan-june02/air 1-18.html/
PBS report on Cheshire, Ohio.

Ohio River Flooding
www.pbs.org/newshour/bb/environment/jan-june97/weather 3-4.html/
In March 1997, the Ohio River crested at its highest level in thirty years, forcing thousands to evacuate.

Ohio River Health
www.wcpo.com/news/2002/local/07/29/rivergrowth.html/
According to samples conducted by scientists, thanks to strong environmental measures the Ohio is now supporting more species of fish than it has in years, including the long-threatened giant paddlefish.

Prairie Ecology
www.grasslandheritage.org/ecology.html/
Information on moisture, temperature, and species of flora and fauna, with an extensive reading list.

Zebra Mussel Information
www.nas.er.usgs.gov/zebra.mussel/
Information on this invasive species, arranged by appearances in Midwestern rivers and lakes.

State Historical Organizations

Each provides information on settlement, geography, history, populations, industry, and other topics.

Indiana Historical Society
www.Indianahistory.org

Illinois Historical Society
www.historyillinois.org

Michigan Historical Center
www.michigan.gov/hal/o,1607,7-160-17445_19273---,00.html

Minnesota Historical Society
www.minnesotahistorycenter.org/exhibits/territory/

Missouri Historical Society
www.mohistory.org

Ohio Historical Society
www.ohiohistory.org

State Historical Society of Iowa
www.iowahistory.org/

Wisconsin Historical Society
www.wisconsinhistory.org/

Videos/Films

Big Picture. St. Louis: Missouri Department of Conservation, 1995. The program stresses the importance of an ecosystem approach to land use issues and discusses the concept of biological diversity by demonstrating how habitats in Missouri are interrelated.

Coal, Corn, & Cows. Madison, WI: Hawkhill Associates, 1985. This program focuses on Illinois, where topsoil must be destroyed in order to mine coal.

Common Ground. Washington, DC: National Audubon Society, Turner Broadcasting System, and WETA, 1987. This program is on ecological balance in the Midwest.

Death of the Dream: Farmhouses in the Heartland. St. Paul, MN: KTCA, 2000. This program was inspired by William Gabler's book on classic midwestern farm houses.

The Flood of '93. Washington, DC: PBS, 1994. This video contains stories from six midwestern public television stations about the flood on the Mississippi River and its tributaries: "When It Rains," by Iowa Public Television; "Who Gets a Levee," by KETC, St. Louis; "A Tale of Two Cities" by WQPT, Moline, Illinois; "Standstill" by KTCA, St. Paul; "Hard Rain" by KTCA, St. Paul; "Letting the River Win" by Wisconsin Public Television.

The Plow that Broke the Plains. Davenport, IA: Blackhawk Films, c.1936. This is an old but classic look at the furrowing of the plains in the region.

Museums and Living History Exhibits

Chicago Botanical Garden
1000 Lake Cook Road
Glencoe, IL 60022
(847) 835-8227

Cranbrook Institute of Science
P.O. Box 801
Bloomfield Hills, MI 48303-0801
(248) 645-3204

Dickson Mounds Museum
10956 N. Dickson Mounds Road
Lewiston, IL 61542
(309) 547-3721

Detroit Zoological Institute
P.O. Box 39
Royal Oak, MI 48068
(248) 398-0903

Eiteljorg Museum of American Indians and Western Art
500 West Washington Street
Indianapolis, IN 46204-2707
(317) 636-9378

Historic New Harmony
P.O. Box 579
New Harmony, IN 47631
(812) 682-4488

Living History Farms
2600 11th Street

Urbandale, IA 50265
(515) 278-5286

Maplewood Nature Center
2659 E. 7th Street
Maplewood, MN 55119
(651) 738-9383

Midwest Museum of Natural History (opening 2004)
P.O. Box 185
Sycamore, IL 60178
(815) 895-9777
Email: information@mmnh.org

Museum of Transportation
3015 Barrett Sta. Road
St. Louis, MO 63122
(314) 965-8007

The New Detroit Science Center
5020 John R. Street
Detroit, MI 48202
(313) 577-8400

Ohio River Museum
601 Second Street
Marietta, OH 45750
(740) 373-3717 or (800) 860-0145

Ohio Village
1982 Velma Avenue
Columbus, OH 43211
(614) 297-2300 Museum

Schingoethe Center for Native American Cultures
Aurora University
347 S. Gladstone Avenue
Aurora, IL 60506-4892
(630) 844-5512

Science Center of Iowa
4500 Grand Avenue
Des Moines, IA 50312
(515) 274-6868

St. Louis Science Center
5050 Oakland Avenue
St. Louis, MO 63110
(314) 289-4474

University of Iowa Museum of Natural History
10 Macbride Hall
Iowa City, IA 52242
(319) 335-1822

ETHNICITY

Brian W. Beltman

The heartland of the United States, once the agricultural breadbasket of the nation and now a complex mix of residential, commercial, and industrial interests more urban than rural, teems with people of great ethnic diversity and manifold cultural attributes. The endless process of new people and cultures entering the region graphically speckles the landscape seemingly in a random way and always in a state of flux. Yet patterns and characteristics emerge from the population jigsaw puzzle formed by different people from different points of origin who make the Midwest a place they have called home—some for a long time, some for a shorter duration, some displacing others, some merging with others, and all part of a process that reflects both change and continuity and underscores ethnic and cultural heterogeneity.

AMERICAN INDIANS

Before the arrival of Europeans, the indigenous population of the Midwest displayed distinctions and variety. Among the numerous Native American groups were the Erie, Potawatomi, Miami, Mingo, Ottawa, Wyandot, Shawnee, Delaware, Illinois, Kaskaskia, Kickapoo, Sauk and Fox (Meskwaki), Winnebago, Menominee, Ojibwa (Chippewa), Santee and Yankton Dakota (Sioux), Iowa, Missouri, Osage, and more. These people were not bound by a common language, identical social customs, a single political arrangement, shared religious beliefs, or a basic pattern of survival and sustenance. None of the native folk resided in tipis. Some found shelter in large wooden longhouses capable of holding a family clan; others lived in small wickiups covered by slabs of bark or woven mats of long grass. Many groups lived in a woodlands environment in the eastern and northern parts of the Midwest or on the grasslands of the prairie plains found farther west. In both areas they practiced traditions of dwelling in small settlements sustained primarily by farming and supplemented by hunting and fishing. Throughout the greater Ohio

Valley they raised maize, squash, beans, and other garden crops on fertile plots close to streams or rivers that provided adequate moisture for seasonal harvests of foodstuff. In the Great Lakes vicinity where wetlands abounded, Indian farmers concentrated on rice production. Hunting game was always secondary to farming. In areas near rivers and lakes, fishing was often a more dependable complement to farming than was hunting. The Hollywood stereotype of Indians mounted on horseback chasing bison was completely incongruous with midwestern Native American life. More typically, tending small cornfields, gathering berries, and harvesting a few deer and elk were rudimentary to their sedentary existence.

Preservation of Territoriality

Survival required concerted attention to food production and acquisition, but Native Americans also interacted with each other as distinctive ethnic groups in ways that evidenced clear concepts of territoriality dividing their areas of occupancy. Fierce rivalries raged between tribes or nations, fueled by quests for power or outright conquest, or arising from ritualistic campaigns against a foe as part of rites of passage into adulthood or as the means to attain prestige and status. In short, all was not peaceful among different indigenous populations. For example, the Erie Indian nation along the southern shores of Lake Erie numbered about 14,000 people by 1600. Although they were sedentary farmers of the eastern woodlands area who focused on the daily needs of self-preservation, they showed some aggressive cultural traits, such as the use of poisoned arrows and the building of villages with defensive palisades. They were traditional enemies of the Iroquois League to the east, and in 1656, after one of the most relentless and destructive Indian wars, the Erie were almost exterminated by the Iroquois. The surviving captives were either adopted or enslaved by their conquerors.

The Europeans Enter Tribal Territory

Ethnic tensions among the American Indians intensified with the arrival of Europeans and the flourishing of the fur trade. The Iroquois frequently battled with various Algonquian-speaking tribes in Ohio country such as the Delaware, Miami, Ottawa, and Shawnee after 1650 as part of the so-called Beaver Wars that lasted from 1630 to 1700. In the Beaver Wars, Indians contested for control of the habitats of fur-bearing animals that were of value in the trade with Europeans. Trade also introduced many new goods and utensils into native cultural life, made the Indians rise to a new level of technology, turned subsistence hunters into commercial hunters, and merged them into a symbiotic relationship with invasive white traders. Woolen blankets, iron kettles, and manufactured tools enhanced their well-being; guns and liquor left a more mixed legacy. The fur trade was inextricably tied as well to empire-building by European powers that pulled different tribes and nations into their orbits of influence. As a result, Native Americans often became pawns to imperial clashes between the French and the English in the seventeenth and eighteenth centuries, and their cultures were drawn into international wars that were not of their own choosing but in which they participated ferociously for whatever gain they might achieve through alliance. In particular, the French and Indian Wars, which ended in 1763, swept Ohio Valley natives into a cauldron of violence; new armaments devastated their villages and decimated their populations.

The fur trade also set in motion physical displacement of one group by another, for the fur trade exploited a resource-limited commodity that required geographic expansion of the fur fields in order to sustain itself. Native procurers of the furs, after harvesting one area of fur-bearing animals into near extinction, thus ranged westward in search of new fur resources. As hunters moved westward, so did their villages, all pressed by the continual settlement of more whites along the Atlantic seaboard. Like dominoes, one group of indigenous people placed pressure on a neighboring group. As a result of Iroquois expansion into the Ohio Valley after 1650, the Shawnee pushed against the Miami who, in turn, crowded the Kickapoo, the latter two shifting westward into southern Wisconsin and northern Illinois. In Michigan the Ojibwa displaced the Sauk and Fox from the Saginaw Bay region as well as the Potawatomi just to the south of them into Wisconsin, thus crowding the resident Winnebago and Menominee. The Ojibwa also eventually drove the Dakota (Sioux) from the Great Lakes woodlands, ultimately making the Dakota an invader of the upper Great Plains.

Displacement and dispossession of native ethnic groups from traditional homelands ever farther into the interior of the Midwest had become a geographic and economic pattern even before the time of the American Revolution. American independence from England forced Native Americans to accept new political patterns that threatened their cultures even more than during the colonial era. The new United States defined indigenous folk as conquered people—"domestic dependent nations" in the legal term—since they had, with few exceptions, sided with the English during the American Revolution.[1] Treaties between the upper Ohio Valley tribes and the new American government on the Atlantic seaboard in the 1780s were harsh and restrictive, and required the Indians to recognize the ultimate sovereignty of the United States—to which the native cultures objected. Under the leadership of Little Turtle (1752–1812), a Miami chieftain, several tribes (Miami, Potawatomi, Shawnee, Wyandot, Ottawa, Kickapoo, Delaware, and Ojibwa) formed a defensive confederacy and opted for war with the overbearing United States. Twice, in 1790 and 1791, the confederacy's warriors mauled the white man's army, so badly on the second occasion that the battle, near the eastern fork of the upper Wabash River, stands as a record-setting defeat (over 690 casualties) for the American army by an Indian foe. But in 1794, opposed by a third, better trained armed force under General Anthony Wayne (1754–1796), the confederacy was militarily beaten at the Battle of Fallen Timbers, and native delegates signed the punitive Treaty of Greenville the next year that formally put them in a subordinate legal position to the government of the United States. The losers also had to forfeit a considerable land base to the winners, which greatly weakened their ability to remain culturally strong and to physically support their populations.

White Assaults on Native People

The late eighteenth century was only a prelude to the escalating frontal assault on midwestern native people. By the mid-nineteenth century, indigenous cultures approached their nadir in terms of strength, identity, and even resiliency. After 1800, powerful frontier politicians such as William Henry Harrison (1773–1841),

William Clark (1770–1838), Lewis Cass (1782–1866), and others curried political popularity in the emerging territories and states of the Midwest by crafting treaty after treaty with the Indians that diminished their landholdings and weakened their cultural integrity while opening new tracts of farmland to white settlers. By 1809, unrelenting treaty-making by Harrison dispossessed the tribes of the Indiana Territory of so much land that it provoked Tecumseh (1768–1813), a Shawnee headman, into appealing for a pan-Indian response. He urged his red brothers to unify in order to stop inexorable land-grabbing and white expansion into the midwestern heartland. Tecumseh and his brother Tenskwatawa (1775–1837), a Shawnee shaman or "prophet," were only modestly successful in assembling an armed confederacy to resist white encroachment, but the American military response led by Harrison proved overwhelming at the Battle of Tippecanoe in 1811. This red–white conflict then merged into the western theater of the War of 1812, and the Indians, as allies to the British, reaped a whirlwind of defeat and destruction. More punitive treaties followed, and more land cessions ensued, ending tribal claims and facilitating white occupancy.

Cultural duress for midwestern indigenous groups intensified during the Jacksonian Era. In 1830, legislators in Congress passed the Removal Act with the full support of the popular frontier politician, former Indian-fighting general, and now President Andrew Jackson (1767–1845). This law required all American Indians east of the Mississippi River to relocate west of it so that the eastern half of the United States was free of the "red problem." Through persuasion, threats, bribery, treaties, and military coercion, the tribal groups experienced refugee deportation from their ancient homelands. They also endured disease, starvation, repeated physical dislocation, armed attacks, and unspeakable emotional and psychological upheaval as part of a process that lasted nearly twenty years before it was completed. Except for the uprising of the Winnebagos in 1827 led by Red Bird (c. 1788–1828) and the resistance of the Sauk and Fox in 1832 led by Black Hawk (1767–1838), most demoralized Indians of the Midwest suffered their fate with resignation and compliance. Each and every one endured a private "trail of tears," and the survivors lived through a cultural travail that no superlatives can define.

Something of a last-gasp stand erupted in Minnesota in 1862 when the Santee Dakota under the leadership of Little Crow (c. 1818–1863) battled white civilians and soldiers.[2] A treaty of 1851 had relegated the Dakota to a reservation in the southwestern portion of Minnesota and promised annual annuities in trade and supplies from the federal government. Not content with the limited land reserve and suffering physically and materially because of the government's repeated failures to honor treaty obligations, the Dakota retaliated by attacking frontier settlements in the western valley of the Minnesota River and its tributaries. They killed backcountry residents as well as

Santee Dakota under the leadership of Little Crow (c. 1818–1863). Courtesy Library of Congress.

some hastily dispatched troops. Terrified whites abandoned their farms and villages such as New Ulm and St. Peter and fled toward Forts Ridgley and Snelling. At Fort Snelling near St. Paul, Colonel Henry Sibley (1811–1891) formed an opposing force of over 1500 combatants that within a month countered the Dakota advance. Rather than face certain arrest and execution, Little Crow and hundreds of Dakota vacated to Canada. But scores of other warriors were captured, and after a trial in St. Paul held amid emotional demands of nothing less than extermination of the native perpetrators, 306 Dakota were sentenced to be hung at Fort Snelling. In the end, President Abraham Lincoln (1809–1865) commuted the sentences of all but thirty-eight men.

The Results of Removal and Resistance of the American Indians

Removal or resistance made Native Americans in the Midwest a nearly vanished people in the larger population portrait of the region, but remnants of former cultures persisted in isolated pockets and found sanctuary in reservations formed by the federal government. This program officially began in 1851, as in the case of the Dakota, but did not materialize fully in the Midwest until after the Civil War. It generally affected only a small number of remaining groups, primarily the woodlands natives of upper Michigan, Wisconsin, and Minnesota, but it also involved the importing of more eastern-based tribes into the midwestern region as a function of the earlier removal policy. Federally designated reservations ultimately included the following: in *Michigan*, Bay Mills, Grand Traverse, Hannahville, Huron Potawatomi, Isabella, L'Anse, Lac Vieux Desert, Little River, Little Traverse Bay, and Sault Ste. Marie; in *Wisconsin*, Bad River, Forest County Potawatomi, Ho-Chunk, Lac Courte Oreilles, Lac du Flambeau, Menominee, Stockbridge-Munsee, Oneida, Red Cliff, Sokagon Chippewa, and Saint Croix; in *Minnesota*, Bois Forte, Fond du Lac, Grand Portage, Leech Lake, Lower Sioux, Mille Lacs, Minnesota Chippewa, Prairie Island Dakota, Red Lake, Sandy Lake, Shakopee Sioux, Upper Sioux, and White Earth; and in *Iowa*, Meskwaki. These reservations became rural enclaves where traditional cultures were redeemed from the brink of extinction in the late nineteenth century. Here aboriginal identity, cultural personality traits, and the security of a common-held land base endured and indeed enabled these Native Americans to prevail into the twenty-first century. To be sure, reservations carry weighty burdens of poverty, low living standards, high unemployment, poor health and educational services, and other social disadvantages. Indeed, some critical observers compare the quality of life on reservations to that of refugee camps in Third World countries in an attempt to get governmental agencies to do a better job of taking care of its "domestic dependent nations." Here, too, are found gaudy casinos doing a thriving business to capture the white man's trade, an ironic reversal of the historic fur trade exchange that in the past often worked to the Indians' disadvantage. Yet reservations continue to provide cultural islands for the First Americans amid a sea of other indifferent people with their own cultural priorities. These "oases" safeguard cultural continuity and allow treasured traditions and a sense of community to flourish despite pressures to change. Thus the Indians have been able to survive economically and politically in the greater mainstream of society.

The American Indians in the Midwest Today

Other Indians have found their communal and cultural needs met in the context of the large urban centers of the Midwest. In Chicago, Minneapolis, Milwaukee, Detroit, and other cities, dispersed tribal affiliates, who have integrated largely into the white workforce and have been seemingly absorbed into a multicultural society through intermarriage and homogenized educational systems, still find innovative ways to reassemble as a collective people. In this way, they provide each other with practical mutual support and remind themselves that they are uniquely aboriginal, even as they labor to sustain their livelihoods and families in the white man's world. Ceremonial powwows, traditional craft festivals, spiritual gatherings, health and legal assistance, language study, and more are part of this urban scene. Today, Native Americans continue to balance the forces of traditionalism and modernism. Whether to remain true to the old ways, accommodate to new, or somehow practice some of both, these options are sources of factionalism among American Indians, but the choices also give a dynamic quality to their lives and ensure their cultural vitality into the twenty-first century.

THE INFLUX OF NORTHERN EUROPEANS

During most of its first century the United States was primarily a rural society with an agricultural economy. For the Midwest these dual traits clearly defined the region well into the mid-nineteenth century even as urban-industrial developments began emerging. Beginning in the 1780s, an irrepressible population stream from eastern settled areas flowed into the nation's heartland as the federal government steadily opened new lands to white occupancy. For the first three or four decades, the settlers were mainly of colonial ancestry—new generations born of American parents with roots traceable to English origins and, in a more limited sense, to German Palatines who had resided in Pennsylvania for a generation or two. In addition, a scattering of French Canadians who pursued the fur trade came into the northern Great Lakes region and shifted in time to the growing timber industry of the vast northern woodlands. The French colonial imprint on St. Louis and Sainte Genevieve in Missouri also lingered in the early nineteenth century, and the lead mining district centered on Washington County remained a cohesive French settlement west of the Mississippi for many decades. Aside from a few international transplants, however, the majority of early settlers in the Midwest were people of American stock, not newly arrived immigrants from foreign lands.

In the 1820s and 1830s, the first hint of a dramatic demographic shift in the peopling of the Midwest was discernible, as some bold forerunners of immigrant origins made their way to the north shore of Lake Erie and along the great riverine arteries of the Ohio and Mississippi—to growing population centers such as Cleveland, Cincinnati, and St. Louis. These early immigrants were few in number and mainly Anglo or Germanic in origin. Some were "radicals" who left homelands where emigration was often considered an act of disloyalty and who were willing to relocate to far-flung, unsettled places in chancy communities in the Midwest or to remote frontier farming areas of the interior. For example, in 1817 a group of German religious separatists under the leadership of Joseph Baumeler (d. 1853) founded the village of Zoar in Ohio. In the 1820s and 1830s Cornish,

Welsh, and Irish miners gravitated to the newly opened Galena lead mining region of southwestern Wisconsin and northwestern Illinois. In the late 1830s Carl Walther (1811–1887) spearheaded a colony of German pietists in Perry County, Missouri, and subsequently started the Lutheran Church-Missouri Synod. And in 1840 German Catholics settled in Dubois County in southwestern Indiana to establish a long-lived German ethnic enclave. Such early arrivals heralded an ethnic diversity infusing into the population as a whole.

The German Wave

By the 1840s and 1850s, the trickle became a free-flowing river of transplants from Northern European sources. English arrivals continued to keep the nation's population primarily Anglo, but several other immigration waves added new currents into the mainstream. Germanic folk from distinct provinces—Saxony, Württemberg, Bavaria, Mecklenburg, Hanover, Westphalia, Pomerania, and Prussia—as well as German-speaking residents from the Austrian-Hungarian Empire and Switzerland—migrated to growing market centers such as St. Louis, Milwaukee, and Cincinnati as laborers, shopkeepers, and artisans. These three cities formed a virtual German triangle in which the culture of the Old Country was replicated. By 1860, 47 percent of all German-born in the United States lived in this area. German skilled laborers—bakers, blacksmiths, butchers, carpenters, masons, and tailors—plied their trades often within the confines of German American urban neighborhoods. German *braumeisters* produced a sudsy beverage that made Milwaukee famous. German folk socialized in beer gardens, enjoyed their traditional polka music and dances, celebrated Oktoberfest while dining on bratwurst and sauerkraut, and shared in the hardy spirit of *gemütlichkeit* (cozy friendship). They actively participated in secular German athletic or singing clubs (Turnverein and Liederkrant) as well as in Protestant, Catholic, or Jewish religious organizations. Though divided by different faiths, in areas where these folk concentrated, the German-language reigned uniformly on the street. Given the vast number of people of Germanic affiliation settling in the Midwest, countless German-language newspapers and other

German American hatmakers in Milwaukee factory. Photo courtesy of Milwaukee County Historical Society.

Turnverein is the German word for gymnastics. *Turners* was the Anglicized name for German social clubs in the United States. Courtesy Cincinnati Museum Center, Cincinnati Historical Society.

printed material came off the presses for local and regional readers. And in both their public and parochial schools German Americans used their mother tongue for instructional purposes. By the late nineteenth century persistent use of German in local schools provoked a nativist backlash against this practice and led to bilingual instruction and ultimately to English-only during the era of World War I, when Germany became a wartime enemy and things German lost popularity. Indeed, reflecting the psychology of war, anti-German sentiment caused wieners to be renamed hot dogs, and sauerkraut, liberty cabbage.

Long before this time, however, some social critics in the 1850s had already worried that Wisconsin might become a "Germanized" state with Milwaukee its "German Athens." Yet in fact, few of these ethnic settlers, though proud of their German heritage, thought of themselves in national terms or aspired to any reimposition of that kind of nationhood. Rather, they clustered locally in narrowly defined ethnic enclaves based on Old Country local affiliations tied to rural neighborhood networks or parish and church membership. For example, Westphalia farmers transplanted their agricultural and rural social life onto farms and hamlets in St. Charles County, Missouri, just west of St. Louis.[3] German-speaking Swiss, who were members of a government-approved emigration society, founded the community of New Glarus in 1845 in Green County, Wisconsin, that still thrives today as a midwestern tourist attraction. Amish and Mennonite populations with strong German origins located across northern Indiana and Ohio in Allen, Elkhart, Lagrange, Adams, Wells, Wayne, Holmes, and Tuscarawas counties. Germanic farmers such as these tended to persist on the land across several generations, but they also proved to be quick and successful students of American methods of commercial agriculture. They abandoned Old World farm village settlement patterns to live on dispersed farmsteads and partake fully in progressive, mechanized farming practices.

Many German immigrants were of rural peasant origins, and to these the fertile soils of the Midwest beckoned irresistibly. The Pre-emption Act of 1841 and the Homestead Act of 1862 signaled that America offered a nearly free-land program to those willing to immigrate and wanting to farm. These liberal land policies made the goal of property ownership a viable reality for immigrants, in contrast to circumstances in Europe where that objective remained little more than a dream. German-born farm families thus took up the land in county after county from Ohio to Missouri and north into Wisconsin, settling in innumerable rural villages with German place names. A brief sampling suggests the pattern: in *Ohio* were Berlin, Bremen, Dresden, Frankfort, Gnadenhutten, and Schoenbrunn; in *Indiana*, Darmstadt, Haubstadt, Munster, Otterbein, and Schnellville; in *Illinois*, Belleville, Bismarck, Bremen, Darmstadt, Hamburg, German Valley, Millstadt, New Badin, Palatine, and Teutopolis; in *Iowa*, Germantown, Guttenberg, Holstein, Oelwien, Remsen, Schleswig, and Westphalia; in *Missouri*, Barnhart, Bismarck, Freidheim, Hermann, Wentzville, Wittenburg, and Weingarten; in *Minnesota*, Cologne, Karlstadt, Kerkhoven, New Germany, New Ulm, Olmsted, Potsdam, and Zimmerman; in *Wisconsin*, Berlin, Dousman, Germantown, New Berlin, New Holstein, Rhinelander, and Shullsburg; and in *Michigan*, Dryden, Frankenmuth, Frankfort, and Westphalia. German festivals persist to the present in those small communities, where residents can trace their lineage back five or six generations or more before finding the ancestor who was foreign-born. Some German Americans own centennial family farms on which a family patriarch established first title by way of a homestead certificate.

Irish Immigrants

Irish peasants and townsmen were on a coincidental immigrant path with the Germans. Decades of political oppression and property control by English landlords had institutionalized poverty and tenancy within the political economy of the Irish, and rampant population growth strained the nation's resources to the point that emigration became a societal relief measure. In the mid-1840s, the infamous potato blight brought starvation where there had been all-too-familiar hunger into the lives of thousands of ordinary Irish residents. Desperation that only the refugee knows made the Irish abandon their abused homeland for the promise of a surely better life in America. Most of these immigrants, often with limited resources, made it to the northeastern coastal region of the United States and stayed there. Others with meager resources to spare also added to growing inland urban centers, working their way into the Midwest as construction workers on canal and railroad projects and ultimately finding moorings in cities, small towns, and farms. In Detroit they created a distinctive ethnic neighborhood known as Corktown, and in Chicago enough Irish day laborers found menial work helping to build the infrastructure of that burgeoning city that by 1850 an estimated one-fifth of its urban population was Irish. Irish workers also toiled on the wharves and aboard steamboats on the Mississippi, Ohio, and Great Lakes. Irish women often hired out as chambermaids, cooks, and nannies. And on streets frequented by the Irish, a Paddy's Pub or Kelly's Keg offered a place to bend an elbow, share some blarney, enjoy boisterous companionship, and exchange stories about the pitiful life left behind in Ireland.[4]

Although most Irish settled in large cities, some Irish workers headed to the copper mining counties of Houghton and Marquette in Upper Michigan in the 1850s or found jobs as sawyers and log-rollers in the timber business of the northern woodlands. Other rural Irish, as low-skilled hands laying track, followed rail lines into the interiors of midwestern states and subsequently secured small acreages to farm. Here they resumed farming traditions and raised crops and livestock without the nagging fear of recurring blight, malnutrition, or famine. In particular, the Illinois Central Railroad served in the 1850s as both employer and conduit for Irish workers who returned to farming the land as they had turned "the sod" in Ireland. Kane County southwest of Chicago and McLean and Randolph counties in central Illinois all attracted Irish settlers. Later, Father John Ireland (b. 1838), archbishop of the St. Paul diocese, collaborated with railroad companies in Minnesota to promote rural colonization of the Irish in the southwestern part of that state, but with mixed success. Rural Irish concentrations also developed in Monroe County, Iowa, and Shannon and Oregon counties, Missouri.

Wherever Irish families rooted, Catholic priests followed to start parishes and community life for the immigrants. Some Irish Americans also quickly became involved in local politics since they had no language barrier to overcome; they proved skillful in the rough and tumble politics of urban precincts and emerging machine politics. Through political quid pro quo practices, Irish bosses repaid the support of ethnic constituents by helping secure jobs, housing, and other social and economic needs. The combined strength of their avid participation in politics and their religious solidarity alarmed some observers. Natives in the 1850s focused menacingly on Irish Catholics as a powerfully dangerous element in the mainstream of American society that needed reining in. Against this religious bigotry and political competition, the Irish battled to retain a semblance of their ethnic heritage through St. Patrick's Day parades and celebrations while aggressively Americanizing to secure a place for themselves socially and politically. Irish Americans were also subsequently instrumental in the organized labor movement to secure better working conditions and win the right of unionization.

Scandinavian Immigration

After Germans and Irish, immigrants from Sweden, Norway, and Denmark formed a third bloc of ethnic settlers in the nineteenth-century Midwest.[5] Scandinavians were predominantly rural in their points of origin and places of relocation, and they were almost totally Protestant. Prior to the Civil War, Scandinavians made only a start at migrating to the heartland; their high tide of resettlement occurred during the postwar decades. At first, family groups of small farmers seeking more fertile and larger tracts of land than their agriculturally limited homelands could provide dominated the immigration flow. Later, landless rural laborers and eventually urban singles surpassed the earlier category of migrants. The lure of land led most Scandinavians to the grain farms of the Midwest. Swedish farmers went largely to northwestern Wisconsin and northeastern Minnesota along the St. Croix River as well as to Henry, Knox, and Winnebago counties in Illinois and Montgomery, Jefferson, and Boone counties in Iowa. Some Swedes, like the Irish, worked in the booming lumber camps of the northern timberlands of the Great Lakes region, and others found employment in the coal mines of south-central Iowa alongside immigrants from the British Isles. Norwegian agriculturalists settled mainly in south-central and southwestern Wisconsin, east-central and northwestern Minnesota, and northeastern Iowa. In Dane and Vernon counties, Wisconsin, tobacco farming became an almost exclusively Norwegian endeavor. Danes relocated to localized rural concentrations in Shelby and Audubon counties, Iowa; in Brown, Waukesha, Waupaca and Polk counties, Wisconsin; and in Freeborn County, Minnesota.

Although chain or serial migration—in which migrants, bound by family ties or by neighborhood or church networks, followed one another to a new country like links in a chain—occurred across ethnic groups, the phenomenon was especially prevalent among Scandinavians. This produced identifiable ethnic enclaves, often centered on a Lutheran church, whose congregation had been members of a parental church in the Old Country that was gradually transplanted over the years to a New World location. In concentrated pockets these ethnics attained a critical mass to support foreign-language newspapers, academies and colleges, and strong church-centered community life. Norwegians in Decorah, Iowa, started Luther

Danes made Elkhorn, Iowa, a distinctive ethnic town with Tivoli Fest in May and Julesfest in November. Courtesy Iowa Tourism Office.

College, and in Stoughton, Wisconsin, they annually celebrate Syttende Mai, Norwegian Independence Day. In Minnesota, Swedes at St. Peter began Gustavus Adolphus College, and in Northfield, St. Olaf College. Danes made New Denmark, Wisconsin, and Elkhorn, Iowa, distinctive ethnic towns, Elkhorn displaying a landmark Danish windmill breaking the prairie horizon.

Scandinavians, though largely focused on agricultural pursuits in the heartland, also presented an urban dimension. In particular, Racine, Wisconsin, became the most Danish city in America, and many Danes there found employment in the J.I. Case agricultural implement company or the Mitchell Wagon Works. Swedes eventually made Chicago the second largest Swedish city in the world. Here in Andersonville lived numerous wageworkers, both skilled and unskilled, who eked out an existence in textile factories, construction projects, and the railroad industry as they struggled for integration into the bustling Illinois metropolis.

Immigrants from the Netherlands

Dutch Americans kept an enduring loyalty to their sense of "Dutchness." Decorative windmills and tulip gardens flourish as Dutch icons on the American landscape. Dez Waan Windmill, Holland, Michigan. Courtesy Travel Michigan.

Among the Northern Europeans who settled in the Midwest, comparatively few Dutch comprised conspicuous pieces in the region's ethnic mosaic. The initial Dutch immigrants arriving from 1846 to the late 1850s were frequently conservative Calvinist Reformed congregants who had abandoned a homeland where religious liberalism invoked unwelcome change. They were also largely small farmers and rural laborers seeking economic opportunity overseas because at home agricultural and industrial modernism was increasingly marginalizing these folk during the second half of the nineteenth century. Many Dutch immigrants were led by clerics who transplanted their followers to compact ethnoreligious colonies in Allegan and Ottawa counties, Michigan; Fond du Lac and Sheboygan counties, Wisconsin; Marion and Sioux counties, Iowa; and in Chicago and its southern rural rim. Such places, magnets for subsequent immigration, sustained ethnic enclave growth and cultural persistence, both fed by the powerful influences of religious solidarity, kinship communication, and resulting chain migration linkages. The Dutch prevailed mainly as farmers in the woodlands and on the prairie plains where they also established small towns as rural service centers and places to build their churches and schools. Some also found mostly blue-collar employment in service capacities in Chicago and the furniture factories of Grand Rapids, Michigan. Dutch Americans remained ethnically distinct through persistent language retention, endogamous marriage, fidelity to their Reformed religious traditions (though Dutch Catholics and Jews were part of their immigration stream as well), geographic compactness in thriving full-service colonies, and enduring loyalty to their sense of "Dutchness."[6] This loyalty ultimately expressed itself in regionally famous Tulip Festivals in Holland, Michigan, and in Pella and Orange City, Iowa. In these towns decorative windmills and tulip gardens flourished as Dutch icons on the American landscape.

Belgians in the Midwest

From the Netherlands' low country neighbor of Belgium came another immigrant stream of comparatively modest size and focused resettlement in the Midwest. Southern Belgians who spoke French and Walloon were generally small farmers and agricultural laborers emigrating in search of farmland. In response to aggressive advertising by shipping companies, some began moving to Sheboygan County, Wisconsin, in 1853 to settle temporarily among the Dutch. Hearing of a small French-speaking parish located to the north near Green Bay, these Belgians relocated to the Door Peninsula in northeastern Wisconsin. Here they acquired farmland and formed a distinctive ethnic island in Door, Kewaunee, and Brown counties, where communities named Brussels, Namur, and Rosiere recalled the homeland. To the present, this area remains the nation's largest rural Belgian settlement in the United States, and residents of Brussels still celebrate "Belgium Days" each July. Flemish-speaking Belgians from the northern part of the nation also relocated to the Midwest from 1880 to 1920. Many were artisans such as carpenters and cabinetmakers as well as glassblowers and lace makers. They tended to settle in Detroit when that city's industrial and manufacturing growth provided employment opportunities for skilled finishers on construction projects, in glassworks, and in transportation factories. Small pockets of Belgians also settled in Michigan City, Indiana; Moline, Illinois; and in Lyon, Lincoln, and Redwood counties of southwestern Minnesota.

Most Belgian Americans were Catholic. In an urban area like Detroit, they joined in worship with other ethnic Catholics such as German or French, but on the Door Peninsula their population base was sufficient to establish their own parishes and parochial schools. For the Belgians, like other groups, religion reinforced ethnicity, and in their churches they celebrated the kermiss, a traditional autumn harvest festival. Belgians also built unique roadside chapels in the countryside of the Door Peninsula to serve rural communicants who lived too far from parish churches to attend regularly.

Finns, the Last Scandinavian Immigrant Group to America

Like the Dutch and Belgians, Finnish immigrants were comparatively few in number but highly regionalized in their midwestern settlement pattern. Beginning in the 1880s and continuing until World War I, the Finns were the last Scandinavian group to come to America. As in the Netherlands, agricultural change in Finland produced a large, poor, landless class of peasants, but in addition, Finns experienced political discrimination and compulsory military service within the Russian Empire. Finnish immigrants thus sought to escape oppression and secure available farmland still vigorously advertised by midwestern states. By the late nineteenth century, however, the only sizable tracts that were affordable were also the most marginal for farming purposes. These lay in the cutover region of northern Wisconsin and Minnesota and the Upper Peninsula of Michigan, where, in the wake of depleted timber stands, acres could yet be homesteaded. Here the Finns brought their families, carved out small farms, built Finnish-style log cabins, and tried to coax a living from soil that critics contended grew only stumps and rocks. Some Finns also found employment in the last days of the lumber industry, in fishing and shipping on the Great Lakes, and in iron and copper mining located in Marquette, Houghton, and Keweenaw counties, Michigan, and in St. Louis County, Minnesota. Regardless of occupation, most Finns endured seasonal incomes and barely eked out a living. As a result, after 1900 they were ripe for the political activism of the rising labor movement. During the 1907 Mesabi iron range strike, nearly three-fourths of the strikers were Finns, along with Poles, Greeks, Italians, Irish, and others. Many Finnish farmers, miners, and lumberjacks subsequently joined the Industrial Workers of the World and subscribed to its socialistic agenda because they did not experience the promised benefits of booming capitalism. This flirtation with radical political and economic alternatives was not long-lasting, although many Finns would continue to miss out on the American Dream. Finnish Americans also established an ethnic legacy by forming farmers' cooperatives for mutual survival; some of the nation's largest cooperative organizations arose in northern Wisconsin.

People from Eastern Europe and Lands Rimming the Mediterranean Sea

Although immigration from Northern Europe to the United States continued during the late nineteenth and early twentieth centuries, points of origin for many new residents shifted to Southern and Eastern Europe as well as to nations bordering the eastern Mediterranean Sea between 1880 and 1920. Italians, Greeks, Czechs, Slovaks, Poles, Hungarians, Lithuanians, Romanians, Serbians, Croatians, Slovenes, Eastern European Jews, Armenians, Arabs, and others poured into the Midwest. Many newcomers came more boldly as single individuals, less as part of nuclear or extended family groups; and often they arrived with few resources but ready hands, strong backs, and ambition born of need. Although most came from rural peasant backgrounds and few had much experience beyond the traditions of agricultural life, by the late nineteenth century the option of taking up virgin farmland, as earlier waves of immigrants had done, was severely limited since the vast acres of the heartland were already claimed. Thus, they gravitated to the burgeoning cities in search of economic opportunity, endured the congestion and squalor of teeming urban ghettos, and found work where they could in the rising industrial sector.

Italians

Although Italians were not widely dispersed across the Midwest, they did form heavy concentrations in Chicago, St. Louis, and later Detroit. These predominantly male immigrants were mainly from the countryside of southern Italy. Some proved to be short-term workers who in time repatriated to Italy with accumulated savings, thus gaining notoriety as "birds of passage," but many also moored permanently in the new land.[7] A minority were skilled artisans—stonecutters, glaziers, and painters—but the vast numbers were manual laborers who superseded the Irish in expanding the railroad network, paving streets, digging sewer lines, and constructing the ever-taller buildings that crowded city centers. Some found jobs in the limestone quarries and coal mines of Indiana or as truck garden farmers on the outer fringes of Chicago. Others peddled goods from pushcarts, operated small grocery stores, meat markets, or delicatessens, or started spaghetti factories or haberdasheries. Still others found an ethnic niche in the occupational structure as barbers, catering with great finesse to their male clientele. Many Italians came to America as ethnic contract laborers through arrangements made by a *padrone* who extorted salary kickbacks. These contractors were usually fellow immigrants, only slightly more adapted to American ways, who manipulated their countrymen while assisting them into the new occupational and residential environment. As a result, Italians endured low-paying jobs and poor living conditions in urban ethnic enclaves.

Areas known as "Little Italy" emerged within several midwestern urban conglomerates. Through chain migration, highly localized village compatriots transplanted from the Old to the New World to recreate Italian neighborhoods. Such urban clusters, however, always included a mix of folk from other ethnic backgrounds including Germans and Irish, for example. Nonetheless, in the Cicero subdivision of Chicago near Hull House, in Murray Hill in Cleveland, on "The Hill" in south St. Louis (the home of Yogi Berra), and among the Third Ward of Milwaukee could be found a clear preponderance of Italians, speaking their language on the street and socializing among their own kind. Survival here meant that all able-bodied male family members labored in the workforce, including children at an early age. In this context, education received short shrift, and few Italian youth received a high school education prior to 1920. In contrast to the Irish, whose wives and daughters cleaned, washed, and cooked for gentry, most Italian women remained at home attending to domestic needs, their labor often crucial in keeping the family intact.

Although most Italians were Catholic, the Church was of mixed social importance, apart from providing important sacramental rituals; some immigrants carried anticlerical cultural baggage that modified their involvement in Church affairs. Moreover, the American Catholic hierarchy was largely dominated by the Irish, which did not quickly offer a warm welcome to the Italian faithful. In addition, communal and fraternal organizations were not particularly prevalent among Italians as was the case with Germans, for their cultural tradition favored a family-based sense of individualism that undergirded local camaraderie. But Italian Americans did form mutual aid societies to provide short-term benefits to the unemployed or to families suffering from sicknesses or injuries and in dire need. Thus, local Galileo or Garibaldi societies became institutional support structures. In addition, among immigrant groups, political participation by Italian Americans was comparatively low because they were shut out by earlier arriving Irish and Germans. And since most were unskilled or semiskilled, few entered the early, trade-oriented labor movement. Later, however, as unionization included noncraft workers, Italians participated in its benefits as well as its confrontations with management. Ultimately, when significant numbers of Italian Americans found employment in the early twentieth-century automobile industry, they took up residence in Detroit and satellite communities.

Although Italians were not widely dispersed across the Midwest, they did form heavy concentrations in Chicago, St. Louis, and later Detroit. Eighth-grade Italian Americans in typing class, c. 1920–1930. Italian American Collection, Special Collections Department, the University Library, University of Illinois at Chicago.

Czechs and Slovaks

Beginning in 1848, some Czech politicos fled to America to escape oppression by Austrian Hapsburg rule in their home regions of Bohemia and Moravia, followed by small farmers suffering from the economic hardships of agricultural depression in the late nineteenth and early twentieth centuries. Early Czech residents capitalized on the Homestead Act and established agricultural footholds along Lake Michigan in Kewaunee and Manitowoc counties, Wisconsin; Caledonia, a community north of Racine, was the first major Czech farming settlement. Later, Czechs farmed in Adams, Richland, and La Crosse counties of central and western Wisconsin, while still others worked in the lumber industry or eked out a living on farms in the cutover of northern Wisconsin in Price, Taylor, Langlade, and Oconto counties. Czech farmers also migrated to scattered rural hamlets in Iowa—Spillville, Protovin, Solon, Traer, Clutier, and Vining—and in Minnesota—New Prague, Ely, and Litomysl. Many Czechs, however, also established urban concentrations in Chicago, Cleveland, St. Louis, Milwaukee, Detroit, and Cedar Rapids, Iowa. The Chicago neighborhood of Pilsens became a center of Czech life, and the city eventually was home to some 100,000 first- and second-generation Czech Americans who were largely employed in steel mills and glass factories. Indeed, by 1890, Czechs were the fifth largest ethnic group in Chicago.

Closely akin to Czechs were ethnic Slovaks who immigrated to the United States beginning in the 1880s. As unskilled laborers, they headed for the heavy industrial regions of iron and steel production and associated coal mines. They concentrated in the area from Youngstown to Cleveland, Ohio. Oil refineries, chemical plants, and steel mills in East Chicago and Gary, Indiana, also attracted many Slovaks to establish residency there.

Czechs and Slovaks came to the Midwest as family units and quickly reestablished vibrant family life. In their ethnic enclaves, the street language was Czech and Slovak, brass bands played polka music in dance halls and for community concerts, and residents celebrated "Bohemian Days" with beer and kolaches (a prune-filled pastry). Czech breweries flourished—the Pilsen and Budweiser brands are Czech names—and gave competition to German brewers. Religiously, the Czechs arrived primarily as Catholics, but once in the New World perhaps as many as 50 percent left the Church because they associated it with the oppressive state religion of the Hapsburg Empire. Thus, Czech Americans were divided between Catholics and Protestants, and many communities had dual church organizations. Some Czechs and Slovaks, however, opposed church affiliation of any kind and became self-styled freethinkers. The freethinkers were instrumental in establishing fraternal and benevolent societies aimed at preserving ethnic heritage and providing social assistance, civic involvement, and health insurance policies. In 1854, the Czechs and Slovaks in Ripon, Wisconsin, for example, formed the Czech-Slavonic Benevolent Society to provide social services to immigrants and the poor. Another organization was the Sokol, a gymnastic club formed in Cedar Rapids in 1873 that promoted physical fitness, held annual picnics, and sponsored a masquerade dance known as the Sibrinky on the Monday before Ash Wednesday.

The Polish

Polish-speaking immigrants came from Germany, Austria-Hungary, and Russia, beginning in the 1850s and cresting after 1900. Polish peasants from small villages knew only the seasonal rhythms of farming, yet their economic plight under three strong European empires led them to seek butter on their bread in the alien environment of American industrial cities.[8] In the Midwest, Polish population centers developed in Chicago, Milwaukee, Detroit, and Cleveland, but early German Poles were fortunate enough to pioneer on the land in isolated pockets, and other Poles carved out ethnic enclaves in middle-sized cities such as Hamtramck, Michigan, and Superior, Wisconsin. The Iowa coalfields attracted some Poles as well as other southeastern Europeans. Two special rural regional concentrations of Polish Americans developed in Portage County, Wisconsin, and in the Fox River Valley of Wisconsin from Oshkosh to Green Bay. The Wisconsin villages of Polonia, Pulaski, Krakow, and Sobieski all hark back to the homeland.

Virtually devoid of skills for urban workplaces, Polish Americans took the low-paying jobs in manufacturing plants, warehouses, and shipping and freighting facilities. Poles were by definition Polish Catholic and fiercely so, which put them at odds with the American Catholic hierarchy, precipitated numerous internecine church quarrels, and led to the establishment through schism of the Polish National Catholic Church in 1904. In turn, Polish Americans strongly supported ethnic parochial schools that upheld their religion and their native language, thus prompting attacks on those institutions for retarding acculturation. Similarly, Polish nationalism applauded the formation of an independent Poland after World War I. This Old World orientation helps explain a lack of Polish participation in local politics, even in Chicago where one out of eight residents claimed Polish ancestry by 1920. Not until that year was the first Polish American elected to Congress by the Chicago constituency.

Eastern European Jews

More than the Poles, Eastern European Jews could claim a variety of national origins. Prior to 1880, most Jewish immigrants to America were German, but thereafter their countries of origin included Russia, Austria, Romania, Hungary, Poland, Ukraine, and more.[9] Although Jews invariably indicated their mother tongue was Yiddish, they also recorded that they spoke various national languages such as Russian, German, and Polish, as well as regional dialects. Jews came to the Midwest like other immigrants to better their material and emotional lives, but they also sought refuge from severe persecution by Eastern European governments that restricted their political and religious rights, physical movement and residency, and occupational and educational opportunities. So great was the desire to flee oppression that Jewish immigrants came to the heartland to stay; like the Irish, few repatriated to the Old World. Again like the Irish, Jewish men and women came in nearly equal gender proportions, often with fathers and older sons arriving first to prepare the way and women and other children following shortly after to reconstitute family life.

Although New York and other northeastern cities received the bulk of Jewish newcomers, midwestern cities garnered their share as well. By 1920, about a tenth of the populations of Cleveland and Chicago were Jewish; many other cities had smaller Jewish minorities as well. Coming from rural, small-village backgrounds, they joined the working poor of the large cities, concentrated in ethnic enclaves, crowded in five- to six-story tenements with often only one toilet per floor and no hot water. Families occupied small three- or four-room apartments and frequently took in additional roomers and boarders to help pay the rent. In such environments, disease could flourish and crime festered. In their distinctive urban ghettos Yiddish-speaking Jews observed the Sabbath, performed the bar mitzvah ceremony, ate kosher food, worshiped in synagogues, and celebrated special holidays such as Passover, Rosh Hashanah, Yom Kippur, and Hanukkah. Invariably, such activities aroused suspicion and evoked general anti-Semitic animosity as well as specific discriminatory practices with respect to employment, membership in social clubs, school attendance, and more.

Most Jewish immigrants worked in manual occupations. Early-arriving German Jews created a stereotypic niche in American folklore as itinerant peddlers traveling the countryside selling an array of goods from a back-pack, or, when more established, from a horse-drawn buggy. Later-arriving Eastern European Jews were more likely to be day laborers, taking whatever work was available at a street corner gathering from a passing employer in search of a few unskilled workers. Apart from this, their skill at needle crafts fitted them well for the emerging mass production industry of ready-to-wear clothing. With the perfection of the sewing machine by Isaac M. Singer (1811–1875), the garment industry expanded tremendously and provided employment for Jewish men, women, and their children. Although these garment workers labored long, dreary hours in cramped, stuffy quarters, the infamous "sweat shops" provided meager opportunities that left the family intact and produced a survival income. To be sure, children's education was often delayed in the process, wages were below standards, and exploitative bosses were callous and demanding in the extreme. Jewish Americans were also visible on the urban landscape as retailers—butchers, bakers, grocers, tailors, and more. As a case in point, by 1880, all retail clothing stores in Columbus, Ohio were owned by Jews. Others used their well-developed talent as entertainers, actors, and musicians along Chicago's Great White Way by the 1890s.

The west side of downtown Chicago in the vicinity of Maxwell Street served as the original settlement area for Eastern European Jews in the Midwest. Here social life often reflected affinity among folk of the same village or rural neighborhood of their country of origin. A castelike division long remained between well-established German Jews, who moved south of Chicago's central business district into Washington Park, Hyde Park, and South Shore, and newly arriving Eastern European Jews. But the Eastern European Jews, having different national origins, also tended to segregate into separate communal neighborhoods with distinctive community lives of their own such as Douglas Park, Albany Park, Humboldt Park, and Lakeview. Intermarriage between Jews of different nationalities was as rare as marriage between Jew and Gentile. The synagogue and rabbi were central to the cultural life of many devout Jewish Americans, whether orthodox or reform, Ashkenazic (European) or Sephardic (Mediterranean), and provided a source of much needed support for struggling families in urban ghettos. Historic K.A.M. Isaiah Israel Temple in Chicago originated from congregational organizations predating the Civil War; Temple Beth-El was formed in 1871 after the great Chicago fire. In addition, secular organizations, or local Jewish committees, were also formed to provide communal services, secure jobs for newcomers, arrange financial aid for the sick and needy, establish death benefits and cemeteries, and generally offer a security net for strangers in an alien land. After 1900, the Jewish Federation of Metropolitan Chicago and its fund-raising arm, the Jewish United Fund, supported multipurpose social welfare agencies to serve Chicago Jews.

Despite poverty and slum living, Jewish Americans prevailed in realizing a better life. Their religious tradition emphasized high standards of cleanliness in terms of hygiene and food preparation, which translated into healthiness and lower death rates for Jews compared to others in the tenements. A strong family institution meant less desertion of families by fathers, and alcoholism was never a serious problem among Jews as it was among some other ethnic groups. Jewish parents also prized education for their children. Every effort was made to get children in schools, attain literacy, and instill an appreciation for formal learning that was the key to prospective upward social mobility. By 1920, Jewish intellectuals were obtaining college degrees and participating in the professions of law and medicine.

Hungarians

Another contingent of Eastern European people, known as Magyars, originated exclusively from Hungary. Escaping ever-worsening economic conditions in their homeland, Magyar men with no industrial skills began to immigrate in large numbers after 1880. They took low-paying jobs in dirty, dangerous working conditions, and they spent little and saved as much as possible to send money back home for the eventual transfer through serial migration of relatives and friends. Although repatriation was high among Magyars, as it was among Italians, more stayed to form families and communities. Many Magyars settled in the heavy manufacturing sectors of northern Ohio from Toledo to Youngstown and worked in steel foundries, shipyards, and cabinet factories. In particular, the Buckeye Road area of east Cleveland anchored a significant Hungarian American settlement. Ethnic churches, both Protestant and Catholic, as well as mutual support associations, served the social and cultural needs of these people.

Established Hungarian ethnic enclaves, such as Cleveland's, were infused in the 1930s and 1940s by refugees from the Nazi regime, many of whom were Jews, and later by displaced persons fleeing Soviet oppression after the unsuccessful Hungarian Revolution of 1956. As a result, from 1945 into the 1970s, "Little Hungary" in Cleveland was vibrant with Hungarian-language radio stations, an ethnic daily newspaper called the *Szabadsag*, and a responsive local Democratic Party machine that served its constituents and promoted Hungarian cultural events.

Greeks

Greek immigration to the Midwest did not begin in earnest until the 1890s. Even if the opportunity had been available, most Greeks had little interest in pursuing a livelihood in farming, for making a living from the soil in their native land was associated with nonproductive toil. Greeks thus came to the cities of the north-central United States to find employment in a wide range of industrial occupations. Greek immigrants were disproportionately male, and in time over half repatriated to their native land. But whether "birds of passage" or true transplants, they found jobs on railroad construction gangs, in the meat-packing plants of Chicago, and in the copper and iron mining district of northern Michigan and Minnesota. Consequently, Greeks were somewhat dispersed in their settlement pattern, but, except for mining and rail line activities, most of them secured urban occupations. Greek American entrepreneurs started shoeshine stands that evolved into income-producing parlors. Some opened sandwich shops offering inexpensive, common fare to white-collar professionals in downtowns. Still others became fruit and candy vendors who might expand their operations to sell an array of confectioneries. Within distinctive Greek American neighborhoods, such as Greektown in the heart of Detroit or west of the Chicago Loop, there also appeared Greek-run grocery stores, wine shops, and coffeehouses catering to their countrymen.

Greek neighborhoods achieved their unique cultural identity amid the urban conglomerates of multiple ethnic enclaves through establishment of Greek Orthodox churches. By forming Orthodox congregations, the Greeks introduced a new faith into the pluralistic American religious pantheon. Often the initiative for church formation began with devout lay people wanting the spiritual and social support offered by a parish. Once organized, the laity then secured a priest though the church hierarchy from Greece. Church ritual and use of the Greek language fortified the strong sense of "Greekness" exhibited by some immigrants and expressed through loyalty to family, parish, neighborhood, Greek customs and traditions, and endogamous marriage patterns.[10] More secular Greeks joined Greek American Progressive Associations that promoted use of the English language, mixed marriages, and less religious orthodoxy. Nonetheless, these Greek Americans, too, continued to value and take pride in their Greek cultural heritage, through festivals and foods as well as through celebration of their ancient classical legacies.

Greek-born Pantelis L. Cafouros owned the Paradise and Devil's Cafe, Indianapolis, c. 1910. Courtesy Indiana Historical Society.

Arabs

After 1900 people from the eastern rim of the Mediterranean Sea joined the throngs of immigrants settling in the Midwest. Initially, these were mainly Christians from Syria and the region that became Lebanon, although at least one small pocket of Lebanese Muslims settled near Cedar Rapids, Iowa, in the 1870s to farm. Later, in 1934, they built a mosque that is now the oldest standing mosque in North America. The great majority of eastern Mediterranean immigrants were non-Muslim, single males who earned subsistence income as peddlers. These itinerant salesmen canvassed the countryside and plied the streets of big cities. First on foot, later on horseback or in wagons, ultimately in automobiles, the peddlers sold costume jewelry, spices and food ingredients, pots and pans, perfumes and notions, linens and rugs to eager rural and urban patrons who welcomed the exotic salesman and his other-than-ordinary wares. In order to make sales, successful peddlers adopted English and excelled in the All-American tradition of salesmanship. Many matured into suppliers of other peddlers or opened retail shops. And with a degree of solvency and stability in hand, they exercised the mechanics of chain migration to bring over their kith and kin and begin to form families.

In time, significant numbers of Arab Americans, some Christian, some Islamic, gravitated to Detroit, where the automobile industry offered a different kind of economic opportunity. As workers on assembly lines, these immigrants would make the Motor City the largest Arab American city in the Midwest and second in the nation to Los Angeles. Indeed, the South End of Dearborn, Michigan, has become the leading Arab American cultural center in the United States.[11] Since the 1950s, Chicago has also experienced an influx of Arab Americans who trace their ancestry to the nations of North Africa as well as Saudi Arabia, Jordan, Palestine, Yemen, and other Mideastern nations. Many came to escape the recurring Arab-Israeli conflicts and ceaseless tensions ravaging the region. Others initially arrived as students of higher education who stayed in the United States as part of the professional workforce. Although the majority of modern Arab Americans are Christian, the Muslim minority has been significant. These latter Arab Americans have replicated bulwarks of their cultural identity by building mosques, engaging imams for their worship, and observing the religious requirements of the month of Ramadan through purification and fasting that ends with the celebration of Eid al-Fitr.

THE INTERNAL MIGRATION OF AFRICAN AMERICANS TO THE MIDWEST

Beginning in the last two decades of the nineteenth century after the failure of Reconstruction and increasing by almost twofold with each passing decade through the era of World War I, African Americans exited the South en masse to populate the urban industrial centers of the Northeast and Midwest. In the 1920s, over three quarters of a million blacks relocated northward—an internal migration that exceeded the international inflow of Irish during the famine decade of the 1840s. With this singular movement of one group of people from one region of the nation to another, the demography of the Midwest, which prior to this had absorbed a vast number of residents from different national and ethnic origins, now became increasingly biracial as well as multiethnic. And its cultural diversity was decidedly enhanced.

It should be noted, however, that the presence of African Americans in the heartland preceded this influx by a half century or more. The five eastern states of the Midwest—collectively known as the Old Northwest—were legally proscribed from allowing the institution of slavery by the provisions of the Northwest Ordinance of 1787, but some slaveholders brought blacks in bondage, euphemistically called registered servitude, from the slave South across the Ohio River into southern Illinois. This introduced African Americans into the subregion known as "Little Egypt." Indeed, the state constitution of Illinois in 1818 did not outlaw this surrogate slavery, and the next year legislators enacted a harsh slave code. Proslavery sentiment grew strong enough in the 1820s to seek an amendment to the state constitution to legalize slavery, but this effort failed.

Across the Mississippi River lay the area that became Missouri, where slavery had been practiced since French colonial times. Missouri was not subject to the Northwest Ordinance, and military and civilian slaveholders brought slaves into this region when it was still a territory. The Compromise of 1820 recognized Missouri as a slave state within the Union, and with that the area's biracial character was firmly established. Although the plantation economy was never part of Missouri's past, numerous blacks worked on white-owned farms, in the lead mines, amid the river traffic on the Mississippi and Missouri, and as urban "house slaves" and craftsmen. By 1820, about one-sixth of the state's population was African American; by 1860, they still exceeded 10 percent of the total.

In Missouri and other midwestern states, a small but significant number of "free persons of color" also made up the population mix. Some of these were mulattoes—often the children of slave owners and slave mothers—who ultimately achieved manumission through owners' wills. Others were former slaves who traveled the "underground railroad" northward across the Ohio River from the slave South to freedom in distant, protected communities such as those in Cass County, Michigan, and Racine and Milwaukee counties, Wisconsin. Not all free blacks were welcome north of the Ohio, however. The state census of Indiana recorded about 11,000 Free Negroes in 1850, which led legislators the next year to attempt to amend the state constitution to bar any more free blacks from settling in the state. Similarly, Iowa lawmakers erected legal barriers to keep out free blacks and deny them basic constitutional rights. In a sharp reversal, however, in 1868, under the protection of the Fourteenth Amendment, black children could attend public schools in Iowa, and black males were allowed to vote in anticipation of passage of the Fifteenth Amendment prohibiting disenfranchisement on racial grounds. By 1880, black men could serve in the Iowa state legislature. Although "free persons of color" in every way lived in narrowly circumscribed contexts, lacked basic civil rights, endured irregular day labor and poor living conditions, and were marginalized to near inconspicuousness amid white society, many of them attained literacy, and they knew the ethos of freedom. Given this head start, however limited, it was from their ranks that the leadership cadre of African American society ultimately came, such as the early founders and supporters of the National Association for the Advancement of Colored People (NAACP) as well as the first black legislators, professionals, and white-collar workers.

Post–Civil War Emancipation

Post–Civil War emancipation slowly set in motion the internal migration of blacks, at first within the South, and then by the late nineteenth century out of the South northward. Initially, these voluntary migrants tended to be young adult males in search of jobs, as they left behind rural agricultural poverty, a void of economic opportunity, and pervasive segregation laws and widespread discriminatory practices commonly known as Jim Crow in the South. Later, agricultural crises caused by the boll weevil and worsening race relations in the South after 1900 invigorated the internal migration of African Americans, as did the ever-increasing demand for blue-collar workers in the industrializing cities across the Midwest. By the early twentieth century, whole families surged northward. Some of these were classic nuclear families, but more were cross-generational, extended families or single-parent families, often maternally headed. Most were moving to join kinfolk already settled and tenuously employed, yet offering an opportunity for a better level of existence than was possible in the deep South.[12]

At first, prior to 1900, African Americans, in relatively small numbers, faced comparatively few restrictions in most midwestern cities, although a color line always limited access to schools, public accommodations, jobs, and social interaction. They found employment requiring few skills and ranking low in social status: waiters, barbers, domestic hired help, day laborers on construction projects, railroad employees, and ditch diggers. A few secured skilled craftsmen tasks as blacksmiths, carpenters, or bricklayers. At first, too, residential segregation was not so pronounced; in Chicago, Detroit, and the lakefront cities of southern Wisconsin, the great majority of blacks lived "invisibly" on back streets in mixed neighborhoods where whites were the "visible" preponderant. Some early migrants from the South rose to middle-class status in the Midwest, a few achieved political offices in municipal and state government, and a rarer few served the medical needs of their race as doctors and dentists.

Racism in the Early 1900s

After 1900, with the ever-greater northward relocation of rural, southern African Americans, who essentially comprised a massive, poorly educated, impoverished underclass in the South, racial lines between blacks and whites in the Midwest also solidified and created deepening social cleavages. Factories from the agricultural implement manufacturers in Davenport, Iowa, and Moline, Illinois, to the steel mills of Gary and South Bend, Indiana, and Toledo and Youngstown, Ohio, from the meat-packing plants of Swift and Armour in Chicago to the Pullman railroad car works in Indiana and the automobile assembly lines in Detroit—all attracted African Americans in droves. As second-generation white ethnics moved up and out of the heavy manufacturing sector and as federal laws restricting immigration of the foreign-born took effect in the 1920s, industrial companies like the Gary Works of United States Steel Corporation relied on blacks to make steel. By 1930, almost 18,000 blacks lived in Gary, 17 percent of the city's population. Yet these same industries instituted discriminatory employment practices in which blacks were the last hired and first fired. And everywhere rigid job barriers aimed to keep blacks in unskilled labor or service categories. Residential segregation laws appeared in urban centers, relegating African Americans to neighborhoods strictly defined by color. Social barricades prevented blacks from participating in public events and public places. The Ku Klux Klan organized in the Midwest, especially in Michigan and Indiana, by the time of World War I and gained regional popularity as it promoted restrictive laws, political disfranchisement, and pathological hatred of African Americans. Blacks also incurred the wrath of other ethnic workers with whom they competed for entry-level jobs or whom they replaced as cheaper wage-earners or even strike-breakers.

As racial tensions built, invariably violence ensued. In 1917, East St. Louis, Illinois, experienced a bloody mayhem between white and black workers in which dozens of blacks died. In 1919, an incident on the Chicago lakefront sparked a week of violence that killed twenty-three blacks and fifteen whites and left over 500 injured. In the summer of 1920 employers in Duluth, Minnesota (where statewide African Americans represented less than 1 percent of the total population) hired job-hungry black workers to weaken local union strength and defuse the threat of a strike. In furious retaliation, a white mob lynched three black circus hands totally unconnected with the labor conflict on a Duluth main street to send a chilling signal to African Americans that racial divides could be crossed only at great risk.

The Great Depression of the 1930s caused a hiatus in the regional northward flow of blacks, but it resumed vigorously during and after World War II to populate further the large northern urban ghettos in South Chicago and inner Detroit, from Kansas City and East St. Louis to Cincinnati and Cleveland, from Milwaukee to Akron. They worked in the booming war factories that converted to production of consumer goods with the return of peace. Some acquired jobs in municipal and state government as policemen, fire-fighters, bus drivers, and utility workers; others entered the federal postal service or broke into the ranks of white-collar professionals such as accountants and teachers. But most blacks lived apart as second-class citizens for years. Every sizable midwestern urban center witnessed the emergence of a segregated African American community, where disparities in education, housing, public health, job opportunities, and political involvement were transparently obvious.

"Separate but Equal": Educational Repression and Opportunity

From 1896 to 1954 African Americans endured the legal legacy of "separate but equal" with particular respect to schooling, but this hollow protection meant that education for blacks was anything but equal to that for whites. Halfway through this era, in 1930, the average African American acquired six years of schooling, compared to ten for whites. The landmark case of *Brown v. Board of Education* in 1954 formally ended discriminatory treatment in the nation's educational structure, but mandated school integration still took more than a few years to implement in the large midwestern urban school systems. Despite the long-term structural disadvantages, black youth began increasingly to attain high school diplomas from the 1920s on, and with the help of the G.I. Bill following World War II more than just the African American elite could attend colleges. By the 1960s, more black students were going to white colleges than to the historic black institutions in the Midwest such as Wilberforce University in Ohio or Lincoln University in Missouri.

The Civil Rights Acts of the 1960s

On the heels of educational change came political change with the Civil Rights Act of 1964 and Voting Rights Act of 1965. Exercise of full citizenship privileges by African Americans, in turn, stirred angry backlashes among whites and other ethnics less enthusiastic about the prospect of "liberty and justice for all" when it included blacks. Protests escalated in blue-collar neighborhoods across the Midwest, particularly aimed at the cultural changes invoked by school integration, busing, and the general mixing of races. Black Power advocates such as the Black Panthers responded with strident rhetoric and radical organizational tactics. Dramatic court cases such as that of the "Chicago Eight," which mixed racial politics with antiwar protest, threatened Middle America with the specter of a complete breakdown of law and order. Protests grew ever more violent, and by 1966 through 1969 cities such as Detroit, Cincinnati, Chicago, St. Louis, and others experienced wholesale race warfare with neighborhoods in flames, armed soldiers in the streets, and violence and chaos never before known in the urban Midwest. Detroit suffered the nation's worst riot in 1967 with forty-three people killed, hundreds wounded, thousands arrested, and millions of dollars worth of property damaged or destroyed. Racial cleavages climaxed in fiery purges in some cities before racial bridges could be constructed.

In the meantime, blacks did take advantage of new, legally enforced educational, economic, and political opportunities that reflected a new spirit of assertiveness and effectiveness, one with more substance than style. Strategy evolved from street confrontation to establishment politics. By 1974, the racial balance had shifted to give blacks a majority in Detroit, and Coleman Young, a black state senator, became the Motor City's first black mayor. In 1980 Gary, Indiana, had a black mayor, Richard C. Hatcher, who used federal funds to revitalize the city center. As with their leaders, so African Americans en masse generally began rising from their previously limited social base and moved into the American middle class and its socioeconomic milieu. With this trend emerged a renewed African American ethos of self-determination, rather than accommodation, that found expression in a significant expansion of black-run businesses and services, black professionals and artists, and black celebrities and sports figures. Yet for all who experienced upward social mobility in the last quarter century, a vast number of have-nots remain unable to cross socioeconomic class lines or to overcome racial impediments. For all too many black midwesterners, Martin Luther King Jr.'s dream continues to be only that.

Black Cultural Heritage in the Midwest

Despite internal migration and resulting social change, African Americans, like many other ethnics who settled in the Midwest, did not by any means merely acculturate over time into a homogeneous cultural mainstream defined by a larger host. Blacks always carried with them and continually created their own distinctive cultural heritage, whether rooted in the survival tactics necessary to cope with slavery or born of the hardships and challenges of enduring in urban ghettos of the Midwest. Three basic social structures—family, church, and language—illustrate the efforts of African Americans to culturally persist and in the process exhibit Black Pride.

It is axiomatic that the black family in slavery and in freedom has been an institution under relentless duress. In slavery, the awful prospect of sale of man or woman could arguably have thwarted the likelihood of nuclear family formation and, if formed, crushed its vitality. In freedom, forced mobility for purposes of employment or a long-term lack of strong male role models continued to weaken a traditional nuclear family. Yet the black family unit has survived, frequently as a matriarchal social entity or in an extended kinship arrangement across three or more generations and with a kith community of practical support and sustenance. Although family may be broadly construed in an African American context, its perpetuity remains sure in the present in varied frameworks such as single parents, foster parents, grandparents, and traditional father and mother dual parenting.

This importance of family is one of several significant activities among African Americans that are, if not unique, at least distinguishing among their cultural patterns. Often lacking a written historical record of their ancestry, blacks nonetheless make great efforts to recapture their seemingly ephemeral past. In search of their roots, they rise to the challenge of documenting their ancestral lineage and flesh out the barebones structure with details provided by rich anecdotal evidence to depict the attributes and values of their people. It is a quest about character and cultural identity as much as a genealogical exercise. Blacks also participate enthusiastically in annual reunions to reassemble a much-scattered family. Because of the regional internal migration pattern from South to North (and back again), the reunions often entail long-distance traveling with shared transportation by various small groups for economy to reunite a large clan at an appointed place. Reunions thrive on camaraderie promoted by good food, fellowship, and other forms of family fun. Because of highly extended family connections, black reunions can include hundreds of people from neighboring towns, cities, and states. They are gala events to reinvent yearly the circle of family. And at funerals, in essence a special reunion, the gathering of family is repeated and re-bonded amid the ritual of grieving.

A second social structure of African American culture has been the importance of church. If the family is the heart of African American life, the church is its living soul. It has long been the focal point of black social development and remains the primary institutional affiliation for most blacks. During slavery, a "concealed church" operated informally or clandestinely to nurture hope and salve the physical and emotional wounds of a people in bondage. Within loosely organized cells, slaves found mutual support and celebrated events such as christenings, marriages, burials, and other rituals. The church of slaves was a mix of white missionary influence, African folk tradition, and adaptive innovation, and it offered a heartfelt religious experience, a place to sing spirituals and dance for God, and a Balm of Gilead. It served to console and to inspire. In slavery's aftermath, the church provided racial uplift, a practical shelter from racial terrorism, and an enduring bulwark for a besieged minority amid an indifferent or hostile majority.

Today the church that African Americans are part of continues to be a vibrant spiritual and social organization for a faith-based people. Black churches provide all-purpose humanitarian aid by feeding the hungry, housing the homeless, inspiring political involvement, encouraging civil rights activism, and being the crucible for black leadership whether cleric or secular. Churches support Head Start, day care, thrift stores, summer youth programs, health and medical assistance, and recreational activities. Since the 1980s with the rise of mega-churches that serve 2,000 or more parishioners and rely heavily on a high-tech, robust style of worship to captivate the youth audience, the broad interests of African Americans have been significantly advanced by the ability of the big churches to marshal resources in money and manpower to fund and staff a wealth of philanthropic strategies and programs. Thus, the Eastern Star Baptist Church of Indianapolis boasts a membership of 7,000 with a staff of fifty, and its ministries include care cells, drill teams, girl scouts, a mass choir, a recreational program, and special outreach efforts directed to groups with demographic and special needs.[13] These mega-churches span denominational lines to encompass African American Muslims, Assemblies of God, Methodist Episcopalians, and Baptists, but many more are evangelical, nondenominational churches. At the same time, small resilient congregations remain the norm within the black community. Regardless of size, churches give blacks a sense of community even as they materially and spiritually shape and sustain culture.

Language and its communication form a third category by which African Americans reassert their uniqueness. Imported as slaves or born into a context virtually devoid of formal education, they adopted English speech patterns that used African-derived words, some shortcuts in diction and grammar, and different syntax and cadence. Some words took on different meanings or served as codes when used by blacks both as slaves and free persons. The rhetoric of the civil rights movement as well as the lyrics of contemporary rappers continues this phenomenon of an evolving language influenced by racial developments. Similarly, blacks of the last generation or two have increasingly returned to the use of African names for themselves and their offspring. Nothing is perhaps more personal or defines one's identity more precisely than one's name. When that designation eschews Anglo or American common names and relies on African names, this speaks volumes about the strength of cultural heritage and self-perception. Finally, blacks use their language most expressively through storytelling, a special cultural practice, often by women, that honors values and ideals deemed socially important or transmits oral traditions, family history, and racial customs from one generation to another. Accordingly, raconteurs who are part of black storytelling associations located in Chicago, Detroit, and Cleveland each year entertain countless children named Nafeesa, Rushawnda, Laquandra, Quashima, and Rahsaan in schools or at public festivals with tales told in a dramatic vernacular manner that recall Mother Africa, relate an inspirational or humorous event with which rapt listeners can empathize, or speak universally to social justice and racial equality. Versatile use of language upholds African American mores and heritage and adds to the cultural diversity of the Midwest.

THE INMIGRATION OF LATINOS AND CARIBBEAN AMERICANS TO THE MIDWEST

Following the tandem global crises of the Great Depression and World War II, a cycle of immigration into the Midwest resumed. However, the points of origin for the new streams of immigrants were no longer Europe but Western Hemispheric homelands—at first Mexico and Puerto Rico and in time other occidental Hispanic cultural hearths as well. And with the Midwest rapidly transitioning from a predominantly rural region to a much more mixed rural/urban landscape, the incoming transplants headed to both the countryside and the city, although they ultimately added more to the urban conglomerates of the heartland.

Mexicans

The immigration of Mexicans into the Midwest essentially began during World War II when the military siphoned manpower from the workforce and employers faced labor shortages. Under the federal bracero program with Mexico begun in 1942, contract laborers were allowed into the United States under certain living and working conditions at specified minimum wages to keep wartime emergency production activities at full throttle. Most Mexicans were of rural background with elemental agricultural know-how. In the Midwest, specialized agricultural commodities not yet processed by machinery required timely and seasonal attention to provide food for the nation in time of war and later in peace as well. In particular, western Michigan farmers were engaged in commercial production of cherries, apples, peaches, tomatoes, melons, grapes, strawberries, celery, and more. At first these farmers used migrant workers of Mexican descent from Texas called Tejanos, but soon workers directly from Mexico became part of the seasonal stream northward to perform the stoop labor of fruit and vegetable farming. Many were granted temporary work permits, sent money to their kinfolk back home, and annually repatriated to their homeland. In the early 1950s, many were also illegal entrants subject to deportation and mass expulsions. All were poor, short-term workers comprising itinerant families in which every member, if physically able (and sometimes not), tended the perishable crops, lived in substandard housing, sacrificed even minimal educational instruction, and knew no security beyond income for another day or two. The most ambitious and hard-working individuals were trying to capitalize in classic immigrant tradition on economic opportunity that might also provide a foothold for permanent relocation and a better life in the Midwest. The rise of corporate canneries in the Midwest—Green Giant, Del Monte, Libby's—intensified the growth of fruit and vegetable agriculture and increased the demand for farm workers, even as the government ended the bracero program in 1964 and tried to crack down on illegal alien immigration. Labor needs spread from Michigan to other midwestern states where truck gardening flourished, and new businesses such as nurseries, greenhouses, and sod farms arose requiring manual laborers. With these jobs available, Mexicans were able to transition from itinerants to long-term residents, and their children subsequently became Mexican Americans with citizenship rights. Thus, another group of foreign-born ancestry repeated the process of expanding the ethnic pluralism of the Midwest.[14]

In addition to rural occupations, urban centers presented entry-level, low-skilled jobs for Mexicans, from street utility work and construction projects to hotels, restaurants, and domestic service. In Chicago, for example, early arrivals prior to World War II found jobs with the railroad industry and meat-packing houses, but by the 1950s an array of blue-collar jobs in manufacturing and processing drew Chicanos in large numbers. By the 1990s, Chicago had the largest Mexican American population in the Midwest and ranked fourth in the nation among cities with a Chicano minority. By 2000 Chicago was second only to Los Angeles. These urban dwellers lived in a distinct residential district on the city's near west side adjacent to Downtown and the South Loop, where earlier other immigrants such as Poles and Czechs had once concentrated. Displacement of one immigrant group by another, a common pattern of urban residential change, thus established a barrio in the Pilsen and "La Villita" (Little Village) areas of South Side Chicago that is now 90 percent Chicano.

Central to Mexican American culture is the family, a close-knit circle of relationships and social activities. Chicano family size, at five, six, or more members, is larger than that of other ethnic groups, although acculturation is moderating this closer to the American norm. Other comparative cultural attributes of Mexican Americans include a traditional family structure of male bread-winners and female homemakers, a low divorce rate, low high school graduation by women, and little college attendance by men. In addition, loyalty to the Catholic Church is exceptionally strong among Chicanos, and devotion to its religious rituals and traditions permeate daily life with the celebration of Mass and church festivities as well as dependence on the leadership and counsel of local priests. Whether in Chicago, Detroit, Cleveland, Milwaukee, or the south St. Louis area, Mexican Americans also display their ethnicity and solidarity through their annual Mexican Independence celebrations on September 16 and Cinco de Mayo festivals on May 5, when they hold parades, dance to mariachi music, and enjoy traditional food. Finally, strong retention of the use of Spanish among Mexican Americans also undergirds their culture. Initially, this language persistence placed some Chicanos at social and economic disadvantages and even stigmatized them as a group of "inferiors," but the continual influx of Spanish-speaking people beyond Mexican Americans has led to the proliferation of bilingual programs in schools, on public signs, and through a wide array of advertising and instructional materials. Spanish-language newspapers, magazines, and television and radio stations are standard media across the contemporary Midwest.

Puerto Ricans

During the 1960s amid persistent concern about illegal immigration by Chicanos and other Latinos, another population flow channeled into the Midwest. Continual demand for manual workers encouraged Puerto Ricans, who since 1917 were recognized as citizens of the United States and thus immune from attacks against illegal aliens, to head for areas in Michigan where the sugar beet industry beckoned to laborers with some knowledge about the production of this tuber. From this beginning with a small core of Caribbean male farm workers, there followed in time-honored fashion the coming of Puerto Rican families by way of chain migration. Some gravitated to Detroit, drawn by the prevalence of the large black cultural influence there, and within the southwestern sector of the city a new ethnic community of Puerto Rican islanders emerged. The greatest concentration of the Puerto Rican population in the last quarter of the twentieth century in the Midwest, however, occurred in the industrial corridor extending from the Chicago metropolitan area into northwest Indiana.[15] Indeed, Chicago is second only to New York City as the largest Puerto Rican population in the country, which underscores the decidedly urban settlement pattern of this group. In 1990 Chicago had over 125,000 Puerto Ricans, living mainly in the Humboldt Park/West Town/Logan Square area of the city. Cleveland and Akron, Ohio, also register a total of at least 20,000 Puerto Ricans.

Prior to 1980, Puerto Ricans were categorized as an underclass hopelessly mired in poverty, but recent occupational and educational changes have improved this group's economic standing. As a group they are a relatively young population, securing jobs in technical, sales, and administrative support positions and improving their high school attainment levels. Perhaps as many as two-thirds of this population cohort are now ambitious members of the American middle class, although the remaining component continues to live below the poverty line. As with other Hispanics, the importance of family, the pervasiveness of Catholicism, and the household use of the Spanish language remain pillars of their ethnic cultural identity.

Latinos from Central and South America and the Caribbean

Particularly since the last decade of the twentieth century, observers have commented on the "browning of the Midwest," given the rapid increase of the general Hispanic population that extends beyond Mexican Americans and Puerto Ricans to include Latinos from Central and South American and the islands of the Caribbean.[16] This "browning" is especially evident in the subregion hugging the lower end of Lake Michigan and extending west to the Mississippi and east into northern Indiana and Ohio and southern Michigan. By 2000 one out of five residents of Cook County, Illinois, was Hispanic. Nearly 50,000 Hispanics live in Detroit, although Pontiac leads the state of Michigan as the municipality with the largest proportion (13 percent) of its population counted Hispanic. In small Iowa and Minnesota cities such as Storm Lake, Marshalltown, Denison, Albert Lea, and Worthington, where meat-packing plants exist, Hispanics form an important (and controversial) part of the local workforce. The fast-growing Hispanic population now represents the largest minority within the nation, surpassing African Americans in this ranking, and in the Midwest Hispanics number about 2.6 million. Their regional impact on the Midwest as a whole cannot be underestimated.

RECENT VOLUNTARY MIGRANTS AND REFUGEES INTO THE MIDWEST

Post–World War II globalism unleashed international migration flows on an unprecedented scale as people crossed national boundaries as well as oceans in an unending search for economic opportunity or personal fulfillment. Political, social, and economic change in the modern world broke down old cultural parochialisms and kept people restless and migratory. Many were eager to attain ambitions wherever possible. Moreover, with former colonial controls dissolving worldwide to create emerging nations even while patterns of new political oppression remained as real as ever in various corners of the world, some disadvantaged groups responded to religious, ethnic, or tribal pressures and purges by relocating away from theaters of conflict and exploitation. In sum, by the last third of the twentieth century, migrants from Third World nations joined the multinational influx into the Midwest to add yet another demographic layer to the region's population mix.

Asians

Much of the recent immigration from Asian nations into the Midwest dates from 1965, when the Immigration and Nationality Amendments Act revised the discriminatory national origins quota system of the 1920s, which essentially sought to preserve an Anglo-Saxon ethnic majority in the United States. For Asians the quota policy had generally amounted to complete exclusion, explicitly so in the case of the Chinese and Japanese since 1882 and 1924, respectively. The 1965 law established a limit of 20,000 persons per year from any one country in the Eastern Hemisphere. Under the new program, Asians from India, Pakistan, Taiwan, China, Japan, the Philippines, and South Korea could now relocate into the heartland as voluntary migrants in search of greater economic opportunity.[17]

Asian Indians and Pakistanis

Often the first Asian Indian arrivals were single males who took entry-level jobs as taxi drivers, gas station operators, mass transit vendors, and hotel service workers. Later-arriving professionals with substantial educational training secured employment in the health services as doctors, nurses, and anesthesiologists as well as in the computer industry as programmers and software technicians. It is estimated that Asian Indians also manage or own about half the motels nationwide, thus establishing a strong role in American's hostelry business. The process of family reunification enlarged this ethnic cohort and created a family-based demographic structure for the cultural group. To some degree, the Asian Indian population in the Midwest can be geographically plotted by locating Hindu and Sikh temple sites.

Japanese Lamp Lighting Festival, Como Park, St. Paul, Minnesota. Courtesy Minnesota Tourism.

Hindu places of worship exist in Aurora and Lemont in the Greater Chicago area, in Troy, Canton, and Pontiac in the Greater Detroit area, in Cincinnati and in Minneapolis. Sikh worship houses are found in Palatine (Illinois), Indianapolis, St. Louis, Columbus, Minneapolis, and Ferndale and Madison Heights in Greater Detroit. A sufficient number of Indians in Chicago's West Rogers Park neighborhood led them to express their ethnic identity and sense of community by renaming part of Devon Avenue after Gandhi. Interestingly, this prompted a number of Pakistani businessmen in an adjoining area to have their neighborhood named after Jinnah, the founder of Pakistan.

Japanese

Until 1980, few Japanese were located in the Midwest, but with the influx of Japanese corporate operations Japanese businessmen and their families have established a presence in the large urban centers of Illinois, Ohio, and Michigan. By 1990, just over 40,000 Japanese Americans lived in these three states. Moving to where companies opened new offices explains some economically driven relocation, but other Japanese chose to migrate to be part of, according to their perception, the more open society existing in America, particularly with respect to opportunities for women. Some Japanese youth attracted to American culture came as students and entered the workforce as young professionals in specialized disciplines or as operators of small Japanese-owned stores and businesses. With comparatively high levels of education, most of today's Japanese Americans are favorably positioned economically in the American mainstream.

Chinese

Like the Japanese, the numbers of Chinese in the Midwest were not appreciable until after 1980. Although by 1970 Chicago ranked fourth in Chinese population in the United States, the ethnic group in the city numbered only 14,000. With the official recognition of the People's Republic of China by the United States in 1979, the quota of 20,000 persons from mainland China was added to that quota already applied to Taiwan, and the Chinese population base expanded. Some Chinese also originated from other Asian nations, or they were second-, third-, or fourth-generation Chinese Americans moving internally from the West or East coasts into the heartland. In the Midwest, Illinois, Michigan, and Ohio cities were the migrants' primary destinations. In 1990 almost 90,000 Chinese lived in these three states. Traditional Chinatowns were not the norm in the Midwest as on the coasts. Detroit once claimed a small Chinatown in the 1930s, but by the mid-1990s its 25,000 Chinese Americans no longer resided in such an ethnic enclave. Although a portion of Chicago's Loop area is denoted as a Chinatown, it exhibits an ethnic heritage mainly to attract tourists. It offers Chinese cuisine, groceries, and gift shops rather than a residential settlement. Generally, recent Chinese Americans have dispersed residentially into neighborhoods that correspond to the middle-class income levels of these usually well-educated and professionally employed migrants. They can be found in apartment complexes of central Chicago, but also in the suburbs. Nonetheless, the presence of Chinese Americans still supports the emergence of clustered business areas that cater to Chinese and other Asians.

Filipinos

Filipinos are the second largest Asian group in the United States after the Chinese, and a significant midwestern concentration is located in Illinois, mainly in Chicago. Filipinos comprise the largest number of immigrant professionals coming to America; many are nurses, doctors, and other medical technologists. Most arrive with English proficiency and high levels of education that allow them to integrate into the socioeconomic mainstream more easily than other groups. They also tend to be less clustered in ethnically identified enclaves. The vast majority of Filipinos are Catholic, and as part of that multicultural religious organization, they meld into existing parishes of urban America.

Koreans

Koreans came to America under the provisions of the 1965 immigration law, but they also reflected a refugee status that derived from the Korean War in the 1950s. War brides and orphans made up two categories of early immigrants. Interestingly, the Twin Cities metropolitan area in Minnesota has the greatest population of adopted Koreans in the nation on a per capita basis. A desire for freedom and security from the ongoing political threat from North Korea coupled with the hope of economic improvement motivated other immigrants by the 1970s. A densely populated nation, South Korea produced an oversupply of college graduates that its domestic economy could not absorb and who appreciated the advantages of a democratic society. Some of these well-educated Koreans immigrated to the United States, only to find that language and cultural barriers frustrated their ability to work in the fields for which they were trained, such as engineering and nursing. Many became self-employed entrepreneurs, operating dry-cleaning businesses, liquor stores, grocery markets, and photo shops. In the 1980s, estimates placed 95 percent of Chicago dry-cleaning enterprises under Korean ownership. Ethnic networking and kye rotating credit associations (community organized financial institutions) greatly assisted entry into these small-business enterprises. By 1990, over 40,000 Korean Americans resided in Illinois. Most of them are Protestants, and many worship in Korean community churches.

Vietnamese, Laotians, and Cambodians

Recent Asian Americans from the mainland countries of Vietnam, Laos, and Cambodia clearly represent refugee culture groups.[18] They found political asylum in the United States in the wake of American withdrawal from Vietnam and subsequent communist takeover in that country in 1975, as well as the tangential chaos in Laos and Cambodia that continued into the 1980s. Initially, Vietnamese immigrants consisted of pro-Western elites, often well-educated professionals with military backgrounds and Catholic affiliation, who feared communist reprisals. By 1980, a wave of "boat people" fleeing the nationalization of businesses or political indoctrination programs dominated the migration flow to the United States. Still later, the Hmong of the northeastern highlands of Laos, lowland Laotians, and Cambodians—three peoples who endured genocidal warfare in their homelands that drove them to temporary United Nations refugee camps in Thailand—participated in resettlement programs to the United States under the 1980 Refugee Act. This law increased the quota for refugee admission and allowed for emergency exceptions for certain groups under dire conditions and in need of sanctuary.

In the Midwest the largest core settlements of mainland Southeast Asians lay in the states of Minnesota and Wisconsin, with Illinois and Michigan accounting for smaller concentrations. By 1990, nearly 90,000 Southeast Asians resided in these four states. The Hmong population is especially pronounced in the metropolitan areas of St. Paul and Minneapolis, in Milwaukee, and in the lesser urbanized Wisconsin counties of Marathon, La Crosse, Eau Claire, Brown, Sheboygan, and Outagamie. Church organizations and civic associations in Minnesota and Wisconsin were particularly active as sponsors assisting initial resettlement efforts, and the strong sense of clan and family ties of the Hmong encouraged ethnic clustering and kinship reunification to further the growth of the midwestern enclaves. Similarly, concentrations of Cambodians gravitated to the Twin Cities and Chicago. Although the Vietnamese established a presence in these large population centers as well, they registered a more dispersed residency in other urban places such as Grand Rapids, Michigan; Kansas City and St. Louis, Missouri; Columbus, Dayton, and Cleveland, Ohio; and Des Moines, Sioux City, and Davenport, Iowa.

Minneapolis-St. Paul exemplifies the classic ethnic inner-city enclave where the Hmong, Vietnamese, and Cambodians have created a vibrant Southeast Asian community.[19] They occupied public housing units and low-rent apartment complexes along major downtown transportation corridors in blighted areas associated with urban economic decline. But the influx of Southeast Asians created a demand for ethnic businesses. Small grocery stores, restaurants, bakeries, clothing shops, and other establishments opened, which enabled members of these cultural groups to become employed despite linguistic and occupational prerequisites. Businesses and residences coexist in the same neighborhood to create a clear culturally defined community. And within this community a host of local Mutual Assistance Associations were formed to provide aid in a variety of social and economic adaptation needs.

Religious affiliation provided another support system for these immigrants, who suffered great loss and anguish through the refugee experience. Their practices range from observance of traditional Taoism, Buddhism, Confucianism, and animism to conversion to Catholicism, Lutheranism, and other Protestant loyalties that reflect the influence of sponsoring church organizations. Whatever the association, spiritual activity underscores ethnicity through reliance on the worshipers' native language, leadership by ethnic pastors or priests, and a blending of cultural traditions and values into a mix of old and new religious experiences. Thus, the Vietnamese continue to celebrate the Old World religious holiday of the Tet New Year and have turned it into a successful public event within their New World church experience. Similarly, the Hmong of the upper Midwest observe their lunar

New Year during the American Thanksgiving week in a corresponding devotional manner. The Hmong of Kansas City, Missouri, still recognize the importance of ancestral and nature spirits that were part of their traditional animistic belief system, but some have also embraced the concept of the Christian Trinity as more powerful than the Old World spirit forces and rely on prayer and massage therapy in addition to shamanistic rituals to treat various illnesses and anxieties.

Eastern Europeans

In addition to Asians, refugees from other parts of the world have come to the Midwest in search of sanctuary and new beginnings. Following World War II and within the context of the Cold War, a series of special relief legislation in 1948, 1953, 1957, and 1960 permitted particular groups of "displaced persons" from Eastern Europe to enter the country. For example, between 1956 and 1958 Hungarian professionals and intellectuals fled their homeland after a failed political revolution against Soviet domination was summarily crushed, and many joined existing Hungarian ethnic communities in the heartland. Similarly, a resurgence of Czech immigration occurred in 1968 amid an era of communist rule when a brief cultural revolution led by Alexander Dubček permitted a window of opportunity for hundreds to leave. Many of these were skilled and educated middle-aged emigrants, and some gravitated to Czech communities in the Midwest. More recent refugees from Southeastern Europe immigrated into the Midwest in the wake of the breakup of Yugoslavia in 1992. Most of these were Bosnians who settled quickly into ethnic enclaves that dated from the nineteenth century when Serbs, Croats, and Slovenians were part of the immigration stream pouring into the major industrial cities of the Midwest and finding work in the steel mills and meatpacking houses. These enclaves in Chicago, Toledo, Detroit, Milwaukee, and St. Louis had already received Yugoslavian refugees during the immediate post–World War II era when communist rule was established under Tito. Then the "displaced persons" were primarily Eastern Orthodox Serbs and Catholic Croats. After 1992, Muslims originating from Bosnia formed a third cultural group of this ethnic potpourri. By 1999, for example, the Bosnian population in St. Louis was 8,000; of this number 7,000 were Muslims. In the Midwest, the highest single concentration of Serbs, Croats, and Bosnian Muslims is located in an urban neighborhood near 185th Street in eastern Cleveland. Bosnians in Des Moines now number about 3,000. Waterloo, Iowa, has 4,000, many of whom work in the meat processing industry.

Salvadorans, Nicaraguans, and Guatemalans

Beginning in the late 1970s, a multinational stream of Central American refugees flowed into the United States, including residents from El Salvador, Nicaragua, and Guatemala, where civil wars uprooted people. In particular, Guatemalans found their way into the Midwest. Indeed, they now represent the third largest Hispanic group in Chicago, possibly numbering 60,000 or more.[20] They came to the heartland as political and economic refugees in three waves. In the late 1970s and early 1980s, middle-class urban activists who resisted Guatemala's military government fled political repression. In the late 1980s, Mayan peasants who supported guerrilla insurgents escaped the government's subsequent ethnic campaign aimed at destroying villages, forcing displaced persons into reeducation camps, and carrying out genocidal purges. And in the 1990s, the general population poor who left their homeland's devastated economy emigrated more as economic refugees than as political refugees. Many Guatemalans were undocumented immigrants who entered the United States through the exploitive and extortive services of a *coyote* (a handler or guide hired by immigrants to slip them across borders). As illegal aliens, they often settled among Mexican Americans and other Hispanics seeking anonymity to avoid detection by the Immigration and Naturalization Service.

Guatemalans in Chicago cluster in many small and separate neighborhoods throughout the city's North Side. Their heaviest concentrations are in the Uptown-Ravenswood area and a bit farther west in the Albany Park vicinity. They tend to live in crowded apartments and rooming houses. They accept low-paying jobs in hotels and restaurants as maids or busboys, or they find domestic employment as nannies or handymen. As day laborers, men often work as carpenters, roofers, or landscapers without job security or unemployment benefits. Many immigrants come as single men or as components of incomplete families. Once in a new location and they are receiving an income, many send remittances back home to their families and make great efforts to achieve family reunification, which is extremely costly. Family separation and delayed reunion place great stress on their family structure, but the family as a social unit remains strong.

The Guatemalan refugees suffer manifold physical health problems such as malaria, parasites, and malnutrition incurred through insufficient food and shelter and poor sanitary conditions. And those who have endured extreme violence prior to emigration suffer mental health problems. Precarious subsistence in resettlement locations, underemployment, fear of deportation, and lack of access to social services such as Medicare because of their alien status only compound their health problems. Despite limited assistance from both Roman Catholic and Protestant social services groups, Guatemalans remain a group under duress in the heartland.

Africans

In the last twenty years, refugee admissions have increasingly included people from African nations. The Refugee Act of 1980 established a low limit of 1500 persons per year from Africa to the United States in part because international policy was encouraging Africans to relocate in other African nations and in part because of domestic fears of uncommon diseases being introduced into the country. By 2001, however, this annual quota had increased to 20,000. According to the U.S. Department of State, during the intervening two decades, over 125,000 African refugees from twenty-five countries have attained permanent resettlement in the United States, including 40,000 Somalis, 35,000 Ethiopians, and lesser numbers of Sudanese, Liberians, Zairians, Rwandans, Ugandans, Angolans, and more. Of this list, the Somalis in particular have found a haven in the Midwest.[21]

Following the overthrow of dictator Siad Barre in 1991, civil war erupted in Somalia, and warring factions plunged the country into chaos with rival clans raiding villages, plundering the countryside, and dislocating thousands of refugees, many of whom fled to Kenya. Starting in 1993, resettlement of some displaced persons began to various locations within the United States, including Georgia, California, Minnesota, and Ohio. Minneapolis–St. Paul quickly became a favored destination for Somalis because of its attractive urban job market, low housing costs, and responsive refugee service agencies. Employment was available in the meat-packing industry and in electric manufacturing plants, and Lutheran social services as well as other organizations were particularly active in assisting in re-settlement and in meeting basic human needs. Some Somalis came directly from refugee camps in Kenya, but many also relocated from California and Georgia. By 2002, Minnesota had the largest concentration of Somalis in the United States with an official tally of 11,200, although Somalis consider this figure a gross undercount and estimate their population as high as 20,000 to 30,000. Minneapolis ranks first in the nation among cities with a Somali population. From the Twin Cities in Hennepin and Ramsey counties where approximately 9,000 Somalis live, they have diffused outward into the great metropolitan area that includes parts of Dakota and Anoka counties as well as to other smaller cities and towns such as Rochester, St. Cloud, Owatonna, and Marshall. Somalis have also followed job opportunities in meat-processing plants across the state border from the Twin Cities into nearby St. Croix and Barron counties, Wisconsin, in the towns of Hudson and Barron. Separate from this upper midwestern gathering of Somalis is the second largest concentration of this ethnic group located in Columbus, Ohio. Here the city's low unemployment and low cost of living have attracted an estimated population ranging from 13,000 to 16,000, although the official count places Columbus second to Minneapolis in rank. Somalis have also relocated to Milwaukee, Des Moines, and St. Louis.

In Minneapolis, the Somalis have their ethnic gathering place known as Suuqa Karmel, a mini-mall on Pillsbury Avenue, where they can be found clad in vivid-colored African clothing, conversing in Somali, enjoying various sweet and pungent smelling dishes of spiced rice, fried liver, or goat meat, and as Muslims, visiting a nearby prayer room to recite their Islamic prayers. The Somalis in Minneapolis have a strong network of organizations and support groups—the Somali Women's Association, the Somali Community of Minnesota, the Somali American Friendship Association, and the Confederation of Somali Community in Minnesota—that serve the immigrants' needs as well as educate the host community about those needs. Like other immigrants, the Somalis exhibit a long-standing cultural tradition of loyalty to family, and many try to assist family members remaining in Africa by sending remittances to relatives. This transfer of money to the homeland has created a special problem for the Somali. In the wake of September 11, 2001, some critics have accused the Somali of providing financial support for Al-Itihaad al-Islamiya, a fundamentalist Islamic group based in Somalia suspected of having connections to Osama bin Laden's terrorist network, al-Qaida. Government officials did shut down one money wiring service in Minneapolis. A few Somali were victims of alleged hate crimes. Distancing themselves from accusations of terrorist affiliations remains a current concern of Somali support groups.

CODA

It is no cliché to observe that the United States is a "nation of immigrants" and that, in turn, the region of the Midwest shares in this vital attribute of the national character. Sustained immigration layered over an indigenous native population of significant variety has produced a mixed society of people reflecting different nationalities, cultures, and perspectives in the nation's heartland. That diversity rests on continual crops of newcomers to the Midwest from Third World points of origin as well as fourth-, fifth- and sixth- (or more) generation progeny of nineteenth- and early twentieth-century migrants who cherish their cultural heritage and remember their ethnic roots, whether European, African or Native American. The resulting polyglot society makes the Midwest an endless ethnic kaleidoscope rich with multicultural diversity and ever fascinating with its continual fluctuation.

RESOURCE GUIDE

Printed Sources

Allen, James P., and Eugene James Turner. *We the People: An Atlas of America's Ethnic Diversity.* New York: Macmillan, 1988.

American Immigration. 10 vols. Danbury, CT: Grolier Educational, 1999.

Archdeacon, Thomas J. *Becoming American: An Ethnic History.* London and New York: The Free Press, 1983.

Bodnar, John. *The Transplanted: A History of Immigrants in Urban America.* Bloomington: Indiana University Press, 1985.

Buenker, John D., and Lorman A. Ratner, eds. *Multiculturalism in the United States: A Comparative Guide to Acculturation and Ethnicity.* Westport, CT: Greenwood Press, 1992.

Ciment, James, ed. *Encyclopedia of American Immigration.* 4 vols. Armonk, NY: M. E. Sharpe, 2001.

Daniel, Roger. *Coming to America: A History of Immigration and Ethnicity in American Life.* New York: HarperCollins, 1991.

Dinnerstein, Leonard, and David M. Reimers. *Ethnic Americans: A History of Immigration.* 4th ed. New York: Harper & Row, 1999.

Glazier, Ira, and Luigi De Rosa, eds. *Migration across Time and Nations: Population Mobility in Historical Contexts.* New York: Holmes & Meier, 1986.

Holmquist, J. D. *They Chose Minnesota: A Survey of the State's Ethnic Groups.* St. Paul: Minnesota Historical Society Press, 1981.

Johnson, Daniel M., and Rex R. Campbell. *Black Migration in America.* Durham, NC: Duke University Press, 1981.

Lehman, Jeffrey, ed. *Gale Encyclopedia of Multicultural America.* 2nd ed., 3 vols. Farmington Hills, MI: Gale Group, 2000.

Levinson, David, and Melvin Ember, eds. *American Immigrant Cultures: Builders of a Nation.* 2 vols. New York: Simon & Schuster, 1997.

Macdonald, John S., and Leatrice D. Macdonald. "Chain Migration, Ethnic Neighborhood Formation, and Social Networks." *Milbank Memorial Fund Quarterly* 42 (January 1964): 82–97

Madison, James H., ed. *Heartland: Comparative Histories of the Midwestern States.* Bloomington and Indianapolis: Indiana University Press, 1988.

McKee, Jesse O., ed. *Ethnicity in Contemporary America: A Geographical Appraisal.* 2nd ed. Lanham, MD: Rowman & Littlefield, 2000.

Oswalt, W. H., and S. Neely. *This Land Was Theirs: A Study of North American Indians.* 5th ed. Mountain View, CA: Mayfield, 1996.

Sowell, Thomas. *Ethnic America: A History.* New York: Basic Books, 1981.

Thernstrom, Stephen, ed. *Harvard Encyclopedia of American Ethnic Groups.* Cambridge, MA: Harvard University Press, 1980.

Vecoli, Rudolph J., and Suzanne M. Sinke, eds. *A Century of European Migrations, 1830–1930*. Urbana: University of Illinois Press, 1991.

Web Sites

Center for the Study of Upper Midwestern Cultures
www.csumc.wisc.edu

Ethnic Groups in Wisconsin
www.wiscinfo.doit.wisc.edu/mkilibrary/ethn-his.html

First Nations Histories
www.tolatsga.org
Articles on Indian tribal groups

Indiana: Ethnic History
www.iprw.edu/ipfwhist/indian/ethnic.htm

Iowa Folklife
www.iowaartscouncil.org

Max Kade Institute for German-American Studies
www.csumc.wisc.edu/mki

Michigan Ethnic Heritage Studies Center
www.cla.wayne.edu/eliweb/english_pages/community_organizations/
center_mi_ethnic_hert.html

Organization that publishes the Michigan Ethnic Directory.

Wisconsin's Ethnic Settlement Trail
www.accesslink.com/west
Tourist guide to ethnic heritage sites in Wisconsin.

Videos/Films

Of the many films featuring specifically ethnic midwestern experiences, three stand out:

Vardalos, Nia, and John Corbett. *My Big Fat Greek Wedding*. Directed by Joel Zwick. 2002. DVD and videocassette. 95 min. New York: HBO Home Video, 2003.
von Sydow, Max, and Liv Ullman. *The Emigrants*. 1971. Directed by Jan Troell. Dubbed English-language version, 151 min. [Burbank, CA]: Warner Home Video, 1994.
von Sydow, Max, and Liv Ullman. *The New Land*. 1972. Directed by Jan Troell. Dubbed English-language version, 159 min. [Burbank, CA]: Warner Home Video, 1994.

Organizations, Museums, Special Collections

Illinois

Balzekas Museum of Lithuanian Culture
6500 S. Pulaski Road
Chicago, IL 60629
Phone: (773) 582-6500
Fax: (773) 582-5133

Email: editor@lithuanianmuseum.org
www.lithaz.org/museums/balzekas/

Chicago Historical Society
Clark Street at North Avenue
Chicago, IL 60614-6071
Phone: (312) 642-4600
Fax: (312) 266-2077
www.chicagohs.org

DuSable Museum of African-American History
740 East 56th Place
Chicago, IL 60637
Phone: (773) 947-0600
www.dusablemuseum.org

Ethnic Heritage Museum
1129 S. Main Street
Rockford, IL 61101
Phone: (815) 962-7402
www.artcom.com/Museums/nv/af/61101-14.htm

Goethe-Institut
150 North Michigan Avenue, Suite 200
Chicago, IL 60601
Phone: (312) 263-0472
Fax: (312) 263-0476
www.goethe.de/uk/chi/enindex.htm

Hellenic Museum and Cultural Center
801 W. Adams Avenue, 4th Floor
Chicago, IL 60607
Phone: (312) 655-1234
Fax: (312) 655-1221
www.hellenicmuseum.org

Instituto Italiano di Cultura
500 N. Michigan Aveue, Suite 1450
Chicago, IL 60611
Phone: (312) 822-9545
Fax: (312) 822-9622
www.iicch.org/english.htm

Mexican Fine Arts Center Museum
1852 W. 19th Street
Chicago, IL 60608
Phone: (312) 738-1503
www.mfacmchicago.org

Oriental Institute
University of Chicago
1155 E. 58th Street
Chicago, IL 60637
Phone: (773) 702-9514
Fax: (773) 702-9853
www-oi.uchicago.edu/OI/default.html

Polish Museum of America
984 North Milwaukee Avenue
Chicago, IL 60622
Phone: (773) 384-3352
Fax: (773) 384-3799
pma.prcua.org

Spertus Museum (of the Spertus Institute of Jewish Studies)
618 S. Michigan Avenue
Chicago, IL 60605
Phone: (312) 322-1747
www.spertus.edu/museum.html

Swedish-American Museum Center
5211 North Clark
Chicago, IL 60640
Phone: (773) 728-8111
Email: Museum@samac.org
www.samac.org

Ukrainian Village in Chicago
Ukrainian National Museum of Chicago
721 N. Oakley
Chicago, IL 60612
Phone: (312) 421-8020
Email: info@ukrntlmuseum.org
www.ukrntlmuseum.org

Indiana

Eiteljorg Museum of American Indians and Western Art
500 W. Washington Street
Indianapolis, IN 46204
Phone: (317) 636-WEST (9378)
www.eiteljorg.org

Historic New Harmony, Inc.
Director: Connie Weinzapfel
P.O. Box 579
New Harmony, IN 47631
Phone: (800) 231-2168
Email: harmony@usi.edu
www.newharmony.org

Iowa

African American Historical Museum and Cultural Center of Iowa
55 12th Avenue, SE
P.O. Box 1626
Cedar Rapids, IA 52406-1626
Phone: (319) 862-2101
Fax: (319) 862-2105
www.blackiowa.org

Danish Immigrant Museum
2212 Washington Street
P.O. Box 470
Elk Horn, IA 51531-0470
Phone: (712) 764-7001 or 1-(800)-759-9192
Fax: (712) 764-7002
Director: Dr. John Mark Nielsen
Email: director@danishmuseum.org
www.dkmuseum.org

German American Heritage Center
712 W. 2nd Street
P.O. Box 243
Davenport, IA 52805
Phone: (563) 322-8844
Email: director@gahc.org
www.wiu.edu/users/mfbdw/gahc_web/index.html

The National Czech & Slovak Museum & Library
30-16th Avenue SW
Cedar Rapids, IA 52404-5904
Phone: (319) 362-8500
Fax: (319) 363-2209
www.ncsml.org

Pella Historical Village
507 Franklin Street
Pella, IA 50219
Phone: (641) 628-4311
Fax: (641) 628-9192
Email: info@pellatuliptime.com
www.pellatuliptime.com

Michigan

Charles H. Wright Museum of African-American History
315 E. Warren Avenue
Detroit, MI 48201-1443
Phone: (313) 494-5800
Fax: (313) 494-5855
www.maah-detroit.org

Holland Museum
31 W. 10th Street
Holland, MI 49423
Contact: Maude Jouppi
Phone: (616) 394-1362 or (888) 200-9123 (toll free)
Email: hollandmuseum@hollandmuseum.org
www.wowcom.net/commerce/museum/index.shtml

Michigan Historical Center
702 W. Kalamazoo Street
Lansing, MI 48909-8240
Phone: (517) 373-3559

TDD (800) 827-7007
www.michigan.gov/hal/0,1607,7-160-17445_19273---,00.html

Michigan State University Museum
Campus, West Circle Drive
East Lansing, MI 48824-1045
Phone: (517) 355-7474
www.museum.msu.edu

Minnesota

The American Swedish Institute
2600 Park Avenue
Minneapolis, MN 55407
Phone: (612) 871-4907
Email: information@americanswedishinst.org
www.americanswedishinst.org

Czech and Slovak Sokol
383 Michigan Street
St. Paul, MN 55102
Phone: (651) 290-0542
www.sokolmn.org

Immigration History Research Center
University of Minnesota
College of Liberal Arts
311 Andersen Library
222-21st Avenue South
Minneapolis, MN 55455-0439
Phone: (612) 625-4800
Fax: (612) 626-0018
www1.umn.edu/ihrc

Missouri

Nance Museum
P.O. Box 292
Lone Jack, MO 64070
Phone: (816) 697-2526
Email: pjnmuseum@worldnet.att.net
home.att.net/~pjnmuseum/book.html

Negro Leagues Baseball Museum
1616 E. 18th Street
Kansas City, MO 64108-1610
Phone: (816) 221-1920
Fax: (816) 221-8424
www.nlbm.com

Ozarks Afro-American Heritage Museum
Fr. Moses Berry
Curator, OAAHM
P.O. Box 265
Ash Grove, MO 65604

Phone: (417) 672-3104
www.oaahm.org

St. Charles Historic District [no address listed]
Greater St. Charles Convention and Visitors Bureau
Phone: (800) 366-2427
www.historicstcharles.com
www.cr.nps.gov/nr/travel/lewisandclark/stc.htm

State Historical Society of Missouri
1020 Lowry Street
Columbia, MO 65201-7298
Phone: (573) 882-7083
Fax: (573) 884-4950
www.umsystem.edu/shs/

Ohio

African American Museum
1765 Crawford Road
Cleveland, OH 44106
Phone: (216) 791-1700
Fax: (216) 791-1774
Email: ourstory@aamcleveland.org
www.aamcleveland.org

The National Afro-American Museum and Cultural Center
P.O. Box 578
1350 Brush Row Road
Wilberforce, OH 45384
Phone: (937) 376-4944 or (800) 752-2603
Director: Vernon Courtney
www.ohiohistory.org/places/afroam

Ohio Historical Center
1982 Velma Avenue
Columbus, OH 43211
Phone: (614) 297-2300 Museum
(614) 297-2621 Group Tours
(614) 297-2510 Archives-Library
Fax: (614) 297-2233
Contact: Sharon Antle
www.ohiohistory.org/places/ohc

Sauder Village
22611 State Route 2
Archbold, OH 43502
Phone: (800) 590-9755
www.saudervillage.com/home/default.asp

SunWatch Indian Village
2301 West River Road
Dayton, OH 45418-2815
Phone: (937) 268-8199
Fax: (937) 268-1760
www.sunwatch.org/special_events.html

Underground Railroad Museum
The Underground Railroad Foundation
P.O. Box 47
Flushing, Ohio 43977
Phone: (740) 968-2080
Email: ugrrf@ugrrf.org
Curator: John S. Mattox
www.ugrrf.org

Wisconsin

Old World Wisconsin
S103 W37890 Highway 67
Eagle, WI 53119
Phone: (262) 594-6300
Email: oww@whs.wisc.edu
www.wisconsinhistory.org/oww

The Wisconsin Historical Museum of the Wisconsin Historical Society
Capitol Square at 30 N. Carroll Street
Madison, WI 53703
Phone: (608) 264-6555
Email: museum@whs.wisc.edu
www.wisconsinhistory.org/museum/visit.asp

Libraries/Archives

For each state, contact the state historical societies or their respective Web sites for further information and more specific links to county or local level research or library facilities.

Center for the Study of Ethnic Publications, Kent State University
The Immigration History Research Center, University of Minnesota

Festivals

Belgium Days
Brussels, WI, in July

Cinco de Mayo festivals
Numerous urban areas in the Midwest, on May 5

Columbus Day festivities
Italian communities in the Midwest, October 11

New Year celebrations
Among the Vietnamese and Hmong in Minneapolis-St. Paul

Oktoberfest
Many towns and cities across the Midwest

Polish Festival
Milwaukee, WI, three days in June

Tulip Festival
Holland, MI, Pella, IA, and Orange City, IA, in May

FASHION

*Joseph W. Slade, Jennifer
A. Scott, and Schuyler Cone*

Often derided for limping in the footsteps of trendsetter cities like New York and Los Angeles, midwestern fashion has come to be regarded as something of an oxymoron. Attitudes toward fashion are steeped in the Midwest's work ethic and its conservative ideals. Midwesterners have usually (but not always) worn clothing that visually communicates simplicity, a quality associated with republican ideals of liberty and equality. But if fashion mediates human performance and interaction—with each other and with culture and physical environment—then midwesterners turn out to be much more aware of fashion than is commonly thought. Because the first Europeans in the region came looking for furs for the salons of Paris, one might claim that fashion triggered the fabulous economy of the Midwest, but despite the undeniable importance of the fur trade to early America, to do so would be hyperbolic. Suffice it to say that midwesterners have always understood that fashion is related to their sense of time and place.

This chapter traces the history of fashion and dress in the midwestern states of Illinois, Indiana, Iowa, Missouri, Minnesota, Michigan, Ohio, and Wisconsin. From the outset, midwesterners responded to their physical surroundings and their cultural life, with their cultural life embodied in the social institutions that were themselves influenced by the environment. They designed, adapted, and made their clothing not only to meet their needs but also to reflect their values, customs, and ideals—in short, to symbolize their regional identities. A sense of place is actually easier to discuss than other aspects of clothing. For whom do people dress? It seems likely that they dress in part for themselves, by asserting an image, regional or otherwise, with which they identify. But they also dress to impress others, to assert membership in a group, to conform to aesthetic and ideological protocols of a class, to follow custom or fad, or to send a variety of social, economic, or political messages. Women can dress for other women, and men for other men, to establish position, rank, and status. At a basic level of discourse and understanding, people dress to attract sexual partners, a function probably closest to the core of fashion. Like people everywhere, midwesterners have always dressed at least some of the time to mate, and thus they have subjected their appearance to standards of beauty and desire that are socially and biologically constructed. An early emphasis on practicality left plenty of room for sexuality signaled by many degrees of tastes and manifested in styles from sober to ostentatious. Midwesterners have never lacked flair.

Because fashion is so integral to human experience, it can be approached from pyschological, social, economic, and historical perspectives. For our purposes, fashion may be classified into four broad historical categories according to types of evolving and overlapping social and technological organization: folk society, agrarian society, urban industrial society, and mass society. Members of folk societies generally adhered to forms of dress and adornment that were simple and functional, the product of technologies usually referred to as crafts. Early midwestern Indians and to a degree early European settlers in the region fall into this category. People in agrarian societies specialized their labor, becoming farmers and herders, for example, in order to maximize their resources. They consumed what they extracted from nature, but they also developed better implements and techniques that over time resulted in surpluses that could be sold and traded. Midwestern farm communities in Ohio and Illinois reflected these economies in both food and clothing. Although members of midwestern agrarian societies made their own materials and their own clothing as forms of "cottage industries," they also sold what they did not need for themselves. During the nineteenth century, the Midwest emerged as a leader in the provision of raw materials—not just furs, but wool and vegetable fibers such as flax—for textile factories first in England and, only slightly later, for mills in New England.

By the 1830s, midwestern farmers could ship their raw materials eastward over rapidly expanding transportation routes and purchase finished cloth in return. America's Industrial Revolution, at first centered in New England, gradually transformed the nation into a more urban industrial society that soon included the cities in the Midwest. As the transformation reshaped lifestyles in a more modern image, changes in dress accelerated and diversified so that people could be identified by the "fashions" of their occupations—as blue- or white-collar workers, with subdivisions such as farming, manufacturing, business, and teaching. Department stores sprang up in Chicago and Cincinnati and St. Louis to merchandize ready-made clothing in standardized sizes. The hallmark of a mass society, our final rough historical phase, was increased mass production of goods—and clothing—for all sectors of the economy. Cottage industries largely disappeared, to be replaced by a homogenization that still permits individual uniqueness in clothing, all of which becomes available through intensively capitalized retail department stores, specialty shops, catalogue companies, and Web-based firms.

As the region evolved through the four stages of society, residents adopted fashions that were markers for popular images of midwesterners. And while to the rest of the world their images might have seemed stereotypical, the people of the Midwest deliberately dressed in accordance with their ideals and their politics. In so doing they set some trends for the nation, in particular in much publicized movements espousing "dress reform."

NATIVE AMERICAN FOLK DRESS

Native Americans in the Midwest also evolved through folk, agrarian, urban industrial, and mass societies, and their dress changed primarily because indigenous people came into contact with Europeans. Cross-cultural contact, in fact, often generates change in fashion, as members of one group attempt to impress or emulate the other group.

Early Indian folk dress was simple, natural, and functional, sometimes consisting of a blanket wrapped around the body. Later, it evolved to become highly decorative handmade clothing embellished with natural materials. Necklaces made of bones, stones, beads, feathers, and furs, worn in a variety of ways and arrangements, were a source of status and pride. Indian dress usually represented meaning, perhaps a story that recalled a significant event in the life of the individual, or just a color preference. Benjamin Drake's (1794–1841) *Life of Tecumseh* (1841) chronicles the appearance of Blue Jacket (c. 1740–1808), a Shawnee warrior and diplomat, whose name reflects his characteristic dress. In fact, many Shawnee typically wore a blue shirt, along with red and yellow feathers, red cloth leggings held up to a belt by straps, and a white blanket with blue stripes that completed the ensemble.

The dress of Native American tribes in Indiana and Illinois probably influenced that of other midwestern tribes. Illinois tribal dress included a buckskin cloak, a trade shirt, and feathers. In Indiana, the Miami nation favored a buckskin shirt with beaded fringe and fur mantle. In 1840, a traveler named John McIntosh commented on the Indian style in *The Origin of the North American Indians*:

It has always been observed that all the various tribes have a close resemblance in their dress; that of the North Americans in their original state, consists entirely of furs and hides; one piece is fastened round the waist, which reaches the middle of the thigh, and another larger piece is thrown over the shoulders. The stockings are of skins, fitted to the shape of the leg; the seams are ornamented with porcupines' quills; their shoes are of the skin of the Deer, Elk, or Buffalo, dressed for the most part with the hair on; they are made to fasten at the ankles, where they have ornaments of brass or tin, about an inch long, hung by thongs. The women are all covered from the knees upwards. Their shifts cover their body, but not the arms. Their petticoats reach from the waist to the knees; and both are of leather. Their shoes and stockings are not different from those of the men. Those men who wish to appear gay, pluck the hair from their heads, except a round spot of about two inches diameter on the crown of the head; on this are fastened plumes of feathers with quills of ivory or silver. The peculiar ornaments of this part are the distinguishing marks of the different nations. They sometimes paint their faces black, but more often red; they bore their noses and slit their ears, and in both wear various ornaments. The higher ranks of women dress their hair sometimes with silver in a peculiar manner; they sometimes paint it. They have generally a large spot of paint near the ear, on each side of the head, and not infrequently a small spot on the brow. These People, it is true, have made several improvements in their dresses, since they commenced to receive European commodities.[1]

To most early whites intent on acquiring land, American Indians all "looked alike." Trappers and hunters who resided among tribes, however, could instantly distinguish one tribe from another by their silhouettes and adornments.

Individuals might invent new articles of clothing when inspired by visions and dreams. When clothes held a particular spiritual meaning, they would not be copied by others in the tribe but rather respected as unique expressions. In general, however, the Indians followed the dictates of custom rather than fashion, which, then as now, called for appreciation of and by their friends. They therefore wore what they saw on the members of their own or other tribes, or, after European contact, on people of another culture. If the collision of cultures is a stimulus to fashion, then Native-American sensibilities were no exception. Gradually, they adopted the silhouettes of the Europeans they encountered in settlements and forts, but they also modified their own dress so as to impress the aliens.

Consider the war bonnet, the stereotype of a thousand western movies. Originally, distinguished Sioux warriors wore bonnets composed of eagle feathers to signify singular prowess in battle. Though varied in style and meaning, war bonnets were taken up by numerous other tribes during the late nineteenth century. Often, when we think of Indian attire, we think of the bonnets as emblems of courage and majesty. That image, spread by media around the world, is still cherished as the sign of a warrior. When McIntosh made his observations, the war bonnet as worn by some eastern tribes had already been admired by colonists. Thus reinforced by cross-cultural approval, the spectacular head-dress quickly replicated westward. The decorative dress of the Plains Indians and many of their neighboring nations who came in contact with midwestern tribes thus underwent aesthetic changes over the next fifty years, as fashion, like the frontier, moved west.

To similar ends, Native Americans took advantage of many new materials suddenly available to them during the eighteenth and nineteenth centuries. From traders they bought beads, metals, and cloth for accessories and apparel. These they fashioned into designs that represented their own heritage or emulated those valued in commerce. For example, designs in Oriental rugs or expensive textiles brought by white settlers inspired intricate Indian designs in beadwork. In some cases, Native Americans simply wore European clothes, reinterpreting them by adding items of their own. An Indian elder might don a hybrid costume consisting of a frock coat, a "wearing" blanket tightly wrapped around shoulders and

Bad Wound, Sioux chief, wearing war bonnet, c. 1899. Courtesy Library of Congress.

torso, and several necklaces. Native Americans in white men's clothing quickly became visible in settlements. The brilliantly colorful costumes often associated with elaborately staged ceremonies and dances came later in the nineteenth century, when economically disadvantaged Indians needed to attract tourists. As always, fashion follows power, even among cultures we designate "folk."

Eventually, of course, the displaced originals generated a renewed—or "retro"—interest. Not until the mid-twentieth century did white Americans rediscover Indian artifacts in earnest. Ironically, in that phenomenon of reciprocity that so often governs fashion, their popularity for the white counterculture may have pushed American Indians in the 1960s toward pride in more authentic (i.e., simpler) traditional dress. Fascination with heritage breeds historical research, which in turn can focus on period appearance as an index of cultural values. Pre-European contact Native American dress seemed to embody a free, physically active, healthy lifestyle. Asking questions about the specific arrangements of garments, accessories, and ornaments elicited information about the beliefs of those ancestors valorized as having lived in harmony with nature. By contrast, white people of the 1960s appropriated and reinterpreted tribal dress as fashion statements of their own. Beadwork and quillwork, weavings, blankets, and leather items from midwestern Indian nations attracted a wider group of middle-class consumers, and still do. Today, "western" and "midwestern" mail-order houses (such as Shepler's of Wichita) and American Indian foundations and businesses sell jewelry, belts, shirts, blankets, moccasins (like Minne-tonka, made in Minnesota), and other items of "traditional" design that are largely disconnected from their original context. To many Americans today, American Indian dress is beautiful, artistic, and dense with cultural meaning, though the consumers rarely understand the symbolism. Where fashion is concerned, however, such considerations are never the whole point. Fashion feeds on novelty, and in the case of modern appropriation of what once was marginal, the borrowing has come full circle.

FASHION ON THE MIDWESTERN AGRARIAN FRONTIER

Early Europeans quickly discovered the suitability of Native American dress to the wilderness in which they found themselves. Seventeenth-century French fur trappers working their way down to the midwestern interior from the Great Lakes, far from European settlements, quickly intermarried with indigenous women and adopted local dress almost as a matter of course. The surveyors, scouts, and pioneers in the Northeast Territory after 1787 also appreciated the virtues of Indian garb. Tough, durable, inexpensive clothing was a response to the physical rigors of the environment and perfectly acceptable to the inhabitants of relatively primitive frontier settlements on their way to becoming agrarian societies. Here isolation and economics dictated clothing that was utilitarian and available. Like Indians, settlers might combine a hunting shirt, deerskin trousers, and moccasins with a waistcoat of European manufacture.

Cincinnati's first *Directory*, issued when it proclaimed itself a city in 1819, describes the dress code for midwestern settlers of the 1790s: "The men wore hunting shirts of linen and linsey-woolsey, and round these a belt in which were inserted a scalping knife and tomahawk. Their moccasins, leggings and pantaloons were made of deer skins. The women wore linsey-woolsey manufactured by themselves."[2] Linsey-woolsey was a poor-quality coarse cloth woven from a linen warp with woolen filling that could be bulked for warmth, creating a plump, not to say shapeless, silhouette.

Outside centers of commerce, letters and diaries from the early years of the midwestern frontier say little about rural clothing, which was doubtless taken for granted rather than admired for its own sake. Period drawings and painting are more helpful. Again, the rule was improvisation and pastiche: veterans of the American Revolution often sported the remnants of military uniforms they had been issued, at least until they became threadbare, supplementing them with buckskin trousers and linsey-woolsey shirts. Their spouses favored simple gray full-length linsey-woolsey all-season dresses, over which they might layer a woolen cloak.

The first settlers in the Midwest, mostly of German, English, Scots, and Irish background, came from New England, the Mid-Atlantic colonies, and the Upland South, bringing with them garments that they soon abandoned in favor of utilitarian outfits. Few Americans of substance were among them, since the whole point of migration was to improve one's lot. Powdered wigs for men and women were already on their way out, especially among lower-class settlers traveling to the new territories, and so were hoop skirts, which had been supplanted by simple cotton or woolen dresses with much more slender silhouettes. Accustomed to knee-length pants over heavy stockings (as seen in pictures of George Washington and original colonists), and to flat-collared shirts over doublets, men suddenly plunged into clearing forests and plowing fields found that these were easily torn and dirtied. They replaced them with full-length trousers and collarless shirts with long sleeves for protection against the sun. If the more affluent settler still owned a long tailcoat, cinched slightly at the waist, perhaps brocaded, he found the ornate sleeves got in the way of axes, hoes, and pruning-hooks. Instead, farmers adopted deerskin or cotton jerkins for warm weather, sturdy woolen jackets for cold. When these improvised clothes wore out, they were patched or replaced piecemeal with local materials, occasionally homespun.

The Frugality of Dress for Nineteenth-Century Midwesterners

The mythos of the frontier has enshrined homespun cloth as a symbol of frugality, simplicity, and self-reliance, in part because people in the original seaboard colonies briefly engaged in making it, first out of necessity and then as an act of defiance against British exploitation of the Americas as a captive market. But it was common in the Midwest mainly during shortages. The War of 1812, for instance, interrupted cloth imports from English textile mills, but New England mills soon took up the slack. In any case, the labor required to produce homespun was hard, beyond the capacity of farm wives beset with other chores. Weaving required some sort of loom, too large and costly for primitive one-room homes; spinning flax into linen, even if the family owned a spinning wheel, was time-consuming. Making a dress or shirt from ready-made cloth was far easier, and that was standard practice. It is important to remember that even homemade clothing of the period was expensive and that few settlers owned many outfits. A wardrobe would consist of two shirts (wool for winter, linen for summer) and one pair of trousers for the men; a dress that resembled a smock, a skirt that was actually a petticoat, and a shift that served as undergarment for the women; and hand-me-downs for the children. Drawers and chemises were also important for both sexes, and the housewives could make these in their spare moments. Everything was altered, renovated, handed around among family members, or sold to others. As Daniel Boorstin observes, buying second-hand clothes was not disreputable, and such surplus was available at general stores and county fairs.[3]

Paintings and photographs of the nineteenth century, while they often depict the handsome outfits of leading town citizens, provide constant reminders of the care that ordinary rural people took of their garments. To judge from these representations, midwesterners wore aprons to protect clothing during much of the day. Housewives were rarely without full-length coverings that shielded dresses from spills in the kitchen, splatters from swilling the hogs, or tears from chopping wood or pumping water. Shopkeepers, blacksmiths, butchers, bartenders, and tradesmen wore heavy, nearly impervious leather aprons. Sunday-best to a farmer or workman was often just his cleaner shirt. Hats and caps were ubiquitous for men and women, and they came in all shapes (e.g., military tricornes, riverboat caps, flat-brimmed hats, and sun bonnets), sizes, and materials from leather and fur to cloth and straw. Suspenders held up trousers; belts fastened jackets and shirts because buttons were rare and buttonholes were difficult to craft. All purpose, all-weather coats were plentiful, sweaters were not. Wool was preferred because it lasted longer than cotton. Shoes and boots were expensive and blocky rather than stylish. In any case, most early settlers could not afford them, and instead wore homemade moccasins or "shoepacks," ankle-length moccassins with heavy soles, stuffed with deer-hair or leaves for comfort. Boys dressed like men, save for being mostly barefoot in warm weather, clad in crude long-sleeve collarless white shirts atop loose trousers held up by galluses. Girls copied their mothers, perhaps substituting a hair-ribbon in place of a bonnet. All this aside, rural mothers and daughters devoted as much effort to making themselves pretty for social gatherings as their city counterparts, often donning a colorful shawl for such occasions.

Style-consciousness increased among less-well-to-do women when colors became available. Factories in Massachusetts began turning out dyed cloth in calico patterns in the 1830s, and midwestern women seized upon to it to replace the prevailing grays. By the 1850s, simple dresses of calico appeared everywhere in the Midwest. They were relatively easy to make, serviceable, and inexpensive. Typical calico dresses had small, simple white collars with a little ribbon bow at the neck. Religion exerted relatively small influence on dress in rural areas. Presbyterians and Episcopalians tended toward more formal attire, while low-church denominations such as Baptists and Methodists were more casual. Only closed faiths enforced dress codes vigorously. The Amish, for instance, prescribed modes for men and women that they still adhere to today. For others, the desire to assimilate, always a factor in fashion, usually prevailed. Generally speaking, save in large ethnic conclaves in northern cities, immigrants quickly bowed to prevailing custom. Midwesterners of the period looked down on ethnic dress; they advised immigrants from Europe to discard the sometimes colorful national garb that made them stand out and switch to "proper," practical clothes.

URBAN-INDUSTRIAL FASHIONS

The rebuilt environment resulting from the closely connected forces of urbanization and industrialization brought changes in dress. Urban factory and business districts nestled against residential sectors and civic spaces. While dim factory floors might be packed with machines operated by rows of ill-clad workers, office buildings had larger rooms, wider passageways, cleaner air, and furniture appropriate for outfits of light colors or delicate fabrics worn by members of a swelling professional corps. Tenements for laborers were cramped, with whole families crammed into single rooms, but middle-class houses boasted parlors for receiving guests; here women and men felt they should be nicely dressed. Large new public buildings afforded citizens opportunities to mingle and to impress friends and strangers with their sense of taste in clothing. After the Civil War, indoor gas lighting, followed in a few decades by electric illumination, extended the hours when midwesterners could see and be seen by others; evening parties and balls called for elegant dress. Out of doors, sidewalks and lawns in cities, unlike those in farming communities, provided level walking surfaces that would not dirty beautiful skirts and trousers. Garments provided clues to status and power; like urban dwellers everywhere, midwesterners in Chicago, Detroit, and St. Louis unconsciously adopted a fashion calculus for assessing passersby on the streets. In short, the artifice of cityscapes increased the range of clothing worn by inhabitants of different classes, and stimulated experimentation in apparel for those who could afford it.

General Trends in the Nineteenth Century

In the early industrial era, affluent citizens of Ohio River towns could embellish their appearance as early as 1811, when steamboats making frequent stops brought fancy cloth for merchants, seamstresses, and tailors. Wealthy families hired either traveling or live-in seamstresses, or took their cloth to a professional tailor as population growth made those professions commonplace. Steamboats brought not only nattily dressed riverboat gamblers sporting cravats and floral waistcoats but also women of easy virtue whose fashion sense inspired locals to muted emulation. For a brief period lasting until the end of the 1820s, well-turned out men and women in Cincinnati adopted the Empire style. This they borrowed from the court of Napoleon (1769–1821), whose courtiers in turn modeled their hair and clothing on the classical Greeks and Romans. Napoleon, who agreed to the Louisiana Purchase in 1803, enjoyed high regard in the Midwest. Cincinnati ladies attended parties dressed in their simple but expensive version of French gowns with low necklines and high waists, the latter tightened with drawstrings or ribbons, there to meet men who had carefully brushed their hair to resemble the locks to be found on Greek statues. As urbanization in the 1830s and 1840s accelerated the pace of fashion, those styles yielded to tight-waisted, full-skirted dresses flared over layers of petticoats. A decade later, dressmakers stiffened the petticoats into crinolines for more dramatic effect, making these underskirts out of horsehair, wire, or light wooden struts.

Statehood boosted regional consciousnesss of fashion. By 1858, Iowa, Michigan, Minnesota, and Wisconsin had joined Indiana, Illinois, and Ohio to make up the new region of the "Middle Border" states, and men began to groom themselves for politics. The cutaway long-tail coat (which eventually evolved into formal evening wear) gave way in Chicago, St. Louis, and Milwaukee to the knee-length, fully skirted redingote, or frock coat, whose silhouette conveyed a substantial look appropriate to increasingly sedentary professions. The full outfit featured the double-breasted coat over fawn-colored trousers, accented with a black satin vest, a black or white cravat, and a top hat. Especially favored by lawyers, it has come down to us in the many representations of Abraham Lincoln (born in Kentucky but matured in Illinois, 1808–1865), who wore a much plainer version with a lack of panache that masqueraded as humility. So ingrained was this image of Middle Border integrity that the signature suit helped Lincoln win his 1858 debates with the far more dapperly dressed Stephen Douglas (1813–1861), the already-citified "Little Giant of the Prairie," whose jacket lapels sported the velvet then in vogue in the Senate, and it helped to keep "Honest Abe" electable. Other midwestern presidents, though hardly fashionplates, also learned to dress for success. The military uniform, on such heroes as Ulysses S. Grant (Ohio, 1822–1885), William Henry Harrison (Indiana by way of Virginia, 1773–1841), and Benjamin Harrison (Ohio, 1833–1901), was iconographic. The dullness of Rutherford B. Hayes (Ohio, 1922–1893), James Garfield (Ohio, 1831–1881), William McKinley (Ohio, 1843–1901), and William Howard Taft (Ohio, 1857–1930) was manifest in a sober style that spoke quietly of Ohio probity. The image did not always run deep, of course. An electorate weary of World War I voted Warren G. Harding (Ohio, 1865–1923), the apostle of "normalcy," into office precisely because he seemed to be what Americans today would call just a "suit," but he pretty much destroyed the state's reputation for integrity. Celluloid collars on Herbert Hoover (Iowa, 1874–1964) reinforced his standing as an upright engineer who might fix the economy of an industrial society sliding into the Great Depression. Though himself always carefully tailored, usually in double-breasted suits, polka-dot bow ties, and panama hats, Harry S Truman (Missouri, 1884–1972) actually failed as a Kansas City, Missouri, haberdasher before entering politics. The suits he offered were too expensive for midwesterners caught in the throes of the Depression.[4]

To be sure, fashion marked the extremes of social class, at least for a time, as disparities of income grew during the surges of industrialization. Workingmen clung to simple trousers, overalls, shirts, and caps that would not catch against tools as the region made a gradual shift from hand-work to machine-work, from shop to factory, from agrarian to industrial economy. Their wives made their own and their children's clothes, or bought cheap garments from company stores in Detroit and in Gary, Indiana. The upper classes of the Midwest, to the extent that they thought of themselves as such, rarely went to great lengths to dress the part. In the 1870s, bustle gowns appeared with exaggerated rears and flounces below tight, lace-trimmed bodices; they were worn mostly in promenades, especially at Easter, which became an annual consumer fashion festival promoted by manufacturers beginning in about 1873 (see, for example, the lavish Easter illustrations in *Harper's Weekly* of April 26, 1873). Gay Nineties fashions were more modest in the Midwest than in the urban centers of the East. Only women in theatrical circles in downtown Chicago or in the less staid haunts of the truly rich in Detroit's Grosse Pointe squeezed themselves into whalebone corsets to slim their waists into "hour-glass" silhouettes and push their powdered breasts above low-cut necklines. The most alluring of these costumes, slighty scandalous because they gave the illusion of lingerie worn on the outside, were too daring for Columbus and Indianapolis. On the other hand, aniline dyes, the product of the region's chemical plants, did add more hues to new wool and cotton blends, and these were welcomed. Accessories included huge feather-bedecked hats, parasols, and coats with elaborate gussets, lace, piping, and furbelows whose sheer expense could be equated with respectability. Though generally plainer, men's clothing could also be a bit flamboyant during the 1890s. Frockcoats grew heavier and fancier in the torso, with lapels that highlighted ruffled shirts, neckcloths, and cravats; the effect resembled a bird's plumage, puffed at the neck.

The Leveling of Fashion in the the Early Midwest

A leveling of fashion had already begun to erase class stratification, which had never been too emphatic in the Midwest in the first place. The effects of the Industrial Revolution on clothing were divergent but generally democratic, especially on the growing middle class. As early as 1830, a middle-class woman reading an issue of *Godey's Lady's Book* (1830–1898) could commission a seamstress to duplicate a dress she saw in its pages, albeit with plebeian modifications appropriate to the region, or try to copy one herself. Other magazines carried illustrations—"fashion plates"—of the latest styles on the coast, most of them too elaborately decorated by midwestern standards, but riveting to subscribers who wished to keep up. Later midwestern women's magazines such as *Ladies' Home Journal* (Des Moines, Iowa) (1893–present) and *Woman's Home Companion* (Cleveland and Springfield, Ohio) (1874–1957) offered fashion columns and patterns as well (see the section on "Newspapers and Magazines" in the chapter on **Literature**).

Far from urban centers, midwestern women could alter what they saw or turn to a local dressmaker who sold limited versions of her own designs, again usually more subdued than the extravagant eastern models whose manufacturers used yards of cloth to absorb the increased output of wool, cotton, muslin, and silk by American textile mills. The economics were bleak for seamstresses. *Godey's Lady's Book* in 1854 reported that a widow supporting her two children by sewing piecework cut by a tailor would receive seven cents for a shirt, twelve for trousers, and twenty for a jacket.[5]

According to U.S. census statistics, most dressmakers in the late nineteenth century were single, native-born, working-class white women. They worked in their homes or in commercial buildings. Alone or in concert with sisters, mothers, daughters, and nieces, they created unique garments of great beauty. In 1897, Cincinnati city directories listed over fifteen hundred women as dressmakers, perhaps only a percentage of the actual number who worked on the side and did not report it because of female employment's vulgar connotations. Often they chose their profession because it was the only reasonably artistic endeavor open to them; certainly it did not pay that well. (The Cincinnati Museum of Art has recovered a good deal of information about the lives and products of Cincinnati's dressmakers.) Hard work for a professional, sewing at home by amateurs was harder still, especially as fashion favored tighter-fitting clothes with more precise seams and lines. Drafting schemes for making the task easier, including proportional scales with instruction booklets, proliferated in the Midwest; the collective number of patents for clothes drafting systems issued to people in the Midwest outnumbered those in other regions. Needless to say, these were gendered innovations. As Claudia Kidwell points out, "no suggestion was ever made that a man not engaged in this trade could use such a system to cut his own clothes."[6] In the 1860s and 1870s, in yet another innovation, firms such as Butterick's and DeMorest's began selling sized patterns by mail to homemakers in remote areas of Iowa and Minnesota. Patterns allowed the recipients to sidestep elaborate "systems," but it could still take them weeks to finish a fashionable dress. Standardization of sizes was key. It not only permitted women to make their own clothes with less effort, but it also rationalized the ready-made industry. In 1880, Daniel Ryan published *Human Proportions in Growth*. Its widely accepted, authoritative charts included measurements of the human body for various ages and sizes, making it possible to standardize ready-made clothes using statistical profiles.[7]

The Beginnings of Ready-Made Clothing

Standardized sizes, coupled with evolving machinery, doomed the cottage industries of independent tailors and seamstresses. The sewing machine invented in 1846 by Elias Howe (1819–1867) and the automated versions devised between 1851 and 1865 by Isaac Singer (1811–1875) transformed clothing and economic patterns as hand-tailoring gave way to machine manufacture. For example, travelers in 1857 noted that the tailors of Pomeroy Ohio, who had congregated in this coal-shipping river town, "executed all kinds of work in the tailoring line with neatness and dispatch." As steamboats brought more and more machine-produced goods to the landing below Court Street, the tailors tried to hold onto their local customers. Many went out of business, but others expanded their shops to include ready-made clothing from upriver, a strategy that did not always succeed. In 1886, the writer Henry Howe (1816–1893) visited Pomeroy, after an absence of forty years and witnessed the end of a boom-and-bust cycle that would become familar throughout the Midwest. Pomeroy's former population of 5560 had fallen to 4726 as Pittsburgh cut into the market for Ohio's bituminous coal, but the coal-dust and smoke from its smokestacks still hung in the air.[8] The town's dressmakers, milliners, and tailors were eking out a living from the remaining Welsh and German miners, who were just as apt to buy ready-made goods.[9]

The most significant impetus to ready-made clothes was the Civil War, when the necessity of cladding thousands of troops spurred machine-processing of what had previously been piecework. Government contractors, many of them dishonest, turned out shoddy woolen jackets and trousers in Yankee Blue, together with belts and caps and other accoutrements. During the war, the uniforms were simply sized small, medium, and large; soldiers of many shapes hemmed and tucked these as best they could. By contrast, officers in nearly all the state regiments took their uniforms to tailors for custom fitting. The war moved clothing industries away from small towns like Pomeroy to large population centers where cheap power and cheap labor were available.

Sweat shops spread through Chicago, which became the midwestern home of ready-made clothing manufacturers. There, in venues similar to those now located on the Pacific Rim of Asia, workers toiled in appalling conditions—poor ventila-

During the Civil War, the uniforms were sized simply small, medium, and large; soldiers of many shapes hemmed and tucked these as best they could. Corbis.

tion, dim light, low wages—to clothe larger and larger numbers of their fellows. One of the most important Chicago manufacturers was Hart, Schaffner, and Marx, founded in 1872. By 1897, it had become the most recognized clothing manufacturer in the industry. Labor unrest peaked in 1910 when Hannah Shapiro, frustrated with her wages and working conditions, walked out of the Hart, Schaffner, and Marx factory where she was employed as a pocket sewer. Within three weeks, almost 40,000 workers were on strike. Shapiro and Bessie Abramowitz (Hillman) spearheaded what became known as the Hart, Schaffner, and Marx Strike of 1910, the largest and most successful strike until that time and a key event in the American labor movement.

The Early Midwestern Retail Economy

The products of those factories fueled a racing midwestern retail economy that was itself boosted by heavy industry on the edges of the Great Lakes, as workers poured into the region to take jobs in steel mills and agricultural processors. Urban midwesterners discovered the joys of shopping for new garments that fit right off the rack. Dry-goods and department stores appeared in all major cities of the Midwest. The first department store in the Midwest seems to have been established in the 1840s by a Canadian company, Mackinac, headquartered in Montreal but with a storehouse and retail outlet at Michilimackinac, Michigan.[10] But it was Marshall Field who began the Midwest's large-scale mercantile movement. In 1852, Marshall Field's started as a dry-goods retailer on Lake Street in Chicago and was renamed Marshall Field & Company in 1881. It was the first store with a bridal registry, thus beginning what has become an international wedding tradition. Other notable department stores followed, many of which bought up chains or conglomerations. In 1902, for example, George Dayton opened Goodfellows in downtown Minneapolis. A year later, the name changed to the Dayton's Dry Goods Company, the foundation of today's Target Corporation.

Competition with department stores, but especially with smaller dry-goods stores, came from the great midwestern mail-order houses. Montgomery Ward, the first mail-order retailer, opened in 1872 in Chicago. By the 1890s, it had become an empire catering especially to the needs of women. It was followed by Sears and Roebuck (1886), also headquartered in the Windy City. Isolated farm families throughout the Midwest eagerly awaited the quarterly Sears catalogs filled with goods of every description, including ready-made clothes of all types. Because Sears bought in volume and commissioned its own products from manufacturers, the catalogs caused prices to drop, earning the company the nickname "the great price maker." Small-town dry-goods retailers fought lower-priced mail-order houses just as they had fought the "monopolistic" department stores, especially on the issue of ready-made clothes, by burning copies of the Montgomery Ward and Sears Roebuck catalogs in town squares.[11] Mail orders continued to rise.

A regional manufacturer cashed in on the phenomenon. Founded in 1895 in Oshkosh, Wisconsin, OshKosh B'Gosh, Inc. grew quickly from a small-town producer of adult workwear. The company began making pint-sized versions in the early 1900s, so that children could dress like their fathers. However, it was not until Miles Kimball, a local mail-order firm, featured a pair of children's overalls in its national catalog that sales of the item took off. OshKosh B'Gosh expanded distribution into specialty and department stores, eventually becoming an international marketer of children's clothing and accessories.

Expanding industry, commerce, and population swelled demand for and affected styles of clothing. Beginning in the 1880s, clothes designed for active women desperate or brave enough to challenge the stigma of working outside the home included a "suit," a sack coat over a practical skirt that could be worn separately with a shirtwaist blouse that soon became universal on shopgirls, office workers, and schoolteachers in Wisconsin, Minnesota, and Michigan, as well as further south. As more and more women moved into diverse pursuits, their garments became lighter-weight and looser, and were purchased ready-made from racks; wage-earning women had little time or extra money to spend on fittings. Clothes for businessmen and middle-management-level males put cut and fit above ornament, color, and display. In both single- and double-breasted models, the suit gradually took on its modern iteration, the sack coat over trousers that varied in silhouette, but changed little until the 1960s.

Mass-Produced Fashions in the Midwest

Chicago remained the clothing manufacturing center of the Midwest for only a short time. Today most clothing is made in California or in eastern states; of the midwestern states, only Michigan still turns out significant volume. Chicago is still a major distribution hub, however. Jobbers and retail-store buyers flock three times a year to fashion shows (the most popular and lucrative is "The National Bridal Market") at the city's gigantic Merchandise Mart. Chicago nonetheless has historically served as the fashion arbiter of the region. That was confirmed in the Roaring Twenties, when the city's flappers and gangsters became national trendsetters. During the 1920s, partly in reaction to the short-lived hobble skirt that restricted movement, young, boyish-looking women danced to the city's famous jazz in the city's speakeasies decked in bobbed hair, long necklaces, and straight, unfitted dresses that bared the knees. Women in rural areas of Iowa, Indiana, and Ohio were less likely to adopt such provocative styles, not to mention the cigarettes that completed the outfit, but bolder souls in the cities of those states occasionally outraged their parents and propriety. Ironically, when Prohibition spurred the bootlegging of spirits smuggled across the Canadian border into isolated towns in the midwestern north, it also made criminals into fashion exemplars surreptitiously admired even by brokers in the Chicago Commodities Exchange. Midwesterners were captivated by Al Capone's (1889–1947) penchant for pin-striped suits, and by the stylish outfits that Bonnie Parker and Clyde Barrow adopted to rob midwestern banks. The Midwest's work ethic aside, the era elevated ersatz glamor and fashion accessories into amusing self-parody, the premise behind Bob Fosse's musical *Chicago*. National media propelled other clothing fads originating in the Midwest. Seen in newsreels, midwesterner Charles Lindbergh's (1902–1974) leather jacket generated a minor industry because the citizen wearing such a jacket while driving an automobile could imagine himself flying planes across the Atlantic.

Dresses grew longer during the Depression; the economic catastrophe hit the Midwest hard, especially in the western edges that abutted the Dust Bowl. Here one saw the "Hoover Apron" or "Hooverall," named after the first president born west of the Mississippi. The "Hoover Apron" was a kind of wraparound house dress handed out by city relief agencies to the unemployed. Feedsack clothing was also a midwestern symbol of tough times. Originally promoted by grain companies selling seed to farmers, it was sometimes all that a family could afford. At the very least it could be made into undergarments. During this time, men's shirt collars grew longer and more pointed, attached rather than celluloid add-ons, while their overcoats grew heavy, functional, and protective. The sea of fedora hats moving along streets in Milwaukee and Des Moines as men searched for work seemed gray and grim.

Hems were shortened again during the 1940s, when waists grew tighter and shoulders broader (thanks to padding), but such ensembles competed against the popularity of blouses and slacks. Women wore blouses and slacks as they joined assembly lines at the Midwest's steel and automobile plants retooled to produce tanks, planes, and jeeps for World War II. Nylons disappeared, but after the war unleashed pros-

Easter Sunday fashions, Chicago, Illinois, 1941. Courtesy Library of Congress.

perity, synthetics returned with a vengeance, as crinolines and lingerie. Fashions evolved more swiftly: close-fitted short-length sheath dresses in the 1950s, A-lines and shifts (see the next section, "Dress Reform in the Midwest") in the early 1960s, and mini-skirts in the second half of that decade. During the same period, the men's fashion scene contented itself with a shift to Ivy League suits (natural shoulders, narrow lapels) and bermuda shorts for leisure wear. Moustaches, long hair, and beards appeared on *au courant* midwestern males, who also discovered a fondness for colored shirts and bright wide ties. "Leisure suits," the product of manufacturers with too much polyester in their warehouses, had more staying power in the Midwest than elsewhere. Fortunately, by 1980, they had disappeared into closets and landfills. The real god of the counterculture was Levi Strauss, whose jeans poured into the Midwest from California, to be worn with homemade tie-dyed blouses and shirts.

Since the 1960s, fashions and fabrics for both men and women have varied enormously, but the one constant has been a long-term national trend toward casual rather than formal styles. It is tempting to claim that midwestern preferences drove that trend, but it seems more accurate to credit the growth of an information and service economy whose digital workstations and active fieldwork encourage more comfortable clothes. Even so, three midwestern fashion vernaculars stand out. The first is a preference for active leisure wear that has grown out of the midwestern passion for sports. Sporting attire took hold in the Midwest early (see the chapter on **Sports and Recreation**). Hunting, for example, carried its own cachet. Oliver Hazard Perry (1817–1864), a native of Ohio named for the famous victor of the Battle of Lake Erie, for thirty years (1836–1855) maniacally hunted deer in the Cass River marshes of Michigan and kept meticulous diaries of his kills. For his exploits he invented a sort of broadcloth union suit, a long tunic over tight trousers, that was widely copied by hunters.[12]

In 1869, the link between midwestern fashion and sports was forged when America's first professional baseball team took its name from the clothes the players wore—the Cincinnati Red Stockings. The nation adopted the Cincinnati style of uniform but not the hat. Midwesterners liked what came to be known as the Chicago pill-box, a hat with a short visor and a flat top horizontally striped like a layer cake. By 1900, however, the forerunner of today's rounded-crown, large-visored cap, originally popularized by the Brooklyn Excelsiors, had swept the leagues.[13] Off the football field, Red Grange (1903–1991), three-time All-American at the University of Illinois and later a player for the Chicago Bears (1925), along with and the Four Horsemen of the Notre Dame team, popularized the full-length raccoon coat and the camel hair polo coat, both of which—along with the whisky flasks associated with them—were soon prized by often-drunk midwestern fans. Today, midwestern football, baseball, hockey, basketball, and automobile racing teams license their logos on apparel ranging from jackets and t-shirts to ball caps and shoes. Fans buy them to identify with their heroes, especially for celebrated regional contests such as the annual football match between the University of Minnesota and the University of Wisconsin, whose rivalry inspires paroxysms of loyalty manifested in exhibits of team colors and symbols.

The second midwestern fashion vernacular is the work uniform. Some of these uniforms have been upscale: Boeing Air Transport, for example, introduced the first airline stewardesses in glamorous high-fashion skirts and jackets on its Chicago to San Francisco route in 1930. More commonly, midwestern work clothes have been straightforwardly utilitarian, expressions of the work ethic of its agricultural and industrial heritage. At some point, overalls, the long-bibbed trouser, emerged as a signature garment. No one seems to know where it originated, but it appears in protomodern form in the eighteenth century; nineteenth-century iterations, cut from the familiar blue and white striped bolts of heavy cotton, required buttons, rivets, or eyelets as fasteners that were not widely available until the 1840s. The all-purpose work suit soon sported specialized watch and pencil pockets, tool loops, and various trappings suitable to carpenters, farmers, train engineers, factory workers, and just anybody else who worked with his or her hands. Rosie the Riveter cheerfully donned it in the 1940s.

Those traditions survive in the work clothing manufactured by Carhartt, Inc., of Dearborn, Michigan. Founded in 1889, Carhartt offers a full line of authentic outdoor wear that has set industry standards for quality, toughness, and

Although common work wear for farmers, overalls are also worn by people in all walks of life throughout the country. Getty Images/PhotoDisc.

durability. In addition to pants, shirts, jackets, overalls, and vests, Carhartt manufactures accessories such as caps, gloves, and socks. Although some of its clothing is made of denim, most of it is made of duck, a rugged, canvaslike material derived from 100 percent cotton suitable for farming, ranching, construction, commercial fishing, logging, and telephone line rigging. The company's coverall and insulated coverall, the shorter, boxy "chore coat," and work trouser can be recognized around the nation by their butterscotch color.

Fashionable variations of the overall—in lighter materials and brown stripes, for instance—are sold by midwestern firms such as OshKosh B'Gosh and The Gap (headquartered in Columbus, Ohio). For workers in peripatetic service sectors, such garments epitomize health, freedom, and practicality—midwestern values. Mutations include accessories sometimes called "nomadic architecture," the construction of wear designed to accommodate items and equipment that have become integral to professional and personal lifestyles: ladies and men's purses, waist packs, fanny packs, pockets and pouches for pagers, calculators, and cell phones, briefcases for laptop computers, back- and chest-packs for carrying infants.

The third midwestern fashion vernacular is the regional conviction that clothes, at base functional rather than ornamental, should also be inexpensive. Midwesterners have long taken pride in homemade copies or cheap knockoffs of designer styles from elsewhere, and discount merchandising continues to govern midwestern fashion. In 1962, four discount merchandisers opened in the Midwest: Target, Kohl's, Meijer Thrifty Acres, and Kresge's. Kohl's, founded by the Kohl family in Milwaukee, Wisconsin, in 1962, quickly became one of America's fastest-growing department stores. Target grew from the Dayton Company's policy of offering discounted clothing. In 1990, Target acquired Marshall Field's of Chicago. The first Meijer Thrifty Acres opened in Grand Rapids, Michigan. In Detroit, Kresge, originally a dime store, became mass-market discounter K-Mart. In the now-familar midwestern pattern by which mail-order firms challenge stores, the following year (1963), Gary C. Comer, a former advertising copywriter and avid sailor, founded Lands' End in Chicago. The first full-color catalogue of 1975 featured thirty pages of sailing equipment and two pages of clothing. Two years later, clothing took up thirteen of forty pages. Now located in Wisconsin, Lands' End is the nation's top online seller of apparel and has been purchased by a Sears Roebuck struggling to regain its prominence. Millions of Americans have bought these essentially midwestern clothes.

DRESS REFORM IN THE MIDWEST

Although these vernaculars have had generalized impact, midwesterners have also more than once deliberately attempted to influence American dress. Despite the desire of urban dwellers to be *au courant*, practicality in dress surfaced early in the Midwest as a strong cultural value. In some sectors, it verged on obsession, most notably when it stimulated calls for "dress reform" of women's attire. The first radical attempt to alter female apparel in the United States took place in the early nineteenth century in the heart of the Midwest, in the utopian socialist community of New Harmony, Indiana. The Harmony Community, founded in 1815 by George Rapp (1757–1847), was purchased in 1825 by Robert Owen (1771–1858), who continued the "New Harmony" community's experiments in idealism. One initiative was to free women by exchanging unhealthy corsets and easily soiled sweeping skirts for pantaloons.[14] A ditty in *The New Harmony Gazette* encapsulates the community's stance on fashion:

> No more ribbons wear, nore in rich dress appear. . . .
> This do without fear, and to all you'll appear
> Fine, charming, true, lovely and clever
> Thought the times remain darkish—
> Young men will be sparkish,
> And love you more dearly than ever.[15]

The New Harmony Community adopted a shortened dress with full trousers as early as 1824. After Owen began promoting the costume as a statement of gender equity in 1827, pantaloons spread to utopian communities such as Oneida in upstate New York and to spas and resorts as well. Midwestern colleges and universities also climbed on the bandwagon. Faculty and students at Oberlin College, whose radical politics included higher education for both women and blacks, endorsed dress reform. The *Oberlin Covenant* (1833) announced that "we will denounce all the world's expensive and unwholesome fashions of dress, particularly tight dressing and ornamental attire."[16] Pantaloons rapidly became associated with incipient campaigns for women's rights. Widely lampooned, and something of an aberration, the pantaloon experiment foreshadowed the struggles of feminist reformers against a mainstream that wanted clothing to signify and reinforce the subordinate roles assigned to women.

Not surprisingly, midwesterners were receptive to yet another reform garment, the bloomer (actually created by Elizabeth Smith Miller), which impressed its supporters with its practicality and convenience. Advocates extolled its simplicity and modesty as both moral and patriotic. In the spring of 1851, *The Hancock Journal* of Findlay, Ohio, praised Amelia Bloomer's (1818–1894) courage in wearing the short dress and full trousers. In summer, the magazine noted that the new dress was being received favorably in midwestern cities such as Cincinnati and Adrian, Michigan. In July, the journal reported that a young woman in Findlay had worn bloomers in public. *Sibyl, a Review of the Follies, Errors, and Fashions of Society*, Bloomer's journal published under the auspices of the National Dress Reform Association, offered still more accounts of sightings in Ohio.[17]

Bloomers appealed to cranks and faddists as well, including Ellen G. White (1827–1915), founder of the Seventh Day Adventist Water Cure, a sort of religious spa in Battle Creek, Michigan. At first, White rejected the bloomer on the grounds that one's religion should determine one's appearance, regardless of alleged issues of health. White's Testimony #10 (1863) recounts a vision from God, in which the Deity forebade Adventist women to wear reform dress. After a visit to James Caleb Jackson's water-cure establishment in New York, however, she changed her mind. As she traveled from church to church in the Midwest, she began peddling patterns for reform dresses of her own design. Eventually she published her ideas on the model reform dress in several tracts, including *How to Live* (1865) and *The Dress Reform* (1868).[18]

The most notorious health faddist, also in Battle Creek, went even further. J. H. Kellogg (1852–1943), the director of the Battle Creek Sanitarium who espoused daily high colonics and other dubious regimens, developed a "practical" dress system for women and men, and frequently lectured on the subject before the Michigan State Medical Society. His system foregrounded healthy underwear: for males, a union suit; for women, tights for cold weather, a combination suit to replace drawers and chemise, and a divided skirt with attached or detachable "freedom waist." In addition, he prescribed a gown form that served as a lining for women's outer dress. Such attire, coupled with sexual abstinence, the eating of Graham crackers named for his friend Sylvester Graham (1794–1851), and Kellogg's recommended daily regimens, would ensure healthy bodies.

In the late nineteenth century, dress reform took on greater respectability, and many midwestern advocates for women's rights, temperance, and other causes added their efforts to the campaign. During the 1870s, Ohio gave birth to two grassroots movements. The first began as the Northern Ohio Health and Dress Reform Association, in South Newbury.[19] The second started in 1874 when the American Free Dress League held its first meeting in Painesville; it lasted three years under the leadership of Mary Tillotson (1816–?). Because of negative press reports linking the bloomer with women's rights, Tillotson jettisoned the name, replacing it with a new label: the Science Costume. As Tillotson's example indicated, Ohio progressives generally avoided the politically charged issue of women's suffrage and instead promoted reform dress as an issue of women's health.

In the spring of 1851, *The Hancock Journal* of Findlay, Ohio, praised Amelia Bloomer's courage in wearing a short dress and full trousers. In summer, the magazine noted that the new dress was being received favorably in midwestern cities such as Cincinnati and Adrian, Michigan. Courtesy Library of Congress.

The Chicago World's Fair of 1893, in addition to showcasing designs from around the world in the Women's Pavilion, also called attention to the regional dress reform movement. The National Council of Women advised women to wear one of three approved styles while visiting the White City: the Syrian Costume, the gymnasium suit, and the American Costume. The Syrian Costume featured a "divided skirt," with the fabric of each leg gathered at, but bagging over, the ankle. The gymnasium suit included a trouser to be worn with extra high shoes. The American Costume combined a short skirt, shirtwaist, or jacket with matching leggings or straight-cut trousers. Trousers were particularly appropriate for strolling through outdoor events along the Fair's midway, said the Council, but could double as practical business attire as well. Mainstream resistance to trousers nevertheless remained strong, in part because many women felt strange in them, despite the Council's advice on how to wear them with confidence.[20] The barriers to dress reform, Frances Parker argued in *Dress, and How to Improve It*, were the reformers' lack of conviction and their inability to understand the irrational nature of fashion, which obeys its own mysterious, collective mandates. As a result, they should aim not just at common sense and comfort, but also beauty.[21] That women's dress remained a hot-button topic is evident in the region's fondness for transvestism. As just one example, Mark Twain has Huck Finn and the Duke and Dauphin dress in women's clothes in *Huckleberry Finn* (1884). By 1930, transvestite revues would annually tour the cities and rural fairs of the Midwest.[22]

As yet another—more recent—instance of failed dress reform, Betsy Bloomingdale, a wealthy New York socialite looking for a feminist alternative to burning brassieres, attempted during the 1970s to spark a fashion trend based on the midwestern "house dress," a comfortable, loose-fitting dress made of cotton or cotton-polyester fabric. Bloomingdale added ruffles and flounces, renamed the result a "Day Dress," and promoted it—unsuccessfully, at least on the scale she had anticipated—at Bonwit Teller's, Saks Fifth Avenue, and, of course, Bloomingdale's.

HISTORIC AND ETHNIC FASHIONS

Reimagining or reinterpreting older garments is still popular. In addition to the Day Dress, midwestern boutiques stock nostalgic versions of the Missouri River Boatman's Shirt, the Prairie Dress, the Quilted Skirt, and the Walking Skirt. Surprises abound in museums: the Western Reserve Historical Society in Cleveland maintains a collection of regional maternity clothes whose styles evolved noticeably from 1830 to the present, a phenomenon perhaps explained by the Midwest's obsession with family values. Greenfield Village, near Detroit, Conner Prairie in Indiana, and other outdoor museums and parks throughout the region dress their staffs in period costumes for the edification and delight of tourists.

In some areas, religion still dictates dress. In Grabill, Indiana, at the heart of Amish country, Souders' Home Center displays flat black hats and button-fly trousers, along with bolts of solid-color cloth and parts for treadle sewing machines. The Amish believe that plain clothes encourage humility and separation from the outer world; clothing is thus an expression of their faith. Old Order Amish women and girls in Amish communities in Ohio, Indiana, and Wisconsin wear modest dresses made from solid-color fabric with long sleeves and a full skirt with hems halfway between knee and floor. They put up their never-cut hair in a bun at the back of the head. If married, they cover their heads with white prayer cloth; if unmarried, they

1890s dress on display in the Granville Lifestyle Museum, Ohio. Courtesy Ohio Tourism.

use black. Amish women do not wear jewelry. Men and boys wear dark-colored shirts, black socks and shoes, and black felt or straw broad-brimmed hats. Shirts have buttons, but coats are held together with hooks and eyes. After they marry, Amish men grow beards without moustaches. Boys cut their hair in bangs; adult males part theirs in the middle, and let their hair cover their ears.

Large concentrations of Jews in Chicago and suburbs such as Skokie can buy clothing appropriate to different Jewish movements. Hasidic Jewish men wear suits of black gabardine made from 100 percent wool (no blends with linen or cotton). Most distinctive are the tsit-tsit, or knotted ritual fringes attached to an undergarment so that they spill out visibly at the waist. Outdoors, they wear black broad-brimmed hats trimmed with fur; indoors they adopt the kepah or skullcap, often made of velvet (unlike the Orthodox Jews who prefer knitted kepah). On the Sabbath and High Holidays, they may wear a white kittel, or robe, tied at the waist. Unlike Muslim girls, unmarried Hasidic women do not cover their heads, but married women always do, using either a wig or a small scarf. Women dress modestly, in dresses that cover arms and knees, and always wear them with stockings. Local stores stock many styles of kepah and talit, a ritual shawl with tsit-tsit worn by women as well as men in the more liberal Reform and Conservative movements.

Many Muslims in the Midwest also emphasize modesty. Depending on their country of origin, some men may wear long shirtlike garments over baggy trousers, but most wear business suits or casual American clothing, though rarely with the keffiyeh, or head scarf, to be found in, say, Arab countries. Women in veils and chadors, the loose cloaks that mask the contours of the body and envelope the head, tend to stand out on city streets. In the months following September 11, 2001, Muslim leaders in Dearborn, Michigan, one of the largest American Arab communities, cautioned women who dress in Islamic scarves, long sleeves, and long skirts to avoid public places.

Thanks to folk festivals, ethnic organizations, and family and public celebrations, midwesterners can also find ethnic dress from past and present, part of the rich polyglot culture that is their regional heritage. Ethnic clothing figures more visibly in some communities than in others, of course. Along Devon Avenue in Chicago, sari shops sell traditional Indian garments, but such shops can be found all over the Midwest because of significant immigration, widespread dispersal, and the growing economic clout of citizens from India and Pakistan. Among the Indian American enclave in Ames, Iowa, for example, traditional weddings are common. The groom wears sandals and a loose, light-colored cotton tunic and trousers, somewhat eclipsed by the bride, whose skin is anointed with saffron, her body clad in a brilliantly colored sari, her head, face, and neck ornamented with gold jewelry. Park visitors in major cities in all eight states during spring and summer can

Reenactment Clothing

Historical reenactments are popular throughout the Midwest. Examples include "The Mountain Man Rendezvous" in Minnesota, Lewis and Clark reenactments in Missouri, and Civil War reenactments in all of the midwestern states. "Festival Retailing" has become a successful business as catalogs and vendors provide reenactors with the clothing and accessories necessary to take part in events. Many reenactors make their own clothing and accessories, paying strict attention to authenticity as they copy period dress. Reenactment clothing transforms contemporary dentists, office workers, insurance salesmen, and mechanics into nineteenth-century farmwives, ruffian canalboatmen, intrepid trappers, and Yankee and Rebel Civil War soldiers.

often spot outdoor weddings whose participants sport "old country" finery. Japanese brides, faces powdered, hair lacquered, arrayed in beautiful kimonos, elevated on high-heeled wooden sandals, marry equally natty grooms in front of festively garbed guests during cherry blossom season in Chicago and Minneapolis, for example. Vietnamese American brides in cheogsams, the colorful split to the waist dress worn over white trousers, pose for portraits with their extended families.

Ethnic festivals have become big business in the Midwest because they attract so many tourists, a fact recognized by The Costumer's Manifesto, a web site (costumers.org) that offers information and advice on clothing of virtually every ethnic group in the United States, with links to organizations such as the Greek-American Society. Here festival participants can find books, illustrations, and commercial sources for ethnic dress. So common are Steuben Day parades and Oktoberfests that the Indiana German Heritage Society offers detailed information on what to wear for those invited to a German festival. According to the Society, the conventional images are "the stereotypical Bavarian Dirndl for the gals and white shirt and Lederhosen for the guys." These are just "costumes," whereas authentic German dress, or "tracht," reflects the actual heimat, or regional home, of the wearer. Variations in dresses, trousers, hats, bonnets, and vests abound, and participants choosing their outfits should be guided by their research and their budgets; the important thing is to affirm one's heritage.[23]

That principle motivates most midwestern ethnic groups. On Syttende Mai at Stoughton, Wisconsin, the largest Norwegian Independence Day (May 17) celebration held outside of Norway, the city honors its Norwegian roots with parades, folk dancing, quilt shows, Norwegian foods, and Norwegian costumes. Male revelers don knitted caps and embroided jackets closed with brightly colored belts. The women's more elaborate costumes feature a long dress, usually blue, over which is layered a full-length red and white apron embroidered with Norwegian symbols, the whole ensemble surmounted by a high, fringed, circular headdress tied in place with gay ribbons. In New Glarus, Wisconsin, women clad in modified dirndls, long-sleeved dresses, yellow aprons, and fanlike headdresses gaze approvingly at the leather suspenders and mountaineer shorts of male yodellers celebrating the heritage of "America's Little Switzerland." Pulaski Day parades in Polish American communities such as Cleveland, or in the annual Polish Fest in Milwaukee or the Polish Easter in South Bend, Indiana, feature marchers dressed in embroidered tunics and caps, often led, somewhat incongruously, by Police Department Emerald Society bands, whose bagpipers wear Irish kilts. Swirling skirts, serapes, and sombreros highlight dances at the Cinco de Mayo celebration in Milwaukee and other cities. The market generated by large numbers of Hispanics throughout the region has made Urban Latino shoes "cool" for mainstream midwesterners as well; popular brands are Queremos Rock!, Havanna Knight, LaLa Feminista, and Maria Me.

Similarly, the street wear of African American musicians has led to widespread adoption of hip-hop and rap fashions such as baggy jeans and untied sneakers, which can be seen on youthful whites and blacks in clubs throughout the Midwest, just as dashikis took hold back in the 1960s and 1970s. Indianapolis has put historical markers at the site of Madame C.J. Walker's cosmetics business, once the largest African American–owned enterprise in the United States. Walker (nee Sarah Breedlove, 1867–1919) invented hair straighteners and skin lighteners for a market shaped by racial discrimination; as is so often the case, yesterday's embarrassment is today's vogue.

CONTEMPORARY REGIONAL FASHION

The contemporary fashion scene in the Midwest is much like that of the rest of the country, primarily because television and the movies have helped to homogenize clothing styles, even as they foreground celebrities whose fans emulate their clothing, hairstyles, and postures. Mass production of clothes has made possible many choices, and discount stores have brought them within the range of virtually everyone. Although some urban socialites shop for clothes in New York, Paris, and Milan, they rarely have to travel further than the nearest mega-mall, where most of the nation's upscale chains have branches. Similarly, up-to-date hairdos, brand-name cosmetics, and exotic fabrics are within the reach of almost everybody; it is the rare midwestern town without both a beauty parlor and a dry cleaner. Entrepreneurs cater to fashion extremes. Tattoo and piercing parlors and "goth"

Advertisement for Madam C. J. Walker hair products for African Americans, 1920. Courtesy Library of Congress.

(gothic styles manifested in clothing borrowed from characters in horror movies) shops and barbers versed in African American and punk trends cluster on the campus drags of midwestern colleges and universities, and on most of those campuses Halloween is a major occasion for dressing up.

Available choices aside, the inexorable trend is toward a casualness that erases traditional clothing markers of class. Many midwesterners think of Americans on the two coasts as unnecessarily concerned with style, and dress instead for comfort and productivity. They seem inclined to shop for larger wardrobes of cheaper clothes rather than invest as their parents might have in a few expensive outfits. That would appear to be the case even with the large number of women who have entered the workforce. Such women now have more outfits, it seems, though not necessarily enough leisure to wear them, and those garments seem more and more all-purpose. In some cases, strong regional conservatism acts as a brake on extravagance and daring. (Perhaps there is just a touch of Victoria's Secret escapism on weekends; the chain is now owned by The Limited of Columbus, Ohio.) Yet even among the more liberal, the most popular clothes would appear to be slacks and shorts, T-shirts and blouses, sweaters and sandals. Soccer moms show up at their children's games in the same ski jackets they wore to work. Men and women routinely wear jeans not only to hardware stores and schools, but also to restaurants, concerts, and churches. Only in the downtown office districts of major cities such as Chicago, Minneapolis, Springfield, and Cedar Rapids is professional business wear to be found on significant display. To be sure, ultra-casual ensembles betray subtle semiotics read differently by young and old, male and female, conservatives and innovators: what appears sloppy to a parent may hold nuanced meaning for a child trying to fit in with her peers. Stylistic preferences have always conveyed messages, but they may be less obvious in a mass culture.

Just how much midwestern sensibilities have contributed to this leveling of traditional fashion sense is unclear. Indifference to elegance is not quite the same as an impulse toward democracy. It does seem plausible, however, that midwesterners dress down because they like to, and if they justify their tastes in terms of the region's valorization of equality and practicality, then that explanation will have to do.

RESOURCE GUIDE

Printed Sources

Agins, Teri. *The End of Fashion: How Marketing Changed the Clothing Business Forever.* New York: First Quill, 2000.

Amneus, Cynthia, et al. *A Separate Sphere: Dressmakers in Cincinnati's Golden Age, 1877–1922.* Lubbock: Texas Tech University Press, 2003.

Batterberry, Michael, and Ariane Batterberry. *Mirror, Mirror: A Social History of Fashion.* New York: Holt, Rinehart, and Winston, 1977.

Benson, Susan. *Counter Cultures: Saleswomen, Managers, and Customers in American Department Stores, 1890–1940.* Urbana: University of Illinois Press, 1986.

Cunningham, Patricia A., and Gayle Strege. *Fashioning the Future: Our Future from Our Past.* Columbus: Department of Consumer and Textile Sciences, Ohio State University, 1996.

De la Haye, Amy, and Elizabeth Wilson, eds. *Defining Dress as Object, Meaning, and Identity.* Manchester, UK: Manchester University Press, 1999.

Dress: The Journal of the Costume Society of America. Published since 1975 by the Costume Society of America, www.costumesocietyamerica.com/dress.htm.

Earle, Alice Morse. *Two Centuries of Costume in America: 1620–1820.* 1903. Reprint. 2 vols. New York: Dover, 1970.

Filene, Adele, and Polly Willman. *The Costume Society of America Bibliography: 1974/1979.* N.p.: Costume Society of America, n.d.

Galloway, William Albert. *Old Chillicothe: Shawnee and Pioneer History: Conflicts and Romances of the Northwest Territory.* Xenia, OH: Buckeye Press, 1934.

Hall, Lee. *Common Threads: A Parade of American Clothing.* Boston: Little, Brown, 1992.

Hartman, Sheryl. *Indian Clothing of the Great Lakes, 1740–1840.* Rev. ed. Liberty, VT: Eagle's View Publications, 2000.

Ley, Sandra. *Fashion for Everyone: The Story of Ready-to-Wear, 1870–1970's.* New York: Scribner's, 1975.

Martin, Richard. *The St. James Fashion Encyclopedia: A Survey of Style from 1945 to the Present.* Detroit: Visible Ink Press, 1997.

McIntosh, John. *The Origin of the North American Indians.* New York: Nafis & Cornish, 1843.

Mulvey, Kate. *Decades of Beauty: The Changing Image of Women, 1890s–1990s.* New York: Facts on File, 1998.

Olian, JoAnne. *Everyday Fashions of the Fifties as Pictured in Sears Catalogs.* New York: Dover Publications, 2002.

———. *Everyday Fashions of the Forties as Pictured in Sears Catalogs*. New York: Dover Publications, 1992.

———. *Everyday Fashions of the Sixties as Pictured in Sears Catalogs*. New York: Dover Publications, 1999.

Oliver, Valerie Burnham. *Fashion and Costume in American Popular Culture: A Reference Guide*. Westport, CT: Greenwood Press, 1996.

Racinet, Albert. *The Historical Encyclopedia of Costumes*. New York: Facts on File, 1988.

Rafert, Stewart. *The Miami Indians of Indiana: A Persistent People 1654–1994*. Indianapolis: Indiana Historical Society, 1996.

Ribeiro, Aileen. *Dress and Morality*. New York: Holmes and Meier, 1986.

Rowley, Laura. *On Target: How the World's Hottest Retailer Hit a Bull's-Eye*. New York: John Wiley, 2003.

Schreier, Barbara. *Becoming American Women: Clothing and the Jewish Immigrant Experience, 1880–1920*. Chicago: Chicago Historical Society, 1994.

Shaw, William Harlan. *American Men's Wear, 1861–1982*. Baton Rouge, LA: Oracle Press, 1982.

Twyan, Robert W. *History of Marshall Field and Company, 1852–1906*. Philadelphia: University of Pennsylvania Press, 1954.

Web Sites

Carhartt, Inc.
P.O. Box 600
5750 Mercury Drive
Dearborn, MI 48126
Phone: (800) 833-3118
www.carhartt.com

Folkwear Patterns
2000 Riverside Drive #3
Asheville, NC 28804
Phone: (888) 200-9099
Email: info@folkwear.com
www.Folkwear.com

Folkwear offers patterns that are reproduced from authentic historical and ethnic garments.

The Merchandise Mart Chicago
Suite 470
The Merchandise Mart
Chicago, IL 60654
Phone: (800) 677-6278
www.merchandisemart.com/mmart/merchmart.html

The Chicago Merchandise Mart hosts fashion shows in conjunction with trade shows such as "STYLEMAX" (http://www.mmart.com/stylemax/) or "The National Bridal Market" (www.merchandisemart.com/nationalbridalmarket/) show.

National Public Radio
635 Massachusetts Avenue, NW
Washington, DC 20001
Phone: (202) 513-3232
www.npr.org

NPR has broadcast a program called "Present at the Creation: Overalls."

Sears, Roebuck, and Co.
3333 Beverly Road
B5-336B
Hoffman Estates, IL 60179
Email: invrel@sears.com
Phone: (800) 349-4358
www.sears.com

Videos/Films

Clothing Workers Strike of 1910. Chicago: The Illinois Labor Historical Society, 1979.

Institutes and Museums

Cincinnati Art Museum
953 Eden Park Drive
Cincinnati, OH 45202
Phone: (513) 721-ARTS
www.cincinnatiartmuseum.org/separatesphere/index.html

The Cincinnati Art Museum features an exhibit on "A Separate Sphere: Dressmakers in Cincinnati's Golden Age, 1877–1922."

Eiteljorg Museum of American Indians and Western Art
500 West Washington Street
Indianapolis, IN 46204
Phone: (317) 636-9378
www.eiteljorg.org

Historic Costume and Textiles Collection
Ohio State University
College of Human Ecology
The Geraldine Schottenstein Wing
175 Campbell Hall
1787 Neil Avenue
Columbus, OH 43210
Email: costume@osu.edu
Phone: (614) 292-3090

Human Ecology Collection
The Education, Human Ecology, Psychology and Social Work Library
The Ohio State University
110 Sullivant Hall
1813 North High Street
Columbus, Ohio 43210
Leta Hendricks, Human Ecology Bibliographer/Librarian
Email: hendricks.3@osu.edu
Phone: (614) 292-2075
Fax: (614) 292-8012
www.hec.ohio-state.edu/hendrick/

Indianapolis Museum of Art
4000 Michigan Road
Indianapolis, IN 46208-3326
Phone: (317) 920-2660
www.ima-art.org/

The Indianapolis Museum of Art features permanent collections of African, American, Asian, and European textiles and costumes.

The School of the Art Institute of Chicago
37 South Wabash
Chicago, IL 60603-3103
Email: studenthelp@artic.edu
Phone: (312) 899-5100
www.artic.edu/saic/art/

The School of the Art Institute of Chicago features an annual fashion show.

The Truman Presidential Museum & Library
500 W. U.S. Highway 24
Independence, MO 64050
Phone: (816) 268-8200 or (800) 833-1225
www.trumanlibrary.org.

Western Reserve Historical Society
10825 East Boulevard
Cleveland, OH 44106-1777
Phone: (216) 721-5722 Ext.232
Fax: (216) 721-0645
www.wrhs.org

Western Reserve Historical Society has an exhibit on maternity clothes from 1830 to the present.

Organizations

Costume Society of America
P.O. Box 73
Earleville, MD 21919
Email: national.office@costumesocietyamerica.com
www.costumesocietyamerica.com/welcome/

International Textile and Apparel Association
P.O. Box 1360
Monument, CO 80132
Email: info@itaaonline.org
www.itaaonline.org

Textile Society of America
P.O. Box 70
Earleville, MD 21919-0070
Email: tsa@dol.net
Phone: (410) 275-2329
http://textilesociety.org/

The Textile Society of America, Inc. provides an international forum for the exchange and dissemination of information about textiles worldwide, from artistic, cultural, economic, historic, political, social, and technical perspectives.

FILM AND THEATER

Rodney Hill

The powerful antiwar song, "With God on Our Side," by the great midwestern poet Bob Dylan (born Robert Allen Zimmerman in Duluth, Minnesota) points up a couple of key contradictions about the Midwest and our culturally inflected ideas of it. Traditionally, midwestern settings in theater and film have been employed to evoke instantaneously certain "core American values," including Christian morality—more often than not of the Protestant variety. Against such mythologizing, Dylan employs irony in calling his country "the Midwest" and in juxtaposing man-made "law" with the eternal notion of "God." The sociocultural landscape of the United States is as varied as its topography, with progressive havens not only on the two coasts but also in college towns across the country, offset by bastions of conservatism in the South and the Midwest, as well as in small towns on the coasts. Thus, there is no singular "American" set of values (indeed, not even a monolithic "midwestern" ethos), apart from the fundamentals laid out in the Constitution. It is also ironic that the powerful media of motion pictures and theater have helped to define and mythologize the "American experience"—especially during the twentieth century—largely by way of midwestern stereotypes, despite the strong ties of both media to the East and West coasts.

Typically, when one thinks of American film, California immediately springs to mind, for Hollywood is one of the world's capitals of filmmaking. For those who prefer the more "arty" variety of American film, New York is an important center, where graduates of New York University and Columbia University offer alternatives to the Hollywood mainstream and where "boutique" distributors like Wellspring and Kino bring the best international films to American screens. Still, the level of film activity outside these major cultural centers has increased steadily in the past few decades, not only in terms of specialized exhibitors, festivals, and "small," independent productions but also the making of big studio films. The Midwest has not been left out of these growing trends, as we shall see.

From the very birth of the cinema in the 1890s, the Midwest has provided locales for shooting films of various stripes, including early, short "slices of life" as well as fictional films. Furthermore, even during the heyday of the studio system, when Hollywood held a virtual monopoly on American film production, the midwestern heartland was a perennial backdrop for stories involving idealized depictions of Americana. However, singling out a distinctly midwestern influence can be tricky, for what seems to be important in these films is the depiction of small-town or rural America. Nonetheless, for purposes of conciseness and focus, we will confine ourselves to the films that deal specifically with the midwestern states of Illinois, Indiana, Iowa, Michigan, Minnesota, Missouri, Ohio, and Wisconsin. This chapter examines some of the more common trends in those representations and how they have changed in recent years.

As far as the theater is concerned, even today the New York stage holds sway in terms of "legitimate" productions. Typically, in most other U.S. cities, the biggest theatrical events are usually touring productions of Broadway shows. Still, as early as the 1830s, midwestern cities like Chicago were developing theatrical identities of their own, with varying degrees of success. And owing partly to the often overlooked ethnic diversity to be found in the Midwest, alternative theatrical practices have been an important cultural force in the region for more than a century.

FILM: BEGINNINGS

In the early days of cinema, from the 1890s until about 1910, the center of the film business in the United States was New York City, but the films themselves were being shot all over the country. Most of these early, short films have been lost, and others survive primarily in archives, not readily accessible. It is therefore quite difficult to make very far-reaching generalizations about depictions of the Midwest in early cinema, but thanks to the efforts of the American Film Institute, we do at least have access to titles and some descriptions of the early films shot *in* the Midwest. Most of these films are "actualities"—that is, scenes of events taking place in the real world, usually not staged for the camera—divided here into a number of categories, according to their general subject matter: street scenes; scenic landscapes; political celebrities; sports and leisure; technology and industry, including agriculture; civic pride and institutions, including the military; and cultural events and the arts. A few early examples of fictional, narrative shorts were also shot in the Midwest.

Film historian Tom Gunning argues persuasively that actuality films and narratives in the early period have more in common than this rather bipolar, seemingly mutually exclusive division might suggest. Gunning suggests that early film was primarily a "cinema of attractions," more akin to fairground spectacle than to older narrative forms such as the theater and the novel (or to later, more sophisticated documentary forms).[1] Certainly, the "cinema of attractions" is evident in each category mentioned here, for these films offered audiences (particularly those in more isolated, rural areas) stimulating views of people, places, and things that they might never have seen otherwise. Indeed, reading through some of the descriptions of these films, one can imagine a carnival barker hawking the exhibitions: "See! The Prince of Prussia visits Chicago! See! World championship boxing match!" and so on.

Street scenes from the Midwest generally depict the hustle and bustle of city life, typically at busy intersections or in crowded shopping districts. An exemplar in this category is *View of State Street*, shot in Chicago in 1903. The distributor's catalog describes "this famous thoroughfare, as viewed from a street car. . . . This picture takes in both sides of the street and shows the throng going and coming, the people crossing the streets, the various sky-scrapers, [horse] teams, the immense stores, the elevated railroad and the famous dead man's curve." A few films depict the more picturesque, serene side of life in midwestern cities, such as *Lincoln Park*, shot in Chicago in 1900, which shows "the most beautiful part of the park," shot from a moving automobile. Chicago did not have a monopoly in this category, as is illustrated in the June 1900 film, *Public Square, Cleveland*, which offered a "panoramic view of a busy spot in one of America's inland cities."[2]

Apart from midwestern cityscapes, some early films also showcased the natural, *scenic beauty* to be found in the region. *Cuyahoga Gorge*, a 1901 film from the American Mutoscope and Biograph Co. depicts a panoramic view near Cleveland, as seen along the line of the Northern Ohio Traction Company. Another film, *On the Cleveland and Eastern Railway* (1900), shows "an interesting railroad panorama through a section of picturesque country in Ohio." Similarly, in 1903 *The Dells of Wisconsin* offered "another panoramic view full of life and action" of an area that still draws the tourist trade, some hundred years later.

Midwestern sporting life in these early films ranges from the breathtakingly gripping to the quotidian. A November 1900 film shot in Chicago, *Gans-McGovern Fight*, was billed by its distributor as the only motion picture then on the market depicting a genuine prize fight, "and the only film which represents the Brooklyn Terror, Terrence McGovern, actually engaged in one of his most famous fights." Offering a different sort of spectacular appeal, the film *A Hot Time on the Bathing Beach* (c. 1901) showed the famous Alaska Beach near Chicago. The Selig catalog description promises "for a bathing and swimming picture this is the real thing; lots of ladies and gentlemen in swimming with their real bathing suits on." A series of films shot in Missouri in 1904 depicts local sporting endeavors; titles include *Basket Ball, Missouri Valley College*, *Gymnasium Work/Physical Culture*, and *Kindergarten Ball Game/Kindergarten Dance*. Shot in St. Louis in 1904, *Panorama of Race Track Crowd* offered "a splendid view of the great throng who witnessed the running of the World's Fair Handicap."

Indeed, the World's Fair of 1904, the Louisiana Purchase Exposition in St. Louis, was a cultural watershed in the Midwest (note the 1943 Hollywood film, *Meet Me in St. Louis*, discussed later), and quite a few films document the sights and festivities of the event. For example, *Parade of Floats, St. Louis Exposition* was described as "a splendid picture showing a parade of decorated floats, representing various nations on the Grand Lagoon . . . the Cascades, Festival Hall and its picturesque surroundings in the background. . . . The floats come very near to the camera and a very fair view of the occupants is given."

Similarly, a series of circus films came out of Cincinnati in 1900, including *A Four-Horse Circus Act*, *A Somersault on Horseback*, and *Water Babies* (in which two toddlers, aged two and four, row about in miniature boats). The "famous Milwaukee Carnival" of 1903 was also memorialized on film, with such short subjects as *Floral Parade* and *Fools Parade*, which "shows the great Bon Ami club of Milwaukee, as they appeared in their outlandish costumes."

Civic pride informed early midwestern films showcasing local clubs and groups, perhaps to foster local self-esteem, but also to promote themselves to outsiders. For example, at least three separate films were released focusing on an 1896 parade in Canton, Ohio (hometown of William McKinley), featuring the local Americus Club, the Sound Money Club, and the Elkins Cadets, respectively. *County Democracy*, from 1898, features some of Chicago's top political leaders of the day marching in a parade; other films similarly show off that city's police and fire departments. In addition, films of *military drills and parades* seem to have constituted an especially popular genre of the period.

Another sort of boosterism is evident in the numerous early films devoted to *agriculture*, which remained an economic mainstay of the region during this era. It was not the family farm, however, that received the most attention from the cinema, but rather the business of agriculture and livestock. Dozens of films depict the famous Chicago stockyards, for example, including such titles as *Sheep Run*, *Chicago Stockyards* (1897), *A Texas Steer* (1898), and *Chicago Fat Stock Parade* (1901).

A fascination with *industry and modern technology* marks a number of films shot in midwestern locales. Railroads and trains captivated audiences from the very beginning of cinema, as evidenced by the popularity of the 1895 French film *Arrivée d'un train à la Ciotat* (*Arrival of a Train*) and the many knockoffs produced in its wake. In a way, the railroad (still a relatively new phenomenon at the time) is an ideal icon of modernity, as it embodies the power of technology to reshape the ways people live and communities interact, and these notions come across in quite a few films. For example, *Giant Coal Dumper* (1897) "shows how a full carload of coal is loaded . . . every thirty seconds at the great Erie Railroad Docks" in Cleveland, Ohio. The sheer delight that many of these films seem to take in the thoroughly modern phenomenon of the railroad is epitomized in a 1903 catalog description of the film *Pioneer Limited*:

> a most wonderful train . . . the fine train of the C. M. & St. P. at Morton Grove [Illinois], traveling at the rate of 78 miles per hour; you see it in the distance when suddenly, with a swish and a swirl, it is past; then you see a team crossing the track, being led by teamsters, when—look out—here comes another train on the next track, going the opposite direction; will it hit the wagon? No, it is a very narrow escape.

This rather explicit confrontation between modernity (the trains) and older ways of doing things (the mule team) surely was not lost on audiences of the time.

Films of *celebrities* in the Midwest during the early period take place, as one might expect, almost exclusively in big cities like Chicago. What might be initially surprising to a modern-day reader, however, is that the "celebrities" in these films seem almost always to be politicos. (Certainly, thanks to phonograph parlors, middle-class midwesterners would have been familiar with musical stars such as Enrico Caruso, but films depicting such personalities were usually shot in New York, not the Midwest.)

Probably the biggest political celebrity of the time with a midwestern connection was President William McKinley. A number of films from 1896 document parades and rallies in McKinley's hometown of Canton, Ohio, during his first campaign for the presidency. Later, after McKinley's assassination, every American film company offered extensive coverage of the funeral proceedings in Canton, with perhaps the most thorough series coming from Edison, in seven separate films that could be shown in sequence, with "dissolving effects" between each film: *Arrival of McKinley's Funeral Train at Canton, Ohio, Taking President McKinley's Body from Train . . . , President Roosevelt at the Canton Station, Panoramic View of the President's House . . . , Funeral Leaving the President's House and Church . . .* , and so on.

Similarly, quite a few short films document a visit to Chicago by another political celebrity, Prince Henry of Prussia, in 1902–1903. For example, *Prince Henry at Lincoln's Monument* shows His Highness, accompanied by Robert Lincoln, a Chicago attorney and descendant of the late president, both paying their respects at the monument. Another film, *Parade through Chicago Streets*, promises "a wonderfully clear picture of the prince and unquestionably the best [that] has been secured from any camera."

Most of these films seem to emphasize the pageantry, pomp, and/or solemnity of the occasion rather than the midwestern locations per se. One interesting exception deals with nonpolitical (indeed nonhuman) "celebrity": *Deadwood Coach* (1903) depicts the famous coach that ran through the Midwest in the days of the western expansion, as it was drawn through the streets of Chicago during Buffalo Bill's Wild West Parade.

The many early actualities (depictions of real events with little or no narrative structure, presented for the sheer fascination of the subject matter) should not suggest that narrative films were not being produced during the early period. Indeed, they were. Film scholars generally agree that between 1903 and 1906, narratives overtook actualities in American cinema. One likely explanation for this shift has to do with simple economics: exhibitors required a steady supply of new films, and short, staged narratives were far cheaper and easier to make than actualities (which required travel to specific locales). However, the bulk of narrative filmmaking in the United States at the time took place in and around New York—hence the focus here on actuality films made in the Midwest.

Still, a few examples of narrative filmmaking in the Midwest may be found during this early period. An 1898 film from Chicago, *Stealing a Ham*, straddles the sometimes blurred line between fiction and nonfiction. The film's depiction of a "thief" pilfering a ham from the back of a cart was actually shot in the yards of Swift & Co. The yard watchman witnesses the crime and pursues and captures the thief. Another film from the same year, *Street Fight and Arrest*, is more clearly "an arranged scene worked out very effectively," in which two "rowdies" fight in the streets of Chicago, drawing a crowd of onlookers. The police arrive, subdue the combatants, and cart them off to jail. Narratives shot in midwestern locations toward the end of the early period include *Lost in the Soudan*, a Tom Mix picture from 1910, shot in Dune Park, Indiana; and *County Fair* (1910) from Galena, Illinois. Unfortunately, as is the case with much of early cinema, very little further information is available on these titles.

THE CLASSIC HOLLYWOOD PERIOD: 1910s–EARLY 1960s

It may seem a bit odd to group American films from the 1910s through the early 1960s together. However, by the 1910s narrative had become the dominant form in American cinema, and the movie business already had begun to mature into a vertically integrated industry, with standard modes of production and stylistic norms. In their landmark book, *The Classical Hollywood Cinema*, David Bordwell, Janet Staiger, and Kristin Thompson show that these conventions remained fairly consistent for several decades, despite technical changes such as the coming of sound, color, and wide-screen.[3]

Furthermore, when one considers (as far as possible)[4] the films depicting midwestern life made during these decades, certain story patterns emerge that are not tied to particular years or technical advances. Some of these narrative tendencies include films depicting a simple, "wholesome" way of life; all-American sports figures; contrasts between rural and city life; the world of industry and enterprise to be found in big cities like Chicago; the corresponding urban underworld; Civil War dramas; tales of legendary characters; other historical films; and genres such as social-problem films and family melodramas. Of course, many of these tendencies continue to the present day. Thus, although this section focuses primarily on films made between the silent era and the early 1960s, it also includes a few recent examples.

"A Simpler Time and Place"

Films that characterize the Midwest as essentially a simple, wholesome place seem to have had their heyday during the 1930s and 1940s. Often these films take place in some unspecified past, when life was "simpler" and "more innocent"—in other words, a fondly (mis)remembered time and place that probably never existed, certainly not as Hollywood depicted it. One obvious explanation is that perhaps such films provided escape from the woes of the Great Depression and then from World War II. Films of this ilk abound, offering an idyllic look at small-town American life, as in *It's a Wonderful Life* (1946); but here we will limit ourselves to films that specify midwestern locations for their versions of *Anytown, USA*.

One prime example is one of Walt Disney's lesser-known feature films, *So Dear to My Heart* (1949). It tells the story of a young boy named Jeremiah (Bobby Driscoll), who lives on an Indiana farm with his grandmother (Beulah Bondi) and uncle (Burl Ives). Jeremiah dreams of taking his black lamb, Danny, to the state fair. His grandmother tries to dissuade him because there is not much demand for black wool. But with the encouragement of his uncle and some animated animals, Jeremiah decides to follow his heart.[5]

Disney himself, it should be noted, was a midwesterner, born in Chicago and schooled at the Kansas City Art Institute, where he met fellow animator Ub Iwerks. Together they formed a company and made their first films in Kansas City. No doubt his midwestern roots informed Disney's world-view, which has attained larger-than-life status through the hundreds of films, television programs, and other properties created by the Walt Disney Company, not to mention the theme parks, which themselves offer a sort of idealized "midwestern" experience.

Another film featuring child protagonists is *Our Vines Have Tender Grapes* (1945), written by Dalton Trumbo. Seven-year-old Selma and five-year-old Arnold live on neighboring farms in Wisconsin, where Selma has been put in charge of looking after a newborn calf. Aside from a couple of budding romances among the adults, the biggest event in the simple world of the film seems to be the building of a new barn at a nearby farm.

Similarly, in *Home in Indiana* (1944) a troubled lad is sent to live with his aunt and uncle on a horse farm in Indiana. Though initially he is not happy about the arrangement, his love of horses and his plans to race a young colt give his life meaning. He also finds romance with a tomboyish local girl who shares his love for horses.

Set in Iowa, the Rodgers and Hammerstein screen musical, *State Fair*—first filmed in 1933 (with Janet Gaynor and Will Rogers) and again in 1945 and 1962[6]—revolves around a farming family and their participation in the eponymous fair in Des Moines. Dad enters one of his prize hogs in competition, while Mom bakes one of her famous mince-meat pies for the baking contest. Their son enters the auto races, and both he and his sister meet promising new flames at the fair.

In the comedy *Earthworm Tractors* (1936), another light-hearted look at life down on the farm, Joe E. Brown plays a tractor salesman in Peoria, Illinois. Because of his total lack of knowledge about farming and tractors, he has a particularly tough time selling to the grouchy lumberman Johnson. But inspired by Johnson's beautiful daughter, he perseveres.

A more somber tone permeates *Happy Land* (1943), a mostly forgotten film in which Don Ameche plays Lew Marsh, a pharmacist in a small Iowa town. When Lew learns that his son, Rusty, has died in the war, the ghost of Lew's father appears and takes him on a journey into the past. Together, they relive Rusty's childhood years through his early adulthood, and "Gramps" finally reassures Lew that "Rusty died a good death." While seemingly offering consolation to audiences facing the actual or potential loss of their young loved ones to the war in Europe, at least one commentator has suggested an underlying, critical tone in the film.[7] This is not surprising when one considers that screenwriter Dalton Trumbo went on to write the powerful antiwar novel, *Johnny Got His Gun* (1939), about a young man who is rendered paralyzed, blind, deaf, and mute by his war injuries.

Another sophisticated, rather dark approach to the "simple life" of the American Midwest comes to us from one of the few true giants of the American cinema, Orson Welles. Himself a midwesterner (from Kenosha, Wisconsin), Welles chose a midwestern family drama for his second feature film, *The Magnificent Ambersons* (1942). Based on Indiana native Booth Tarkington's novel, the film chronicles the downfall of an aristocratic midwestern family at the turn of the twentieth century; but on a larger scale the film mourns the passing of a way of life. While *Ambersons* avoids the sort of whitewashing of the past evident in some other films cited here, it does suggest convincingly that many aspects of life *were* simpler and perhaps more desirable than in the present day. The automobile acts as a central metaphor in the story, not merely for technological change but for the shifts in morality and social interaction brought about by such change. In one of the film's most memorable vignettes, a horse-drawn streetcar pulls up in front of a large house and waits patiently while the woman who lives there comes down to catch it; while the car waits, the passengers disembark to stretch their legs, light their pipes, and so on. In voice-over, Welles as the narrator reminisces fondly about such an era, when people seemed to have the time for such leisurely politesse, noting the irony that as modes of transportation get faster, we seem to have less time to spare and less patience for each other.

Rarely has midwestern life been depicted in a more sardonic fashion than in the works of Mark Twain; film adaptations of his novels date back well into the silent period. One source cites a 1907 film of *Tom Sawyer*, but if such a film existed it would not have been longer than about ten to twelve minutes, the norm for narratives at the time. A 1917 version of *Tom Sawyer* features Jack Pickford, younger brother of Mary Pickford and a movie star in his own right. Director William Desmond Taylor followed up with a sequel the next year, entitled *Tom and Huck*; then in 1920 Taylor directed a feature film version of *Huckleberry Finn*. All told, Twain's *The Adventures of Tom Sawyer* has been adapted to film at least eight times, as has *Adventures of Huckleberry Finn*.

One of the clearest examples in film of the "pure, simple, midwestern life" comes in *The Music Man* (1962), starring Robert Preston and Shirley Jones. Preston originated the role of Professor Harold Hill on Broadway in 1957, in Meredith Wilson's stage musical, which ran for 1375 performances.[8] Based in part on Wilson's own childhood experiences in Iowa, *The Music Man* relates the story of con-man Hill's arrival in the small town of River City, Iowa. There he intends to run his usual scam of selling musical instruments and band uniforms to all the boys in town, under the pretext of forming a boys' band. After collecting the money, and before the merchandise arrives, Hill plans to leave and go on to the next town, where he can repeat the same swindle. Marian (Shirley Jones), the local librarian, discovers Hill's plot; but she does not expose him because she has fallen in love

Scene from the film *The Music Man* (1962). Photofest.

with him. Although Hill's initial plans do not include romance, he ultimately decides to stay with Marian in River City and face the consequences of his actions. One of Hill's early musical numbers warns that there is "trouble, right here in River City," but the film and play make it fairly clear that the only real trouble has been brought about by Hill himself. It seems that the worst thing to be exposed in River City is the gossip and underlying hypocrisy that no doubt plague any town, small or large.

"This Sporting Life"

Hand-in-hand with the often pure, down-home portrayal of the Midwest in classical Hollywood films is the valorization of sports heroes. Such clichés as "Mom, apple pie, and baseball" are the stuff Hollywood dreams are made on, and a significant number of films set in the Midwest deal with sports and sportsmen.

Perhaps the archetypal example lies in *Knute Rockne All-American* (1940), with Pat O'Brien as the legendary coach of Notre Dame's "fighting Irish." This biopic, set largely in Indiana and Chicago, contains the quintessential pep-talk, in which the title character urges the team to play this game "for the Gipper" (Ronald Reagan). Interestingly, the film also employs a number of patriotic symbols, including the Statue of Liberty and West Point Military Academy.

More sports heroics are to be found in *The Kid from Cleveland* (1949), in which the real-life Cleveland Indians (including legendary Hank Greenberg) come to the aid of a troubled young fan who poses as an orphan in order to get close to the team. Forty years later, the Cleveland Indians once again figure prominently in the plot of a Hollywood film, but this time in an entirely fictionalized capacity, in the comedy *Major League* (1989). In that film, the team's owner dies, leaving the Indians in the hands of a young widow who hates Cleveland and wants to move the team to Miami. The only way she can do so, however, is through an escape clause stipulating that the team may move from Cleveland if annual attendance drops below 800,000; so the new owner tries to put together the worst team possible, with none too surprising results.

Oddly enough, one of the more melodramatic baseball pictures of the 1940s is based on real life. *The Stratton Story* (1949) has James Stewart playing Chicago White Sox pitcher Monty Stratton, whose record-breaking career in the major leagues came to an abrupt end after a hunting accident cost him his right leg. Despite this grave setback, Stratton continued to pitch in the minor leagues for several years. Stratton's story is parodied briefly in Woody Allen's *Radio Days* (1987), in which a radio announcer tells of a pitcher who first lost a leg, then an arm, and finally his eyesight, but who continued pitching despite all obstacles.

The notorious Chicago White Sox team of 1919, accused of throwing the World Series, informs two baseball pictures of the late 1980s. In *Field of Dreams* (1989) an Iowa corn farmer (Kevin Costner) hears a voice that inspires him to build a baseball diamond in the middle of his cornfield. There, the ghosts of "Shoeless" Joe Jackson and the other seven "Black Sox" members appear to him. John Sayles's *Eight Men Out* (1988) offers a dramatization of the events surrounding the "Black Sox" scandal, casting the human drama in the context of labor relations and organized crime.

Other baseball-related films set in the Midwest include: *It Happens Every Spring*

(1949), in which Ray Milland invents a baseball that is repelled by wooden bats; *Fireman, Save My Child* (1932), with Joe E. Brown as a fireman, inventor, and local baseball show-off; and Joe E. Brown again in *Elmer the Great* (1933), in which the title character is reluctant to leave his hometown of Gentryville, Indiana, despite the recruiting efforts of the Chicago Cubs.

In addition to football and baseball, auto racing figures prominently in several films set in the Midwest, chiefly at the famous Indianapolis Speedway. In *The Crowd Roars*, a 1932 film by Howard Hawks, racing champion Joe Greer (James Cagney) returns to his hometown to compete in a race. When another driver is killed in the contest, Joe loses his nerve, and his brother ends up winning. As Joe's career takes a downturn, his brother's spirals upward. This film was remade scene-for-scene in 1939 as *Indianapolis Speedway*, using the same racetrack footage.

In *Speed* (1936), Terry (James Stewart) and Frank both work for an auto company in Detroit, Terry as the chief auto-tester and Frank as an engineer. The two colleagues compete for the attentions of Jane (Wendy Barrie), who works in the company's publicity department. In order to test a new carburetor that Frank has designed, they enter a car in the Indianapolis 500.

Clark Gable stars in *To Please a Lady* (1950) as a tough-ridden racecar driver who lives under a cloud of doubt after possibly having caused the death of another driver. Barbara Stanwyck co-stars as a strong-willed columnist who eventually helps him through his troubles. Other racecar dramas set in the Midwest include *Straightaway* (1933), *Red Hot Tires* (1935), written by future studio exec Dore Schary, *Road Demon* (1938), *Fever Heat* (1969), about stock-car racing in Iowa, and *Winning* (1969), in which Paul Newman must choose between his loved ones and the pursuit of his dream: winning the Indianapolis 500.

Rural/Urban Opposition

One of the most common tropes in films dealing with the Midwest is the contrast between rural or small-town America and life in the big city. Quite a few such films center on down-home protagonists who move to the city, where they face various crises, often of a moral nature. This formula goes back well into the silent era. For example, in the western, *The Money Corral* (1919), cowhand Lem Beason (William S. Hart) wins a shooting contest at a rodeo. As a result, railroad president Gregory Collins hires Beason to return to Chicago with him to take charge of security for the railroad. Once there, Beason encounters a level of criminal activity he has not known before, and he struggles not to let it get the best of him.

Similarly, *A Perfect Lady* (1918) offers the tale of a moral reformer from Kansas who goes head-to-head with sin in the burlesque halls of Chicago; and in *The Small Town Guy* (1917), the title character falls victim to a con-artist and blackmailer in Chicago. A more humorous example lies in *The Rebellious Bride* (1919), a comedy that contrasts mountain life in the Ozarks with that of St. Louis.

"Midwesterner moves to the city" became a classic American plot setup, if repetition and longevity are any indication. Betty Grable's signature film, *Pin-Up Girl* (1944), has the eponymous character leaving the small Missouri town where she has been the sweetheart of virtually every military man on the local base, heading for New York to pursue a fantasy career in the USO. In actuality, she goes into a government service job, but her vivid imagination leads her into an unlikely romance with a bandleader, as well as other complications.

Mervyn LeRoy's *Big City Blues* (1932) gives us three days in the life of an Indiana man who inherits money and heads for New York City. There he falls for a chorus girl (Joan Blondell), whom he meets through his cousin, and ends up in the wrong place at the wrong time. When a young woman is killed at a party in his hotel room, our man is the chief suspect. Similarly, in *So This Is New York* (1948), a midwestern man is dragged to New York City by his wife and sister-in-law, who have delusions of grandeur when it comes to life in the big city. There, three rather broadly drawn characters take advantage of them in one way or another: a con man, a jockey, and a rich but dubious Rudy Vallee.

A famous variant on this theme may be found in *The Great Gatsby*, in which midwesterner Nick Carraway, now living on Long Island—not exactly the big city, but populated largely by well-off city folk—becomes fascinated with his high-society neighbor, Jay Gatsby. Carraway's midwestern origins are used to underscore his initial naïveté, and his gradual disillusionment is key to the story's development, as he realizes Gatsby's possible links to organized crime. F. Scott Fitzgerald's celebrated 1925 novel was filmed at least three times, in 1926, 1949, and 1974.

Another common incarnation of this plot device is in the familiar story of the small-town girl (usually) who wants to break into show business. She gets her big chance, and moves to the big city, often New York, to pursue her dreams. Examples include: *Strike Up the Band* (1940), in which Judy Garland and Mickey Rooney dream of joining the Paul Whiteman Orchestra; *Presenting Lily Mars* (1943), also with Garland; *Sing, Baby, Sing* (1936), starring Alice Faye and set in Kansas City; *Second Fiddle* (1939); *Juke Joint* (1947); and *The Rat Race* (1960), in which a midwestern musician (Tony Curtis) tries to make it big in New York, with the help of a dance-hall girl (Debbie Reynolds) who is down on her luck. This formula, repeated often enough, arguably portrays the Midwest and small towns in general as places from which one needs to escape. Although this may be reassuring for city-dwellers, comforted by the fact that they live in the most "desirable" environs, it may also result in unfair and narrow conceptions about the Midwest, such as the well-known but perhaps exaggerated idea among New Yorkers and Californians that they are separated geographically by a vast cultural wasteland. Of course, this stereotype is no more accurate than the one that casts the Midwest as the American ideal incarnate.

The city–country contrast works the other way round in films as well, with characters from the big city finding themselves in rural or small-town midwestern settings. An early example can be found in *The Clean-Up* (1917), in which the publicity agent for a traveling burlesque troupe returns to his hometown of Weston, Illinois, in order to drum up some advance publicity for the coming show. He runs into heavy opposition from the "Purity League," until the leader of that group finally admits to having seen the show in New York. This suggests a somewhat nuanced approach to the big-city/small-town distinction in terms of morality, as the protagonist is a local boy returning home, and the small-town voice of morality seems to have been drawn to the very "evils" he decries.

In *June Bride* (1948), Linda and Carey (Bette Davis and Robert Montgomery) are editor and correspondent, respectively, for a New York women's magazine. For

The Films of Oscar Micheaux

Between 1919 and 1948, the independent African American filmmaker Oscar Micheaux (1884–1951) wrote, produced, and directed forty-four feature films in the United States. Denied many opportunities because of his color, this Metropolis, Illinois, native carefully invested the money he earned working as a shoeshine boy, farmhand, and Pullman car porter in the purchase of South Dakota farmland. As his land speculation began to pay off, he branched into writing and publishing, selling his first novel, *The Conquest* (1913), door to door in South Dakota. He wrote several detective stories, several set in Chicago. When the Lincoln Film Company tried to option his *The Homesteader* (1917), Micheaux went door to door again for capital to start the Micheaux Book and Film Company in order to make the country's first African American movie himself. Shot in Winner, South Dakota, by Micheaux's Chicago crew, *The Homesteader* (1919) made enough money to finance more films. His *Within Our Gates* (1920) attacked D. W. Griffith's *Birth of a Nation*, in part by inverting Griffith's scenes of interracial conflict. This took courage, especially since race riots had erupted across America in 1919, but Micheaux took full advantage of the controversy, learning to market his films to black audiences in much the same way he had sold his novels, by securing agreements in advance from African American theaters. Micheaux intended his films to "uplift the race" by creating a mature black cinema free of stereotypes. His characters were flawed but real; his films boldly depicted interracial romance, dealt with African American skin color bias, and exposed religious hypocrisy. On Micheaux's screen, African Americans exhibited the broad diversity and rich experience to be found in every culture. He seized on new technologies, shooting his first "talkie," *The Exile*, in 1931, and experimenting with jump cuts and novel narrative strategies. Didacticism in films such as *God's Step Children* (1938), *Lying Lips* (1939), and *The Notorious Elinor Lee* (1940) diminished his audience, but in retrospect his efforts seem to have been ahead of their time. The Oscar Micheaux Festival, held every year in Gregory, South Dakota, recognizes the kinds of talent he pioneered, as does the Oscar Micheaux Award, given annually to an independent filmmaker by the Producers' Guild of America.

an upcoming issue, they travel to Cresthill, Indiana, to interview their "bride of the month" for June. The bride's family consists of an array of small-town stock characters: the chummy grandpa who distills his own whisky, the fawning mother who is thrilled at the prospect of her daughter's becoming "famous," the bride who aspires to be a model and thus escape her small-town existence, the rebellious younger sister who votes Democrat. For their magazine feature, Linda and Carey undertake to refashion the family home, to make it more palatable to a "sophisticated" New York audience. They replace the wallpaper, the drapes, and even a bust of Julius Caesar that had been a treasured family gift, all implying none too subtly that when it comes to good taste, New York has it in spades over the midwestern "hinterlands."

Even some films made outside the dominant Hollywood studio system focused on similar themes. Such was the case with at least two films by Oscar Micheaux, the first known African American feature filmmaker. His 1919 film, *The Homesteader*, based on his own novel from 1913, deals with city life in Chicago contrasted with small-town/country life in South Dakota. Micheaux remade the film in 1931 as *The Exile*.

Industry and Enterprise

From the late nineteenth and early twentieth centuries, factories and mills have played central roles in the economies of numerous small towns and big cities alike in the Midwest. So it seems natural that this milieu would supply the backdrop for at least a few Hollywood dramas. *The Magnificent Brute* (1936) stars Victor McLaglen as Big Steve, who arrives in an Ohio town to work in a steel mill. He soon develops a rivalry with Bill Morgan, another mill worker, as they vie for the affections of a local woman. As an outsider, Steve becomes a suspect when some money (collected to help the widow of one of the mill workers) is stolen, and the town turns against him.

In *I Loved a Woman* (1933), an art student leaves Greece to run his father's meat-packing plant in Chicago. His social-climbing wife chides him for his concerns about his workers and the cleanliness of the plant's meat. He eventually sacrifices his ideals and sells tainted meat to the Army during the Spanish-American War.

An idealized vision of the "American Dream" is offered in the aptly titled *An American Romance* (1944), directed by King Vidor. Brian Donlevy plays an immigrant who works his way up from the iron mines and steel mills of Michigan to become a successful industrialist.

Another enterprise that figures prominently in films about midwestern cities, especially Chicago, is the newspaper business. *Call Northside 777* (1948) stars James Stewart as a relentless *Chicago Tribune* reporter determined to find the truth about an accused cop-killer. (See a more thorough treatment of this film in the following section.)

Based on a play by Ben Hecht, *The Front Page* (1931) centers around the professional friendship between editor Walter Burns (Adolphe Menjou) and ace reporter Hildy Johnson (Pat O'Brien). When Johnson announces he is leaving the paper to get married, Burns begins scheming to keep him on board. When Earl Williams, a convicted killer scheduled to be hanged, escapes from prison, the possibility of a major "scoop" presents itself when Williams turns up in Johnson's office. The film was remade in 1939 by Howard Hawks, in the most well-known incarnation of the story, *His Girl Friday*. That film transforms Hildy Johnson into a woman (Rosalind Russell) and adds a back-story of romance between Johnson and Burns (Cary Grant). Billy Wilder remade *The Front Page* in 1974, with Walter Matthau as Burns and Jack Lemmon as Johnson. In each of the three versions (as with *Call Northside 777*), through fierce determination the midwestern protagonist not only gets the "scoop" but also ends up saving the life of a condemned man.

The Underbelly of Urban Life

In films that focus on midwestern cities like Chicago, one of the most common and long-lived plot elements is the underworld of prostitution, drugs, organized crime, and gangsters. A notable example is *Chicago*, originally produced on the New York stage in 1926 as a satirical comedy, then revived and revamped as a stage musical by John Kander, Fred Ebb, and Bob Fosse in 1975. The second version subsequently was revived on Broadway at the turn of the twentieth-first century and adapted as a motion picture starring Renee Zellweger, Catherine Zeta-Jones, and Richard Gere in 2002. The first film version of *Chicago* appeared in 1927, a silent comedy-drama; then in 1942 another film version called *Roxie Hart* featured Ginger Rogers in the title role. *Chicago* satirizes show business, the media, and corruption in the legal and penal systems, as convicted murderers become front-page celebrities and go on to rather successful stage careers after their release from prison.

The trend of depicting the criminal element in midwestern cities dates back as early as 1916, with *The Little Girl Next Door*, a film about the connections between racketeering and the white slave trade in Chicago. According to copyright descriptions, the film was based in part on actual testimonies of women who were forced into prostitution.[9] Other examples into the 1920s include D.W. Griffith's *That Royle Girl* (1925), a film now believed to be lost. In this film, Joan Royle, a beautiful but naive model from the slums, falls for Fred Ketlar, the leader of a dance band. When Fred's estranged wife Adele is murdered, Fred is arrested and convicted of the crime; but Joan believes that the real murderer is Baretta, a gangster who was keeping Adele as his mistress.

Most famously, a cycle of crime films emerged in the 1930s from Warner Brothers, some of which were set in the Midwest. *The Public Enemy* (1931) chronicles the rise of Tom (James Cagney) and Matt from petty crooks to Chicago mob leaders during the Prohibition era. Tom's moral failings are contrasted with his brother Mike's respectable living after service in the Great War. Despite the efforts of Mike and his mother to put Tom on the right path, a rival gang eventually kills Tom after he takes revenge for Matt's murder.

Likewise, in *Little Caesar* (1931), Rico Bandello (Edward G. Robinson) is a small-time hood who carefully plots his rise to power, eventually becoming Chicago's top mob boss. However, fate catches up to Rico, and he dies pitifully after being gunned down in an alleyway. A couple of years later, Warner Brothers released a bit of a send-up on its own brand of gangster film with the crime-comedy, *The Little Giant* (1933). Edward G. Robinson stars again, this time as a Chicago gangster who, when Prohibition is repealed, heads to the West Coast to infiltrate California high society. Other Warner Brothers gangster-related films set in the Midwest include *The Widow from Chicago* (1930) and *Kansas City Princess* (1933).

All the major studios followed suit with their own entries in the gangster genre. United Artists brought us *Scarface* (1932), starring Paul Muni as Tony Camonte, a character (loosely based on Al Capone) who rises to power in the Chicago mob after helping to kill his former boss. A 1983 remake by Brian De Palma, starring Al Pacino, transposes the action to present-day Miami. De Palma revisits Capone and the Chicago mob in his 1987 film, *The Untouchables*. Other examples include *Underworld* (1927), directed by Josef von Sternberg and starring George Bancroft; *Yellow Contraband* (1928), a gangster melodrama about heroin trafficking; and *Car 99* (1935), a film about gang bosses, bank robbery, and police corruption in Michigan, starring Fred MacMurray.

By the 1940s and 1950s, the gangster film had been replaced to a large extent by the *film noir*. This cycle of literally and emotionally dark films dealt with wartime and postwar malaise, urban decay (both physical and moral), and corrupt authority figures; some examples are set in the Midwest. Tyrone Power plays a believable con man in *Nightmare Alley* (1947), a classic *film noir* that runs the gamut from a carnival setting to the wood-paneled suite of a corrupt psychiatrist in Chicago. Power uses his good looks and screen presence to command empathy from the audience, despite his morally flawed role. Strong supporting cast members include Joan Blondell and Colleen Gray (who would later appear in Stanley Kubrick's *The Killing*).

Another well-known *film noir* set in the Midwest is *Call Northside 777* (1948), an example of what the critic J. P. Telotte has identified in his *Voices in the Dark* as a documentary-like tendency in certain *noir* films. Based on a series of articles written for the *Chicago Tribune* by James P. McGuire, the film follows reporter P.J. O'Neal (James Stewart) as he reopens a decade-old murder case. As O'Neal begins to believe in the innocence of a man convicted of killing a policeman, he meets with increasing resistance from authorities unwilling to be proved wrong.

Another film set in Chicago bears a quintessential *noir* title: *Dark City* (1950),

Scene from the film *The Untouchables* (1987). Photofest.

directed by William Dieterle. In this film, Charlton Heston plays Danny Haley, a bookie whose operation is shut down and who then cons a gullible out-of-towner named Arthur Winant into gambling away $5,000 that isn't his. When the distraught Winant commits suicide, his shadowy, protective older brother comes looking for revenge, and Danny begins to feel his dark fate closing in.

Midwestern History in Cinema

Several Civil War dramas produced by Hollywood take place at least partly in the midwestern states, whose loyalties were split between the Union and the Confederacy. In *The Copperhead* (1920), President Abraham Lincoln asks a small-town Illinois farmer to infiltrate a secret organization of Confederate sympathizers, known as the Copperheads. Because of his involvement with the group, the man's family brands him a traitor, not knowing the true nature of his mission. He dies in the line of duty, and only years later do his relatives and friends realize the sacrifice he made for the Union.

Similarly, in *The Crisis* (1916), a St. Louis lawyer and his fiancée separate because of their convictions. He is on the side of the Union, and she is a Confederate sympathizer. This trope of loved ones being torn apart is rather common in the Civil War mythos, most often articulated in terms of "brother fighting brother," and it resonates particularly in midwestern settings. Yet another film dealing with such conflict is *The Sting of Victory* (1916), which specifically enacts the "brother against brother" scenario. In a variation on the theme, *The Arizona Kid* (1939) pits friend against friend. Roy Rogers plays a Confederate officer stationed in Missouri who is charged with quashing outlaw gangs operating under the pretense of service to the Confederacy. When Roy captures the McBride Gang, which includes his old friend Dave, his loyalties are put to the ultimate test.

The films set in the Civil War era depict a number of legendary American characters from the period, chief among them the martyred President Abraham Lincoln, who spent his young adulthood in Illinois. Lincoln's early life is portrayed most notably in two films made within a year of each other: *Young Mr. Lincoln* (1939) and *Abe Lincoln in Illinois* (1940). Henry Fonda as the young Lincoln in John Ford's film brings a quiet self-assuredness to the role, and the film's plot hints at the inevitability of Lincoln's rise to greatness. Some commentators, however, consider the signature Lincoln performance to be that of Raymond Massey in *Abe Lincoln in Illinois*, a role he originally played on stage in 1938. That film elevates Lincoln to Christ-like status, suggesting that he sacrificed his life for the good of the country.

Other legends that emerged after the Civil War, figures of "the Wild West," actually have midwestern roots. In *Annie Oakley* (1935), Barbara Stanwyck plays the sharpshooter from Ohio who lands a job in Buffalo Bill's Wild West Show.[10] A Broadway stage version of the story, *Annie Get Your Gun*, was produced in 1946 by Rodgers and Hammerstein, with music and lyrics by Irving Berlin and book by Herbert and Dorothy Fields. The show, which starred Ethel Merman, ran for 1147 performances. A film version of the musical was released in 1950, with Betty Hutton as Annie, a role initially given to Judy Garland. Buffalo Bill turns up again in *The Plainsman* (1937)—a film set partly in St. Louis—as do Wild Bill Hickok (Gary Cooper) and Calamity Jane (Jean Arthur).

A more notorious legend was Jesse James, and at least three silent feature films were made about his life in Missouri. *Jesse James under the Black Flag* (1921) chronicles his involvement with Quantrill's Raiders, a band of guerrillas in Missouri led by William Clarke Quantrill, who attacked Union sympathizers during the Civil War. A sequel, *Jesse James as the Outlaw* (1921), depicts his return to Missouri after the hostilities. Despite his desire to settle down to a peaceful existence, James is drawn into a life of crime and is eventually killed. In 1927 another film appeared based on his life: *Jesse James*, written by the famous scenarist Frances Marion, one of the most prominent women in the silent film industry. In the 1939 version of *Jesse James*, set in Missouri and Northfield, Minnesota, Tyrone Power plays Jesse, with Henry Fonda as his brother, Frank James. Fritz Lang filmed a sequel in 1940, *The Return of Frank James*, one of the most intelligent westerns of the era, again with Fonda. Another 1939 film, *Days of Jesse James*, has singing cowboy Roy Rogers infiltrating the James gang in an attempt to solve a bank robbery. All told, more than thirty feature films recount the Jesse James legend, sometimes portraying him as villain, sometimes as hero/victim.

The figure of Jesse James—a midwesterner who is more often associated with "the West"—points up the problematic nature of the distinction between West and Midwest. The states that we now consider as "midwestern" once constituted the westernmost "frontier" of the United States. As the American conquest of territory continued on westward, the region took on the identity of "gateway to the West." Indeed, in a number of western genre films, starting in the silent period, the Midwest is depicted as a place of transit, through which one passed on the way to the West.

For example, in *Days of Daring*, a Tom Mix western from 1920, the hero is a mail rider from Illinois who heads for California with his sweetheart during the gold rush of 1849. Another "western" from 1920, *Lahoma*, based on a novel by J. Breckenridge Ellis, concerns homesteaders in Kansas City, Missouri, and Oklahoma. *Step on It* (1922), starring Hoot Gibson and set in Kansas City, deals with the familiar western trope of cattle rustling. In *Wells Fargo* (1937), set partly in St. Louis, Joel McCrea plays one of the famed courier service's early riders, who becomes a staunch supporter of rapid U.S. expansion westward. More films that feature midwestern settings in the tale of western settlement include *Rock Island Trail* (1950), *Saginaw Trail* (1953), and the epic *How the West Was Won* (1962).

Other aspects of midwestern history are depicted in silent films such as *Indiana* (1916; also known as *The Birth of Indiana* and *Historic Indiana*), which tells the story of the founding of that state. Similarly, *Barriers Burned Away*, a 1925 melodrama directed by W. S. Van Dyke, chronicles the great Chicago fire of 1871, a topic that would resurface later in films of the sound era, including *Sweepings* (1933) and *In Old Chicago* (1937), the fictional story of two sons of Mrs. O'Leary, whose cow was purported to have started the great blaze. Set in 1803 around the imminent purchase of the Louisiana Territory, *Old Louisiana* (1937) deals with a thwarted plot to smuggle guns into St. Louis and thus take control of the territory.

Other Genres

Other genres that feature the Midwest as a key setting range from social-problem films to family melodramas. Based on the famous Upton Sinclair novel, *The Jungle* (1914) deals with the horrendous conditions in Chicago's meat-packing plants at the turn of the twentieth century, as well as the formation of labor unions in that industry. Perhaps equally disturbing to audiences of the time were the problems addressed in *And the Children Pay* (1918), which tackles prostitution, illegitimacy, and birth defects.

Family melodramas of the silent period set in Chicago include *Adam's Rib* (1923), directed by Cecil B. DeMille. In this film, a prominent businessman spends all his time at the office, at the expense of his family's emotional needs. His wife (Anna Q. Nilsson) seeks creature comforts elsewhere, and their adult daughter ends up taking the blame in order to protect her mother's reputation.

Of all the great MGM musicals, *Meet Me in St. Louis* (1944) is one of the darkest, and as such it also works as a family melodrama. It also implicitly contrasts midwestern city life with the "big city" of New York. The upper-middle-class Smith Family has four daughters, two of them on the verge of adulthood. Esther (Judy Garland) falls in love with "the boy next door," who barely seems to notice her at first. Her older sister, Rose, is anxiously awaiting a proposal from a young man who is away at college in New York. Meanwhile, their father learns that he is to be transferred, to head up the New York office of the firm in which he is a junior partner. This bit of news throws the family into turmoil, as they face the possibility of having to leave their beloved home in St. Louis and miss the upcoming 1903 World's Fair to boot. Although the action never actually takes us to New York, that city looms in the background, at once threatening and promising. However, when Mr. Smith finally realizes the damage that a move to New York might inflict on his family, he decides that they should stay in St. Louis, where, after all, there is plenty of opportunity and excitement.

CHANGING APPROACHES TO THE MIDWEST IN FILM

By the mid-1950s, Hollywood began to take a bolder, franker approach in general to topics such as sexuality, drug use, crime, and corruption, and this change applied to films dealing with the Midwest as well. Among the most important factors contributing to this shift were two landmark Supreme Court cases. One in 1948 (*U.S. vs. Paramount Pictures, et al.*) forced the major studios to sell off their theater holdings in an attempt to put an end to monopolistic practices and allow independent filmmakers, distributors, and theaters to participate more fully in the industry. In the other (the so-called *Miracle Case* in 1952), the High Court declared for the first time that motion pictures were protected under the First Amendment's guarantee of freedom of expression. The combined results of these two cases included the eventual demise of the studio system as it had existed since the late 1910s and the abandonment of the Production Code, the industry's self-imposed system of censorship.

Furthermore, as international films (primarily from Italy and France) gained popularity among sophisticated audiences, Hollywood found it economically necessary—in order to compete not only with foreign films, but also with the groundswell of independent American films—to abandon the kinds of naïve depictions that had been *de rigeur* in previous decades. In the view of film critic Donald Lyons, "The heartland of America has served as inspiration, stimulus, and backdrop for as much innovative cinema as either coast. In many respects, films set outside the New York or Los Angeles areas have been more radical than work [depicting] the cultural centers."[11]

A Darker, Wider Underbelly

Whereas the *film noir* of the 1940s tended to locate the "dark side" of the Midwest in big cities like Chicago and Detroit, films of the 1950s and 1960s extended that underworld into suburban and small-town settings, rejecting earlier sentimental or comic characterizations of them. In the famous crop-duster scene in Alfred Hitchcock's *North by Northwest* (1959), Roger Thornhill (Cary Grant) waits at a remote crossroads in rural Illinois to meet with a man he does not know. The setting becomes more and more surreal and isolated, until a previously innocuous crop-duster comes after Thornhill, swooping down on him and spraying machine-gun fire dangerously close by. As in a number of Hitchcock's films, an initially tranquil, stereotypically benign setting turns nightmarish with little warning.

The only film directed by legendary actor Charles Laughton, *The Night of the Hunter* (1955) takes the *film noir* out of its usual gritty, urban setting, into small towns and rural areas of the Midwest. Ben Harper has killed a man for $10,000 and hidden the money. Only his two children, Pearl and John, know where the money is stashed, and Ben has sworn them both to secrecy. As Ben awaits execution, his cellmate, "Preacher" (Robert Mitchum), tries unsuccessfully to learn the whereabouts of the loot. When Preacher is released from prison, he seeks out Ben's family and charms his widow, Willa (Shelley Winters), into marrying him. When she threatens to leave Preacher, after discovering his true nature and motives, he kills her and takes charge of the two children. They run away, and he pursues them relentlessly across the countryside. They find refuge at the homestead of a kind, elderly woman (Lillian Gish) who proves to be a formidable match for Preacher. One of the most visually stunning examples of *film noir*, *The Night of the Hunter* portrays the Midwest as potentially a place of great idyllic beauty, but it also points up the fleeting nature of peaceful existence and the constant threat of dark forces out to disrupt that tranquility.

In Otto Preminger's *Anatomy of a Murder* (1959), an army lieutenant (Ben Gazzara) stationed in upper Michigan is accused of murdering a man thought to have raped the lieutenant's wife (Lee Remick). His attorney (James Stewart) must unravel the details of the two crimes, amidst a web of hidden motives and questionable loyalties. For the sake of local character and authenticity, Preminger decided to shoot the film on location in Marquette, Michigan, described in the *New York Times* as a windswept land of lakes, streams, and trees—a deceptively placid backdrop for such a relatively lurid tale.[12]

Stanley Kubrick's *Lolita* (1962), adapted from the controversial novel by Vladimir Nabokov, chronicles the life of a professor, Humbert Humbert (James Mason), who settles in a university town in Ohio. Against this wholesome backdrop emerges a lurid tale. Humbert eventually marries a widow, Charlotte Haze (Shelley Winters), in order to be near her pubescent daughter, Lolita (Sue Lyon). After Charlotte's accidental death, Humbert has Lolita to himself, but he soon realizes that another sexual predator, Clare Quilty (Peter Sellers), is trailing them. Fear and jealousy eventually lead Humbert to track down Quilty and shoot him dead. For a film to deal frankly with such a taboo subject as pedophilia was far from common in Hollywood at the time, and the small-town midwestern setting makes the treatment even more compelling.

One of the most famous films about evil in the heartland is all the more unsettling because of its basis in real-life events. Richard Brooks's *In Cold Blood* (1967), adapted from Truman Capote's book, relates the anguished tale of two small-time hoodlums from Missouri (Robert Blake, Scott Wilson) who invade a Kansas farm in the dead of night, expecting to steal thousands of dollars. Finding no money, they murder the farmer, his wife, and their two teenaged children, with little apparent motive beyond the abortive robbery. The history of the true crime, still so hard to fathom, haunts the local community to this day, as so many people there knew the family of victims. The film continues to pack a powerful punch, as evidenced by an internationally successful restoration and theatrical re-release in the fall of 2003.

Other horrific crimes committed in the Midwest have found their way into famous novels and films. A notable example is the case of Ed Gein, a psychotic Wisconsin man whose dreadful story was transformed into Robert Bloch's novel and Alfred Hitchcock's film, *Psycho* (1960). In that film, however, the action is transposed to Arizona and California.

A more recent, but fictional, example lies in Jonathan Demme's Oscar-winning *The Silence of the Lambs* (1991), about a psychopath called Buffalo Bill who kidnaps and murders young women across the Midwest. Clarice Starling (Jodie Foster), an FBI agent based in Chicago, is assigned to the case, and she must interview another (incarcerated) serial killer, Dr. Hannibal Lecter (Anthony Hopkins), in order to piece together Buffalo Bill's profile. In all of these tales, whether or not based on true crimes, one of the most horrifying elements is the incongruity between the heinousness of the acts and the stereotypes of the Midwest as an "all-American" locale. In other words, we seem to be most frightened by the idea that "this could happen *here*."

The Midwest, Warts and All

Of course, the cinema need not be horrifying in order to challenge established views of the Midwest, and there is a long tradition of dramatic films that take a "warts and all" approach to the region. Based on a novel by Sinclair Lewis, *Elmer Gantry* (1960, Richard Brooks) examines life on the Chautauqua circuit with Sister Sharon Falconer (Jean Simmons), an immensely popular evangelist who takes her tent revivals around the rural Midwest. A salesman and self-professed sinner who has seen and played all the angles, Elmer Gantry (Burt Lancaster) charms his way into Sister Sharon's heart and her organization. With dollar signs in his eyes, the charismatic Gantry aims to take the show to new heights in Chicago and beyond. Like *The Miracle Woman* (1930, starring Barbara Stanwyck), *Elmer Gantry* takes a frank look at the relationships between religion and receipts, manna and marketing, salvation and showmanship. Significantly, most of the figures representing established religion in the film are motivated by greed, power, and the promise of fame. Midwesterners are portrayed alternately as good-hearted folk with simple wisdom, gullible boobs, or fickle sycophants all too willing to turn on their pop idols, Falconer and Gantry, at the first suggestion of impropriety.

By the late 1960s, the cultural landscape of the country had changed, and the Midwest was not left out. Especially among young people (always an important audience for the movies), there was an increasingly urgent awareness of racial injustice, the war in Vietnam, and government corruption. Haskell Wexler's *Medium Cool* (1969) tackles all these issues head-on, and it deftly uses its midwestern setting to complex dramatic effect. A tough TV news reporter named John Cassellis (Robert Forster) specializes in stories about racial tensions and violence in the ghettos of Chicago. He discovers that the network is turning over his tapes to the FBI to help them find suspects among his interviewees. He quits his job in protest and independently covers the 1968 Democratic National Convention in Chicago. Wexler skillfully peppers his fictional world with actual footage of protesters outside the convention, giving *Medium Cool* a quasidocumentary feel and a quality of self-examination (which is also implied in the title, a reference to Marshall McLuhan's theories of "hot" and "cool" media). While covering the Chicago slums, Cassellis befriends a poor woman and her young son who have moved to Chicago from the rural south. In the process of getting to know Cassellis (and falling in love with him), the woman awakens to the burning political questions of the era, issues she had never considered before. In shifting her life from rural isolation to the big city, she has joined a larger community and has matured into a citizen not only of Chicago but of the world. In a time of postassassination cynicism, *Medium Cool* takes a hard look at the role played by the media in the machinations of power in the United States. This surprisingly critical stance is made all the more remarkable by the fact that it was distributed by one of the major studios, Paramount Pictures.[13]

Several other major films of the era also address the issue of race in the Midwest, a subject that had been ignored or glossed over in past decades. Based on a stage play and set in the south side of Chicago, *A Raisin in the Sun* (1961) chronicles the struggles of an African American family to get out of the ghetto. They may have a chance when they inherit $10,000, but the adult son and head of the household (Sidney Poitier) loses part of the money, making their struggle even more difficult. This was one of the first mainstream American films to portray the very real, everyday problems faced by African American families.

In *The Great White Hope* (1970), based on Howard Sackler's stage play, James Earl Jones plays Jack Jefferson, a boxer dealing with the racism and hatred of 1950s midwestern America. Not only is he the first black heavyweight contender, but he is also in love with a white woman. Jefferson must deal with the racial scorn of whites, as well as the ostracism coming from some members of the black community, who feel he has sold out.

The first feature film by the maverick African American director Melvin Van Peebles, *Watermelon Man* (1970) depicts a white bigot in Indiana who wakes up one day to discover that his skin has turned black. The world as he has known it turns against him, and he quickly learns what it means to be the victim of such irrational prejudice as he himself once practiced.

The middle-class, white midwestern American family, long a staple of wholesome Hollywood fare, falls apart in a number of post–1960s Hollywood films, including Robert Redford's directorial debut, *Ordinary People* (1980). The accidental death of their older son devastates Calvin and Beth Jarrett (Donald Sutherland, Mary Tyler Moore), but the tragedy puts a particular strain on the relationship between Beth and her younger son, Conrad (Timothy Hutton). After a suicide attempt, Conrad sees a psychiatrist (Judd Hirsch) who helps him work through his feelings of anger and guilt, but Beth continues to unravel, as the illusions she has constructed for herself shatter one by one. Cast brilliantly against type, Moore plays Beth as being incapable of loving or being loved, and when the ultimately unlikable mother leaves her family, the audience hopes for her redemption only for the sake of Calvin and Conrad.

The breakdown of family relations serves as a springboard from which Jim Jarmusch's dark, minimalist comedy, *Stranger Than Paradise* (1983), goes on to suggest the pointlessness and dull homogeneity of American life. New York City slackers Willie and Eddie (John Lurie, Richard Edson) are surprised and perturbed by the sudden arrival of Willie's cousin Eva (Eszter Balint) from Hungary. Soon growing tired of the two friends and their inane banter, Eva goes to Cleveland to stay with her aunt Lotte (Cecilia Stark). A year later, Willie and Eddie join her in Cleveland and easily persuade her to leave Aunt Lotte and go to Florida with them. Wherever they go, however, the trio find the same bleak, industrial landscapes and the same deep-seated boredom and existential angst. At one point, Eddie remarks that Florida looks just like Cleveland, which looks just like New York; and as though the comment has struck too close to home, Willie tells him to "shut up." For all the traveling in the film (from Hungary to New York to Cleveland to Florida), none of the characters ever seems to really go anywhere.

Another dark comedy set largely in the Midwest is the sublimely kooky *Fargo* (1996), by Joel and Ethan Coen. In this film, a Minnesota car salesman, Jerry Lundegaard (William H. Macy), hatches a plot to have his wife kidnapped so that her wealthy father (Harve Presnell) will pay the ransom. The plan is that Jerry and the kidnappers (Steve Buscemi and Peter Stormare) will then split the take, and his wife will be released relatively unharmed. But as is so often the case in caper films, things go terribly awry. The bumbling crooks get pulled over in Brainerd, Minnesota, by a highway patrolman and then shoot him dead, triggering an investigation by local police chief Marge Gunderson (a role that won Frances McDormand an Oscar) that eventually leads from Minnesota to the kidnappers' home of Fargo, North Dakota. Along the way, Marge ably interviews and interrogates an increasingly colorful array of characters, while juggling personal issues of her own, including a late-term pregnancy. Filmed in various locales throughout Minnesota and North Dakota, *Fargo* might be mistaken as insulting to midwesterners were it not for the fact that the filmmakers themselves hail from Minnesota. As an examination of region, the film sports what Roger Ebert calls "an absolutely dead-on familiarity with small-town life in the frigid winter landscape of Minnesota and North Dakota." Ebert continues, "Then it rotates its story through satire, comedy, suspense and violence, until it emerges as one of the best films I've ever seen."[14]

A general dissatisfaction with "life in the heartland" lies at the core of Clint Eastwood's *The Bridges of Madison County* (1995). In the summer of 1965, photographer Robert Kincaid (Eastwood) happens upon the Johnson farm as he looks for help in finding a local covered bridge for his photo essay. Francesca Johnson (Meryl Streep) is home alone for a few days while her family is away at the Iowa state fair. She agrees to show Kincaid all the bridges in the county, and thus begins their intense, four-day love affair, which turns out to be the romance of their lives. Years later, upon Francesca's death, her children find a diary chronicling her affair with Robert, including her request that her ashes be scattered from the Rosamunde Bridge, as Robert's had been at the time of his death. These discoveries reveal a side of their mother they had never known, and perhaps implicit in the story is the suggestion that behind the most mundane existence may beat hidden passions and repressed desires for a better life.

Independent filmmaker Harmony Korine further explores midwestern repression (or rather what Freud termed the "return of the repressed") in his film *Gummo* (1997), an episodic tale of the bizarre lives of two teenagers in Xenia, Ohio. The boys' antisocial misadventures run the gamut, from sniffing glue, to killing cats, having sex, and associating with a rogue's gallery of odd, sometimes frightening sorts. They include two foul-mouthed six-year-olds; a man who pimps his mentally ill wife to the boys; three sisters whose dream is to become strippers; a 12-year-old gay transvestite who is also a cat killer, and his boyfriend, a black Jewish midget; and a nymphlike skateboarder who wears pink rabbit ears around town—hardly a cast of characters one would expect to see in earlier, idyllic films like *So Dear to My Heart*.

Some of the weirdest depictions of small-town American life have come to us from director David Lynch. Curiously, his one feature film set entirely in the Midwest is also arguably his most mainstream: *The Straight Story* (1999). The aging Alvin Straight (Richard Farnsworth, in his last role) heads from Iowa to Wisconsin to see his critically ill brother. The two have not spoken in years, and for Alvin, making the journey on his own, without anyone's help, becomes a point of honor. Since he can neither drive a car nor afford a bus ticket, he sets out on his riding lawnmower. Along the way he meets an odd assortment of characters, including a runaway teenage girl and a friendly couple who take him in for a few days. These brief encounters offer a taste of the kind of odd tone one normally expects from

Lynch, but as the film is based on a real-life story, it does not veer into the weirdly surreal realms of such nightmarish small-town visions as *Blue Velvet* (1986) and *Eraserhead* (1976).

Set in Detroit, *8 Mile* (2002) tackles such problematic issues as racism, poverty, teen pregnancy, violence, and alcoholism. B-Rabbit (Eminem) is an erstwhile rapper who hopes to overcome all of these problems, if he can only win an upcoming rap showdown. Arguably, *8 Mile* offers a variation on the old Hollywood formula whereby a midwestern kid hopes to make it big in show business.

One of the freshest American films in years, *American Splendor* (2003) examines the seemingly mundane real-life experiences of a Cleveland file clerk, Harvey Pekar (Paul Giamatti). Based on Pekar's autobiographical, sardonic series of comic books, the film skillfully intersperses actual interviews with Pekar himself into the fictionalized depictions of his life. At its foundation, the film dismantles the romanticized ideas of simple, working-class people and idealized midwestern life. It denies us the kind of stereotypical Hollywood ending in which hard work and determination ultimately yield material payoffs or fame in a traditional sense, at the same time that it questions the validity of pursuing such rewards. It is also a profound study not only of American pop culture but also of how the very act of dramatization can be therapeutic for the artist as well as for the audience.

Spoofs and Satires

As early as the 1960s, mainstream films began to lampoon traditional ideas about life in middle America, often providing broader satires of the American cultural landscape. In *Bye Bye Birdie* (1963), life in Sweet Apple, Ohio, turns topsy-turvy when a national TV promotional stunt brings rock superstar Conrad Birdie to the small town. There, he will sing a love song to a local high school girl (Ann-Margret) and then kiss her goodbye, all for the benefit of the cameras of the *Ed Sullivan Show*. The presumably down-home, innocent residents of Sweet Apple are shown to have not only an appetite for fame but also a thinly veiled, burning sexuality that can match anything that Birdie—an obvious parody of Elvis Presley—can dish out.

An unlikely mixing of genres distinguishes the gangster-film send-up, *Robin and the 7 Hoods* (1964), a comedy–crime–musical featuring the "rat pack" (Frank Sinatra, Dean Martin, Sammy Davis, Jr.). Set in Prohibition-era Chicago, the story revolves around two feuding crime lords (Sinatra and Peter Falk) and a corrupt sheriff (Victor Buono), with loose parallels to the story of Robin Hood.

Arguably a spoof on *The Music Man*, and certainly an amusing variation on the well-worn genre of "traveling salesman" jokes, the 1968 film *Did You Hear the One about the Traveling Saleslady?* concerns one Agatha Knabenshu, who arrives in a small town in Missouri to sell player pianos to the locals. When her disastrous sales attempts nearly destroy the town, she befriends an equally bumbling inventor, and together they try to sell his automatic milking machine. But things go sour when a demonstration of the contraption causes a stampede through the town.

Wholesome midwestern holiday traditions become the objects of satire in the charming comedy, *A Christmas Story* (1983). Although much of the film was shot in Ohio, the story is based on novelist Jean Shepherd's (1929–1999) stories of growing up in 1940s Indiana. Ralphie Parker (Peter Billingsley) dreams of his ideal Christmas gift: a Red Ryder air rifle. Despite all his efforts, the adults in the film (including his doting mother, his teachers, and even Santa Claus) try to discourage Ralphie, repeatedly offering the clichéd warning, "You'll shoot your eye out!"

In a more serious vein, Paul Verhoeven's *Robocop* (1987) satirizes the all-too-real problems of crime, police brutality in major cities, and corporate influence over government. In the near future, a crime-ridden Detroit is run by a big corporation, which develops crime-fighting robots. The technology gets out of control, however, as robots begin killing minor offenders. In order to recover from this public relations disaster, the company reconstructs the martyred body of a respected, murdered policeman. The resulting half-human, half-robotic crime-fighter eventually turns on the corrupt government–corporate forces that created him.

The dark, satirical comedy *Heathers* (1989), set in Sherwood, Ohio, is based loosely on screenwriter Dan Waters's own high school experiences in South Bend, Indiana. Critic Donald Lyons suggests that the film's fictitious Westerburg High School and town of Sherwood "allude to *Winesburg, Ohio*, Sherwood Anderson's classic 1919 collection of short stories that amounted to a mosaic of lonely, unhappy lives in a paradigmatic small town."[15] A scathing, brilliantly funny satire on herd mentality, *Heathers* centers around Veronica (Winona Ryder), the newest, reluctant inductee into a vacuous high school clique, "the Heathers," and her nonconformist biker boyfriend, J.D. (Christian Slater). After falling victim to a prank by one of the Heathers, Veronica facetiously wishes her dead, and J.D. is only too happy to oblige. The two of them murder Heather #1 by slipping some Drano into her soda. Horrified yet intoxicated by what they have done, Veronica willingly goes along with J.D. in the murders of two of the school's homophobic football stars. The three deaths are mistaken as suicides, and teen suicide becomes all the rage at the school. Ultimately, Lyons sees *Heathers* as a perverse, even anarchic satire of midwestern life, in the vein of Mark Twain and Ambrose Bierce.

The more raucous comedy *Waiting for Guffman* (1996) offers a rather brutal satire of midwestern cultural life, specifically community theater. In honor of the 150th anniversary of Blaine, Missouri, local director Corky St. Clair (Christopher Guest) prepares an amateur theatrical production based on the town's history. The play's cast includes a local dentist (Eugene Levy), a married couple who work together as travel agents (Fred Willard, Catherine O'Hara), an auto mechanic, and a Dairy Queen waitress. St. Clair, a self-proclaimed "off-off-off-off Broadway" director, invites a renowned New York theater critic named Guffman to see the show, a gambit that seems to be a recipe for disaster.

Since the 1980s, a number of films have countered the conventional wisdom about the Midwest by presenting characters who are anything but conservative, uncultured, or generally uninteresting. The midwesterners of these films possess a certain *savoir-faire*, a hip or "cool" attitude toward the world that lends them a kind of charmed existence.

An emblematic example may be found in the classic comedy *The Blues Brothers* (1980), starring John Belushi and Dan Aykroyd, as the eponymous Jake and Elwood Blues. Set in Illinois, the film has the brothers trying to reassemble their band for a concert to benefit their old school, run by nuns, which is about to be shut down because of back taxes. As they try to fulfill this "mission from God,"

Jake and Elwood leave a trail of enemies and disasters in their wake, but they emerge unscathed and unfazed at every turn. Their imperviousness, combined with their ubiquitous black suits and hats, white shirts, and dark sunglasses, makes the duo the epitome of cool. Thanks to Belushi's and Aykroyd's television stardom, as members of the original cast of NBC's *Saturday Night Live*, the film held particular appeal for young audiences at the time.

Similarly, throughout the 1980s, midwestern film director John Hughes (born in Michigan) targeted teenagers with his comedy–dramas featuring young "brat-pack" actors like Emilio Estevez, Molly Ringwald, Matthew Broderick, Judd Nelson, and Anthony Michael Hall. Many of Hughes' teen films were set in Illinois (where he spent his adolescence), including *The Breakfast Club* (1985) and *Ferris Bueller's Day Off* (1986). In *The Breakfast Club*, five high school students have detention on Saturday morning. Initially, it seems they have little in common: one is a jock, one a "princess," one a nerd, one a tough guy, and one a "goth[ic]" girl. During their afternoon together, however, they go from hating each other's stereotypes to understanding how much they have in common.

In *Ferris Bueller's Day Off*, Matthew Broderick plays an ultra-savvy high school kid who knows all the tricks. He takes a day off from school, pretending to be sick, so that he and two friends can live it up in Chicago. Meanwhile, neither Ferris' sister nor the school principal believes that he is ill, and each hatches various schemes to give Ferris his just desserts. Not only does the film remind one of the old chestnut, "you have to stop and smell the roses," but it also showcases just what a sophisticated and exciting city Chicago is. During their day off from school, the kids go to a Cubs game, have lunch at a posh seafood restaurant, and stand in awe before Georges Seurat's famous pointillist painting, *La Grande Jatte*, at the Art Institute.

In addition to updating images of the Midwest as a hip region, films such as these touched on a need to escape from the general angst and ennui characteristic of "Generation X" teenagers. *High Fidelity* (2000) takes a look at how that generation, years later, is coping with the problems of adulthood. Billed as "a comedy about fear of commitment, hating your job, falling in love and other pop favorites,"

The Films of John Hughes

John Hughes was born on February 18, 1950, in Lansing, Michigan, but moved with his family to Northbrook, Illinois, a suburb of Chicago, in 1963. Fictionalized as Shermer, Illinois, Northbrook would become the home of the Buellers, Donnellys, Bakers, and Griswolds who populate his movies. After working as an advertising copywriter, Hughes began writing for comedians such as Rodney Dangerfield and Henny Youngman, and from there moved in 1979 to an editorship at the *National Lampoon*. While at the magazine, Hughes wrote the screenplay for *National Lampoon's Class Reunion* (1982) and *National Lampoon's Vacation* (1983), and then began directing. During the 1980s, the films he shot for Paramount chronicled adolescence in the Midwest: *Sixteen Candles* (1984), *The Breakfast Club* (1985), *Weird Science* (1985), *Ferris Bueller's Day Off* (1986), and *Pretty in Pink* (1986). His reputation as a wry master of comedy established, Hughes also directed *Planes, Trains and Automobiles* (1987), *She's Having a Baby* (1988), *Uncle Buck* (1989), *Curly Sue* (1991), and *High School Reunion Collection* (2003). His output has been prodigious. Hughes wrote and produced *Some Kind of Wonderful* (1987), *The Great Outdoors* (1988), *National Lampoon's Christmas Vacation* (1989), *Home Alone* (1990), *Home Alone 2: Lost in New York* (1992), *Dennis the Menace* (1993), *Miracle on 34th Street* (1994), *Baby's Day Out* (1994), *101 Dalmatians* (1996), *Home Alone 3* (1997), *Flubber* (1997), *Reach the Rock* (1998), *New Port South* (2001), *Just Visiting* (2001), and *Maid in Manhattan* (2002). Many of these films have been huge successes, and most draw heavily on a midwestern sensibility that manifests itself in laughter at urban pretense. Since 1988, the Hughes Company has released films through Universal and Disney.

the film follows Rob (John Cusack), a thirty-something record-shop owner in Illinois as he tries to come to grips with the fact that he is now undeniably an adult. Rob's "midlife" crisis of sorts stems from his recent breakup with his girlfriend, Laura. Constantly making "top five" lists of bands, albums, singles, and so on, Rob reflects on his "top five" worst breakups, beginning with Laura. Rob's bouts with introspection and fantasy all play out in his store, where his two socially inept clerks (Jack Black and Todd Louiso) exchange pop culture references all day long, acting as constant reminders of how he could turn out if he doesn't "grow up."

DOCUMENTARIES

As mentioned earlier, the shake-up in the American film industry in the 1950s cleared the way for an increase in independent film production, a good measure of which was devoted to documentary filmmaking. Not surprisingly, in the ensuing decades, quite a few documentarians have turned their cameras on the American Midwest and various aspects of life in that region.

One of the most outstanding historically important examples is Robert Drew's *Primary* (1960). Leading up to the 1960 Democratic presidential primary, the film follows John F. Kennedy and Hubert Humphrey as they campaign across the state of Wisconsin, competing for the Democratic nomination. Not only is the film an important chronicle of life on the campaign trail with two legendary politicians, but it is also an important early example of what has been termed *cinema verité* (cinema truth), a new style of documentary filmmaking made possible by lightweight, portable equipment, among other factors.

Wisconsin is the subject of another well-known documentary, *The War at Home* (1979). This film focuses on demonstrations against the Vietnam War during the 1960s and early 1970s at the University of Wisconsin—Madison, which was at the time one of the most politically active campuses in the country. Some commentators have characterized *The War at Home* as one of the most illuminating depictions of the antiwar movement.

Albert and David Maysles, who had worked with Robert Drew on *Primary*, codirected another classic of the documentary genre, *Salesman* (1969). The film follows four door-to-door Bible salesmen through Chicago and other towns as they peddle their wares. Their potential customers are mostly poor or lower-middle class Catholics whose lack of interest suggests that they have better things to do with their money than to buy expensive, ornate Bibles.

Academy Award winner Michael Moore (*Bowling for Columbine*, 2002) made his directing debut with *Roger and Me* (1989), about the closing of a General Motors plant in his hometown of Flint, Michigan, and the resulting devastation in that community. Moore relentlessly (but futilely) tries to interview G.M. president Roger Smith, who closed ten other plants around the country at a time when the company was posting record profits. All told, 30,000 jobs were relocated to Mexico, where labor is much cheaper, presumably in order to net even greater profits. In subsequent film and television work, including his latest film, *Fahrenheit 9/11* (2004), Moore has consistently called into question the motives of big corporations, the level of influence they have in American government, and the impact of the resulting policies on the people of Flint and other ordinary Americans.

One of the most popular documentary features of the 1990s, *Hoop Dreams* (1994) chronicles more than four years in the lives of two inner-city Chicago youths who dream of becoming basketball superstars. Both successfully enter the elite high school where professional basketball star Isaiah Thomas once played, but one of the young men must leave after his first year due to academic problems. The film provides a moving, sometimes jubilant, often tragic, look at inner-city poverty and the desperate dreams to escape it.

Mark Borchardt, a young man from Milwaukee, has another dream: to make movies. *American Movie* (1999) documents his tireless but feckless efforts over the course of three years to complete a short horror film called "Coven." With money borrowed from friends, relatives, and credit card companies, Borchardt struggles to finish his film while at the same time battling his own demons: alcohol, gambling, self-doubt, and a dysfunctional family. The humorous tone during much of the film might lead viewers to mistake it for a "mockumentary" along the lines of *Waiting for Guffman*, but *American Movie* is the genuine article. Furthermore, the humor is balanced by the touching level of humanity that comes through in Borchardt's determination and in the unconditional support he receives from his family and friends, despite the fact that his short film seems doomed to failure.

RECENT FILM CULTURE IN THE MIDWEST

In recent decades, a few key organizations have sprung up in the Midwest with the aim of promoting an alternative film culture. Among them is Facets Multimedia in Chicago, a nonprofit media arts organization, founded in 1975, which provides an extraordinary range of film and video programs. Facets Video, a division of Facets Multimedia, is one of the nation's largest distributors of foreign, classic, cult, art, and hard-to-find videos. Noted film critic Roger Ebert has hailed Facets as "a veritable temple of cinema."

Another organization with an important midwestern presence is the Independent Feature Project (IFP), a not-for-profit service organization dedicated to providing resources, information, and avenues of communication for independent filmmakers, industry professionals, and independent film enthusiasts. It is committed to the idea that independent film is an important art form and a powerful voice in our society. The IFP has branches in Chicago and Minneapolis-St. Paul, as well as in other U.S. cities.

The increase in independent film production in the United States led, from the 1970s on, to substantial numbers of American films being shot each year in locales outside of California and New York. Virtually every state in the union, including all those in the Midwest, now has a film commission whose job it is to entice motion picture producers to come to that state to shoot films and thus stimulate the local economy. In general, film commissions provide producers with information about tax breaks and other incentives, local service companies, talent, technical crews, locations, and other resources necessary for motion picture production. The agencies also notify local actors and technicians about upcoming film shoots, with information on where to send resumes, head shots, and so on.

The Illinois Film Office maintains an extensive list of films and television shows shot in that state, from the 1890s to the present. Thanks largely to Chicago's vibrant film production community, Illinois has seen a particularly high level of feature film production. Major films shot there in recent decades include *In the Heat of the Night* (1967), *The Sting* (1973), *Uptown Saturday Night* (1973), *Cooley High* (1975), *Looking for Mr. Goodbar* (1977), *Damien: Omen II* (1978), *Pennies from Heaven* (1981), *Risky Business* (1983), *Sixteen Candles* (1984), *Grace Quigley* (1984), *Jo Jo Dancer, Your Life Is Calling* (1986), *Manhunter* (1986), *The Color of Money* (1986), *The Untouchables* (1987), *When Harry Met Sally* (1989), *Flatliners* (1990), *Home Alone* (1990), *Backdraft* (1991), *Candyman* (1992), *Wayne's World* (1992), *Groundhog Day* (1993), *The Fugitive* (1993), *The Hudsucker Proxy* (1994), *Natural Born Killers* (1994), *My Best Friend's Wedding* (1997), *He Got Game* (1998), *What Women Want* (2000), *Ocean's 11* (2001), and *The Road to Perdition* (2002).

Similarly, the Indiana Film Commission, a division of the state Commerce Department, acts as a liaison between producers and talent, services, and other government agencies to facilitate feature filmmaking in that state. Well-known films shot at least partially in Indiana include *Brian's Song* (1971), *Breaking Away* (1979), *Hoosiers* (1986), *Eight Men Out* (1988), *Rain Man* (1988), *A League of Their Own* (1992), *In the Company of Men* (1997), and *Pearl Harbor* (2001).

The Iowa Film Commission, a division of the state's Department of Economic Development, emphasizes a number of factors in trying to attract feature film productions. Most prominently, the state offers a wide variety of landscapes and locations, ranging from the Mississippi and Missouri rivers to the lakes of northwestern Iowa, from flat plains to steep limestone bluffs, from the picturesque main streets of small towns to vibrant cities. Among the more than 250 feature films shot in Iowa since 1935, some well-known examples include *F.I.S.T.* (1977), *Country* (1983), *Children of the Corn* (1983), *Starman* (1984), *Noises Off* (1991), *Puppetmasters* (1994), *Twister* (1995), and *The Straight Story* (1998).

Founded in 1979, the Michigan Film Office attracts and assists outside production companies and promotes the growth of the local film community from within. Feature films shot in Michigan since the agency's creation include *Hardcore* (1979), *Continental Divide* (1981), *The Evil Dead* (1982), *Beverly Hills Cop* (1984), *Action Jackson* (1987), *Midnight Run* (1987), *Presumed Innocent* (1989), *Die Hard II* (1990), *True Romance* (1993), *Grosse Point Blank* (1997), *American Pie 2* (2001), *8 Mile* (2002), and *Bowling for Columbine* (2002).

Based in Minneapolis, the Minnesota Film and TV Board seeks to develop the state's film/video production industry as a force for economic and creative growth. The nonprofit organization assists producers of feature films, commercials, industrial videos, television programs, and documentaries, as well as local actors, technicians, and screenwriters. Feature films shot partly or entirely in Minnesota include *Purple Rain* (1984), *Patti Rocks* (1987), *The Mighty Ducks* (1992), *Grumpy Old Men* (1993), *Mallrats* (1995), *Fargo* (1995), *Drop Dead Gorgeous* (1998), and *A Simple Plan* (1998).

The Missouri Film Commission, based in the state capital of Jefferson City, was created in 1983 to promote film, television, video, and cable productions in Missouri. Furthermore, Kansas City and St. Louis have such active film communities as to warrant separate organizations dedicated specifically to promoting filmmaking in those cities: the Kansas City Film Office and St. Louis Filmwire. Missouri's film credits include the following feature films: *Paper Moon* (1973), *Escape from New York* (1981), *American Flyers* (1985), *Mr. and Mrs. Bridge* (1990), *Kansas City* (1996), and *Ride with the Devil* (1999).

As of this writing (2004), the Ohio Film Commission was suffering from a statewide budget crisis; in fact, the position of Film Commissioner had been eliminated. However, at least three regional film offices exist in Ohio: the Cleveland Film Commission, the Cincinnati Film Commission, and the Youngstown Warren Regional Film Commission. Past films shot in the Buckeye State include *The Deer Hunter* (1978), *The Shawshank Redemption* (1994), *Air Force One* (1997), *The Rainmaker* (1997), *Edge of Seventeen* (1998), *The Horse Whisperer* (1998), *Traffic* (2000), *Welcome to Collinwood* (2002), *Antwone Fisher* (2002), and *Sea Biscuit* (2003).

The Wisconsin Film Office, a branch of the Wisconsin Department of Tourism, promotes and facilitates film productions while also serving as an information clearinghouse for the state's film industry. Among the films shot at least partly in Wisconsin are *The Betsy* (1978), *Clash of the Titans* (1981), *Mrs. Soffel* (1984), *28 Up* (1985), *Back to School* (1986, prominently featuring the campus of the University of Wisconsin–Madison), *Hellraiser* (1987), *Meet the Applegates* (1990), *The Big One* (1997), and *The Straight Story* (1999).

DOMINANT THEATER PRACTICES

As with film, theatrical traditions in the Midwest have run the gamut. From the dominant mainstream "legitimate" stage, to radical leftist street productions, these practices form a landscape as diverse as the region itself. Rounding out the topography we find the immensely popular forms of vaudeville and chautauqua, regional repertory theater, and the nonprofit fount of populist creativity that was the Federal Theater Project of the 1930s. As long as there has been a midwestern identity, there has been midwestern theater, and the trends noted here illustrate the richness and variety of its history.

The "Legitimate" Stage

Arguably, the legitimate theater in the United States has always been centered in New York and remains so to this day. Indeed, the highest-profile stage productions in most major cities have usually been Broadway shows on tour. Of course, there are exceptions, and in the Midwest, Chicago has had the most success in creating its own unique, respectable, commercial theater.

Small theaters existed in Chicago as early as 1839, and the city's first major theater was built in 1847; but the real birth of theater culture in Chicago came with the reconstruction of the city after the devastating 1871 fire. An important producer in the late 1800s was David Henderson, who mounted musical spectaculars, many of which toured the United States.

The tradition of successful musical comedies in Chicago ran into the 1910s, and productions such as *The Sultan of Sulu* (1902) and *The Time, the Place, and the Girl* (1907) often toured the Midwest and even occasionally made it to the New York stage. By the 1920s, Chicago was the second most important theater center in the country, with more than twenty theaters operating simultaneously. Ensuing decades saw a decline in Chicago's role as a theater center, possibly owing to overly harsh tendencies in local drama criticism, but more likely attributable to the rising values of the real estate occupied by playhouses.[16]

In recent decades, Chicago's contributions to theater culture have been largely nonmainstream enterprises such as the Goodman Theatre, smaller companies like the Steppenwolf and Wisdom Bridge theaters, and the famous Second City troupe, which generated a nationwide craze for improvisational comedy. Other midwestern cities have established branches of Second City, hoping perhaps to emulate the success of the Chicago original, which over the years propelled many comic actors into the national limelight. An incomplete list would include John Belushi, Dan Aykroyd, Bill Murray, Harold Ramis, Joan Rivers, Alan Arkin, Gilda Radner, Betty Thomas, Robert Klein, Fred Willard, Martin Short, John Candy, Tina Fey, Rachel Dratch, and Chris Farley. One can hardly think of the long-running television program *Saturday Night Live* without acknowledging the number of Chicago comedians who energized the first years of that "New York" show.

Internationally recognized talents who have emerged from Chicago's amateur and professional stages include Geraldine Page and other prominent Broadway figures, David Mamet, Mike Nichols, and Elaine May, Gary Sinise, Joe Mantegna, John Malkovich, and Eugene Levy.[17]

Vaudeville

From the late nineteenth century until the early 1930s, the most widespread professional, commercial stage performance in the United States was vaudeville, and the phenomenon made its mark in the Midwest as well as the rest of the country. Vaudeville in Chicago began around 1882, at Kohl and Middleton's West Side Museum, a dime museum founded by C. E. Kohl and George Middleton. The Kohl–Middleton partnership expanded its vaudeville operations to include the Clark Street Museum, the Olympic Theater, the Chicago Opera House, and the Haymarket Theater. In 1900, Kohl bought out Middleton, and his new partnership with George Castle would dominate early vaudeville in Chicago. Over the next few years Kohl and Castle augmented their holdings with the Majestic Theater, the Academy of Music, the Star Theater, and the Palace Music Hall. In 1919, Kohl and Castle became a part of the Orpheum vaudeville circuit. Other notable Chicago vaudeville houses included the London Dime Museum, Howard's, and the Pekin (black-owned and catering to black audiences).[18]

Vaudeville acts ranged from singers, musicians, and dancers to acrobatic acts, comedic skits, magicians, ventriloquists, and animal acts. Some of the stars of vaudeville, perhaps virtually forgotten today, went on to achieve fame in motion pictures and television; these include Burns and Allen, Buster Keaton, W. C. Fields, the Nicholas Brothers, Rose Marie, and Morey Amsterdam. Vaudeville performers toured the country appearing in theaters controlled by a few key companies, or theater circuits.

The most important consortium of vaudeville theaters in the Midwest and the West was the Orpheum circuit. The first Orpheum theater opened in 1887 in San Francisco, and by 1905 the company had expanded to seventeen theaters, reaching as far east as Chicago. Among the major midwestern theaters of the Orpheum circuit were the State-Lake Chicago and the Orpheum in Kansas City. Altogether, Orpheum controlled twenty-six vaudeville houses in the Midwest, with multiple theaters in Illinois, Indiana, Iowa, Minnesota, Missouri, and Wisconsin, several of which still stand.

Variety noted that at one point the Alexander Pantages circuit was the most important independent vaudeville circuit in the country. Booked out of New York and Chicago, it included theaters in Chicago (the Chateau), Cleveland (the Circle), Columbus (the James), Detroit (the Miles and the Regent), Indianapolis (the Chateau), Toledo (the Rivoli), Kansas City (the Pantages), and Minneapolis. According to *Variety*, "personally, Pantages favored the acrobatic type of act and played at least one on all of his shows."[19]

The B. F. Keith circuit was more powerful in the eastern states, but it did control a few houses in the Midwest, including the Temple in Detroit, the Hippodrome in Cleveland, and B. F. Keith's in Indianapolis. In the mid-1920s, Keith's became more actively involved in the film industry, integrating motion pictures and vaudeville acts in a single program (although that practice dated back at least to the 1910s).[20]

Another circuit active in the Midwest was the Shubert Vaudeville Exchange, an arm of New York's famous Shubert organization. The so-called Shubert Advanced Vaudeville presented two shows a day, seven days a week, in Chicago, Detroit, Cleveland, and Dayton, as well as a few East Coast cities. Finally, the Loew vaudeville circuit included theaters in Chicago (the Rialto), Cleveland (the State), Milwaukee (Miller's), and Evansville, Indiana (the Victory).

Probably the best surviving record of actual vaudeville acts is a series of short films produced by Warner Brothers, starting in 1926, using their then-new Vitaphone sound system. One of the strategies of Warners' move into sound film production (at a time when practically no other studio was even considering sound) was to be able to showcase top vaudeville acts of the day in their movie theaters around the country, by way of these short films with sound.

ALTERNATIVE THEATER PRACTICES

Chautauqua

According to Anthony Slide, chautauqua was in many ways an outdoor form of vaudeville, presenting lecturers and respectable entertainers on a circuit as well run as anything in the vaudeville industry. The concept originated in 1874 with a midwesterner, Lewis Miller of Akron, Ohio, and a Camptown, New York, minister named John H. Vincent, who jointly decided to start a summer school to teach religious values. A similar group formed in Lakeside, Ohio, and as the movement spread it began to attract nondenominational speakers as diverse as Carry Nation, Eugene V. Debs, and Booker T. Washington. Eventually, small-time vaudeville acts found their way into chautauqua, and virtually any act was considered acceptable as long as it provided culture, uplift, or inspiration. The movement flourished in the Midwest and other regions until 1924, when it could no longer compete for audiences with vaudeville, motion pictures, and radio.[21]

Showboats

The singularly American phenomenon of the showboat first appeared on the Mississippi River in 1817, offering a staple of melodrama, musical comedy, and obscure minstrel shows. The phenomenon halted with the onset of the Civil War but resumed around 1869, offering such new attractions as magic, ventriloquism, banjo playing, and vaudeville-style turns between major acts. Showboats could still be found on the Mississippi into the early 1930s, but after the Great Depression only a few survived as curiosities.

Life aboard a midwestern Mississippi River showboat was unforgettably dramatized in the Oscar Hammerstein II and Jerome Kern musical, *Showboat*, based on the Edna Ferber novel and first produced on Broadway in 1927. The original run lasted 575 performances, and the show has been revived on Broadway at least four times. Three film versions were made—in 1929, 1936, and 1951.[22]

ETHNIC THEATER IN THE MIDWEST

Less famous and less commercial than the other theatrical forms discussed so far, ethnic theater played a vital role in the cultural lives of immigrant communities across the Midwest. These performances not only sustained ethnic identity but also enriched the regional arts scene.

Polish American Theater

We can trace Polish American theater, one of the oldest ethnic theatrical traditions in the Midwest, as far back as the 1870s, although the greatest period of Polish immigration into the United States began in the early 1900s. In Chicago in 1873, Gmina Polska (the Polish Community Society) began sponsoring amateur stage performances, with an average of five plays per season, continuing through the 1880s. Soon Polish language theater began truly to thrive in various parts of the United States, including New York and Philadelphia. In the Midwest, Chicago remained the apex of activity, but active Polish stage programs also could be found in Milwaukee, St. Paul, Detroit, La Salle, Illinois, Menominee, Wisconsin, Winona, Minnesota, and Grand Rapids, Michigan.[23]

The Roman Catholic Church played an important financial role in the development of Polish American theater. In Chicago alone more than half a dozen parishes became theatrical benefactors between 1891 and 1915. The Polish American socialist movement also sponsored amateur theater, and there was at least one socialist company in Chicago, the Society of the Free Spirit, that presented plays about class struggle in Poland and in the United States.

Detroit's Polish American theater groups tended to be secular, less political, and semiprofessional, rather than amateur, and more mainstream. Between 1915 and the early 1930s, at least eight such companies produced plays with some regularity, often with two or three groups existing simultaneously. The plays they produced varied from operettas to melodramas, from tragedy to comedy, from traditional Polish works to translated, non-Polish plays (including works of Shakespeare, Schiller, Molière, and Gorky), and perhaps most interestingly, plays written by Polish Americans chronicling the shared immigrant experience. Although a number of the productions seemed simply to offer entertainment as an escape from the problems of everyday life faced by their immigrant, working-class audiences, some took on themes as wide-ranging as antiwar (during World War I), anticapitalist, anti-German, and anti-Russian.

Finnish American Theater

Finnish Americans made up one of the smallest immigrant populations in the Midwest in the early twentieth century, but that community's dedication to the cultural side of life, demanding and supporting an amazing level of dramatic activity, makes it well worth considering here. Theater was one of many functions of Finnish community centers, so every enclave had at least one theater and often more. The labor movement especially used theater spaces as centers of social life, political activity, and education.

Regional theater historian Paul Sporn cites 1910–1930 as the "golden age" of Finnish American theater, with an average of 3,000 performances a year nationwide, to an annual audience of half a million. These are astonishing figures for a community that numbered only 350,000 at the most. These theater groups regularly produced a new play every two, three, or four weeks, in big cities such as Cleveland and Detroit, as well as in smaller towns like Warren, Ohio. Even the very smallest of Finnish enclaves, such as those in Upper Michigan, had theater companies of long tenure that produced several plays a year. All these performances would consistently play to near-capacity houses, according to Sporn. Audiences and performers alike were working class: from the steel mills of Chicago, the iron ranges of Minnesota, the automobile factories of Detroit, and the copper mines of Michigan.

The repertoire had its healthy share of socialist-themed plays, as well as plays by Finnish Americans about the immigrant experience; but the people at the helm of these efforts recognized that too much of such an emphasis would wear thin on audiences. Furthermore, the need to make money called for a wider repertoire. In fact, classics of the Finnish stage made up the bulk of productions, with melodramas, musical plays, and folk dramas rounding out each season.

African American Theater

One of the most important theatrical phenomena for midwestern African American audiences in the twentieth century was the so-called Chittlin' Circuit. Some contemporary commentators consider the term offensive because as it harks back to a pre–civil rights era, when blacks generally were not allowed on the same bill as whites. Nevertheless, the phrase is still used to describe not only the venues featuring African American performers catering primarily to African American audiences, but also the type of programming typically offered there. This included plays, concerts, even minstrel shows, where entertainment and inspiration took precedence over heavy-handed "art" and social commentary. Audiences, especially in the early twentieth century, expected familiar characters, humor, and escapism from these shows, not anger, agitation, or revolutionary messages. The Chittlin' Circuit has grown and continued to thrive, even after the end of segregation in the South and Midwest. It is one of the few places that consistently has offered African American audiences meaningful theatrical representations of their own lives.[24]

A number of other theatrical enterprises have of course also targeted black audiences in midwestern cities, such as the Gilpin Players of Cleveland's Karamu (Swahili for "center of the community") Theater in the 1920s, and the Skyloft

Players of Chicago, founded by Langston Hughes in 1941. Detroit provides a good example. In the mid-1920s, the Urban League of Detroit added a number of cultural clubs, including a dramatic club, to its roster of after-work social activities for the city's working-class black population. The program drew hundreds of participants, adults as well as children, who performed mostly one-act plays for black and white audiences at various locations around the city. Other independent black theater groups in Detroit performed in venues such as the YMCA, offering fare that ranged from *Murder in the Cathedral* to an adaptation of *Hamlet* with songs and dance to dramas by the local playwright Willard Leon Gardner.

THE "LITTLE THEATER" MOVEMENT

This nationwide phenomenon of the 1920s formed the roots of community and regional theater. Little Theaters were local, amateur groups, usually with high-minded ideals expressed in manifestos, driven by the conviction that they could create theater locally that was as good or better than that of the New York stage. The Chicago Little Theater dates from 1911, and the Wisconsin Players in Milwaukee from 1914. The movement spread. By 1925, the National Theater Conference located at Cleveland's Western Reserve University helped guide and coordinate the activities of local theaters around the country.

By the 1930s, however, the revolutionary quality of the movement, and thus its relevance, had diminished. What had been the "Little Theater" movement (with capital *L* and *T*) became community theater, a relatively safe enterprise that offered an evening's entertainment.[25]

Repertory Theater in the Midwest

One of the Midwest's most famous repertory companies, managed by Jessie Bonstelle in Detroit, was variously known as the Bonstelle Playhouse and the Detroit Civic Theater. Between its inception in 1910 and its demise in 1934 (two years after the death of Bonstelle herself), it attracted some of New York's top talent for its leading roles, including Melvyn Douglas, Jessie Royce Landis, and Katherine Cornell. One of the most outstanding features of the Bonstelle company was its sense of community, with the stated goals of giving the public "the best of spoken drama . . . at the lowest possible prices," and particularly of acquainting "the younger generation with the finest of the world's dramatic literature." Audience involvement was also rather important, and Bonstelle initiated one-dollar "sponsorships" that garnered as many as 30,000 supporters annually. Another indication of the group's popularity was that its annual free outdoor performance of Shakespeare's *A Midsummer Night's Dream* regularly drew audiences in the tens of thousands.[26]

By the late 1920s, the Detroit Civic Theater had become a model for other emerging community theaters around the country, and there was hope that the movement would eventually result in a national theater. Such groups laid an important foundation for the work that the WPA's Federal Theater Project would accomplish in the late 1930s.

Left-wing Revolutionary Theater

In the early years of the Great Depression, working-class, revolutionary theater was supported by "John Reed Clubs," Marxist-communist groups formed in most major American cities and some smaller ones, including Chicago, Cleveland, Detroit, Milwaukee, and Youngstown, Ohio. One example was Chicago's Blue Blouse mobile theater, essentially an agit-prop[27] street company that put on as many as three performances a night.

Among other achievements, such productions helped build an audience for the understandably socialist bent that would inform many of the Federal Theater productions to come in the mid- to late-1930s. According to Sporn, in the 1920s and 1930s, "Chicago, Cleveland and Detroit had left-wing theater groups that stimulated local playwrights to dramatize working-class struggles and politics. Their most innovative stagings were achieved in short agit-prop skits and musical farces, the latter relying on popular and folk tunes for their basic material."[28]

The WPA Federal Theater Project

Begun in 1935 as part of the New Deal's Works Progress Administration, the Federal Theater Project (FTP) was designed to provide work for unemployed artists and administrators. At its peak, the Federal Theater gave work to more than 15,000 professionals, and by the time of its demise in 1939 (at the hands of the House Un-American Activities Committee), it had staged over one thousand productions in forty American cities. Midwestern FTP units that lasted for the entire tenure of the program were to be found only in Illinois, Michigan, and Ohio.

Hallie Flanagan, the director of the Federal Theater Project, believed that "for the first time, the professional theatre might also be considered regionally. Under a federal plan, could not all of these various theatres, commercial, educational, and community, in the East, West, North, South, work together?"[29] Flanagan also sought to reach a public that had been overlooked by the legitimate stage. She wrote that the people of the "factory district of Detroit," for example, "like our small Iowa towns in a different way, made up the very backbone of America." These previously overlooked publics, whether they be family farmers or immigrant workers, "had become the American scene," as Sporn puts it,[30] and they were vitally important to the project of the Federal Theater. The FTP canvassed audience opinion after each performance, paying special attention to the responses of labor and community leaders believed to represent the "common" public.

In general, the FTP groups performed a wide range of plays, including many folk-related works in which various ethnic groups could introduce their cultures and customs to each other. FTP projects, like other socialist arts, "tend to idealize their subjects, to portray them in monumental scale." The most profoundly populist effort of the FTP was to produce plays by local writers who had experienced the problems of the common farmer, laborer, immigrant, and the like in the Midwest. The program also put on plays based on local and regional legend and lore. This was a major effort, as the FTP consistently encouraged even the largest and most successful programs, such as the one in Detroit, to stage local plays. Still, some administrators were more concerned with filling houses than with populist ideals, and some even believed that light entertainment was all that

Detroit Federal Theatre Unit of Michigan Works Progress Administration presents *It Can't Happen Here* by Sinclair Lewis, c. 1936–1937. Courtesy Library of Congress.

regional federal theater could reasonably hope to accomplish. As Sporn points out, none of the Detroit unit's twenty-five plays came from the lives of the immigrant workers to whom they were being addressed, but a number of them did stress social issues.

Chicago's Federal Theater Project was atypically cosmopolitan and professional, making it more like a New York or California company. Its most famous production was a home-based creation of its "Negro unit," *The Swing Mikado*. This revamping of Gilbert and Sullivan, using jazz stylistics and a flamboyant but particularly American visual design, was a highly collaborative effort.

In addition to fulfilling its stated goal of providing meaningful jobs, the Federal Theater accomplished at least two other important feats. It spawned a sizable body of professional theater practitioners, and it identified and developed an audience for serious, socially committed drama.

Post–World War II Regional Theater

Historian Gerald Berkowitz characterized the professional American theater at mid-twentieth century as being totally dominated by Broadway.[31] However, we have already seen that there were numerous thriving, regional, amateur theater movements in the Midwest (and indeed around the country), and those efforts continued, post–WPA and post–World War II. Indeed, some existing amateur companies were inspired to elevate themselves to the level of professional theaters, in what Berkowitz calls the Cleveland Play House model:

> The Play House, one of the oldest community theatres in America, had had a professional executive director and business staff since the 1920s but had retained its amateur status even as its activities expanded to include an annual summer Shakespeare festival; it finally made the change in 1958.[32]

Recent productions on the main stage of the Cleveland Play House include *Two Pianos, Four Hands*, the world premiere of *Forest City*, Neil Simon's *The Dinner*

Party, *Vincent in Brixton*, *The Underpants* (adapted by Steve Martin), and *Cookin' at the Cookery: The Life and Music of Alberta Hunter*.

Similarly, Chicago's Goodman Theater, a community theater and acting school affiliated with the Art Institute since the 1920s, formed a professional repertory company in 1969. That company remained, even after the acting school split off to become part of Chicago's De Paul University. Some notable productions at the Goodman since 1969 include *The Canterville Ghost*, *St. Joan*, *The Tooth of the Crime*, *Glengarry Glen Ross*, and *Hurlyburly*. The 1990s saw world premiere productions of *Marvin's Room*, *The House of Martin Guerre*, *Spinning into Butter*, and *Boy Gets Girl*; and classics including *The Iceman Cometh* with Brian Dennehy, *The Night of the Iguana* with William Petersen and Cherry Jones, *Three Sisters*, *The Young Man from Atlanta*, and *Death of a Salesman* with Brian Dennehy.

Conversely, some theaters started out in the 1950s as professional stock companies and later reorganized themselves into nonprofit repertory theaters. In 1963, Milwaukee's Fred Miller Theater (founded in 1954 and named for the head of the Miller Brewing Company) became the Milwaukee Repertory Theater. Since then, the Rep has offered an array of productions ranging from Molière's *Tartuffe* to Brecht's *Mother Courage*, from Chekhov's *Uncle Vanya* to *Marat/Sade*, from Shakespeare to world premieres including Nagle Jackson and Jeffrey Tambor's *All Together Now*, Robert Ingham's *Custer*, David Mamet's *Lakeboat*, Larry Shue's *The Foreigner*, Norman Moses and Wesley Savick's *Wholly Moses*, Kander and Ebb's *2x5x4*, and Mercedes Ellington's *Duke's Place*.

The Guthrie Theater

By the late 1950s, a number of dedicated, energetic individuals and groups had created full-grown regional theaters, with perhaps the most spectacular example being the Minnesota Theater Company (later known as the Tyrone Guthrie Theater) in Minneapolis. Tyrone Guthrie and two associates decided that they wanted to create a professional repertory company, and the location of Minneapolis was chosen somewhat arbitrarily. They did not seek so much to address their theater to a particular community as to find a community that would support their vision for a theater company. Community leaders in Milwaukee were so impressed with Guthrie's plans that the city agreed to build the $2.25 million facility. The largest gift came from the Walker Foundation, which donated not only the real estate where the theater would be built but also $500,000. The smallest, yet much-publicized gift was $6.37, from a Sunday school class in Mankato, Minnesota, some eighty miles away. This contribution was not only hyped in local newspapers but also was commemorated in a short "documentary" film about the fund-raising effort, *Miracle in Minnesota*. This mammoth local support brought a new level of legitimacy and attention to the regional theater movement, and other such theaters sprang up around the country in the 1960s.[33]

Around this time, some university theaters began to step up their programs to a more professional level, in response to concerns raised by funding agencies that such programs were merely "teaching people to teach people." It became necessary, then, for theater departments to ally themselves with existing professional companies or to bring professionals on board as adjunct faculty. For example, the University of Minnesota developed a close working relationship with the Guthrie.

In some cases, what began as a university theater company would evolve into a professional theater. Such was the case with the Loretto-Hilton Center of St. Louis, which grew out of the theater program at Webster College (now Webster University).

Berkowitz characterizes the general tendencies in programming strategies among regional theaters, from the 1960s on, as striking "a predictable balance between the familiar and the challenging."[34] A typical season might include one Shakespeare play, one modern continental classic (probably Shaw or Chekhov), one major American playwright such as Tennessee Williams or Arthur Miller, one crowd-pleaser such as a musical or comedy, maybe one rather avant-garde piece by Pirandello, Brecht, or Beckett, and sometimes even a new American play, possibly even something written locally.

By the end of the 1970s, regional theater had successfully become a part of the American cultural landscape. This was thanks largely to the subscription-based system of ticket sales, which not only fostered regular patronage among audiences but also gave companies the freedom to be a bit more daring in their programming choices. The success of regional theater not only brought drama to audiences who otherwise might never have been exposed to it, but it also gave the theater a vital role in American cultural life that it had not had in well over a hundred years.[35]

MAJOR MIDWESTERN PLAYWRIGHTS

Midwestern playwrights did not attract much attention before the late nineteenth century, when American letters overcame the inferiority complex that had subordinated American culture to that of England and Europe. Two somewhat contradictory tendencies governed the presentation of region on stages. The first, associated with the local color movement of the 1890s, later to peak in attempts by the Federal Theater Project to recover earlier works, celebrated midwestern experiences and values as humane and admirable. The second, associated with the "revolt from the village" period of American fiction during the early twentieth century, viewed small towns as incubators of conservatism and backwardness.

Eugene Walter (b. Cleveland, Ohio, 1874–1941) wrote *Paid in Full* (1908) and *The Easiest Way* (1909), works usually regarded as prefiguring more realistic treatment of small-town life. Augustus Thomas (b. St. Louis, Missouri, 1857–1934) wrote *Mizzoura* (1893) and *The Copperhead* (1917), Civil War melodramas set in Missouri and Illinois, respectively, after a career as a newspaperman in St. Louis and Kansas City. William Vaughn Moody (1869–1910), a native of Spencer, Indiana, wrote a series of verse plays that were vaguely redolent of the region west of Pittsburgh: *The Fire Bringer* (1904), *The Great Divide* (1909), and *The Faith Healer* (1909). Floyd Dell (1887–1969), a Chicago journalist before he became editor of the radical magazines *The Masses* and *The Liberator*, wrote leftist one-act plays such as *The Angel Intrudes* (1918). Rachel Crothers (1878–1958), also from Illinois, wrote many plays dealing with women in the modern world, among them *A Man's World* (1909), *He and She* (1911), *Nice People* (1920), and *Susan and God* (1938). Wisconsin-born Zona Gale (1874–1938), best known for her Pulitzer Prize-winning *Miss Lulu Bett* (1920), a treatment of the effects of a bleak village life on a spinster, also wrote plays that sentimentalized life in Friendship Village; examples are *The Neighbors* (1914) and *Uncle Jimmy* (1921). Another writer from Wisconsin, Hamlin Garland (1860–1940), condemned the slavery of farm life in the Midwest in *Under the Wheel* (1890). Jerome Lawrence (1915–   ) and Robert E. Lee (1918–1984), both of Ohio, authors of *Inherit the Wind* (1955), also based their *Jabberwock* (1972) on the life of Columbus, Ohio, humorist James Thurber (1894–1961). Thurber himself, writing with Elliot Nugent, set *The Male Animal* (1939) in Columbus. For many Americans, of course, the quintessential midwestern drama will always be Meredith Wilson's (1902–1984) *The Music Man* (1957), a musical set in "River City," Iowa, clearly modeled on Wilson's own hometown, Mason City. Wilson's other musicals include *The Unsinkable Molly Brown* (1960) and *Here's Love* (1963), the latter an adaptation of *Miracle on 34th Street*. All of them left the nation humming Wilson's songs.

Many dramatists who gravitated toward the theatrical scene of the East nonetheless drew on their experience before they left, setting their stages in small midwestern towns populated with characters they constructed to represent values they remembered, admired, or despised. The histories of Susan Keating Glaspell (1876–1948) and George Cram Cook (1873–1924) are typical. Born in Davenport, Iowa, the two of them married, then fled what they thought of as small-mindedness; together they founded the Provincetown Players (Massachusetts and New York). Glaspell's own plays pose midwestern ideals against midwestern smugness; her characters tend to be trapped in rusticated isolation. She set *Trifles* (1916), *Close the Book* (1920), *The Inheritors* (1921), and *Chains of Dew* (1922), in Iowa, for instance. After winning a Pulitzer Prize for the nonmidwestern play *Alison's House* (1931), she returned to her region to direct the Midwest Play Bureau of the Federal Theater Project in 1936. Cook wrote plays with Glaspell, then set his *The Spring* (1921) in an Illinois village once inhabited by the tribal chieftain Black Hawk. *The Spring* rejected small midwestern town life. After his divorce from Glaspell, Cook became one of the most distinguished of the nation's stage designers.

Less inclined to draw on their origins, other dramatists aimed at more universal themes for national audiences. Archibald Macleish (1892–1982), from Glencoe, Illinois, wrote *Panic* (1935), *J. B.: A Play in Verse* (1958), and *Scratch* (1971), none of which was dependent on familiarity with his birthplace. Langston Hughes (1902–1967) was born in Joplin, Missouri, and lived as well in Kansas, Illinois, and Ohio. In Chicago, he experimented with plays, the most successful of which is probably *Mulatto* (1935), but they did not evoke much regional sensibility. Even Booth Tarkington (b. Indianapolis, 1869–1946), often identified as a Hoosier writer, tended to stage stories set in far-off places, as in *Monsieur Beaucaire* (1901), about a French duke's adventures in eighteenth-century England; *Seventeen* (1917) is one of his plays that used Indiana characters. Thornton Wilder (1897–1975), born in Madison, Wisconsin, devoted his talents to depicting small-town life in New Hampshire (*Our Town* [1938]) and New Jersey (*The Skin of Our Teeth* [1942]).

Several important playwrights identified with the Midwest were born elsewhere. The New Jersey poet William Ellery Leonard's (1876–1944) *Glory of the Morning* (1912) and *Red Bird* (1923) dramatized encounters between early French trappers and Indians to illustrate the damage that Europeans wreaked on indigenous cultures in the area that became Wisconsin. Born in Kansas, William Inge (1913–1973) spent much of his working life as a drama professor and a critic for the *St. Louis Star-Times* before his success with *Come Back, Little Sheba* (1949), *Picnic* (1953), and *Bus Stop* (1955), all of which dealt with life in small towns swept by change. Born in New York City, Ben Hecht (ca. 1893–1964) moved as a boy to Racine, Wisconsin. Charles MacArthur (1895–1956), born in Pennsylvania but like Hecht a Chicago newspaperman, collaborated with Hecht in writing *The Front Page* (1928) and *Twentieth Century* (1932), both shaped by their journalistic experience in the Midwest. Usually associated with New Orleans and points south, and actually born in Mississippi, Tennessee Williams (1914–1983) spent his formative years in St. Louis. There, after a short stint at the University of Missouri, he worked in a shoe factory and began his career as a dramatist with The Mummers, a local group. After attending Washington University in St. Louis and the University of Iowa, he began turning out one-act and full-length plays for The Mummers before moving to New Orleans. National renown came with the Chicago opening of *The Glass Menagerie* (1944), a poignant story set in a St. Louis being overtaken by modernity. New Yorker Robert E. Sherwood (1896–1955) won one of his Pulitzer Prizes for *Abe Lincoln in Illinois* (1938), which finds clues to the great president's personality in the youth he spent traversing the Midwest. Originally from Tennessee, Lorraine Hansberry (1930–1965) grew up in Chicago. The African American characters in her *Raisin in the Sun* (1957) cope with racism and intolerance in the ghettos of that city. The Midwest is often irresistible to outsiders who find its values enobling or stultifying. George Aiken's (1830–1876) stage version of Harriet Beecher Stowe's *Uncle Tom's Cabin* (1852) is of course partially set in Ohio, a beacon of freedom for the escaped slaves. Although neither was from the Midwest, Countee Cullen (1903–1946) dramatized Arna Bontemps' (1902–1973) *St. Louis Woman* (1946) into a rousing African American musical. Moss Hart (1904–1961) and George S. Kaufman's (1889–1961) *The Man Who Came to Dinner* (1939) finds laughter in the encounter between a New York radio personality and a family in Ohio.

More recently, David Mamet (1947–) has emerged as one of the most prominent serious midwestern playwrights. In 1975, Chicago's Goodman Theatre produced Mamet's *American Buffalo*, whose plot, involving thieves attempting to steal a coin collection, was almost secondary to Mamet's deft use of midwestern language and voices. Mamet followed this enormous success with other urban dramas, most notably *Sexual Perversity in Chicago* (1976), about a couple fleeing the singles scene, and *Glengarry Glen Ross* (1992), about corrupt Chicago real estate entrepreneurs. Like Mamet also a screenwriter, Sam Shepard (1943–), born in Fort Sheridan, Illinois, has become a major writer of subversive drama, especially in *Buried Child* (1979), *Mad Dog Blues* (1971), and *True West* (1980). Vietnam looms large in the plays of Iowan David Rabe (1940–), whose career has explored the effects of trauma on veterans, some of them midwestern: *The Basic Training of Pavlo Hummel* (1971), *The Orphan* (1973), *Boom Boom Room* (1973), *Streamers* (1976), and *Hurlyburly* (1984). Rabe has explored the American psyche through wit, satire, and fantasy. Lanford Wilson (1937–) has achieved fame for such works as *The Hot L Baltimore* (1973) and for the more specifically regional *The Mound Builders* (1975), the story of an archaeological dig. The plays of his Talley tetralogy, however, are his most region-bound. *Talley's Folly* (1979), *Talley & Son* (1985), and *A Tale Told* (1987) all take place on the same night, July 4, 1944, in his boyhood home of Lebanon, Missouri. The fourth play, *The Fifth of July* (1978), takes place the day after.

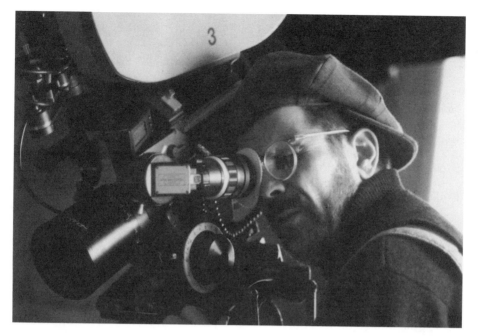

David Mamet. Photofest.

CONCLUSION

We have seen, by way of the plethora of film and theater activity centered in the Midwest, that its cultural life is vastly more varied and complex than one might initially suspect. From the birth of cinema up to the present day, films have employed midwestern settings and themes to reinforce and reinvent our perceptions of the region; and the theater has been an important component of midwestern cultural life from the earliest days of American settlement there. Furthermore, the "midwestern identity," reflected in films and plays about the region, is considerably more nuanced than we sometimes allow. Far from being a homogenized cultural void, inhabited solely by "simple, white-bread folk," the Midwest boasts a rich, heterogeneous, sociocultural landscape that continues to re-present and redefine itself. This dynamism manifests itself in myriad ways, not least in the region's vital ongoing theater and film cultures.

RESOURCE GUIDE

Printed Sources

Berkowitz, Gerald M. *New Broadways—Theatre Across America: Approaching A New Millennium*. Revised edition. New York: Applause, 1997.

Gunning, Tom. "The Cinema of Attractions: Early Film, Its Spectator and the Avant-Garde." In *Early Film*, ed. Thomas Elsaesser and Adam Barker. London: British Film Institute, 1989.

Herron, Ima Homaker. *The Small Town in American Drama*. Dallas: Southern Methodist University Press, 1968.

Internet Movie Database. www.imdb.com.

Lyons, Donald. *Independent Visions: A Critical Introduction to Recent Independent American Film*. New York: Ballantine, 1994.

Merrick, James W. "'Anatomy' Operation Before a Bar of Justice: Screen Version of Book Takes Shape in Authentic Courtroom Setting." *New York Times*, April 12, 1959.

Slide, Anthony. *The Encyclopedia of Vaudeville*. Westport, CT: Greenwood Press, 1994.

Sper, Felix. *From Native Roots: A Panorama of Our Regional Drama*. Caldwell, ID: Caxton Printer, 1948.

Sporn, Paul. *Against Itself: The Federal Theater and Writers' Projects in the Midwest*. Detroit: Wayne State University Press, 1995.

Telotte, J. P. *Voices in the Dark: The Narrative Patterns of Film Noir*. Urbana: University of Illinois Press, 1990.

Tibbetts, John C. "Elastic Soil: Spaces and Places in Movies about the American Middle West," In *Columbia University Companion to American History on Film*. New York: Columbia University Press, forthcoming 2004.

Zeigler, Joseph Wesley. *Regional Theatre: The Revolutionary Stage*. Minneapolis: University of Minnesota Press, 1973.

Selected Filmography

Abe Lincoln in Illinois. Dir. John Cromwell. Max Gordon Plays & Pictures Corp., and RKO Radio Pictures; 1940.

The Adventures of Huckleberry Finn. Dir. Richard Thorpe. Metro-Goldwyn-Mayer; 1939.

The Adventures of Tom Sawyer. Dir. Norman Taurog, George Cukor, H. C. Potter, and William A. Wellman. Selznick International Pictures; 1938.

American Movie. Dir. Chris Smith. Bluemark Productions, C-Hundred Film Corp., and Civilian Pictures; 1999.

An American Romance. Dir. King Vidor. Metro-Goldwyn-Mayer; 1944.

American Splendor. Dir. Shari Springer Berman and Robert Pulcini. Good Machine and Home Box Office; 2003.

Anatomy of a Murder. Dir. Otto Preminger. Carlyle Productions and Columbia Pictures Corp.; 1959.

Annie Get Your Gun. Dir. George Sidney. Metro-Goldwyn-Mayer; 1950.

Annie Oakley. Dir. George Stevens. RKO Radio Pictures; 1935.

The Blues Brothers. Dir. John Landis. Universal Pictures; 1980.

The Breakfast Club. Dir. John Hughes. A&M Films and Universal Pictures; 1985.

The Bridges of Madison County. Dir. Clint Eastwood. Amblin Entertainment, Malpaso Productions, and Warner Bros.; 1995.

Bye Bye Birdie. Dir. George Sidney. Columbia Pictures Corp. and Kohlmar-Sidney Productions; 1963.

Call Northside 777. Dir. Henry Hathaway. 20th Century-Fox; 1948.

Chicago. Dir. Rob Marshall. Loop Films, Miramax Films, and the Producers Circle Co.; 2002.

The Crowd Roars. Dir. Howard Hawks. Warner Bros.; 1932.

Dark City. Dir. William Dieterle. Paramount Pictures; 1950.

8 Mile. Dir. Curtis Hanson. Imagine Entertainment and Mikona Productions; 2002.

Elmer Gantry. Dir. Richard Brooks. Gantry Productions and United Artists; 1960.

Ferris Bueller's Day Off. Dir. John Hughes. Paramount Pictures; 1986.

The Front Page. Dir. Lewis Milestone. The Caddo Co.; 1931.

The Front Page. Dir. Billy Wilder. Universal Pictures; 1974.

The Great Gatsby. Dir. Jack Clayton. Newdon Productions and Paramount Pictures; 1974.

The Great White Hope. Dir. Martin Ritt. 20th Century-Fox; 1970.

Gummo. Dir. Harmony Korine. Fine Line Features and Independent Pictures; 1997.

Heathers. Dir. Michael Lehmann. Cinemarque and New World Entertainment; 1989.

High Fidelity. Dir. Stephen Frears. Dogstar Films, New Crime Productions, Touchstone Pictures, and Working Title Films; 2000.

His Girl Friday. Dir. Howard Hawks. Columbia Pictures Corp.; 1939.

Hoop Dreams. Dir. Steve James. KTCA Minneapolis and Kartemquin Films; 1994.

Huck and Tom. Dir. William Desmond Taylor. Famous Players-Lasky Corp. and Oliver Morosco Photoplay Co.; 1918.

Huckleberry Finn. Dir. William Desmond Taylor. Famous Players-Lasky Corp. and Paramount Pictures; 1920.

In Cold Blood. Dir. Richard Brooks. Pax Enterprises and Columbia Pictures Corp.; 1967.

In Old Chicago. Dir. Henry King. 20th Century-Fox; 1937.

Jesse James. Dir. Henry King and Irving Cummings. 20th Century-Fox; 1939.

June Bride. Dir. Bretaigne Windust. Warner Bros. and First National Pictures; 1948.

The Jungle. Dir. George Irving, John H. Pratt, and Augustus Thomas. All Star Feature Film Corp.; 1914.

Knute Rockne All-American. Dir. Lloyd Bacon. Warner Bros. and First National Pictures; 1940.

Little Caesar. Dir. Mervyn Leroy. First National Pictures; 1931.

Lolita. Dir. Stanley Kubrick. Anya Productions, Harris-Kubrick Productions Seven Arts Productions, and Transwood; 1962.

The Magnificent Ambersons. Dir. Orson Welles. Mercury Productions, and RKO Radio Pictures; 1942.

Major League. Dir. David S. Ward. Mirage and Morgan Creek Productions; 1989.

Medium Cool. Dir. Haskell Wexler. H & J; 1969.

Meet Me in St. Louis. Dir. Vincente Minnelli. Metro-Goldwyn-Mayer; 1944.

The Money Corral. Dir. William S. Hart. William S. Hart Productions; 1919.

The Music Man. Dir. Morton DaCosta. Warner Bros.; 1962.

The Night of the Hunter. Dir. Charles Laughton. Paul Gregory Productions and United Artists; 1955.

Nightmare Alley. Dir. Edmund Goulding. 20th Century-Fox; 1947.

Ordinary People. Dir. Robert Redford. Wildwood and Paramount Pictures; 1980.

Pin-Up Girl. Dir. H. Bruce Humberstone. 20th Century-Fox; 1944.

The Plainsman. Dir. Cecil B. DeMille. Paramount Pictures; 1937.

Presenting Lily Mars. Dir. Norman Taurog. Metro-Goldwyn-Mayer; 1943.

Primary. Dir. Robert Drew. Time Magazine; 1960.

The Public Enemy. Dir. William A. Wellman. Warner Bros.; 1931.

A Raisin in the Sun. Dir. Daniel Petrie. Columbia Pictures Corp.; 1961.

The Return of Frank James. Dir. Fritz Lang. 20th Century-Fox; 1940.

Robin and the 7 Hoods. Dir. Gordon Douglas. Claude Productions, Essex Productions, and Warner Bros.; 1964.

Robocop. Dir. Paul Verhoeven. Orion Pictures Corp.; 1987.

Roger and Me. Dir. Michael Moore. Dog Eat Dog Films and Warner Bros.; 1989.

Roxie Hart. Dir. William A. Wellman. 20th Century-Fox; 1942.

Salesman. Dir. Albert Maysles, David Maysles, and Charlotte Zwerin. Maysles Films; 1969.

Scarface. Dir. Howard Hawks. Caddo and United Artists; 1932.

The Silence of the Lambs. Dir. Jonathan Demme. Orion Pictures Corp.; 1991.

So Dear to My Heart. Dir. Hamilton Luske and Harold D. Schuster. Walt Disney Pictures; 1949.

State Fair. Dir. Henry King. Fox Film Corp.; 1933.

State Fair. Dir. Walter Lang. 20th Century-Fox; 1945.

The Straight Story. Dir. David Lynch. Asymmetrical Productions, Channel Four Films, CiBy 2000, Studio Canal+, Les Films Alain Sarde, the Picture Factory, The Straight Story Inc., and Walt Disney Pictures; 1999.

Stranger Than Paradise. Dir. Jim Jarmusch. Cinesthesia Productions, Grokenberger Filmproduktion, and Zweites Deutches Fernsehen; 1983.

Strike Up the Band. Dir. Busby Berkeley. Loew's Inc. and Metro-Goldwyn-Mayer; 1940.

Tom Sawyer. Dir. William Desmond Taylor. Famous Players-Lasky Corp. and Oliver Morosco Photoplay Co.; 1917.

The Untouchables. Dir. Brian De Palma. Paramount Pictures; 1987.

Waiting for Guffman. Dir. Christopher Guest. All Night Productions, Castle Rock Entertainment, Pale Morning Dun, and Sony Pictures Classics; 1996.

Watermelon Man. Dir. Melvin Van Peebles. Johanna and Columbia Pictures Corp.; 1970.

Wells Fargo. Dir. Frank Lloyd. Paramount Pictures; 1937.

Young Mr. Lincoln. Dir. John Ford. Cosmopolitan Productions and 20th Century-Fox; 1939.

Organizations, Museums, Collections

Bowling Green State University (Ohio)
Popular Culture Library
Leo S. Rosencrans Collection of Chautauqua
Jerome Library, 4th Floor
Bowling Green, OH 43403
(419) 372-2450
www.bgsu.edu/colleges/library/pcl/pcl.html

Chicago Historical Society
Clark Street at North Avenue
Chicago, IL 60614-6071
(312) 642-4600
www.chicagohs.org/collections/film.html
Film and video collections.

Cleveland Play House
8500 Euclid Avenue
Cleveland, OH 44106
(216) 795-7000
www.clevelandplayhouse.com

Facets Multi-Media, Inc.
1517 W. Fullerton Avenue
Chicago, IL 60614
(773) 281-9075
www.facets.org

The Goodman Theatre
170 North Dearborn Street
Chicago, IL 60601
www.goodman-theatre.org

Greater Cleveland Film Commission
www.clevelandfilm.com/

Illinois Film Office
100 West Randolph, Suite 3-400

Chicago, IL 60601
(312) 814-7160
www.illinoisbiz.biz/film/index.html

Illinois State Historical Society
210 ½ S. Sixth
Springfield, IL 62701-1503
(217) 525-2781
www.historyillinois.org

Illinois Theatre Association
1225 W. Belmont Avenue
Chicago, IL 60657
www.iltheassoc.org

Independent Feature Project
Chicago chapter
33 East Congress Parkway, Room 505
Chicago, IL 60605
(312) 435-1825
www.ifp.org/?chapter=3

Independent Feature Project
Minneapolis–St. Paul chapter
401 N. 3rd Street, Ste. 450
Minneapolis, MN 55401
(612) 338-0871
www.ifp.org/?chapter=5

Indiana Film Commission
Indiana Department of Commerce
One North Capitol Avenue
Suite 700
Indianapolis, IN 46204-2288
(317) 232-8829
www.in.gov/film/

Indiana Historical Society
450 W. Ohio Street
Indianapolis, IN 46202
(317) 232-1882
www.indianahistory.org

Iowa Film Office
200 E. Grand Avenue
Des Moines, IA 50309
(515) 242-4726
www.state.ia.us/government/ided/film/html/fronthtml/index.html

Michigan Film Office
P.O. Box 30739
Lansing, MI 48909
(800) 477-3456 / (517) 373-0638
www.michigan.gov/hal/0,1607,7-160-17445_19275---,00.html

Milwaukee Repertory Theater
108 E. Wells Street
Milwaukee, WI 53202
www.milwaukeerep.com

Minnesota Film & TV Board
401 North Third Street
Suite 460
Minneapolis, MN 55401
(612) 332-6493
www.mnfilm.org

Minnesota Historical Society
Moving images collection
345 Kellogg Boulevard West
St. Paul, MN 55102
(651) 296-6126
www.mnhs.org/library/collections/movingimages/movingimages.html

Missouri Film Commission
301 W. High
Room 720
P.O. Box 118
Jefferson City, MO 65102
(573) 751-9050
www.ded.mo.gov/business/filmcommission

Missouri Historical Society
P.O. Box 11940
St. Louis, MO 63112-0040
(314) 454-3150
www.mohistory.org

New York Public Library for the Performing Arts
Lincoln Center
Billy Rose Collection
40 Lincoln Center Plaza
New York, NY 10023-7498
(212) 870-1639
www.nypl.org/research/lpa/the/the.html

Ohio Film Commission
Ohio Division of Travel and Tourism
77 S. High Street, 29th Floor
Columbus, OH 43215
(615) 466-8591
www.ohiofilm.com

Ohio Historical Society
Audiovisual collections
1982 Velma Avenue
Columbus, OH 43211
(614) 297-2300
www.ohiohistory.org/resource/audiovis/

Ohio Theatre Alliance
English/Drama Dept.
Franciscan University
1235 University Boulevard
Steubenville, OH 43952
(740) 283-6245, ext. 2121
www.ohiotheatrealliance.org

State Historical Society of Iowa
600 East Locust
Des Moines, IA 50319-0290
(515) 281-5111
www.iowahistory.org

University of Iowa
Special Collections and Manuscripts Division of the University Libraries
B. F. Keith / E. F. Albee Collection (Vaudeville)
University of Iowa Libraries
Iowa City, IA 52242-1420
(319) 335-5921
www.lib.uiowa.edu/spec-coll/NARR.HTM

Wisconsin Center for Theater and Film Research
Wisconsin Historical Society
816 State Street
Madison, WI 53706
(608) 264-6466
www.wisconsinhistory.org/wcftr/

Wisconsin Film Office
201 W Washington Avenue
2nd Floor
Madison, WI 53703
(800) 345-6947
www.filmwisconsin.org/

Selected Film Festivals (drawn from dozens)

Cedar Rapids Independent Film Festival (April)
Collins Road Theatres
1462 Twixtown Road
Marion, IA 52302

Films exhibited must have ties to Iowa.

Cleveland International Film Festival (March)
230 Huron SW
Cleveland, OH 44113

Open to films of any nationality.

East Lansing Film Festival (March)
P. O. Box 4880
East Lansing, MI 48826

Especially promotes Michigan film.

Heartland Film Festival (October)
200 S. Meridian Street
Indianapolis, IN 46225

Emphasizes humanistic films.

Indiefest (July–August)
P.O. Box 148849
Chicago, IL 60614

Exhibits independent films.

Ladyfest Ohio (May)
P.O. Box 10236
Columbus, OH 43201

Publicizes activist and feminist films.

Motor City International Film Festival (August)
315 E. Warren Avenue
Detroit, MI 48201

Encourages production of films shot in Detroit.

St. Louis International Film Festival (November)
6350 Delmar Boulevard
St. Louis, MO 63130

Open to films of any nationality.

Strictly Midwest Movies and Short Hits (October)
309 SE Oak Street
Minneapolis, MN 55435

Devoted to promoting midwestern independent films.

Underneath Cincinnati (four times a year)
Mockbee Building
Cincinnati, OH 45220

Exhibition of works by local and regional filmmakers.

Women in the Director's Chair International Film and Video Festival (March)
941 West Lawrence
Chicago, IL 60640

Shows works by women around the world.

MIDWESTERN ACTORS, DIRECTORS, AND PLAYWRIGHTS

Actors

Scott Bakula (St. Louis, MO)
Ann Baxter (Michigan City, IN)
Halle Berry (Cleveland, OH)
Richard Brooks (Cleveland, OH)
Drew Carey (Cleveland, OH)
Johnny Carson (Corning, IA)
Hopalong Cassidy [William Boyd] (Cambridge, OH)
Joan Cusack (Evanston, IL)
John Cusack (Evanston, IL)

Doris Day (Cincinnati, OH)
James Dean (Marion, IN)
Ruby Dee (Cleveland, OH)
Walt Disney (Chicago, IL)
Harrison Ford (Chicago, IL)
Clark Gable (Cadiz, OH)
Judy Garland (Grand Rapids, MI)
Betty Grable (St. Louis, MO)
Arsenio Hall (Cleveland, OH)
Anne Heche (Aurora, OH)
William Holden (O'Fallon, IL)
Rock Hudson (Winnetka, IL)
The Jacksons (Michael, Janet, LaToya) (Gary, IN)
Greg Kinnear (Logansport, IN)
Jessica Lange (Minnesota)
David Letterman (Indianapolis, IN)
Karl Malden (Gary, IN)
Frederic March (Racine, WI)
Dean Martin (Steubenville, OH)
Marlee Matlin (Morton Grove, IL)
Bill Murray (Evanston, IL)
Paul Newman (Cleveland, OH)
Sarah Jessica Parker (Nelsonville, OH)
Richard Pryor (IL)
Ronald Reagan (Tampico, IL)
Ginger Rogers (Independence, MI)
Roy Rogers (Cincinnati, OH)
Marion Ross (MN)
Jane Russell (Bemidji, MN)
Martin Sheen (Dayton, OH)
Spencer Tracy (Milwaukee, WI)
Forrest Tucker (Plainfield, IN)
Kathleen Turner (Springfield, MO)
John Wayne (Winterset, IA)
Clifton Webb (Indianapolis, IN)
Richard Widmark (Sunrise, MN)
Gene Wilder (Milwaukee, WI)
Robin Williams (Chicago, IL)
Debra Winger (Cleveland, OH)
Shelley Winters (St. Louis, MO)

Directors

Robert Altman (Kansas City, MO)
Francis Ford Coppola (Detroit, MI)
Howard Hawks (Goshen, IN)
John Hughes (Lansing, MI)
John Huston (Nevada, MO)
Jim Jarmusch (Akron, OH)
Sydney Pollack (Lafayette, IN)
Steven Spielberg (Cincinnati, OH)

Preston Sturgis (Chicago, IL)
Orson Welles (Kenosha, WI)
Robert Wise (Winchester, IN)

Playwrights

George Cram Cook (IA)
Susan Glaspell (IA)
David Mamet (IL)
Paul Osborn (IN)
David Rabe (IA)
Sam Shepard (IL)
Melvin Van Peebles (IL)
Thornton Wilder (WI)
Lanford Wilson (MO)
Meredith Wilson (IA)

FOLKLORE

Ruth Olson

Is there a regional consciousness of the Midwest? Do farmers in the western plains of Minnesota feel kinship with autoworkers in Detroit? Do those who fish the Ohio River express themselves the same way as hunters in the north woods of Wisconsin and Michigan? Do African Americans in the urban setting of Chicago have a connection to rural farming communities in Iowa?

What is "midwestern"? It is a constantly shifting set of perceptions. Just as the boundaries of the Midwest itself are open to debate, so too the idea of what is intrinsically midwestern is always being negotiated and determined by who is telling the story and for what purpose. Few instances of folklore can be considered exclusively midwestern; most of the narrative types, music, traditional practices, and beliefs found in the Midwest can also be seen elsewhere in the country. This makes sense, considering the permeability of the Midwest's boundaries and its history of settlement. Settlers from New England and the Atlantic seaboard brought their traditions with them to the Midwest; southerners did the same. In turn, as the American frontier expanded, midwesterners carried traditions westward. As described below, certain subregions in the Midwest physically, economically, or culturally overlap with eastern, southern, or plains states.

The consciousness of being midwestern is readily evident in the stories that midwesterners tell about themselves and each other, and in the stuff of those stories—the traditional practices, occupational knowledge, and everyday details of life shared within a perceived community. But because of the vast size of the area that people call the Midwest, one can find enormous variety in the flavors, folkways, and symbolic representations and cultural expressions of its residents. While the residents of the East and West coasts might share the spongy notion of the Midwest as a "flyover" zone, populated by overweight rural white people, in fact life in this region is varied and enriched through many different ethnic groups, religions, natural resources, and distinctive geographical characteristics.

Several broad themes emerge within midwestern folklore. First, the indigenous, migrating, and immigrating groups that settled the Midwest have had a pervasive effect on the region's folklore. Residents' interactions with the area's physical features, especially the Great Lakes and other waterways, continue to figure in the region's folklore. Occupations and recreational activities based on natural resources have also provided a good amount of regional folklore.

Second, the Midwest's folklore confirms its image as America's "Heartland"— not only the physical center of the country, but also a transportation hub, with its network of railroads, trucking firms, and airports. In a sense, the Midwest is quintessential America. Its ethnic diversity, its permeability to the other regions around it, its major industrial and agricultural areas—all resonate the larger cultural richness of the United States. Its residents embody core American values—hard work, resilience, integrity. Midwesterners are unpretentious people, with a get-the-job-done attitude, unexciting and perhaps too trusting. At the same time, the region's early identity as an American frontier continues to manifest itself through an appreciation of individualism, and the support and valorization of some forms of rambunctious and unruly behavior. Many of our country's most popular folk heroes—Paul Bunyan, Johnny Appleseed, Mike Fink—emerged from the Midwest's days as a frontier.

But finally, what remains most distinctive about the Midwest is the sheer variety of cultural groups, environments, and residents' experiences. The Midwest is characterized more by local culture than by regional culture. The folklore of the Midwest reveals that for midwesterners, personal and group identity is based on a local sense of place and the everyday details of living in that place. The Midwest contains a number of smaller, occasionally overlapping regions, where the distinct experiences of residents have resulted in a collective awareness, made manifest through stories, ways of living, local knowledge, community events, and other expressions of local culture.

ETHNIC, RECREATIONAL, AND OCCUPATIONAL IDENTITY IN THE MIDWEST

The expanses of the Midwest permitted immigrants to develop ethnic enclaves, where they continued traditions brought from their home countries. But as groups came into contact, they borrowed and adapted traditional elements from each other—from foodways to building techniques to good stories. Over time, cultural contact resulted in new perceptions of ethnic identity. Numerous festivals and calendrical celebrations in the Midwest exhibit the influence of various ethnic groups on the region, as ethnic identity can be particularly pronounced during such occasions. Celebrations allow communities to perform their stories—demonstrating the vitality of existing folk cultures and providing fertile ground for a number of cultural expressions: food; music, dance, and song; decorative arts, seen through clothing and other decorations specific to the event; and stories, sayings, and other verbal arts.

German

Ethnic festivals in the Midwest often maintain cultural traditions by reinterpreting them, or by selecting emblematic ethnic behavior. The large number of

German immigrants in the nineteenth century coming to states like Ohio, Indiana, Missouri, and Wisconsin has assured that many communities in the Midwest host German festivals, especially Oktoberfests, where a number of different traditions are brought together under the pan-ethnic identification "German." The wearing of special clothing (lederhosen), the serving of food identified as "German" (sausage and beer), the emphasis on certain types of music (polka)—all pronounce selected symbols of Germanness as an ethnicity.

Dutch

Many festivals promote ethnic identities that have been associated with particular towns. Since 1929, Holland, Michigan, has celebrated its Dutch heritage in a Tulip Time Festival, which brings in nearly 1 million visitors annually. Tulip Time includes selected emblems of ethnic identity: tulips planted throughout the city; townspeople in Dutch costume washing the street; klompen dancers in wooden shoes; and both a Musiekparade of marching bands and a Kinderparade featuring local children in Dutch costume. Across the Midwest, such ethnic festivals flourish, sometimes in spite of changes in town demographics. Holland's Tulip Time Festival, for example, has come to include a Fiesta celebration, which reflects the growth of the Hispanic population in the town.

A number of communities in the Midwest host German festivals (often as Oktoberfests), where a number of different traditions are brought together under the pan-ethnic identification "German." Courtesy Travel Michigan.

Swiss

A community's celebration of ethnicity may be a complex marriage of pride in heritage and the creation of a tourism industry. New Glarus, Wisconsin, settled by Swiss immigrants in 1845, has since the founding of the town celebrated its Swiss heritage through a number of different events and performances. One of the most spectacular is the staging of Friedrich Schiller's 1804 play *Wilhelm Tell*, which the town has put on annually since 1938, in both English and German. This massive effort, performed out of doors, features intricate costumes, goats, cows, and horses. It requires more than 200 local volunteers, a large portion of the community.

Over the years, New Glarus' various retellings of their story of "Swissness" have reflected the issues of the day. In the town's early years, its ethnic celebrations combined tradition with new American themes, facilitating an internal discussion of the Swiss community's vision of itself. Amid the anti-German sentiment after World War I, when speaking German was frowned upon and so-called hyphenated Americans were called to task for divided loyalties, residents used their celebrations as an argument for their rights as German-speaking Americans. *Wilhelm Tell*, the Swiss story of independence, was an important part of that argument. During the 1960s, as tourism offered prosperity for this small community, the play became more of a spectacle for out-of-town visitors. Around that time, the town began to re-create its built environment to reflect popular notions of "Swissness." Known today as "America's Little Switzerland," New Glarus attracts thousands of visitors, including hundreds of tourists from Switzerland. At the same time, this self-conscious sense of identity has assisted the survival of German language skills and the maintenance of musical and artistic traditions (transformed by time and cross-cultural interactions), assuring the prosperity and cohesion of this community.

African Americans

As a result of the Great Migration from the South in the early decades of the twentieth century, the Midwest is home to many African Americans. One particular event held in Chicago every August, the Bud Billiken Parade, the largest African American parade in the United States, unites diverse groups within this large urban setting by providing a common sense of community and celebrating racial pride and hope for the future. Organized by the African American community, the parade celebrates children and the return to school. The black newspaper *Chicago Defender* began the parade in 1929 to honor the legendary character Bud Billiken. Billiken was the pen name of Willard Motley, who wrote a column for the children's section in the *Chicago Defender* that promoted social awareness and racial pride. Today, Bud Billiken is a symbol of pride and hope for young black people. Marching bands, drum groups, black fraternities and sororities, beauty pageant winners, celebrities, and of course politicians all take part in this large event. The parade attracts over 1 million spectators and 150,000 participants. In 2003 more than 250 organizations were represented and the parade took more than five hours.

Native Americans

Similarly, the powwow is an important gathering for many midwestern Native Americans—a chance to socialize, enjoy different drum groups, and dance. Powwows serve as an intertribal celebration, and often feature competitive dancing and the awarding of prize money in various categories, such as Grass, Fancy, or Traditional dancing. Music at the powwow is provided by a number of drum groups, some of whom may be invited, and others who just show up for the powwow. The "powwow circuit" (the series of powwows spread across the region) is well established in the Great Lakes states, and participants can find a powwow almost every weekend through the summer and into the fall. A powwow typically stretches over a weekend, beginning on Friday night, and contains a number of separate periods of dancing. Powwows can take place in a variety of locations: community halls, school gymnasiums, cultural centers, or traditional grounds on reservations. A powwow is a lively, various event, based on the concept of a circle, with multiple activities taking place from the center of the circle where the drum groups play to the participants dancing around the drum groups, emanating outward to outlying campgrounds or other places for rest and recreation. Typically, the dance grounds themselves are ringed by vendors selling jewelry or other items likely to be of interest to the dancers and audience, and of course food stands featuring fry bread and the ever-popular "Indian taco"—the usual taco ingredients served on fry bread.

Every powwow begins with the Grand Entry, when the dancers enter the dance arena behind the head dancers (honorary positions selected for the powwow), head veterans, and flag carriers as the drum group sings traditional "Grand Entry" songs. Dancers enter the arena in an order that reflects native custom. Male dancers enter by dance category and in order of age. Traditional dancers (noted for their relatively sedate gait and older-style regalia) are followed by Grass dancers (with larger, swooping dance steps and regalia in vivid color combinations: fuchsia, orange, or pink, for example). Next come the Fancy dancers, whose steps and regalia emphasize the performance quality of their dance, acrobatic and colorful. After the men, the women enter, again in order of age, first Traditional, then Jingle, finally Fancy Shawl dancers. In general, the women's dance steps are less energetic than those of the men, reflecting the prized value of modesty.

After the Grand Entry, an elder gives an invocation, providing a spiritual context for the entire event. Often there is also a Flag Song, during which the flags for participating countries and Native nations are raised. An emcee helps to direct the drum groups to play particular songs, so that intertribal dances, in which anyone is free to dance, are interspersed with dances specific to war veterans, or Honor songs (to honor a selected individual), or other specialty dances. The socializing that takes place during the powwow may continue until late at night, as groups gather to sing intertribal "49" songs, more informal songs that may have English lyrics and often are love songs. Powwows provide an important space for many tribal people, not only to meet up with old friends and exchange news and stories, but also more symbolically to express cultural values, both for themselves and for non-Indians, who are always graciously welcomed to the event.

Scandinavians

Another type of circuit is the "lutefisk circuit," the round of lutefisk dinners held at Lutheran churches across the Upper Midwest in the fall. The lutefisk tradition stems from the Scandinavian immigrants who came to the Midwest during the mid-nineteenth century. While for the most part no longer eaten by Norwegians, lutefisk has become a powerful symbol of Norwegian American identity in the Midwest. Often, lutefisk fans will visit several dinners during a season and compare the quality of the various meals they have consumed. Among stalwart Norwegian Americans, the dish also appears on holidays, especially Thanksgiving or Christmas.

Lutefisk is cod that has been dry-preserved. To get it ready for the table, the slabs of dried fish have to be soaked in water, then in lye, and then rinsed in more water. Cooked correctly, it can be soft and flaky; overcooked, it becomes a gelati-

Ole and Lena

While humor in the Midwest is similar to humor in the rest of the country, still there are distinctive jokes that center on the people who have settled here. Thus, ethnic jokes about the immigrants and indigenous people who populate the Midwest can be identified with the region. The Irish Pat and Mike, the Finnish Eino and Toivo, the Polish Stash are stock characters in jokes that sometimes migrate from ethnic group to ethnic group. These ethnic figures might be found universally in folk humor, but in their manifestation in the Midwest, their world is furnished with the familiar accoutrements of the region. Among the best known of these stock characters in the Upper Midwest are the Scandinavians Ole and Lena, sometimes appearing as Swedes, sometimes as Norwegians. Jokes about Ole often are numskull stories, relying on Ole's foolishness for comic effect. Lena, his upstanding wife, is perhaps more bawdy than she should be:

Ole and Lena got married. On their honeymoon trip they were nearing Minneapolis when Ole put his hand on Lena's knee. Giggling, Lena said, "Ole, if you vant, you can go farther!" So Ole drove to Duluth.

Ole wore both of his winter jackets when he painted his house last July. The directions on the can said, "Put on two coats."

Ole, Lena, and Sven were lost in the woods of Northern Minnesota and were becoming desperate. It was winter, the snow was deep, their situation was looking very bleak. Ole dug down into the snow to find some nuts and he found an old lamp. When he rubbed it to get the snow off, a genie came out of the lamp. The genie says, "I am the great genie of Nordern Minnesota and I can grant each of you vun vish."
Ole says, "I vish I vas back on my farm." Poof! Ole was gone. Lena quickly says, "I vish I vas back on da farm vit Ole." Poof! Lena was gone.
Sven was sitting there looking sad and the genie finally says, "Sven, vat is your vish?" and Sven says, "Gosh, I'm lonely. I vish Ole and Lena were back here vit me."

Ole and Lena went to the same Lutheran Church. Lena went every Sunday and taught Sunday School. Ole went on Christmas and Easter and the occasional Sunday. On one of those Sundays, he was in the pew right behind Lena and he noticed what a fine looking woman she was. While they were taking up the collection, Ole leaned forward and said, "Hey, Lena, how about you and me go to dinner in New Ulm next Friday?"
"Yah, Ole, dot vould be nice," said Lena.
So on Friday he picked Lena up and took her to the finest restaurant in New Ulm. When they sat down, Ole asked Lena, "Lena, vould you like a cocktail before dinner?"
"Oh, no, Ole," said Lena. "Vat vould I tell my Sunday School class?"
Ole was set back a bit, so he didn't say much until after dinner. Then he reached in his pocket and pulled out a pack of cigarettes.
"Hey, Lena," said Ole, "vould you like a smoke?"
"Oh, no, Ole," said Lena. "Vat vould I tell my Sunday School class?"
So Ole vas feeling pretty low after that. He was driving Lena home when they passed the Hot Springs Motel. He figured he had nothing to lose. "Hey, Lena," said Ole, "how vould you like to stop at that motel with me?"

"Yah, Ole, that I will do."

Well, Ole drove right back to the motel and checked in with Lena.

The next morning he asked her, "Lena, vat are you going to tell your Sunday School class now?"

Lena said, "The same ting I alvays tell dem. You don't have to smoke and drink to have a good time!"

nous mush that inspires jokes. Warm lutefisk gives off a distinctive smell that some people find quite unappealing. But a lutefisk dinner is more than just the fish. Usually meatballs are available for those who don't like lutefisk. Boiled potatoes are a must, and often rutabagas or peas and carrots are served. Lefse or flatbread accompanies the meal. Lutefisk is often doused with melted butter; some prefer to wrap the lutefisk in their lefse so they don't have to see it while they eat it.

Most significant is the culture that surrounds the dish. For example, at lutefisk dinners, one may see T-shirts sporting such quips as

Lutefisk Cookbook

Lutefisk Surprise: 1. take one lutefisk, 2. get rid of it.

Stories are told of dogs that lift their legs on lutefisk stored out-of-doors; cooks and consumers alike don't notice the difference. The aromatic dish has inspired songs, such as this one sung to the tune of "O Tannenbaum":

O Lutefisk, O Lutefisk, how fragrant your aroma
O Lutefisk, O Lutefisk, you put me in a coma
You smell so strong, you look like glue
You taste just like an overshoe
But Lutefisk, come Saturday
I think I'll eat you anyway.

Hmong

Certainly not unique to the Midwest, but nonetheless important, is a celebration by one of the region's more recent immigrant groups, the Hmong. Their New Year celebration has become an essential regional gathering that allows Hmong Americans a chance to come together and share significant cultural traditions that are becoming relegated to holidays. The Hmong, a tribe of mountain dwellers native to Laos with strong clan loyalties, supported the United States war effort in Vietnam. In the 1970s, after the Americans had left Vietnam, the Hmong began to arrive in the United States as refugees. Many were forced to spend long years in refugee camps in Thailand as they waited to immigrate to the United States. Minnesota, Wisconsin, and Michigan host some of the largest Hmong populations in the United States.

Marking the end of the harvest season, the New Year celebration is the most important holiday in the Hmong cultural calendar. In Laos, this celebration lasted more than a week. In the United States, it usually takes place over a weekend and can draw people from around the region. Hmong Americans celebrate the New Year at different times, but usually around Thanksgiving, especially in the Midwest, where it's more convenient to travel before the snow flies. Celebrants wear ornate outfits with brilliant colors. Women wear elaborately embroidered skirts and tops, decorated hats, and heavy necklaces made of silver. Although men may wear embroidered vests and hats, with a plain white shirt, more often they are dressed in simple black tunics and trousers. Traditionally, it's important to wear new clothing at New Year to celebrate the past year's good fortune and help bring future prosperity. Music, singing, dancing, games, and food are all part of the Hmong New Year celebration. During this time, young Hmong Americans can meet potential spouses by playing a traditional ball-toss game that enables them to talk with and assess their game partners.

The Hmong New Year celebration is an example of a calendrical tradition, albeit one that is scheduled according to the travel needs of its midwestern participants. A number of other calendrical holidays in the Midwest also show the influence of its immigrants. For example, German immigrants introduced both the Christmas tree and the practice of giving gifts at Christmas, traditions quickly incorporated into American culture. In addition, midwesterners celebrate more ethnically specific holidays, such as Dyngus, a holiday still observed in Polish American communities across the Midwest.

Other Ethnic Celebrations

Dyngus was originally an ancient rural Polish custom that took place on Easter Monday and Tuesday. On that Monday, boys would lie in wait for girls, attack them with willow switches applied across their legs, then drench them with water. Tuesday was the girls' turn. These days, it's more common to use only the water—or to forgo these activities altogether in exchange for a good party. In the Midwest, Dyngus Day often includes a polka dance. Other holidays identified with specific ethnic groups have taken on a more expansive character; on St. Patrick's Day, almost everyone chooses to be honorarily Irish. In Chicago, for example, St. Patrick's Day is such a huge celebration that the river is dyed green to commemorate the day.

Then there is the invented holiday of St. Urho's Day, a Finnish joke at St. Patrick's expense, celebrated on March 16. Although there is some contention about its creator (either Sulo Hayumaki of Bemidji or Richard Mattson of Virginia, Minnesota), the legend of St. Urho began to circulate in northern Minnesota in the 1950s. Supposedly, St. Urho chased the grasshoppers out of Finland and saved the grape crop by saying "Heinäsirkka, heinäsirkka, mene täältä hiiteen" ("Grasshopper, grasshopper, go to Hell!"). People celebrate St. Urho's Day by wearing purple and green, and of course imbibing. Other lighthearted activities vary from town to town. In Finland, Minnesota, "Miss Helmi" is crowned on St. Urho's Day; the contestants are all men in women's clothing. St. Urho's Day has grown so popular that it is now celebrated not only throughout the Midwest, but also in Canada and Finland.

CELEBRATIONS AND THE ENVIRONMENT OF THE MIDWEST

Fairs and Competitions

Intermingled with ethnic performances of identity are the celebrations and narratives of people's interactions with the environment of the Midwest. The region's geographical features and abundant resources have greatly affected occupational traditions, as is especially evident through agriculture.

Although county fairs exist elsewhere in the United States, midwestern fairs carry the longest and strongest traditions, because of the significance of agriculture in the Midwest. County fairs are especially important in rural communities because they involve the work of so many local people. From the middle of the summer until after Labor Day, counties across the Midwest hold fairs that typically last from three to nine days. Most of these events take place on permanent fairgrounds, maintained by counties and equipped with livestock barns, exhibit halls, and grandstands. Usually, fairs will also feature a midway, where a carnival from out of town will come in to set up rides, games, and other booths. There may also be commercial exhibitors and food booths run by 4-H or other youth clubs. Casual visitors may come for the midway, but the core of the county fair consists of the exhibitors and the large corps of supporters it takes to sustain their work. Judges, in both the exhibit halls and the show rings; the friends and family who make up the audience; and other community members invested in ensuring that agricultural lifestyles are carried on devote time and attention to encourage young exhibitors. Youths in such clubs as 4-H and the Future Farmers of America (FFA) compete as they exhibit livestock and projects featuring home arts, horticulture, and crafts. Adults also bring goods to be judged competitively, from canned and baked goods to handcrafts and sewing. These competitions reveal the standards and values of the community, as well as inviting neighborly mingling and social diversion. All kinds of activities take place around the stock barns and show ring, as kids hang out with their animals, decorating stalls, organizing informal card games, and taking care of their livestock. Sometimes exhibitors bring in couches and other home comforts for the days they will spend with their animals in the stock barn.

Competitions and the show barns are open during the day, but at night the midway comes to life with rides; often concerts and events meant to draw larger audiences are featured at night. No wonder county fairs have status as the major cultural event in many of the counties in which they are held. Often, they inspire memories; long-term participants fill scrapbooks with pictures, articles, and ribbons from each year. County fairs create kinship as they showcase local talent and resources and provide opportunities for expanding and maintaining social contacts within a larger farming community.

The region's resources are also displayed and celebrated through community festivals, which are endemic to the Midwest. Minnesota has more community festivals between Memorial Day and Labor Day than California; at least 250 towns in Minnesota annually put on festivals.[1] Many community festivals are based on occupation or local resources. Festivals throughout the Midwest pay tribute to apples, pumpkins, potatoes, cranberries, maple syrup, corn, milk, tractors, ice,

State and county fairs are especially important in rural communities because they involve the work of so many local people. Courtesy Iowa Tourism Office.

water, sausages, rutabagas, and other products that make our lives worth celebrating. Quirkier festivals highlight local oddities; Walker, Minnesota, holds an Eelpout Festival to celebrate this repulsively snakelike rough fish. Belleville, Wisconsin, boasts that it is the "UFO Capital of the World" and hosts a UFO Day. Such community events bring people home, both literally and figuratively, connecting residents from small communities even after they have left for urban areas. For such communities, festivals are focal points in the year. They can serve as marketing devices for a town, boosting tourism and helping to create a community identity.

Across the region, festivals share a common structure, usually including most of the following elements: a parade, street dances, a beer garden, festival food, a queen pageant, activities for children, opportunities for business promotion like street sales, and other events like car shows, old-time music, art in the park, or craft shows. During these "marked" times, often things happen that wouldn't be considered normal in everyday life; for example, town leaders might allow themselves to be humiliated in the dunking tank. People might spill out into the street, or drink in the middle of the day, or dress up in special outfits.

The environment has also influenced the recreational traditions of the Midwest. Within the Midwest and its subregions, hunters and fishers have built traditions around certain places and certain game or catches. Duck hunting on the Mississippi, smelting on Lake Michigan, and catching catfish on the Ohio River all carry with them special vocabulary, familiarity with place and time, special skills, special lore—in short, local knowledge. Mert Cowley, the "Jack Pine Poet," writes narrative poems about deer hunting, mostly based on true events. His poetry books offer humor and advice as he tells stories of inexperienced or inattentive hunters, braggarts who meet their comeuppance, terrible camp cooks, and fantastic inventions in aid of the hunter, from inflatable boots to the ultimate deer stand. Elsewhere, he describes another model of hunter: the serious, sober, respectful user of natural resources, who loves and values traditional knowledge and culture. Both *In Camps of Orange* (1993) and *The Ultimate Stand* (1990)—filled with hunting tips, camp journals, photos, and illustrations, as well as narrative poetry about deer hunting—have proved to be very popular within the hunting community.

Recreation in the Midwest includes not only folkways that are regionally distinctive, but also everyday activities that are not unique to the region, but inevitably take on local qualities because they are in practice here.

Occupational Traditions

The lakes and waterways of the Midwest have also affected occupational traditions. Lake Michigan and Lake Superior have rich histories of commercial fishing. This dangerous occupation requires specialized equipment and knowledge, especially of the environment. These concerns help determine much of the subject matter of commercial fishermen's narratives: notable characters and places, humorous episodes, effective fishing technology, and shipwrecks. Many shipwreck narratives focus on lost or seized opportunities to salvage materials. For example, after the *America* sank off Isle Royale in Lake Superior, local fishermen told stories of grabbing free fruit as it floated by—to the point where some fishermen overindulged and could no longer stand to look at a banana.[2]

The Great Lakes have long provided transportation to the Midwest. Native peoples used the lakes to travel, and immigrants also traveled to the Midwest via boat. The Great Lakes continue to be important for transporting bulk goods across the Midwest. The enormous storms on the Great Lakes, especially "the gales of November," have resulted in a large repertoire of stories about shipwrecks. One of the most famous storms was the "white hurricane" of 1913, in which many ships and at least 235 lives were lost. For a week after the storm, farmers along the shores of Lake Huron retrieved the bodies of sailors, many of them battered beyond recognition and coated with ice. A number of strange stories emerged from this tragedy. One told of an unidentified sailor who washed ashore. He had a tattoo with the initials *J.T.* on his arm. A relative alerted the father of John Thompson, who then rushed to the funeral home to identify the corpse. Although the body was battered, he decided it was indeed his son: what he could see of his features was familiar; he had crossed toes like his son; the tattoo was on the left arm as was his son's; scars on the nose and leg matched his son's; the body was missing the same teeth as his son. But in the middle of the funeral, John walked in. Apparently, he had jumped ship and missed the storm. Reading of his own death in the newspaper, he decided to attend his funeral to surprise his grieving relatives.

A more recent famous shipwreck is that of the S.S. *Edmund Fitzgerald*, which went down in Lake Superior in November 1975. The freighter, loaded with 26,000 tons of taconite pellets, was crossing Lake Superior headed to Detroit when she sank during a gale which the captain had identified as one of the worst storms he had been in. All twenty-nine crew members died. In 1976 Gordon Lightfoot wrote "The Wreck of the *Edmund Fitzgerald*," assuring the lasting fame of this tragedy. In the time-honored tradition of ballad-writers, Lightfoot commemorated this significant event by providing a narrative account of the wreck.

Other occupations in the Midwest that rely on its natural resources are logging and mining. The lumber camps and lumberjacks of the nineteenth century contributed enormously to folklore in the Upper Midwest. Typically, lumbering took place in the winter, when the camp crews spent their time either in hard work during the day or lodging together at night, far from the conveniences and social life of town. Nineteenth-century lumbering was indeed a distinctive culture, with its own vocabulary, pastimes, ballads, and stories, especially tall tales. A popular subject was the vermin that the lumberjacks had to deal with. In one story, a lumberjack wanted to spend the night at another camp, but the lumberjacks there wouldn't let him in until he took off all his clothes, which were crawling with bedbugs. During the night, his clothes crawled over to the barn to try to get in where it was warm.

Many songs have been written describing lumberjack life in the Midwest. Humorous or serious, these songs tend to depict the valor of hard work and extraordinary feats. Many ballads tell of particular incidents in the camps. One famous ballad composed in a northern Wisconsin lumber camp in the early 1870s is "The Little Brown Bulls," which describes a log-skidding competition between two teams: McCluskey's big spotted steers and Bull Gordon's little brown bulls. The contest is fueled by the fact that McCluskey is a Scotsman and Gordon is a Yankee:

> Not a thing on the river McCluskey did fear
> As he skidded the logs with his big spotted steers.
> Says Bull Gordon, the Yankee, "You'll have your hands full
> If you skid one more log than my Little Brown Bulls."

As the contest proceeds, McCluskey is overcome with confidence:

> Now the sun had gone down when the foreman did say,
> "Turn out, boys, turn out. You've enough for the day."
> As they scaled them and counted McCluskey did smile
> 'Til the foreman says, "Mac, you're behind by a mile."
>
> The boys then all laughed and McCluskey did swear
> As he tore out by handfuls his long yellow hair.
> So it's fill up your glasses and fill them up full,
> And we'll drink to Bull Gordon and his Little Brown Bulls.

Northern Minnesota, northern Wisconsin, and the Upper Peninsula of Michigan continue to pay tribute to the old lumber camps with resorts and restaurants, statues, parks, and festivals, often named after that most famous of lumberjacks, Paul Bunyan. In spite of the fact that lumberjacks did not tell stories about Bunyan, numerous tall tales related to the exploits of Paul Bunyan have entered the canon of American folklore—the blizzard that caused Bunyan's ox and companion Babe to turn blue; the attack of giant mosquitoes, when Bunyan's work crew were forced to cover themselves with a giant skillet; and the building of a prune stone bridge across Lake Superior.

Mining, whether for coal, taconite, or other ore, has also contributed to midwestern folklore, some of it directly related to the immigrant populations who came to work in the mines. For example, Cornish miners, frequently called "Cousin Jacks" in America, brought with them old stories about Tommy Knockers—dwarflike creatures who lived underground. But the most explicitly midwestern folklore can be found in stories and ballads that commemorate mining disasters and other tragedies. One typical story, turned into a ballad, describes a fire in the St. Paul Mine at Cherry, Illinois, in 1909, when 200 workers were sealed into the mine. After several days, mine inspectors went in to search for corpses. They found one group alive; the miners had survived for eight days without food, water, or light. As they were being led to safety, one of the miners heard that other miners still needed rescue elsewhere in the mine, and he refused to leave. He had to be forced to the surface.

Another famous incident was the fire at the Italian Hall in the copper-mining town of Calumet, Michigan, which took the lives of eighty-four children as miners and their families stampeded to get out. The fire took place during a particularly ugly strike, and it has never been determined who set the fire; the mine operators and the miners' union accused each other. Highly sympathetic to the miners, Woody Guthrie wrote a ballad about the catastrophe. In addition, a number of stories related to the incident developed. In one such story, a Finnish miner escaped harm because he interpreted the whistling of his tea kettle as a bad omen, and thus did not go to the Italian Hall.

Mining and industry are the subjects of much folklore in the Midwest because they have been so essential to midwestern economic life. Midwestern industry has provided a rich environment for folk poetry, which often is used to express the concerns of occupational groups. Autoworkers and other assembly line workers have recorded their boredom and frustration with meaningless work—and have also written humorously about pulling tricks on arrogant bosses or stealing enough parts to build their own cars.

Folklore that documents industrial accidents, mining tragedies, and assembly line boredom has long inspired the labor movement. The Midwest has served an important role in this movement. The Industrial Workers of the World, established in Chicago in 1905, produced writers who used their creative works to support the cause. These anthems were in turn taken up by working people and often supplied with new words to address specific needs. Ralph Chaplin's "Solidarity Forever!" for example, written while he lived in Chicago, continues to be sung in strikes and union halls far beyond the boundaries of the Midwest:

> It is we who ploughed the prairies, built the cities where they trade,
> Dug the mines and built the workshops, endless miles of railroad laid;
> Now we stand outcast and starving 'mid the wonders we have made,
> But the union makes us strong.
>
> Solidarity forever! Solidarity forever! Solidarity forever!
> For the union makes us strong!

AMERICA'S "HEARTLAND" AND THE CREATION OF FOLK HEROES

As the Heartland, the Midwest has played an important part in building the mythology of America and American character. The folk heroes within the Midwest are images of our selves. They tend to possess, often in exaggerated form, the personal traits we value—strength, integrity, resilience, helpfulness, and self-reliance. Within the Midwest there are several types of heroes: real people who have been turned into sentimental folk heroes; characters promoted through popular culture, the much rewritten and re-created heroes we are likely to find in elementary school libraries; regional heroes and characters whose fame is limited to a specific cultural group or area; and culture heroes and tricksters.

Mike Fink, Johnny Appleseed, and Paul Bunyan

At one time, the Midwest was the frontier, and its early folk heroes embody that American experience. Some of the frontier figures especially associated with the Midwest include the keelboatman Mike Fink and the benevolent Johnny Appleseed. Also falling within this category are such fakelore creations as Paul Bunyan.

From the early nineteenth century on, as various modes of transportation made the nation more mobile, Americans delighted in hearing about regional heroes who served as examples of national character. The young republic chose common people for its folk heroes, and told stories that altered these historical figures into legendary characters. These legendary figures grew to share common elements, developed and supported by their audience: the ability to brag with humor and audacity; the use of idiomatic speech that showed independence of spirit and contempt for aristocrats; and the accomplishment of feats involving trickery and the extravagant gestures of tall-tale deeds.

Mike Fink, for example, a keelboatman who worked on two major midwestern rivers, the Ohio and the Mississippi, was promoted as a brawler, a sharpshooter, and an independent thinker. Keelboatmen had to be strong enough to pole their craft back upriver, so stories about keelboatmen reflected their extraordinary effort. They were pictured as strong and hardy, at home on the water, exuberantly open, big drinkers, big fighters, big boasters.

Mike Fink was the quintessential keelboatman. Anecdotes describe him as having a magnificent physique, muscular and weatherbeaten. He was known for his ability to brag and to shoot; hunters nicknamed him "Bang-All." Fink was seen as a trickster as well as a marksman. In one story, he tricks a sheep farmer into supplying provisions for his crew by rubbing snuff on several sheeps' heads and telling the farmer they have a disease. He offers to kill them for two gallons of peach brandy. After dark, he sneaks back to the farm, loads up the dead sheep, and celebrates with the brandy.

Fink was loved by some and held in contempt by others. Many of the stories about Fink celebrate his independence, but others exhibit racism and misogyny. Fink supposedly tested his girlfriend's fidelity by shooting a tin cup from between her thighs. After 1815 Fink headed west. He was killed there in 1822, during a quarrel that provided new fuel for another set of legends about him. The most common story says he was shot in retaliation for "accidentally" killing a friend while trying to shoot a tin cup full of whiskey off his head. Essential to all versions is that Mike Fink died a violent death on the new frontier.

Another real person who generated legends was Johnny Appleseed. Appleseed is popularly pictured as a gentle man who traveled barefoot through the frontier forests of Ohio and Indiana, planting apple trees. Dressed simply, traveling in poverty, staying with pioneer families, acting as a true Christian, and refusing to harm any living thing, he is beloved as a noble toiler in the interest of others. Part of this story is that Johnny never married because his youthful love went west and died before he found her. Supposedly, Johnny peacefully died in 1845 on the Indiana frontier after a lifetime serving humankind in the Ohio Valley wilderness.

Johnny Appleseed's original name was John Chapman (1774–1845). He was born in Massachusetts, of Yankee stock. John Chapman was not a pauper who planted his trees for the good of all, but rather a businessman who accumulated twenty-two properties of nearly 1,200 acres. He was not a hermit, as depicted in legend, but a man who enjoyed company, spending time with a half-sister and her family in Ohio. Folklorist Richard Dorson has pointed out that before the legend of Johnny Appleseed was sentimentalized in written literature, oral tales about him circulated among Ohio pioneer families. However, these stories are very unlike the published accounts we know today. Early oral accounts describe Chapman's stamina. Stories tell of his ability to drink and hint he was a womanizer. One story collected in the Ozarks in 1931 claimed that Johnny dressed like everyone else and wore Choctaw moccasins rather than going barefoot. Johnny also had a wife, a full-blooded Choctaw. She had malaria, and Johnny returned east to get "feverweed" to make a tea to cure her. When he returned with the weed, she and their baby were both dead. Johnny lost his reason, and went around the countryside planting feverweed rather than apple trees. This Ozark story claimed he should be called "Johnny Feverweed," not Johnny Appleseed.

Often the folk heroes we recognize from juvenile literature are inventions of professional writers and public-relations people, not genuine folk groups. The legendary figure of Paul Bunyan dominates the literary landscape of North Woods logging in the Upper Midwest. Unfortunately, there is little evidence that North Woods lumberjacks really told stories featuring Paul Bunyan. Richard Dorson used Paul Bunyan as a prime example of "fakelore"—fabricated folklore attributed to a group that never possessed it.

The story of Paul Bunyan first appeared in print in 1910 in the *Detroit News-Tribune*, in an article titled "The Round River Drive." This story describes Bunyan's efforts to clear a forty-acre plot shaped like a pyramid with pine growing on all sides. When his crew tries to send the logs down the river, they realize the river is round and has no outlet. In 1914 a pamphlet for the Red River Lumber Company featured Paul Bunyan stories interspersed with advertisements; thus, Paul Bunyan was essentially developed as a marketing device. An article published by K. Bernice Stewart and Homer A. Watt in 1916 offers perhaps the only demonstration of Paul Bunyan's presence in oral lore in lumber. Stewart and Watt repeat the exploits of Paul Bunyan during his Round River drive. Other legends describe the enormous size and powers of Babe the Blue Ox, and the huge griddle and other cooking paraphernalia utilized by Bunyan to feed his crew, such as the hot springs he uses to make pea soup. Stewart and Watt claimed the Bunyan legend cycle was typically American—fueled by contests in lying.[3] By the early 1920s Bunyan had

Folklore Institute at Indiana University

It's hard to talk about midwestern folklore without talking about the influential Folklore Institute at Indiana University. This program has had a profound effect on the
collection of folkloric materials in the Midwest and elsewhere, and has helped determine the types of material collected and the collection process used. As early as the
1920s, a number of faculty at Indiana University shared an interest in folklore topics,
particularly Stith Thompson (1885–1976), who played a fundamental role in developing two tools credited with creating a more systematic study of folklore: the tale type
index and the motif index. Known for his work on American Indian tales (*Tales of the
North American Indians*, 1929), which organized tales by tale type rather than by tribe
or culture area, Thompson drew attention to the comparative study of folk materials,
focusing on patterns to discern theories of diffusion. Thompson organized the first
Summer Institute focusing on folklore in 1942. In 1962 Indiana University formally
established the Folklore Institute as an academic department. With two prolific and
influential folklorists at the helm, Thompson and Richard Dorson (1916–1981), the
Folklore Institute produced many of the folklorists who established the serious study
of folklore in the United States. A number of these students documented folklore
within the region of the Midwest.

Richard Dorson has played a seminal role in shaping both the academic and popular notions of American and regional folklore. Before the 1940s, many American folklorists focused on collecting folklore items—songs, stories, games, beliefs—often
without identifying either the people who performed those items or the cultural context in which those performances occurred. Rather than looking for how social process and other forces might affect cultural expressions, folklorists collected static items
more as "survivals" from the past. As a consequence, American folklorists have tended
to focus on ethnic groups and immigrants, and that in turn has influenced their view
of region, often as synonymous with ethnic settlement.

When Dorson's book documenting the cultures of the Upper Peninsula of Michigan, *Bloodstoppers and Bearwalkers: Folk Traditions of the Upper Peninsula*, was published
in 1952, it explored new ground in the study of folklore. His book relied totally on
stories that Dorson had collected from people, rather than from older written accounts.
It also was one of the first to go beyond descriptions of ethnic groups to note key forces
shaping the region: geography and natural resources, settlement patterns, economic
structure, and history. Dorson showed that a number of folk cultures can reside within
one place, and in fact impact each other.[4] *Bloodstoppers and Bearwalkers* served as a
demonstration that folklore is a regional product, a response to residents' experiences
within that place, and that most of the "folkways" or expressions of culture that people
participate in not only maintain traditional elements but also evolve.

By the 1960s, more and more folklorists were reconceiving folklore as a process—a
dynamic, creative response to experience, and the expression of shared beliefs, values,
and experiences. It is now recognized that folklore marks boundaries between insiders
and outsiders, and underscores the experiences shared among insiders. That recognition informs the study of the folklore of specific regions.

national stature. Other writers began to edit and creatively include Bunyan in their
accounts of logging camps. In one instance, a lumberjack memoir was altered to
substitute Bunyan legends for more risqué stories.

Paul Bunyan has displaced authentic midwestern folk heroes in the national
imagination. Lumber camp legends borrowed from the oral tradition and attached

to Bunyan have typically been sanitized to be more appropriate for print and for a popular audience. In contrast, stories collected by folklorists from individuals who actually worked in the logging camps emphasize hard drinking, momentous fighting, unimaginable hardship in the face of freezing temperatures and ubiquitous vermin, indelicate women, and coarse acts, as well as tremendous feats of strength. As Richard Dorson has said, the lumberjack of the North Woods didn't need a Paul Bunyan to exaggerate his already hard-to-believe reality.

Other Midwestern Regional Folk Heroes

Regional folk heroes tend to be associated with specific cultural groups. Every locality has stories of local characters, past and present—not necessarily heroic—who stand out in the community for one reason or another. Local legends about feats of strength are common in both rural and industrial settings. One Wisconsin strongman was Albert Gamroth, a Silesian immigrant who inspired a number of local stories: that he carried a granary to a new location, for example, and could carry more than fifteen grain sacks tied to his back from threshing machine to granary. In another story he swung an ox by its tail.

A number of these characters were lumberjacks. Joe Mouffreau, for example, was a French Canadian who worked in the Upper Peninsula of Michigan (U.P.). Supposedly seven feet tall, with size seventeen shoes, Joe could pull crooked logging roads straight with his yoke of oxen. Another woodsman who cut pine in Michigan in the 1880s and 1890s was the subject of many stories celebrating his ability to fight and work. "Silver Jack" Driscoll was a Canadian-born logger, standing six foot four and renowned for his strength, fighting ability, and reputation as a defender of the weak. Silver Jack, like many lumberjacks, did not go to church but did have a natural reverence for the Lord. He also liked his drink, and in one story he and an opponent under the influence of alcohol fight until they do massive damage to each other, and then drink amiably to God. In another story, he fights another legendary character, Frenchman Joe Fournier, who possessed a double row of teeth and could bite chunks out of the counters in saloons. After a lengthy fight, they drink together in friendship according to the lumberjack code.

Another strongman was a Finnish immigrant in northeastern Minnesota, Otto Walta. Like many of his fellow Finns, Otto tried to homestead a farm in the "cutover region," land littered with stumps left by the timber companies. And like many of his fellows, he occasionally worked as a lumberjack to tide him over financially. Born in Finland in 1875, Otto sailed for America in 1898, perhaps to escape the law, and died in 1959 after spending his last seventeen years in a Minnesota state hospital. He never learned English. Finns in northeastern Minnesota claimed Otto was a man with great capacity for work, able to rip trees out of the ground, carry boulders, and bend thick steel pry-bars so that he could pry pine stumps out of the ground. There are also stories of Otto as a big eater. He was said to have drunk down a twelve-quart pail full of milk, and then refilled it for another gulp. When his neighbor asked Otto to help him drag a bear he had just shot out of the bush, Otto agreed—but first cut into the carcass and devoured four pounds of raw meat. He then proceeded to drag out the bear, and told the neighbor to jump on top if he couldn't keep up. Otto was a prodigious fighter, once defeating ten French Canadian lumberjacks by flinging one man at the rest of his comrades as if he were bowling. At the same time, he was said to have a heart so tender he would not squash bedbugs. He would hitch himself to his plow to save his horse. The Finns who told stories about Otto believed he represented *sisu*, the Finnish term signifying stamina, tenacity, and endurance.

Swedish immigrants in Minnesota had their own hero—Ola Värmlänning. Just as is the case for Otto, the story of Ola's immigration is a bit mysterious. Some say he was the black sheep in his family and was sent away; some say he came because he was disappointed in love. In any case, he came to Minnesota, where stories about him flourished in the late nineteenth century. Ola was both strong and gentle, and had an inordinate love for the bottle. He was often pictured as a joker. One story claims that once when he was flush with funds, he ordered a special train from Minneapolis to St. Paul. People thought a dignitary was coming, and a large crowd gathered at St. Paul Union Depot. They were extremely disappointed to see only Ola get off the train. In another story Ola persuades a policeman to help him move a pig's carcass from a butcher shop and then tells the returning butcher that the cop took the pig. Other times, he locks up a bunch of policemen, or throws them in the Mississippi River if they try to interrupt his fun. His antics gave rise to sayings as well as stories. Other Swedish lumberjacks would reenact jokes told about Ola. Finding a louse on a collar, a lumberjack might tell it to come in where it's warm.

Midwestern Tricksters

The Midwest has its share of tricksters as heroes. Mythological narratives of many cultures feature a culture hero—a being who brings gifts to his/her society to help them survive. In many Native American cultures, the culture hero is also a trickster, a being who embodies the best and worst of human nature. The trickster rebels against authority and breaks taboos, and often is a clown as well as a bringer of culture. One example from the largest native nation in the Midwest is Wenabozho (also called Manabozho or Nanapush), the Ojibwe culture hero and trickster. Wenabozho is lecherous, greedy, lazy, gullible, and quick to anger. He also is very smart and teaches people many things. Telling stories about him occasions laughter, affection, and reflection. Because Wenabozho can be a sacred character, there is a prohibition against telling sacred stories featuring him unless there is snow on the ground. (Many Native American cultures regulate the telling of sacred stories in such ways.) However, some of the Wenabozho stories are not sacred. Some are etiological legends that explain why something is the way it is—why the hell diver (the pied-billed grebe, a bird that plummets straight down) has red eyes, how the Apostle Islands were created. In "Wenabozho and the Birds," greedy Wenabozho tricks ducks into closing their eyes while he sings and they dance, so that he can kill them off without the others knowing, guaranteeing himself a nice meal. Some versions of "Wenabozho and the Birds" are told with a song in the middle, which Wenabozho teaches to the ducks as they dance.

Another Native American trickster is Wakdjunkaga, of the Ho Chunk or Winnebago nation. The Wakdjunkaga cycle collected by Paul Radin (1883–1959) tells an elaborate series of stories in which Wakdjunkaga breaks a number of the most important Ho Chunk taboos, and thus creates humorous situations. In one early episode, he removes his very long penis from the box in which he keeps it and sends it creeping across a lake in order to have intercourse with a chief's daughter. As the cycle progresses, he begins to act less like a joker and more like a culture hero. He travels down the Mississippi River, removing obstacles along the way, killing beings that are molesting humans, and generally making the river safer for his people.

Midwestern Outlaws, Sports Stars, and Politicians

Other legendary figures in the Midwest include gangsters, sports stars, and military leaders. Among the outlaws who are rooted in the Midwest are John Dillinger, Al Capone, and Jesse James. Chicago especially dominates the gangsters' legendary landscape as the site of many famous shoot-outs and denouements. Many local legends circulate in northern Michigan and Wisconsin about gangsters' hideouts and pleasure spots in the idyllic North Woods. Typically, these local stories place gangsters in unexpected places, such as a fishing boat, where they fish with handguns instead of fishing rods.

Perhaps the outlaw who best represents the spirit of the Midwest is Jesse James. Stories about him abound in Missouri, Illinois, Indiana, and Minnesota. The details of his personal life have helped to feed his legend. Often he was depicted as a sort of Robin Hood figure—midwestern farmers liked him because supposedly he only robbed banks and gave to the poor. Jesse Woodson James was born in Clay County, Missouri, in 1847, and northwestern Missouri remained his home territory until his death. His father was a Baptist preacher and his mother was raised in a Catholic convent. Jesse got his start as a criminal during the Civil War, when he participated in the conflict between Kansas and Missouri. Considering banks impersonal and greedy, and bankers "a species of Yankee reptile," he participated in his first armed robbery at age nineteen when, with his brother Frank, he robbed the bank in Liberty, Missouri, in 1866. The James boys went on to rob banks throughout Missouri, Kentucky, and Arkansas. Finally, in the Jameses' famous raid on Northfield, Minnesota, in 1876, citizens fired back, killing and capturing part of Jesse's gang, the Younger brothers. Jesse and Frank went into hiding, but after a few years Jesse tried to rebuild the gang under the name of Howard. Bob Ford, the brother of a former associate, came to live with "Mr. Howard" and killed him in 1882. Ford then toured the country reenacting the murder.

Ballads and legends have kept Jesse's fame alive in oral tradition. *The Ballad of Jesse James* details Bob Ford's act: "that dirty little coward / That shot Mr. Howard / Laid poor Jesse in his grave." Countless tales have reshaped Jesse into a romantic outlaw. Many of the anecdotes collected about James have shown him as kind and generous, uncanny and brave. Various stories depict him saving a black boy from a mob, refusing to rob a preacher, and giving a widow money to pay off a mortgage-holder (whom Jesse promptly robs once the widow has paid him off). Some tales celebrate his trickery: throwing off posses by shoeing his horse backward, or sprinkling the blood of a wild hog to misdirect trackers. Others emphasize his humor: he escorts home a pool player scared of robbers. Other stories suggest that Jesse James was still alive and had taken on a new life. There are still stories in circulation about the location of his buried treasure.

A more sinister trickster was Belle Gunness, an immigrant from Norway, who in the early 1900s settled in northwestern Indiana. Belle was called "the Lady Bluebeard" after it was discovered that she had killed at least one husband and several suitors. She also supposedly killed her own children. Belle was described as a large woman. Neighbors gossiped when she got out of bed quickly after childbirth. Some saw it as an example of "old country" strength, while others found it proof that she had faked the birth and was in fact a man in woman's clothing. After the death of her first husband, Belle began advertising in Norwegian-language newspapers and killed suitors once she had stripped them of their possessions. After her crimes had been revealed, her legend grew. Supposedly, she died in a farmhouse fire. A decapitated body was found in the ruins of the burned house. But the rumor persisted that she had planned her escape by substituting another woman's body for her own and setting the fire. This unresolved ending to the Gunness story has made it serviceable for a number of authors. For some, Belle has become a heroine, a woman who took her destiny into her own hands at a time when men traditionally dominated women.

More recent midwestern heroes—those notable characters who appear in people's stories—reflect the current concerns and obsessions of midwesterners. Vince Lombardi, the revered coach of the Green Bay Packers, has stimulated a series of inspirational stories. Richard J. Daley, mayor of Chicago, also known as "the Boss," ruled the city for many years and became nationally notorious during the 1968 Democratic Convention. He and "the Daley Machine" are the subject of multiple stories and jokes. In one, the pope, the president, and Mayor Daley are in a shipwreck. Because the lifeboat will only hold one person, they decide to vote on who will survive. Daley wins by ninety-eight votes.

Are folk heroes an important part of midwestern identity today? While older heroes like Johnny Appleseed and Paul Bunyan have been absorbed into the national imagination, in everyday life they serve mostly as points of reference, such as restaurant or street names. The stories most likely to be told in casual conversation are of the exploits of local characters—the tough old "river rat" who finds innovative ways to get by, the smart aleck who always has a quick answer, the young woman determined to race stock cars. These local stories, shared among community members, strengthen bonds, express ideals and values, and sometimes gently steer neighbors back to the locally accepted way of life.

REGIONS WITHIN THE REGION

Midwesterners' identity depends upon place. The specificity of the details of everyday life in environments as distinct as the busy streets of Chicago, the cornfields of Iowa, or the hills of southeastern Ohio assures that cultural expressions—language and dialect, reference points within narratives, community events and local knowledge—will vary greatly from place to place in the region. Within the Midwest are a number of smaller, occasionally overlapping regions, formed through geographic location, occupations, environmental factors, settlement patterns, or a combination of these things. Many of these subregions include states outside the Midwest, proof that region doesn't fit within the political constraints of state lines and evidence that the Midwest's boundaries are permeable.

The Bootheel and Appalachian Ohio

Some subregions that cartographers might place in the Midwest bear more cultural connection to the South. For example, migrant workers from Arkansas, Mississippi, and Tennessee who moved into the Bootheel, the southern "heel" of the Missouri "boot," transformed the region into the northernmost land of cotton with a relatively large African American population. The twenty-nine southern and eastern counties in Ohio, about one-third of the state, comprise Appalachian Ohio, where the area's hills and resource-based occupations such as agriculture and coal mining have assured that residents identify more strongly with Appalachian culture than with the concerns of the more industrial western and northern part of Ohio.

The Ozarks

Similarly, the Ozarks, although partially contained within a state-defined notion of the Midwest, bear more resemblance to the South. Found in the highland region of southern Missouri, northern Arkansas, and eastern Oklahoma, the Ozark Mountains have been pictured as a historically isolated region. The majority of settlers there were Scots Irish, with German and English minorities. Overwhelmingly white and Protestant, the Ozarks are also flavored with early interactions between Native American and African American populations. Vance Randolph (1892–1980), the most famous collector of Ozark lore, collected, annotated, and published different folklore genres found in the Ozark region over a thirty-year period. Among the many volumes, both popular and scholarly, that he produced are *We Always Lie to Strangers* (1951) and *Pissing in the Snow and Other Ozark Folk Tales* (1976). Randolph paid particular attention to accurately documenting the stories and songs he heard. As an example, in the story "The Call to Preach," collected in Missouri in 1933, Randolph attempts to capture the dialect of the Ozarks as part of the storyteller's style:

> One time there was a fellow come walking into town, a-hollering how he's going to quit farming and preach the gospel. He was just a big country boy, all pecker and feet, the kind of a fellow that couldn't find his butt with both hands in broad daylight. Anybody could see he didn't know enough to pour piss out of a boot, with directions printed on the heel. But he stood right up in meeting anyhow, and told everybody he had a call to preach.

The story explains how this farm boy saw a message in the sky as he was plowing: smoke forming the two letters *PC*, which he decides means "Preach Christ." However, the preacher, after much thought, tells him it stands for "Plow Corn." The farm boy grumbles, but a trip to the local tavern makes him feel better, and before long he confesses to his drinking companions that he never really did see that message in the sky.

> So then the fellows at the tavern give him a lot more beer, and finally one of 'em says, "What makes you think you're called to be a preacher?" The

country boy just grinned kind of foolish. "Well, I got the biggest prick in the neighborhood," says he, "and a terrible craving for fried chicken."[5]

The irreverence of such stories underlines the spirit of a people willing to poke fun at those more concerned with propriety. It also illustrates the large canon of folk stories seldom sought out and preserved by collectors before Randolph. His efforts to accurately document stories generally considered offensive has provided us with a better representation of the kinds of stories that people actually tell.

Egypt in Illinois

The southernmost part of Illinois certainly displays the influence of its southern settlers. Yet other parts of its history have shaped it into a distinctive region known for its contrariness and its violent past. This subregion is also distinctive because of its name: Egypt. For Illinoisan Egyptians, regional identity is defined by their dialect, their continued sense of connection to the South, economic hardship, as well as their stories of violence—through the presence of the KKK, harsh coal mining companies, union activity, and Prohibition. Towns with related names—Cairo, Karnak, and Thebes—mark the region. One legend about how the region got its name is that during a crop shortage in the nineteenth century, farmers from northern Illinois had to travel to southern Illinois to find corn, just as in the Bible people went to Egypt for corn. Early settlers were hunters and trappers, followed by Scots Irish settlers from southeastern states, and later still joined by Quakers and other religious groups opposed to slavery but still southern in their outlook. During Reconstruction the Ku Klux Klan had a prominent presence in Egypt, as evidenced by legends and stories of that period. Egypt was considered a rough frontier region right into the late nineteenth century.

Coal mining developed into an important factor in the development of Egypt's regional identity. As immigrants from various countries were housed together in company towns, they found themselves united against company oppression through unionization. Various union-breaking activities helped develop the region's bloody reputation. A number of local legends recount the history of these events and others occasioned by gang activity during Prohibition.

Older traditions from early settlers in Egypt have entered the canon of folklore about the region, although they are no longer actively practiced. For example, folklorists and local historians in the region have collected stories and beliefs about New Year's Day traditions in Egypt. Reflecting early British settlement, a number of residents used to observe the tradition of "first footing"—the belief that the first person entering the home after midnight on New Year's Eve would affect the luck of the family for the next year. Traditionally, the preferred "first footer" in southern Illinois would be a man. Many neighbors had an agreement to perform this service for each other and would sometimes bring a gift of food or alcohol to share. The tradition of eating certain foods at midnight on New Year's Eve reflects Egypt's various settlement groups: while black-eyed peas and beans were popular among old-time southern Illinoisans, German immigrants more typically served pickled herring.

Ohio River Valley

One of the determining features of the Midwest is the Ohio River, which flows along the borders of Ohio, Indiana, and Illinois, creating a distinctive cultural life within the Ohio River valley. Long before European settlement, people in the Ohio River Valley sustained themselves through fishing and living off the river. The valley was originally occupied by the Shawnee and the Delaware, but during the seventeenth century French outposts were established there, to be followed by British settlement. Settlers used the river for transportation as well as for sustenance, with vessels that ranged from early-day pirogues to flatboats or keelboats that could carry entire families. Today, a small community of commercial fishermen survives, and many still identify with the houseboat tradition that was part of Ohio River life from the early nineteenth century through the 1950s.

The Ohio River valley is also historically and symbolically significant for African Americans; before the Civil War, the river during times of drought offered opportunities for slaves to cross over to freedom, earning it the name "the River Jordan." The area has a rich history as part of the Underground Railroad. Supposedly the Underground Railroad received its name as a consequence of an incident that took place in Ohio. The legend is that a runaway slave, Tice Davids, slipped across the Ohio River in 1831 and landed in Ripley, Ohio. Although his owner was in hot pursuit, he lost sight of Davids in Ripley; it was, as the owner said, as if Davids had "gone off on an underground railroad." During the development of industry in the area, the Ohio River continued to mark the difference between the Jim Crow South and the urban North. In the river's urban centers of Pittsburgh, Cincinnati, Louisville, and Evansville, blacks still maintain vibrant communities.

Tornado Alley

In the central United States, the warm, humid air in which thunderstorms thrive is especially conducive to the powerful tornadoes that have led to the designation Tornado Alley. Rather than an indication of a true region, the term serves more as a characterization based on a single dominant factor—in this case, weather conditions. While Tornado Alley also includes Texas, Oklahoma, and Kansas, most of this loosely defined area consists of Missouri, Iowa, Illinois, Minnesota, and Wisconsin. As a result, a large portion of the Midwest has a significant repertoire of beliefs and stories about tornadoes.

Many people are familiar with weather lore for recognizing imminent tornadoes: a green sky or a sound like a locomotive. However, shared beliefs and lore about tornadoes are not necessarily accurate. The Osage Indians, native to Kansas, Oklahoma, and Missouri, told settlers that tornadoes would not strike near the confluence of two rivers. Other inaccurate beliefs proliferate: overpasses offer protection; opening windows to equalize air pressure protects the roof; the southwest corner of the basement is the safest place to be; tornadoes don't hit cities. For each of these, documented cases prove otherwise.

Tornado narratives tend to be either about their devastation and the stories of their survivors, or about their capriciousness and the oddities found in the wake of their wreckage. Infamous tornadoes like the Tri-State Tornado (Missouri, Illinois, and Indiana) of March 1925, which killed 695 people and injured another

A large portion of the Midwest has a significant repertoire of stories about tornadoes. Many of these stories focus on the bizarre things that can happen during a tornado. Photo by Steve Nicklas. Courtesy NOAA.

2,027, live on in local and regional stories. One story from that tornado is of a survivor who goes back to the rubble of his house to find a box of unbroken eggs. Another less deadly but still notorious tornado in Belvidere, Illinois, in April 1967 killed thirteen people, many of them children, and injured 300 when it struck the local high school as students were boarding buses. Twelve buses were overturned. One bus driver was killed, but most of the dead were students, who were "tossed like leaves" into adjacent fields.

By far the most repeated tornado stories detail the bizarre results of these natural catastrophes. One common early story exclaimed over winds forceful enough to pluck the feathers right out of chickens. Other stories recount the adventures of cars, mattresses, or other objects carried miles from their original sites or ending up in trees or other unlikely spots; or describe entire homes or neighborhoods destroyed, while a few feet away another building is left untouched. Another frequent theme is that of straws driven through walls or telephone poles, a demonstration of the strength of the winds. The drama of tornadoes tempts exaggeration. In one account, a railroad engine is picked up, turned in midair, and set down on a parallel track facing in the opposite direction. One man's house was so gently lifted that he was unaware it was twenty-five feet in the air. He stepped out the door and seriously injured himself when he dropped to the ground.

The Corn Belt

Another subregion named for a single attribute is the Corn Belt, an agricultural area that contains Ohio, Indiana, Illinois, Iowa, Nebraska, and Kansas. A common story shared among different states in the Corn Belt, for example, is of the farmer who hears booming and popping noises during the night. Fearing that someone has been dynamiting fish in his creek, in the morning he hurries out only to discover that the booming and cracking noises he heard were produced by swelling corn stalks undergoing rapid growth because of rich soil and recent rain.

The Rust Belt and Calumet

The Midwest also contains the Rust Belt, a region that spans the heavily industrial northeastern and midwestern United States, in economic jeopardy because of outdated factories and technologies. The term *Rust Belt* gained wide use in the 1970s as the formerly dominant industrial region became noted for the abandonment of factories, unemployment, outmigration, and overall decline as the nation shifted toward a service economy.

Within the heart of the Rust Belt, the Calumet region stretches from northeastern Illinois to northwestern Indiana, following the southern part of Lake Michigan from South Chicago across the Indiana line to Michigan City. This heavily industrialized subregion gets its name from the Grand Calumet and Little Calumet rivers, which run through the area. During the nineteenth century, in part because it didn't offer good agricultural sites, the region developed slowly. However, by the late nineteenth century, with the railroad coming into the area, the Calumet prospered, and by 1920 it had become one of the world's leading industrial districts, a center for the steel and oil refining industries. Steelworkers there were dubbed "millrats," a term inspired by the ubiquitous presence of rats in the older steel mills. Industrial folklore abounds in the region, from personal stories of job dissatisfaction and accounts of terrible deaths and accidents such as falling into the "slag buggy" (a large pot filled with the hot waste material resulting from making steel), to humorous episodes and descriptions of characters, such as the legendary worker who demolished a Coke machine with a forklift to get the bottle of soda he paid for.

The U.P. of Michigan

Another example of a subregion that lies within a distinctive region of the Midwest is the Upper Peninsula of Michigan (U.P.), contained within the Upper Midwest. Because it is separated from lower Michigan by the Straits of Mackinac, and bordered by Lake Superior, Lake Michigan, and Lake Huron, the U.P. provides natural isolation for the people who live there. The area was historically populated by the Ojibwa, and the great woods and ore deposits brought in a variety of immigrants, from early French, to Cornish, Italian, Polish, Croatian, Serbian, French Canadian, and Scandinavian. When the logging and mining booms ceased in the twentieth century, the residents of the U.P. had another factor that helped to forge regional identity: a poor economy. As the U.P. came to depend more and more on tourism to bring money into the region, residents developed a stronger sense— and sometimes resentment—of more monied outsiders. Natives of the U.P. call themselves "Yoopers" to distinguish themselves from "trolls" or "fudgies" who live below the five-mile-long Mackinac Bridge, the suspension bridge connecting the upper and lower peninsulas.

The Upper Midwest

Yoopers may view their fellow Michiganders as outsiders, but within the larger region of the Upper Midwest, residents see themselves as not only culturally distinct from other regions in the United States, but also discrete from the rest of the Midwest. Stretching from the eastern parts of the Dakotas to the Upper Peninsula of Michigan, and from the northern parts of Illinois and Iowa to the southernmost parts of Ontario, the Upper Midwest contains large concentrations of European Americans—Belgians, Czechs, Dutch, Germans, Poles, Swiss, and various Scandinavians—with significant populations of many other groups, including the greatest cultural variety of Native Americans east of the Mississippi. Weather, the prevalence of certain occupations and resources, shared immigration patterns, and corresponding histories all have helped create strong ethnic traditions and a strong sense of identity, characterized by an appreciation for and dependence on the region's natural resources, especially woods and water.

In the Upper Midwest, talking about weather, particularly winter and the shortness of summer, can be a full-time occupation. Winter helps to organize recreational activities, such as ice fishing, skiing, and hockey, and is a major motif for stories and jokes about coping and survival. A common joke in Minnesota and other northern climes is that the state has two seasons: winter and road construction.

When Richard Dorson collected narratives in black communities in Michigan around 1950 among residents who had migrated from the Deep South, he found a number of accounts of the shock of encountering cold weather. From one teller, he heard about the mule Charlie traveling north to Michigan with his owner. Along their journey they stopped in Missouri, then Indiana. Everywhere they stopped, folks claimed the mule couldn't live in Michigan because it was too cold. Sadly, Charlie was listening. When they finally got to Covert, Michigan, in mid-July, it was the hottest day there in a hundred years. Charlie peeked through the crack of his stable, saw the dry corn popping, and thought it was snow. So he lay down and froze to death.

Residents of the Upper Midwest sometimes exaggerate conditions and features of the region. A good example is the legendary stature of the mosquitoes in the North Woods. Minnesotans claim the mosquito as their unofficial state bird. One joke that demonstrates the ferocity and size of mosquitoes in the North tells of a camper who on his first night out overhears two mosquitoes discussing whether to eat him there or take him home. One mosquito says, "We better eat him here. If we take him home, the big ones will take him away from us." The camper packs up and checks into a motel.

By contrast with these relatively recent tales about life in the Midwest, many based on narrative traditions brought from Europe (such as supernatural legends about ghosts who appear as warnings, or the presence of Old World beings like Norwegian trolls), stories told by the indigenous peoples who have long populated the Midwest are more intrinsically associated with place. Native American tribes—the Dakota, Fox, Ho Chunk, Menominee, Ojibwa, and Potawatomi, to name a few—continue to tell myths, sacred stories that help to explain the people's presence as well as the presence of other things in the region. Many myths are associated with particular places, like Madeline Island, the location where the megis shell appeared to the Ojibwa people on their migration from the Atlantic coast to the Great Lakes, and the heart of Ojibwa homelands in northern Wisconsin. The Ojibwa creation myth tells of a great flood that covered the earth. When Wenabozho asks different animals to dive down and look for earth, Muskrat retrieves a piece of it. Wenabozho forms the new earth, which Turtle offers to bear on his back, and that is why North America is sometimes called Turtle Island. Variants of the earth diver story appear across the world, but this specific story, informed by the local landscape and local knowledge, is the one that carries power for the Ojibwa of the Upper Midwest.

The people of the Midwest are always actively involved in discerning the shifting boundaries of their communities and region. They do so through such cultural expressions as the telling of stories, the sustaining of particular heroes and descriptions of local character, the aesthetic judgment of certain types of skills and objects, and the valuing of certain memories and specific types of knowledge. In all these instances, the details provided through local knowledge and environment make those expressions meaningful to residents.

CONCLUSION: CONTEMPORARY STORYTELLING

Telling personal stories is the predominant contemporary form of storytelling in the Midwest. Personal stories are the most local. They refer to characters, places, and events best known by a small group of people in a local community. Yet such stories are also of interest to a wider audience when they reflect common, recognizable interests and concerns.

That's the case with this story told in 1998 by Harold Hettrick, a raconteur, former game warden, and duck hunter from Wisconsin. As is the case with a good story, Harold has told this one many times, in duck camp and in informal settings with friends, especially when others were recalling severe weather events.

Many stories are told of the Armistice Day blizzard of 1940, which wreaked havoc across Wisconsin, Minnesota, and Iowa. It took many duck hunters by surprise when it swept rapidly down the Mississippi River. Ninety-three duck hunters died. Harold begins his story by describing how beautiful that day was when it began. Temperatures were in the low seventies, and many duck hunters took advantage of the unseasonable November warmth to hunt along the Mississippi wearing nothing heavier than shirts and canvas jackets. By 4 p.m., the storm was ferocious, and the water was too rough for hunters in skiffs on the river to get back to shore. Many hunters were stranded.

Harold was in high school at the time, but still recalls that day with vivid detail:

So they were stranded out there, many in hip boots and waders and small skiffs, small boats, in marshes or on shallow islands above the water line. The wind was coming over, bringing the waves over these islands and these marshes, and as 6 o'clock came, it was sub-zero. They were freezing. They were sheets of ice.

Those who were a little better prepared mentally tried to get to higher ground, an island with a tree on it or something, and gather marsh grass and stick it down their hip boots, their waders, in the sleeves of their jackets, and

Legend Trips

Urban or contemporary legends—those stories that our relatives and friends tell to warn us of the dangers of modern life—are usually spread nationally or internationally, and thus may not reveal much about a particular region. Nonetheless, some contemporary legends—like "The Hook," a story of an escaped maniac with a hook instead of a hand who attacks young couples parking in remote areas for romantic purposes—tend to be told as if they occurred in a specific place, because naming places makes them more believable.

One type of contemporary legend that is especially common in the Midwest is the legend trip. Popular among adolescents, the legend trip involves traveling to a particular site that is the basis for a set of legends—for example, haunted houses, graves, spooklights, or other places where tragedies are supposed to have taken place. Often, adolescents travel to the spot and then tell the stories on site as a way to terrify their uninitiated friends. Other activities might be involved as well, such as touching a forbidden object or entering a haunted house. The stories that develop about a particular site may have nothing to do with the original story or the known facts of an event; in fact, as time passes and more people have experiences as a result of a legend trip, the collection of legends may well grow, and interpretation may change. For example, legends about the Black Angel (a bronze statue that has oxidized over the years) in a cemetery in Iowa City, Iowa, suggest that it was a marble statue turned black by a mother's grief over her child's death; or more recently as a sign of a wife's unfaithfulness to her husband. An origin legend for the Paulding Light, a mysterious set of light spheres in the northern woods near Watersmeet, Michigan, explains that the light is the ghost of a railroad brakeman killed by a train. The Hornet Spooklight, another unexplained light phenomenon near Joplin, Missouri, has been observed since the 1880s and consistently draws visitors.

High school students, and sometimes college students, travel to such sites late at night to "test" the legend. Usually, these sites not only have origin legends but legends of retribution—what will happen if someone scoffs. Such trips are a form of play that helps to cement relationships within the group. When the group is thoroughly scared, they depart, either to continue partying or to go home.

build a nest in their boats by tipping their boats on the side and huddling in and trying to maintain their warmth. Those who were less fortunate that didn't get in, they just froze. . . .

We got home from school at 4 o'clock and the storm was really kicking up and everybody said, "Well, we got hunters out." And we had a lot of duck hunters in those days. So everybody responded to the riverbank, seeing if they could help hunters get in. Or seeing if they could get a larger boat out to go rescue 'em. The only ones who had big boats were the commercial fishermen and they even couldn't get off from shore. They couldn't get enough momentum to head into the waves. So those hunters were out there all night. They froze stiff in the ice, those that were in the water. . . .

There was a lawyer, a young lawyer right out of the university law school who married my neighbor's daughter about the previous year. And she was expecting a baby. And Marv was a good river rat. Because it was a holiday, he didn't have to go to court and practice law so he went hunting. And he got stuck out there in a skiff. . . .

He knew his wife's situation so he tied his gun, his decoys in his boat, the ducks he had killed, he tied those in. Then he rolled the skiff upside down and climbed in and held on underneath this air pocket and waded out to deeper water towards shore where the wind picked the boat up and him and moved him to shore. He'd have never made it right side up but he made it upside down hanging on in the water.

And there was an older lady named Cookwell who lived on the shore where he had started out from and she was worried about him. So she had a roaring fire going and she was walking the shore along with the rest of us waiting to help a hunter come in and when he came in, his boat came in and we didn't know there was a body with it! So we went and pulled the boat up on shore and out of it climbs Marv Fugini. And he was literally a frozen ice stick. We couldn't bend him to walk because his clothes were stiff. So we drug him.

And that older lady Mrs. Cookwell, she really drug. She did much of the pulling. We got him into the kitchen [with the] stove and he thawed out and he went on to the hospital that night and his wife delivered him a son.[6]

This story of duck hunting is an apt conclusion to a discussion of midwestern folklore because it resonates many of its important themes, and brings them into the present. The story integrates many elements of life in the Midwest—a connection to land and waterways, an appreciation of natural resources, a concern for neighbors, and a reflection on midwestern virtues of integrity and responsibility. Ordinary people stand out in this story, and their lives take on a heroic dimension as they are challenged by powerful natural forces. Marv's tough spirit, Mrs. Cookwell's neighborly concern, everyone's involvement in the rescue effort, and the birth of Marv's son celebrate personal and community resilience. Thousands of stories like this are told every day across the Midwest.

RESOURCE GUIDE

Printed Sources

Allen, Barbara. "Regional Studies in American Folklore Scholarship." In *Sense of Place: American Regional Cultures*, ed. Barbara Allen and Thomas J. Schlereth, 1–13. Lexington: University Press of Kentucky, 1990.

Baker, Ronald L. *Jokelore: Humorous Folktales from Indiana*. Bloomington: Indiana University Press, 1986.

Bird, S. Elizabeth. "Playing with Fear: Interpreting the Adolescent Legend Trip." *Western Folklore* 53 (July 1994): 191–209.

Botkin, Ben. *A Treasury of Mississippi River Folklore: Stories, Ballads, and Folkways of the Mid-American River Country*. New York: Crown, 1955.

Bronner, Simon J. *Piled Higher and Deeper: The Folklore of Campus Life*. Little Rock, AR: August House Publishers, 1990.

Danielson, Larry. "Tornado Stories in the Breadbasket." In *Sense of Place: American Regional Cultures*, ed. Barbara Allen and Thomas J. Schlereth, 28–39. Lexington: University Press of Kentucky, 1990.

Dorson, Richard M. *America in Legend*. New York: Pantheon Books, 1973.

———. *American Folklore*. Chicago: University of Chicago Press, 1959.

———. *Bloodstoppers and Bearwalkers: Folk Traditions of the Upper Peninsula*. Cambridge, MA: Harvard University Press, 1952.

———. *Buying the Wind: Regional Folklore in the United States*. Chicago: University of Chicago Press, 1964.

———. *Land of the Millrats: Urban Folklore in Indiana's Calumet Region*. Cambridge, MA: Harvard University Press, 1981.

———. *Negro Folktales in Michigan*. Cambridge, MA: Harvard University Press, 1956.

Kaplan, Anne R., Marjorie A. Hoover, and Willard B. Moore. *The Minnesota Ethnic Food Book*. St. Paul: Minnesota Historical Society Press, 1986.

Langlois, Janet L. "Belle Gunness, the Lady Bluebeard: Narrative Use of a Deviant Woman." In *Women's Folklore, Women's Culture*, ed. Rosan A. Jordan and Susan J. Kalcik, 109–124. Philadelphia: University of Pennsylvania Press, 1985.

Lavenda, Robert H. *Corn Fests and Water Carnivals: Celebrating Community in Minnesota*. Washington, DC: Smithsonian Institution Press, 1997.

Leary, James P. *So Ole Says to Lena: Folk Humor of the Upper Midwest*. 2nd ed. Madison: University of Wisconsin Press, 2001.

———, ed. *Wisconsin Folklore*. Madison: University of Wisconsin Press, 1998.

Lloyd, Timothy C., and Patrick B. Mullen. *Lake Erie Fishermen: Work, Tradition, and Identity*. Urbana and Chicago: University of Illinois Press, 1990.

Loew, Patty. *Indian Nations of Wisconsin: Histories of Endurance and Renewal*. Madison: Wisconsin Historical Society Press, 2001.

Lund, Jens. *Flatheads and Spooneys: Fishing for a Living in the Ohio River Valley*. Lexington: University Press of Kentucky, 1995.

Prosterman, Leslie. *Ordinary Life, Festival Days: Aesthetics in the Midwestern County Fair*. Washington, DC: Smithsonian Institution Press, 1995.

Tanner, Helen Hornbeck, ed. *Atlas of Great Lakes Indian History*. Norman: University of Oklahoma Press, 1987.

Web Sites

Center for Great Lakes Culture
http://greatlakes.msu.edu/

The Center for Great Lakes Culture supports conferences and publications, and offers other opportunities related to the folk cultures of the Great Lakes region.

Center for the Study of Upper Midwestern Cultures
http://csumc.wisc.edu/

This Web site features a number of projects about various ethnic groups and other folk cultures in the Upper Midwest.

Iowa Roots Radio
http://www.iowaartscouncil.org/folklife/iowa_roots/index.htm

This series of radio programs features music, stories, and talk of Iowa traditional artists.

Michigan Traditional Arts Program
http://www.museum.msu.edu/s-program/MTAP/index.html

This Web site describes the activities of the Michigan Traditional Arts Program and provides information on traditional arts for educators.

Missouri Folk Arts Program
http://museum.research.missouri.edu/mfap/

Information about the traditional arts in Missouri.

River of Song
http://www.pbs.org/riverofsong/index.html

Articles and more to accompany the Smithsonian-produced series on music along the Mississippi River.

Traditional Arts Indiana
http://www.indiana.edu/~tradarts/

Information on the traditional arts in Indiana, including back issues of newsletters.

Wisconsin Folks
http://arts.state.wi.us/static/folkdir/index.htm

This on-line artist directory on traditional arts in Wisconsin offers detailed descriptions of art forms and artists and educational material for teachers.

Videos/Films

Wisconsin Powwow/Naamikaaged: Dancer for the People. 2 videocassettes. Smithsonian Folkways Recordings. Producer: Thomas Vennum, Jr., 1996.

Event

The Great Lakes Folk Festival
Michigan State University Museum
West Circle Drive
East Lansing, MI 48824
http://www.greatlakesfolkfest.net/

FOOD

Lucy M. Long

The Midwest usually brings to mind the adjectives self-sufficient, resourceful, rural, bucolic, family-oriented, practical. Midwestern food reflects these characteristics as well—plain and straightforward, hearty and wholesome, food that sticks to your ribs to get you through the day. The public image of midwestern food is one of meat-and-potatoes or casseroles, hearty comfort foods, "like mom used to make." Often bland and basic, midwestern food offers standard ingredients with few spices and few surprises, emphasizing heartiness over healthiness, quantity over quality. Although this image is not completely inaccurate, midwestern foodways traditions also include a wide diversity of regional and ethnic specialties.

Midwestern foodways are perhaps best thought of as layers that can be peeled away one by one. At the core are American Indian and pioneer American (mostly British and German-based) food traditions. A second layer is made up of specific ethnic foods, some of which have blended into the regional foodways, while others have kept their ethnic status. For example, the Amish and Mennonites have maintained distinctive foodways traditions, yet many of their foods and their conceptualizations about food overlap with German American traditions. Immigrants from Scandinavian countries have contributed to the foodways of the northern parts of the Midwest; Appalachian traditions are common throughout the southern parts of the more eastern states. African American migration brought southern traditions, Hispanic migration brought foods from the American Southwest and Latin America, and more recent immigrants from around the world have established communities and restaurants in most urban centers throughout the Midwest. According to one scholar, however, for the most part, "regional conformity has eclipsed ethnic heritage."[1]

The outermost layer of midwestern foodways is composed of public and commercial food traditions. Food production and processing is a major part of the midwestern economy. Ohio, Indiana, Illinois, and Iowa are known as the Corn Belt, whereas southern Indiana, Illinois, and southwestern Wisconsin are part of the

Dairy Belt. Major food brands and restaurant chains have their origins in the Midwest, and mass-produced foods play a significant role in the identity of the region. In fact, midwestern food traditions have come to largely define American food traditions and are frequently referred to as "all-American." Distinguishing midwestern from American food is one of the challenges of this chapter.

NATURAL RESOURCES

The foodways of the Midwest have been shaped by the topography and climate of the region. Four seasons, accessible water sources, rich soil, relatively flat terrain, woodlands, and meadows all offer natural resources that have contributed to a strong agricultural society. Although the region's flat topography is a distinct feature, that flatness appears in varying degrees with rolling hills, bluffs, and even sand dunes (left over from glaciers) breaking up the landscape. The southern parts of Ohio and Indiana are in the foothills of the Appalachian Mountains, while the Ozark Mountains extend into southern Missouri.

A number of other features are also significant to the foodways of the region. Historically, the Midwest contained forests, woodlands, swamps, prairies, meadows, and wetlands, all of which offered plentiful wild game, fruits, nuts, and berries. The soil tended to be rich and fertile and mostly flat—prime farmland. Very cold, snowy winters and hot summers offered one long growing season. Plentiful rain and rivers, wells, and lakes watered towns, farms, and factories. The Great Lakes, the northern boundaries of most of the Midwest, held fish sufficient for commerce and recreation, with walleye and perch particularly famous. Numerous rivers, including the Mississippi, provided fishing, as well as reliable means of transporting goods to markets outside the region. In the early and mid-1800s, a network of canals grew in Ohio. While these did not last long, canal workers, along with railroad workers, brought in ethnic foods.

These geographic features have contributed to a stable, agricultural-based society throughout the Midwest. Family farms were the mainstay, and these raised a variety of crops, frequently being self-sufficient and bringing in small cash through produce stands. Today these farms specialize in single crops, such as soy beans, tomatoes, or corn, and many are being consolidated and bought by farming corporations. Ironically, fresh, locally grown produce is not always easy to obtain. The roadside stands are dying out, and the supermarket chains carry commercially processed foods. To be sure, today's grocery chains also stock fresh foods. Fruit from all over the world—mangoes, star fruit, blood oranges, Asian pears, oroblancoes, cherimoyas, and pepino melons, to name but a few—are now readily available. A growing awareness of regional identity as well as of the health and social benefits of fresh foods has stirred something of a movement to reestablish farmer's markets and to utilize local resources. The Slow Food organization, committed to promoting carefully prepared and leisurely consumed meals, has recently established chapters in midwestern cities.

NATIVE AMERICAN FOODS

Prior to European settlement, the Midwest's natural resources supported abundant hunting, fishing, and gathering for Native American cultures.[2] Woodland tribes built semipermanent dwellings with small gardens to raise corn, beans, and squash that supplemented hunting and fishing.

The Ojibwa of the upper Midwest have been able to maintain their traditional foodways. Like other midwestern Indians, they depended primarily on foods from the wild: berries (strawberries, June berries, raspberries, pin cherries, blueberries), mushrooms, greens (fiddlehead ferns, milkweed stems, watercress, dandelion, pigweed, leeks, camas bulbs, Jerusalem artichokes), nuts (hazelnuts, walnuts), and herbs. They also tapped maple trees for sap that they turned into syrup and sugar. Wintergreen or Labrador leaves were used for tea. Game such as deer, moose, bear, porcupine, beaver, rabbit, muskrat, and raccoon, and birds such as partridge, duck, pigeon, snowbird, and coot made up diets. Turtles, turtle eggs, and seagull eggs were also eaten. Fish was a mainstay and was caught year round, usually with nets and hooks, with spears for ice fishing. Lake Superior supplied trout and whitefish, whereas inland lakes offered northerns, walleye, sunfish, suckers, and bullheads. The Indians preserved fish by smoking or, during the winter, by freezing in snow or in the cold air. A typical snack still eaten today is fish roe lightly fried in a little fat or spread on crackers.

Some tribes in the southern Midwest raised corn, much of which they dried into hominy for use during the winter months as well as for bartering. Wheat flour may have been introduced as a government allotment in the mid-1800s; wheat breads are staples in Native American foodways. The Ojibwa preferred two types. The first is bannock, a heavy, baked biscuit-like dough made of flour, baking powder, water, salt, and lard or bacon fat. The second is fry bread. Made of wheat flour, salt, baking powder or yeast, water or milk, and little or no shortening, fry bread is rolled and cut into shapes with a hole in the middle, then dropped into hot fat. Usually eaten plain or with sugar, jam, or syrup, fry bread could be found among other midwestern tribes, sometimes shaped like a thick, puffy tortilla. This variation is also found in the Southwest, where it may have been introduced by Native Americans returning to their homelands in the Midwest after their ancestors were removed to "Indian lands" further west in the latter 1800s.

European Americans have incorporated into their diets the most distinctive of Indian food: wild rice. Actually the kernel of an aquatic grass, it is the only grain indigenous to North America. The rice grows in the lakes and rivers of the upper Midwest (Minnesota, Michigan, Wisconsin), where it was gathered by the Dakota (Sioux) and Ojibwa. These cultures gave it symbolic meanings and ceremonial uses, and it played a significant role in their foodways. The Ojibwa harvested wild rice by shaking the tall grasses over a canoe. They then parched it lightly and loosened the hulls by gently dancing on them. The kernels could then be boiled in water and eaten with butter or bacon fat, used in breads and soups, popped in hot fat, and eaten either lightly salted or mixed with maple sugar.

Because so many of the food traditions of Native Americans changed with the coming of Europeans and with the loss of open spaces through settlement, their descendants have tried to recover their food traditions and to recognize their contribution to American foodways. The Michigan Folklife Festival in East Lansing, for example, includes Indian food booths selling, among other things, fry bread and a corn and bean stew. Others wrap fry bread around a meat or bean filling with chopped lettuce, tomato, and cheese for an "Indian taco." Restaurants serve wild game with wild rice as Indian regional fare. Minnesota claims wild rice as its official state grain.

FOOD ON THE FRONTIER

In the late 1700s and early 1800s, horseback and wagon trains brought British and German Americans across the Cumberland Gap into Ohio.[3] Others followed the Great Lakes and the many rivers criss-crossing the Midwest. The Homestead Act of 1862 encouraged settlement by offering 160 acres in exchange for five years of continuous habitation.

The frontier presented hardship and deprivation as well as opportunity and abundance. Life there was often harsh, lonely, and unforgiving; unpredictable weather, grasshopper plagues, hailstorms, droughts, and high winds could wipe out the year's crops. Settlers were forced to rely on the local natural resources, which in good times were abundant—wild game (ducks, prairie chickens, turkeys, rabbits, squirrels, occasional deer), fish, and wild berries—plums and cranberries in Wisconsin, persimmons in Indiana, strawberries, raspberries, gooseberries in Ohio and Missouri. Gardens supplied much of the produce for the home: turnips, rutabagas, cabbages, carrots, tomatoes, squash, onions, melons were cultivated from seeds either sent from the East by relatives or carefully hoarded from one growing season to the next. During the winter months, when fresh fruits and vegetables were not readily available, families consumed what they had preserved through salting, pickling, smoking, drying, and later, canning. From family cows came milk and beef, and a hog was usually butchered every fall to provide pork and lard throughout the year. Provisions such as flour, sugar, salt, and coffee that could not be home raised were obtained through the occasional trading post or merchant.

Food was intertwined with every aspect of everyday life for pioneer women. Early cooking equipment was rudimentary, mostly open hearths, which limited methods to boiling, frying, and roasting over an open flame. Cast iron stoves, introduced in the 1830s, improved conditions immensely. They also increased expectations that every housewife would bake and produce bread. Food preserving was challenging; fresh produce and meat could be frozen during winter months but in warm weather needed to be smoked, dried, or canned. Preserving fruits and vegetables required their being boiled down in a large copper kettle over an open flame. Fruit butters, particularly apple but also pear and pumpkin, were made this way, sometimes by group activity lasting several days. A similar process produced catsups made of cucumbers, currants, gooseberries, and other vegetables as well as tomatoes. The general lack of cupboards and sinks in pioneer homes made storage and cleanup difficult. Staples such as flour, salt, sugar, and coffee were stored in wooden barrels (many of which were produced in the oak forests of northwest Ohio) or metal tins in order to be kept dry, while produce was kept in cold storage in cellars or sheds. Rodents and insects constantly threatened stored food.

By the mid-nineteenth century, and probably earlier, midwesterners had begun to acquire some regional consciousness about what they ate and how it should be prepared. Catharine Beecher (1800–1876), daughter of the famous clergyman Lyman Beecher, lived in Cincinnati and Milwaukee. She published a series of books on running households and kitchens, most notably *Treatise on Domestic Economy*, published in 1841 and reprinted annually until 1856. With her sister Harriet Beecher Stowe (1811–1896) she co-wrote another version, *The American Woman's Home: or Principles of Domestic Science* (1869, also frequently reprinted). Beecher's *Miss Beecher's Domestic Receipt Book Designed as a Supplement to Her Treatise on Domestic Economy* (1846), a book of recipes, gave form and ethos to American and midwestern cooking.

An excellent source of frontier foodways is the *Little House on the Prairie* book series written by Laura Ingalls Wilder (1867–1957). Although these are fictionalized accounts of her growing up in Wisconsin, Minnesota, and South Dakota in the second half of the 1800s, they contain insightful descriptions of the role of food in pioneer life. Wilder tells of nearing starvation, of longing for food, but also of eating to her heart's content at feasts and celebrations. She recounts the arduous food preparations that started from scratch with planting gardens and hunting and skinning game and ended with cleaning up.

CONTEMPORARY FOODS—GENERAL PATTERNS

Such sources aside, midwestern food is rarely presented as a distinctive regional cuisine. There is only one survey of the entire region; it was conducted by Barbara Shortridge, a cultural geographer from the University of Kansas. Cookbooks and cooking magazines instead focus on specific ethnic groups, states or cities, communities, churches, families, or restaurants. Few editors recognize a unified midwestern identity within the region. Similarly, scholars have addressed specific areas within the Midwest but have ignored the region as a whole. Much of their research has been used to develop folklife festivals. Festival booklets and exhibits are thus excellent resources for information on midwestern foodways. The following description attempts to identify general regional patterns; information on specific ethnic groups follows.

Typical Midwestern Foods

Shortridge surveyed Minnesota county extension agents, food editors at daily newspapers, geographers at community colleges and universities, and home cooks, asking them "to create a menu for hypothetical out-of-state guests who wanted to eat food representative of the region."[4] She found that the meal of choice was roast beef (with grilled steak second and hamburgers third), potatoes (mashed or baked), green beans, corn on the cob, lettuce salad, and apple pie, served with coffee and milk. No one mentioned the stereotypical jello salads or casseroles, although both are ubiquitous. Tastes tended to be conservative, based on rural, pioneer foodways emphasizing substantial meals served in a "down-home" manner. Many cooks associate place with locally produced crops, yet they also heavily use commercially processed foods. For Minnesota, beef could be replaced by pork and, unexpectedly, fish, probably because of Scandinavian heritages in the state. Turkey and chicken could also substitute for beef, but they were not as popular in Shortridge's survey. By contrast, what is called a casserole elsewhere is a "hot dish" in Minnesota; it consists of a baked mixture of ground beef, macaroni, and tomatoes, or ground beef, tater tots, and a canned cream soup. Wild rice or noodles might also be used, and other meats and vegetables can be substituted as well. Tuna or chicken

The typical Midwest meal often includes beef (roasted or grilled), corn on the cob, and lettuce salad. Getty Images/PhotoDisc.

and noodles with cream of mushroom soup are common in other parts of the Midwest. Vegetables are usually green beans or frozen mixed vegetables (peas, diced carrots, and green beans).

Midwestern meals also rely heavily on starches, frequently including one or more with bread in one meal. Shortridge's survey found that potatoes were the first choice. These were usually mashed, but could also be baked or prepared as potato salad or scalloped with cheese and cream. New potatoes could be boiled and served with butter, parsley, and chives. Horseradish (ground and mixed with vinegar) functions as a frequent relish for potatoes in Minnesota. Rice as a staple is unusual, although wild rice is found at celebratory or heritage meals, particularly among American Indian groups or in Minnesota communities where rice is still harvested. Homemade egg noodles are standard starches in the German and Amish areas of the Midwest and are frequently served with mashed potatoes, as in chicken pot pie in western Ohio (stewed chicken and noodles poured over mashed potatoes). Italian pastas, such as spaghetti and macaroni, have spread throughout the Midwest, served with either a tomato or cheese sauce, but little attention is paid to the subtleties found in traditional Italian cooking. The region can boast some distinctive uses of pasta, however, in Cincinnati chili and the more ubiquitous chili-mac. These dishes are available commercially as well as in the home.

If bread is a staple of every meal, it tends to come in the form of store-bought loaves of white bread. German and Jewish establishments stock dark breads, but these are distinctly ethnic. Homemade and store-bought rolls, buns, and muffins have long been widespread, but bagels became popular through national chains only in the late twentieth century. Bread usually came with butter or margarine and jams and preserves. These last are frequently homemade from locally grown fruits.

The role of vegetables in midwestern cuisine is mixed. Shortridge found that 12 percent of her respondents did not include a cooked vegetable in their meal, and 20 percent did not include a salad. Cookbooks do not emphasize vegetables, and many outsiders comment on the lack of fresh and lightly cooked vegetables in homes and restaurants. My own research, however, has determined that family gardens are ubiquitous and that respondents think vegetables so commonplace as to not be worth mentioning. Shortridge found that "sweet corn" (made famous by Garrison Keillor's radio stories about "Lake Wobegon") was the most popular cooked vegetable, usually served on the cob. Carrots and green beans were numerous, followed to a much lesser extent by peas, baked squash, asparagus, and baked beans. Vegetables were buttered, often boiled. Two distinctive vegetable dishes are tomato pudding and corn pudding. The first is a sweetened bread pudding made with tomato juice or diced tomatoes.

Tomato Pudding

4 cups (about 8 slices) bread cubes
½ cup butter or margarine, melted
1 (15-ounce) can tomato puree
½ to 1 cup firmly packed light brown sugar
1 tablespoon light brown sugar
1–2 tablespoons lemon juice
½ teaspoon salt
⅛ teaspoon pepper

Preheat oven to 350 degrees. Arrange bread in lightly greased 1-quart baking dish; pour butter over bread. In medium saucepan, combine remaining ingredients; bring to a boil. Reduce heat, cover and simmer 5 minutes. Pour over bread cubes; do not stir. Bake 35 to 40 minutes or until top is puffed and dark brown. Makes 4–6 servings.[5]

Corn pudding is a milk and egg custard composed of whole kernels of corn, similar to corn puddings found in the southern United States, except that they seem to use more sugar. Both dishes can be used as desserts because of their sweetness.

Lettuce ("tossed" or "green") was the most common type of salad in Shortridge's survey. Midwesterners like raw vegetables with dips, and sliced tomatoes and cucumbers. Restaurant menus throughout the Midwest offer coleslaw, or cabbage salad, frequently laced with a sugar and vinegar dressing. Guests take layered salads of lettuce, peas, shredded carrots, cheese, mayonnaise, and sour cream to potlucks, or large-group, celebratory meals. Variations top salads with crushed potato chips, or as in a "taco salad," with browned hamburger, salsa, and tortilla chips.

Molded gelatin salads, a stereotyped food of the Midwest, showed up on Shortridge's survey only in casual meals. When they appear at potlucks, they contain marshmallows and fruit rather than vegetables. Interestingly, Shortridge found that pickles were prized; homemade ones are a "source of pride." Pickled beets, green beans, onions, carrots, and cauliflower recur throughout the Midwest, often marketed as a local food, but cucumbers are usual. Fruits, particularly apple sauce, sometimes take the place of vegetables. Home- and commercially canned apples, peaches, pears, and cherries can be side-dishes. Stores in Ohio and Indiana with a strong German heritage market sauerkraut juice. Homemade tomato juice is drunk or forms a base for sauces and soups. Ohio claims tomato juice as its state beverage, not surprisingly given the significance of tomatoes in that state's agriculture.

Midwesterners like desserts with every meal, according to Shortridge's survey. This part of the meal affords the most diversity and innovation. Pie outnumbers other desserts; numerous regional bakeries serve homemade pies, most often made with locally grown fruits—particularly apples, but also strawberries, raspberries, blueberries, cherries, and rhubarb (mixed with strawberries). Less health-conscious pies constructed with mass-produced confections are also popular—M&M's, chocolate chips, candy bars. Ice cream stands alone or tops pies, particularly in dairy-producing areas. Cakes seem less an item of regional heritage, as opposed to cookies that appear during the Christmas season, when family recipes are high-

View of the interior of New Holland Brewing Company, Holland, Michigan. Photo courtesy New Holland Brewing Company/Travel Michigan.

lighted. On the other hand, desserts such as *kolaches* (Eastern European), rice puddings with berries (Scandinavian), and coffee cakes (German) have large followings.

German families have long brewed beer locally throughout the Midwest. Ohio, for example, boasted numerous small home breweries prior to Prohibition. While these breweries have not returned as a family tradition, midwestern beers are distributed nationally especially as micro-brews have taken hold. These have historically been wheat-based, but newer varieties experiment with local ingredients. Unexpectedly, wine is also produced in the Midwest. Soil and climate in Ohio and Michigan on Lake Erie are similar to those in northern Italy, and a number of vineyards and wineries have been developed there. Stifled during Prohibition, these survive as tourist sites as well as wine producers.

Despite the Midwest's reputation for blandness and conformity, specific states, cities, and communities frequently claim distinctive foods. Michigan boasts cherries, Wisconsin cheese, Minnesota the "hot dish" (casserole), the Upper Peninsula of Michigan pasties (turnovers filled with potato and other ingredients), Iowa "loose meat" (boiled ground beef simmered down to a thick sauce and served on buns). Some states have invented symbolic foods. Chocolate and peanut butter confections that resemble inedible buckeye chestnuts are marketed as Ohio Buckeyes. Ohio and Michigan promote maple sugar, which is usually associated with New England as a regional food. With more credibility, both Ohio and Indiana have treated apples

Selected List of Midwest Micro-Breweries

Illinois

- America's Brewpub-Walter Payton's Roundhouse (Aurora): Honey Wheat Ale, Payton Pilsner, Sweeny Stout

- Bent River Brewing Company (Moline): Bohemian Pilsner, Amber Lager, Stout

- Big Horn Brewing (Wheeling): Buttface Amber, Big Red Ale, Total Disorder Porter

- Blue Cat Brewpub (Rock Island): Wigged Pig Wheat, Big Bad Dog, Arkham Stout

- Brewing Company No. 9 (Chicago): Huckleberry Brown, Miami Weiss, Grouper

- Mickey Finn's Brewery (Libertyville): Mickey Finn's Wheat Ale, Mickey Finn's Classic Irish Stout, St. Pat's Irish Ale

- Millrose Brewing (South Barrington): Country Inn Ale, Prairie Pilsner, Panther Ale

- Taylor Brewing Company (Lombard): Voo Doo Raspberry, Darkstain, Northern Light Ale

- Two Brothers Brewing Company (Warrenville): Brother's Best Brown, Monarch, Iditarod Imperial Stout

- Wild Onion Brewing Company (Lake Barrington): Paddy Pale Ale, Bevo Brown Ale, Pumpkin Ale

Indiana

- Alcatraz Brewing Company (West Maryland): Weiss Guy Wheat, Big House Red, Penitentiary Porter

- Black Road Brewery (LaPorte): Bricklayer's Ale, Blueberry Ale, Millennium Lager

- Bloomington Brewing Company (Bloomington): Quarryman Pale Ale, Freestone Blonde, Big Stone Stout

- Duneland Brewhouse (Michigan City): Lighthouse Light, Bubba's Brown, Shoreline Stout

- Indianapolis Brewing (Indianapolis): Dusseldorfer Dark, Dusseldorfer Amber, Stout

- Lafayette Brewing Company (Lafayette): East Side Bitter, Weeping Hog IPA, Black Angus Oatmeal Stout

- Mad Anthony's Brewing (Fort Wayne): Gabby Blonde, Pan Head Red, Big Daddy Brown

- Mishawaka Brewing Company (Mishawaka): Wall Street Wheat, Lake Effect Pale Ale, Four Horsemen Ale

- Three Floyds Brewing (Hammond): Alpha King, Drunk Monk Hefeweizen
- Tucker Brewing (Salem): Smoked Porter, Brown Ale, Blackberry Wheat

Iowa

- Bricktown Brewery (Dubuque): Blackeye Stout, Laughing Ass, Get Fuggled
- Cedar Brewing (Cedar Rapids): Golden Hawk Wheat, Flying Ace's Ale, Sassy Lassy Pale Scotch Ale
- Court Avenue Brewing (Des Moines): Robbie's Rye, Porter Brown Ale, James Polk Porter
- Dubuque Brewing and Bottling (Dubuque): Champions Clubhouse Classic, Big Muddy Red, River Town Brown
- Front Street Brewery (Davenport): Stout
- Millstream Brewing (Amana): Schildbrau, Millstream Wheat, Schild Brau Amber
- Raccoon River Brewing (Des Moines): Vanilla Cream Ale, Bandit IPA, Homestead Red
- Stone City Brewing (Solon): Iowa Pale Ale, Stone Bluff Pilsner, John's Belgian Wit

Michigan

- Arcadia Brewing Company (Arcadia): Battle Creek Reserve, Angler's Ale, Starboard Stout
- Atwater Block Brewing (Detroit): Kruasen Dunkel, Hell Ale, Dunkel Weizen
- Boyne River Brewing Company (Boyne City): 10:30 Ale, Log Jam Ale, Lake Trout Stout
- Brewbaker's (Ann Arbor): Helles German Pale Lager, Chestnut Ale, Raspberry Ale
- Frankenmuth Brewery (Frankenmuth): Old German Dark, Frankenmuth Dark, Frankenmuth German Style Bock
- King Brewing (Pontiac): Honey Bee Ale, Big Red
- Kraftbrau Brewery (Kalamazoo): Munich Red, Bohemian, Doppelbock
- Lansing Brewing (Lansing): Cream Ale, Timberman's Beer
- Michigan Brewing (Webberville): Pale Ale, Stout
- New Holland Brewing (Holland): Paleooza, Kourage, Mad Hatter

Minnesota

- Ambleside Brewing (Minneapolis): St. Cloud Wheat, Unfiltered Pale Ale, Lakeside Cream Ale
- August Schell (New Ulm): Fire Brick, Maifest, Caramel Bock
- Barley John's Brewpub (New Brighton): Rosey's, Little Barley Bitter, Wild Brunette

- Fitger's Brewhouse (Duluth): Mariner Mild, Lighthouse Golden, El Niño Doublehopped IPA
- Great Waters Brewing (Saint Paul): Martin's Bitter, Piper Down Scotch Ale, Hooligan's IPA
- Hops Grillhouse and Brewery (Eden Prairie): Clearwater Light, Alligator Ale, Golden Hammer/Golden Thoroughbred
- Lake Superior Brewing (Duluth): Kayak Kolsch, Split Rock Bock, Winter Solstice Spiced Ale
- O'Hara's Brewpub and Restaurant (St. Cloud): Quarry Rock Red, Pantown Ale, Sid's Irish Stout
- Summit Brewing (St. Paul): Extra Pale Ale, Winter
- Townhall Brewery (Minneapolis): Bright Spot Golden Ale, Hope & King Scotch Ale, Masala Mama Indian Pale Ale

Missouri

- 75th Street Brewery (Kansas City): Cow Town Ale, Good Hope I.P.A., Possum Trot Brown Ale
- Augusta Brewing Company (Augusta): 1856 I.P.A., Tanhauser, Augusta Blonde
- Boulevard Brewing (Kansas City): Unfiltered Wheat, Bob's 47, Bully Porter
- Flat Branch Pub and Brewery (Columbia): Amber Chili Ale, Katy Trail Pale Ale, Scottish Ale
- Morgan Street Brewery (St. Louis): Dobbelbock, Altbier, Krystal
- O'Fallon Brewery (O'Fallon): O'Fallon Gold, O'Fallon Wheat, O'Fallon Light
- Route 66 Brewery & Restaurant (St. Louis): Blackberry Blonde, Scotch Ale, German Wheat Ale
- Schlafly Brewing (St. Louis): Pale Ale, Pilsner, American Lager
- Springfield Brewing (Springfield): Miller Unfiltered Wheat, Bull Creek Brown, Mueller Doppel Bock
- Weston Brewing (Weston): Pale Lager, Irish Ale

Ohio

- The Brew Kettle (Strongsville): Dancin' Bee, Apricot Wit Ale, Milk Stout
- Columbus Brewing (Columbus): Nut Brown Ale, Special Reserve, Black Forest Porter
- Crooked River Brewing (Cleveland): Cool Mule Porter, Settler's Ale, Lighthouse Gold
- Gambrinus Brewing (Columbus): Gambrinus Golden Lager, Augustiner Amber Lager, Bock
- Great Lakes Brewing Company (Cleveland): Dortmunder Gold, The Holy Moses, Conway's Irish Ale

- Lift Bridge Brewing (Ashtabula): Amber Lager, Oatmeal Stout, Continental Pilsner
- Main Street Brewing (Cincinnati): Woody's American Wheat, Over-the-Rhine Raz', Steamboat Stout
- Miami Trail Brewing (Xenia): Golden Ale, Pale Ale, Red Ale
- Samuel Adams Brewing Company (Cincinnati): Little Kings Cream Ale, Midnight Dragon Malt, Big Jug Xtra Malt Liquor
- Western Reserve Brewing (Cleveland): Strong Ale, Amber Ale, English Brown Ale

Wisconsin

- Capital Brewing (Middleton): Gartenbrau Octoberfest, Capital Gartenbrau Dark, Gartenbrau Special
- Gray Brewing (Janesville): Honey Ale, Gray's Classic Oatmeal Stout, Winter Porter
- Green Bay Brewing (Denmark): Amber Ale, Maple Bock
- Jacob Leinenkugel Brewing #1 (Chippewa Falls): Leinenkugel Premium, Leinenkugel Red Lager, Leinenkugel's Red Lager
- Joseph Huber Brewing (Monroe): Berghoff Dark, Berghoff Honey Maibock, Jack Dempsey Stout
- Lakefront Brewery (Milwaukee): Big East, Organic, Fuel Café
- New Glarus Brewing (New Glarus): Uffda Bock, Apple Ale, Belgian Ale
- Slab City Brewing (Bonduel): Esker Ale, Wolf River Wheat, Xena Bock
- Sprecher Brewing (Glendale): Black Bavarian, Mai Bock
- Stevens Point Brewery (Stevens Point): Spud Premium Beer, Point Special, Pont Classic Amber

Compiled by Sayonada Thomas

as cultural icons directly associated with Johnny Appleseed (John Chapman, 1774–1845), who traveled throughout the states planting apple trees).

Kansas City is famous for its barbecue, Cincinnati for its chili (cinnamon-flavored meat sauce on spaghetti topped with beans, shredded cheese, or chopped onions), Chicago for its deep-dish pizza, Milwaukee for its beer. Some foods are specific to neighborhoods within a city. For example, the Italian neighborhood known as The Hill in St. Louis, Missouri, offers toasted ravioli (actually deep fried). Snoot sandwiches (deep fried rings of pig snout) and brain sandwiches are available in the African American areas. St. Louis also boasts the St. Paul Sandwich, made of egg foo yung on white bread. Detroit has coney dogs (hot dogs smothered in chili sauce and other toppings). Parts of the Midwest prefer their own terminology: "pop" for carbonated soft drinks; "mangoes" for green peppers; "pot-pie" for stewed chicken and homemade noodles on mashed potatoes, "chili mac" for chili sauce, meat, and beans mixed with macaroni pasta, "pulled chicken" for chicken stewed, boned, "pulled" apart, and served on hamburger buns.

Milk and soft drinks typically accompany meals. Coffee is the standard morning and after-meal drink, while tea is generally unsweetened and iced. Coffee holds a special place in the upper Midwest, where "egg coffee" embodies Scandinavian practice. Three meals a day typifies the "all-American" meal system, with a hearty meat and carbohydrate-filled breakfast, a lighter lunch (soup and sandwich), and a more formal family meal in the evening. Special occasions are frequently marked with food. Chili, grilled steak, or barbecued chicken, fried fish, sausage, pulled chicken sandwiches,

Buckeyes

1½ sticks softened butter
1 lb. confectioners' sugar
1½ c. creamy peanut butter
1 tsp. vanilla
¼ c. finely chopped nuts (optional)
¼–½ bar paraffin (wax)
8–12 oz. milk chocolate

Cream together all ingredients except paraffin and chocolate and roll into balls the size of a buckeye (about 1 inch). Chill. Then melt the paraffin and the milk chocolate. Dip balls into chocolate mixture with a toothpick, leaving a small area near the top without chocolate to represent a buckeye. Yields 80 to 100 pieces of candy.

Buckeyes are the unofficial state candy of Ohio. This recipe was adapted from various sources.

or picnic fare mark special occasions. Holiday celebrations highlight family recipes, reflecting the high value placed on close-knit extended families, particularly in rural areas. Ethnic dishes also show up at these celebrations—*matzah brie* (matzah fried in scrambled eggs), Hungarian cabbage rolls, *paczki* (Eastern European pastry prior to Easter), pork and sauerkraut (for Thanksgiving and New Year's), lasagna or spaghetti—and are frequently a family's only reminder of their heritage.

Midwestern foodways include the network of activities surrounding the procurement, preservation, preparation, and consumption of food as well as the food items themselves.[6] Historically, food was home-grown or home-butchered, and this is still the ideal in farming communities of the Midwest. Many rural and small-town homes have a vegetable garden in the back yard for raising common vegetables, favorites being tomatoes, cucumbers, lettuce, and beans. Freshly picked produce is often available at roadside stands, many of which sell on the honor system. Neighborhood butchers maintain their customers' loyalty and are a source of local pride; local bakeries thrive even in some urban areas. Most midwesterners today, however, procure their food from commercial groceries and supermarket chains.

Hunting is still frequently a family tradition as well as a form of recreation. Farmers think hunting necessary to protect their crops from deer, groundhogs, and rabbits and their domestic animals from predators such as bears. Many midwesterners feel that hunting is the right of every individual to the country's natural resources. Bow hunting is popular. Many farm families use venison in their meat dishes (such as chili or casseroles); hunting lodges may feature restaurants that specialize in wild game.

Although few families depend upon it for sustenance, fishing is widely popular recreation and ranges from boat fishing on the Great Lakes to fly-fishing in streams and rivers. As is true of hunting, fishing trips are often a family ritual: grandfathers pass along skills and lore to grandchildren; equipment and memorabilia are often artistically displayed in homes; contests and formal organizations center social activities around fishing. Fly-tying, for example, is taught in workshops as well

Dinner, Lunch, and Supper

Some farm families still eat a relatively large and hot meal at noon, called "dinner," to feed those working on the farm, and also a large family meal typically served at 6 P.M., which is always called "supper." Many midwesterners continue to call the evening meal "supper," instead of "dinner," which they equate with "lunch." On Sundays, especially in rural areas and small towns, the Sunday dinner is usually a large family meal at noontime, often served after return from church. In these cases, the supper served on Sunday night is usually a light and informal meal.

as informally. Families frequently stock their freezers with fish and then empty them in spring in a festive "fish-fry." Sometimes part of a family reunion or celebration, fish-fries are also community fundraisers for a church or fire department. In northern climates, ice lake fishers cut holes in the ice through which hooks and lines can be set. In places where the ice holds for an extended time, enthusiasts build small shacks around these holes and furnish them with heaters and other comforts.

Canning and pickling were historical forms of preservation and are still popular today, although they may be done commercially rather than in the home. Standard in rural homes is a separate freezer or second refrigerator, often used for home-grown produce. Smokehouses for fish along the Great Lakes are dying out, replaced by refrigeration and by larger commercial smoking operations.

"All-American" food preparation methods actually reflect the ethnic heritage of early settlement of the region: frying from the Germans; boiling from the British; baking from British and German backgrounds; and grilling possibly from Indians but also from American pioneer life. Tradition notwithstanding, midwesterners are progressive. Numerous inventions for farming and food preparation have come from the region, and many homes boast the latest cooking equipment and gadgets.

The presentation of food—how it is served and the attention paid to its appearance—tends to be informal, "down-home," and comfortable, closer to "Mom's" kitchen than to a gourmet restaurant. This general aesthetic enhances the midwestern conceptualization of food. Food is both nutritional and practical; it should be hearty and filling; it should be plain rather than fancy, and tasty without unusual flavors or ingredients. Midwesterners often describe their approach to food as "straightforward" or "what you see is what you get." Conservative in their tastes, they are slow to try new foodways. On farms, large amounts of food were required as fuel for hard work and to bind large families. Many midwesterners grow up eating their grandparents' cooking. Gender roles in relation to food tend to be conservative as well. Although patterns are now changing, women cook for family celebrations and community potlucks as well as for the everyday meals, while men cook outdoors and for large public gatherings. Girls are expected to learn to cook from other family members, school home-economics classes, or 4-H clubs.

An interesting break in the tendency toward conservatism is the extensive use of commercially processed foods. Canned foods, commercial mixes, and pre-prepared, frozen foods are often incorporated into both daily and celebratory meals. Two of the dishes many midwesterners point to as representing their region depend upon store-bought items—green bean casserole and gelatin salad and dessert molds. These foods may represent a specific generation (women coming into homemaking in the 1950s) rather than a region. The recipes come from women's magazines and commercial packaging (Durkee's fried onions, for example), and the ingredients are easily available throughout the United States. In the 1920s, General Mills, already an institution in the Midwest, invented the friendly—fictitious—Betty Crocker, who dispensed cake recipes and kitchen advice to housewives who wanted to add more zest to their cooking. Not surprisingly, General Mills could usually supply everything the ambitious cooks might need. The annual "Bake-off" competition sponsored by Pillsbury in Minneapolis generates new uses of the company's flours, mixes, and prepared foods.

Eating Out in the Midwest

Early inhabitants of midwestern cities doubtless chose their boarding houses in part on the basis of the quantity and quality of the meals they could expect. European travelers complained that Americans, especially on semifrontiers like Missouri, ate far too fast, wolfing down the contents of their plates with little ceremony. That seemed to be the case even for lunch, as restaurants sprang up in Cincinnati, Chicago, St. Louis, and other commercial centers to cater to store clerks, office workers, and brokers who thronged the streets. These restaurants ranged from storefronts and greasy spoons to diners and substantial halls. Waiters formed unions in St. Louis, St. Paul, and Chicago in 1890, and in Indianapolis and Minneapolis the following year, an indicator of the size and scale of the restaurant industry and its growing professionalism.[7]

As city dwellers became more affluent, they could afford more leisurely evening entertainment in finer establishments, where hors d'oeuvres graced real china, the silverware sparkled, and the linens glowed under bronze gaslight fixtures. Chicago theatergoers in Dreiser's *Sister Carrie* (1900), for example, consume oysters, fish, and elegantly prepared chicken or veal dishes in restaurants along Wabash Avenue. Steakhouses then as now attracted businessmen and salesmen; here beer complemented hearty cuts of beef purchased directly from the stockyards that abutted railroad connections in all of the major cities. Morton's, a Chicago legend, is now an international chain of steakhouses. Gourmet chefs still dominate splendidly appointed rooms in fashionable midwestern downtowns and upscale malls; La Maisonette in Cincinnati, awarded five stars by nearly every travel guide, comes to mind.

Leisurely restaurant meals have long competed with those consumed on the run. More than any other region, the Midwest is responsible for America's identification with fast food. Although one might include in this category snacks such as Crackerjack (1893) and Hostess Twinkies (1930), both Chicago inventions, it was the institutionalization of rapidly cooked and delivered meals that made the greater impact. Post–World War II midwesterners traversing the region's flat landscape in their cars were sped on their way by fast-food chains. Steak 'n' Shake originated in 1934 in Normal, Illinois. Dairy Queen sold its first frozen ice cream concoction in 1938, in Kankakee, Illinois. In 1955, Ray Kroc (1902–1984) opened a hamburger stand in Des Plaines, Illinois, and from there exported McDonald's franchises around the globe. Dave Thomas (1932–2002) established the first Wendy's Old Fashioned Hamburgers restaurant on East Broad Street in Columbus, Ohio, in 1969 (a virtual museum of fast food, it is still there). A year later, Thomas opened a second restaurant in Columbus and attached to it the world's first "Drive-Thru Window." The chains displaced the dozens of roadside eateries, some built in the shape of wigwams or ears of corn, that lined the Dixie Highway and the National Road. Golden Arches also appeared on urban streetcorners, dis-

Battle Creek, Michigan

Now known as the "Breakfast Capital of the World," Battle Creek, Michigan, in the second half of the 1800s was home to Sylvester Graham and John Henry Kellogg, inventors of graham crackers and cold breakfast cereal, such as grapenuts and cornflakes. Both men were Seventh Day Adventists who believed that social reform could be achieved by changing American's food habits. Among other solutions, they promoted abstinence, vegetarian diets, and the use of whole grain breads. Kellogg, a follower of Graham, advertised his cereals as a cure for mental as well as physical ills.

pensing calories that soon became visible in the increased waistlines of their consumers.

ETHNIC TRADITIONS

Immigrants to the Midwest brought their foodways with them. If new arrivals could not duplicate ingredients from home, they adapted familiar recipes to locally available foods or established local sources to supply them. Generations later, families maintain traditional foodways within the general context of midwestern life. Ethnic foods not only make appearances at old-country holidays but also join the turkey at Thanksgiving.

British, Irish, Scottish, Welsh, Cornish Foodways

British traditions, one of the foundations for colonial American foodways, were carried into the Midwest as well.[8] These traditions involved ideas of what constituted a healthy and satisfying meal (meat with a starch and a vegetable completed with a sweet dessert; foods presented separately and in whole pieces), definitions of what were edible meats and plants, taste preferences (dairy, sweets), porridges made of available grains, and hearty breakfasts. Across much of the Midwest, these food traditions now seem "all-American" and are not celebrated as ethnic. Some communities, families, and organizations, however, do practice distinctive food traditions from the British Isles and Ireland. One Irish-English-American family in Toledo, Ohio, recalls eating "bubble-and-squeak," "bangers-and-mash," and "Yorkshire puddings," not realizing that these were not everyday foods for their neighbors.

English traditions appear at tea rooms, some of which advertise themselves as English.[9] These serve a variety of teas along with scones, biscuits (which Americans would call cookies), and dainty finger sandwiches made of watercress, cucumber, or salmon on cream cheese. Scones have recently become popular and are now available in numerous coffee shops and bakeries, often with Americanized flavors and ingredients (such as cranberry, blueberry, or pecan). Welsh foods are rare, although several towns in central and western Ohio have a strong Welsh heritage.[10] Food traditions, along with language, names, religion, and distinctive singing, are continued there. Among the distinctive foods are sausages and oatcakes (thin, sweet crackers made of oats), and "Welsh cakes," a kind of cookie or scone, filled with currants, baked on a griddle. These are sometimes sold at renaissance fairs and Celtic festivals. Immigrants from Cornwall settled the Upper Peninsula of Michigan in the early 1800s, bringing their traditional pasties with them.[11] These potato-filled turnovers were a hearty lunch for men working in the mines, and were soon borrowed by the Finnish immigrants, eventually becoming symbolic of the Upper Peninsula in general.

Scottish foods rarely appear except at special events specifically celebrating Scottish ancestry.[12] Burns Night is a popular Scottish holiday in the United States. Held on January 25, it celebrates the birth of poet Robert Burns, born in 1759. The primary food served is the infamous *haggis*, a meatloaf-like pudding made of oatmeal, chopped liver (lamb or beef), and other ingredients (beef suet, beef heart, lamb shoulder, whisky) that is steamed inside a cow's bladder or sheep's stomach. (An ovenproof bowl covered with tin foil is an acceptable alternative.) This is served with great ceremony: it is usually "piped in," carried on a tray followed by a bagpiper. Someone reads a poem by Burns, "Address to a Haggis," and the *haggis* is dramatically cut open. The meal can also include "cock-a'leekie" (chicken stewed with leeks), "tatties and neeps" (mashed potatoes and turnips), "tipsy laird" (sponge cake, biscuits, jam, and spirits), or trifle. Haggis has been adapted to American tastes in recipes that leave out some or all of the animal parts. The Shriners' organization in Toledo, Ohio, celebrates Burns Night with *haggis*, but many of their pipers are actually of Polish heritage.

Hogmanay, Scottish New Year's, is celebrated on December 31 and traditionally involves giving special foods to the "first-footers," the individuals first stepping into one's house: bottles of whisky, *bannocks* of oatcake, shortbread, and *blackbun* cake (a type of fruitcake soaked in whisky and aged for several weeks). Scottish-made whiskys are world-renowned and are served throughout the Midwest regardless of one's ethnicity. Large, public "gatherings of the clans" occur at Highland Games held in a number of places in the Midwest, notably Oberlin, Ohio. These festive events include Scottish dance, music, and sporting competitions rewarded with shortbread cookies and sausages. Scottish dance clubs, along with other Scottish social organizations, sometimes offer "fry-ups," an informal meal of fried sausage (including traditional black and white puddings), bacon, eggs, potato cakes, toast, and broiled tomatoes. The Welsh and Irish prepare a similar meal.

Irish immigration to the Midwest peaked in the mid-1800s as a result of the potato famines.[13] Irish labor helped build the canals and railroads of the Midwest, and established Irish enclaves in a number of midwestern cities, especially Chicago, Cleveland, and Milwaukee. Traditional Irish foodways fit easily into the established pioneer American patterns of potatoes and bread with meat, either separate or stewed (Irish stew of mutton/beef and potato, onion, carrot), bland spices, and milk and butter. The Irish fondness for cabbage blended with already established German foodways. The Irish also established pubs in every urban center in the Midwest, and although these pubs reinforced stereotypes of Irish ethnicity, they were actually centers of Irish music and socializing. Most pubs offered informal Americanized foods (fried potatoes, hamburgers, sandwiches, "fish and chips"—fried fish pieces with French fries) along with Irish beers and whisky, and introduced Americans to the heartier stouts and ales of the British Isles. Irish food is always available on St. Patrick's Day (March 17), one of the only ethnic holidays celebrated nationwide and across ethnicities in the United States. On that day, even non-Irish restaurants now offer a "Jigg's Dinner" (boiled dinner of corned beef, cabbage, potatoes, and carrots served with soda bread). Patrons seek green beer from pubs that open early in the morning. Irish foods show up at the numerous Irish and Celtic festivals found throughout the Midwest, although these tend to focus on potato, sausages, and fish and chips. *Feiseanna* (competitions of dance, music, oratory, art) feature Irish biscuits and products from Ireland. Stores carry

When Samuel Kingan immigrated from Northern Ireland to America in 1862, he opened a meatpacking plant in Indianapolis. Courtesy Indiana Historical Society.

homemade soda bread around March 17. As is the case with many watered-down ethnic traditions, only one variety is generally available—a sweetened cakelike bread made with white flour and currants or, if Americanized, raisins.

German, Amish, Mennonite, and Swiss Traditions

Germans were the largest non-English speaking group settling the English colonies (over 100,000 escaped wars, high taxes, and religious disputes in their homeland during the 1600s and 1700s), and German culture is one of the foundations of midwestern culture. German foodways, however, are generally not identified in the Midwest as such,[14] because they have become mainstream. Items such as sausages, breaded cutlets, sauerkraut, and potato dishes have translated easily into American tastes. Moreover, because German ethnicity became private and hidden for four decades (1917–1957) following the two world wars, during which time German culture was considered suspect in the United States; German names were not used for foods, and dishes that were obviously German were not offered publicly. The dominance of southern German food in the American diet can be traced to the publication in 1931 of *The Joy of Cooking* by Austrian American Irma S. Rombauer. (Later editions were published with her daughter, Marion Rombauer Becker.)

Recent interest in ethnic heritage as well as the celebration in 1983 of 300 years of German immigration to the United States has led to the founding of new restaurants and associations that offer German food. Many of these are tourist venues within historically German neighborhoods. For example, the German Village in Columbus, Ohio, boasts several German restaurants, as does Frankenmuth, Michigan, advertised as a town offering year-round celebrations of German culture.

The most popular German foods are bratwurst, strudel, and beer, served at

German immigrants brought their traditional foods to America. Courtesy Cincinnati Historical Society.

Oktoberfests, German beer gardens, and polka events. German midwestern food-ways rely heavily on vinegar both as a flavoring and as a preservative (particularly in pickling and sauerkraut); on melding of sweet and sour tastes in sauces (as on cabbage slaw and potato salad with vinegar and sugar dressing) and marinades for meat; on varieties of sausages; on homemade noodles; on heavy, rich desserts; and even on the home brewing of beer.

Many nineteenth-century German immigrants were farmers, known for their orderly and well-run farms as well as their self-sufficiency. They raised pigs, and they used every part of the animal. Headcheese was made from hog's head; hocks and feet were pickled; brains were fried (sometimes with eggs); tripe was used in stews; and sausage was made from pig's blood. Stewed chicken feet added flavor to soups. Potatoes (fried, mashed, boiled, or dumplings) appeared at every meal. Canning, as with most pioneer families, was a major form of preservation; German families put up their home-canned meats, pickles, and sauerkraut. They also made their own cottage cheese, noodles, and root beer. Germans in the upper Midwest collected wild horseradish as a condiment for meats and potatoes.

Beer, traditionally homemade among early German immigrants, accompanied most meals. Although those traditions have died out, *Rathskellers* and *Brauhauses* in most midwestern cities offer German beers on tap, and frequent customers often keep their own *steins* (mugs) on the shelves. German restaurants foreground a "beer garden" area. Typical is Minneapolis's Black Forest Inn, whose menu lists the *Hausplatte* (*sauerbraten* aspic, *rippchen*, *bratwurst*, and Polish sausage served with red cabbage sauerkraut and potato salad), *hasenpfeffer* (German-style rabbit), and four different tortes. Their best known dessert, Black Forest torte, is a triple-layered chocolate cake with cream cheese filling with cherries between the layers and a whipped cream frosting.

Bratwurst

German butchers and sausage-makers thrived in the Midwest; numerous family-run businesses survive today. *Bratwurst*, made of pork, veal, and eggs, grilled and served on a crunchy hard roll with chopped onion, sauerkraut, ketchup, and/or mustard, is seen everywhere in the Midwest, with Wisconsin claiming it as "soul food." Sheboygan, Wisconsin, has held a Bratwurst Day every summer since 1953, serving it with rye bread and beer. Numerous other festivals, especially "Oktoberfests," also feature bratwurst. Sometimes however it is served simply as a celebratory food not tied to German heritage. Midwesterners favor many varieties of *wurst* (sausage), which they consider the German ancestor of the all-American hot dog.

Heavy, dark German breads have been replaced by store-bought white breads, but rye and pumpernickel breads are still available from specialty bakers or baked at home for special occasions. Also found in midwestern grocers and delis are several varieties of potato salad (*Kartoffelsalat*). Some German confectionaries offer marzipan (almond paste made from ground almonds, sugar, egg whites, and vanilla) made into shapes and painted, dipped into chocolate, and decorated. Marzipan is also rolled into a thin sheet and draped over a cake as icing. Some German foods have become Americanized: *wiener schnitzel*, for example, is served as breaded veal or pork cutlet, and *rouladen* have become "roll 'em ups." Sauerkraut has entered mainstream American cuisine, although the custom of drinking sauerkraut juice seems to persist only in German areas of the Midwest.

German foods appear at holidays, particularly Christmas. Pre-Christmas baking produces numerous cookies and tortes; Christmas dinner features goose with bread stuffing. New Year's Day calls for pork and sauerkraut with caraway seeds, a dish that sparkles at Thanksgiving in the Midwest as well. Among Germans in Minnesota, Sunday dinner may include *sauerbraten* (a roast marinated with juniper berries), chicken, or *wiener schnitzel*; dumplings or *spätzle*, creamed vegetables, and a sweet and sour salad. Saturday night supper might feature cold, sliced sausage, dark bread and cheese, fruit *kuchen*, and homemade beer.

German food traditions frequently overlap with those of the Amish and Mennonites, which are religious subcultures as well as ethnic groups.[15] Both originated from the Anabaptist movement of the early 1500s in Switzerland, with the stricter Amish splitting off in 1693. Although their food traditions reflect their migration histories and join some of the other prevalent ethnic traditions in the region, Swiss and Russian as well as German, their food holds a distinctive place in the tourism and public stereotypes of the Midwest. The word "Amish" is a marketing tool, denoting plain but tasty home-cooked fare utilizing local agricultural resources and implying produce organically grown on family farms and old-fashioned processing.

The Amish have maintained distinct and separate cultural traditions and communities over the years. Often identified by their horse-drawn buggies, they maintain strict social boundaries between believers and nonbelievers. The majority of the 150,000 Amish living in North America today reside in Ohio (Holmes County has the largest number), northern Indiana, and Iowa. Often referred to as the "plain people," they avoid eating with outsiders, and their food reflects their philosophy of family- and farm-based simplicity. Their food is home-raised, closely tied to the seasons, and hearty enough for the physical labor involved in farming. Meals emphasize meat with starch and other carbohydrates. Breakfast is frequently cornmeal mush or other cooked cereals with eggs and fruit or juice. A typical dinner includes noodles or potatoes, meat (often fried), and home-canned vegetables, with bread and dessert. A lighter meal would be soup, cheese or bologna, and fruit. Whole grain breads and cereals are staples, and cakes and cookies complete most meals. Dairy products (milk, cheese, cottage cheese, yogurt, ice cream) come from the family cow, and Amish-produced cheese is carried by most grocers throughout the Midwest.

Old-order Amish do not have electricity in their homes, relying on wood or kerosene stoves for cooking and on ice boxes, spring houses, or basements for cool storage. The most common means of preserving vegetables, fruits, and meats is home-canning, which has produced a profitable tourist industry. Fruit jams and preserves, pickles (cucumbers, beets, garden vegetables), and relishes sell well. Homemade sausage is also widely marketed, particularly bologna made without the casing, and Amish chickens are promoted as healthier to eat than other commercially produced brands. Amish pies, made either with local fruits or with various creams and sugars, are renowned. Their "Shoo fly" pies are made of brown sugar, syrup, and butter; "fry pies" are a turnover variation with fruit filling. The Amish themselves often shun Amish food at Amish restaurants in Ohio and Indiana, however, "Midwestern heritage" restaurants also offer Amish dishes.

Unlike the Amish, Mennonites do not maintain separate lifestyles and do not constitute a subculture; instead, Mennonites frequently run food-related businesses that emphasize social and environmental responsibility in food choices. For years, their stores were frequently the only source for alternative "health foods" and for vegetarian items in the rural Midwest. Bluffton, Ohio, and Goshen, Indiana, are home to Mennonite colleges that train entrepreneurs in such businesses and supply international foods for Mennonite missionary activities. Mennonites run fresh produce markets and family-oriented restaurants. One of the best known pie shops in Toledo, Ohio, is owned by Mennonites. Many Mennonites in western Ohio also emphasize their Swiss ethnicity, sponsoring festivals and historical societies.

Although frequently lumped together with German, Swiss foodways have also contributed to midwestern culture. Swiss who immigrated to central Ohio in the mid-1800s were skilled in cheese-making and dairying: several small cheese factories still produce high-quality specialty cheeses. New Glarus, Wisconsin, is an enclave of Swiss ethnicity where businesses offer representative German-Swiss foods. New Glarus was established in 1845 for unemployed textile workers who quickly learned dairy farming and cheese-making. Now a tourist site of Swiss-American ethnicity, New Glarus holds festivals, restaurants, and breweries. Small, European-style food shops there specialize in cheese fondue, *wiener schnitzel* (pan-fried veal), onion soup, homemade sausages (*landjaeger*, *Kalberwurst* made of veal and milk, *mettwurst*, and *bratwurst*), locally made and imported cheeses (Swiss, Gruyère, butterkase), breads, cookies (*bratzeli*, anise *springerli*, and *sandbisson*), and pastries (fruit tarts, honey cakes, puff pastries, and *stollen*).[16]

African American Foodways

African American foodways in the Midwest are found primarily in urban areas where southern blacks found employment in the Great Migration of the 1920s.[17] St. Louis, Detroit, and Chicago are probably the best known black communities, famous for music as well as for establishments serving "soul food." These restaurants offer "southern" cooking: fried chicken, fried catfish, cornbread, greens (frequently, collard greens cooked with ham hocks), hominy grits (corn soaked in lye, dried, and ground), homemade biscuits, and dried beans (pintos, field peas, black-

Distinctive African American cooking includes cornbread, rice, cole slaw, and sweet potato pie. Corbis.

eyed peas). Pot liquor, the liquid left over from boiling greens, functions as broth or gravy. Distinctive to African American cooking are sweet potato pie, red beans and rice, ribs, and a liberal use of hot sauce and spicy peppers.

A number of African American foods generally appear only at private functions because they either require expert, time-consuming preparation skills, or they are considered socially marginal. Chittlin's or chitterlings (small intestines of pigs), tripe, pig tail, hog maw, chicken necks, possum (boiled and then baked with sweet potatoes), brains with scrambled eggs are not standard fare in American cooking. African American fare that has become mainstream includes baked macaroni and cheese, spaghetti and meat sauce, potato salad, cole slaw, numerous cakes (particularly pound cake), pies, and puddings (banana is a favorite). Some foods are too humble for the general public, such as crumbled hoe cake in buttermilk, which is common in Minnesota. Rice, a mainstay of much African American cooking, sets it apart from potato-oriented midwestern cuisine. Sweet potatoes (baked, mashed, in pie) are also associated with African Americans. Buttermilk became a common ingredient because many African Americans have a genetic intolerance to fresh milk.

Cans of "soul food" items line shelves in ethnic sections of grocery stores, especially collard greens, field peas, and hominy. It shares a number of ingredients with Mexican food: beans and rice, hot sauce and chili peppers, corn meal, and hominy as well as tripe and various pig parts. In many parts of the Midwest, African Americans sell barbeque on the street from specially designed trucks, offering barbequed chicken and ribs with corn bread or biscuits, baked beans, potato salad and cole slaw (both made with a mayonnaise dressing), and corn on the cob.

Scandinavian and Nordic Traditions—Norwegian, Swedish, Danish, Finnish

Immigrants from Norway, Sweden, Denmark, and Finland have contributed significantly to the food cultures of the northwestern and northern parts of the Midwest.[18] Although some foodways have remained distinctive to specific cultures, many have blended into a pan-Scandinavian cuisine shared by members of various Scandinavian ethnicities as well as non-Scandinavians in those regions. Stores stock foods from all of the countries, and public food events as well as family meals include items from different groups in one menu.

Aesthetic protocols among all groups mandate that "colors and textures are contrasted in culinary pairings: lutefisk and meatballs, sweet relishes and jellies with hearty meats or delicate fish, and the brightly colored condiments and berries against the white or subdued major colors."[19] Cookies are "never overly sweet but are rich in cream," and are decorated only with a bit of powdered sugar. Typical foods are fruit soups, meatballs, dried cod and pickled herring, rye and flat breads, headcheese and sausages, milk puddings, potatoes, open-faced sandwiches, cookies, and pastries. *Ris a l'alamande* is a festive and popular Christmas dessert. Each Scandinavian subculture gives these items its own spellings and emphasizes some items over others. Christmas Eve features a large festive meal where coffee is important as a drink and as an accompaniment to socializing. Church coffees and suppers figure largely in social life. The Scandinavian smorgasbord or buffet, traditionally associated with Christmas, has been adopted by the American mainstream.

Norwegian food in the Midwest is often symbolized by *lutefisk*, salt-preserved codfish, soaked in lye, rinsed (usually repeatedly over three weeks), then boiled or steamed and served with melted butter and boiled potatoes.[20] Its taste and appearance (large and gelatinous) have made it the subject of jokes and a test of ethnicity. Although it used to be a staple of the Norwegian diet, lutefisk now appears primarily at Christmastime. Cod prepared in a variety of styles is a favorite. *Torskklubbene* or codfish clubs were established in the upper Midwest after World War II as cultural organizations promoting Norwegian sports, food, and social networks.

Lefse usually accompanies lutefisk and appears at any public celebration of Norwegian ethnicity. A round, flat bread, *lefse* is cooked on a griddle and turned with a wide stick designed for that purpose. Although Norway has developed many varieties, the Minnesota version is made of mashed potatoes, salt, shortening, and flour. It is eaten with meals, plain or with butter and sugar, or as a snack, wrapped around a filling, such as herring, cheese (goat-milk cheese, referred to in Minnesota as "Norwegian peanut butter"), potatoes, meatballs or *lutefisk*.[21]

Kransekake is another food associated primarily with Norwegian Americans (*kransekage* in Danish, *kranskaka* in Swedish). A pastry tower as tall as 18 inches, made of baked rings of almond paste, sugar, and egg whites, it appears at weddings, birthdays, and anniversaries. A *julekake* (yeast sweet loaf with citron) is usually purchased for Christmas. Norwegian cookies, like other Scandinavian cookies, are rich and buttery and come in a variety of shapes and preparations. The basic ingredients are flour, butter, eggs, sugar, and cardamom. Favorites are *fattigmann* (with sweet cream and deep fried), *goro* (cognac or vanilla and baked on an iron in rectangular shapes with a religious scene stamped onto the dough), *kringler* (anise oil), *sandbakkels* (chopped almonds), *krumkake* (thin dough rolled into cones), and *rosetter* (deep fried in wheels or flower shapes).

Another distinctive Norwegian food is *klubb*, a boiled dumpling made of potatoes, flour, salt, and water. A traditional type, *blodklubb*, used pork blood, sugar, and rye flour. Also notable is *rommegraut*, a porridge made of sweet cream, flour, warm milk, salt, sugar, and lemon juice. This food is cooked for several hours into a pudding, frequently stirred with a *tvare* (a whisk made of the top of an evergreen tree) and served with melted butter, sugar, and cinnamon (chopped egg is used in Norway). In the upper Midwest, it is the main course and is accompanied by *akevitt* (schnapps) and festive sandwiches or sausages.

Swedish immigrants to the Midwest in the nineteenth century also settled in the northern and western areas. Their food traditions closely resemble those of the Norwegian Americans, drawing on the sea and the dairy for soups, potatoes, fish, and porridge for the pioneer diet.[22] American foods, particularly pork, have been incorporated since early settlement. Though not celebrated outside Swedish midwestern communities, the most distinctive holiday is Santa Lucia Day (December 13), which commemorates the Italian saint, Lucia, who provided food to starving Swedes. Wearing a candle headring and white gown, the eldest daughter serves a breakfast of saffron-flavored *lussekatter* buns (baked in an "s" shape), coffee, and sometimes ginger cookies.

Swedish foods in the Midwest shade toward creamy and mild with pickles (beets, cucumbers, herring) and red items (beets, lingonberries, red currants) providing contrast. Fresh dill adds flavor. Distinctive dishes include meatballs with a cream gravy, *bruna bonor* (brown beans baked in a sweet-sour sauce), *potatiskorv* (potato sausage), headcheese, ring liver sausage, and *kram*, a thickened fruit pudding made with whatever fruits are available. Soups are traditional—pea, cabbage, ox-tail, chicken, noodles or dumplings, and fruit—as are a variety of breads, including *limpa* (rye bread), *knackebrod* (crispy hardtack), pumpernickel bread, and *lefse*. Fish is a part of most meals, most often herring (often pickled), dried cod or *lutefisk* but with cream sauce or mustard gravy, anchovies, and whitefish. Different grains (rice, rye) make up *grot* (mush) cooked in butter and milk. Rye *grot*, when cold, is cut in slices and fried in butter. Thin, crispy pancakes topped with symbolic lingonberries crushed in sauces, preserves, and jellies, fill breakfast plates.

In contrast to other Scandinavian immigrants to the Midwest, the Danish did not come to America to escape poverty or adversity, and thus were less inclined to assimilate quickly. This may explain the unusual continuity between foods found today in the Midwest and foods found in Denmark.[23] Social clubs, churches, and language camps and schools have helped to ensure the survival of Danish culture in the United States. Like other Scandinavians in the Midwest, Danes prize thrift and simplicity in their foods. They emphasize fish, soups, breads, and pastries. Unique to Danes, however, is a reliance on fresh vegetables, including parsley, carrots, peas, kale, new potatoes (boiled, served with butter and parsley), and cucumbers (as pickles served with meats and on sandwiches). They also prefer fresh ocean fish rather than salted cod and *lutefisk*. Fresh *torsk* (cod) is a favorite, served with a cream or mustard sauce. Tables carry herring, anchovies, eel, freshwater fish (frequently smoked), and a Danish treat: rolled fish fillets filled with parsley, oysters, and mushrooms.

Danish immigrants brought with them a fondness for *smorrebrod*, open-faced sandwiches. Breads support different toppings (rye for most, but white for shrimp, salmon, and cheese, and crisp flat breads for cheeses). Elaborate toppings (smoked eel, flaked crab, raw scraped steak, scrambled eggs, *rullepolse*, pickled herring, salami, liver pate, sausages, cheeses), specific garnishes (lemon twist, beet pickles, cucumbers, orange or grape slices), and several sauces (relish, curry, sugar, horseradish, mayonnaise) spice the *smorrebrod*. Imported Danish cheeses are also used—Havarti, bleu, and Camembert. The Danes eat sandwiches in a given order (fish to chicken or egg to meat to cheese).

Other distinctive Danish American foods are *medisterpolse*, a sausage made of pork with no grains or potatoes added, and *rullepolse*, a meat roll of lamb shank and pork loin seasoned with pepper, cloves, and onions. Marinated in saltpeter and salt for ten days, it is served thinly sliced on rye bread. Four types of soup are traditional. Uniquely Danish are vegetable soups that include fresh kale, cauliflower, peas, and celery, meat and fish broths (usually with dumplings), and milk soups thickened with rice, barley, or buckwheat. Their favorite soup is buttermilk soup, made with tapioca, fresh lemon, and orange juice concentrate. Fruit soups (*sodsuppe*) are pan-Scandinavian, although the Danish incorporate any kind of available fruit, canned or dried.

Finns immigrated to the Midwest, especially to the Upper Peninsula of Michigan and to Minnesota,[24] because the climate was similar to that of their homeland—a short growing season and cold winters with abundant ice and snow. Wild game, fish, and berries were standard in the immigrants' diet, as were root vegetables (potatos and rutabagas) and milk. Finns in the Midwest are known for their hearty and thrifty but mild soups, stews, casseroles, rice puddings, whole grain breads, coffee, hot cereals, and rutabagas. Finns eat rutabagas raw, boiled, mashed, cubed, or in casseroles with or without potatoes. A festive version is *lanttulaatikko*, made of mashed rutabagas, eggs, milk, and nutmeg. They also add rutabagas to pasties, a Cornish turnover of meat, potatoes, carrots, and onions that Finnish miners borrowed from fellow immigrants. Pasties have become associated with Finns in the Upper Peninsula.

Bread forms the basis of every meal, with rye, barley, and whole wheat flours predominating. The most ethnic type is *rieska*, a large, flat, round rye loaf with a large hole in the middle. Hard flatbreads are mostly store-bought. *Pulla*, a braided sweet bread of white flour, eggs, and cardamom, perks up breakfast or snacks, and is elaborated at holidays with raisins, dates, or nuts. Finns give *pulla* as a gift to neighbors at Christmastime throughout the Midwest.

Milk is ubiquitous as a drink, as a food in itself, as an ingredient in cooking, as

Pasties

Pastry dough

4 cups all-purpose flour, spooned into cup
2 teaspoons salt
1 cup chilled lard or vegetable shortening
½ to 1 cup cold water

1. Measure flour and salt into medium-sized bowl. Cut lard into small pieces and drop on top of flour mixture. Using sharp knives, pastry blender, or finger tips work lard and flour until mixture resembles crumbs.

2. Stir in cold water slowly, adding only enough to hold dough together in a ball. Wrap dough in plastic and refrigerate about 15 minutes before rolling out.

3. Dough can be made 2 or 3 days in advance, wrapped well in plastic, and refrigerated. Allow to stand at room temperature for 1 hour before rolling out for pasty.

Filling

1½ pounds round steak, cut in ¼-inch pieces
2 cups finely diced onions
1½ cups grated rutabagas (or carrots)
3 cups diced potatoes
⅓ cup butter, cut in small pieces
1 teaspoon salt
½ teaspoon black pepper

To assemble 8 medium-sized pasties:

1. Divide pastry into 8 equal pieces. Keep covered until needed.

2. On a lightly floured board roll out each piece into a 9-inch round. Layer ⅛ of meat and each vegetable down center of round, in the same order as listed. Top with pieces of butter and salt and pepper.

3. Brush edge of circle lightly with water. Fold edges to center and crimp or flute together to provide a tight seal. Cut a small vent in each side of crimped edge. Can be prepared ahead, covered well, and refrigerated until needed. Can also be frozen, well wrapped, at this point.

4. Bake in oven preheated to 400°F until crust is golden, 55–65 minutes. Serve warm or at room temperature.[25]

a topping for hot cereal, or as an addition to coffee. Older Finnish Americans soured it into *Viili* and *Piima* (similar to yogurt). *Uunijuusto*, called "squeaky cheese," required the milk of a cow that had just calved. Eaten plain, it was added to coffee in cubes. Many soups use a milk base, as do *riisipuuro* (rice pudding) and *pannukakku* (oven pancake). Whipped cream appears frequently in desserts.

The dried, salted cod of the Norwegians gets a mixed reception from the Finns, but salt salmon is so common it is referred to as "Finnish gold."[26] Finnish dishes include *mojakka*, a fresh fish stew with onions, potatoes, allspice, pepper, and water or milk broth, and *laxlada*, a casserole of potatoes, cream, and salmon. Because the Finns prefer fresh fish, fishing (along with hunting) is still an important family tradition. Ice fishing, particularly on the Great Lakes, owes its development to the Finns (and Native Americans).

Coffee warms both formal and informal socializing; Finnish Americans pride themselves on their coffee-making skills. Breads and desserts accompany coffee events as well as meals. Finnish Americans have created few ethnic cookies, opting instead for puddings—bread, rice, custard, often with berry toppings. *Ilmapuuro* (air pudding) made of farina cooked in cranberry juice, and beaten until it triples in volume, seems to be distinctively Finnish.

Eastern European Foodways

Eastern Europeans settled in urban centers in the eastern and central parts of the Midwest in the late 1800s; their foods have now entered the midwestern mainstream.[27] Their "peasant" foods—hearty, inexpensive, for everyday eating—feature fish, particularly herring and pike, pork, sausages, cabbage, mushrooms, potatoes, beets, apples, rye and flavorings (paprika, vinegar, sour cream, horseradish, poppy seeds, caraway seeds, allspice, butter) in now familiar dishes (sauerkraut, cabbage rolls, paprika gravies, dark breads). Midwesterners dote on their butter cookies and festive baked pastries.

Czech and Slovakian

Immigrants from Czechoslovakia settled primarily in Michigan, Wisconsin, Illinois, and Iowa, coming in large numbers to urban areas such as Chicago, Milwaukee, Detroit, and Cedar Rapids, where they established many Czech and Slovak restaurants and bakeries. Czech food is often influenced by that of its neighbors, especially the Austrians, Hungarians, and Germans: "Their original Slavic taste for souring foods with sour cream, lemon, vinegar or green grapes is greatly influenced by the schnitzel from Vienna, the goulash from Hungary and sauerkraut from Germany."[28] Among favorite Czech foods are *kolaches* (soft yeast pastries, filled with fruit), beer or pork with sour cream, and excellent rye bread.

Hungarian

Hungarian food in the Midwest is similar to Polish American food.[29] Paprika gravy (lard, paprika, garlic; chopped green peppers, onions, and tomatoes; chicken and beef stock, salt, pepper, and sour cream) is basic. Stuffed green or red peppers are variations on cabbage rolls. Hungarian dumplings resembling German *spätzle* figure in soups or as a side dish.

One of the best known restaurants in the Midwest is Hungarian—Tony Packo's in Toledo, Ohio. Started in 1932 by Tony Packo, the son of Hungarian immigrants, as a sandwich and ice cream shop, it served a sausage on a bun with Tony's original spicy meat chili sauce, promoted as the "Hungarian hot dog." It became famous in the 1970s because of the television show *M.A.S.H.*, which featured Toledo native Jamie Farr. Celebrities passing through Toledo began stopping by the family-run restaurant to sign their names on hot dog buns. Over 1,000 signed hot dog buns now line the walls of the restaurant. The restaurant's menu includes Americanized Hungarian foods. Chili plays an active role—as sauce on taco chips (with sour cream and cheese as a "chili Sunday"), hot dogs, French fries ("chili cheese fries"), and dumplings ("chili-mac") or as soup. Another culinary innovation of the restaurant, fried green pickles, has a large following. The restaurant also lists authentic Hungarian dishes: stuffed cabbage, chicken paprikash, sausage platters, paprika dumplings, chicken soup with dumplings, and strudel: "the kind of pastry our Hungarian grandma would make. A paper thin, flaky crust brimming with apple, cherry, or special fruit filling. Add whipped cream or ice cream, a taste sensation you'll never forget." Tony Packo's pickles (peppers and cucumbers) and chili sauce are sold in most groceries in the Midwest.

Polish

Most mainstream groceries and moderately ethnic restaurants in the Midwest carry Polish food.[30] The typical menu appears in an announcement issued by the Bowling Green University Dining Hall: "Enjoy a taste of Poland as we celebrate St. Joseph's Day on Friday, March 19. We will serve authentic Polish kielbasa, sweet and sour cabbage, chicken paprika and *pierogies*." The Dining Hall added cabbage rolls, cabbage and apples, and Polish stew (kielbasa, chicken, mushrooms, cabbage, onions, paprika). Students found the meal familiar and compared it to Mom's cooking.

Galumkis (usually called stuffed cabbage or cabbage rolls) enclose ground beef and pork with rice in cabbage leaves simmered in water. Some recipes call for sauerkraut and tomatoes, others for sour cream in the broth. These 2 by 3 inch packages enliven family celebrations; seasoning recipes are closely guarded. Chicken paprika consists of simmered boneless chicken breasts in a paprika and sour cream sauce, served over dumplings or noodles. Polish Americans make kielbasa from whatever meats are available, seasoning it with salt, black pepper, marjoram, summer savory, allspice, garlic, and paprika. They then grill them like hot dogs, serving them in buns with ketchup and mustard, relish, and chopped onions. Along with kielbasa, *pierogies* are the most popular Polish food in the Midwest. These small dumplings contain any combination of mashed potatoes, onions, cheese, cabbage, sauerkraut, and ground meat. Boiled, then fried lightly in butter and topped with fried onions, they are available frozen in most supermarkets.

Mushroom and barley soup (*krupnik polski*) is essential to traditional Christmas Eve dinners. *Oplatki*, thin wafers stamped with religious pictures or symbols, delight friends and family. Commercially available during the Lenten season in Illinois and Indiana is *paczki*, a festive doughnut filled with jelly or fruit (prune or apricot).

South Slavic

Immigrants from southern Slavic cultures (Croats, Slovenes, and Serbs from the former Yugoslavia) settled in Minnesota in the early 1900s, working in meat-packing industries or in the iron mines.[31] Slavic women frequently ran boarding houses, incorporating American food patterns as well as presenting their own. Slavic foodways resemble those of other Eastern Europeans but show a definite Turkish influence (stuffed vegetables, soured milk, yogurt, cheese curds, thin pastry dough) as well as Mediterranean (pasta, polenta or corn-meal mush, browned butter, garlic sauce, and baked dishes using eggplant, zucchini, or potatoes). Dishes still found today include homemade sauerkraut, sausage, wine, and whole-animal barbeques. Bean dishes (pinto, kidney, and roman dressed with salt, pepper, and oil) are plentiful. Other hot vegetables carry seasonings of browned butter or a roux (*prezganje* or *ajmpren*). Browned, crispy breadcrumbs top noodles, dumplings, or vegetables. Family pastries—*potica*, a rolled pastry; *strudel*, a thin pastry dough filled with fruit; *flancati*, a fried dough; and *krofe*, similar to a yeast doughnut—are heavily sweetened. The flavors of milk dishes, bread (made with white flour), and soups (vegetables in brown roux, doused with vinegar) range from sweet to sour.

Greek Traditions

Greek immigrants began settling in the Midwest in the early 1900s, frequently opening small food shops and restaurants.[32] Their traditions drew on both Middle Eastern (rice, lentils, chickpeas, yogurt, lamb, cinnamon, nutmeg, strong coffee) and Mediteranean foods (seafood, citrus fruits, tomatoes, leafy vegetables, pork, and wine). Some of their dishes easily fit with midwestern foods, while retaining a distinct Greek identity—stews, bean and lentil dishes, egg-lemon sauce, *pastitsio* (baked macaroni and meat), and *moussaka* (eggplant and meat casserole). Mint, cinnamon, and nutmeg flavor meat dishes; parsley, dill, oregano, and basil are staples. Greek restaurants are scattered throughout midwestern cities. Signs advertising *gyros*, lemon-flavored chicken and rice soup, "Greek salad" (greens with feta cheese, whole olives, and olive oil dressing), spinach and cheese pies, and *baklava* (walnut and honey-filled *phyllo* dough) entice street traffic. Family or church-based events center on roast lamb, followed by Greek coffee, *ouzo* (raisin, fennel, and anise brandy), and a variety of sweets. A significant Greek contribution to Midwestern foodways is Cincinnati chili,

Cincinnati Chili

Sauce:

1. Add 1 to 1½ pounds of lean ground beef to 6-ounce can of tomato paste, 6 cups of water, and secret spices (paprika, cinnamon, salt, garlic, chili pepper).

2. Stir with fork and bring to a boil. Then simmer uncovered for 1-1½ hours, stirring occasionally.

Serving Style:

Two Way: chili sauce on spaghetti

Three Way: spaghetti topped with chili sauce, grated cheddar cheese

Four Way: spaghetti topped with chili sauce, grated cheddar cheese, chopped onions

Five Way: spaghetti topped with chili sauce, grated cheddar cheese, chopped onions, beans

Or put sauce on hot dog in bun; top with onions, cheese, and mustard.

invented by a Macedonian immigrant[33] and made distinctive by its use of cinnamon. The practice of stacking toppings can be found in creations such as Coney dogs sold by Greeks in Detroit.

Italian Foodways

Immigrants from southern Italy first came to the Midwest during the mid-1800s.[34] Southern Italian cooking has defined Italian food for most Americans—pasta from semolina flour, tomato and olive oil sauces, and pizza (in contrast to the egg pastas, rice and corn, and cheese and butter sauces of the north). Similarly, garlic, oregano, and basil have become standard Italian-midwestern spices. Pork sausage, ham, chicken, and veal are the usual meats, although the prevalence of beef in the Midwest has perhaps encouraged the popularity of "Italian meatballs" and *braciolis* (ham, cheese, and vegetable-filled beef rolls). Fish played a large part in the immigrant diet, and still does today, although squid, octopus, and eel have been relegated to festive, ritual meals (such as Christmas Eve's "seven dishes from the sea" dinner). Fresh vegetables bolster Italian cooking, and many families still have big home gardens (growing mainly tomatoes, squash, peppers, and herbs)—sometimes to the dismay of neighbors who feel that produce should only be grown privately in back yards. In the past, vegetable peddlers were usually Italians.

Although spaghetti and pizza bear little resemblance to their originals, they retain their Italian ethnic associations for many in the Midwest. A list of ethnic restaurants in northwest Ohio, for example, identifies all pizza places as Italian. Numerous varieties of pizza toppings are usually available, many of which stray from original Italian aesthetics (which never mixed cheese with anchovies), including dessert pizzas made of cookie dough, sometimes topped with sweetened cream cheese or whipped cream and fruit slices.

Mexican/Hispanic Foodways

Hispanic food in the Midwest comes from two sources.[35] The "Tex-Mex" food traditions brought by migrant workers beginning in the early 1910s introduced tacos, tortillas, rice and beans, and chili peppers as seasoning and as side dishes. Partly because of the marginal social status of these migrants, midwesterners viewed their foods somewhat suspiciously. As a result, Mexican food did not become widely popular outside Hispanic populations until mainstream fast food restaurants such as Taco Bell or ChiChi's adopted "safer," blander versions. Americanized versions of Mexican food are now ubiquitous in the Midwest, with tacos, burritos, and tortillas (sold as "wraps" with a wide range of fillings) even available in school cafeterias. "Mexican fried ice cream" (ice cream wrapped in pastry and deep fried) stands out on menus.

Some foods, however, are available only within the Mexican community. These include *menudo* (tripe soup, thought to be a good cure for hangovers) or *barbecoa* (pit-roasted cow head). *Tamales* play a special role in Hispanic culture. Their preparation tends to be a family (mostly women's) affair involving several days of work; they are often given as gifts at Christmastime. On the other hand, midwestern gourmets can prepare *mole*, a sauce made of chocolate, chiles, anchovies, sesame seeds, salt, and garlic, which is usually poured over steamed chicken for festive meals. Entrepreneurs now promote *chicherrones*, fried pork rind, as an alternative to carbohydrate-laden potato or corn chips.

"Authentic" food is available at Hispanic-run restaurants, grocery stores (both ethnic and mainstream), and family events, such as *Quinceañeros* (girls' fifteenth birthday celebrations), confirmations and first communions, and community gatherings. Mexican-run bakeries offer ethnic pastries and cookies, and most cities have one or more tortilla "factories." Church fairs and *Cinco de Mayo* (May 5) celebrations often dispense homemade Mexican food to the general public. Although some restaurants and festivals are starting to offer more variety, the foodways of other Hispanic and Latino groups tend to be included with Mexican. Immigrants from Puerto Rico, Panama, Guatemala, and other Central and South American countries frequently highlight their food traditions at cultural festivals and celebrations.

Asian (Chinese, Korean, Japanese) and Southeast Asian (Vietnamese, Filipino, Hmong, Thai) Foods

Asian foods in the Midwest were historically defined by Chinese restaurants. Only in the final decades of the twentieth century did foods from other Asian cultures as well as different provinces in China develop a following. Almost every urban center has at least one Chinese restaurant, and most supermarkets now carry some Asian foods. Minneapolis-St. Paul and Chicago are particularly well known for their clustered Asian communities and restaurants. Hmong (from Laos) and Korean immigrants run farms in Minnesota and Michigan that specialize in Asian produce. Some foods, such as *tofu*, green tea, and bean sprouts have been embraced by vegetarians, and others, such as *chop suey*, *teriyaki* sauce, *wonton* (with cream cheese filling), and egg rolls have been adapted to mainstream midwestern diets. *Ramen* noodles (packaged dry noodles with sauce originally from Korea and Japan) are universal snacks on campuses and are the basic ingredient for a popular salad made with chopped cabbage, green peppers, and sweet vinaigrette dressing.

The earliest Chinese immigrants to the Midwest came around 1870 from other areas of the United States where anti-Chinese movements were active.[36] Chicago and St. Louis were the first cities with Chinese populations, most of whom worked in groceries, restaurants, or laundries. They were mostly southern Chinese featuring Cantonese cooking. Natural flavors, rice, seafood, oyster sauce, *hoisin* sauce, shrimp paste, black beans, and subtle sauces highlighted stir-fried and steamed dishes. Some of these foods quickly became American favorites, especially fried rice, egg rolls, egg foo yung, potstickers (steamed and pan-fried dumplings), wonton (boiled, fried dumplings), and sweet and sour pork. *Dim sum*—pastries and dumplings historically served in teahouses in China—was transformed into a brunch sampler in the United States. While considered haute cuisine in China, Cantonese food is inexpensive and is easy to prepare in the Midwest. The stereotypical dish is *chop suey* (meaning "mixed pieces"), stir-fried veggies with bits of meat and a sauce of soy sauce, oyster sauce, and cornstarch. A farmer's dish in southern China, it was introduced in California in the mid-1800s, Americanized, and brought to the Midwest.

Only Illinois, Michigan, Missouri, and Ohio have significant numbers of Chinese residents. Since the 1960s, however, more recent immigrants from mainland

China, Taiwan, and Hong Kong, most of whom are educated white-collar workers, have opened restaurants throughout the urban Midwest. These present a wider variety of Chinese cuisines than formerly. The spiciness of Szechuan cuisine—including peppercorns, chili peppers, hot and sour soups—does not always suit midwestern tastes. Wheat for noodles, pancakes, and dumplings forms a substrate for northern (Peking) dishes, notably, mu shu pork (pancakes wrapped around a filling), Mongolian hot pot, and Peking Duck. Fried chow mein noodles are available commercially. Eastern Chinese cuisines feature rice (Fukien Province) as often as wheat (Shanghai) and tend to be sweet; chefs simmer meat in soy sauce for a red tint. Most Chinese restaurants tend to mix the regional styles. Special holiday foods available from ethnic groceries during the Chinese New Year and the mid-autumn harvest festival (Mooncake Festival) include steamed and baked cakes and buns. A recent innovation in restaurants is sweetened cream cheese-filled fried wontons.

Japanese food first appeared in the Midwest in Japanese steak houses where chefs flourish knives over food cooked at the table.[37] They slice beef and chicken and then add *teriyaki* sauce, rice, and American side dishes. *Sushi*, popular on both U.S. coasts, infiltrated the Midwest at the end of the 1990s. Deli sections of supermarkets now carry *maki-sushi*, or rice rolls wrapped in *nori* (dried sheets of seaweed). Midwesterners also like the "California roll," a vegetarian sushi made with avocado, cucumber, and carrot in rice rolled in sesame seeds. Housewives complement this packaged sushi with soy sauce, *wasabi* (spicy horseradish paste), and thin slices of pickled ginger root.

Like the Japanese, Koreans appeared in the Midwest in the latter half of the twentieth century when they opened pan-Asian grocery stores, produce markets, and restaurants,[38] though all-Korean menus were unusual outside cities with large Korean populations. To most midwesterners, Korean cuisine is *kimchi*, a cabbage and turnip "pickle" fermented with garlic, salt, shrimp paste, and chili peppers; its memorable odor rarely appeals to American tastes. Since seafood stews and other dishes are also too "exotic" for midwesterners, Korean restaurants emphasize dishes that have proven successful: *chop chae* and *bulgogi*, ribs, *bibimbop*, and *mandoo*. Frequently, the *kimchi* is Americanized into a less spicy version.

Since the 1970s, in the aftermath of the Vietnam War that brought many Southeast Asian immigrants to America,[39] midwesterners have learned to enjoy Vietnamese, Cambodian, Thai, Laotian, and Hmong (hill tribes from Laos) foods. Thai restaurants have recently blossomed in most midwestern cities, and Thai sauces and dishes fill shelves in mainstream supermarkets. *Pad Thai* (rice noodles tossed with shrimp, chicken, tamarind sauce, cilantro, lime, and chopped peanuts), chicken and lemongrass soup, and coconut-based curries have been particularly successful in the Midwest. Vietnamese food has also been translated into American restaurant fare, partly because proprietors can emphasize both the strong Chinese influence that makes it familiar to Americans and the French influence (asparagus, green beans, and potatoes, as well as some preparation and presentation methods) that makes it elegant (and attractive to vegetarians). Noodle soups and spring rolls (wrapped in lettuce and other greens) have become American favorites. Classic Cambodian and Laotian foods also carry strong French influence, but midwestern variations draw more on the rural, peasant backgrounds of many immigrants. Hmong meals have remained private, family-oriented affairs, although large communities in Minnesota support ethnic farms and groceries. All these strains employ rice (both long grain and short-grain, glutinous), noodles, coconut, mango, lime, lemongrass, fresh basil and coriander, peanuts, taro root, fish and pork, and soybean products. Soy sauce, however, is usually replaced by a fermented fish sauce (*nuoc mam* in Vietnamese).

Filipino food, though Southeast Asian, displays a strong Spanish influence in its ingredients and in certain dishes. For example, flan (egg and milk custard) appears as a dessert, and milk and cheese are a part of the Filipino American's everyday diet. Filipino food is rarely available commercially in the Midwest.

Middle Eastern Foodways

Middle Eastern food rolled into the urban Midwest in two waves.[40] Lebanese Christians began establishing communities in the 1880s, and immigrants from various Arab nations (primarily Muslim) began coming in the 1940s. Detroit now has the largest Arabic population outside the Middle East. Some newcomers worked as food peddlers, or in small groceries and food stands, perhaps because small food businesses were common back home. Detroit citizens quickly learned to enjoy stuffed vegetables, sesame, olives, dates, cardamom, mint, anise, rose water and honey-flavored desserts, nuts (almonds, pine nuts, pistachios), and garbanzo beans. *Halal* stores lining the streets in Chicago's Arab neighborhoods follow Muslim dietary laws. Along with alcohol, Muslims also prohibit pork, substituting lamb and mutton. Foods prepared according to these rules are considered *halal*. Arabic tradition also features thick, strong, sweet coffee, frequently offered as a ritual of friendship and unity.

Middle Eastern foods sold at the local Kroger's stores are a staple of vegetarian diets. Pita bread covered with *hommus* (ground chickpeas and sesame seeds), Americanized with additional ingredients (spinach, jalepeno pepper, roasted red pepper, garlic, and onion) is now lunch for midwestern clerks and professionals. Now largely free of ethnic associations, pita bread increasingly encloses peanut butter and jelly, and tuna salad. Detroit and Chicago delis advertise *tabouli* (parsley, bulgar wheat, olive oil, lemon juice) and *falafel*—fried chickpea patties in pita bread, usually with *hommus*, cucumber, tomato, and a yogurt sauce. An American variation is "falafel pizza," in which toasted slices of falafel are floated in feta cheese on top of pita instead of inside it. Now well within the midwestern mainstream are shish kebabs (grilled cubes of meat and vegetables on a skewer) served as appetizers (bite-size cheese, vegetables, and meat) or as dessert (pieces of fruit). Packaged mixes for couscous (bulgar wheat) and rice pilafs with both Middle Eastern and American flavorings are stocked next to premium rice at most supermarkets.

The long-established Lebanese community of Toledo, Ohio, boasts several Middle Eastern restaurants, bakeries, carryouts, and grocery stores. The Tiger Bakery touts "healthy and delicious Mediterranean home-made food prepared fresh-from-scratch." Their catering menu includes color photographs of each dish, including *fatoosh* (cucumber, tomato, toasted pita bread pieces, parsley salad), *shish tawook*, and *shish kafta* (grilled chicken or beef on sticks); grape leaves, *fatayer* (meat, spinach or cheese pies—actually tarts with *phyllo* dough), rice *pilaf*, and a wide variety of baklava.

Jewish Foods

Jewish American food in the Midwest[41] displays two main cultural traditions—Ashkenazi (German and East European) and Sephardic (Mediterranean and Middle Eastern). Both follow *Kashrut* dietary laws, and distinguish between private and public (open to non-Jews) food traditions. Like the Muslims, Jews avoid pork; ingredients are often available at Middle Eastern groceries.

In the 1880s, Jewish immigrants began concentrating in midwestern urban areas, where they opened delicatessens that carried Kosher foods, carryout sandwiches, and pre-prepared side dishes. A reputation for high-quality meats, "exotic" food items, and European dark breads attracted a non-Jewish clientele. One can scarcely find a block in Chicago without a deli, and Jewish restaurants cater to such prominently Jewish suburbs as Skokie. That pattern is visible in many cities. Nationally known Zingerman's Delicatessen started in Ann Arbor, Michigan, in 1982, selling traditional Jewish foods and sandwiches of corned beef and pastrami, free range chicken and turkey, homemade chopped liver, smoked fish, and chicken salad. Since 1992, Zingerman's has shipped traditional breads and pastries throughout the Midwest and now worldwide, offering American originals, Jewish rye, European countryside breads, and sweet specialty breads. Other Jewish foods are eaten privately in the home, particularly among Orthodox Jews practicing *Kashrut*, and for ceremonial meals. Most groceries carry items for the Passover seder (particularly *matzah* "crackers," which now come in different flavors), along with stereotypical foods such as gefilte fish, *matzah* ball soup, pickled herring, chopped liver, *knishes* (potato, meat, or cheese dumplings similar to *pierogi*), and potato or noodle *kugel* (a casserole, the noodle version often sweet with raisins or cream cheese).

Foodways of Other Ethnicities

By the year 2000, urban areas in the Midwest had become home to significant international populations. So many refugees settled in Lansing, Michigan, that a local editor gathered recipes from areas as disparate as Kosovo, Somalia, Sudan, Cuba, Afghanistan, Colombia, Kurdistan, and Laos into a volume called *A Taste of Freedom*.[42] Restaurants specializing in various cuisines are on the increase, and mainstream restaurants seem to be broadening their menus to include familiar (frequently Americanized) ethnic dishes. The educational outreach efforts of cultural organizations, schools, museums, and historical and culinary societies have familiarized midwesterners with ethnic traditions. In addition, stores carry ingredients needed for ethnic cooking so that families can more easily continue their food traditions.

COMMERCIAL AND PUBLIC FOODWAYS

Both corporate and family-run businesses bring food "from the field to the table." Processing plants clean and package locally grown and trucked-in produce. A plant in McClure, Ohio, for example, processes radishes grown in the South, while nearby Heinz factories process local tomatoes into ketchup. The Minnesota-based Jolly Green Giant distributes canned vegetables and fruits nationally, and Battle Creek, Michigan, houses three major cereal companies: Kellogg, Post (a division of Kraft), and Ralston. Types of industry come and go. Once infamous in the 1800s and early 1900s for its butchering industry and cattle yards, Chicago is now about to lose Fannie Mae candies (going out of business in 2004).

Successful midwestern restaurant chains sell millions of basic, home-cooked, family-oriented meals. Perkins ("with no surprises") has franchises in thirty-five states, most of which are located in the Midwest. Bob Evans Restaurant and General Stores, started in Rio Grande, Ohio, now has over 550 franchises, promising "hearty homestyle meals" with "farm-fresh goodness and friendly service." Their menus picture the public image of midwestern food: hearty breakfasts of eggs, sausage, hotcakes, sausage gravy, home fries, and freshly baked biscuits; lunches of soups and sandwiches; and dinners of steak, chicken, pork chops, or fish with two "savory sides" and a roll.

Midwestern food traditions are displayed, celebrated, and, in some cases, invented in festivals throughout the year. Many festivals feature a single crop, such as apples, pumpkins, cherries, or potatoes; others celebrate a dish based on local produce or heritage, such as apple butter, cheese, sauerkraut, bratwurst, or pork-a-leans (pork patties, Wood County, Ohio). Some festivals highlight local fauna, such as muskrats, walleye, or perch, as hunting and fishing legacies. Others combine food and local history. Ohio and Indiana, for example, abound with Johnny Appleseed festivals. Although food festivals are not unique to the Midwest, many communities in the region stress the strong ties between midwestern identity and farming.

Midwest towns support farmers' markets as cultural and social centers as well as outlets for local produce. Photo by Vito Palmisano. Courtesy Travel Michigan.

THE FUTURE OF MIDWESTERN FOOD

Trends in midwestern food seem to be following similar trends seen in other parts of the United States. On one hand, the number of ethnic foods available, many of them adapted to midwestern tastes, has increased; so has openness to more authentic versions as the foods become familiar. On the other hand, more organizations now recognize place-based food traditions. Perhaps as an outgrowth of interest in local history and family genealogy, enthusiasts have generated interest in culinary history, promoted environmental and health concerns with food production and preservation, and helped develop culinary tourism. Towns support farmers' markets as cultural and social centers as well as outlets for local produce. The surge in the use of food for economic development and for tourism is encouraging producers and consumers to innovate, as well as to honor culinary artifacts from the past.

RESOURCE GUIDE

Printed Sources

Adams, Marcia. *Heartland: The Best of the Old and the New from Midwest Kitchens*. New York: C. Potter, 1991.

Allen, Brigid, ed. *Food: An Oxford Anthology*. Oxford: Oxford University Press, 1994.

The American Heritage Cookbook and Illustrated History of American Eating and Drinking. New York: American Heritage, 1964.

Brown, Linda Keller, and Kay Mussell. *Ethnic and Regional Foodways in the United States: The Performance of Group Identity*. Knoxville: University of Tennessee Press, 1984.

Camp, Charles. *American Foodways: What, When, Why and How We Eat in America*. Little Rock, AR: August House, 1989.

Carlson, Barbara. *Food Festivals: Eating Your Way from Coast to Coast*. Detroit, MI: Visible Ink Press, 1997.

Counihan, Carole M., ed. *Food in the USA: A Reader*. New York: Routledge, 2002.

Cummings, Richard Osborn. *The American and His Food: A History of Food Habits in the United States*. Chicago: University of Chicago Press, 1940.

Davidson, Alan. *The Oxford Companion to Food*. Oxford: Oxford University Press, 1999.

Fertig, Judith M. "The Midwest." In *Encyclopedia of Food and Culture*, edited by Solomon H. Katz, 454–457. New York: Charles Scribner's Sons, 2003.

———. *Prairie Home Breads*. Boston: Harvard Common Press, 2001.

———. *Prairie Home Cooking*. Boston: Harvard Common Press, 1999.

Gabaccia, Donna R. *We Are What We Eat: Ethnic Food and the Making of Americans*. Cambridge, MA: Harvard University Press, 1998.

Geffen, Alice M., and Carle Berglie. *Food Festival: The Ultimate Guidebook to American's Best Regional Food Celebrations*. New York: Pantheon Books, 1986.

Haber, Barbara. *From Hardtack to Home Fries: An Uncommon History of American Cooks and Meals*. New York: Penguin Books, 2002.

Hess, John L., and Karen Hess. *The Taste of America*. Urbana: University of Illinois Press, 2000.

Hope, James, and Susan Failor. *Bountiful Ohio: Good Food and Stories from Where the Heartland Begins*. Bowling Green, OH: Gabriel's Horn, 1993.

Humphrey, Theodore C., and Lin T. Humphrey, eds. *"We Gather Together:" Food and Festival in American Life*. Ann Arbor, MI: UMI Research Press, 1988.

Jones, Evan. *American Food: The Gastronomic Story*. 3rd ed. Woodstock, NY: Overlook Press, 1990.

Kaplan, Anne R., Marjorie A. Hoover, and Williard B. Moore. *The Minnesota Ethnic Food Book*. St. Paul: Minnesota Historical Society Press, 1986.

Kreidberg, Marjorie. *Food on the Frontier: Minnesota Cooking*. St. Paul: Minnesota Historical Society Press, 1975.

Lockwood, Yvonne, and William Lockwood. "Continuity and Adaptation in Arab American Foodways." In *Arab Detroit: From Margin to Mainstream*, edited by Nabeel Abraham and Andrew Shryock, 515–549. Detroit, MI: Wayne State University Press, 2000.

———. "Pasties in Michigan's Upper Peninsula: Foodways, Interethnic Relations, and Regionalism." In *The Taste of American Place: A Reader on Regional and Ethnic Foods*, edited by Barbara G. Shortridge and James R. Shortridge, 21–36. New York: Rowman & Littlefield, 1998.

Long, Lucy. "Apple Butter in Northwest Ohio: Food Festivals and the Construction of Local Meaning." In *Holidays, Ritual, Festival, Celebration, and Public Display*, edited by Cristina Sanchez-Carretero and Jack Santino, 45–65. Alcala, Spain: Universidad de Alcala, 2003.

————, ed. *Culinary Tourism*. Lexington: University Press of Kentucky, 2004.

Pillsbury, Richard. *No Foreign Food: The American Diet in Time and Place*. Boulder, CO: Westview Press, 1998.

Prosterman, Leslie. *Ordinary Life, Festival Days: Aesthetics in the Midwestern County Fair*. Washington, DC: Smithsonian Institution Press, 1995.

Root, Waverly, and Richard de Rochement. *Eating in America: A History*. New York: William Morrow, 1976.

Shortridge, Barbara G. "Ethnic Heritage Food in Lindsborg, Kansas, and New Glarus, Wisconsin." In *Culinary Tourism*, edited by Lucy Long, 268–296. Lexington: University Press of Kentucky, 2004.

————. "Not Just Jello and Hot Dishes: Representative Foods of Minnesota." *Journal of Cultural Geography* 21, no. 1 (2003): 71–94.

Shortridge, Barbara G., and James R. Shortridge, eds. *The Taste of American Place: A Reader on Regional and Ethnic Foods*. Lanham, MD: Rowman & Littlefield, 1998.

Smith, Jeff. *The Frugal Gourmet Cooks American*. New York: Avon Books, 1987.

————. *The Frugal Gourmet on Our Immigrant Ancestors*. New York: William Morrow and Company, 1990.

Tannahill, Reay. *Food in History*. New York: Crown, 1989.

Trillin, Calvin. *American Fried*. New York: Penguin Books, 1975.

Vennom, Thomas, Jr. *Wild Rice and the Ojibway People*. St. Paul: Minnesota Historical Society Press, 1988.

Walker, Barbara M. *The Little House Cookbook: Frontier Foods from Laura Ingalls Wilder's Classic Stories*. New York: HarperCollins, 1979.

Wilson, David Scofield, and Angus Kress Gillespie, eds. *Rooted in America: Foodlore of Popular Fruits and Vegetables*. Knoxville: University of Tennessee Press, 1999.

Journals

Digest: An Interdisciplinary Review of Food and Foodways

Food and Foodways

Gastronomica

Journal for the Study of Food and Society

Journal of the American Folklore Society

Midwest Living

Web Sites

Check Web sites for each state's tourism department as well as the following:

Amish culture and foods
www.amish.net/lifestyle.asp

Chinese food
www.chinesefood.about.com

Mennonite culture and foods
www.anabaptists.org/history

Mennonite culture and foods
www.mhsc.ca/mennos/cfood.html

Michigan's Mitten of Plenty
www.michigan.gov/mda/0,1607,7-125--77200--,00.html

Microbreweries
www.beertravelers.com/micros/

Videos/Films

Lucy Long and Tony Howard. *Stirring Up the Past: The Grand Rapids Applebutter Fest*. Bowling Green, OH: WBGU-TV, 2001.
PBS Home Video. *A Hot Dog Program*, 1999.

Festivals

Illinois

Bagel Fest
Last weekend in July
Mattoon, IL (50 miles south of Champaign)
Contact: Mattoon Chamber of Commerce, 1701 Wabash Avenue, Mattoon, IL 61938
Phone: (217) 235-5661

Burgoo Festival
Second Sunday in October
Utica, IL (100 miles southwest of Chicago)
Contact: LaSalle County Historical Society, P.O. Box 278, Utica, IL 61373
Phone: (815) 667-4861

Hog Capital of the World Festival
Labor Day weekend
Kewanee, IL
Contact: Kewanee Chamber of Commerce, 113 E. 2nd Street, Kewanee, IL 61443
Phone: (309) 852-2175

International Horseradish Festival
First weekend in June
Collinsville, IL (8 miles east of St. Louis)
Contact: 211 West Main Street, Collinsville, IL 62234
Phone: (618) 344-2884

National Sweet Corn Festival
Second weekend in August
Mendota (80 miles west of Chicago)
Contact: Medota Chamber of Commerce, P.O. Box 620, Mendota, IL 61342
Phone: (815) 539-6507

Indiana

Hot Dog Festival
Last weekend in July
Frankfort, IN (30 miles north of Indianapolis)
Contact: Frankfort Main Street, 301 E. Clinton Street, Frankfort, IN 46041
Phone: (317) 654-4081

Johnny Appleseed Festival
Third full weekend in September
Fort Wayne, IN

Contact: Johnny Appleseed Festival, Fort Wayne Parks and Recreation Dept., 705 E. State Street, Fort Wayne, IN 46805
Phone: (219) 427-6003

Ligonier Marshmallow Festival
Labor Day weekend
Ligonier, IN (20 miles south of Elkhart)
Contact: Ligonier Chamber of Commerce, P.O. Box 121, Ligonier, IN 46767
Phone: (219) 894-4113

Persimmon Festival
Last full week of September
Mitchell, IN (35 miles south of Bloomington)
Contact: City of Mitchell, P.O. Box 2, Mitchell, IN 47446
Phone: (812) 849-2152

Popcorn Festival
Saturday after Labor Day
Valparaiso, IN
Contact: Valparaiso Popcorn Festival, Inc., 204 E. Lincolnway, P.O. Box 189, Valparaiso, IN 46384
Phone: (219) 464-8332

Iowa

Iowa State Fair
Runs for 10 days, traditionally ending two weeks before Labor Day
Contact: Iowa State Fair Authority, Iowa State Fair, P.O. Box 57130, Des Moines, IA 50317-0003
www.iowastatefair.org

Pumpkinfest
First weekend in October
Anamosa, IA
Contact: Anamosa Chamber of Commerce, 124 E. Main Street, Anamosa, IA 52205
Phone: (319) 462-4879

Michigan

Cereal Festival
First weekend in June
Battle Creek, MI
Contact: Greater Battle Creek/Calhoun County visitors and Convention Bureau, 35 W. Jackson Street, Battle Creek, MI 49017
Phone: (616) 962-2240

Harrison Mushroom Festival
Second weekend in May
Harrison, MI
Contact: Harrison Chamber of Commerce, P.O. Box 682, Harrison, MI 48625
Phone: (517) 539-6011

National Asparagus Festival
Second weekend in June

Shelby, Hart, MI (70 miles northwest of Grand Rapids)
National Asparagus Festival, P.O. Box 153, Shelby, Michigan 49455

National Cherry Festival
Week following July 4
Traverse City, MI (185 miles north of Lansing; on Lake Michigan)
Contact: National Cherry Festival, P.O. Box 141, Traverse City, MI 49684

National Mushroom Hunting Championship
Mother's Day weekend
Boyne City, MI (200 miles north of Lansing)
Contact: Boyne City Chamber of Commerce, 28 South Lake Street, Boyne, MI 49712
Phone: (616) 582-6222

Minnesota

Minnesota Wild Rice Festival
July weekend
Kelliher/Waskish, MN
Contact: Wild Rice Festival Committee, Kelliher, MN 56650

Rutabaga Festival
Fourth weekend in August
Askov, MN
Contact: Askov City Offices, 6369 Merchant Street, Askov, MN 55704
Phone: (302) 838-3616

World's Championship Booya Competition
First Saturday in October
South St. Paul, MN
Contact: Booya Competition, 44 6th Avenue South, South St. Paul, MN 55075
Phone: (612) 455-4273

Missouri

American Royal Barbecue
First weekend in October
Kansas City, MO
Contact: American Royal Complex, 1701 American Royal Court, Kansas City, MO 64102
Phone: (816) 221-9800

Ozark Ham and Turkey Festival
Third Saturday in September
California, MO (20 miles west of Jefferson City)
Contact: California Chamber of Commerce, P.O. Box 85, California, MO 65018
Phone: (573) 796-3040

Pecan Festival
First weekend in October
Brunswick, MO (65 miles east of Kansas City)
Contact: Pecan Festival, 211 E. Broadway, Brunswick, MO 65236
Phone: (816) 548-3636

Wurstfest
Third full weekend in March
Hermann, MO (60 miles west of St. Louis)
Contact: Wurstfest Committee, 312 Market Street, Hermann, MO 65041
Phone: (800) 932-8687

Ohio

Circleville Pumpkin Show
Third weekend of October
Circleville, OH (25 miles south of Columbus)
Contact: Circleville Pumpkin Show, P.O. Box 288, Circleville, OH 43113
Phone: (740) 474-7000

Grand Rapids Apple Butter Fest
Second Sunday in October
Grand Rapids, Ohio (15 miles west of Toledo)
www.applebutterfest.org

Ohio Honey Festival
Second weekend in August
Hamilton, OH (25 miles north of Cincinnati)
Contact: Ohio Honey Festival, Inc., P.O. Box 754, Hamilton, OH 45012
Phone: (513) 868-5891

Zucchini Festival
Third weekend in July
Eldorado, OH (25 miles northwest of Dayton)
Contact: Zucchini Festival, P.O. Box 136, Eldorado, OH 45321
Phone: (513) 273-2791

Wisconsin

Applefest
First full weekend in October
Bayfield, WI
Contact: Bayfield Chamber of Commerce, P.O. Box 138, Bayfield, WI 54814
Phone: (800) 447-4094

Burger Fest
First Saturday in August
Seymour, WI
Contact: Home of the Hamburger, Inc., P.O. Box 173, Seymour, WI 54165
Phone: (414) 833-2517

Chocolate City Festival
Third weekend in May
Burlington, WI (thirty miles southwest of Milwaukee)
Contact: Burlington Area Chamber of Commerce, 112 E. Chestnut Street, P.O. Box 411, Burlington, WI 53105
E-mail: administration@ChocolateFest.com

Eagle River Cranberry Fest
First weekend in October
Eagle River, WI

Contact: Eagle River Area Chamber of Commerce, P.O. Box 1917, Eagle River, WI 54521
Phone: (715) 479-6400

Fry Bal Festival (Scandinavian Summer Solstice)
Third weekend in June
Ephraim, WI
Contact: Ephraim Business Council, Ephraim, WI 54211
Phone: (414) 743-4456

Great Wisconsin Cheese Festival
First weekend in June
Little Chute, WI (thirty miles south of Green Bay)
Contact: Great Wisconsin Cheese Festival, 1940 Buchanan Street, Little Chute, WI 54140
Phone: (414) 788-7390

United Festivals (various ethnic groups living in Milwaukee)
June through September
Milwaukee, WI
Contact: Greater Milwaukee Convention and Visitors Bureau, 501 Kilbourn Avenue, Milwaukee, WI 53203
Phone: (414) 273-3950

Organizations

Association for the Study of Food and Society
www.nyu.edu/education/nutrition/NFSR/ASFS.htm

Culinary Historians of Chicago
www.culinaryhistorians.org/links.htm

Michigan State University Museum (Great Lakes Folk Festival)
www.museum.msu.edu/home

Slow Food (international organization)
www.slowfoodusa.org

Midwestern Restaurants

Bob Evans Restaurant
www.bobevans.com

Perkins
www.perkinsrestaurants.com

Tony Packo's Restaurant, Toledo, Ohio
www.tonypackos.com/history.html

Zingerman's
www.zingermans.com

LANGUAGE

Beverly Olson Flanigan

American regional cultures are distinguished by a number of factors: modes of living, occupational patterns, folk traditions, foods, music, dress, and social customs. But it could be argued that language and dialect differences mark regions and cultures more indelibly than any other factor; they indicate where people have come from, whom they affiliate with, and how they see themselves in the wider array of Americans. Language differences are more resistant to change, and at the same time they announce loudly and clearly who we are. This chapter will delineate some of these differences by tracing the history of language in the Midwest under three headings: the original Native American languages in the region, the various immigrant languages brought in after the settlement of what were first called the Northwest and Louisiana Territories, and the dialects of American English that finally took root in the eight-state region.

NATIVE AMERICAN LANGUAGES

From an estimated total of 2,000 languages spoken by the indigenous peoples of North America at the time of the first European explorations, approximately 200 remain, according to Ives Goddard of the Smithsonian Institution.[1] Of these, John D. Nichols has claimed that twenty-seven are spoken, in varying degrees of fluency, in the Midwest. One-third of these languages have no native speakers (Miami, Huron, Mohican, and Wyandot, among others); another third have fewer than 100 native speakers (including Omaha and Osage); and five are approaching language death (including, in our region, Delaware and Ioway). Only five languages in the eight states of this region have more than 1,000 speakers; these are Ojibwe (or Ojibway, also called Chippewa), Ottawa, Cherokee, Winnebago, and Dakota Sioux. The most commonly used is Ojibwe, an Algonquian language spoken by some 25,000 to 40,000 speakers in Michigan, Wisconsin, Minnesota, and four Canadian provinces; almost 6,000 of these live in our eight states. About 2,000

Table 3. American Indian languages spoken at home in midwestern states

Numbers of Speakers by Language Family

	Michigan	Ohio	Indiana	Illinois	Missouri	Iowa	Minnesota	Wisconsin
Algonquian languages	1315	148	87	90	76	559	3822	1899
Fox	-	-	-	9	1	545	2	15
Menomini	-	-	-	16	-	-	17	535
Ojibwe/Chippewa	858	29	31	37	56	9	3704	1123
Ottawa	378	-	-	5	-	-	11	20
Potawatomi	57	-	21	9	4	-	15	166
Shawnee	-	64	29	-	-	-	-	16
Siouan languages	53	59	66	101	93	207	761	1159
Dakota/Sioux	53	59	36	80	78	119	669	75
Omaha	-	-	-	-	-	69	4	-
Winnebago	-	-	21	-	-	9	84	1084
Iroquouian languages	202	258	128	61	295	83	15	494
Cherokee	109	239	128	61	293	83	15	43
Oneida	42	-	-	-	-	-	-	429
Athapascan/ Eyak languages	87	173	73	115	120	-	34	11
Navajo	80	153	66	115	96	-	34	11

Source: Characteristics of American Indians and Alaska Natives by Tribe and Language, 2000. See U.S. Census at http://factfinder.census .gov/home/aian/index.html.

Note: Only those languages with 50 or more speakers in any one state are listed. All languages are native to the region except Navajo, which represents in-migration of speakers from the Southwest. Data are based on self-reporting.

tribal members are thought to be monolingual in Ojibwe, most of them being in Canada; self-reported speakers of all Native languages in the United States are generally bilingual.[2] (See Table 3 for a list of major Native American Indian languages still spoken in the eight-state region encompassed in this volume.)

According to Nichols, attempts to revive regional languages have been more or less successful. More than twenty colleges teach Ojibwe, but some of them prohibit writing in the language, presumably because they believe "authentic" learning should be for oral use only, as in earlier periods of use. Ojibwe is also mandated for use in some reservation courtrooms. The Dakota dialect of the "Sioux" language is also taught in some colleges, including the University of Minnesota and tribal colleges in South Dakota. However, as the languages are used by increasingly older people, facility and fluency will continue to decline and English will replace them as the only language used by ever fewer bilingual speakers. This is not an unusual situation in many countries of the world, where formerly colonial languages have become first the lingua francas of disparate groups needing a means of communication across language communities and ultimately the primary (i.e., first or native) language of those communities. Attempts at revival (or revitalization) that fail to involve the family, the schools, and especially literacy training, as well as oral instruction, are doomed to becoming sterile academic exercises in the preservation of "quaint" folk languages.[3]

Nonetheless, the imprint of the indigenous languages is still present in the countless state, city, town, and river names of the region. *Michigan, Ohio, Illinois* (the French spelling of one of the Miami tribes), *Wisconsin, Minnesota, Iowa*, and *Missouri* (also adapted by the French, via either Canada or Louisiana) are all derived from Native words; *Indiana*, the sole English-named state, is "the land of the Indians."

The imprint of the Native American languages is present in countless midwestern place names. View of the great treaty held at Prairie de Chien, Wisconsin, September 1825. Courtesy Library of Congress.

Des Moines is named for the French abbreviation for a Native tribe labeled derogatorily "Moingweena" (i.e., "dung face") by the neighboring Peoria tribe; a similar derogation that stuck is the French term "Sioux," abbreviated from the Ojibwe label "Nadowessi," applied to their Dakota enemies and meaning "snakes." The source of *Chicago*'s name is debated, but it appears to be derived from Native words for "skunk" or "(skunk-like) smelly onion." More favorable regional labels include *Milwaukee* ("good land or place for meeting"), *Minnetonka* ("large water"), *Minnehaha Falls* ("water flowing from eyes," i.e., tears—not "laughing water"), *Minneapolis* (a blend of Dakota "water" and Greek "city"), *Ohio* ("beautiful river"), and of course *Mississippi* ("big river") and *Missouri* (*oumissourit*, the people of "big watercraft," i.e., canoes). The *Appalachians* were named after a Native tribe in Florida (in Spanish, the "Apalache"); the term was picked up by the French as a name for the mountain range extending partway into eastern Ohio in our region. Farther west, the *Ozarks* were the region *aux arcs*, abbreviated from "toward the Arkansas (Indian tribe)." (*Arkansas* itself is named for the French plural for the tribe, hence the final –*s* is silent; *Kansas* is named for the same tribe, with final -*s* pronounced.)[4]

These and countless other Indian names have been changed variously, as these examples show, to fit an increasingly anglicized vocabulary and pronunciation system, just as they were once changed to fit French or Spanish systems. Ironically, their adoption and continued use has become a matter of pride in the honoring of our indigenous peoples, the first immigrants to the continent, even as the native populations and their languages are in decline.

IMMIGRANT LANGUAGES

Other languages were brought into the Midwest, as in the East, by successive waves of immigration. French and English were the first, of course, but German, Dutch, and Scandinavian languages quickly followed. French came into the midwestern states from Quebec in the East and across the northern border with the Canadian voyageurs; they brought with them such terms as *shivaree* (for the banging of pots and pans outside the bedroom of newlyweds) and *booya* (a stew, presumably from *bouillabaisse*). A number of the forts established during the Seven Years' War of the French and Indians against the British (1756–1763) evolved into French-named communities, especially in Michigan, northern Ohio, Indiana, and Illinois. French settlements along the Mississippi River from Minnesota through Iowa and Wisconsin to Missouri maintained French-speaking communities well into the nineteenth century. Marietta (named for Marie Antoinette), Sault Ste. Marie, Prairie du Chien, Marquette, Detroit, Lafayette, Terre Haute, and St. Louis are only a few such communities that either retained only the French name or maintained enclaves of native speakers. In time, the pronunciation of these place names became unfamiliar to American-born residents; thus, Versailles (in Indiana, Ohio, and probably elsewhere) became "Versaylies," and Sainte Géneviève, Missouri, became "Saint Gennaveeve." Belpre, Ohio, originally "Belle Prairie," was clipped to accommodate English /r/ pronunciation; Bellefontaine, Ohio, became "Belle Fountain"; and Des Moines became "Da Moyne." Such processes are common all over the world, of course, as foreign words are nativized.

Nineteenth-Century European Immigration

As French was superseded by English, so other European languages entered the area as the new country expanded beyond the original thirteen colonies into the Northwest Territory and then the Louisiana Purchase. The American English of the Midwest illustrates how successive waves of immigration mark the distinct histories of these varied groups.

German Languages

German was probably the earliest European language brought westward after the Revolution. It arrived from Pennsylvania first via descendants of pre-Revolutionary families and later via Amish, Mennonite, and other Anabaptist emigrants from Europe seeking religious freedom on the frontier. Historian Steve Keiser reports the presence of Mennonites in Ohio by 1799 and of Amish by 1803, with successive groups moving on to Indiana, Illinois, and Iowa. These groups, unlike the pre-Revolutionary Germans before them and the mid-nineteenth-century Germans after them, wished to maintain a separate lifestyle and economic system from those of surrounding communities. They shunned the language of "the English" as intruding upon their freedom. Their schools used German as the medium of instruction and the subject of literacy training, and it was the language of religion, economy, and cultural life as well. The largest Amish communities anywhere in the world are found in Ohio. According to Keiser, Mennonites began to give up German even before the twentieth century, but the Amish have maintained a stable bilingualism in English and the "Deitsch" (or "Pennsylvania") variety of German into the twentieth-first century. However, as men leave farming and women take on jobs in town, Deitsch is used less frequently, especially by younger people, and a diglossic, or domain-based, split between the language of work and the language of home and religion is becoming more evident. As this diglossia progresses, changes in Deitsch are occurring in pronunciation shifts, word formation simplification, and even syntactic structure.[5]

Germany has continued to send immigrants to America and the Midwest; to this day, more Americans claim German ancestry than any other single na-

Diglossia

Charles Ferguson defines diglossia as the balanced use of two varieties of one language in distinctly separate and socially agreed upon spheres of behavior. Thus, High German would be used in school, work, and civic affairs, while Low German would be used at home, in friendship groups, and in religion. The definition has recently been expanded to include the social division of two different languages as well, and the divisions may vary across domains of use. An example would be the use of Latin (or Hebrew, or Arabic) in a religious liturgical rite and English in the sermon or homily.[6]

tionality. (For the latest census data on immigrants and language use in the United States, go to www.census.gov/population/cen2000/phc-t20/tab05.pdf.) Like other immigrants, these new Americans sought to maintain their German language for one or two generations before yielding to the general pattern of bilingual shift: The newcomer generation speaks the ancestral language almost exclusively, except for necessary contacts in work and civic spheres; the first-born American generation is bilingual in the old language and English, especially after it enters school; and the third generation in the new country is almost exclusively English-speaking, to the point where it no longer finds value in transmitting the ancestral language to its own children. Only Spanish and, among nonimmigrant languages, Navajo, persist into the fourth generation and beyond. For a time, German-speaking "Bunds" were popular social clubs in places like Cincinnati and Milwaukee, and several urban schools provided instruction solely in German or in bilingual English-German programs. Most of these programs are gone now, and German is taught in "ethnic mother tongue" programs, often after school or in summer camps, in an attempt to pass on some knowledge of the heritage language, however fleeting, to descendants of the immigrants. Food terms remain, however; beer and *bratwurst* (or "brats"), *sauerkraut* and *lebkuchen* are standard favorites regardless of ethnic origin.[7]

The Dutch Language

Dutch has undergone the same processes of dialectal change and shift to English, although communities remain in Michigan, Illinois, and Iowa where even fifth-generation Dutch Americans still speak the language fluently. Here, too, gender, locale, and religion play a large role in the maintenance of Dutch. Men, especially in rural areas, and members of the Dutch Reformed church find what Peter Trudgill has called "covert prestige" in using Dutch, much as the Amish do in their use of Deitsch. Nonetheless, although Holland, Michigan, became famous for its Dutch tulips, *koekje* eventually became cookies and *krullers* became common American doughnuts.[8]

Scandinavian Languages

The Scandinavian languages were first brought to the Midwest in the 1820s (Swedish settlements had been established earlier in the Delaware Valley). With famine and overpopulation spreading throughout Europe in the mid-nineteenth century, as many as one-half of the population of Norway left for America, and Swedes, Danes, and Icelanders were not far behind. Settling for the most part in rural areas, these immigrants retained their native tongues in family, work, and religious domains, though inevitably these related languages became mixed with each other and with English in what Einar Haugen has called a new "hybrid" variety. Thus, food terms like *fruktsuppe*, *kringles*, *lutefisk*, and *lefse* retained, more or less, their Scandinavian pronunciation, while adapted or mixed words like *travla* ("to walk"), *farmhus* ("farm house"), *julekard* ("Christmas card"), and *vel av* ("well off") reflect blending and shifting in word formation and sound. This Americanized Norwegian became a part of the everyday vernacular of the first and second-generation speakers. The tone system of Norwegian was also transmitted in the distinctive intonational "lilting" pattern that marked these speakers and subsequent generations as having Scandinavian heritage even when knowledge of the ancestral languages faded in the traditional shift pattern described earlier. Such residual sound patterns are not unique to this group, of course. Hispanic and Latino descendant groups often retain phonological markers of their heritage languages, and Slavic and German and other groups may do so as well. These eventually become part of the regional dialects of particular areas, so that even speakers who don't share the ancestral background of the dominant first immigrants pick up these features and spread them throughout the region. Large metropolitan areas like Chicago and Minneapolis have Slavic and Scandinavian features, for example, even in residents who don't have those ancestries.[9]

IMMIGRATION IN THE TWENTIETH AND TWENTY-FIRST CENTURIES

Later arriving language-heritage communities in the Midwest came to flee religious persecution, economic hardships following the world wars, and governmental oppression, whether from czarist Russia, Nazi Germany, or Asian communism. Whether these recent immigrants maintained their native languages depended on the degree to which they were isolated from English speakers, desired a cohesive or even separatist identity, and, most important, followed the needs and wishes of their children and grandchildren.

European Immigrant Languages

Immigrants from Eastern Europe brought numerous languages to the region. About 7.5 percent of Illinois' population claims Polish ancestry, as does 8.6 percent of Michigan's residents and 9 percent of Wisconsin's people. Notable among these communities is Hamtramck, Michigan, where Poles constitute 60 percent of the population of 16,000 or so, and about 1,000 of them still speak Polish.[10] Others include immigrants, old and new, from the former Yugoslavia (Slovenians, Serbs, Croatians, and Bosnians), many of whom came to Chicago, Cleveland, and Detroit a hundred years ago and continued to come after the Balkan wars broke out in the 1990s. Czech emigrants, predominantly from Bohemia, in the former western Czechoslovakia, also came to the Midwest, settling on farms in Minnesota, Iowa, and elsewhere. (The Czech composer Antonín Dvořák wrote his *American Quartet* while spending a summer with the Czech immigrant community in Spillville, Iowa). These Slavic peoples brought with them their ethnic foods, including *kielbasa* and *kolaches*; and they left Americanized place names like New Prague ("New Prayg") in Minnesota. (Contrary to the myth perpetrated by a television ad of some years ago, however, Wausau, Wisconsin, was not named for Warsaw, Poland.)

Italian immigrants, though more numerous in the East, have settled in the Midwest largely in Michigan, Illinois, and Ohio, where they average 4.5 to 6 percent of the total population in each state; they constitute less than 4 percent of the population in the other five states of the region. However, their numbers range between 7.5 percent and 12 percent in the Cleveland area, and as high as 20 percent in the coal mining and manufacturing region that extends from Pittsburgh into eastern Ohio. Robert Di Pietro has documented how early Italian immigrants

Italian American railroad construction workers resting in front of a boxcar, c. 1920s. Courtesy Italian American Collection, Special Collections Department, University of Illinois at Chicago.

adapted both English and their many Italian and Sicilian dialects, producing such lexical items as *aisiskrima* and *medicina*.[11]

The Hungarian heritage is maintained in South Bend (Indiana), Detroit and Calumet (Michigan), Chicago, Cleveland, and Toledo, among other places. Hungarianized borrowings from English like *káré* (for "car") and *drájvol* ("drive") were once common. However, even this "Hunglish" is virtually gone now, despite the influx of new immigrants after the 1956 revolution in Hungary, except in food terms like *goulash*.

Of less than half a million Finnish-heritage people in the United States, about 213,000 live in Michigan (chiefly in the Upper Peninsula) and Minnesota (in the Iron Range district). Smaller numbers settled in Wisconsin, Ohio, Illinois, and Indiana (in descending order). In these six states, only 8,000 or so still speak Finnish, and most also report speaking English "very well." Thus, the likelihood that Finnish will persist much longer is, as in other bilingual communities moving toward English monolingualism, very small.[12]

Your Linguistic Family Tree

Investigate your linguistic heritage by interviewing one or more family members: your parents, grandparents, great-grandparents, children. What languages did they speak? with whom? in what states or countries? Did any of them speak more than one language? If so, why and where? If they have immigrated to this country (or another), how many of them have retained their original family languages in the new land? Were they teased or mocked for using those languages in school or business? Have they passed them on to you and your generation? If not, why not? Ask them about their attitudes toward the "Old Country" languages, and try to get them to reminisce about using them!

Personal interviews are best, but you can also look for old family letters, diaries, Bibles, and so on, for more evidence of ancestral language use. Have fun with this; you and your relatives may discover languages you never knew existed in your family tree!

Other language communities with even smaller numbers include Yiddish, notably in Cincinnati, where Lubavitcher Hasidic Jews from New York still use Yiddish, often in a diglossic relationship with Hebrew. But only imperfect learning of Yiddish occurs now. Greek families in Columbus number 800, twice the number in 1950, and about 60 children are enrolled in Greek Language School. However, few are fluent in Greek, and English-Greek mixes are common: A boy might be sent to the *bekkery* or the *groceria*, with an extra *quotti* to buy a *milsekki* or an *ice creemy*. Of the half million Armenian descendants in America, most live in California and on the East Coast, but almost 16,000 live in Michigan, with smaller numbers in Cleveland; of these, only 175,000 still speak Armenian.[13]

The only Celtic language to survive transplantation to the Midwest was Welsh; the two Gaelic languages, Scots Gaelic and Irish, largely remained in the East. All three languages are virtually absent in the present generation. (Irish immigrants, and the mixed ethnic group called Scots-Irish, came to America in greater numbers than any other national group except Germans, but most of them spoke English upon arrival or before they moved westward from the East.) Welsh immigrants came to the coal mines in Ohio, in particular, and the Bob Evans Farm near Rio Grande (pronounced "Rye-oh Grand") preserves that legacy as well as sausages and white gravy. Ironically, it is next door to Gallipolis, "city

Gallipolis, "city of the Gauls," was founded by exiled French aristocrats after the Revolution of 1789. Courtesy Ohio Division of Travel and Tourism, www.DiscoverOhio.com.

of the Gauls," founded by exiled French aristocrats after the Revolution of 1789. More numerous now are the descendants of Dutch/Flemish-speaking Belgians; separated from their language compatriots in Holland after the redivision of the Lowlands, they left French-dominant Belgium for the rich farmlands of the Midwest.

Latin American Immigrant Languages

In spite of this apparent decline in the retention of immigrant languages in the Midwest, some languages are actually on the increase. These include Spanish, several Southeast Asian languages, and, among African languages, Somali and Sudanese Arabic. Spanish has been here the longest, at least since the Depression, and also shows the largest increase in speaking use, with continuing waves of both immigrant and migrant families swelling the ranks of communities where Spanish is the dominant language even as the fourth generation of Americans of Hispanic heritage switches increasingly to English. Over 10 million people in the United States reported speaking Spanish in the home in the 2000 census; of these, over

1.25 million are in Illinois (almost 11 percent of that state's population). In Michigan, 247,000 persons reported speaking Spanish in the home, and in Ohio the number was 213,000, with much smaller numbers in the other five states of the Midwest (see Table 4).[14]

Not all of these new Americans are dominant in Spanish, since the younger generations increasingly use English. Nonetheless, the growth of extended families by successive waves of immigration ensures the survival of Spanish-language use in bilingual families to a degree not seen in earlier immigrant communities. The cohesiveness of communities, especially in urban areas, and the value placed upon the use of Spanish in home, church, and other cultural activities are reflected in the desire of families to have their American-born children taught Spanish even in the face of English dominance. Bilingual education in English and Spanish is offered in large urban areas like Chicago and Cleveland, and some cities, like Columbus and Minneapolis, have Spanish immersion schools where both Spanish-heritage children and non-Hispanic children can learn Spanish through instruction that phases in English only after initial subject-matter learning for three to five years is done solely in Spanish. Cincinnati, Milwaukee, and other cities offer similar programs in French and German. Moreover, even when the inevitable shift to English occurs and their Spanish is no longer "authentic," young people often self-consciously adopt and exaggerate Hispanicized pronunciations of English words in an affirmation of their cultural heritage. Thus, they may substitute tense vowels for lax ones (Spanish has only tense [long] vowels), as in "That's so beeg" and "He didn't do no-ting." This has created a generalized Chicano or Latino English used throughout the United States but most particularly in urban areas with large concentrations of Latino Americans, such as Los Angeles, New York, and, in the Midwest, Chicago.[15]

Asian and African Immigrant Languages

Filipino speakers have been coming to the United States since the end of World War II, but other Southeast Asian groups have immigrated in large numbers only since the 1970s. Refugees arrived first, numbering more than 1.3 million after the Vietnam War; immigrants have followed, with about 10 percent of the present total of 1.5 million settling in the Midwest, the vast majority (some 75,000) in Minnesota, Wisconsin, and Illinois. Of these, 41 percent are Hmong speakers (most in the Minneapolis-St. Paul area), about 33 percent are Lao and Thai speakers, and the rest are Cambodian, Vietnamese, and Filipino. The continued cohesion of Hmong, Cambodian, and Lao communities, even as American-born generations increase, has led to considerable maintenance of their languages. However, heritage language programs, including summer camps and free neighborhood classes, are not uniformly successful, especially when literacy is not emphasized and were not even common in the home countries until the 1950s. Vietnamese immigrants do not tend to live in enclave communities and therefore have the poorest chance of maintaining their language. However, bilingualism is likely to continue in these populations for some time.[16]

Somali refugees from the civil wars of the 1990s have settled mainly in the Minneapolis and Columbus areas, as have Sudanese immigrants, most of them speaking Arabic as a second language. (It is estimated that 20,000 to 30,000 Somalis now live in Columbus; Minnesota has over 43,000 Africans of Sub-Saharan descent, in-

Table 4. Principal languages spoken at home in the midwestern states

Number of Speakers and Percent of State Total Population

	Michigan	Ohio	Indiana	Illinois	Missouri	Iowa	Minnesota	Wisconsin
English only	8,487,401	9,951,475	5,295,736	9,326,786	4,961,741	2,578,477	4,201,503	4,653,361
	91.6%	93.9%	93.6%	80.8%	94.9%	94.2%	91.5%	92.7%
All other languages	781,381	648,493	362,082	2,220,719	264,281	160,022	389,988	368,712
	8.4%	6.1%	6.4%	19.2%	5.1%	5.8%	8.5%	7.3%
Spanish	246,688	213,147	185,576	1,253,676	110,752	79,491	132,066	168,778
	2.7%	2.0%	3.3%	10.9%	2.1%	2.9%	2.9%	3.4%
Other European languages	303,122	296,816	126,530	640,237	97,816	49,032	110,644	124,719
	3.3%	2.8%	2.2%	5.5%	1.9%	1.8%	2.4%	2.5%
Asian/Pacific languages	104,467	84,658	36,707	248,800	41,970	25,335	103,520	61,447
	1.1%	.8%	.6%	2.2%	.8%	.9%	2.3%	1.2%

Source: U.S. Census, Profile of Selected Social Characteristics, 2000. See at http://factfinder.census.gov/servlet/BasicFactsTable. Self-reported data on degree of language proficiency were tallied but are not included in this summary table.

Note: American Indian and African languages were not tallied in this table.

cluding Somalis and Sudanese.) However, Arabic has an older history in the Detroit-Toledo area, dating back at least a century to Lebanese and other Levantine immigration. Earlier immigrants shifted to English in the usual pattern, with over one-third attrition of Arabic in just one generation. Later groups, usually of Muslim identity, have tried to maintain Arabic longer, particularly through the teaching of Classical Arabic for reading and religious purposes. However, the Somali and Sudanese communities usually arrive with no literacy in any language, and instruction in Arabic in special schools, such as the International Academy Charter School in Columbus, is of limited success when the children often confuse their own native tongues with the artificial print Arabic they learn by rote. Aleya Rouchdy has predicted that a new American Arabic dialect will emerge within the Arab diaspora, one that will not be understood in the home countries, just as Americanized Norwegian and Hungarian are not always understood in Europe.[17]

Issues of language maintenance and shift are therefore very real in all immigrant communities and no less so in midwestern America. How long an ancestral language can be maintained for normal and vital use in all, or even some, domains before it diffuses into a "mixed" variety and finally succumbs to the majority language of the new country is the central question. Lack of contact among different language groups, ongoing replenishment of a first-language community by new immigrants, and maintenance of distinctive ethnic, religious, and cultural identities all contribute to language retention.

The typical pattern of acculturation and eventual assimilation of new groups into a larger host country with hundreds of years of absorbing and leveling of disparate peoples behind it militates against such retention, even among communities with long-held convictions of separateness like those of the Amish, Hasidic Jews, and Islamic Arabs. In time, the new groups, like those who came before, will tend to speak like the "mainstream" inhabitants of a particular region; this is as true in the Midwest as it is in the urban enclaves of New York or Boston or New Orleans or San Francisco. It is to those regional differences that mark the dialects of midwestern English that we now turn.

DIALECTS OF AMERICAN ENGLISH IN THE MIDWEST

A brief review of American dialect research might be useful before looking at English in the Midwest. Dialect research in the United States began in the 1930s with the intention of producing a Linguistic Atlas of the United States and Canada. Regions were sampled according to age and educational levels of selected informants, who were interviewed by fieldworkers to elicit regional lexical items, grammatical structures, and pronunciation forms. Maps were drawn with isoglosses between major lexical, grammatical, and phonological divisions. Four major areas were distinguished: New England, Northern, Midland, and Southern; the West was, and still is, under study, with subdivisions being delineated up to the present. The Midland region has already been subdivided into North Midland and South Midland. Although the exact boundary between the two subareas is disputed, speech differences appear distinctive enough to warrant discussion. The Midwest spans three of these areas: Northern, North Midland, and South Midland. Minnesota, Wisconsin, Michigan, and the northern portions of Iowa, Illinois, Indiana, and Ohio all fall into the Northern dialect region; the four last-named states (and all of Missouri) also have sizable Midland areas. Features of these dialect areas will be discussed in the following section.[18]

The North

Like all dialect regions, the northern part of the United States east of the Mississippi is characterized by distinctive vocabulary, grammar, and pronunciation forms. Lexical items commonly used in the northern tier of the Midwest include *eaves troughs*, *green pepper*, *pail*, *bag*, *firefly*, *crayfish* (or the misnomer *crabs*), *frying pan*, *shades*, *faucet* or *tap*, *ski cap*, *see saw*, and *Trick-or-Treat*, among the more hotly debated terms. Soft drinks are *pop* in most of the North, although large urban areas are switching to *soda*. Localisms not uniformly used throughout the area include *bubbler* for "drinking fountain" (in northern Illinois and Wisconsin), *hard road* (paved, in Illinois), *hawk* (the winter wind in Chicago), *Devil's Night* (the night before Halloween in Detroit and elsewhere), *devil's strip* (the "berm" or grass strip between sidewalk and curb, in Cleveland and Akron), *loose-meat sandwich* (barbecued meat in Iowa), and *uff da* (expression of disgust in Scandinavian Minnesota, akin to *oy* in the East).[19]

Grammatical constructions like *wait for* (someone), *quarter to* or *quarter past* (when telling time), and full verbal forms like "want to get off or go out" and "needs to be washed or done" (alternating with "needs washing" or, more rarely, "needs doing") are commonly used. "Negative *anymore*" is almost exclusively used, as in "It never rains anymore." So-called standard past tense and past participle forms are preferred, including *did*, *came*, *saw*, *have done*, *had come*, and *has seen*, although variants include *done*, *come*, and *seen* for past tense. Phrases like "sick to the stomach" and past tense verbs like *dove* and *woke (up)/awoke* are used in the Northern area at least as far west as Minnesota and the Dakotas, in contrast with "sick at the stomach," *dived*, and *waked*, which are still common, though receding, in the Midland. A form often noted, particularly in Minnesota and Wisconsin but also in Chicago, is the use of a verb followed by *with*, as in "Do you want to come with?" The presumed "error" is the lack of a noun object of the preposition, and the usage is uniformly derided outside the region. However, dialectologists suggest the true origin of this construction is the two-part verb common in German and the Scandinavian languages brought to the Upper Midwest. Thus, German *mitkommen* would be separated in a sentence to produce *komm mit*. In other words, *mit* (English *with*) is a so-called verb particle, not a preposition, and therefore it does not require a following noun object (see McDavid and McDavid, 1960). A related expression is "Where's it at?" which is used throughout the Midwest (and indeed, throughout the country). The final preposition/particle is only used if the WH word is contracted, presumably for intonational balance; "Where is it?" would generally not include this form.[20]

The "Yoopers" of the Upper Peninsula (U.P.) of Michigan are known for their use of the French Canadian tag "eh?" at the end of utterances, and they share in some Canadian pronunciations as well, such as "da" for *the*; a license plate holder seen recently read "Don't forget to visit da U.P. now, eh?" However, many residents of Minnesota and Wisconsin also use /d/ for the "th" sound, as do New Yorkers and others throughout the English-speaking world. It is the confluence of such forms with others, in particular vowels, that distinguishes one region from another. So-called Canadian raising of diphthongs (combinations of a vowel with *y* or *w*, like *aye*, *oy*, and *ow*) is common the farther north one goes in all three midwestern states: *right* is more rounded to sound like "royght," and *out* is increasingly "owt" or even "oot."

Most notably, pronunciation in the Northern dialect region, from Vermont to Minnesota, has traditionally differentiated the central vowels in words like *cot* and *caught*, *Don* and *dawn*, and *hock* and *hawk*. (Spelling masks the fact that each of these words contains only one vowel sound.) William Labov and other linguists note that this distinction, or lack of it, is one of the key diagnostic features of American dialects. In the past half century, the distinction has begun to be lost as the merger of these two central vowels spreads northward and westward from the Midland region.

Thus, in the eight midwestern states which are the focus of this volume, the merger to one sound, the "short o" vowel of *cot*, is already virtually complete in Minnesota and Iowa. However, in the northern and southern tiers of Ohio, Indiana, and Illinois, most of Missouri, and almost all of Michigan and Wisconsin, the distinction is still made.[21]

Other pronunciation features include the use of contrasting vowels in words like *field* and *filled*, *sale* and *sell*, *pool* and *pull* (and *pole*), and *pin* and *pen*. We shall see how these sets are becoming merged in the areas of the Midwest designated by dialectologists as "Midland." One merger has long been established in the entire eight-state region, however; *Mary*, *merry*, and *marry* are all pronounced the same, unlike their differentiated forms in Boston, New York, and some other parts of the East and South. Only *bury* seems to vary within our region, between rhyming with "Mary" or "hurry." One set of vowels that has flip-flopped in usage is that in *for* and *far*; in St. Louis and the Great Plains they tend to be either reversed or to merge toward the low vowel of "car." Words like *roof* and *root* are traditionally pronounced with short (or nontense) vowels in the North, although self-conscious speakers in urban areas, particularly those with more education or in frequent contact with people from other regions of the country, increasingly try to use the long (or tensed) vowels. This is especially the case with *creek*, which traditionally was pronounced "crick" in the North.

A very distinctive vowel change is occurring in a string of cities along the Great Lakes from Buffalo to Cleveland to Detroit to Chicago to Milwaukee and perhaps all the way to Minneapolis. Called the Northern Cities Vowel Shift by William Labov, it marks this "Inland North" off even from the rest of the Northern dialect region. The "short a" vowel in words like *bath* is first moved slightly up and to the front of the mouth, and then other vowels also move in a clockwise rotation pattern, with upward movements forcing other vowels downward and back. The result is that *bad* sounds like "bed," *locks* sounds like "lacks," *Ann* rhymes with "Ian," *been* (= bin) and *milk* sound like "ben" and "melk," *Debbie* sounds like "Dubbie," and *busses* sounds like "bosses." Thus (overheard in a taxicab), "in Chicaehgo Ellanoy the White Saex are doing great!"

Pockets of ethnic or racial populations, whether large or small, have additional words and pronunciations, not to mention grammatical forms like the above-mentioned "come with" and "needs washed," which have old origins but persist because of familiarity and tradition or because they serve as group identity markers. These may include borrowings like *Bund* for German-speaking clubs, and numerous words and code-mixed blends used in Hispanic and Latino communities, like *biper* (beeper), *chileando* ("chilling out"), *maicrogüey* (microwave oven), and *pullóver* (T-shirt). These tend to be the same in all dialect regions, however, and pronunciation in these communities also tends to be the same throughout the country, as long as the user groups are sufficiently large and cohesive to allow for the dispersion and continuance of such forms through successive generations. We have seen such "inherited" words and pronunciations in the Scandinavian and German settlement areas. Distinctive pronunciations and, to some extent, grammatical forms are also found in extended and semi-isolated American Indian communities, especially in Minnesota, Wisconsin, and the Dakotas. Final consonants are often deleted, and consonant clusters may be broken up with an inserted vowel: *firs'*, *ol'es'* (oldest), *don'*, *moderen* (modern), and *childern* have been attested, as has the common *innit* (isn't it).[22]

The Midland: North and South

The Midland, as noted earlier, is a wide swath of distinctive, transitional, and overlapping linguistic features. The North Midland extends from New Jersey through Pennsylvania into central Ohio, Indiana, and Illinois. The South Midland follows the broad Ohio River Valley to the Mississippi River. Cross-cutting this area diagonally in eastern Ohio is the Appalachian Plateau, with features partly South Midland and partly Southern. West of the Mississippi, a "general" West Midland blends features from these divisions. Most of Iowa and Missouri share North Midland and South Midland features (with the exception of the Ozark Highlands of Missouri, where an extension of Appalachian English is spoken), and they have been found in varying degrees all the way to the Pacific coast.

Since the South Midland is sharply distinguishable from the North, it might be best to begin with this region and note contrasts and overlaps with the North Midland area in between. Vocabulary items common in the South Midland and especially the Ohio Valley include *eaves spouts* (and, more recently, *gutters*), *mango* (for green pepper), *bucket*, *sack*, *lightning bug*, *crawdad*, *skillet*, *blinds* (on rollers), *spigot*, *toboggan* (a winter cap), *groundhog* (= woodchuck), *briggity* (= uppity), *ornery* (pronounced "awn'ry" in Missouri and the Ohio Valley), and *Beggars' Night* (for "Halloween"). Some of these, however, now alternate frequently with the northern or more "urban" forms cited earlier, especially in the North Midland. A *potluck* dinner in the North may be called a *pitch-in* in Indiana or a *carry-in* in parts of Illinois and Ohio. Soft drinks are *pop* in most of the Midland, except in Missouri, where *soda* (or "sody") *pop* is common. A Southern term that's beginning to creep into the South Midland, especially Indiana, is *coke*—used generically for all types and colors of soft drink.

The use of *mamaw* and *papaw* for grandparents (or *mawmaw* and *pawpaw*, the latter sometimes reserved for great-grandparents) is still common, however, even in young people's speech. In researching dialects in the Ohio Valley, Robert Dakin found other distinctive terms for food items and farm implements still used in the 1960s. Some of these terms may still be used in rural areas but are disappearing with the loss of a farming economy: *clabbered milk*, *ridy-horse*, *pallet*, *barn lot*, *coal oil* (= kerosene), *snap and butter beans*, *middlin meat* (= salt pork), *peckerwood*, *woods colt*, *branch* (= creek), *soft peach*, *snake feeder* (= dragon fly), *poke*, *polecat*, and *johnny cake*.

Phrases still heard occasionally include "lay out of school," "a little (or "fur") piece" (vs. *piece*, *piecing* = snack, snacking), "to hull (or shuck) beans," and "right smart." Using *quarter till* for telling time is by far the standard practice in this area (vs. *quarter of* or *to*), as is the distinction between *wait on* (someone who doesn't come) and *wait for* (someone who eventually does come).[23]

Grammatical forms include the plural *you all* (not *y'all*), *youse*, and *you'ns*, as well as the possessive *you all's*. Reduced phrases are common, including *want off*, *want out*, *over top of*, and *upside*, as well as *needs washed*, *corrected*, *done*, and so on (vs. *needs to be washed* or *needs washing*). "Positive *anymore*" contrasts with the exclusively negative usage in the North but is actually more common in the North Midland and the West Midland than in the South Midland: "It rains all the time anymore" (= nowadays). Vernacular past tense forms are common, including *he come*, *I done it*, and *I knowed it*, as well as the perfective past *I done seen him*; and the past tense of the *be* verb is often regularized: *I/she was, you was, we/they was*. The subject relative pronoun is occasionally absent, as in "He's the man stole my car"; and a personal dative pronoun is sometimes added, as in "I'm gonna get *me* a new car soon." Contracted *there's* is commonly used with both singular and plural nouns, in both North and South Midland ("There's ten people in the room"). Singular nouns of measurement may be used with plural meaning: *ten mile, five bushel, six foot, two pound*; and an *a*-prefix before a progressive verb is still used by older and rural people: "He was a-dancin', they come a-runnin'." In the Ohio Valley and the Appalachian Plateau, some also use *whenever* to mean point-of-time *when*, as in "Whenever my father died, I was sad."

Change is occurring in the use and comprehension of some of these structures, of course. A survey by Beverly Flanigan of the grammatical usage of college students revealed that sentences like "My hair needs washed," "He bought two pair of pants," "The cat wants out," and "I need you to understand" were widely used and understood, suggesting that these once localized forms are becoming more widespread. However, "He went a-hunting" and "There was a man told me about it" were overwhelmingly rejected for personal use or even recognition of others' use. Students often report that their grandparents or "the farmers down the road" use these forms but that they themselves do not.[24]

Pronunciation features include the merging of *cot* and *caught*, *Don* and *dawn*, and *hock* and *hawk* throughout the Midland region, though the merged vowel is slightly more backed in the South Midland (with a resulting British-like pronunciation of words like *pot* and *hot*). Thus, *collar* rhymes with *caller* and sometimes, in the South Midland, *color*. Three other mergers advancing throughout the South Midland have led to the rhyming of *steel* with *still*; of *pool* (and sometimes *pole*) with *pull*; and of *sale* with *sell*. A feature spreading throughout General Midland is the fronting of vowels in words like *coat* and *go* ("ca-oat" and "ga-o") and in *boot* and *due* ("be-oot" and "dyoo"); in the North these vowels sound like "oh" and "ooh." But distinctive in the South Midland are some Southern features that have migrated northward to overlap with North Midland forms. Among these is the tensing of short (or lax) vowels in words like *fish*, *push*, and *special* ("feesh," "poosh," "spayshul"). In addition, *greasy* is pronounced "greazy," and an intrusive /r/ is added to *wa(r)sh*, /l/ is inserted in *draw(l)ing*, and /t/ is added to *across(t)*. The use of monophthongs for diphthongs in *I*, *buy*, *fire*, and *tired* (to rhyme with "ah," "bah," "far," "tarred") and of diphthongs for monophthongs in *dog*, *saw*, and *tall* (the gliding sound in "dawg," "saow," "towel") is common in areas close to the Ohio River but more rare farther away from the river. Another Southern English feature, the merger of *pin* and *pen* so that both sound like "pin," is also heard in the river valley. Substituting a glide /w/ for final /l/ (as in *boil* and *tall*) and adding a "dark" /l/ after a final low back vowel (as in *saw(l)* and *mamaw(l)*) are also frequently produced. Disyllabic words containing glides are sometimes reduced to monosyllables, as in *sewer*, *Stewart*, and *Newark* ("sore," "stort," "nerk"). Names ending in *-i* may be pronounced with a final "uh" sound; thus, *Missouri* and *Cincinnati* may sound like "Missoura" and "Cincinnata." The "ee" ending tends to be Northern, while the "uh" ending tends to be Midland and is thought to have been influenced by Scots-Irish pronunciation forms in the Midland. Finally, stress on the first syllable in words like *insurance*, *umbrella*, and *Detroit* is common in the South Midland but less so in the North Midland.[25]

The lexical, phonological, and grammatical features described above will continue to change. Overlap and transition will likely occur, particularly in vocabulary items, as urbanization and orientation increase toward centers of culture, entertainment, and other out-

Dialect Research

The best guide to doing family and community-based dialect studies is an article by Roger W. Shuy, "Dialects: How They Differ," excerpted from his monograph, *Discovering American Dialects*, published by the National Council of Teachers of English in 1967 and reprinted in *Language: Readings in Language and Culture* (6th ed.), edited by V. Clark, P. Eschholz, and A. Rosa (New York: St. Martin's Press, 1998). This is a very readable introduction to the facts of dialect differences and how to study them, with sections on potential pronunciation, lexical, and grammatical features to consider. Tests of potential differences, checklists of vocabulary items (pop vs. soda, pail vs. bucket, etc.), and tests of differences in prepositions, plurals, past participles, and so on, are included for easy (and legal) copying. A questionnaire on biographical and residential facts is also suggested.

When interviewing friends and family, it is important to create a relaxed and informal atmosphere, since natural vernacular speech is best elicited when people are not overly self-conscious about "how they sound." Tape-recording should be as nonintrusive as possible, and topics should be comfortable and familiar. Informants might be asked to talk about their childhood, favorite games and sports, travels, and (only at the end) attitudes toward their own speech and that of others. Group discussions often create the best and most informal talk, but too many voices on a tape can be confusing.

Tapes may be transcribed or not, but the ultimate goal should be to make copies available to informants. They make wonderful family and community oral histories, regardless of the linguistic interpretation of them that one may or may not wish to make.

side focal areas. However, pronunciation features and grammatical forms will change much more slowly and in more restricted population groups. Furthermore, Labov has shown that the influence of General Southern speech (used south of the states focused on in this volume) is growing, so that monophthongizing and diphthongizing rules, as well as tensing and laxing processes, will likely continue to compete with Northern forms in the pronunciation of Midland speakers. As these forms migrate to urban areas with their users, they will become part of the rich matrix of English dialects that typically characterizes large cities. Indeed, the presence of South Midland and Appalachian English is already noticeable in Cincinnati, Dayton, Columbus, Akron, Ypsilanti, and Indianapolis. (It has been estimated that by 1930 about 30,000 residents of Ohio were of Appalachian origin.) These South Midland patterns should therefore be regarded not as relic forms, but rather as evidence that traditional, if less prestigious, features are still alive and well.[26]

Geographic space is only one dimension in the complicated patterning of language use. Fundamental to any study of dialect variation is the role of education, social class, economic opportunity, ethnicity, and gender, and these are important in the study of English in the Midwest as well. As people in any region acquire secondary and higher education, for example, they become influenced by those language forms considered by schools to be prestigious. And as they move from working-class to middle-class socioeconomic status, those prestige forms become linked with access to power and wealth. Linguists who study the use of language in everyday life have long known that women tend to be conservative in speech. In an effort to gain social and economic power for themselves and their children, they adopt language forms that have greater prestige in society than do their more "homespun" vernacular forms. In other words, they try to use, and to insist that their children use, "standard" grammar, nonlocal vocabulary terms and pronunciation that conforms as much as possible to urban speech, typically that of the increasingly influential large urban areas around Columbus, St. Louis, and such western cities as Denver, Seattle, and San Francisco. The older centers of influence, like Boston, New York, Philadelphia, and Chicago, are less regarded as "prestigious" and more often thought of as "marked," that is, as having idiosyncratic features of pronunciation that are no longer considered models of "standard" American English except in their own regions. Thus, while "General American English" is analytically a meaningless term, an idealized combination of presumably central (or even North Central) dialect features, it may emerge in coming decades as an appropriate term, at least for those parts of the country west of the Mississippi.

Although not all midwesterners use all of the vernacular forms discussed here, many use some of them, especially in rural and small-town areas. Older people tend to use them more than younger people, and men are more likely than women to use vernacular grammar in particular. While education and outmigration are promoting the adoption of nonlocal vocabulary and grammar, pronunciation is more resistant to change. However, even vowels can vary with education, occupation, age, gender, and degree of identification with local culture and tradition. Furthermore, tests of perception, as opposed to production, show that exposure to other dialects through increased outside contact may lead not only to changes in the quality of those vowels productively but also to listeners' comprehension of vowels, even in their own area.[27]

As Walt Wolfram and Natalie Schilling-Estes have shown, distinctive vernacular forms may spread and become more self-consciously used in a "contrahierarchical" move to reaffirm local and regional, and even ethnic and class, identity. The growing popularity of country and bluegrass music has familiarized "outsiders" with Southern and Appalachian English, and the blues and rap (or hip-hop) music have made African American English a comfortable, if not always authentic, medium of communication among young people of diverse ethnic and national origins. In the Midwest these varieties are also becoming influential, in the last mentioned case principally because of mass migration to the North and especially to urban areas during the Great Depression and after World War II. Thus, Chicago, Detroit, Cleveland, Milwaukee, Indianapolis, and St. Louis (arguably a southern city anyway) are now major centers of black language and culture; the large urban areas of Minnesota and Iowa are not far behind.[28]

African American English

This summary of dialect variation in the Midwest must not end without a discussion of the linguistic features of African American English (AAE). Unified less by region than by a sense of historical and contemporary social group identity, Black English is remarkably uniform across the United States, with variations based largely on educational and class consciousness rather than on where one is from. Thus, current AAE slang is for the most part uniform across the country, and it may or may not be shared, or even understood, by other communities. Examples are "bro" or "brah" = brother, "bad" = good, and "phat" or "da bomb" = really good. Pronunciation features are also shared by many blacks regardless of region, although many of them are derived from the southern English of the plantation era and are still common among whites in the South. Most salient are the deletion of /r/ everywhere except before a vowel, leading to near rhymes in words such as *god* and *guard*, *saw* and *sore*; and the reduction of consonant clusters, as in *passed* (where the final /t/ sound is lost after /s/) and *tests* (where three consonants are reduced to two or even one: "tes"). Many other groups evidence similar deletion patterns, but research has shown that frequencies of deletion are greater in the African American speech community. Other phonological features include the merging of the vowel sounds in *pin* and *pen* so that both sound like "pin," and the replacement of some of the "th" sounds with either /t/ or /d/, as in "dis" and "wit," or with /f/ or /v/, as in "wif" and "bruvver." Deletion of /l/ may occur also, so that *told* (or *toll*) and *toe* rhyme and *help* and *hep* rhyme. This process also occurs in other dialects, especially in the South and the South Midland (e.g., in southern Ohio). Finally, diphthongs may be reduced, particularly before /l/, so that *boil* and *boy* both sound like "bawh."

In grammar, AAE, like many other dialects, uses multiple negatives (sometimes as many as four or five in a single sentence, all intensifying the negative meaning), perfect forms for past tense (as in "he done it" and "they come yesterday"), and the ubiquitous "ain't." Most distinctive, however, are a few grammatical rules that have no parallel outside AAE and are therefore often completely misunderstood. Two usages of the "be" verb, in particular, cause confusion: In AAE, when "be" is used in its infinitive or unconjugated form, it implies an ongoing or habitual state or action (as in "He be working" = he's employed); when "be" is omitted altogether, it signals a momentary, or present, state (as in "She nice" and "He working" = at this point in time). Negating these two states is also marked differently: "He don't be working" vs. "He ain't working" or "she ain't nice." Inverting subject and verb is also common, as in "Ain't nobody told me that" and "He asked could he go." Finally, the meaning of "been" and "done" may be distinctive: "She's been married" with regular stress implies that she is no longer wed, while "She's BEEN married" (with stress on the auxiliary verb) means she has been wed for some time and still is. "Done," in addition to its common use in simple past tense, may also mean completed or intensified action, as in "He done did it" or "I'm done sick of this job."[29]

These last grammatical rules are understood, if not used, by virtually all blacks who have had even limited contact with the general African American community, and their frequency and predictability of use depend not on region but on social class, education, profession, and, to some extent, age and gender. It is true that a northern black like the rock star Prince, who grew up in a middle-class Minneapolis family, may sound like any other Minnesotan at home, but he can also switch to AAE, using some, if not all, of its features, when he chooses to do so. This kind of "code-switching" is as prevalent in bidialectal speakers as it is in bilingual speakers.

The question of whether AAE should be allowed, or even used, in the classroom has been debated since the 1960s, but it was raised again in the so-called Ebonics controversy in Oakland, California, in the late 1990s. Linguists, and teachers concerned about their students' attitudes toward schooling as well as their academic achievement, take a positive stance on this issue. They view Black English Vernacular, as they do all home vernaculars, as an authentic vehicle of social communication and not as a "substandard" variety to be condemned and prohibited. Indeed, using the vernacular has been found to help students "bridge the gap" between their home language and the language of the schools, and it affirms their right to have two ways of speaking and, in effect, two identities as they prepare for the world beyond school.

A court case involving the rights of African American children to use their own dialect as a bridge toward Standard English was settled, in favor of the children, in Ann Arbor, Michigan, in 1979. The decision ordered the Martin Luther King Elementary School to educate its faculty on the nature of AAE so that they could better understand the dialect children bring to school from home.[30] This does not mean that teachers need to learn to speak AAE, but it does insist that they come to understand its principles so that they can approach their students' learning problems, especially in reading, with the tools to facilitate acquiring "standard" pronunciation and grammar as well as the spelling conventions that encode that standard. Indeed, such an approach would be valuable for all educators, and for society in general, as we debate the many varieties of English spoken in this ever-enlarging "melting pot." An attitude of acceptance of all dialects as equally valid—Black English, Appalachian English, Hispanic English, Vietnamese English, Arabic English, and others—would go a long way toward promoting the acceptance of all the varied groups that make up America.

CONCLUSION

This overview of the language varieties spoken in the Midwest must also mention the prospects for change and continuity in the three aspects of language we have focused on: pronunciation, grammar, and vocabulary. Vocabulary will continue to change and expand, as it always has, through borrowing of useful words and phrases from other languages and innovation of new terms, particularly slang and jargon, found to meet the needs of various groups. Both processes tend to occur nationally rather than only regionally. Even Valley Girl Talk and hip-hop slang travel across the country rapidly today. Grammar, too, tends to stabilize as education and class mobility (not to mention geographic mobility) reduce barriers between social groups. However, nonstandard verb forms persist, in part because they become rooted in early childhood but also because they signal social group cohesiveness and identity in in-group interaction.

Pronunciation will always reflect regional roots, basically because it is difficult to change one's accent after adolescence but also because accent announces "home" more than either lexicon or grammar does. In a large and diverse country such as ours, this identification with place appears to be more and more important, in part to distinguish oneself from others in an immediate and salient way. The assumption that the media, or mass education, or class consciousness will erase accent differences is a myth. Even the presumably accent-free Broadcast English takes on the accents of regional news centers and their affiliates. In the Midwest, this means Chicago English, or Minneapolis English, or St. Louis English, or Columbus English. Style, diction, and lexicon are similar, to be sure, but the sounds of the region persist, even with minor and gradual changes. The leavening of such distinctive features with the varieties spoken by African Americans, American Indians, and the many new immigrant groups who continue to arrive will only enrich the speech of the Midwest and the nation as a whole.

RESOURCE GUIDE

Printed Sources

General Works

Allen, Harold B. *Linguistic Atlas of the Upper Midwest*. 3 vols. Minneapolis: University of Minnesota Press, 1973–1976.

Bartelt, Guillermo. *Socio- and Stylolinguistic Perspectives on American Indian English Texts*. Lewiston, NY: Edwin Mellon Press, 2001.

Baugh, John. *Black Street Speech*. Austin: University of Texas Press, 1983.

———. "Bridging the Great Divide." *Language Magazine: The Journal of Communication and Education* 2, no. 7 (March 2003): 39–44.

Boas, Franz. *Introduction to Handbook of American Indian Languages*. 1911. J. W. Powell, "Indian Linguistic Families of America North of Mexico." 1891. Reprint, Lincoln: University of Nebraska Press, 1966.

Cassidy, Frederic G., and Joan Hall, eds. *Dictionary of American Regional English (DARE)*. 4 vols. Cambridge, MA: Belknap Press, 1985–. Projected five-volume series.

Deloria, Ella C. *Dakota Texts*. Vermillion: University of South Dakota Press, 1978.

Dillard, J. L. *Black English*. New York: Random House, 1972.

———. *A History of American English*. New York: Longman, 1992.

Ferguson, C. A., and S. B. Heath, eds. *Language in the USA*. New York: Cambridge University Press, 1981.

Flanigan, Beverly Olson. "American Indian English in History and Literature: The Evolution of a Pidgin from Reality to Stereotype." Ph.D. diss. Indiana University, 1981. Ann Arbor: University Microfilms International.

———. "Bilingual Education for Native Americans: The Argument from Studies of Variational English." In *On TESOL '83: The Question of Control*, edited by Jean Handscombe et al., 81–93. Washington, DC: Teachers of English to Speakers of Other Languages, 1984. Also in ERIC Documents, ED 233 605.

———. "Different Ways of Talking in the Buckeye State." *Language Magazine: The Journal of Communication and Education* 1, no. 11 (July 2002): 30–34.

Gordon, Matthew J. "Straight Talking from the Heartland." *Language Magazine: The Journal of Communication and Education* 1, no. 1 (January 2002): 35–38.

Hoover, Herbert T., Karen P. Zimmerman, and Christopher J. Hoover. *The Sioux and Other Native American Cultures of the Dakotas: An Annotated Bibliography*. Westport, CT: Greenwood Press, 1993.

Labov, William, Sharon Ash, and Charles Boberg, eds. *Phonological Atlas of North American English*. New York: Mouton de Gruyter, in press. Preview of maps available at www.ling.upenn.edu/phono_atlas/home.html.

Marckwardt, Albert H. *American English*. New York: Oxford University Press, 1958.

———. "Principal and Subsidiary Dialect Areas in the North-Central States," *Publications of the American Dialect Society* 27 (1957): 3–15.

Metcalf, Allan. *How We Talk: American Regional English Today*. New York: Houghton Mifflin, 2000.

Northrup, Jim. *Walking the Rez Road*. Stillwater, MN: Voyageur Press, 1993.

Perry, Theresa, and Lisa Delpit, eds. *The Real Ebonics Debate*. Boston: Beacon Press, 1998.

Rickford, J. R., and R. J. Rickford. *Spoken Soul*. New York: John Wiley, 2000.

Ronda, James P., and James Axtell. *Indian Missions: A Critical Bibliography*. Bloomington: Indiana University Press for the Newberry Library, 1978.

Smitherman, Geneva. *Black Talk: Words and Phrases from the Hood to the Amen Corner*. Boston: Houghton Mifflin, 2000.

———. *Talkin That Talk: Language, Culture, and Education in African America*. New York: Routledge, 2000.

St. Clair, Robert, and William Leap, eds. *Language Renewal Among American Indian Tribes*. Rosslyn, VA: National Clearinghouse for Bilingual Education, 1982.

Theisz, R. D., ed. *Buckskin Tokens: Contemporary Oral Narratives of the Lakota*. Aberdeen, SD: North Plains Press, 1975.

Vizenor, Gerald. *The People Named the Chippewa*. Minneapolis: University of Minnesota Press, 1984.

Wolfram, Walt, and Donna Christian. *Dialects and Education: Issues and Answers*. Englewood Cliffs, NJ: Prentice Hall Regents, 1989.

Wolfram, Walt, Carolyn Adger, and Donna Christian. *Dialects in Schools and Communities*. Mahwah, NJ: Erlbaum, 1999.

Zentella, Ana Celia. *Growing Up Bilingual*. Oxford: Blackwell, 1997.

Additional Reading

Alvarez, Lizette. "It's the Talk of Nueva York: The Hybrid Called Spanglish." In *Language: Readings in Language and Culture*, edited by V. Clark, P. Eschholz, and A. Rosa, 483–488. 6th ed. New York: St. Martin's Press, 1998.

Baker, Colin. *Foundations of Bilingual Education and Bilingualism*. 3rd ed. Clevedon: Multilingual Matters, 2001.

Boyce, Heather. *Language Attitudes and Classroom Practices: In or Out with Arabic, English, and Somali?* M.A. research paper, Ohio University, Athens, 2003.

Bright, William. "Native American Placenames in the Louisiana Purchase." *American Speech* 78 (2003): 353–362.

Christian, Donna, Walt Wolfram, and Nanjo Dube. *Variation and Change in Geographically Isolated Communities: Appalachian English and Ozark English*. Tuscaloosa: University of Alabama Press, 1988.

Dakin, Robert F. "South Midland Speech in the Old Northwest." *Journal of English Linguistics* 5 (1971): 31–48.

Dégh, Linda. "Hungarians." In *Peopling Indiana: The Ethnic Experience*, edited by R. M. Taylor and C. A. McBirney, 224–242. Indianapolis: Indiana Historical Society, 1996.

Di Pietro, Robert J. *Language Structures in Contrast*, rev. ed. Rowley, MA: Newbury House, 1978.

Ferguson, Charles A. "Diglossia." *Word* 15 (1959): 325–340.

Fishman, Joshua. *Handbook of Language and Ethnic Identity*. New York: Oxford University Press, 1999.

Flanigan, Beverly Olson. "American Indian English and Error Analysis: The Case of Lakota English." *English World-Wide* 6 (1985): 217–236.

———. "'I Might Could Be Polylectal': Report from the Mid-American Field." *Ohio Uni-*

versity Working Papers in Linguistics and Language Teaching 15 (1996): 103–121. Athens: Department of Linguistics, Ohio University.

———. "Mapping the Ohio Valley: South Midland, Lower North, or Appalachian?" *American Speech* 75 (2000): 344–347.

Flanigan, Beverly Olson, and Franklin Paul Norris. "Cross-Dialectal Comprehension as Evidence for Boundary Mapping: Perceptions of the Speech of Southeastern Ohio." *Language Variation and Change* 12 (2000): 175–201.

Fought, Carmen. *Chicano English in Context*. New York: Palgrave Macmillan, 2003.

Goddard, Ives, ed. *Handbook of North American Indians*. Vol. 17: *Languages*. Washington, DC: Smithsonian Institution Press, 1996.

Greppin, John A. C. "Armenian in Cleveland." Paper presented at the State Linguistic Profiles Conference, Columbus, OH, May 2001.

Hankey, Clyde T. "Notes on West Penn-Ohio Phonology." In *Studies in Linguistics in Honor of Raven I. McDavid, Jr.*, edited by Lawrence M. Davis, 49–61. Tuscaloosa: University of Alabama Press, 1972.

Haugen, Einar. *Bilingualism in the Americas*. Publication of the American Dialect Society 26. University: University of Alabama Press, 1956.

———. *The Norwegian Language in America: A Study in Bilingual Behavior*. 2nd ed. Bloomington: Indiana University Press, 1969.

Hirvonen, Pekka. "Finnish in the Upper Midwest." Paper presented at the State Linguistic Profiles Conference, Columbus, OH, May 2001.

Joiner, Judge Charles W. *The Ann Arbor Decision: Memorandum Opinion and Order and the Educational Plan*. Arlington, VA: Center for Applied Linguistics, 1980.

Keiser, Steve Hartman. "Research Findings on Deitsch (Pennsylvania German) in Ohio." Paper presented at the State Linguistic Profiles Conference, Columbus, OH, May 2001.

Kerek, Andrew. "Hunglish in Ohio." *The New Hungarian Quarterly* 33 (1992): 140–143.

Kontra, Miklós. "Hungarian(s) in the Midwest: Select Bibliography." Paper presented at the State Linguistic Profiles Conference, Columbus, OH, May 2001.

Kretzschmar, William A., Virginia G. McDavid, Theodore K. Lerud, and Ellen Johnson, eds. *Handbook of the Linguistic Atlas of the Middle and South Atlantic States*. Chicago: University of Chicago Press, 1994.

Kurath, Hans. *Studies in Area Linguistics*. Bloomington: Indiana University Press, 1972.

———, ed. *Linguistic Atlas of New England*. 3 vols. Providence, RI: Brown University Press, 1939–1943.

Kurath, Hans, and Raven I. McDavid, Jr. *The Pronunciation of English in the Atlantic States*. Ann Arbor: University of Michigan Press, 1961.

Labov, William. *Language in the Inner City*. Philadelphia: University of Pennsylvania Press, 1972.

———. *The Study of Nonstandard English*. Champaign, IL: NCTE, 1970.

———. "The Three Dialects of English." In *New Ways of Analyzing Sound Change*, edited by Penelope Eckert, 1–44. New York: Academic Press, 1991.

———. "The Triumph of the Southern Shift." Paper presented at the Southeastern Conference on Linguistics, Norfolk, VA, April 1999.

Labov, William, and Bettina Baker. Individualized Reading Program, University of Pennsylvania. Available at: www.ling.upenn.edu/~wlabov/UMRP/UMRP.html.

Labov, William, Sharon Ash, and Charles Boberg. *Phonological Atlas of North American English*. New York: Mouton de Gruyter, forthcoming. (Preview available at: www.ling.upenn.edu/phono_atlas/home.html.)

Lance, Donald M. "The Pronunciation of *Missouri*: Variation and Change in American English." *American Speech* 78 (2003): 255–284.

Linguistic Society of America. "Resolution on Ebonics, 1997." Available at: www.lsadc.org/ebonics.htm.

McDavid, Raven I., and Virginia G. McDavid. "Grammatical Differences in the North Central States." *American Speech* 35 (1960): 5–19.

Morgan, Terrell A. "Field Report on Spanish in Ohio." Paper presented at the State Linguistic Profiles Conference, Columbus, OH, May 2001.

Nichols, John D. "The Indigenous Languages of the Midwest." Paper presented at the State Linguistic Profiles Conference, Columbus, OH, May 2001.

Pappas, Panayiotis A. "Greek in Columbus." Paper presented at the State Linguistic Profiles Conference, Columbus, OH, May 2001.

Pederson, Lee. *Linguistic Atlas of the Gulf States*. 7 vols. Athens, University of Georgia Press, 1986–1992.

Plichta, Bartek. "Aspect in American Polish." Paper presented at the State Linguistic Profiles Conference, Columbus, OH, May 2001.

Ramos-Pellicia, Michelle. "Spanish Phonology of Lorain, Ohio." Paper presented at the State Linguistic Profiles Conference, Columbus, OH, May 2001.

Ratcliff, Martha. "Southeast Asian Languages in the Midwest." Paper presented at the State Linguistic Profiles Conference, Columbus, OH, May 2001.

Rouchdy, Aleya. "Arabic in the Midwest." Paper presented at the State Linguistic Profiles Conference, Columbus, OH, May 2001.

Schaengold, Charlotte. "Yiddish in Cincinnati." Paper presented at the State Linguistic Profiles Conference, Columbus, OH, May 2001.

Shuman, Amy, and Norma Mendoza-Denton. "On Language, Ethnicity, Heritage, and Identity." Paper presented at the State Linguistic Profiles Conference, Columbus, OH, May 2001.

Shuy, Roger W. *Discovering American Dialects*. Champaign, IL: National Council of Teachers of English, 1967.

Thomas, Erik R. "Vowel Changes in Columbus, Ohio." *Journal of English Linguistics* 22 (1993): 205–215.

Trudgill, Peter. *On Dialect: Social and Geographical Perspectives*. New York: New York University Press, 1983.

U.S. Bureau of the Census. Available at www.factfinder.census.gov/home/saff/main.html.

Van Marle, Jaap. "On the Divergence and Maintenance of Immigrant Languages: Dutch in Michigan." Paper presented at the State Linguistic Profiles Conference, Columbus, OH, May 2001.

Veltman, Calvin J. *Language Shift in the United States*. New York: Mouton, 1983.

Wolfram, Walt, and Natalie Schilling-Estes. *American English: Dialects and Variation*. London: Blackwell, 1998.

Fiction

Eggleston, Edward. *The Hoosier Schoolmaster*. New York: O. Judd, 1871. Nineteenth-century Indiana speech.

Morrison, Toni. *Beloved: A Novel*. New York: Knopf, 1987. African American English portrayed by an Ohio-born author.

Rolvaag, Ole E. *Giants in the Earth*. New York: Harper, 1929. Norwegian American life on the midwestern prairie.

Twain, Mark. *The Adventures of Huckleberry Finn*. New York: Charles L. Webster and Co., 1885. Authentic Missouri and Mississippi/Ohio Valley speech.

Videos/Films

American Tongues. Produced and directed by Louis Alvarez and Andrew Kolker. 45 and 56 min., videocassette and 12-page print guide. New York: Center for New American Media, 1986. The best video introduction to American dialects; expurgated and full versions.

Barbershop. Directed by Tim Story, 2000. 102 min., DVD. MGM Home Entertainment, 2003. Vernacular African American English-speaking community on Chicago's South Side.

Barbershop 2: Back in Business. Directed by Tim Story, 2004. 106 min., DVD. MGM Home Entertainment, 2004. Sequel to *Barbershop*.

The Business of Fancydancing. Directed by Sherman Alexie, 2003. 103 min., DVD. Wellspring Media, 2003. Authentic representation of the prosodic and intonational English speech of young "Rez" Indians.

Dances with Wolves. Directed by Kevin Costner, 1990. 181 min., videocassette. Orion Home Video, 1991. 236 min., 2 DVDs. MGM Home Entertainment, 2003. Extensive Sioux dialogue in the Lakota dialect, related to the Dakota dialect of Minnesota and Wisconsin.

The Emigrants. Directed by Jan Troell, 1971. 151 min., videocassette. Svensk Filmindustri. Warner Home Video, 1994. Swedish production based on the novel by Vilhelm Moberg; dubbed into English but retains the intonational contours of the translated Swedish.

Escanaba in da Moonlight. Directed by Jeff Daniels, 2000. 92 min., videocassette and DVD. Monarch Home Video, 2002. Authentic "Yooper" speech of Michigan's Upper Peninsula.

Fargo. Produced by Ethan Coen, 1996. 98 min., videocassette and DVD. Upper Midwest/Minnesota Norwegian-influenced speech.

The New Land. Directed by Jan Troell, 1972. 159 min., videocassette. Svensk Filmindustri. Warner Home Video, 1994. Swedish production based on the novel by Vilhelm Moberg; dubbed into English but retains the intonational contours of the translated Swedish.

NYPD Blue, Season 1. An ABC-TV Production, 1993. 1078 min., 6 DVDs. Twentieth Century Fox Home Entertainment, 2003. The supposedly New York cop Andy Sipowicz in this TV series is played by Chicagoan Dennis Franz, whose speech reflects the Northern Cities Vowel Shift.

Polish Wedding. Directed by Theresa Connelly, 1998. 107 min., videocassette and DVD. Twentieth Century Fox Home Entertainment, 1998. Comedy set in Polish American Detroit.

Web Sites

Center for Applied Linguistics.
www.cal.org/twi/FAQ.htm

Linguistic Society of America. "Resolution on Ebonics, 1997."
www.lsadc.org/ebonics.htm

Position paper on the Ebonics, or Black English, controversy, by the largest professional organization of linguists; includes bibliography.

Talk of the Nation series. Produced by National Public Radio, 1999.
www.npr.org/features/feature.php?wfId=1002839

Segments include interviews with William Labov, Walt Wolfram, Penny Eckert, Allan Metcalf, and others on language and dialect variation.

Organizations

American Dialect Society
c/o Duke University Press
Durham, NC 27708
(919) 687-3602
www.americandialect.org

Linguistic Society of America
1325 18th Street, NW
#211
Archibald A. Hill Suite
Washington, DC 20036-6501
(202) 835-1714
www.lsadc.org

Raven I. and Virginia G. McDavid Collection
Robert E. and Jean R. Mahn Center for Special Collections
Alden Library
Ohio University
Athens, OH
(740) 593-2710
www.library.ohiou.edu/libinfo/depts/archives/index.htm

Language data for Michigan, Ohio, Indiana, Illinois, Wisconsin, Kentucky, and Ontario. Includes two smaller collections: (1) data donated by Timothy C. Frazer and Roger W. Shuy on Illinois and Michigan; and (2) data analyses by Robert F. Dakin for *The Dialect Vocabulary of the Ohio River Valley*, 3 vols. (Ph.D. diss., University of Michgan, 1966).

LITERATURE

*Joseph P. Bernt,
Joseph Csicsila,
Patrick S. Washburn,
and Edward S. Watts*

In 1925, in the first comprehensive history of books in the early Midwest, Ralph Leslie Rusk wrote of the dominance of England and the eastern states in the region formerly called the "West": "Nowhere was the exchange more uneven than in literature. There, the whole force of a tradition centuries old bore in one direction. Notwithstanding occasional protestations of sectional loyalty, western writers kept their faces turned toward the East and toward England."[1] Rusk's title, *The Literature of the Middle Western Frontier*, implies that, after 1840, the "frontier" had moved out of the Ohio Valley, affirming the westward-moving frontier thesis advanced by Hector St. John de Crèvecoeur (1735–1813) in 1786, Frederick Jackson Turner (1861–1932) in 1893, and R.W.B. Lewis in 1961.

As it moved, however, the "settlement" left in the frontier's wake began to protest eastern and English cultural dominance more than only "occasionally."[2] Furthermore, westerners' claims were not "sectional"—defined as in opposition to the national culture, like the Confederacy—but rather "regional"—cognizant of *both* the area's place-specific difference *and* its entanglement in the nation. In fact, midwestern literature dates from the sense of alienation and ambivalence generated between 1833 and 1860, which might be called the colonial period of the Midwest. By "colonial," we mean that this period was defined by a combination of external cultural coercion, local imitativeness, and the simultaneous effort to escape the narrow options of assimilation or resistance. The later midwestern regionalist Hamlin Garland (1860–1940) called all American literature before 1860 "colonial," and we use the term in the same way.[3] Because the "force of tradition" is often less overbearing in nonliterary forms, much of the best colonial midwestern writing appeared in genres that were not generally considered creative and as such will occupy the beginning of the current chapter.

As Rusk notes, however, around 1840 a transition occurred in midwestern writing as the region shifted from frontier to settlement. After 1840, writers and other cultural spokesmen and women, especially those who gravitated to Cincinnati, more often attempted to transcend mere geographic distance to define "local" writing. In the process, they tried to develop a literature that did more than extend or transfer to the Midwest the language, images, and forms established in the East and England, resulting in what might be called "Literature in the Midwest." On the contrary, they hoped to create a literature that reflected the experiences, languages, demographics, memories, and hopes specific to the growing and changing region, creating a true "Midwestern Literature" in the period before the Civil War.

These cultural conditions also led publishing companies in the Midwest to pioneer new forms of newspaper and magazine journalism, which today reach a large national audience. Currently, despite the concentration of American papers in New York and Los Angeles, nineteen of the hundred largest circulation daily newspapers in the United States are located in the Midwest, six in Ohio alone; and the eight states in the region are home to nearly 600 consumer and more than a thousand specialized business magazines attesting to the Midwest's commercial traditions. Among publishers and editors especially responsible for the development and the innovation of midwestern journalism were Robert Abbott, Gardner Cowles, Jr., Wilford Fawcett, Hugh Hefner, John H. Johnson, Gertrude Battles Lane, Robert McCormick, Joseph Medill, Edwin T. Meredith, and E. W. Scripps. In the Midwest, newspapers emerged to serve a wide range of readers (black and white, English speaking and polyglot), most notably abolitionists, pro-slavery northerners, social progressives, and isolationists opposed to U.S. involvement in World War II. Magazines in the region range from national consumer titles with multimillion circulations; to niche magazines for snowmobiling, knitting, automobile collecting, vegetarians, and E-Bay collectors; to trade magazines for restaurant managers, quarry operators, alcohol distributors, and machine shop owners; to agricultural titles for fruit growers and beekeepers. This rich journalistic history in the Midwest began with newspapers well before the Civil War.

Since the Civil War, the Midwest, more than any other geographical region of the United States, has shaped and defined the character of American literary art yet it has continued to struggle in some sense for a distinct identity altogether independent of the other major literary regions of the United States. Large portions of the Midwest's geographical territory are variously ascribed to the East, South, and West in literary histories and anthologies as often as the origins of its greatest writers are forgotten. Yet despite such historical impediments, the Midwest enjoys a long and varied tradition in American literature and a claim to more than its fair share of America's most celebrated literary figures.

For example, the Midwest's long history as a setting in American fiction, which began with the nation's earliest writers of note, including James Fenimore Cooper and Washington Irving, extends to the most contemporary authors, such as Charles Johnson and Sandra Cisneros. In these works, the Midwest provides an ideological space for the presentation of distinctly American themes: community, identity, self-fulfillment, race. The Midwest also possesses a rich tradition for technical and linguistic experimentation in American literature. In fact, many of the literary artists who have been credited with fundamentally shaping the appearance and character of American writing, such as Mark Twain, Paul Laurence Dunbar, Sherwood Anderson, Toni Morrison, and David Mamet, are from the Midwest. Add to all of this the long list of acclaimed writers who call it home, including half of the American authors awarded the Nobel Prize for Literature in the twentieth century, and the Midwest enjoys arguably the most enviable legacy in all of American literature.

MIDWESTERN LITERATURE BEFORE 1860

In 1836, the Cincinnati-based editor, poet, and abolitionist William Davis Gallagher (1808–1894) wrote of the inability of western writers and journals to maintain themselves financially because of eastern literary dominance:

> The conclusion, then, is that the familiarity of western men with grand subjects of composition, breeds contempt therefor; that stranger and distant persons write about them better, their ignorance of the subject giving an originality to their statements, quite novel and pleasing; and finally, that the people of the West acquiesce in and encourage the state of things brought about by this faith, by neglecting western literary enterprizes, and giving their money for the periodicals and papers of the east.[4]

Although Rusk is correct in noting a change in regional identity after 1840, Dr. Daniel Drake's broadsides of 1833 and 1834 began the process and Gallagher echoed his sentiments.[5] Drake (1785–1852), alarmed in 1832 by both the Nullification Crisis and the Black Hawk War, perceived the nation dividing into the polarized sections of North and South. He saw in each designs to dominate the "West," as the Midwest was then known, and demanded that it resist attaching itself to either. Only strong regional culture and confident literary self-assertion, Drake and his companions argued, could offset the destructive northern and southern efforts to claim the mantle of national representativeness.

Regionalism—unlike both sectionalism and nationalism—is less monolithic and grandiose, and therefore a bad fit for "the grand subjects of composition." Life in the settlements often was hardly a "grand subject." Moreover, when a "grand subject"—such as Indian Removal or Wars of Conquest—presented itself, westerners were more likely to regard it as destructive embarrassment than as the stuff of epic literature. Yet eastern writers persisted in imposing epic-sized narratives on western experience in texts in which westerners themselves saw very little of their own lives. For example, while William Cullen Bryant (1794–1878) could imagine centuries of midwestern history in a brief poem, Cincinnati poet Charles Jones (1815?–1851) could offer a more immediate meditation on the haunting presence of Indian mounds as towns were growing around them. Midwestern writing, then, began as a series of intertextual responses to inaccurate images imposed from other places.

Midwestern writers resisted the images imposed on their region. Eighteenth- and early nineteenth-century eastern writing usually portrayed it as a safety zone—having been spared the violence of the Revolution and the turbulence of early Republic politics, with "no inveterate systems to overcome," in the terms of the Rev. Manasseh Cutler (1742–1823), spokesman for the Ohio Company.[6] Midwesterners knew that their home shared little with the *tabula rasa* of Enlightenment fantasy and began writing to correct this misrepresentation. However, because their views often ran counter to popular literary conventions, it was difficult for young writers to find publishers willing to invest in book-length publications. Many of the texts studied in this section first appeared in western periodicals, most of them destined for bankruptcy within a few years. This can be seen in each of the antebellum genres addressed in this chapter. Their efforts to distinguish midwestern literature characterize the region's effort to resist absorption into what James Hall (1793–1868) called "the universal Yankee nation."

Travel Writing and Ethnography

Beginning in the mid-seventeenth century, the Midwest was first described in print by French and Spanish explorers. For the entire two hundred years covered here, Europeans continued to travel through the region and write about it. Often, their observations of both the indigenous populations and the white settlers influenced the developing fields of ethnography and sociology. Early visitors from Europe include Captaine Jean Bernard Bossu (1720–1792), Louis Hennepin (ca. 1650–1690), Thomas Pownall (1722–1805), and Charles Johnston (1719–1800); in the nineteenth century, Charles Dickens (1812–1870), Harriet Martineau (1802–1876), Frances Trollope (1780–1863), Alexis de Tocqueville (1805–1859), and others. Notable eastern Americans include George Catlin (1796–1872), Henry Rowe Schoolcraft (1793–1864), Jedediah Morse (1761–1826), Margaret Fuller (1810–1850) and Charles Fenno Hoffman (1806–1884), not to mention innumerable missionaries and speculators, many of whom published their stories. Eastern and European travelers, especially prior to the Revolutions of 1848, were decidedly interested in the region's experiments in combining commercial capitalism with democratic politics. Usually they were disappointed: when they found the frontier to be a much messier place than they had hoped, they faulted the new community, not the unrealistic Enlightenment ideals they brought with them. Nonetheless, the hope that the Midwest was a *tabula rasa* upon which rational dreams of restarting human history often informed the perspectives of both European and Eastern travelers. A number of idealists, from Robert Owen (1771–1858) to the British Chartists, traveled to the Midwest and published their accounts as "Letters," a common label for travel writing.

Of European travelers to the Midwest, Charles Dickens is perhaps the most famous. As did Trollope and Tocqueville, Dickens concentrated on Cincinnati when he published *American Notes* (1842). Largely responsible for the image of the primary city of the Old Northwest as "Porkopolis," Dickens was appalled at the young city's filth, noise, and lack of what he considered culture. Although Trollope and Tocqueville were both more encouraged by the spirit of democracy afoot, they shared Dickens' notion that Cincinnati was far behind the East, not to mention Europe. Other Europeans were not so eager to leave. Of these, Morris Birkbeck (1764–1825), founder of the English Colony in Illinois—an early experiment with cooperative settlement—particularly stands out. His *Letters from Illinois* (1818) is notable for its realistic description of the Illinois frontier in the decades prior to Indian Removal.

Among easterners, Schoolcraft stands out. His travel writing, along with the massive *Algic Researches* (1839), by sheer bulk nearly offset the racist baggage he bore: he constantly worked to ferret out the Christian underpinnings of Ojibwe culture, setting the tone for the Eurocentric basis of professional anthropology.[7] On the other hand, Timothy Flint's *Recollections of the Last Ten Years* (1826) is at once more typical and more intriguing for its role in separating a midwestern perspective from eastern views. Flint (1780–1840) came west as a missionary in 1815. Like both Joseph Badger (1757–1846) and James Handasyd Perkins (1810–1849), who also describe the Midwest as anything but a *tabula rasa*, Flint traveled broadly through Ohio, Indiana, Illinois, and Missouri and met a vast array of peoples. Flint (whose fiction and history-writing are discussed below) described a region often at odds with itself, as expectations diverged from reality and as a diverse group of immigrants brought with them their own religions, traditions, and languages. Most telling is the book's concluding section, written as Flint returned to Massachusetts to meet with publishers, where he documents the divergence of East and West.

The most important travel book written by a westerner is Henry Marie Brackenridge's *Views of Louisiana* (1814). The oldest son of Hugh Henry Brackenridge (1748–1816), the multilingual and cosmopolitan Henry Marie (1786–1871) produced an intriguing account of a journey to the far western settlements along the Missouri River. His extensive commentary on the rich riverine environment of the "American Bottom" includes a detailed description of the mounds at Cahokia, Illinois. Equally interesting are the eight editions of Zadok Cramer's (1773–1813) *The Navigator* (1801–1815). Although the book served initially as a guide for settlers navigating their flatboats down the Ohio, it became far more, especially in its appendices and addenda, growing into a fragmented, uneven, energetic, and curious book that, appropriately enough, seems precisely suited to the complex communities it describes.

The study of American travel writing has come to be viewed as providing an important barometer of national attitudes toward a great number of subjects.[8] Travel writing about and from the antebellum Midwest also testifies to the region's diversity and to the conflicts central to the establishment of regional identity. Furthermore, its ubiquitous consumption by readers on both sides of the Atlantic Ocean as well as both sides of the Appalachian Mountains suggests that the region was first encountered in ways that foretold its coming role as both prospective paradise and troubled colony.

Captivity Narratives

Often the first writing from the midwestern frontier was in the form of a narrative of Indian captivity. Recently, scholars such as June Namias, Michelle Burnham, and Christopher Castiglia have established the centrality of this genre to the origins of American literature in general, and this was certainly true of midwestern writing as well.[9] In the two-volume *Selections of Indian Captivity* (1811), Archibald Loudon (1754–1840) collected a vast number of these, focusing especially on the Indian Wars of the 1790s, but extending back to the French and Indian War. In the "contact zone" of the frontier, the midwestern captivity narrative articulates the many layers of destabilization intrinsic to life in the colonies. The most important of these is John Tanner's *A Narrative of the Captivity and Adventures* (1828), a book lauded by the editor and author Benjamin Drake in Cincinnati. The book tells the story of how Tanner (1780–1847?), captured as a boy in southern Ohio, spent the majority of his adult life as a fully acculturated Ojibwa working in the northern Great Lakes region. Tanner's account, though transcribed by Edwin James, Schoolcraft's chaplain, is considered authentic by most modern scholars and, as such, a strikingly rich source for understanding the northern frontier.

Loudon's collection, like John McClung's (1804–1859) *Sketches of Western Adventure* (1832), is far more typical than Tanner's, because the stories they recreate are *not* captivity narratives in the strictest sense. Both are full of the captivities of soldiers and others associated with the military during the "Indian" wars: POWs were far more common than long-term residential tribal adoptees. The focus of POW narratives is too often on the details of torture, cannibalism, resistance, and escape. Aside from Tanner, Mary Jemison (1743–1812), James Smith (1737–1812), and Daniel Boone (1734–1820)—all of whom spent time as captives in what is now eastern Ohio—and many others contributed narratives that tell of acculturation and adaptation on the western frontier. As early as the eighteenth century, no lesser figures than Cadwallader Colden (1688–1766) and Benjamin Franklin (1706–1790) were astonished by the realization that most white captives preferred native life to reentry into Anglo-America. The narratives dictated by various captives bear out this unexpected phenomenon.[10]

Nonetheless, the sensationalism of "captivity" (more precisely of captivity without acculturation) served as a narrative foundation for much of the literature—fictional or otherwise—that found the broadest readership east of the Appalachians.

Biography and Autobiography

Especially among writers in and around Cincinnati, it became imperative to create a pantheon of western heroes whose greatness would lend grandeur to regional culture. In the East, many of the best-selling books were the biographies, memoirs, and autobiographies of prominent leaders of the Revolutionary era—Weems' biography of George Washington, for instance. Moreover, the political biography was central to any electoral campaign. On both accounts, westerners found the path to legitimacy through mimicry. Biographies of Daniel Boone were ubiquitous, the best being Timothy Flint's *Biographical Memoir of Daniel Boone, the First White Settler of Kentucky* (1833). Similarly, William Henry Harrison's presidential campaigns of 1836 and 1840 generated a slew of books. Along more regionalist lines, Benjamin Drake's two Indian biographies—*The Life and Adventures of Black Hawk* (1838) and *Life of Tecumseh* (1841)—offer devastating critiques of American policy and activities with regard to Native Americans. As such, they go beyond mimicry such as Flint's and move toward a more localized way of thinking about the region and its peoples: Drake (1794–1841) included Indian, settler, immigrant, *and* eastern voices in his compilation of evidence.

Black Hawk (1767–1838) himself was the subject of the most important autobiography as well. His autobiography, *Life of Ma-ka-tai-me-she-kia-kiak, or Black Hawk*—as translated and transcribed by Antoine Le Claire (b. 1797) and published by John Patterson (1805–1890) in 1833 (as opposed to the later editions that Patterson corrupted)—stands as a strikingly original text. Most scholars agree that Black Hawk's voice, despite his illiteracy and unfamiliarity with the conventions of life-writing, emerges as authentic, a tribute to Le Claire's skills. Typically, however, Le Claire, a mixed-blood, was removed with Black Hawk west of the Mississippi and later settled in Davenport, Iowa. The book itself ranges into auto-ethnology, testimony concerning the war, treaty history, and personal narrative of a man whose intra- and interracial experiences brought him into contact with Spanish, French, British, and American colonial presences. Le Claire also describes contact and combat with the Sioux, Shawnee, Ojibwe, and dozens of other tribal groups. The book therefore reflects the region's striking instability, an instability that destabilizes our concept of the "indigenous." For example, Black Hawk opens by noting that his grandfather was born in lower Canada and came west with the Sauk to Illinois, where they defeated the Kaskaskias. That is, while the Sauk were indigenous to North America, they were not native to the Mississippi Valley.

Establishing indigeneity was a central theme in white autobiography as well. Daniel Drake's *Pioneer Life in Kentucky* (1848; rpt. 1870) articulates the standard narrative of western boyhood—"growing up with the country." The themes of local knowledge, community-building, friendship with fading natives, and familiarity with nature are all there, and all for the purpose of imagining such whites as the natural heirs to the land. These books, located somewhere between memoir and autobiography, were doubtless the foundation of the postbellum emergence of the "frontier childhood" genre practiced by Ohio's William Dean Howells (1837–1920), Missouri's Mark Twain (1835–1910), and many others.

Local History and Culture

Starting with the Whiskey Rebellion (1794), "westerners" were aware of their misrepresentation in the national story and undertook to correct such false images by calling for self-consciously local textuality. For most of the era in question, Pittsburgh, at the head of the west-flowing Ohio River, was considered "western" in the days before rail and steam when "drainage was destiny," as were northern sections of Kentucky. In William Findley's (1751–1821) *History of the Insurrection* (1795) and Hugh Henry Brackenridge's *Incidents of the Insurrection* (1796), the authors responded in official reports on the Rebellion to representations of themselves and their neighbors as illiterate, ignorant semi-savages. They wisely perceived that the interregional causes of the Rebellion itself were connected to the eastern dominance of the nation's print culture. The same patterns of misrepresentation and resistance characterize the writing generated by the War of 1812 and the Black Hawk War. Kentucky's Robert Breckenridge McAfee (1784–1849) in *A History of the War in the West* (1815) and Cincinnati's Isaac Galland's (1790–1858) *Chronicles of the North American Savages* (1835) represent important attempts to distinguish a local perspective that was often at odds with American history as written east of the mountains.

Starting in the 1830s, local historians began producing self-consciously regional histories of their states and of the Old Northwest. Salmon P. Chase's (1808–1873) *A Sketch of the History of Ohio* (1832), Caleb Atwater's (1778–1867) *A History of the State of Ohio* (1838), James H. Lanman's (1812–1887) *History of Michigan* (1839), John B. Dillon's (1808–1879) *A History of Indiana* (1859), and, in Illinois, two separate *Histories of Illinois* by former governors John Reynolds (1789–1865; 1844) and Thomas Ford (1800–1850; 1854) set a standard for engaging narrative historiography. Moreover, their common motivation always seems entangled in ongoing political issues. For example, Chase's later involvement with abolitionism is foreshadowed by his early efforts to distinguish free Ohio from slaveholding Kentucky, a conflation typical in eastern representations of the "West." More important, historians also became interested in regional self-definition—set against the polarization of North and South—demonstrating the first local efforts to distinguish the Midwest from other regions. Among these works, Flint's *The History and Geography of the Mississippi Valley* (1833), A. M. Hart's (1814–1879) *History of the Mississippi* (1853), and A. W. Patterson's (c. 1840–1880) *History of the Backwoods* (1843) best show how midwesterners responded to the sectional crisis by taking the middle path. Their interest in place was neither sectionally partisan nor uncritically national. By acknowledging the entanglement of local and national (and immigrant) presences in the region, they resisted the destructive vortex of antebellum antagonism.

One other volume is notable in this category: William Warren's *History of the Ojibway People* (1852; 1888) reflects its author's complex identity. Descended from Ojibwe, French, and British lineages, Warren (1825–1853) wrote a tribal history that became, in a sense, a history of the many peoples of the upper Mississippi Valley, especially Wisconsin, Minnesota, and the Upper Peninsula of Michigan. Warren's lucid style and candid approach make it an especially accomplished work. Unfortunately, Warren, just twenty-eight years of age, died from tuberculosis before seeing the book to press, and so his plans for future books on the Ojibwe died with him. Nonetheless, his efforts to merge regional and racial history stand, with Tanner's and Drake's books as the most important efforts not only to establish a history of midwestern subjects, but also to find a regionally appropriate means of writing local history.

Creative Writing

In fact, this mixed method informs William H. Venable's (1836–1920) *The Beginnings of Literary Culture in the Ohio Valley* (1891), a singularly important work. Venable's mixture of history, criticism, and biography seems uniquely suited to the shape-shifting development of his subject. Nonetheless, as Venable documents, Cincinnati was the center of midwestern literary activity during this era. Although other midwestern locales produced the occasional author or journal, most of these eventually found their way to Cincinnati. Lexington, Louisville, Columbus, and Detroit all fall into this category. Only St. Louis, and the writers surrounding the weekly *Reveille* (John Robb [1813?–1856] and Joseph [1802–1882] and Matthew Field [1812–1844]), sustained literary activity. However, their work was deliberately southern, striking a kinship with the humorists of the Old Southwest. Furthermore, while the stage was very active, very few antebellum plays by midwesterners have survived and so will not be addressed here. Neither Venable, Rusk, nor Watts found any locally penned drama worthy of notice.[11] As to the healthier market in midwestern fiction, local novels also struggled with finding a voice. Short stories, however, generally fared better. Poetry was the most successful form of early midwestern creative writing.

Usually in settlement colonies, two genres, distinguished by the gender of the targeted readers, are imported from the metropolis: the adventure tale and the settlement narrative. The male-based adventure stresses conquest, racial conflict, and, of course, triumph, although it often betrays a measured ambivalence—the marginality of James Fenimore Cooper's (1789–1851) Natty Bumppo of the Leatherstocking novels, for example. Targeting female readers, the settlement narrative takes up where the adventure tale ends and chronicles the complex processes of home- and community-building. Each, however, is highly episodic, and, in the episodes, each often borrows from the other (mini-adventures in settlement narratives and vice versa), but the distinction is still useful and revealing. In midwestern writing, the adventure template was Cooper's Leatherstocking novels and the settlement template was Caroline Kirkland's (1801–1864) *A New Home—Who'll Follow* (1838), set on the Michigan frontier. Starting from these, midwestern writers moved from imitation toward originality. However, this achievement occurred almost exclusively in short fiction, while the novels rarely transcended generic conventions.

Adventure Tales

Most midwestern literary histories begin with Hugh Henry Brackenridge's *Modern Chivalry* (1792–1815), an American frontier version of *Don Quixote*. Brackenridge, a Pennsylvanian mentioned above for his writings on the Whiskey Rebellion, is viewed as the author of the first midwestern novel, an argument made by Daniel Drake in 1833 and William T. Coggeshall (1824–1867) in 1860. A few other fictional representations appeared before 1820; however, like *Modern Chivalry*, they were mostly in the satirical pre-Romantic vein. After Cooper popularized frontier-based fiction, writers such as William Snelling (1804–1848), Robert Montgomery Bird (1806–1854), and Chandler Robbins Gilman (1802–1865) capitalized on the interest in "adventures" set in the Midwest. Midwestern writers followed this trend as well. From Cincinnati publishers came a torrent of such narratives: James Hall's *The Harpe's Head* (1833), Edmund Flagg's (1815–1890) *Francis of Valois* (1843), Thomas H. Shreve's (1808–1853) *Drayton* (1851), and Timothy Flint's *Francis Berrian* (1826), *George Mason* (1829), and *The Shoshone Valley* (1830) offer similar variations on the Cooperian narrative. While the Cooperian narrative certainly thrived in the colonial setting, its interest is intrinsically extra-local: the adventure narrative purges the frontier of its unassimilable elements and sanitizes the space of future white settlement.

Only in short fiction did many of these same writers break from the adventure tale's assumption that the violence of the conquest period had in fact sanitized the region. The recalcitrant backwoodsmen, French settlers, mixed-race figures, and unredeemed captives of short narratives remain and complicate the smooth ascendance of white commercial society. For example, Hall's short fiction exemplifies the venture into less stable terrain. His most famous story, "The Indian Hater" (1828), was rewritten as "The Pioneer" in 1834. Whereas the first emphasized the tragic necessity of frontier violence, it concludes by affirming the ultimate righteousness of white conquest by coloring the pathological Indian-Hater as a mere leftover. However, in "The Pioneer," a far more complex story, Hall introduces French and Indian characters and, in the end, has the Indian-Hater's sister—a captive since a girl and now a squaw and a mother—refuse reentry into the white world. The story ends with the Indian-Hater donning the hair-shirt (literally).

Between 1828 and 1834, Hall had resisted and witnessed the Black Hawk War. Another of that war's critics, and one of Hall's closest friends, Benjamin Drake, collected his stories in *Tales and Sketches from the Queen City* (1838). The pair's resistance, in response to the East's heavy-handed actions, contributed to a midwestern resistance to eastern cultural dominion as well. Later antebellum fiction such as Coggeshall's *Easy Warren and His Contemporaries* (1856) redirected this energy into feminism, temperance, and, most powerfully, abolition. However, by the 1850s, the Cooperian frontier was a distant memory, and the adventure narrative, having served both its purposes, faded. In fact, the most lasting character in midwestern fiction in this vein—Ohioan Edward Judson's (1822–1886) recurring "Ned Buntline" character—satirized the standards of this anachronized form, yet retained huge popularity.

Settlement Narratives

Caroline Kirkland's *A New Home* was based on her brief residence on the Michigan frontier. After she returned to New York, her book found its way back to Pinckney, where her former neighbors were angered by her satirical representation of their slow and absurd ascent toward the national standard of sentimental domesticity. This model of female enclosure was then being propagated by writers like Lydia Sigourney (1791–1865) and Catherine Beecher (1800–1878). Not surprisingly, the book helped Kirkland start the popular magazine *Hearth and Home*, and she became a primary spokeswoman for the cult of female domesticity in Victorian America. Such is the purpose of the settlement narrative in a colonial setting: assimilation and familiarization. Her imitators included, in Illinois, Eliza Farnham (1815–1864) in *Life in Prairie-Land* (1846) and, in Wisconsin and Chicago, Juliette M. Kinzie (1806–1870) in *Wau-Bun* (1856). In both, the eastern woman creates "that home feeling" by training the wives of the settlers in the ways of homemaking and republican motherhood.[12]

In Cincinnati, women writers, ironically, sustained careers by implicitly discouraging other women from doing the same. Maria Collins (ca. 1850), Alice Dumont (1794–1857), E. N. Dupuy (1814–1881), and, especially, Caroline Lee Hentz (1800–1856) all wrote readable novels in this vein. Similarly, male writers Frederick Thomas (1806–1866), George Prentice (1802–1870), and James Handasyd Perkins all produced novels (some only in serialized form) that juxtapose eastern manners and western communities. Among their ascendant eastern values was the removal of women from economic activity outside the home, and marriage too often becomes the culmination of each novel's plot. Nonetheless, the implicit feminism in the definition of republican motherhood suggests a subtle subversiveness in this genre, an ambiguity linked to regional identity by Alice Cary (1820–1871).

Both Cary sisters, Alice and Phoebe (1824–1871) but particularly Alice, manipulated the settlement narrative to challenge the conventions of both region and gender. Although Alice published three collections of her poetry and wrote three novels, only *Married, Not Mated* (1856) comes close to the quality of her short fiction. Her best writing, like Hall's, was her short fiction. In her two Clovernook books (1851 and 1853), Cary assembled stories that had been published initially in both Cincinnati and the East, often in abolitionist journals. Although she is not explicitly abolitionist, her views of gender suggest a parallel liberatory mission through intertextual commentary: young frontier girls brought into contact with the domestic world of the New York women's magazines. The smarter girls, of course, learn not to measure themselves against such inappropriate standards. More often, however, the rhetoric of conformity does more harm than good, and the westerners are made to feel unworthy of inclusion in Victorian America.

Just as Washington Irving's (1783–1848) *Sketch-Book of Geoffrey Crayon* (1819) might express the new nation's relationship to old England by stressing fragmentation and inconsistency, so might we view the prominence of the short story in the relationship of the Midwest to eastern publishing centers. With the short story's emphasis on incompleteness and its unwillingness to strive toward an epic scope, it reflects—on a formal scale—the colonial condition of the region that produced it. By noting both a connection with and a space between local subjects and the textual convention, it strives for a place-specific textuality.

Poetry

Along the same lines, little extended epic or extended verse was published by pre-1860 midwesterners, even though those forms maintained national popularity in poems set in the Midwest but written in the East. In Longfellow's (1807–1882) *Hiawatha* (1855), the setting on the Great Lakes implies a lost epic past—gone long before the arrival of the whites—that serves to legitimize settlement. Similarly, in Walt Whitman's (1819–1892) "Song of Myself" (1855), references to the West reflect the same expansive national vision of simplicity and fecundity that informed the nation's visionary poetry dating back to the Connecticut Wits—David Humphrey's (1752–1818) "Poem on the Happiness of America" or Joel Barlow's (1752–1812) "Vision of Columbus." In either case, the Midwest is a big farm, devoid of history and ripe for the replanting of national dreams and myths. As was the case with fiction, midwestern writers would have an ambivalent relationship to these powerful national images of the region's assigned place in the nation.

Both of these perspectives—and many more—are represented in Coggeshall's massive 1860 collection *The Poets and Poetry of the West*. Professional and comprehensive, Coggeshall collects the work of 152 poets from twelve midwestern states (including Kentucky), and ranges from the obscure (Cincinnati's Salmon P. Chase as a poet?) to the well known (Phoebe Cary and a very young William Dean Howells). The contributors—all of whom are introduced with generous headnotes—range from itinerant laborers to professional men of letters. Generally, however, the poetry can be sorted into two categories: the natural/personal and the public/historical. Although the Midwest produced no Poe or Dickinson with regard to formal experimentation, many proficient antebellum poets were working within established verse-forms with a high degree of competence and, occasionally, with an interest in localizing a poetry suited to the region.

The Natural and the Personal

The most famous poet in this category is fictional and very bad: Mark Twain's Emmeline Grangerford in *Adventures of Huckleberry Finn* (1885). Although Coggeshall's collection reprints some verse by her real-life parallel, Emeline H. Johnson, most of the poetry that uses a midwestern natural setting as a reflection of personal feelings is much better and not quite so morbid. Johnson's popular verse might be represented by the following:

Ah! That dew at dawning day,
From the bough will melt away;
And those stars, which beam so bright,
And that love-inspiring light;
All must vanish with the night,
And flowers will droop and die,
Ere another day glides by;
And those skies so darkly blue,
In an hour will change their hue
Even now these things decay
Where's thy love then?—passed away![13]

Johnson's morbid theme and unmediated use of the sympathetic fallacy make her the poetic equivalent of what Nathaniel Hawthorne called the "scribbling women" who ruled the antebellum literary market. Twain's satire, however, more effectively deflates the bathos of such verse.

Whereas the Midwest was as guilty as any other region in the overpublication of overwrought poetry, some poems rise above the standards of the inherited convention. For example, Frederick Thomas—better known as a novelist—and Julia Dumont provide quite lucid expressions of the link between the tumultuous weather of the Ohio Valley and the extremes of temperament inherent to the romantic perspective. However, each generally works within the conventions of the genre, a telling lack of originality best shown in their use of iambic hexameter couplets, a line well suited to the strictures of the newspaper columns where their poetry often first appeared.

If there is a "lost" poet in this vein, it is Otway Curry (1804–1855). An associate of William Gallagher, Curry ranged quite broadly in subject matter: he could easily link the darker and lighter elements of Romanticism in brief poems on both public and private subjects. "Autumn Musings," "The Eternal River," and "The Lore of the Past" stand out in Coggeshall's collection for their experimental versification. Although Curry worked mostly within the confines of standard diction, he seemed to be reaching for a vernacular versification, swinging between blank verse and rhyming sequences with great ease, especially in "The Lore of the Past." Curry, more than the others, transcended the sympathetic fallacy that characterizes so much mediocre mid-nineteenth-century poetry by moving toward a more naturalistic description of nature's indifference and by seeking to use poetic lines as rough-hewn as the natural setting they mean to describe. His poetry also stands out for his linkage of nature to the political tumult of the times, the subject of the next section.

Historic and Public Poetry

Some of the most effective agitation of the antebellum period was done in public verse. Although a novel by a woman who lived in Cincinnati gets most of the credit (*Uncle Tom's Cabin* by Harriet Beecher Stowe [1811–1896]), on a daily basis Americans in every region were assailed with political arguments set to verse. Some of the best midwestern poetry was written in this propagandistic vein. Earlier, this often had to do with Indian affairs. Charles Jones's eponymous poem of Tecumseh, for example, rejects the "vanishing Indian" convention: "Though not a dirge / Is thine, beside the wailing blast / Thy name and fame can never die / Whom freedom loves will live forever." Written during Indian Removal, Jones's poem aims to use poetry to tell his white readers that Tecumseh's heroism stands in stark contrast to their greedier goals. While Jones indulges the "noble savage" myth, within the context of Removal his voice was confrontational. Other poets similarly mined local history to critique the colonial "imitativeness" that they viewed as dominating too much of the region's economics, politics, and culture.

More often, economic issues, including slavery, were the subject of these poems. William D. Gallagher deserves credit for many things, but his abolitionist and activist poetry is his greatest accomplishment. He might be linked to Whitman in that, while each attempted to merge activist and artistic elements of the medium, Whitman was the radical in terms of form and Gallagher, in politics. For example, in Gallagher's "Radicalos," the title character is an egalitarian avenging angel:

> Where obey the fettered millions;
> Where command the fettering few;
> Where the chain of wrong is forging,
> With its red links hid from view;
> And he standeth by the peasant,
> And standeth by the lord,
> And he shouts, "Your rights are equal!"
> Till earth startles at the word.

Other poems reflect Gallagher's opinions about labor conditions, slavery, and feminism. In his 1841 collection of western poetry, superseded by Coggeshall's in bulk and quality, Gallagher nonetheless focused on other poets interested in the public "work" of verse.

Antebellum midwestern poetry should be remembered more as artifact than as art. However, in an age when each was equally valued, this accomplishment should not be dismissed. The best poetry mixed form and function to serve two purposes: first to make midwestern readers aware that good poetry need not come from Boston; and, second, to affirm that the local issues of their lives could resonate with the grandeur lent by poetic endeavor.

In 1859, William Turner Coggeshall stated more explicitly the regionalism behind his work as an editor. In "The Protective Policy in Literature," he excoriated the eastern literary establishment's efforts to exclude western writers as it defined "American Literature" as a significant subject for scholarly attention. To overcome this prejudice, Coggeshall recognized that the colonial midwesterners must decolonize themselves in a way that would reflect the motivation of the best writing described above: "The people of the West will win scornful censure, unless they encourage, with pen and purse, with good will and good words, instrumentalities which are competant to individualize a Western Literature. . . . To learn that it is nobler to develop new thought than to circulate old; that the capacity to produce is grander than that which enjoys."

NEWSPAPERS AND MAGAZINES IN THE MIDWEST

The decolonization advocated by Coggeshall was actually accomplished by editors in newspapers and magazines. On June 10, 1847, J.K.C. Forrest, James J. Kelly, and John E. Wheeler published the first issue of the *Chicago Tribune* on a hand press, printing 400 copies, hardly a notable beginning. The entire newspaper, from the newsroom to the composing room, was located in only one room, and two of the three owners quickly left the business. Yet, over the next century, the *Tribune* established itself as not only the most significant paper in the Midwest but also one of the most important in the United States; editors Joseph Medill (1823–1899) and Robert McCormick (1880–1955) drove the paper passionately and left an indelible stamp on American journalism. But while the *Tribune* occupied center stage in the Midwest after its founding, other papers also were important, ranging from abolitionist publications to black newspapers. Giants such as Edward Wyllis Scripps (1854–1926) and Joseph Pulitzer (1847–1911) also commanded attention, as they should have, outside of Chicago. It was an eclectic mix that resulted in a powerful press.

American newspapers existed long before the Midwest was settled as the frontier rolled west. As settlers streamed into the Midwest in the late 1700s and early 1800s, many of them in covered wagons, they brought not only plows but also hand-operated printing presses, which they quickly used to start newspapers. Many of these papers appeared in towns along waterways because these were the important "highways" on the frontier, and nearby communities became trading centers and markets as well as social gathering places for their regions. The Ohio River was the major source of commerce in the early Midwest, but early publishers also moved their wares along the Wabash, Muskingum, Scioto, Maumee, Cuyahoga, and Mississippi rivers.

Thus, it was no surprise that the first newspaper in the Midwest may have been in an Ohio River town, Cincinnati, where the *Centinel of the North-Western Territory* began publishing in 1793, only six years after the Northwest Territory had been approved by Congress. Other early papers, also along water routes, were the *Indiana Gazette* in Vincennes in 1804 and the *Missouri Gazette* in St. Louis in 1808. Subscribers frequently paid editors in flour, beef, pork, or corn.

As historian William E. Huntzicker has noted, the editors of these early papers had much to gain in rising income and expanded influence from making their papers a success. And as towns prospered, the number of newspapers increased dramatically. A St. Louis paper exclaimed in 1829 that frontier papers were becoming as "thick as blackberries in the spring," which was clearly evident a year later in Cincinnati, where there were seven weekly newspapers and two dailies.[14] As newspapers blossomed all over the Midwest, they occasionally took different forms, spurred on by an insatiable appetite for news. In Iowa, for example, which did not have its first newspaper until 1836, there were at least three handwritten papers in the small frontier town of Washington between 1844 and 1854, when a printed paper was finally established.

Midwestern Journalism and Progressive Politics

But the demographic and geographic position of the Midwest between slave and free states meant that not all newspapers were welcome. In 1836, James G. Birney (1792–1857), a Danville, Kentucky, slave owner, crossed into Ohio, let his slaves go, and relocated his mild abolitionist paper, the *Philanthropist*, in Cincinnati because it had not been received well in his home town. An angry mob, however, promptly destroyed his printing press and ransacked Cincinnati's black neighborhoods; and he barely escaped. In 1837 and in 1841 mobs again raided the printing office, but Bailey kept publishing until 1846 when he and his wife moved to Washington, D.C., and started the abolitionist *National Era*, which serialized *Uncle Tom's Cabin*, America's most famous political novel, from 1851 to 1852, as the author composed it. Further west Elijah Lovejoy (1802–1837), who published a Presbyterian abolitionist paper, the *Observer*, in Alton, Illinois, became a martyr for the anti-slavery cause in 1837, when for the fourth time a mob destroyed his press. Former President John Quincy Adams (1767–1848) noted that Lovejoy's murder sent "a shock as of an earthquake through the continent." Today the annual Elijah Lovejoy Award for Courage in Journalism memorializes him by recognizing journalists who do their jobs despite great danger.[15]

After the Civil War, midwestern newspapers gave up partisan reporting. The *Chicago Tribune* helped lead the trend. When Joseph Medill (1823–1899) and five partners took over the *Chicago Tribune* in 1855, he turned the paper into an outspoken enemy of slavery, a pro-Union advocate, and a leading proponent of the Republican Party, of which he was one of the western leaders. An early supporter of Abraham Lincoln, of Illinois, he reported the future president's speeches and praised them in editorials. In 1874, after several years in public service, Medill took over complete editorial and financial control of the newspaper and over the next twenty-five years developed a format that made the *Tribune* into what today would be considered a modern newspaper. It actively covered Chicago, and departmentalized the news into specific areas such as city, foreign, financial and commercial, books, religion, sports, and women. Furthermore, it was not afraid to take editorial positions independent of the Republican Party. All of this increased circulation, made it the most influential newspaper in the Midwest, and put the *Chicago Tribune* on the path to national greatness.[16]

Further west, another great publisher was emerging in St. Louis, whose 1870 population of 310,864 made it the nation's fourth largest city, bigger than Chicago. Joseph Pulitzer, born in Hungary, came to the United States in 1864 when he was recruited by agents for the Union Army. After the Civil War, with little money and limited language skills, he drifted to St. Louis and had a number of brief jobs before he was hired as a reporter on a leading German-language daily paper, the *Westliche Post*, in 1868. Ten years later, after a career including being elected to the Missouri State Assembly, being admitted to the District of Columbia bar, and making considerable money through shrewd business deals, he bought the bankrupt *St. Louis Dispatch* for $2,500 and three days later combined it with the *Post* to form the *Post-Dispatch*. Its chief innovation was a public promise to "serve no party but the people."[17] It constantly crusaded in the public interest, attacking a gas company, a lottery racket, a horse-car monopoly, and insurance fraud. It also bordered at times on the sensational.

In St. Louis Pulitzer introduced what became known nationally as "New Journalism" and modeled newspapers as we know them today. "Never drop a thing until you have gone to the bottom of it," he exhorted his staff. "Continuity! Continuity! Continuity until the subject is really finished."[18] In 1883, Pulitzer brought his crusading journalism to the *New York World* and scaled further sensational heights in the Yellow Journalism period of the 1890s. In 1917, six years after his death, the prestigious Pulitzer Prizes were established from a $2 million gift that he had made to Columbia University.[19]

While Pulitzer was establishing himself in St. Louis, a third midwestern giant of the 1800s started out modestly. Edward Wyllis (better known as E. W.) Scripps bought one share of a newspaper, the *Detroit News*, owned by his brother James (1835–1906), for $600 and became circulation manager in 1873. Five years later, with the help of two brothers and a sister, he started the *Cleveland Press*, and in 1883, now making $10,000 a year, he took over a struggling penny paper that became the *Cincinnati Post*. By the end of his life, when he was worth $50 million, he had started or acquired forty-eight newspapers and launched four newspaper chains as well as the United Press wire service, two syndicated services, and a newsreel company. Besides establishing one of the earliest chains in the country, thereby contributing significantly to a trend that increased from one in ten papers being in a chain at the beginning of the twentieth century to four out of five today, Scripps also drew national attention by experimenting with two adless papers, starting the *Day Book* in Chicago in 1911 and the *Philadelphia News-Post* a year later. Both failed, although the former came within $500 a month of breaking even before it closed in 1917.[20]

Unlike Medill and Pulitzer, who liked newspapers with large circulations in big cities, Scripps targeted the working class in smaller but growing industrial cities. He declared himself the "people's champion," and once said, "The first of my principles is that I have constituted myself the advocate of that large majority of people who are not so rich in worldly goods and native intelligence as to make them equal, man for man, in the struggle with individuals of the wealthier and more intellectual class." Thus, he considered his papers a "schoolroom," and he set about teaching his readers with interesting, easily read stories. He supported labor unions and collective bargaining and boasted that his papers reflected a "spirit of protest." This was summed up in his motto, "Whatever is, is wrong." In brief, he considered himself a "damned old crank" who was in rebellion against society, an editorial philosophy that was a huge success.[21]

Scripps' emphasis on protest fit the times. Public indignation over a wide variety of societal ills, from unsafe conditions at meatpacking plants to prostitution to city governments in league with criminals, helped spawn the famous muckraking era, largely at magazines, in the first decade of the 1900s. Continually aligning themselves with the Progressive movement, Scripps' newspapers joined the *Milwaukee Journal* (founded in 1882) in backing Progressive political candidates from both major parties. Later, in the late 1940s and 1950s, the *Journal* achieved fame for taking on Joseph R. McCarthy (1908–1957), the junior senator from Wisconsin, criticizing both him and the techniques he used ruthlessly trying to expose Communists at the start of the Cold War.

Joining in at the end of the muckraking era with their own protest were black newspapers. Leading the way, and drawing national attention to itself, was the *Chicago Defender*. After earning a law degree, only to be told that he was "a little too dark" to succeed as an attorney and also finding the unionized print industry closed to him despite his training as a printer, Robert Abbott (1868–1940) decided to start the *Defender* in 1905. He began modestly, writing his paper on a pad in his landlady's home and taking the pages to a printer. With a black population of 40,000, Chicago was a good location even though the city had several other black papers; within five years, the *Defender* had a circulation of 10,000. At that point, looking for a way to increase circulation dramatically to offset a lack of profitable advertising, Abbott decided to model his paper after the yellow journalism of Pulitzer and William Randolph Hearst in New York. Thus, he made the *Defender* the country's first mass appeal black newspaper. His front-page news about crime and discrimination played under "race angling" banner headlines, with the Ku Klux Klan being particularly targeted. Black newspapers in the Midwest and elsewhere quickly followed suit, and the black press changed forever, becoming far more radical.[22]

Over the next ten years, the *Defender* became the largest and most influential black newspaper in the country. It became particularly famous for its campaign encouraging blacks to leave the South and come north, where there were more and better job opportunities, by running train schedules to Chicago, columns on proper etiquette for black workers in the North, and numerous testimonial letters. A number of southern towns, infuriated as hundreds of thousands of blacks left the region during the 1910s, blamed the *Defender* for the exodus and passed ordinances banning the sale of black newspapers within their city limits. Abbott, however, enlisted the aid of one of the most respected groups of black workers, the porters who worked on the sleeping cars of trains; they hid bundles of papers on the trains and tossed them out in the countryside before the trains reached the towns. The *Defender* kept circulating in the South, and the ordinances were rendered largely useless.[23]

Midwestern Magazines Lead Modern Moods

Magazines arrived in communities across the Appalachians nearly as soon as did newspapers, but until the Civil War they tended to be moralistic, literary, religious, short-lived, and easily moved from one city or state to another. Predecessors of what would in the twentieth century become a prosperous midwestern magazine industry were first established across the Appalachians in Lexington, Kentucky, where the *Medley, or Monthly Miscellany* was published during 1803. In 1812 Thomas T. Skillman (1786–1833) started three short-lived religious publications in Lexington before he launched the *Western Luminary*, a religious journal that lasted in Lexington for ten years before Eli Taylor purchased it in 1835 and moved it to Cincinnati. Cincinnati had fewer periodicals than Lexington before 1825, but a literary and professional culture was developing there in the 1820s and 1830s. John D. Goodman (1794–1830) published six issues of the *Western Quarterly Reporter of Medical, Surgical, and Natural Science* during 1822 and 1823; and John P. Foote (1783–1865) published the *Cincinnati Literary Gazette* in 1824 and 1825.[24]

Specialized Magazines

The focus of magazines gradually but clearly shifted from the religious, political, and literary topics that dominated as settlement of the Midwest began to practical subjects that reflected the region's agricultural foundation and growing industrial economy following the Civil War. By 1900, farm journals as well as farmers were flourishing in Iowa. *The Iowa Homestead*, founded as the *Northwestern Farmer and Horticultural Journal* in Dubuque in 1856, survived until 1929.[25] The *Western Farm Journal* published from 1870 to 1897 in Des Moines; and the *Iowa Farmer*, edited for several years by the first Secretary of Agriculture, James Wilson (1835–1920), was published in Cedar Rapids from 1878 to 1892. Henry C. Wallace (1866–1924) purchased the *Iowa Farmer* in 1892 and moved it to Des Moines, where it became the nationally influential *Wallace's Farmer*, continuing today with a circulation of 63,000.[26] The *Iowa Tribune*, founded in Des Moines in 1878 as a Greenback Party magazine and edited for a decade by 1880 Greenback presidential nominee General James B. Weaver (1833–1912), ultimately was given to Edwin T. Meredith (1876–1928) in 1895 and became the financial base for his *Successful Farmer* and *Better Homes and Gardens*.[27]

Still, to an extent in reaction against industrial and commercial change in the United States, two influential magazines emerged at the end of the nineteenth century and the beginning of the twentieth in the Midwest that contributed their voices to the nation's literary development, albeit for less than three decades. These were *Reedy's Mirror* and *Midland: A Magazine of the Middle West*.

Between 1891 and 1920 *Reedy's Mirror* grew from a floundering St. Louis weekly to a national vehicle for progressive American politics and modern American poetry. The magazine began as the *Sunday Mirror*, covering gossip, politics, the arts, and entertainment in St. Louis, but even large infusions of cash barely kept it alive until 1903, when editor William Marion Reedy (1862–1920) inherited the enterprise from a disenchanted owner. Reedy saved the magazine, which he had edited since 1893, by blending midwestern political activism with midwestern literary innovation. (See discussions of the vernacular tradition and the Chicago Renaissance, below.) An "independent Democrat" who often contributed a third of an issue's content, Reedy wrote reformist editorials such as "What's the Matter with St. Louis?," which antedated muckraker Lincoln Steffens' (1866–1936) famous 1903 exposé of Minneapolis, *The Shame of the Cities*. But the magazine, renamed *Reedy's Mirror* in 1913, is best known for publishing poems by midwestern innovators such as Edgar Lee Masters (1868–1959), Vachel Lindsay (1879–1931), Edwin Arlington Robinson (1869–1925), and Carl Sandburg (1878–1967)—along with poems by rising stars from elsewhere, including Robert Frost (1874–1963), Babette Deutsch (1895–1982), Edna St. Vincent Millay (1892–1950), and Ezra Pound (1885–1977)—until the magazine folded in 1920 following Reedy's death.[28]

By contrast, *Midland: A Magazine of the Middle West* (1915–1933), began in Iowa City when students associated with the English department at the University of Iowa sought to create a noncommercial midwestern journal of literature and commentary published in the amateur spirit. Founding editor John Towner Frederick

(1893–1975) expressed a regional ethos in expecting literature to treat life experience. Although the most prominent writers of the early decades of the twentieth century did not appear in *Midland*, in part because contributors received no payment, writers from the region, such as Iowan Ruth Suckow (1892–1968) and Chicagoan James T. Farrell (1904–1979), along with easterners such as Mark Van Doren (1894–1972), published stories and poems in its pages. *Midland*'s influence extended beyond its subscribers because the annual anthology series *Best Short Stories* and *Boston Transcript* series, compiled by Edward J. O'Brien (1890–1941) and William Stanley Braithwaite (1878–1984), respectively, reprinted its fiction and poetry each year. This recognition, together with Henry L. Mencken's (1880–1956) assertion that *Midland* was "probably the most important literary magazine ever established in America," inspired Frederick in 1930 to relocate to Chicago, seek new investors, and become (as its revised subtitle promised) *A National Literary Magazine*. It lasted until mid-1933 before succumbing to the economic realities of the Great Depression.[29]

Much more successful was a third magazine, *Poetry: A Magazine of Verse*, founded by Harriet Monroe (1860–1936) in 1912. Developed to claim Chicago's place as an artistic center, *Poetry* sought writing that expressed the vitality of modern life and looked to the present instead of the past for poetic language, subjects, and forms. No magazine wielded greater influence on twentieth-century poetry. Its first issue featured two works by the young Ezra Pound (1885–1972); within a few years Sandburg, Lindsay, and other poets of the "Chicago school" had joined Missourians T. S. Eliot (1888–1965) and Marianne Moore (1887–1972), and such other literary innovators as H.D. (Hilda Doolittle, 1886–1961), Amy Lowell (1874–1925), William Carlos Williams (1883–1963), and William Butler Yeats (1865–1939) in launching literary Modernism and declaring Chicago the modern poetry center of the world. Today *Poetry* is still published in Chicago, now under the aegis of the Poetry Foundation, established in 2003 with a gift of approximately $100 million, the largest single donation ever made to a literary association, from philanthropist Ruth Lilly (1891–1973), wife of Indiana pharmaceutical businessman Eli Lilly (1885–1977).

General Interest Magazines

The age of the modern magazine, based on the symbiotic rise of advertising and mass production techniques in the late nineteenth century, brought forth three extremely successful national general-interest magazines in the Midwest. Those were *Woman's Home Companion*, published by Crowell Publishing Company in Springfield, Ohio; *Better Homes and Gardens*, published by Meredith in Des Moines, Iowa; and *Look*, published by Cowles Magazines and Broadcasting first in Des Moines and after 1940 in New York. For a brief period between 1925 and 1927, they were joined by *Time* magazine, which Henry R. Luce (1898–1967) moved from New York to Cleveland.[30]

The roots of *Woman's Home Companion* were in Cleveland, where brothers S. L. and Frederick Thorpe started *Home* in 1874 as a cheaply printed magazine of fiction and household departments. After Frederick Thorpe died in 1877, S. L. took over another Cleveland magazine, *Little Ones and Home*, and merged it with *Home* to form *Home Companion: A Monthly for Young People*. In 1866, after several changes in ownership and a move to Springfield, Ohio, *Home Companion* became the *Ladies' Home Companion*. By 1897, it had added serial fiction, more coverage of fashion and food, and more illustrations to become one of the leading magazines serving women and the home, with circulation approaching 300,000. To distinguish itself from the competing *Ladies' Home Journal*, it became the *Woman's Home Companion* in 1897; the successive editorships of T. J. Kirkpatrick, former newspaperman Joseph F. Henderson (1852–1916), and Arthur T. Vance (1872–1930) remade the women's magazine into a family magazine with an emphasis on public affairs, crusades against child labor, and short stories by noted authors, including Wisconsin-born Hamlin Garland. The magazine maintained some regional ties after the editorial offices were moved to New York and Kirkpatrick sold his interest in the publishing house in 1901.

Under editor-in-chief Gertrude Battles Lane (1874–1941), who took charge in 1911, when the *Companion* had a circulation of 564,000, the magazine attracted presidents and other notables as contributors. Eleanor Roosevelt (1884–1962) regularly contributed a page in the 1930s, when Midwestern fiction writers were especially prominent: Edna Ferber (1887–1968), Kathleen Norris (1880–1966), Willa Cather (1873–1947), Sherwood Anderson (1876–1941), Ellen Glasgow (1874–1945), and Sinclair Lewis (1885–1951). Circulation reached 3 million in 1938. Following Lane's death in 1941, *Woman's Home Companion* continued to prosper until the mid-1950s; however, it lost publishers Crowell-Collier $3 million in 1956, and the magazine was closed with the January 1957 issue. The company's companion magazine, *Collier's*, was closed at the same time. Crowell-Collier had already closed *American Magazine*, its other major publication, with the August 1956 issue.[31]

Better Homes and Gardens can be traced back to 1902, when Edwin T. Meredith started *Successful Farming* on a shoestring in Des Moines. With the help of his spouse, Edna C. Elliott Meredith (1879–1969), he built *Successful Farming* into one of the most important farm magazines in the nation, based on an editorial formula of providing practical instruction in efficient farming techniques. A century later, Meredith Corporation continues to publish *Successful Farming*, which now boasts the largest paid circulation of all agricultural magazines. After serving as Wilson's Secretary of Agriculture, Meredith turned in 1922 to publishing a similar magazine of practical advice for the growing number of homeowners in cities and the expanding suburbs. Begun as *Fruit, Garden and Home*, in 1924 it became *Better Homes and Gardens*. By the time of Meredith's death in 1928, *Better Homes and Gardens* had become the first magazine to reach 1 million in circulation without relying on fiction or fashion. Rather, the focus was on tested recipes, landscaping techniques, letters from readers, gardening, home designs and improvements, and large illustrations. In 1930, the magazine published the still popular *My Better Homes and Gardens Cook Book*, the first of many branded publications, products, and services the Meredith Corporation continues to offer its readers.[32] Today Meredith's stable of titles includes sixteen related monthly magazines, including its former competitor, *Ladies' Home Journal*, published in New York, as well as numerous special interest publications. Except for *Successful Farming*, most of these were added in the 1980s and 1990s and have circulations from about 465,000 to more than 1 million. *Better Homes and Gardens* now has a circulation approaching 8 million, and its revenues rank fifth among consumer titles.

While Henry R. Luce was planning *Life* magazine in 1936, Gardner Cowles, Jr. (1903–1985), also was developing a picture-magazine concept in Des Moines. After George H. Gallup's (1901–1984) studies conducted for the Des Moines *Register and Tribune* in 1925 found that readers favored photographs over text, Vernon Pope—who would become *Look*'s first editor—experimented with series of photographs that told stories in the paper's Sunday rotogravure section. These picture series were so popular that they were syndicated to other newspapers in 1933 while Cowles began planning *Look* and trading ideas with his friend Luce. Drawing on *Register and Tribune* staff and resources, the first issue of *Look* was published in January 1937, just two months after the first issue of *Life* appeared. After ten months, circulation reached 1.7 million. In 1940, the magazine moved from Des Moines to New York. Within ten years *Look* grew from its midwestern roots to become a magazine that mixed a serious approach to world and national affairs with sports, entertainment, science, and fashion. While remaining a photojournalism magazine, it also presented long articles by such national and international figures as Walter Lippmann (1889–1974), Ernest Hemingway (1899–1961), C. P. Snow (1905–1980), Adlai Stevenson (1900–1965), Archibald MacLeish (1892–1982), Gloria Steinem (b. 1934), and Bertrand Russell (1872–1970). When television threatened its advertising base during the 1950s and 1960s, *Look* competed with other general interest magazines to expand circulation. By 1963 it had 7 million subscribers and $74 million in advertising, the second highest revenue of any magazine in the United States. Ultimately, *Look* produced itself into bankruptcy as competition with television, and the increasing costs of paper, printing, and particularly postage (for distributing more than 5 million copies for subscribers) overtook revenues. *Look* ceased publication in October 1971, slightly more than a year before *Life*'s last weekly issue in December 1972.[33]

Niche Publishing

The Midwest also is home to several nationally important, highly successful niche magazine publishing ventures. In St. Louis, *The Sporting News* thrived by covering major league baseball beginning in the late nineteenth century and continuing into the twenty-first century. Madison has been home to *The Progressive* magazine and its liberal agenda since 1909, when Wisconsin Senator Robert La Follette (1895–1953) founded it as *La Follette's Weekly*. In Chicago, Johnson Publishing produced two of the first and most popular magazines to target African American readers, *Ebony* and *Jet*; and Playboy Enterprises published *Playboy*, the best-selling men's magazine in the world. In Minneapolis, Fawcett Publications—starting after World War I with a mimeographed sheet of bawdy jokes—published a range of imitative magazines that targeted working-class readership, and Lens Publishing compiled the *Utne Reader*, the largest circulation magazine of leftist, alternative writings in the country.

The Sporting News was just one of many periodicals in the late 1800s launched to exploit the popularity of baseball, but it was the one that actually profited and has survived into the twenty-first century. Albert H. Spink started the magazine in 1886 after Charley Comiskey's (1859–1931) St. Louis Browns won the American Association pennant. Charles C. Spink (d. 1914), Albert's brother, served as the magazine's business manager and took over the enterprise in 1897. *The Sporting News* heavily promoted the American League, and today its content still emphasizes baseball over coverage of other sports.[34]

In starting *La Follette's Weekly* in 1909 at 409 East Main Street in downtown Madison, La Follette sought to establish "a magazine of progress, social, intellectual, institutional." For ninety-five years in these same offices, *The Progressive* has maintained this mission as the liberal or progressive—some might say radical—voice on issues of democracy, peace, civil rights, environmental concerns, and social justice at home and abroad. In its early history, this journal of opinion advocated an end to child labor, called for women's suffrage, resisted entry into World War I, and denounced the Palmer Raids of the red-scare era of the early 1920s as it did McCarthyism following World War II. *The Progressive* also has opposed, throughout the twentieth century, U.S. military ventures abroad in Southeast Asia, Central and Latin America, and the Middle East. Most famously, *The Progressive* has consistently opposed nuclear weapons. This stance led to the controversial publication in November 1979 of "The H-Bomb Secret: How We Got It and Why We're Telling It" by Howard Moreland, which the U.S. government used a preliminary injunction to suppress for six months. By deciding to drop its case against publication of Moreland's article, the Department of Defense avoided losing what would have been the nation's most important prior-restraint case pitting issues of national security and weapons secrecy against the First Amendment right to publish information derived from publicly available materials. Contributors to *The Progressive*, past and present, make up a who's who of socialist, progressive, and liberal intellectuals, journalists, and politicians. In its pages have appeared Jane Addams (1860–1935), Helen Keller (1880–1968), Jack London, Upton Sinclair (1878–1968), Lincoln Steffens, George Orwell (1903–1950), Martin Luther King, Jr. (1929–1968), James Baldwin (1924–1987), I. F. Stone (1907–1989), Edward Said (1935–2003), Barbara Ehrenreich (b. 1941), Nat Hentoff (b. 1925), Adlai Stevenson, J. W. Fulbright (1905–1995), Molly Ivins (b. 1944), Howard Zinn (b. 1922), Noam Chomsky (b. 1928), Ralph Nader (b. 1934), Ramsey Clark (b. 1927), Susan Douglas (b. 1950), George McGovern (b. 1922), Russ Feingold (b. 1944), Paul Wellstone (1944–2002), and Dennis Kucinich (b. 1946).[35] The large number of midwesterners in the list testifies to the region's activist tradition of reform.

In 1942, John H. Johnson (b. 1912) borrowed $500 and founded the largest company publishing magazines for African Americans. Johnson's idea was to give his readers magazines with the same editorial formulas that had proven successful with mainstream readers. With the help of Ben Burns (1913–2000), a *Chicago Defender* journalist, he gathered articles to include in *Negro Digest*, much as Lila (1889–1984) and DeWitt Wallace (1889–1981) did in creating *Reader's Digest* two decades earlier. His success with this first venture encouraged Johnson to launch other magazines. In 1945 he recruited freelancers to help him produce initial issues of *Ebony*, a picture magazine modeled on the success of *Life* and *Look*. The success of *Ebony* showed advertisers the importance of the African American market—a lesson they had already learned during the war from the black press. This success led Johnson Publications to create additional titles: *Tan* for women in 1950 and *Jet*, a vest-pocket news magazine, in 1952. Johnson Publications later experimented with *Ebony, Jr.* Johnson's company today continues to publish *Ebony* for 1,720,000 subscribers and *Jet* for 952,000 subscribers.[36]

Hugh H. Hefner (b. 1926) left the University of Illinois hoping to publish a men's magazine similar to sophisticated *Esquire*, a smart magazine he admired and which offered him his initial job in its Chicago promotion office. When *Esquire* wanted to transfer him to New York, however, Hefner turned down the opportunity because the offered raise was $5 under his demand. Instead, he remained in Chicago; much as Johnson had done, he borrowed $600, and sold $7,000 of stock to friends. With this he put together the December 1953 issue of *Playboy* on his kitchen table, and printed 70,000 copies of this first issue with a cover price of fifty cents. Without a financial base, Hefner's first issue needed a gimmick in order to succeed; the gimmick was the now famous "Playmate of the Month" pinup of Marilyn Monroe stretched out nude.

From this first issue forward, Hefner changed the "girlie" image of the pinup from lower-class bawdiness to the embodiment of the girl next door, the girl that sophisticated young men aspired to date. Not until the early 1970s did *Playboy*—forced by the competition of more explicit images in *Penthouse* and the even more graphic images in *Hustler* that Larry C. Flynt (b. 1942) founded and first published for two years in Columbus, Ohio—include a full-frontal nude. Following the lead of *Esquire*, Hefner included quality fiction from the beginning and, during the 1960s and 1970s, culturally and socially important interviews and nonfiction for his upscale readers. Offering as much as $2,000 for a short story, *Playboy* attracted fiction by such authors as John Steinbeck (1902–1968), Vladimir Nabokov (1899–1977), William Saroyan (1908–1981), Bernard Malamud (1914–1986), Isaac Bashevis Singer (1904–1991), Joyce Carol Oates (b. 1938), Ray Bradbury (b. 1920), James Baldwin, Erskine Caldwell (1903–1987), Arthur C. Clarke (b. 1917), and Paul Theroux (b. 1941). The *Playboy* interviews have included a wide range of personalities and viewpoints; Miles Davis (1926–1991), John Lennon (1940–1980) and Yoko Ono (b. 1933), Ayn Rand (1905–1982), Anita Bryant (b. 1940), and Jimmy Carter (b. 1923) have all been interviewed. To this mix, Hefner added a stable of cartoonists, the Playboy Advisor on sexual matters, the Playboy Forum discussing the Playboy Philosophy, and the omnipresent Playboy Bunny logo that has become a brand as internationally recognized as the Coca-Cola script or the Nike swoosh.

A peak circulation of 7 million copies was reached with the September 1972 issue, and thereafter declined significantly to just over 3 million today. On its fiftieth anniversary, *Playboy* still ranked thirty-sixth in total annual revenue, earning $179,526,000.[37] Playboy Enterprises has scaled down, too, in areas other than circulation. By the 1980s Hefner gradually turned over control of the *Playboy* empire to his daughter. Christie Hefner (b. 1952), cutting overhead, has recast the organization into strictly a media company by selling off her father's legacy of Playboy clubs, casinos, hotels, and the luxurious seven-story offices on Michigan Avenue. Playboy Enterprises now resides in a custom duplex on the top of the American Furniture Mart in Chicago.[38]

Two other magazines among the region's many others deserve special mention. *Utne Reader*, based in Minneapolis, has since 1984 tapped the softer new-age aspects of the midwestern populism responsible for the success of La Follette's

Progressive magazine. Named after Eric Utne, founding editor and publisher who put the first issues together on the kitchen table, *Utne Reader* today attracts 230,000 subscribers by gathering what it considers the best, most significant materials from alternative and independent media sources along with original articles for readers actively seeking personal growth and social change. Among magazines sustaining the Midwest's commercial traditions, *Chicago* magazine stands out. With a circulation of 200,000, *Chicago* is arguably the most successful city magazine in the nation. From its origin in 1952 as a program guide for the local classical music radio station, WFMT, it gradually added entertainment and feature articles, including a mix of investigative reporting and service journalism. Under editor Hillel Levine, *Chicago* has covered city slumlords, the lives of Chicago's working poor, urban terrorism, and Cook County politics, and become a model for city magazines across the nation.

MIDWESTERN LITERATURE AFTER 1860

The practical and editorial traditions established by Midwestern newspapers and magazines in the nineteenth century also nourished imaginative literature after the Civil War. In addition to providing publishing outlets for aspiring writers, journalism gave employment and an ad hoc education to writers from Samuel L. Clemens (Mark Twain, 1835–1910) onward. Ohio-born William Dean Howells spearheaded American Realism from his editor's chair at the *Atlantic*. Many authors who shaped the Chicago Renaissance doubled as journalists. Whether they remained in the region or moved elsewhere, however, midwestern writers after the Civil War built on regional foundations of setting, character, and language established in the antebellum period. On these foundations they established a modern literary heritage of stylistic and formal innovation second to none.

Like their predecessors, post–Civil War authors struggled to represent the Midwest as they experienced it. The Midwest existed in the literary imagination of early nineteenth-century New England writers merely as a wilderness region—what Judith Yaross Lee's introduction to this volume describes as the "Hinterland" interpretation of the Midwest—of both exaggerated brutality and idealized independence. This seemingly paradoxical characterization emerged from the desire of early American Romantic writers—for instance, James Fenimore Cooper in *The Prairie* (1827) and Washington Irving in *A Tour on the Prairies* (1835)—to envision the Midwest chiefly as a new Eden threatened by both the immigrant farmer and the westward expansion of eastern civilization. By the middle of the nineteenth century, when decades of migration had populated the Great Lakes region and the valleys of the Ohio and Mississippi Rivers, and midwesterners themselves had assumed the mantle of portraying their region in poetry and fiction, depictions of the Midwest showed more sympathy for the agrarian society of the frontier. Henry Nash Smith (1906–1986) documents this evolution in his seminal treatment of the American West, *Virgin Land* (1950), and reports that the brutish frontier "squatters" of Cooper and Irving were eventually displaced in American literature by the desperate but mostly admirable midwestern granger, or homesteader, of Caroline Kirkland (1801–1864), Alice Cary (1821–1871), and Edward Eggleston (1837–1902).[39] A native of Ohio, Cary is credited by scholars and literary artists alike, including Smith and Eggleston, as the first writer in American letters to present the Midwest honestly and authentically. Cary's poetry and prose, with their realistic depiction of the harshness of life in an agricultural society, led the way for later authors' characterization of the midwestern men and women whom she calls "poor hard-working folks."

Edward Eggleston, who spent his youth in southern Indiana, built on Cary's pioneering realism efforts. In such novels as *The Hoosier Schoolmaster* (1871), *The End of the World: A Love Story* (1872), and *The Circuit Rider* (1874), he introduced regional forms of dialect into midwestern prose. "Lay it on good," advises Pete Jones, antagonist and principal advocate of classroom corporal punishment in Eggleston's first novel. "Don't do no harm. Lickin' and la'rnin' goes together. No lickin', no la'rnin'!" In addition to the realistic detail that vernacular afforded his work, Eggleston's experiments with language also transformed the image of midwesterners from worn, yet persevering, frontier farmers into citizens of a unique rural folk culture by focusing on larger communities and rooting their dialect in a common heritage.

From another perspective, Eggleston's experiments with language can also be understood in light of nineteenth-century literary politics that gave midwesterners "so little to lose" in their radical departures from conventional literary practices.[40] Regarded as outside the mainstream of the Eastern literary establishment, midwesterners may have felt freer to stray from its norms. In either case, with the rise of Eggleston's vision of an autonomous midwestern culture, we may see the beginnings of what Judith Yaross Lee terms the Heartland vision of the Midwest that counters the image of the Hinterland. Although Eggleston's fiction by no means ignores the crudeness of frontier life—some critics would even argue that it preserves aspects of the region's reputation for savagery and wildness[41]—his midwestern communities, unlike the sparsely populated homesteads of earlier works, possessed well-defined histories, often stretching back several generations, that provided a regional tradition for their distinctive speech patterns and rituals.

Eggleston's realistic studies of Midwest village life also initiated what is now occasionally referred to as the "Hoosier School" of literature. This minor turn-of-the-century midwestern literary movement was characterized by works with romantic plots celebrating homely virtues and whose ranks eventually included poets Will Carleton (1845–1912) and James Whitcomb Riley (1849–1916) and novelist Booth Tarkington (1869–1946). Ultimately, however, through the work of writers such as Cary and Eggleston, the Midwest defined itself independent of the West as it developed for the first time the makings of an identity all its own.

Hamlin Garland and the six stories that comprise the first edition of his *Main-Travelled Roads* (1891) established the Midwest, once and for all, as a major American literary region. In works such as "Up the Coule," "A Branch Road," and "Under the Lion's Paw," the Midwest and its distinct agrarian society emerge unambiguously heroic in the face of widespread degradation and suffering brought about by successive decades of natural disasters and oppressive economic conditions. Garland's interest in Populist politics of the 1880s and 1890s clearly shaped his artistic vision, and in fiction, poetry, and such autobiographical works as *A Son of the Middle Border* (1917) and *A Daughter of the Middle Border* (1921) he sharpened the realistic depictions of hardship characteristic of Cary's work and combined them with the more salient features of Eggleston's experiments in local color. He sought partly to effect social change for the farming communities of the

Midwest and partly to undermine broadly held romantic notions of life on the farm by emphasizing the harshness of the labor and the isolation of the granger. Championed by William Dean Howells and other eastern establishment literati, Garland's brand of realism, which he termed *veritism*, eventually garnered an international audience for midwestern literature.

Late Nineteenth-Century Poetry

The most memorable poetry produced by midwesterners in the final few decades of the nineteenth century came from two writers whose reputations were built on their use of dialect in verse. James Whitcomb Riley enjoyed enormous popularity in his own lifetime with the publication of his first book, *The Old Swimmin' Hole and 'Leven More Poems* (1883). In this and later volumes, Riley established himself as among the most determined advocates of dialect in literature. Though later dismissed by critics, even mocked in recent years for his excessively vernacular style, there can be little doubt that Riley approached the use of dialect with a seriousness of purpose and design, as he makes clear in his famous defense of the practice titled "Dialect in Literature":

> Equally with the perfect English, dialect should have full justice done it. Then always it is worthy, and in Literature is thus welcome. The writer of dialect should as reverently venture in its use as in his chastest English. . . . The real master must not only know each varying light and shade of dialect expression, but he must as minutely know the inner character of the people whose native tongue it is, else his product is simply a pretense—a willful forgery, a rank abomination.[42]

Indeed, Riley saw the use of dialect as essential to any truthful, authentic depiction of midwestern culture. And due in large part to Riley's extremely popular poetry, his brand of "Hoosier" dialect became a hallmark of late nineteenth-century midwestern literature.

Paul Laurence Dunbar (1872–1906), like Riley, also forged a literary reputation through dialect verse. Yet Dunbar's case is fundamentally different from Riley's in at least two respects. First, even though Dunbar was born in Ohio and lived much of his short life there, his poetry is more often associated with the "Plantation School" movement, a brand of nineteenth-century American literature that tended to treat nostalgically the antebellum slave culture of the South. Scholarship of the last forty years has challenged the validity of such an association between Dunbar and writers of the "Plantation School," noting in particular the presence of irony in his seemingly disparaging portraits of African American culture. Ironic or not, however, Dunbar's style has all the same been linked historically to—whether as participant in or critic of—this brand of southern writing. Thus, Dunbar's work is routinely identified with a geographical region thoroughly beyond the borders of the Midwest. Second, Dunbar's own attitude toward dialect in literature seems to have been more ambivalent than Riley's. Early on, Dunbar was encouraged by the likes of William Dean Howells to express lyrically the full experience of "Negro" life, idioms and all. Dunbar followed that advice and went on to produce several volumes of poetry comprised of such memorable works as "A Negro Love Song"

(1895), "An Ante-Bellum Sermon" (1895), and arguably one of his most his popular poems, "When De Co'n Pone's Hot" (1896):

> When de worl' jes' stahts a-spinnin'
> Lak a picaninny's top,
> An yo' cup o' joy is brimmin'
> 'Twell it seems about to slop
> An' you feel jes' lak a racah,
> Dat is trainin' fu' to trot—
> When yo' mammy says de blessin'
> An' de co'n pone's hot. (ll. 5–12)

Throughout the 1890s, Dunbar's dialect verse had been lauded by Howells and other influential literati as innovative and experimental. His vernacular cadences seemed fresh and accurate, and the detailed descriptions robust and vibrant. Yet despite all of the acclaim and success, critics believe that Dunbar may have felt confined by his reputation as a dialect poet. "We Wear the Mask" (1895) and "Sympathy" (1899), with its famous line "I know why the caged bird sings!", have been read by modern scholars as self-revealing laments about the constraints of critical expectation and commercial typecasting that led to the neglect of his poetry in standard English. Nevertheless, Dunbar was a pioneer on several fronts at a time when American poetry languished for lack of innovation, and he stands today as among the most accomplished and highly celebrated literary figures of his time.

Plainspoken Midwestern Writers

In the years between the publication of Alice Cary's *Clovernook; or, Recollections of Our Neighborhood in the West* (1852) and Hamlin Garland's *Prairie Folks* (1893), the Midwest saw many of its greatest writers leave the region and produce work abroad. Some midwesterners, however, such as Abraham Lincoln (1809–1865), always managed to convey a sense of their frontier heritage through a style marked by biblical undertones and plain-spoken language, and peppered with homespun witticisms. Garry Wills' *Lincoln at Gettysburg* (1992), the book-length study of Lincoln's 272-word speech at the dedication of the Gettysburg battlefield cemetery on November 19, 1863, takes particular note of Lincoln's revolutionary American style when compared to the speeches and orators of his day. Carl Sandburg even described the Gettysburg Address as "one of the great American poems."[43] Indeed, Lincoln's ten-sentence speech does invite comparisons with the midcentury American-language experiments of Walt Whitman's *Leaves of Grass* (1855). From the memorable biblical echoes of Lincoln's opening line—"Four score and seven years"—to the understated, rhetorically uncomplicated assertions of the middle paragraph—"We are met on a great-battlefield of that war. We have come to dedicate a portion of that field, as a final resting place for those who here gave their lives that that nation might live. It is altogether fitting and proper that we should do this"—to the speech's epic but linguistically egalitarian close—"that government of the people, by the people, for the people, shall not perish from the earth"—the Gettysburg Address relies on none of the Augustan syntax, none of the grand speechifying gestures, none of the ornate prose that had come to be as-

A Sampling of Midwestern Accents

Midwesterners' pleasure in the sound of regional voices has led to an abundance of vernacular writing, especially imitations of speech known in the style called *mock-oral*. Some notable examples are as follows:

George Ade (Indiana, 1866–1944), author of musical comedies such as *The College Widow* (1904), was better known for his humorous books on country characters who spoke in a racy vernacular. These include *Fables in Slang* (1899), *People You Knew* (1903), and *Hand-Made Fables* (1920).

Though born in Detroit, Nelson Algren (1909–1981) became famous for novels depicting the lives of Polish underdogs on the mean streets of Chicago, first in *Never Come Morning* (1942) and then in *The Man with the Golden Arm* (1949). His ear for language also gave authenticity to his novel of the New Orleans underworld, *A Walk on the Wild Side* (1956).

Erma Bombeck (1927–1996), initially a columnist for the Dayton *Journal Herald*, syndicated her humor column nationally for many years. She satirized domestic life from the standpoint of an exhausted, exasperated housewife in barely expurgated prose. Her books, which collected or expanded her columns, include *The Grass Is Always Greener over the Septic Tank* (1976), *If Life Is a Bowl of Cherries, What Am I Doing in the Pits?* (1978), *Motherhood: The Second Oldest Profession* (1983), and *A Marriage Made in Heaven . . . , or, Too Tired for an Affair* (1993).

Poet Gwendolyn Brooks (1917–2000) chronicled life in the African American Chicago neighborhood where she grew up, most beautifully in *A Street in Bronzeville* (1945). She won the Pulitzer Prize for *Annie Allen* (1949), a verse treament of the maturation of a black girl during World War II. Other notable works include *Maud Martha* (1953), *The Bean Eaters* (1960), and *Selected Poems* (1963).

Chicago journalist Peter Finley Dunne (1867–1936), editor of *Collier's* Magazine (1918–1919), indulged his social and political humor as author of a series of books featuring Mr. Dooley, a Chicago barkeep, who critiqued politicans, events, courts, and cultural issues with a sharp wit not at all masked by a rich Irish brogue that entertained readers for two decades. The first book in this series was *Mr. Dooley in Peace and in War* (1898) and the last, *Mr. Dooley on Making a Will* (1919).

As a journalist first for the *Denver Tribune* and then for the *Chicago Tribune*, Eugene Field (Missouri, 1850–1895) wrote humorous columns in a spare, vernacular prose that anticipated Modernism, collected in *The Tribune Primer* (1881) and *Culture's Garland* (1887). Volumes of verse such as *A Little Book of Profitable Tales* (1889), *With Trumpet and Drum* (1892), and *The Holy Cross and Other Tales* (1893) established him as a sentimental poet of childhood. Field is best remembered for the sentimental poems "Little Boy Blue" and "Dutch Lullaby" ("Wynken, Blynken, and Nod"), both set to music, and for the occasional off-color verse such as "When Willie Wet the Bed."

Ben Hecht (1894–1964), born in New York but reared in Wisconsin, became a Chicago journalist and member of the Chicago group of writers he promoted in the little magazine, *Chicago Literary Times* (1923–1924). *Erik Dorn* (1921), *Gargoyles* (1922), *1001 Afternoons in Chicago* (1922), and *Tales of Chicago Streets* (1924) all celebrate the rowdy romance of the city, as did his autobiography, *Gaily, Gaily* (1963). His plays, *The Front Page* (with Charles MacArthur, 1928) and *20th Century* (1932), became notable motion pictures.

Garrison Keillor (b. 1942), the most famous son of Lake Wobegon, Minnesota, the quintessential American small town, was actually born Gary Keillor in Anoka and originally sought to be a poet. He turned to prose shortly after publishing his first poem,

"Some Matters Concerning the Occupant," in the July 1968 *Atlantic* and was already a regular contributor to *The New Yorker* magazine when he began broadcasts of *A Prairie Home Companion* for Minnesota Public Radio in 1974. Thirty years later, his prodigious imagination has not been exhausted by the skits and tall yarns that constitute the myth of Lake Wobegon, a backwater in the Upper Midwest "where all the women are strong, all the men are good-looking, and all the children are above average." While continuing to write about Minnesotans for his weekly radio show, broadcast nationally since 1982, he has also published novels and short stories, beginning with *Happy to Be Here* (1981) and *Lake Wobegon Days* (1985) and most recently, *Lake Wobegon Summer, 1956* (2001) and *Love Me* (2003).

Born in New York State, David Ross Locke (1833–1888) surfaced in Ohio as a printer and journalist. His humorous letters on political subjects, signed Petroleum V. (for Vesuvius) Nasby, began to appear in 1861 in the Findlay [Ohio] *Jeffersonian* that Locke edited. Ostensibly a Copperhead minister supporting the South in the Civil War, Nasby so undermined the southern cause that President Lincoln read the letters to his cabinet. Scurrilous, inept, and illiterate, Nasby reveled in bombast made funnier by grotesque spelling and assorted stupidities, and kept commenting on current events long after the war ended. Locke began collecting the letters in 1864 (*The Nasby Papers*) and parlayed their success into the editorship and later ownership of the Toledo *Blade*.

Wisconsin journalist George Wilbur Peck (1840–1916) wrote comic political articles in Irish dialect, collected as *Adventures of One Terence McGrant* (1871). As owner of the Milwaukee *Sun*, Peck wrote columns on his boyhood adventures as a prankster. Published as *Peck's Bad Boy and His Pa* (1883) and in other volumes, they launched Peck's political career, first as mayor of Milwaukee (1890–1891) and then as governor of Wisconsin (1891–1895).

Jean (Parker) Shepherd (1929–1999), like Garrison Keillor a radio raconteur, turned his childhood experiences in Hammond, Indiana, into humorous broadcasts and stories. His *Christmas Story* (1983), a tale of midwestern schoolyard misadventures, has become a classic motion picture, but his fans also prize his novel *In God We Trust: All Others Pay Cash* (1967), and the stories and essays in *Wanda Hickey's Night of Golden Memories and Other Disasters* (1972) and *The Ferrari in the Bedroom* (1973); all draw on Shepherd's wry regional sensibilities.

Although he wrote novels and plays on diverse subjects, Booth Tarkington (1869–1946) seemed to be *A Gentleman from Indiana* (1899). *Penrod* (1914), *Penrod and Sam* (1916), *Penrod Jashber* (1929), and *Little Orvie* (1934), comic novels about boys, achieved immense popularity; *The Magnificent Ambersons* (1918) and *Alice Adams* (1921) were the most renowned of his mannered novels of middle-class life in the Midwest.

sociated with the popular "Old World" oratorical style of public speaking in the nineteenth century.

The closing sentences of the First Inaugural Address demonstrate even more precisely Lincoln's ear for simple cadences and vernacular rhythms. An early draft of the speech written by William Seward concludes: "I close. We are not, we must not be, aliens or enemies, but fellow-countrymen and brethren." Lincoln, however, revised the passage to read: "I am loth to close. We are not enemies, but friends. We must not be enemies."[44] In Lincoln's hands the reference to "Aliens and enemies" is trimmed to "enemies," and "countrymen and brethren" is reduced to the more vernacular "friends." It is interesting to note, too, that Seward's and Lincoln's versions of the passage are both sixteen words long, but Lincoln's seems more concise because of its simplicity of style, reliance on monosyllables, and absence of conventional rhetorical phrasing. Like the writing of other nineteenth-century American authors who were born and spent their formative years in the Midwest, Lincoln's prose reflects a fidelity to the language and cultural experience of small-town prairie life on the midwestern frontier. Well into the twentieth century, midwesterners continued to prize the region's heritage of "plain talk," which former president Harry S Truman of Missouri made his personal trademark.

Mark Twain

Others who left the region, such as Mark Twain, occasionally returned to the stuff of their midwestern origins for the materials of fiction and autobiography. The St. Petersburg of *The Adventures of Tom Sawyer* (1876) and *Adventures of Huckleberry Finn* (1885) as well as the settings of "The Man That Corrupted Hadleyburg" (1899) and *No. 44, The Mysterious Stranger* (written 1902–1908, published 1969) are all thinly veiled portraits of Twain's boyhood home of Hannibal, Missouri. Twain was also the first writer to use the language and setting of the Midwest in his work to transcend the limitations of regional boundaries and forge a distinctive and enduring national character for American literature itself. His Mississippi River Valley, with its middle American towns, its range of middle American types, and its variety of middle American landscapes, evolved over time into an emblem of national cultural identity. This appropriation of Twain by the larger national consciousness has been so thorough, so complete, that Twain himself is almost never considered in the context of his region or as an author of midwestern people and places. He is, of course, more regularly regarded as a writer of American people and places—perhaps *the* writer of American people and places.

Twain's use of his adolescent Midwest experiences—what Henry Nash Smith termed the "Matter of Hannibal"[45]—began in earnest with his quasi-autobiographical reflection "Old Times on the Mississippi," serialized in *The Atlantic Monthly* in 1875. Mostly styled as a coming-of-age narrative, "Old Times" also inaugurates Twain's experiments with midwestern language in a midwestern setting. The piece opens memorably:

> When I was a boy, there was but one permanent ambition among my comrades in our village on the west bank of the Mississippi River. That was, to be a steamboatman. We had transient ambitions of other sorts, but they were only transient. When a circus came and went it left us burning to become clowns; the first Negro minstrel show that ever came to our section left us all suffering to try that kind of life; now and then we had a hope that, if we lived and were good, God would permit us to be pirates. These ambitions faded out, each in its turn; but the ambition to be a steamboatman always remained.[46]

What we encounter here is something entirely new in mainstream American literature. The events of the narrative are conveyed to the reader not in a "written" language but in a spoken voice—we seem to hear the prose as we read—and the voice we hear is distinctly midwestern. There are, to be sure, small remnants of genteel prose in this early piece by Twain, but syntactical constructions such as "there was but one" and phrasings like "transient ambitions," are mostly functions of the frame-narrative technique hidden just below the surface of "Old Times" that help to emphasize through juxtaposition the free vernacular language in expressions like "burning to become" and "suffering to try." As Twain moves further into "Old Times"—particularly in the lyrical description of the town coming to life as the steamboat approaches—he gradually increases the frequency and intensity of the colloquial speech. Moreover, the broader attitude of Twain's narrator, as many critics have noted, seems also to reflect a "vernacular sensibility." That is to say, the aspiration to become a steamboatman itself (as opposed to that of lawyer, doctor, poet, statesman, or any of the more conventional and refined professions) signals the cultural consciousness of ordinary folk.

Arguably the greatest experiment in American literary language of the nineteenth century came in Twain's 1885 masterpiece, *Adventures of Huckleberry Finn*. As Twain claims in the novel's "Explanatory" (and scholarship has corroborated[47]) no fewer than seven distinct and distinguishable varieties of dialect are employed in *Huckleberry Finn*. The two most central, Huck's "ordinary 'Pike County' dialect" and Jim's "Missouri negro dialect," are, as matter of geography, midwestern. And insofar as the "voices" of Huck and Jim contribute fundamentally to the novel's acclaim in the minds of many subsequent authors and critics as the true beginning of an "American" literature—one recalls, for example, Ernest Hemingway's declaration that "all modern American literature comes from one book by Mark Twain called *Huckleberry Finn*"[48]—then one could make a case that an authentically "American" literature was born in the vernacular cadences of the midwestern voice.

The timeless opening passage of *Huckleberry Finn* embodies much of the stunning achievement of Huck's voice: "You don't know about me, without you have read a book by the name of "The Adventures of Tom Sawyer," but that ain't no matter. That book was made by Mr. Mark Twain, and he told the truth, mainly." Victor Doyno's excellent study of the manuscript points out that Twain returned to the first few lines of the novel at least three times, making minor alterations until he got Huck's voice just right.[49] What originally read as "You will not know," Twain revised first to "You do not know" and then to "You don't know." The final version, with its contracted predicate, transforms an initially stiff and overly grammatical representation of dialogue into the voice of a living, breathing illiterate midwestern boy. But more than that, the genius of Huck's voice lies in the fact that his colloquial speech is presented through the syntactical arrangement of the words instead of through the comic misspellings and the intrusive dialect of earlier writing, including that of the "Hoosier School." The communication of vernacular language chiefly through idiom and its rhythms is just one of Twain's foundational contributions to American literature, and as Hemingway observed, it marks nothing short of a transformation in the way American writers envisioned their art.

Beyond Twain: Other Midwestern Literary Artists of the Late Nineteenth Century

Another group of writers visited the Midwest from other parts of country and transformed their experiences into literary art. Harriet Beecher Stowe, though born in Connecticut, spent her twenties and thirties in Cincinnati, Ohio, and that experience unquestionably contributed to the conception of *Uncle Tom's Cabin* (1852), which is set partly in the Midwest and urges a reformist agenda later identified as midwestern. A final group departed (a few only temporarily) and forever remained principally associated with other regions of the country, among them William Dean Howells (Ohio; 1837–1920) with the East; Charles Chesnutt (Ohio; 1858–1932) and Kate Chopin (Missouri; 1850–1904) with the South; and Ambrose Bierce (Ohio; 1842–1914?), Dan DeQuille (pen name of William Wright; Ohio and Iowa; 1829–1898), and Frank Norris (Illinois; 1870–1902) with the West. Though Howells occasionally drew on Midwest settings for scenes within larger works—*A Modern Instance* (1882), for example, places action in Indiana and *The Leatherwood God* (1916) in Ohio—and recollected the region in his four autobiographies, he relied almost exclusively on the East and Europe for the settings of his fiction. Chesnutt, too, periodically remembered the Midwest in work written during his years as a Cleveland legal stenographer but more often placed the action of his stories and novels in the South.

Scholars have recently begun to recognize the profound ideological impact writers such as Chesnutt and Dunbar had on twentieth-century African American authors. Langston Hughes, who was born in Missouri and graduated from high school in Cleveland, was central to the success of the Harlem Renaissance, the first fully self-conscious literary movement by African Americans, in the decades following World War I. He would, of course, later relocate to the burgeoning artistic community in New York City where he produced works like "The Negro Speaks of Rivers" and "Mother to Son." But the achievement of Hughes, Countee Cullen, and Zora Neale Hurston had its true cultural foundations in the breakthrough careers of nineteenth-century African Americans, especially Chesnutt and Dunbar. Although the *renaissance* of African American literature was centered in Harlem, New York, its *nascence* was in the Midwest.

Early Twentieth-Century Midwestern Writers

The midwestern tradition in American literature, as it had developed throughout the nineteenth century, might be said to have culminated early in the twentieth century in the novels of Willa Cather (1873–1947). Through *O Pioneers!* (1913), *The Song of the Lark* (1915), and *My Antonia* (1918) as well as numerous shorter prose pieces, the Midwest actually assumes the aspect of a cosmos writ small, populated by a range of completely realized and complex character types. Cather fully humanizes midwesterners, for in her work they belong to different classes, hold diverse beliefs, and hail from a multitude of origins. Cather's treatment of the land itself is also far more complicated than that of her predecessors, as in her fiction the soil of the American prairie seemingly possesses the ability to redeem as often as it would destroy. In Cather's hands, the Midwest and its inhabitants finally transcend the sometimes stereotyped categories of weary granger or quaint hayseed and instead embody supple identities that evolve naturally over the course of a narrative.

With the Midwest in full possession of a distinct, complex identity all its own by the turn of the century, a yearning arose among the artists of the region to establish a geographic base for their creative efforts. And following the World's Fair of 1893, Chicago began to experience a rush in artistic activity. This unprecedented surge inaugurated what became known as the Chicago Renaissance. Writers such as Theodore Dreiser (1871–1945), Floyd Dell (1887–1969), Sherwood Anderson (1876–1941), Edgar Lee Masters (1868–1950), Carl Sandburg (1878–1967), and Vachel Lindsay (1879–1931) sensed that because the Midwest had emerged unquestionably as the American Heartland, the country's cultural center ought to be established there within the region—and in that region's grandest city. Several important publications were founded in Chicago in the years just before World War I: Harriet Monroe's (1860–1936) *Poetry* (1912) and Margaret Anderson's (dates unknown) *Little Review* (1914), to name just two, which helped to establish the Chicago Renaissance as an internationally significant movement. The individuals associated with this group of authors, while holding diverse beliefs and writing about an array of topics and themes, by and large shared three fundamental traits. First, the writers of the Chicago Renaissance were generally committed to the Midwest as a setting for their work. Second, they seemed to focus in one way or another on the growing urbanization and industrialization of American society and the accompanying loss of traditional rural values. Third, many of these writers sought to employ a simplicity of language that both reflected the cadences of ordinary midwestern speech and recognized—some more sympathetically than others—the centrality of the middle and working classes to the life of the region. As the Midwest's first codified literary movement, the Chicago Renaissance did much in the early years of the new century to nurture the region's growing international reputation for artistic excellence.

Satiric Portraits of Small-Town Life

The story of the Midwest in American literature in the first half of the twentieth century seems to be essentially threefold. A number of writers, particularly early in the century, present the Midwest in poetry and prose through mainly satiric portraits of small-town life. Edgar Lee Masters' *Spoon River Anthology* (1915), for instance, is occasionally credited with inaugurating what esteemed critic Carl Van Doren labeled "the revolt from the village," as it contrasts the disillusionment of recent generations with the vigor and pioneering spirit of the original settlers to the region, and so documents the spiritual degeneracy of midwestern culture. But it is more accurate to say that Masters' work critiques the pettiness and sham wholesomeness of midwestern village life. In so doing, Masters advances a tradition launched in the nineteenth century with Mark Twain's biting portraits of St. Petersburg and Hadleyburg and Hamlin Garland's sometimes equally devastating commentaries on small-town midwestern folk. *Spoon River Anthology* deserves credit for transporting this motif of late nineteenth-century midwestern realism into twentieth-century literary Modernism. Written in flat, prosaic rhythms, the poems of Masters' volume are composed as a series of epitaphs from the gravestones of lonely, frustrated midwestern souls whose lives seem to have been largely wasted. Masters' "characters" demonstrate, one after the other, a longing for communal sympathy but show no signs of offering any to others. The collective portrait of the Midwest in *Spoon River Anthology* is certainly distressing but not altogether condemning. Throughout the volume, Masters actually echoes some of the isolation and severity of the Midwest found in mid nineteenth-century literary depictions of the region, reviving a sense of its pathos even as he surveys its darker, more unsettling depths.

Sherwood Anderson's *Winesburg, Ohio* (1919) remains perhaps the most enduring chronicle of disconnect and frustration within the seemingly tranquil communities of middle America. His tales are populated by "grotesques"—individuals whose principal relationship to each other lies in the warped sensibilities that they attempt to keep well concealed from public view. In one sense, then, it might be said that Anderson's achievement consisted of simply doing in prose what Masters had begun to do in verse. Indeed, both authors exploit a stylistically spare, stripped-down rural, middle-class diction in their writing; both focus on the ugliness and despair that partly define midwestern life; and both invite consideration of the ways that modern life has eroded and transformed the "Heartland" values of the agrarian Midwest. But in addition to all of that, Anderson's writing also turned away from nineteenth-century tropes and looked resolutely forward. Consequently, Anderson exerted considerable influence on the next generation's major literary figures. For fellow midwesterner Ernest Hemingway, Anderson partly provided a model for what would become Hemingway's characteristically understated prose style. For William Faulkner, Anderson partly provided the inspiration for the southern novelist to focus on his own "little postage stamp of native soil."[50] In this regard, it might be claimed that midwestern literature—through the work of Sherwood Anderson—fundamentally shaped American literary Modernism and all that it influenced later in the twentieth century.

In novels such as *Main Street* (1920), *Babbitt* (1922), *Arrowsmith* (1925), and *Elmer Gantry* (1927), Sinclair Lewis stepped up the attack on "the village" and exposed the stultifying effect that the sham culture of small Midwest towns could have on an individual whose true potential might have been nurtured and realized in larger, more vital metropolitan areas. In *Babbitt*, for example, well-to-do real-estate partner George F. Babbitt, living in the smugly booming, midsized, midwestern city of Zenith, enjoys a successful career, but his is a domestic existence devoid of grace. Babbitt's neighborhood is lovely enough, standardized and conventional to the extreme, but he dimly realizes the hollowness of his life. At forty-six he begins to rebel through a series of sexual, political, and moral acts. In the end, however, after his closest friend Paul Riesling, a musician turned roofing salesman, has been jailed for murder and Babbitt's own business is threatened, Babbitt sinks back into his Good Citizens' League life and his earlier brand of domestic conventionality. In the end, fearing ostracism above all, Babbitt whimpers, "They've licked me; licked me to a finish!" as the novel comes to a searing close. Throughout the 1920s, Lewis garnered the growing admiration of H. L. Mencken (1880–1956) and other critics of the "booboisie" (Mencken's term) as Lewis laid bare in book after book the herd mentality and discomforting realities of mid-American middle-class culture. In 1930, Lewis became the first American to receive the Nobel Prize for Literature, and his view of the Midwest as the Hinterland was enshrined as well.

The revolt was sustained by other regional expatriates. Ring Lardner (1885–1933), a native of western Michigan who wrote from a vantage point in New York, also situates many of his sardonic tales of twisted small-town folk in the rural hamlets of the Midwest. A story like "Haircut," arguably his best-known story of this kind, compresses all the dullness and cruelty of the most enduring midwestern "attacks on the village" into a single work. James Thurber (1894–1961), celebrated short fiction writer for *The New Yorker* magazine, looked back at his home town of Columbus, Ohio, with comic condescension. In "The Secret Life of Walter Mitty" (1939), easily Thurber's most celebrated story, the docile and mercilessly henpecked protagonist escapes the dreariness and monotony of his work-a-day middle-class life through fantasy. The story introduced the now-archetypal character Walter Mitty to American literature and thus the term *Walter Mittyish* to the American vernacular.

The Midwest as Refuge from the Modern World

A second group of writers in this period portrays the Midwest as an idyllic refuge or retreat from the chaos and desolation of the modern world. Ernest Hemingway, born in Oak Park, Illinois, is best remembered for his classics of high Modernism, novels with foreign settings, including *The Sun Also Rises* (1926), *A Farewell to Arms* (1929), and *For Whom the Bell Tolls* (1940). Nonetheless, Hemingway locates the acclaimed Nick Adams stories of *In Our Time* (1925) in the wilds of northern Michigan, where at last his protagonist attempts to search for the semblance of inner peace after his violent war experiences in Europe. "Indian Camp," "Up in Michigan," and the collection's best known tales, "Big Two-Hearted River: Part I" and "Big Two-Hearted River: Part II," document Nick's gradual recovery from the mental and physical wounds he suffered during World War I. Not at all coincidentally, his recovery takes place in his retreat amid the natural world of the upper Midwest:

> Nick looked down into the pool from the bridge. It was a hot day. A kingfisher flew up the stream. It was a long time since Nick had looked into a stream and seen trout. They were very satisfactory. As the shadow of the kingfisher moved up the stream, a big trout shot upstream in a long angle, only his shadow marking the angle, then lost his shadow as he came through the surface of the water, caught the sun, and then as he went back into the stream under the surface, his shadow seemed to float down the stream with the current, unresisting, to his post under the bridge where he tightened facing up into the current.
>
> Nick's heart tightened as the trout moved. He felt all the old feeling.[51]

Ernest Hemingway. Courtesy Library of Congress.

The profusion of nature here—embodied in the references to the bird, the fish, the stream, and the sun—provide a constant, nearly overwhelming sense of the pastoral. This complex of images, clearly a source of solace to Nick (note the extraordinary level of concentration informing his observations), is juxtaposed to absence of such solace—in other words, the trauma of war—brilliantly veiled by Hemingway behind statements like "It had been a long time since. . . ."

and "He felt all the old feeling." The description of Nick's suffering as implied by such references is also an excellent illustration of Hemingway's hallmark "iceberg" prose style, his ability to provide just the tip of an idea, leaving to readers to infer the larger unstated meanings through rereading and imaginative participation in the text.

Similarly, in *The Great Gatsby* (1925), fellow Modernist expatriate F. Scott Fitzgerald (1896–1940) of St. Paul, Minnesota, envisions the Midwest as a place to which Nick Carraway might return after his harrowing summer in New York among Jay Gatsby and the Buchanans. Following Gatsby's death, Nick recollects the Midwest in ways that are a deliberate ideological expansion of the slightly prescribed agrarian landscapes of Cary, Garland, and Cather: "That's my middle-west—not the wheat or the prairies or the lost Swede towns but the thrilling, returning trains of my youth and the street lamps and sleigh bells in the frosty dark and the shadows of holly wreaths thrown by lighted windows on the snows."[52] Many of Fitzgerald's shorter works, including "The Ice Palace" (1920) and "Winter Dreams" (1922), further contribute to Fitzgerald's mostly affirmative winter-scaped vision of the Midwest. But more generally, Fitzgerald, like Hemingway, sketched his "middle west" as a "Heartland" space that generates hearty, idealistic adolescents who leave their homes only to return years later to rediscover the nurturing simplicity of the farms, streams, and frozen boulevards of their youth. Though written much later in the century, the poetry of Ohioan James Wright (1927–1980) at times implies a comparably affirmative vision of a pastoral Midwest through quasiromantic descriptions of the natural world in poems such as "Stages on a Journey Westward" (1963), "Arrangements with Earth for Three Dead Friends" (1963), and "Lying in a Hammock at William Duffy's Farm in Pine Island, Minnesota" (1963).

Midwestern Urban Literature in the Twentieth Century

A final cluster of twentieth-century authors depicts the Midwest through vast portraits of metropolitan city life. Many of the best known works by Theodore Dreiser, Carl Sandburg, Richard Wright (1908–1960), and Saul Bellow (b. 1915), to name only a few, are set in large midwestern urban areas, and together they demonstrate the degree to which the original idea of an agrarian Midwest has diminished in the twentieth century. Regarded as "the greatest chronicler of America's cities" and remembered for his "mastery of urban psychology,"[53] Theodore Dreiser was really the first American author to write outside the nineteenth-century American tradition and produce work that was of a more modern age. Of course, the fact that his first novel, *Sister Carrie* (1900), was published in the first year of the twentieth century adds to the sense that Dreiser contributed to the inauguration of a new era, but his reputation as an American literary vanguard obviously rests on much more. He brought forward the depiction of individuals living in urban environments initiated by earlier writers such as Howells, Henry James, and Stephen Crane. By self-consciously portraying the vastness of the city as a microcosm in which the processes of a deterministic universe play themselves out, Dreiser demonstrated ultimately that individuals exert little or no control over their fate. In doing so, he quickly garnered the reputation of being the most thorough practitioner of turn-of-the-century American literary naturalism.

Sister Carrie, for example, documents the story of Caroline Meeber, a midwestern girl full of unformulated desires who at eighteen leaves her home in rural Wisconsin to find work in the grand metropolis of Chicago. What Carrie finds upon her arrival in the metropolis is drab and hopeless beyond belief. Everything from the abstract dreariness of her sister's home to the depressing sweat shop conditions of the shoe factory in which she finds employment leads Carrie to drift into a succession of passionless relationships. However, through a series of events—some accidental, some coincidental, but very few intended—Carrie rises in the world in spite of the immorality that Dreiser deliberately attaches to nearly everything that happens to her. In this sense, then, the story of Carrie and her lovers is a study of the mechanical process of success and failure—a process that to Dreiser as a naturalist writer appears unrelated to moral or ethical behavior. George Hurstwood, a restaurant-bar manager whom Carrie meets in Chicago, deserts his family, steals ten thousand dollars, and flees to New York with Carrie, promising marriage. But eventually overcome with remorse, he decides to return the money and, thus, begin a new life with Carrie. His decision to turn a "new leaf" notwithstanding, Carrie abandons him and through a string of happy accidents she becomes a theatrical star while Hurstwood sinks to ruin and eventually commits suicide. Success and failure are, in the end, according to Dreiser in this novel and such other of his works as *Jennie Gerhardt* (1911) and *An American Tragedy* (1925), both aspects of a morally indifferent universe.

Carl Sandburg's depiction of the midwestern urban experience differs decidedly from Dreiser's. In *Chicago Poems* (1916), particularly the volume's best-known poem, "Chicago," Sandburg offers a more balanced, affirmative portrait of the city:

Hog Butcher for the World,
Tool Maker, Stacker of Wheat,
Player with Railroads and the Nation's Freight Handler;
Stormy, husky, brawling,
City of the Big Shoulders. . . . (ll.1–5)[54]

Fundamentally indebted to Walt Whitman for his sense of subject, style and vision, Sandburg stated that his goal as a literary artist was to celebrate America's working classes in poetry that they could read and comprehend. Like Whitman, he wrote in simple language fashioned into long lines of verse free from the constraints of rhyme and meter, and like many of his midwestern predecessors, he wrote in cadences that approximated the rhythms of vernacular speech. But even if Sandburg's affirming and compassionate portraits of the masses fail to present the folk as fully realized human beings (as many recent critics have asserted) there is actually much to congratulate him for. As Cary Nelson has explained, Sandburg ultimately sought to articulate types, not distinct individuals, in order to "make these types available to a popular audience—not so that they could be regarded with self-congratulatory empathy but so that they could be reoccupied with a newly politicized self-awareness."[55] Sandburg, in other words, called for the working classes of America's urban centers to "celebrate themselves" in a grand poetic gesture of political activism. Indeed, this spirit informs practically all of Sandburg's writing, including his epic biographies of Lincoln, *Abraham Lincoln: The Prairie Years* (1927) and *Abraham Lincoln: The War Years* (1939), the latter earning him the Pulitzer Prize in History in 1939. Lincoln's appeal to Sandburg as a biographical subject has its roots in what he would have viewed as a kinship between fellow midwesterners with a penchant for political reform and a proclivity for regional vernacular expression.

Richard Wright and Saul Bellow, both heavily influenced by Dreiser's work, also took up the task of depicting the realities of midwestern city life. Wright's study of Chicago's urban dwellers in *Native Son* (1940) is ultimately drawn from the perspective of the consummate outsider, the racially marginalized Bigger Thomas. In Wright's hands, life in the city is even bleaker than in Dreiser's. To all of the naturalistic force of cosmic determinism bearing down on the characters of *Sister Carrie*, Wright adds the pressures of race, with its sociological and psychological effects on black and white individuals alike. Bigger, Mary, Jan, and Max, to name only a few, are trapped in the great machine of society chiefly by virtue of their participation in stereotyped reactions to racial difference. Although Saul Bellow was born in Canada and is Jewish, he has spent his entire career battling labels that would identify his perspective as that of an "outsider." While fellow midcentury Jewish writers like Joseph Heller and Philip Roth were attracting enormous critical interest to their novels promoted as examinations of Jewish identity, Bellow nevertheless classified himself unrelentingly as an American artist before all else. In *The Adventures of Augie March* (1953), Bellow explores the slums of Dreiser's and Wright's Chicago, and despite the superficial cheerfulness of his protagonist, he, too, emerges with a similarly hopeless impression of the effects of the urban environment on the individual. Biographer Robert Kiernan points out that later novels by Bellow, including *Henderson the Rain King* (1959), *Herzog* (1964), and *Humboldt's Gift* (1975), concentrated more and more on the role of ideas in the

Richard Wright (right), shown here with Orson Welles. Photofest.

modern consciousness—so much so that many consider Bellow currently to be America's foremost intellectual writer. Bellow was awarded the Nobel Prize for Literature in 1976.

Midwestern Playwrights

In addition to producing many of the twentieth century's most acclaimed American novelists and poets, the Midwest can lay claim to several of the most important playwrights of the last 100 years. Born in Davenport, Iowa, Susan Glaspell (1876–1948), for example, fostered early twentieth-century American drama. Glaspell's early work was in prose fiction. She generated a number of regionalist short stories at the turn of the century, tales largely written in the vein of realism but often showing signs of formulaic sentimentality, which were first published in a variety of women's magazines and then later collected in *Lifted Masks* (1912). After publishing a few novels, Glaspell met and married George Cram Cook, who was associated with both the Chicago Renaissance through friend Floyd Dell and later the highly influential dramatic group Provincetown Players, which eventually gave rise to the likes of Eugene O'Neill and Edna St. Vincent Millay. Glaspell's contemporary reputation rests on her experimental plays written between 1916 and 1922 while associated with the Provincetown Players, among them the regularly anthologized one-act drama *Trifles* (1916). A play such as *Trifles* exhibits the influence of late nineteenth-century European drama on Glaspell. Though realism marked her earlier short fiction, the work of the Provincetown Players era presents a more despairing consciousness, often focusing on the desperate, subjugated lives of women in rural midwestern settings. The opening scene description of *Trifles* typifies Glaspell's darker, less mawkish dramatic vision:

> The kitchen in the now abandoned farmhouse of John Wright, a gloomy kitchen, and left without having been put in order—unwashed pans under the sink, a loaf of bread outside the bread-box, a dish-towel on the table—other signs of incompleted work. At the rear the outer door opens and Sheriff comes in followed by Country Attorney and Hale. The Sheriff and Hale are men in middle life, the Country Attorney is a young man; all are much bundled up and go at once to the stove. They are followed by the two women—the Sheriff's wife first; she is a slight wiry woman, a thin nervous face. Mrs. Hale is larger and would ordinarily be called more comfortable looking, but she is disturbed now and looks fearfully about as she enters. The women have come in slowly, and stand close together near the door.[56]

The "gloomy" rural setting, the physically and spiritually worn individuals, the pervading sense of despondency established here at the beginning of the play seem reminiscent of Alice Cary's "The West Country" while they intimate the anguish and frustration throughout such later midwestern works as *Spoon River Anthology* and *Winesburg, Ohio*. Today perhaps only the reputation of Eugene O'Neill figures more prominently than Glaspell's in early twentieth-century American drama, and her stature owes much to the regional sensibility in her plays.

At midcentury, the American theater seemed dominated by the work of Tennessee Williams and Arthur Miller. In their long shadows emerged Chicago playwright Lorraine Hansberry. With *A Raisin in the Sun* (1959), Hansberry became the first African American woman to have a play produced on Broadway as well as the first African American recipient of the prestigious New York Drama Critics Circle Award for Best Play of the Year, beating out Williams' *Sweet Bird of Youth* and O'Neill's *A Touch of the Poet*. Set in the urban squalor of Chicago's south-side slums, *A Raisin in the Sun* compares well with Richard Wright's *Native Son*. Even though the play garnered unprecedented praise from black *and* white audiences early on, Hansberry remained ambivalent about *Raisin*'s success in clarifying the deeper issues at stake for African Americans on the eve of the civil rights movement. Instead of appreciating the work as a critique of institutional racism, the public and many reviewers seemed all too ready to accept the play's apparent endorsement of Pollyannaish optimism, as the ending presents a now-healed Younger family determined to move to the white suburbs. What Hansberry knew was that none of the larger problems looming over the Younger family—and, thus, African American culture—were really resolved in the end: not least the matter of how to handle the inevitable opposition to suburban integration facing the Youngers once they take up residence in their new still-all-white neighborhood, to take just one example. Despite these tensions, Hansberry's play remains a milestone in the Midwest's continuing contribution to American literature and arguably belongs to that cluster of three or four works consistently hailed as classics of American drama.

More recently, fellow Chicagoan David Mamet has taken up the mantle of acclaimed midwestern playwright. Through works like *Sexual Perversity in Chicago* (1972), *American Buffalo* (1975), *Glengarry Glen Ross* (1983), *Speed the Plow* (1988), and *Oleanna* (1992), Mamet has reinvigorated the midwestern writer's reputation for experimentation with idiom. Speech is at the center of all of Mamet's writing—both in the sense of what is being said as well as how it is being said. Critics have almost universally maintained that his representation of vernacular speech is flawless. But, paradoxically, to read or recite Mamet's dialogue properly seems to be nothing short of an acquired skill. The myriad pauses and repetitions that Mamet painstakingly orchestrates throughout his plays are often even more essential to the meaning of a conversation than the ideas conveyed by the words themselves. Moreover, the implied family ideal, the fading of communal bonds, and the pursuit of the American Dream amid the urban landscape—all hallmarks of nineteenth- and twentieth-century midwestern literature—are themes that figure prominently in Mamet's body of work. All said, Mamet may be the most thorough incarnation of the midwestern legacy in contemporary American literature.

Contemporary Midwestern Writers

Recent trends indicate that contemporary authors are utilizing not one or two but the entire range of long-established authorial attitudes toward the Midwest in their work. Midwesterners Toni Morrison (b. 1931), Charles Johnson (b. 1948), Rita Dove (b. 1952), Sandra Cisneros (b. 1954), and Louise Erdrich (b. 1954) are among those writers who treat the region's various legacies—American Indian cultures, agrarian social systems, differing small-town mentalities, larger urban environments—as a collective, wholly integrated heritage by situating the present always in a broader sociohistorical context of the past. Recipient of the Nobel Prize for Literature in 1993 and a multiple best-selling author, Toni Morrison is probably the most celebrated midwestern writer living today in terms of both critical acclaim and popular success. Morrison was born in Lorain, Ohio, a small town on the shore of Lake Erie west of Cleveland. The enormity of her current international reputation as an important American writer makes it possible to forget how heavily her work relies on her native region for setting and materials. Four of her novels (some critics might argue these are also her four most significant books) are set entirely or almost entirely in the Midwest: *The Bluest Eye* (1970), *Sula* (1973), *Song of Solomon* (1977), and *Beloved* (1987). In one sense, of course, Morrison, as many writers before her, simply places her fiction in her own native soil. In another sense, however, Morrison's fictive

Toni Morrison. Photofest.

settings suggest her recognition of the fact that the Midwest is especially well suited for dealing with questions related to the legacies of racism in American culture. Burdened by none of the reductive commonplace historical associations made with the North (i.e., abolitionist activism, fighting the Civil War to free the slaves) and South (i.e., slaveholding, fighting to defend the practice of slavery), the Midwest can be viewed as a "borderland" region between North and South where characters like Pecola Breedlove, Sula Peace, Milkman Dead, and Sethe explore with Morrison's audience themes of race and injustice simultaneously inside and outside regional historical paradigms.

The current generation of midwestern authors, many of whom have already begun to receive prestigious awards for their writing, share a keenness for literary experimentation and an awareness of individual cultural legacies within the context of a larger regional and national history. Charles Johnson is perhaps the most eclectic midwestern writer to emerge in the last twenty years. Hailed as the heir to Ralph Ellison's brand of writing that positions the black experience within the American experience, Johnson has produced novels, also like Ellison's, that are expressions of a highly intellectual, highly philosophical mind. In experimental works like *Faith and the Good Thing* (1974), *Oxherding Tale* (1982), *The Sorcerer's Apprentice: Tales and Conjurations* (1985), and *Middle Passage* (1990), for which he won the National Book Award, Johnson combines phenomenology, Eastern religious thought, American folklore, and fantasy to explore themes of individual and collective consciousness. Johnson's fiction is often narrated within the classical comic mode, which provides his writing with an unmistakable quality of freshness especially in light of the tendency toward the tragic in so much contemporary African

American literature. Along with close friend Ishmael Reed, Johnson is considered the preeminent black male voice in American literature today.

If Johnson represents the male perspective in contemporary African American writing, then Rita Dove is one of its strongest female voices. Born in Akron, Ohio, Dove was the first African American named Poet Laureate and the first since 1950 to win the Pulitzer Prize for Poetry. Critics often describe Dove as a poet with an "inclusive sensibility," a trait in keeping with midwesterners' often misunderstood "niceness." Her writing, in other words, is inclined to pull individuals out of their more limited racial and cultural contexts in the process of exploring common human concerns. "As an artist," Dove notes, "I shun political considerations, and racial or gender partiality."[57] Her 1989 poem "Pastoral" is indicative of this broader vision for African American writing.

The narrative voice in "Pastoral" invokes several levels of archetypal empathy between artist and audience as it transgresses lines of race and gender throughout the poem. Although the first stanza depicts the supremely feminine experience of nursing, the second stanza closes with the nearly equally exclusive masculine experience of lying beside a first lover. Between the two images, Dove creates something of a circuit of imaginative empathy that allows both male and female emotive access to one another's experiential knowledge. Within the context of the pastoral episode identified both in the title and the events of the poem, Dove manages to lift her work into realms that seem to transcend specific cultural understandings. Even though her writing frequently situates itself squarely within the African American literary tradition of acting in response to social injustice, Dove more often seeks to undermine monolithic cultural constructs and in doing so has fashioned for herself a niche within contemporary American writing.

Sandra Cisneros and Louise Erdrich, both graduates of the esteemed Iowa Writers' Workshop master of fine arts program in the 1970s, have in recent years established reputations for themselves as the voices of historically marginalized communities of the Midwest. In both poetry and fiction, Cisneros surveys the Hispanic experience in the United States, often highlighting the realities of violence, racism, and oppression her young protagonists face as they mature in their conspicuously nurturing homes within the Mexican American enclaves of urban America. Her widely acclaimed novel, *The House on Mango Street* (1984), and her 1987 collection of verse, *My Wicked Wicked Ways*, in particular, juxtapose these forces of a hostile social environment and the supportive milieu of family and community. Louise Erdrich has emerged since 1984 as one of the strongest midwestern Native American voices in contemporary American writing. In that year she published *Jacklight*, her first collection of poetry, as well as *Love Medicine*, her first novel, which was awarded the prestigious National Book Critics Circle Award. Set on the Turtle Mountain Reservation, where her grandmother had been tribal chairperson, Erdrich's stories trace the lives of individuals of Chippewa heritage as they struggle with conflicts that arise out of the gradual historical merging of Anglo and Native American culture. A gifted stylist, Erdrich, like Cisneros, presents her writing in experimental forms that possess the unique quality of engaging her readers rather than alienating them.

The Midwest has indeed contributed mightily to American literary history. As a setting, this region has furnished American writers with an evolving ideological landscape for more than two hundred years. Over the last century and a half, its authors have developed a tradition of formal and linguistic experimentation unrivaled by any other geographical area in the United States. From the simple cadences and vernacular rhythms of Lincoln and Twain to the dialect verse of Riley and Dunbar to the formal departures of Cisneros and Erdrich, midwesterners since the Civil War have defined many of the most recognizable and salient features of American literature itself. In fact, the Midwest has produced some of the nation's finest poets, novelists, and playwrights, including five of the ten Americans awarded the Nobel Prize for Literature in the twentieth century. In addition to those authors already mentioned, the Midwest also lays claim to the likes of T. S. Eliot (1888–1965), Zitkala Sa (née Gertrude Simmons, 1876–1938), William Vaughn Moody (1869–1910), Vachel Lindsay (1879–1931), Zona Gale (1874–1938), John Dos Passos (1896–1970), Hart Crane (1899–1932), Tillie Olsen (b. 1913), and William S. Burroughs (1914–1997). Given such enviable credentials, there is little hyperbole in the broader conclusion that midwestern literature really *is* American literature. The region's current crop of acclaimed authors, particularly its varied and profound minority writers, suggests that the Midwest will continue setting the course and defining the character of American literary art in the twenty-first century and beyond.

RESOURCE GUIDE

Printed Sources

Midwestern Literature

Donald, David, and Frederick A. Palmer. "Toward a Western Literature, 1820–1860." In *Lincoln Reconsidered: Essays on the Civil War Era* by David Donald, 167–186. New York: Vintage, 1956; 2nd ed. New York: Vintage Books, 1989.

Greasley, Philip A., ed. *Dictionary of Midwestern Literature*. Bloomington: Indiana University Press, 2001.

Kolodny, Annette. *The Land Before Her: Fantasy and Experience of the American Frontier, 1630–1860.* Chapel Hill: University of North Carolina Press, 1984.

MidAmerica. East Lansing, MI: Midwestern Press, Center for the Study of Midwestern Literature [Michigan State University], 1978–present.

Midwestern Miscellany. East Lansing, MI: Midwestern Press, Center for the Study of Midwestern Literature [Michigan State University], 1974–present.

Nemanic, Gerald. *A Bibliographical Guide to Midwestern Literature*. Iowa City: University of Iowa Press, 1981.

New, W. H. "Colonial Literatures." In *New National and Post-Colonial Literatures*, edited by Bruce King, 102–119. New York: Oxford University Press, 1996.

The Old Northwest. Oxford, OH: Miami University, 1975–1992.

Poetry. Chicago: Modern Poetry Association, 1912–present.

Primavera. Chicago: Salsedo Press (c/o University Feminist Organization, Ida Noyes Hall, 1212 E. 59th Street, Chicago, IL 60637), 1975–1996, 1998–present.

Rusk, Ralph Leslie. *The Literature of the Middle Western Frontier*. 2 vols. New York: Columbia University Press, 1926.

Seelye, John. *Beautiful Machine: Rivers and the Republican Plan, 1755–1825*. New York: Oxford University Press, 1991.

Venable, W. H. *Beginnings of Literary Culture in the Ohio Valley: Historical and Biographical Sketches*. Cincinnati, OH: Clarke, 1891.

Vinz, Mark, and Thom Tammaro, eds. *Inheriting the Land: Contemporary Voices from the Midwest*. Minneapolis: University of Minnesota Press, 1993.

Watts, Edward. *An American Colony: Regionalism and the Roots of Midwestern Culture*. Athens: Ohio University Press, 2002.

Weber, Ronald. *The Midwestern Ascendancy in American Writing*. Bloomington: Indiana University Press, 1992.

Woolley, Lisa. *American Voices of the Chicago Renaissance*. DeKalb: Northern Illinois University Press, 2000.

Magazine and Periodical Publishing

Endres, Kathleen L., ed. *Trade, Industrial, and Professional Periodicals of the United States*. Westport, CT: Greenwood Press, 1994.

Endres, Kathleen L., and Therese L. Lueck, eds. *Women's Periodicals in the United States: Consumer Magazines*. Westport, CT: Greenwood Press, 1995.

Fackler, Mark P., and Charles H. Lippy, eds. *Popular Religious Magazines of the United States*. Westport, CT: Greenwood Press, 1995.

Finkle, Lee. *Forum for Protest*. Cranbury, NJ: Associated University Presses, 1975.

Ford, James L. C. *Magazines for Millions: The Story of Specialized Publications*. Carbondale: Southern Illinois University Press, 1969.

Forsyth, David P. *The Business Press in America: 1750–1865*. Philadelphia: Chilton, 1964.

Gussow, Don. *The New Business Journalism: An Insider's Look at the Workings of America's Business Press*. San Diego, CA: Harcourt Brace Jovanovich, 1984.

Janello, Amy, and Brennon Jones. *The American Magazine*. New York: Abrams, 1991.

Lueders, Bill. *An Enemy of the State: The Life of Erwin Knoll*. Monroe, ME: Common Courage Press, 1996.

Mott, Frank Luther. *A History of American Magazines*. 5 vols. Cambridge, MA: Harvard University Press, 1957–1968.

Nourie, Alan, and Barbara Nourie, eds. *American Mass-Market Magazines*. Westport, CT: Greenwood Press, 1990.

Paine, Fred K., and Nancy E. Paine. *Magazines: A Bibliography for Their Analysis, with Annotations and Study Guide*. Metuchen, NJ: Scarecrow Press, 1987.

Peterson, Theodore. *Magazines in the Twentieth Century*. 2nd ed. Urbana: University of Illinois Press, 1964.

Riley, Sam G., and Gary W. Selnow, eds. *Regional Interest Magazines of the United States*. Westport, CT: Greenwood Press, 1991.

Rusk, Ralph Leslie. *The Literature of the Middle Western Frontier*. 2 vols. New York: Columbia University Press, 1926.

Sloane, David E. E., ed. *American Humor Magazines and Comic Periodicals*. Westport, CT: Greenwood Press, 1987.

Smith, Reed. *Samuel Medary and "The Crisis."* Columbus: Ohio State University Press, 1995.

SRDS Business Advertising Source, Part 1.

SRDS Consumer Magazine Advertising Source.

Swanberg, W. A. *Pulitzer*. New York: Charles Scribner's Sons, 1967.

Taft, William H. *American Magazines for the 1980s*. New York: Hastings House, 1982.

Tebbel, John. *An American Dynasty: The Story of the McCormicks, Medills and Pattersons*. Garden City, NY: Doubleday & Co., 1947.

Tebbel, John, and Mary Ellen Zuckerman. *The Magazine in America, 1741–1990*. New York: Oxford University Press, 1991.

Terrell, Martin. "The *Chicago Defender*'s Great Northern Drive." Master's thesis, Ohio University, 1991.

Trimble, Vance H. *The Astonishing Mr. Scripps: The Turbulent Life of America's Penny Press Lord*. Ames: Iowa State University Press, 1992.

Waldrop, Frank. *McCormick of Chicago: An Unconventional Portrait of a Controversial Figure*. Englewood Cliffs, NJ: Prentice-Hall, 1966.

Washburn, Patrick S. *A Question of Sedition: The Federal Government's Investigation of the Black Press During World War II*. New York: Oxford University Press, 1986.

Wendt, Lloyd. *Chicago Tribune: The Rise of a Great American Newspaper*. Chicago: Rand McNally, 1979.

Web Sites

The Chicago Renaissance
www.chipublib.org/digital/chiren/

The Dunbar Project: Exploring the Life and Legacy of Paul Laurence Dunbar
www.ohiou.edu/crhc/dunbarmain.htm

Minnesota Author Biographies Project
http://people.mnhs.org/authors/index.cfm

Modern American Poetry
www.english.uiuc.edu/maps/

Pioneering the Upper Midwest: Books from Michigan, Minnesota, and Wisconsin, ca. 1820–1910
http://memory.loc.gov/ammem/umhtml/umhome.html

Videos/Films

And the Earth Did Not Swallow Him. Directed by Severo Pérez. 99 minutes. Distributed by Facets Video, Kino on Video, 1999. Videocassette. Adaptation of Tomas Rivera's novel exploring the Latino migrant workers traveling from Missouri to Michigan.

Beloved. Directed by Jonathan Demme. 172 minutes. Burbank, CA: Touchstone Pictures, 1998. Videocassette and DVD. Adaptation of Toni Morrison's Pulitzer Prize-winning novel about a woman who made her way from slavery to a free life in Ohio and will do anything to keep her children from being reenslaved.

"The Black Press: Soldiers Without Swords." Stanley Nelson, director. Half Nelson Productions, 1999.

"Colonel Robert McCormick." A&E Television Network, 1998.

The Great Gatsby. Directed by Jack Clayton. Screenplay by Francis Ford Coppola. Starring Robert Redford and Mia Farrow. 144 minutes. Hollywood: Paramount Home Video, 1991. Videocassette. Adaptation of F. Scott Fitzgerald's jazz age novel about midwesterners in Long Island society.

Mark Twain. Directed by Ken Burns. Produced by Dayton Duncan and Geoffrey C. Ward. 220 min. Burbank: PBS Home Video, 2001. 2 videocassettes or 1 DVD. Documentary about the life and writing of Samuel Langhorne Clemens.

Native Son. Directed by Jerrold Freedman. Coproduction of PBS's American Playhouse. 112 min. Stamford, CT: Lightning Video, 1986. Videocassette. Adaptation of Richard Wright's novel about an angry black youth, Bigger Thomas, in 1930s Chicago.

A Raisin in the Sun. Directed by Daniel Petrie. 128 min. 1961. Reissued, Culver City, CA: Columbia Tristar Home Video, 1999. Videocassette and DVD. Sidney Poitier,

Claudia McNeil, and Ruby Dee star in Lorraine Hansberry's drama about a Chicago family's attempt to find/make meaning in their lives.

The Secret Life of Walter Mitty. Produced by Samuel Goldwyn. Directed by Norman Z. McLeod. Starring Danny Kaye and Virginia Mayo. 110 min. 1947. Reissued, New York: HBO Video, 1991. Videocassette. James Thurber's short story of a henpecked husband.

Recordings

Carl Sandburg Reading His Poetry. Recorded March 21, 1958, in New York City. Caedmon, 1962. TC 1150. LP analog, 33[T] rpm.

Dove, Rita. *Selected Poems.* 90 min. Random House Audio, 1993. RH 314. Sound cassette.

Dunbar, Paul Laurence. *I Know What the Caged Bird Feels: The Best Loved Poems of Paul Laurence Dunbar.* Read by Ameria Jones. Masterbuy Audio Books, 1997. 964559366. Sound cassette.

Hemingway, Ernest. *The Short Stories.* 2 vols. 10 hours. Read by Stacy Keach. 1953. Reissued, Simon & Schuster Audio, 2002. 10 compact disks.

Lardner, Ring. *Best Short Stories.* Read by Daniel Grace. 12 hours. Books on Tape, 1977. 8 sound cassettes.

Masters, Edgar Lee. *Spoon River Anthology.* Performed by Julie Harris. 58 min. Caedmon. TC 1152. Sound cassette.

Festivals and Events

James Wright Poetry Festival, Martins Ferry, Ohio. Early spring.
www.eastern.ohiou.edu/events/jwright/jwfhome.htm

Midwest Literary Festival, Aurora, Illinois. September.
Sherman Jenkins or Mike O'Kelley
(630) 897-5500
http://midwestliteraryfestival.com

Ohio University Literary Festival, Athens, Ohio. May.
English Department
(740) 593-2838
www.english.ohiou.edu/litfest/

Organizations

Many midwestern writers receive close attention from individual author societies meeting annually in May or June under the aegis of the American Literature Association. For a complete list, see www.americanliterature.org.

Iowa Writers' Workshop
University of Iowa
102 Dey House
507 N. Clinton Street
Iowa City, IA 52242-1000
(319) 335-0416
www.uiowa.edu/~iww

The Poetry Foundation
(formerly MPA, Modern Poetry Association)
1030 N. Clark Street, Suite 420

Chicago, IL 61610
(312) 787-7070
www.poetrymagazine.org/toc_mpa.html

Society for the Study of Midwestern Literature
David D. Anderson
Department of American Thought and Language
Michigan State University
East Lansing, MI 48824-1033
(517) 355-2400

Museums and Special Collections

Historical societies and university libraries in each state have major literary manuscript collections. Authors' birthplaces and homes can be visited in every city and many small towns. Archival and manuscript collections relating to midwestern authors are especially abundant at the following libraries:

Harry Ransom Humanities Research Center
University of Texas, Austin
21st and Guadalupe
P.O. Box 7219
Austin, TX 78713-7219
Phone: (512) 471-8944
Fax: (512) 471-9646
www.hrc.utexas.edu/home.html

Henry W. and Albert A. Berg Collection of English and American Literature
The New York Public Library
Fifth Avenue and 42nd Street, Room 320
New York, NY 10018-2788
(212) 930-0802
E-mail: brgref@nypl.org

The Newberry Library
60 W. Walton Street
Chicago, IL 60610-7324
(312) 943-9090
www.newberry.org

MUSIC

Richard D. Wetzel

Before the nineteenth century, America's coastal metropolises—New York, Boston, Philadelphia—were the nation's centers of greatest musical significance. As westward migration increased, cities formed in the Midwest and soon boasted bands, orchestras, choral societies, theaters, and concert halls that rivaled those in the East. By 1850 much of America's musical vitality and creative impetus were being generated in the heartland. The secular and religious music of indigenous peoples, European immigrants, African Americans, and others took root in the Midwest. Their music sometimes retained its distinctiveness and sometimes coalesced to form new styles and genres. Among the latter were nineteenth-century parlor music, ragtime, blues, Kansas City jazz, country and western, and rock and roll. These styles, and the people who created them and whose performances and recordings enriched America's musical culture, are the subjects of this chapter.

MUSIC OF INDIGENOUS PEOPLES IN THE MIDWEST

An overview of music in the Midwest rightly begins with an introduction to the music of its indigenous peoples. Of the estimated more than 1,000 Indian tribes who once lived in North America, the most prominent of the Midwest were the Shawnee, Miami, Wyandot, Ojibwa (Chippewa), Menominee, Cherokee, Crow, Delaware, Dakota, and Sioux. Despite some differences in their music, they shared a common musical aesthetic: the belief that songs preexist and are given through dreams or visions. A song was a mystical and religious *gift* to an *individual*, not the creation of a "composer." It was also inseparable from the spirit, power, or "medicine" (called *orenda* by the Iroquois, and *manido'* by the Ojibwa) of the object, creature, or phenomenon it was about or that inspired it, and this power was transferred to the individual when the song was "received."

Frances Densmore, an early ethnomusicologist who studied the music of the Ojibwa and Menominee in the Great Lakes region, says the first song to be received was the boy's *vision song*: "Every Indian boy, at the age of about twelve years, was expected to fast for several days and watch for the dream or 'vision' in which he saw his individual 'spirit helper,' and usually received a song from that source. In later years, when he wished to receive 'spirit help,' he sang the song and also performed certain prescribed acts."[1]

This perception of the origin and use of music has no parallel in European American culture. Native American music served a practical function—for example, to cure the sick or ensure a successful hunt or battle. It was performed by medicine men, and much of it had religious significance. Indian music was rarely performed without dancing and—except in love or courting songs, lullabies, and children's game songs—treats spiritual experience, dance, singing, and drumming as integrated and inseparable.[2]

The study of Indian music by qualified, objective scholars came slowly, and early European Americans had difficulty accepting it as music. Some, hearing Indian music for the first time, thought they heard the same song being sung over and over. Missionaries regarded Indian songs as a "persistent phase of heathenism." Typical of the latter was the Reverend David Jones (1736–1817). A minister from New Jersey, Jones spent approximately a year as a missionary among the Shawnee and Delaware Indians in what would become the state of Ohio. After hearing and watching three Shawnee *Monneetoes* [*sic*] he wrote:

> Their noise was shocking. . . . Each had a false face, and all dressed in bearskin with the hair on, so that the only resemblance of their species [humanity] consisted in walking. The foremost had a red face, with a prodigious long nose, and big lips; the others had black faces with long chins resembling bears. All had cased tortoise shells, with artificial necks—grains of corn are put into these, to make a gingle [*sic*]—and many other trinkets are used to complete the noise. . . . In short their looks, voices and actions were such, that it was thought if they had got their samples from beneath [Hades], the scene could not be much exceeded.[3]

What Jones witnessed was a Bear Dance common to most eastern tribes. Indians admired the black bear's physical appearance and quasi-human qualities. It could stand upright, walk on full foot with five toes, and use its forepaws somewhat like a human hand. It could be playful, but was a fast runner and fierce fighter. By "receiving" a song about the bear, the Indian acquired its spirit.[4]

While European Americans considered this idea superstitious, it is quite the opposite. Nothing was supernatural to the Indian, as we understand that term. The words to Indian songs show that they felt a union and communion with animals, whom they addressed as brothers, as well as with trees, rain, and thunder, and all objects and creatures through the mysterious power they shared with them.[5]

As the Indians were removed from the East and became part of American myth and lore, nineteenth-century Americans romanticized them. Popular songs (called parlor songs), poetry, and novels of the time (especially the novels of James Fenimore Cooper) portrayed the Indian as a noble savage, the victim of the white man's cruelty and greed. William Cumming Peters' song "The Spotted Fawn" (Cincinnati, 1845) tells of the tragic massacre of "Spotted Fawn, the Red Chief's only child," and her betrothed, "gallant young White Cloud," on their wedding day. The villains were white men who "through the forest, stealthily . . . came in wrath . . . and blood was in their path." All musical elements of the song are European American, and pieces like this, as well as more ambitious orchestral compositions purportedly based on "Indian melodies" (e.g., Edward MacDowell's *Indian Suite*), helped call attention to Native American music but did little to expand knowledge of its styles or the social, religious, and cultural contexts in which it was used. Some European Americans believed that Indian music was useful only when its melodies and rhythms were incorporated into large works for orchestra or chorus. When songs were performed as solos, they were often given elaborate piano accompaniments.[6]

Ethnographic scholarship by Densmore, Bruno Nettl, and Gertrude P. Kurath has placed Indian music in its social and religious contexts, and related it to other western folk music. The development of the phonograph early in the twentieth century contributed to the accurate study of Indian music because none of the native peoples possessed a music notation system.

In terms of general stylistic features, Indian music is monophonic (unharmonized melody), although it is rarely sung without the accompaniment of drums and other percussion instruments. When women sing with men the voices are an octave apart; accompanying percussion instruments create heterophony. Melodies often begin high and end low, and the last note is frequently the lowest note in the melody, although it may not be the "keynote." Range is not wide, and the Ojibwa, Iroquois, and Creek songs collected by Densmore, Kurath, and Nettl are largely confined to one octave. Modern notation shows that minor thirds occur frequently, especially descending. Repeated notes are pervasive. Wide leaps are uncommon. Fractional or microtonal pitches limit the usefulness of modern musical terms, especially the European American perception of the term *scale*.[7] Some melodies suggest sophisticated awareness of the overtone series and diatonic chord patterns. Others seem confined to a single, pivotal tone around which one or two notes move below or above it. In spite of these patterns, the performance of Indian melodies on tempered instruments (e.g., piano) produces a distorted interpretation. Indian song texts, similarly, defy translation or paraphrasing. Nevertheless, numerous Indian melodies and texts have been adapted for use as hymns in various Christian church hymnals as well as in school textbooks.

Rhythm is generally more significant than melody in Indian music. Among the Ojibwa of White Earth, Leech Lake, and Red Lake reservations in Minnesota, "the idea of song" resides in its rhythm.[8] Vocal accent determines the length and shape of a rhythmic pattern; repetitions of one pattern and combinations of different patterns create metric units.

Given their supernatural power and origin, most individual songs were ceremonial and largely vocal, although flutes, whistles, and percussion instruments of multiple shapes and sizes were made from wood, bone, and pottery. These were played primarily by men. The most common instrument used to accompany singing was the single-headed frame drum. The rhythmic complexity of the song developed because the song and drum beat did not move at the same speed.

Indians prefer chorus singing over solo singing. Among the Ojibwa a leader may begin a song, but will quickly draw others into it in order that their *orenda* may supplement his own. Unlike the European American singer, the Indian sings with mouth slightly open and teeth lightly separated and makes little use of the lips. The resultant tone is forced and nasal, and singers cultivate a fast vibrato. There is much sliding and gliding between pitches, and songs often end with shrill exclamatory vocables ("wah—hee, hee, hee!").

Dances are divided into sections, each having a distinctive song and movement, and are usually begun by a leader or leaders who may shake rattles and wave feather fans and engage the gathering with antiphonal calls. Other dancers may form a line behind them and respond to their movements. If there are two lines, men are in one and women in the other. Lines generally form circles and move counter-clockwise.

Choreographic motions are energetic and varied, in time with a continuous drum beat. Iroquois moves studied by Kurath include stepping in place, shivering, the lunge and shiver, crouch and hop, clapping, heel-bump, shuffle, pivot, twist, stomp step, and jump, among many others. Motions are designed to evoke specific spirits or achieve specific results, such as the Sun Rite or Rain Dance, or (as in the Bear Dance) they mime the motions of a particular animal.

THE EUROPEAN INFLUX: CHURCH MUSIC

The European immigrants who arrived in increasing numbers beginning in the seventeenth century traveled in small sailing vessels that had room for essentials only; fashionable musical instruments they may have known (harpsichords, lutes, organs, viols, and various wind instruments) were left behind. Early musical activity by European immigrants was largely vocal and served both social and religious functions. The Psalms, the only acceptable texts to Protestants (especially those who followed John Calvin's teachings, regardless of national origin), were paraphrased and rhymed, and sung to stark homophony with little use of counterpoint. More complex motets, anthems, and cantatas with their arias and recitatives were impractical.

Among the most important New England influences were hymnbooks (Psalms plus new religious poems) that opened with Prefaces or Lessons—brief pedagogical methods—from which the fundamentals of music could be learned. The forum for using these books was called the singing school. Both had their precursors in Europe but were nonetheless made distinctively American. Called "oblongs" or "end-openers" because of their format, the hymnbooks (also called tune books) were frequently written not in traditional notation but with note shapes that indicated the pitches of the syllables (wedge = fa, circle = sol, rectangle = la, diamond = mi) so that one could learn to sight sing by memorizing the sound of the shapes without having to learn the notes in the various scales and keys. Dozens of singing masters expanded upon this idea, designing their own more exotic note shapes. Some added half-moons, traditional note shapes with slashes drawn through them at various angles, or numbers rather than note-heads. Each innovator claimed that his system was easier to use than those of his predecessors and competitors. The systems had various generic names, among them shape notes, buckwheat notes, and patent notes.

Three- or four-voice homophonic settings gave the melody to the tenor and incorporated brief imitative passages. The desired sound was nasal and ringing. Titles of midwestern collections emphasized American identity: N.D. Gould's *National Church Harmony* (Boston and Cincinnati, 1832) and Allen D. Carden's *Missouri Harmony* (Cincinnati, 1834) were typical. Singing schools were conducted by peripatetic singing masters who held classes in schools, taverns, and churches. Indeed, early religious, cultural, and social life in America was largely shaped by itinerant and often self-taught masters: circuit-riding preachers, portrait painters, schoolmasters, and tinkers of various kinds, who generally boasted at least two skills or crafts (the schoolmaster was often a singing master, and the portrait painter produced signs).

While little documentation survives, we can assume that the French trappers and fur traders who traveled the rivers and lakes of the Midwest during the eighteenth century sang chansons popular in their native country, and Roman Catholic priests who established missions certainly employed Gregorian chants in their celebration of Office and Mass. The earliest musical ensembles in Indiana appear to have been those of a German religious communal society, George Rapp's Harmony Society, located at New Harmony between 1815 and 1824. Midwest culture, generally, was an international mixture throughout this period.

The earliest music in the Midwest with a truly American flavor came from the East as pioneers brought with them their favorite songbooks, choosing from the hundreds available to them from publishers in Boston, Philadelphia, and New York. The midwestern market expanded rapidly, in part because of the religious awakenings, revivals, and then the Sunday School movement that characterized American religious life of the eighteenth and nineteenth centuries. With the growth of towns and cities came private schools, academies, seminaries and convents, and ultimately public schools, although the latter were strongly resisted by Roman Catholics and others who objected to being taxed for mass education. Music was important in the curricula of all of them.

Music of the Roman Catholic Church was especially significant in the Midwest, and the Catholic Normal School of the Holy Family was established in 1871 in St. Francis, Wisconsin, a suburb of Milwaukee, to train teachers for parochial schools. When Polish and Slovenian immigrants augmented the predominantly German Catholic population in the nineteenth century, Milwaukee became a center of the Caecilian movement in America. Initiated in Europe, the Caecilian movement sought to restore Gregorian chant and Renaissance music to the liturgy. One of the founders of the Catholic Normal School at St. Francis, John B. Singenberger, formed the first Caecilian group in the United States in 1873.

By the 1830s Cincinnati was the musical hub of the Midwest. Eastern musicians ridiculed shaped notes, but they lost little popularity as the nineteenth century wore on. Further, Cincinnati soon had a Musical Fund Society, patterned after the one in Philadelphia; an Eclectic Academy of Music, where Timothy Mason introduced the Pestalozzian system of teaching music and where concerts were given by an orchestra of twenty-four players; and a Sacred Music Society that performed Haydn's *Creation* and Handel's *Messiah*, and gave concerts with the famed Germania Orchestra that visited the city in 1853 and 1854. By that time no visiting artist, regardless of stature, could ignore Cincinnati.

SECULAR MUSIC OF THE NINETEENTH CENTURY: PARLOR MUSIC, THE MINSTREL SHOW, BANDS, AND RAGTIME

As theaters and public concert halls appeared in American cities in the eighteenth century, secular and sacred music diverged. By the time midwestern musical culture began to flourish, American styles modified European harmonies, rhythms, and texts, and indigenous genres were emerging. The emancipation from European music was under way, but so-called serious American composers and performers throughout the nineteenth century lamented the absence of a national music and tradition, and they self-consciously traveled to Berlin, London, and ultimately Paris to study and legitimize their artistic credentials. American and European critics spoke disparagingly of music composed in America, and until the early decades of the twentieth century, saw nothing worthy of the term "American music." They were looking in the wrong places and using inappropriate criteria.

The industrial revolution brought about refinements in the mechanisms of musical instruments, especially the piano. The first prominent piano maker in the Midwest was D. H. Baldwin (1821–1899), who established himself in Pike's Opera House in Cincinnati and went on to become an enduring force in the industry, ultimately sharing international dominance with an immigrant German piano builder in New York, William Steinway (1835–1896).

But purchasing a piano required a considerable investment of money, and the instrument had significance beyond musical entertainment. As a piece of furniture, it symbolized middle-class status, and it became the centerpiece in the inner sanctum of the American home, the parlor. Whether they lived in small towns or on isolated farms, nineteenth-century Americans had to entertain themselves, and they did so in the parlor. Their talents and training were generally modest, but their enthusiasm was unbounded and created a huge market for vocal and instrumental music now known as parlor music.

Marches, waltzes, cotillions, quadrilles, polkas, variations on opera arias, folk melodies, and popular songs were published in single sheets and collections. Most featured practical and easily mastered arrangements. Publishers arose in Cincinnati (W. C. Peters & Sons; John Church, Jr.), Chicago (Root & Cady; Higgins Bros.), St. Louis (Balmer & Weber; J. J. Dobmeyer & Co.; Compton & Doan), Cleveland (S. Brainard & Co.; Holbrook & Long), Lafayette (Patrick & Crose), Milwaukee (H. N. Hempsted), Detroit (H. D. Sofge), Madison (John Luck), and other cities of the Midwest. By 1870 Milwaukee alone had fourteen music publishers and retail music stores.

The most popular genre was the sentimental song, whose texts touched the hearts of middle-class Americans. Verses of unrequited love portrayed women as angelic figures located somewhere between earth and heaven; other songs extolled the sanctity of motherhood, recalled childhood and objects of the past ("Old Dog Tray," "The Old Arm Chair," "The Old Oaken Bucket"), mourned death (especially the deaths of children and mothers), and invoked quasi-religious subjects replete with metaphors of moonlight, dreams, flowers, streams, lakes, and trees. The music employed simple rhythms, melodies in narrow range, and harmonies comprising a few easy chords.

Famous works in the genre are "Open Thy Lattice, Love," "Come Where My

Love Lies Dreaming," and "Gentle Lena Clare" by Stephen Foster (1826–1864), whose brief residence in Cincinnati was artistically formative and led to his professional association with his early publisher, W.C. Peters (1805–1866). Foster's melodic style is indebted to the English ballad and the Italian aria, but its spirit is hauntingly American, and it is a spirit that emanated from the Midwest, not the East.

The distinction between European concert music and parlor music was especially acute in the Midwest, where, in spite of the preponderance of German immigrants, there was less inclination to imitate and be intimidated by European masterpieces. (There was, for example, no midwestern counterpart to the academic, pro-European *Dwight's Journal of Music*, published in Boston from 1852 to 1881.) Further, parlor music often served a pedagogical function: the numerous "professors" who both composed and taught it (e.g., Charles Grobe, 1817–1879) did much to shape the fledgling musical culture upon which later American achievements and institutions were built.

More important, the strain-structured marches and harmonically simple song forms of parlor music (not complex and contrapuntal European sonatas) provided the building blocks of a soon-to-appear truly American music, ragtime. And there was a final irony: much of the parlor music played and studied in the Midwest, and ridiculed by East Coast critics, was published in cities in the East. Midwesterners wanted a music that spoke to their time and place. To them, music that failed to do this, regardless of its sophistication, was irrelevant.

Minstrelsy

When a distinctive American music appeared it fused a multitude of national traditions—a process possible only in America—and the most essential musical ingredients came from Africa, brought here by slaves. The mixing of traditions began in a curious genre called the minstrel show. As a musical and theatrical genre, the American minstrel show is a social, political, and cultural embarrassment, if not a scandal; at the same time it stands as the earliest and most far-reaching achievement in the creation of a native American music: jazz. Jazz is possibly the only music that can be called a truly universal music. It would have been slower to develop—perhaps it would never have developed—without the minstrel show.

The minstrel show integrated African American and European American musical elements for the first time. Further, its combination of humor, satire, dance, and sentimental songs appealed to a large part of the American populace, while its syncopated rhythms and snappy tempos quickly became part of a broad and general musical expression and vocabulary. The music of America was enriched, but at the expense of the African American, who was parodied and denigrated in its jokes, songs, and dances.

The river cities of the Midwest were significant to minstrelsy's birth and dissemination. Steamboats on the Ohio, Mississippi, and Missouri rivers were floating theaters. Interracial encounters on board and at shore gave minstrel shows their dialogue, humor, song lyrics, characters, and plots. All revolved around a ludicrous distortion of the personality and intellect of the black, sometimes portrayed as a rural character ("Jim Crow") and other times as an urban dandy ("Zip Coon" or "Dandy Jim").

During the 1820s, Thomas Dartmouth "Daddy" Rice (1808–1860) toured the

Ohio River towns with circuses, performing short entr'actes that were the prototype of the minstrel show.[9] He blackened his face with burnt cork, wore ragged and tattered clothes, spoke and sang in the pseudo-dialect of the plantation slave, and danced grotesque steps and movements that combined African American folk dance with the Irish jig. He became especially famous for an act he created called "Jim Crow," reportedly the first solo act by a blackface performer.[10]

Dozens of "Jim Crow" songs were written in imitation of Rice's original, and publishers issued them with piano accompaniments. The following verse is a typical Jim Crow lyric.

> When Jim Crow is president
> Of dis United State
> He'd drink mint jewlips
> An swing pon a gate.[11]

Minstrel show performers provided their own accompaniment as they sang and danced. Instruments included the tambourine, four-string banjo (an instrument with African roots), homemade rhythm instruments called bones that produced a unique tapping, rattling sound, and fiddle, played in a manner called "roaring." The exotic and energetic musical sounds framed fast-paced jokes that ridiculed politicians and pretentious intellectuals and touched on gender and racial issues. The whole was presented by a buffoon character who spoke in a pseudo-Negro dialect and who, in spite of his portrayed poverty and ignorance, ironically emerged as a paragon of folk wisdom.

The scandalously racist minstrel show integrated African American and European American musical elements for the first time. Courtesy Library of Congress.

Dramatic and musical elements were expanded in the 1830s and 1840s, the minstrel's classic period, and the productions became longer, more varied, and sectional. Ohio native Daniel Decatur Emmett (1815–1904) made important contributions to the genre, and is rightly called the father of classic minstrelsy, although the concept originated with British musicians Charles Dibdin (1745–1814) and Charles Matthews. Emmett played fiddle, fife, drums, and banjo, and in 1843 formed the Virginia Minstrels, a quartet that became internationally known and the model for dozens of similar ensembles that toured America. Some troupes were active well into the twentieth century.

Emmett was a skilled instrumentalist, dancer, and songwriter. It is difficult to say which of the more than 100 songs attributed to him are folk songs that he adapted and which ones he actually composed, but there is no doubt about the authenticity of his most famous one, "In Dixie's Land," written in 1859 as a "walk-around," by then the customary finale to the minstrel show. An abolitionist, Emmett was chagrined when the song became the marching song of the Confederacy.

Minstrel Show Dancing

Some elements of the style can be traced to the Irish jig, British folk dances and hornpipes, and the dances of American riverboat men, frontiersmen, and mountain men of the Midwest and West. A particularly acrobatic step, called the "kneel"—a sudden drop to one knee, then more steps and a drop to the other knee—may have originated in Indiana.

Most influential, however, were dances of plantation African Americans. The covers and lyrics of hundreds of published song sheets describe blacks doing "heel solos" (the precursor of tap dancing), leaps with outstretched arms (called the "pigeon wing"), and strutting steps (called the "turkey trot"), among many others. Song texts indicate where certain steps occurred and suggest how they were done:

> He twist round de ancle,
> And he flatten on de heel,
> And he makes a mighty hole—
> When his foot gib a wheel.
>
> Here is the Jay bird wing!
> And the back action spring.

Perhaps the most curious tradition to be incorporated into minstrel show dancing was that of the religious sect called the Shakers. Shaker settlements were numerous in the East, but the Midwest also had established communities. A pre–Civil War painting by C. Winter shows minstrels imitating Shaker dance movements.[12]

Perhaps the most novel aspect of the minstrel show was the dancing that accompanied songs and instrumental numbers. Shuffling and stomping steps, body twists, bizarre leg positions and high-stepping kicks, angular motions of arms and elbows, the use of hands and fingers, props (especially hats), and the speed of the dancers' movements together formed a repertory of motion unknown to any previous dance tradition.

Negative racial and religious implications aside, minstrelsy was a tightly unified choreographic, dramatic, and musical entertainment that addressed political and social issues of its time, and it resonated with a large part of both rural and urban America before the Civil War. Minstrelsy also provided the choreographic models and attitude for the acceptance of the numerous lively social dances that appeared in the twentieth century, among them the Charleston and its successor, the jitterbug.

Popular Dance in the Nineteenth Century

The most popular entertainment during the nineteenth century was the social dance, also called an assembly or ball. Sometimes held after a theater production, a ball could last as long as eight hours and comprised a succession of cotillions, quadrilles, and similar line dances (square) that alternated with couple dances (round), among them the waltz, polka, schottisch, mazurka, and galop. Unlike the rowdy atmosphere of the minstrel show, the ball was characterized by modesty, propriety, and politeness, not only in its European dance steps and movements, but also in conversation and dress. For the ladies, the latter was often determined by fashions illustrated in the most recent issue of *Godey's Lady's Book*.

The degree of formality varied, and in the Midwest dances after about 1840 assimilated regional folk influences ("calling" replaced the dancing master), but a common format prevailed. The ball began with a march during which the couples promenaded around the room. A succession of dances followed, alternating duple and triple meter dances. The polka became a favorite after 1840. The waltz, brought to America by German and Austrian immigrants, was first viewed as too "wanton," but was accepted by 1830. If the occasion was ceremonial, "To Anacreon in Heaven" was certain to be played. Originally an English drinking song, the tune was later adapted to the text "The Star-Spangled Banner," and in the twentieth century it became the national anthem of the United States. The ball ended with the song "Sweet Home."

The public lives of Americans, including those who lived in its midland, were regulated by rules of social etiquette. Many can be inferred from the cover art on nineteenth-century popular sheet music. Manuals on correct ballroom behavior were an essential part of every up-to-date home library, and instructed ball-goers to dance "with modesty, neither affect to make a parade of your knowledge; refrain from great leaps and ridiculous jumps, which would attract the attention of all toward you."[13]

Bands in the Nineteenth Century

Just as the piano in the home parlor was the symbol of a family's middle-class status, the presence of a band in a nineteenth-century American town distinguished it as a real community. Bands gave dignity and color to social, political, and cultural ceremonies and were the object of civic pride. They allowed Americans to indulge their fascination with things military, although by the middle of the nineteenth century the connection of many "regimental" bands to actual military units had become tenuous. The military association was not surprising, since the American band tradition had its foundation in the colonial period when most towns and hamlets maintained small ensembles of about ten musicians to provide music for their militia units. The Morrill Act of 1862 required courses in military training at midwestern land-grant colleges. Military ceremonies called for music, and uniformed sixteen-piece brass bands to U.S military specifications sprang up at universities across the Midwest after 1865.[14]

It is estimated that in the decade before the Civil War there were more than 3,000 bands, with more than 60,000 members, active in the United States. Some were supported by taxes from "band laws," levied by states to provide free public concerts. An early civic band was established in Naperville, Illinois, in 1859.

As bands increased in number some became professional or semi-professional "business bands." They toured throughout the United States and Canada, playing a varied repertory of opera overtures, popular songs, and contemporary dance music. Two noted ones in the Midwest were Russel Munger's Great Western Band of St. Paul and Christopher Bach's Band of Milwaukee. While professional bands dominated the limelight in the latter part of the nineteenth century and well into the twentieth (Gilmore, Sousa, Liberati, and Pryor, among many others), it was amateur bands that kept the quasi-military band movement alive and vital for such a long time.

American businesses and industries made substantial contributions to the maintenance of bands with both financial support and other inducements. Newspapers commonly carried advertisements seeking a person with a given business or manufacturing skill, with the stipulation that he also be a competent performer on an instrument. Many factories had their own bands. Probably the most distinguished cornet soloist to come out of the Midwest was Bohumir Kryl (1875–1961). Born in Prague, he immigrated to the United States at age fourteen and settled in Indianapolis. He was employed by the When Clothing Company to play in the company-sponsored band. He also studied with another midwestern cornet virtuoso, Fred Weldon, director of the 2nd Regiment Band of Chicago. Kryl ultimately became a cornetist in the most famous of all bands, Sousa's.

By 1889 *Harper's Weekly* estimated that more than 10,000 military bands were active in the United States.[15] Most were in the eastern and midwestern states. Among bands in the Midwest were the Elgin Watch Factory Band of Elgin, Illinois, with an ensemble of seventy-six musicians under the leadership of Professor J. Heckler; the Cleveland Gray's Band; the Toledo City Band; the Metropolitan Band of Dayton; and the Kansas City Band.

The twentieth century saw continuing increase in the number of bands as fraternal and veterans' organizations (Elks, Masons, American Legion, Veterans of Foreign Wars) and the Salvation Army, among others, swelled their ranks. These bands were all-male organizations, although female soloists (vocalists, harpists, violinists) might appear in concerts with them. There were, however, all-female bands, among them Helen May Butler and her Ladies Brass Band, which appeared at the Minnesota State Fair in 1909.

Midwestern educational institutions early joined the band movement. A brass band formed at the University of Indiana in 1832. Soon after their founding the University of Michigan (1817) and Notre Dame University (1842) also had bands. Hundreds of universities and colleges in the Midwest are renowned today for their excellent bands and wind ensembles, and many regularly commission works from composers throughout the world. When music became part of public education, bands were included in the curricula. Elementary school bands were active in Columbus, Ohio, as early as 1892.

Ragtime

Midwestern contributions to popular music blossomed with ragtime, which Rudi Blesh, its leading authority, calls "the first native music thoroughly to encompass the contradictory American spirit" and "to include in creation and performance both of the races, Black and White": "It issued in its origins from no Caucasian majority but from the deprived American minority of dark-skinned people. And it came from no conservatories nor, even, from studios however humble. It bloomed in the lurid nights of those inner cities of the 90's, the infamous redlight districts of brothels, saloons, casinos and wine rooms."[16] The time and place of ragtime's origin are obscured by its association with and possible derivation from the cakewalk, the walk-around of the minstrel show, the racist "coon songs" heard in vaudeville theaters, the syncopated music of traveling circus bands, spirituals, work songs, and country blues. Although ragtime is commonly viewed as a piano medium, Scott Joplin's (1868–1917) "The Entertainer" was dedicated to James Brown and His Mandolin Club, and "The Cascades" is "Respectfully Dedicated to Kimball and Donovan, Banjoists." And while its birthplace is assumed to be New Orleans, in its classic stage ragtime was nurtured and flourished in the Midwest.

Among the earliest pieces called ragtime in print were Chicago bandleader William H. Krell's "Mississippi Rag" (Chicago, 1897); black pianist Tom Turpin's (1873–1922) "Harlem Rag" (St. Louis, 1897); Joplin's "Original Rags" (Kansas City, 1899); and what would become the defining piece of the genre, Joplin's "Maple Leaf Rag" (Sedalia, Missouri, 1899). Prior to this rags were known as "jig piano." Anecdotal comments suggest that the music was performed almost two decades before it appeared in print. W. C. Handy (1873–1958), the composer of "St. Louis Blues," apparently heard something like ragtime in a café in Memphis around 1880. Compositions by America's first internationally known pianist-composer, Louis Moreau Gottschalk (1829–1869), a Creole born in New Orleans, suggest that the sounds that came to characterize ragtime emerged even earlier. Of particular interest are his *Bamboula* (1844) and *Le Banjo* (1854), whose syncopated rhythms fascinated Frederick Chopin and Franz Liszt when Gottschalk played for them in Paris.

The creators and performers of ragtime came from diverse places. A few outstanding ones among the many were Scott Joplin from Texarkana, Texas, who spent his most formative years in Sedalia, Missouri; Tom Turpin, who was born in Savannah, Georgia, but moved to St. Louis at an early age; and James Scott (1886–1938), born in Neosho, Missouri. Their contributions to the genre changed American music forever. In fact, the features of the music and the freedom with which they are treated comprise a musical embodiment of American democratic ideals.

The distinctive features of ragtime piano composition are the constant use of rhythmic syncopation ("ragging") in the melody, which is played with the right hand; and the steady, even pattern of bass-chord figures played by the left. The effect suggests the plucking sound of a plantation banjo. The left-hand motion requires the performer to "stride" or "jump" from a low bass note to the appropriate chord in the middle register. Thus, the free approach to rhythm and accent in the right hand is held in check by the steady pulse of the left. The resulting "oompah" effect is similar to that created by the tubas and horns in a march for band, leading some to suggest that ragtime came into being when band scores were reduced for performance on the piano.

Ragtime was not intrinsically improvisatory, as jazz would be, although performers probably incorporated additions and changes in repeated performances. The rhythmic characteristics of ragtime have their origin in African American music (such as "Patting Juba," a song-dance tradition practiced by slaves at Congo Square in New Orleans before the Civil War), but the scales and harmonies are

European American. There are fewer "blue notes" or "bent pitches" than in spirituals and field hollers, and most rags are in major keys and 2/4 time.

Rags can therefore be accurately expressed in traditional music notation. This was significant to the dissemination and popularization of ragtime early in the twentieth century and to the involvement of white musicians in its creation and performance. Many whites were introduced to ragtime at the World's Columbian Exposition at Chicago (1893) and the Louisiana Purchase Exposition at St. Louis (1904). Ragtime was not part of the latter, but a contest in the tenderloin district drew leading composers and performers to the city at that time.

During the 1880s and 1890s, towns and cities in the Midwest were magnets for ragtime players. Ethnic and racial mixing (especially of Germans and African Americans) in St. Louis, Indianapolis, Chicago, Kansas City, and Cincinnati brought together the disciplined European techniques of the one and the free and energetic rhythms of the other. These cities were connected by the railroads, and ragtime pianists could easily move from Tom Turpin's Rosebud Café in St. Louis to Johnny Seymour's Bar in Chicago, and to Frenchman's in New Orleans, to mention a few among many locations where the new music flourished and where players congregated, picked up new pieces, and shared playing techniques.

A small town in Missouri called Sedalia was, for a time, the hub of the ragtime world. On roughly the same latitude as St. Louis but in the western part of the state, Sedalia was a prosperous community of 15,000 that was established in 1860 and served as a Union military post during the Civil War. Rudi Blesh and Harriet Janis provide a colorful description of the town, once a candidate for state capital, that was the home to the annual state fair, several railroads, and a seamy district that nourished ragtime:

> It was not the respectable Sedalia that supported the beginnings of what was to become the classic ragtime. East Main Street, with its honkytonks, clubs, and bawdy houses, was the patron of syncopated music. Such was the Negro's position in our society that it was inevitable that this rich new vein of music should be previewed for white America in whorehouses. In the tenderloins—and nowhere else—there was entrée for these musical originators; but in the tenderloins at least were the free and easy conditions, the ready money, and the freedom for a pianist to play pretty much as he pleased. . . . So there existed in Sedalia and throughout the country, a large class of Negro—and some white—pianists, many of them highly gifted and all of them close to the source of folk music.[17]

Sedalia had several bands, among them the white twelve-piece Independent Band and the eighteen-piece Sedalia Military Band. But the best band in the city was the black twelve-piece Queen City Concert Band. Scott Joplin, who later gave the city a permanent niche in the annals of American music as the king of ragtime, played second cornet in this band and was also a member of a vocal quartet. Other members of the concert band were Sedalia workmen and businessmen. While in Sedalia, Joplin lived for a time with the family of Arthur Marshall (1881–1956), composer of "The Pippin-a Ragtime Two Step," and both took music courses at George Smith College for Negroes, operated by the Methodist Church. The ragtime center of Sedalia was the Maple Leaf Club, where black and white gamblers played cards and pool to syncopated piano barbershop music by black performers.

Ragtime flourished in dozens of similar clubs throughout the Midwest, and an all-star cast of composer-performers emerged. In addition to Joplin, Turpin, Marshall, and Scott were Louis Chauvin (1881–1908), born in St. Louis and reputedly the best player of them all; Scott Hayden (1882–1915), a native of Sedalia and Joplin's pupil; Artie Matthews (1888–1959), a star on the St. Louis scene who later turned to classical music and church music; and Joe Jordan (1882–1971), born in Cincinnati but who also rose to fame in St Louis.

Rags were a staple in publishers' catalogs between 1908 and 1916 across the region. Prominent in Indianapolis were Isodor Seidel, Will B. Morrison, Warren C. Williams, and J. H. Aufderheide. The latter published "classic" rags by May Aufderheide, Julia Niebergall, Paul Pratt, J. Russel Robinson, and Russell Smith. In Chicago, F.J.A. Forster issued rags by Raymond Birch; Victor Kremer Co. and Will Rossiter, the latter self-proclaimed "the Chicago Publisher," published rags by Joplin and Tom Turpin; Arnett-Delonais Co. published Joe Jordan and Percy Wenrich; Wenrich was also published by Frank K. Root & Co. Charles K. Harris, who by 1915 added to his copyright note "British Rights Secured," published Charles Hunter. In Kansas City, Carl Hoffman published Joplin's first rag to be printed, "Original Rags," in 1899. Will L. Livernash Music Co. issued rags by Clarence Woods, whose "Sleepy Hollow Rag" gives instructions for using the piece for dancing. Cincinnati publishers issued no fewer than 110 ragtime works, most by local composers, among them Homer Denny, Henry J. Fillmore, Albert Gumble, Clarence M. Jones, Louis H. Mendel, and Floyd H. Willis. Among the numerous Cincinnati publishers were John Arnold, Great Eastern Publishing Co., Groene Music Publishing Co., Joseph Krolage Music Publishing Co., and Mentel Bros. Publishing Co.[18]

St. Louis, however, reigned supreme in the Midwest in the number and quality of its ragtime composers and performers, as well as in the number of its publishing houses, including S. Simon, Val. A. Reise Music Co., Syndicate Music Co., Robt. De Yong & Co., and Stark Music Co.

While not the first to publish ragtime, John Stark (1841–1927) must be acknowledged the single most important influence in the dissemination of the music. His belief in ragtime as a valid native music (he coined the term "classic rag"), his generous dealings with composers, and his high-quality printing set him apart in a competitive industry in which these attributes were rarely found. Stark's catalog is distinguished by the numerous works by Scott Joplin it contains. The cover to "The Cascades" (1904) bears a handsome portrait of the composer, an unusual gesture in the direction of racial tolerance and equality at a time when most ragtime sheet covers consisted of racial caricatures. Stark's cover of "Peacherine Rag" (1901) calls Joplin "the King of Ragtime Writers." "The Chrysanthemum" (Stark, 1904) is subtitled "An Afro-American Intermezzo." This must surely be among the earliest examples of that politically sensitive term in print. Arthur Marshall, Louis Chauvin, Joseph Lamb (the white rag composer from New Jersey and Joplin protégé), Artie Matthews, and James Scott were all published by Stark.

Stark continued publishing rags long after jazz emerged and overshadowed it. Late protests against the changing tastes may have prompted his addition of the following note to the John Stark imprint around 1920: "Publishers of Ragtime that is Different," and the issuing of James Scott's "Don't Jazz Me-Rag-I'm Music," published by Stark Music Company in 1921.

Ragtime and Dance

Published rags were often called "rag time march and two step," and their performance by bands with varied and sometimes unusual instrumentation suggests a continuation of the earlier tradition of marches in the nineteenth-century social ball. Other dance terms found with rag titles are "dance characteristic," "slow drag," "rag time waltz," "cake walk," and "cake walk march."

Among the rags subtitled "Dance Characteristic" are an assortment of "animal dances," some of which are also called "Dance Grotesque." These are exotic dances with roots in earlier African American dance styles, such as the buck and wing. (Louis Chauvin was reportedly an adept dancer of the buck and wing.) Also popular among early dances was the buzzard lope. Animal dances were the models for later socially acceptable dances, among them the turkey trot, eagle rock, and one-step. The latter was reportedly introduced around 1912 by the dance team Vernon Castle (1887–1918) and Irene Castle (1894–1969). The tango rhythms of Joplin's "Solace" (Seminary Music Co., 1909) show the influence of Latin music on ragtime.

The slow drag, a sensuous couples dance, was an important precursor of the modern social two-step. The partners embraced and rotated their hips while standing, moving slowly in a motion known as the "grind." James Scott's "New Era Rag" (Stark, 1919) is parenthetically called "Dance" and the cover shows couples dining and dancing. A note on Clarence Woods' "Sleepy Hollow Rag" (Will L. Livernash, 1918), a virtuosic work with extraordinary attention to dynamics and articulation, advises, "This number can be played for anything except a waltz by slightly altering the style and tempo."

The ragtime era ended with Joplin's death in 1917. New Orleans and Chicago jazz overshadowed it, and ragtime pianists joined jazz ensembles. Strong revivals followed, however, during World War II and again in the 1970s. The film *The Sting* (1973; music adapted by Marvin Hamlisch) featured Joplin's rags in the sound track and generated new recordings by, among others, Joshua Rifkin, Itzak Perlman, André Previn, and William Bolcum. The latter, a distinguished composer at the University of Michigan, composed a number of rags, among them "Seabiscuits Rag" (1970).

JAZZ IN THE MIDWEST

The minstrel show, bands, country blues, and ragtime were largely a part of the musical culture of rural and small-town America, sustained and spread by traveling musicians. Although jazz drew heavily from these styles, it was a product of urban America. Ragtime eventually rose above the risqué nocturnal environment of its origins, moved quickly into print, and entered the musical entertainment scene of mainstream America. Jazz, by contrast, emerged in the ghetto, was almost impossible to notate, and emphasized spontaneity and improvisation in performance. Its initiators and innovators were often relegated to subculture status.

The Roaring Twenties were the heyday of Chicago jazz. The city was the nation's bootleg alcohol capital during the Prohibition era, and musicians found employment in its numerous speakeasies. Trumpet "King" Joe Oliver (1885–1938) moved there from New Orleans in 1918 and formed his own band in 1920. Other New Orleans musicians joined him, among them Honore Dutry (1892–1937), trombone; Warren "Baby" Dodds (1894–1959), drums; Johnny Dodds (1892–1940), clarinet; Edward "Kid" Ory (1886–1937), trombone; and Louis Armstrong (1901–1971), trumpet. The pianist in Oliver's band was Lillian "Lil" Hardin (1898–1971), who came to Chicago from Fisk University. She was the first prominent woman in jazz and in 1924 married Louis Armstrong. She recorded with Oliver's bands as well as with Armstrong's small ensembles (Hot Five, Hot Seven) and later formed and recorded with her own band.

Few recordings were made in New Orleans, and the first jazz recordings made by the white, internationally famous Original Dixieland Jazz Band (1917) and the Louisiana Five (1918), while historically significant, have an element of parody about them. The authentic New Orleans sound had a four-layered texture: clarinet played a high counter-melody to the cornet, which carried the melody in the middle; trombone provided scale runs, slides, and smears in the tenor register (called "tailgate trombone"), while the tuba laid down the beat. Percussion and banjo might reinforce the beat. This was "outside-music," closely related to street band music and without piano. The prevailing sound is known as "collective improvisation," so-called because each instrument operates in its own register or range, and the instrumental colors and rhythms together form an aural mosaic or musical kaleidoscope. The characteristic beat is called "flat four."

The textbook Chicago sound, by contrast, was "two-beat": the meter was 4/4 but there was a strong accent on beat one and a weaker, secondary accent on beat three. The piano was a regular part of the ensemble, and the players retained the ragtime left-hand oompah pattern, which either created or added density to the two-beat effect. Other features of New Orleans style were retained, but the bands gradually got larger: King Oliver added a second cornet-trumpet when he brought Armstrong up from New Orleans in 1922. Clarinetists doubled on saxophone (Oliver's Dixie Syncopators, working at Chicago's Plantation Café in 1925, had three alto players who doubled on clarinets and soprano saxophone), the brass bass or tuba ultimately gave way to the upright string bass, guitar replaced banjo, and section-work augmented and eventually replaced collective improvisation. For some time, however, the transplanted New Orleans musicians retained pride in their place of origin, and Oliver, Kid Ory, and others probably continued to play in a basically New Orleans style and identified themselves with their roots by calling their bands and ensembles "Creole jazz bands."

The indigenous white Chicago musicians (the north side of Chicago was white, the south side black), influenced by the music of the New Orleans musicians, further defined a "Chicago style." Jazz historian Frank Tirro, however, rightly cautions against oversimplifying the origins of Chicago jazz: "Chicago had a ragtime—and perhaps Jazz—tradition before the well-known New Orleans musicians arrived in the late teens. Jazz did not arrive in Chicago via the Mississippi riverboats—the Mississippi does not flow through or near Chicago."[19] Tirro points out that the Illinois Central Railroad brought jazz musicians "from widely divergent backgrounds" to Chicago and that all contributed to the emerging Chicago style.

Among the prominent white musicians to move from New Orleans to Chicago were the New Orleans Rhythm Kings. Jelly Roll Morton (1890–1941), a Creole, recorded with them in the early 1920s. Such mixed-race performances occurred in a studio, not in public. Before World War II, the arts and entertainment, like almost everything cultural, social, and political in America, were segregated. White musicians might, at some risk to their safety, venture into the black section of Chicago, St. Louis, or Detroit to listen to black musicians; black musicians might entertain all-white audiences at a given venue. But blacks and whites did not perform together. Their influence on each other—influence ran in both directions—was largely achieved through recordings until Chicago clarinetist Benny Goodman (1909–1986) organized integrated groups.

Bix Beiderbecke and Friends

The Midwest embraced jazz with incomparable enthusiasm and energy. Traditionalists condemned it. The noted cornetist-teacher Herbert Clarke (1867–1945) called it "music from hell," but hundreds of young musicians defied their teachers and learned to play jazz by listening to so-called race records. Two prominent labels were OKeh Record Company (originally OkeH) and Pace Phonograph Corporation, later called Black Swan, the first black recording company. Other companies were Paramount (located in Port Washington, Wisconsin), Victor, Columbia, Brunswick, and Gennett (located in Richmond, Indiana). These companies entered the jazz market after it had shown itself to be very profitable. (In 1920 OKeh issued Mamie Smith's [1883–1946] "Crazy Blues," which reportedly sold 800,000 copies; the other companies became competitive in the jazz market around 1923.)

Among the leading young white Chicagoans were Bix Beiderbecke (1903–1931), cornet, and members of the so-called Austin High School Gang: Jimmy McPartland (b. 1907), trumpet; Dick McPartland, banjo; Frank Teschemacher (1906–1932), saxophone; Lawrence "Bud" Freeman (b. 1906), saxophone; Dave Tough (1908–1948), drums; Joe Sullivan (1906–1971), piano; and Floyd O'Brien (1905–1968), trombone. They recorded under various names, among them the Wolverines, the Jungle Kings, and the Charles Prince Orchestra. Other white musicians included Eddie Condon (1904–1973), banjo; George Wetling (1907–1968), drums; Joseph "Wingy" Manone (b. 1904), trumpet; Charles "Pee Wee" Russell (1906–1969), cornet; Milton "Mezz" Mezzrow (1899–1972), clarinet; Francis "Mugsy" Spanier (1906–1966), cornet; Benny Goodman, clarinet; Gene Krupa (1909–1973), drums; Jimmy Dorsey (1904–1957), clarinet and saxophone; and Tommy Dorsey (1905–1956), trombone. They refined their jazz skills in Chicago and recorded there or at the Gennett Studio in Richmond, Indiana. Not all were native Chicagoans (the Dorseys were from Pennsylvania; Beiderbecke was born in Davenport, Iowa; Condon was from Goodland, Indiana), yet the mixture of black and white, as well as midwestern tastes and traditions, resulted in what Tirro aptly calls "a flood of Jazz activity."

This activity was not confined to recordings and speakeasies. The numerous dance halls and clubs throughout the Midwest and the excursion boats on the Great Lakes employed large bands; among the prominent ones were those formed by Jean Goldkette (1899–1962), Charlie Straight, Glen Gray, Frankie Trumbauer, and

Bix Beiderbecke. AP/Wide World Photos.

especially Paul Whiteman (1890–1967), who was somewhat inappropriately called the "King of Jazz."

These musicians and numerous others would dominate jazz and commercial music for decades, forming their own bands and expanding the interest in jazz through performances and recordings and through collaborations with songwriters and vocalists drawn to Chicago, among them Hoagy Carmichael (1899–1981) and Bing Crosby (1904–1977). Carmichael, a native of Bloomington, Indiana, wrote dozens of hit songs, most notably "Star Dust" (1929), which was recorded more than 1,100 times and was translated into thirty languages.

The contributions made to early jazz by Benny Goodman, Gene Krupa, the Dorsey brothers, and other Chicagoans—black and white—were great, but a special place in the annals of jazz must be given to Beiderbecke, whose creative genius typified the Jazz Age. Burdened by a learning disability that kept him from developing facility in reading music, disappointed by a nonsupportive and disapproving family, and plagued by alcoholism that ended his life at age twenty-eight, he nevertheless achieved a level of proficiency as a jazz innovator and interpreter exceeded only by Louis Armstrong.

Kansas City Jazz and Swing

The mixing of musicians of varied musical and social backgrounds in the Midwest in the 1920s and 1930s had a softening effect on the original blues-oriented hot style. Black and white musicians helped make jazz respectable. For example, Doc Cooke (1891–1958) and Dave Peyton (1885–1956), two black Chicago bandleaders, insisted that their sidemen be able to read music. The classically trained pianist Jean Goldkette owned the Greystone Ballroom in Detroit when jazz was becoming "peppy dance music in a contemporary style" and was moving from taverns and cabarets into ballrooms.[20] Born in France but raised in Greece and Russia, Goldkette operated more than twenty bands by the late 1920s and employed Beiderbecke, Trumbauer, the Dorsey brothers, and Eddie Lang (1902–1933). Ballrooms proliferated in the 1930s, now known as the Swing Era, when thousands of sidemen were employed in hundreds of ensembles. The players, twelve to twenty or more, were grouped in sections: trumpets (2–4), trombones (2–4), saxophones (2 altos, 2 tenors, 1 baritone, some or all doubling on clarinets), and rhythm (drum set, including snare, bass drum, tom-toms, and an assortment of cymbals, played with sticks and brushes). Piano, string bass, and guitar (replacing the banjo) were part of the rhythm section but could also function melodically.

Big bands were by their very size dependent upon written arrangements and were brought into being, as it were, by a new "performer"—the arranger. While some arrangers were band leaders or sidemen, others were specialists who composed and arranged for but did not usually perform with bands. Outstanding in this category was Ohio-born Billy Strayhorn (1915–1967), who arranged and composed for the Duke Ellington Orchestra. The most commercial bands featured sentimental ballads. The sound was characterized by saxophones played with a wide vibrato and brasses that played precisely on the beat; the rhythm was square (called, among other things, "Mickey Mouse"). Their arrangements, which contained little or no place for improvisation or the spirit of the blues, appealed to middle class whites. For example, the bands of Sammy Kaye from Cleveland, who formed his first ensemble in the early 1930s while a student at Ohio University (Athens), enjoyed a regional reputation before television brought him national prominence in the 1960s.

Tommy Dorsey, Gene Krupa, Jimmy Dorsey, and Benny Goodman formed another category: bands that programmed music for middle-class whites but could also generate more rhythmic interest because they and their sidemen were skilled jazz soloists. Goodman eventually and rightfully became known as the "King of Swing." He was among the first to perform and record regularly with black musicians, among them pianist Teddy Wilson (1912–1986) and Chicago vibraharpist Lionel Hampton (b. 1913). Texas-born trombonist and blues singer Jack Teagarden recorded with a black ensemble, including Louis Armstrong, in 1929, and in the same year Eddie Condon recorded with pianist Fats Waller (1904–1943), but these were exceptions to the rule.[21] To this list might be added trombonist Glenn Miller (1904–1944), who was born in Clarinda, Iowa, but received most of his early training in Fort Morgan, Colorado.

All bands catered to an audience obsessed with dancing. The early exotic fast dances gave way to the Charleston, then the Lindy and jitterbug (the distinction between the latter two is vague and disputed), which alternated with slow, couples dances, the most basic of which were called, among other things, the box step and the businessman's bounce.

A third band type was rhythmically more exciting. Most bands in this category were black. Their arrangements made greater use of blues forms (the twelve-bar pattern was most common), and they attempted to retain the collective improvisation that characterized New Orleans jazz. They also left more space in their arrangements for solos, and their sidemen were uniformly acknowledged to be the best in the jazz world.

Like most other swing bands, these ensembles relied on the "riff," a rhythmic-melodic figure that supported the harmonic background of the arrangement and gave it its drive. The riff functioned in a call-and-response pattern originating in the African American spiritual, the drone or ostinato of blues accompaniments, and the accent displacement of ragtime. By tossing one or more riffs back and forth between the sections, the arranger achieved orchestral color and variety.

In the 1920s and early 1930s, Kansas City bands exhibited more of that indefinable element—swing—than bands in the East. Particularly distinctive were those formed by Benny Moten (1894–1935)—later the Count Basie Orchestra—Andy Kirk (1898–1992), Harland Leonard, and Jay McShann (b. 1909). An important training center for musicians in their bands was Lincoln High School, where the remarkable Major N. Clark Smith (1877–1933) was bandmaster.

Kansas City musicians made unique contributions to swing, infusing into arrangements elements of the blues and recalling features of New Orleans jazz when other bands were comparatively commercial. Because of the corrupt Pendergast political machine that ignored state and federal laws, Kansas City "roared" during the 1930s while the rest of the country succumbed to the Great Depression. It was also a final stopping place or turnaround point on the Theater Owners Booking Association (TOBA) circuit. Actors, dancers, and musicians booked by TOBA often found themselves broke and stranded until they were "re-routed, disbanded, or re-formed, so that there was always a pool of talent at liberty in Kansas City to give tone to its night life and show business status."[22]

Kansas City was a world within a world in American show business, and the shows on the TOBA circuit perpetuated racist stereotypes. At the same time TOBA provided expanded visibility and exposure for black musicians, dancers, and actors, among them Butterbeans and Susie (Jody Edwards, 1895–1967; Susie Hawthorn, 1896–1963) and Rubberlegs Williams. By bringing blues singers such as Ida Cox (1896–1967), Ma Rainey (1886–1939), and Bessie Smith (1894–1937) to Kansas City, TOBA fostered their influence on local singers such as Ada Brown, Mary Bradford, and Julia Lee. TOBA promoted a "black vaude-

Benny Moten and Kansas City Swing

If not the best of the Kansas City groups, Benny Moten's achieved the most attention, in part because of the tragic manner in which his career ended. A fine ragtime pianist, he worked in a trio, then a sextet, and made his first recordings on the premiere race record label, OKeh, in 1923. Prior to this Kansas City was dominated by ragtime and brass bands, but Moten's career coincided with the city's transition to jazz, as documented in his recordings.

Moten's first recordings were blues, mixing the New Orleans collective improvisational texture with riffs and improvisatory solos. The Kansas City style, with sections playing riffs as the central element, emerged in the recordings from 1924 and 1925 by the newly formed Benny Moten Orchestra, but its total realization took time and the addition of new players, among them pianist William "Count" Basie (1904–1984), who joined Moten in 1929, and bassist Walter Page (1909–1957), who joined in 1931.

Between 1923 and 1932, Moten developed and spread the Kansas City style through tours and engagements in ballrooms and theaters in New York, Philadelphia, and other eastern cities. The band made its final, definitive recordings for Victor in Camden, New Jersey, in December 1935. Tragically, Moten, who was then at the pinnacle of his career, died during a tonsillectomy. The ensemble was ultimately taken over by pianist Bill Basie and became the Count Basie Orchestra. It remained the model of Kansas City swing until Basie's death in 1984.

ville," which, like the earlier minstrel show, perpetuated racial stereotypes while providing a performance venue for African American artists.

Finally, Kansas City was the center from which territorial bands, small ensembles frequently made up of excellent musicians, fanned out and worked small towns and rural areas of Texas, Oklahoma, Nebraska, Wyoming, Kansas, and Missouri. Their playing displayed ongoing contact with the blues, ragtime, and New Orleans jazz. Leaders of large bands kept their eyes on territorial bands, frequently cannibalizing them—hiring away their best players. The number of such bands was legion, and most fell into obscurity, but they were the "schools" for such jazz greats as Ben Webster (1909–1973), Lester Young (1909–1959), Buster Smith, Oran "Hot Lips" Page (1900–1957), Hershel Evans (1909–1939), and William "Count" Basie. Kansas City was also the home training ground for musicians who would shape post-swing jazz of the 1940s and 1950s, notably alto saxophonist Charlie Parker (1920–1955) and trumpeter Miles Davis (1926–1991), the masters of bebop and cool, respectively.

Not surprisingly, this milieu produced the most remarkable jazz pianist of the twentieth century: Art Tatum (1910–1956). Born in Toledo, Ohio, Tatum was legally blind. He attended the Toledo School of Music, where he studied scores in Braille, but taught himself largely by playing piano rolls and listening to recordings. He raised jazz piano technique to an unprecedented level, using both hands equally and playing at uncanny tempos. He expanded the harmonic vocabulary of the standard stride piano repertory (Broadway and Tin Pan Alley tunes) and created a style distinctly his own. One could argue that Charlie Parker's virtuosic technique was an attempt to equal on the saxophone what Tatum achieved on the piano. Parker's legacy was especially evident in two later Chicago pianists, Lenni Tristano (1919–1978) and Herbie Hancock (b. 1940).

Art Tatum. Photo by Hulton Archive/Getty Images.

Tristano was an avant-garde jazz musician whose music defies classification (his playing style was neither bop nor cool, the predominant styles of the 1950s and 1960s). His most significant contribution to jazz may have been as a teacher. His students included Chicago alto saxophonist Lee Konitz (b. 1927) of the Miles Davis Nonet and the Stan Kenton Orchestra. Hancock established the first school for jazz musicians in New York in 1951, and achieved prominence as a pianist in the Miles Davis Quintet.

Efforts to revive swing after World War II met with limited success. Some of the better sidemen and arrangers turned to Hollywood and composed scores for films. Notable among midwesterners was Cleveland-born Henry Mancini (1924–1994), whose successes include TV and film scores, notably *Peter Gunn* and *The Pink Panther*. Chicago-born Quincy Jones (b. 1933) composed TV scores for *Ironsides, Roots, The Bill Cosby Show*, and *Sanford and Son*, among many others.

Bebop and cool, the jazz styles that emerged from swing and were in some respects rebellions against it and the racial and economic inequalities it represented, were largely East and West Coast music. Both were small-ensemble jazz, although cool exemplar Miles Davis (born in Alton, Illinois) who made recordings with Charlie Parker and Dizzy Gillespie in the late 1940s, made his most definitive recordings with larger groups, notably his Nonet, for which Gil Evans made outstanding arrangements in the cool style. Like bop, cool explored extended harmonies, but tempos were less aggressive; performers played slightly behind the beat (called "lag-along" or "laid-back"), and more of the repertory was arranged. Cool, like bop, was music to be listened to, not danced to, and a large, predominantly white audience developed among college students.

The models for the many bop and cool saxophonists were Coleman "Bean" Hawkins (1904–1969), from St. Joseph, Missouri, and Lester "Prez" Young (1909–1959), a sideman with the Kansas City Moten and Basie bands. Trombonist J. J. Johnson (b. 1924), who hailed from Indianapolis, worked with Count Basie, Miles Davis, and Stan Kenton (1911–1979). Fusions of bop, cool, and swing can be heard in the solos of many jazz artists of the second half of the twentieth century, and in the recordings of many big bands that continued to operate through the 1950s and 1960s, notably those of Milwaukee native Woody Herman (1913–1987). Efforts to compose jazz using classic forms resulted in an intellectualized style called "third stream," a term coined by composer-scholar Gunther Schuller (b. 1925). Miles Davis and J. J. Johnson experimented in Third Stream in concerts and recordings. Cincinnati native George Russell (b. 1923) composed in this style and published a book on jazz theory titled *The Lydian Chromatic Concept of Tonal Organization for Improvisation* (1959).

POPULAR SONG IN THE TWENTIETH CENTURY

While ragtime and jazz celebrated the mutual influence of avant-garde black and white musicians in the Midwest, popular song of the early twentieth century reflected more conservative, white, middle-class virtues. The genre, whose prototype was created in Tin Pan Alley, an area of West 28th Street in New York City, reached midwesterners through local music stores and publishers who served as distributors for New York companies. In 1900, for example, Tin Pan Alley's E. T. Paull Music Co. reached the Chicago market through F.J.A. Forster Co.,

Lyon & Healy, and National Music Co., and the Milwaukee market through Rohlf-ing Sons Music Co. Lyrics took up contemporary themes of great significance to midwesterners: progress and invention, gender roles, war, and prohibition. As the home of the Wright brothers and the nation's rail hub, the Midwest provided audiences for Fred C. Roegge and Berte C. Randall's "That Aeroplane Rag" (New York and Detroit: Jerome H. Remick Co., 1911) and Stanley Murphy and Henry I. Marshall's "On the 5:15" (New York and Detroit: Jerome H. Remick & Co., 1914).

Popular lyrics replaced regional themes with more universal topics as commercial recordings and radio created a national music scene, yet heartland values remained salient. Midwesterners' faith in farm and family received national attention in the 1939 film *The Wizard of Oz*, whose most famous song, "Over the Rainbow" (music and lyrics by Harold Arlen and E. Y. Harburg), launched the career of a young singer-actress from Grand Rapids, Minnesota, Judy Garland (Frances Ethel Gumm, 1922–1969). In the 1940s and 1950s songs that portrayed America as a land of innocence, prosperity, and equality found their embodiment in another midwestern singer-actress, Doris Day (née Kappelhoff, b. 1924), from Cincinnati, Ohio. Day played the wholesome "girl next door" in most of her thirty-nine films; her hit songs—including "Sentimental Journey" (1944), "If I Knew You Were Comin' I'd've Baked a Cake" (1949), and "Qué Será, Será" (1955)—conveyed heartland verities.

By contrast, Cole Porter (1891–1964), from Peru, Indiana, rejected the middle-class values of the Tin Pan Alley tradition along with his own midwestern origins. Instead, prefiguring late twentieth-century rock and hip-hop, Porter imbued his lyrics with double entendres and references to drugs and sex. Porter's sophisticated lyrics and music—written mainly for revues, Broadway shows, and films, and frequently with a specific singer such as Fred Astaire, Bing Crosby, Grace Kelley, or Ethel Merman in mind—include "Love for Sale" (1930), "Anything Goes" (1934), "Make It Another Old Fashioned, Please" (1942), and "True Love" (1956).

Another rejection of Tin Pan Alley came from midwestern musicians who invoked masculine values in "covers" (new interpretations of songs recorded earlier by other artists, frequently with limited success) of country and folk songs from the West and South. Chicago-born singer-songwriter Frankie Laine (b. 1913) made a career of such masculine songs as "Mule Train" (1949), "High Noon" (1952), and "Moonlight Gambler" (1957). Bandleader-singer Vaughn Monroe (1912–1973) of Akron, Ohio, who gained broad popularity through his *Camel Caravan* radio show, recorded covers of "Riders in the Sky" (1949) and other folk songs.

FOLK AND ETHNIC MUSIC IN THE MIDWEST

Midwestern interest in "roots" music came with migrations of the 1920s, and Illinois-born poet Carl Sandburg (1878–1967) published 280 songs in one of the nation's first folk song collections, *The American Songbag*, in 1927. Recordings and films featuring Burl Ives (1909–1995), from Jasper County, Illinois, popularized folk music further. Ives, who acquired a formal music education (Eastern Illinois State Teachers College and New York University), recorded extensively for Decca and Columbia, and was especially known for his signature song, "Wayfaring Stranger," also the name of his 1940–1942 CBS radio show. A second folk revival in the 1950s and 1960s was led in part by the Old Town School of Folk Music on Chicago's near-North Side. From its opening in December 1957 under the leadership of singer Win Stracke (1908–1991), the Old Town School united performing, learning, and listening. The school hosted concerts by nationally known performers, including locals such as Big Bill Broonzy, launched the careers of students such as Bob Gibson (1931–1996) and Bonnie Koloc, and enabled many thousands of students—6,000 per week in recent years—to make their own music.

Before 1950 the styles now called country and western, bluegrass, and, more generically, Nashville, were programmed by radio stations with fixed and limited broadcasting areas. WLS in Chicago had its *National Barn Dance* (produced by John Lair), and Cincinnati had WCKY, a 50,000 watt, clear channel station that programmed country and western records for four or five hours a day. WLW (Cincinnati) featured the *Renfro Valley Barn Dance*, which was to midwestern listeners what Grand Ole Opry was to Nashville. At Emery Auditorium, a center of Cincinnati broadcasting, performers included Cowboy Copas (1913–1963), Hawkshaw Hawkins (1921–1963), Louis Marshall "Grandpa" Jones (b. 1913), and disc jockey, songwriter, and singer Wayne Raney (b. 1921), all of whom recorded for the local King Records label.

"Hillbilly music," as it was sometimes facetiously called, was first aimed at rural audiences, but after World War II it was increasingly assimilated into the popular mainstream. Midwestern country western performers included Cincinnati-born Roy Rogers (originally Leonard Slye, 1911–1998) and Pee Wee King (originally Julius Kuczynski, b. 1914) from Abrams, Wisconsin, who incorporated midwestern waltzes and polkas into country music. King was a backup musician for the singing cowboy Gene Autry in films of the early 1930s, then formed his Golden West Cowboys with fiddler-singer Redd Stewart. In 1937 the band joined the Grand Ole Opry. King was also a songwriter. His "Tennessee Waltz" (1947) was recorded more than 300 times and sold about 40 million records.

Irish, Polish, Hungarian, Czech, Russian, Greek, Turkish, German, Italian, Scandinavian, and Jewish music, among others, continue to be widely performed in midwestern cities, especially in Wisconsin, Michigan, and Minnesota. Solo and group performances of ethnic music are often heard at fairs and folk festivals. The preservation of vocal music from these traditions is dependent upon the continued use of native languages, which becomes increasingly rare as a consequence of acculturation. But instrumental ensembles, such as the Greek *kompania* and *bouzouki*, Turkish *Tamburitza*, and the ubiquitous Polish polka bands remain popular. The accordion and concertina are common to most ethnic traditions, but many employ instruments specific to their native countries.

Jewish klezmer music, an eclectic style that combines traditional folk music with classical music and jazz, became especially popular in the United States around 1970. Since Jewish Americans emigrated from culturally divergent countries (Spain, Russia, Germany, countries of central Europe, Egypt), the mixture of linguistic and musical elements is particularly rich. Klezmer music is ensemble music intended for dancing, and weddings are the common venue for its performance. Melodies are primarily in minor mode and built on pentatonic scales. The clarinet often functions in a virtuosic capacity in klezmer ensembles, such as the Yiddishe Cup Klezmer Band of Cleveland. Hebrew Union College in Cincinnati promotes the study and preservation of Jewish music of many styles and traditions, including cantorial music.

Repudiation of the eastern music industry gradually fostered a new kind of popular song. In the midwestern tradition of labor activism, Chicago-born James Petrillo (1892–1984), the powerful president of the American Federation of Musicians and namesake of Chicago's Grant Park bandshell, required major recording companies to pay a fee for all discs produced. Decca agreed in 1943, and RCA and Columbia held out until November 1944, but recording companies reasserted themselves by turning away from instrumental music. Big bands, which had emerged across the Midwest as outgrowths of the region's school and community bands, never recovered from this blow; by the late 1940s, vocalists dominated popular music. Soon a disenchanted, disenfranchised subculture, weary of corporate domination of the industry, racial discrimination, and hackneyed and worn-out musical and lyrical clichés, began a cultural revolution. It challenged not only the traditional concept of the form and content of song lyrics and music, but also the way music and recordings were produced and sold. Important centers in this development were in the Midwest, and the stylistic point of departure was black American music, especially Chicago blues.

BLUES IN THE MIDWEST

It is often suggested that the closing of Storyville, the notorious red-light district in the French Quarter of New Orleans where ragtime flourished and elements of jazz first appeared in the playing of cornetist Charles "Buddy" Bolden (1877–1931), forced musicians to seek employment elsewhere. But the riverboats moving up and down the Mississippi had bands to entertain their passengers with music for listening and dancing long before the closing of Storyville in 1917. New Orleans musicians, many of whom were Creoles, notably Lemott Ferdinand Joseph "Jelly Roll" Morton, had also begun spreading the new music before that time. The musical, cultural, racial, and sociological requisites to create jazz came together in New Orleans more than anywhere else, but the music quickly followed the Mississippi River and the railroads north, where further incubation took place and where most of the earliest recordings of the new music were made. "Father of the Blues" W. C. Handy first heard the blues in the Mississippi Delta, but one of his earliest compositions was "St. Louis Blues" (1914).

Employment in meat-packing plants in Chicago attracted blacks from the South, as did the automobile industry in Detroit. The blues came up the river especially during the so-called Great Black Migration (1910–1930), when an estimated 1 million African Americans moved to the North, more than 50,000 to Chicago alone. During that time the blues mixed with ragtime and became a determining and enduring element in jazz. However, the blues retained its own expressive integrity and styles even while it influenced jazz. Country, urban, rhythm and blues, and gospel, among others, became and continue to be viable genres separate from jazz. Jazz, too, evolved into styles with distinctive features, the major ones being New Orleans, Chicago, big band and swing, bebop, cool, funky (hard bop), third stream, free jazz, and fusion. The spirit of the blues was important in shaping all of them.

Both country (Mississippi Delta) and urban (classic) blues became powerful social and cultural forces in the Midwest, especially in Chicago, St. Louis, and Detroit, in the 1920s and 1930s. Country blues (sometimes called "the Devil's spirituals") had its roots in spirituals, work songs, and field hollers. The classic formula uses a three-line rhymed stanza, in which the first two lines have similar or repeated lyrics and thus give the singer time to improvise the third, over an instrumental accompaniment of twelve bars in 4/4 time in a basic harmonic progression of I, IV, and V chords. Growing out of the poverty and racism of the Deep South, the lyrics of country blues lament hard times, troubled relationships, alcoholism, crime, and prison life. Sexual symbolism and metaphors and references to voodoo charms and magic are common, as in the classic "Hellhound on My Trail" by Robert Johnson (c. 1912–1938), the so-called King of the Delta Blues. Often autobiographical in origin, the songs are performed with tremendous feeling, emphasized by "blue" notes and a gritty style. The performers are usually men (although there have been notable women) who accompany themselves most often on guitar in a style called "bottleneck" or "slide" to produce blue sounds while moving up and down the strings. Prominent in the accompaniments are ostinato patterns reminiscent of the ritual music of the Ewe, Ashanti, Yoruba, and other tribes of Africa.

Among the early performers were Charlie Patton (1881–1934), Willie Brown, Papa Charlie Jackson (1890–1938), Blind Lemon Jefferson (1897–1929), Huddie Ledbetter (1889–1932), and Robert Johnson. These pioneers, as well as the next generation, were all born in the South, but they did most of their recording in the Midwest. Chicago first attracted wide attention as a center for blues in Papa Charlie Jackson's "Maxwell Street Blues" (recorded 1926), performed with a banjo strung like a guitar. But by the 1930s midwestern black communities like East St. Louis, Illinois, midway between North and South, were producing a wealth of homegrown blues talent such as Chuck Berry (b. 1926) and Ike Turner (b. 1931) and his wife, Tina Turner (b. 1939).

Midwest record labels diffused the blues throughout the nation. After the surprise success of the first blues vocal recording, "Crazy Blues" by Cincinnati-born Mamie Smith in 1920, OKeh Records of New York directed its production toward "race records" and opened a recording studio in Chicago under the direction of former Storyville pianist Richard M. Jones (1892–1945). OKeh's innovative on-location recordings, beginning in 1922, captured important jazz and blues performances in St. Louis, Kansas City, and Detroit, and beyond the region. Charlie Jackson recorded the first country blues, "Papa's Lawdy Lawdy Blues," with banjo accompaniment for Paramount Records in Chicago in 1924. After World War II, Chicago's Chess Records, which had signed Muddy Waters (1915–1983), became the world's most influential blues label.

Though it lacked the industrial pull of Chicago, Cincinnati also attracted blues artists through its position on the Ohio River, an important North-South border. The same year that Charlie Jackson made his first recording, Cincinnatian Sam Jones (a.k.a. "Stovepipe No. 1," c. 1890s–?) sang "Pitiful Blues," "Six Street Blues," and "Them Pitiful Blues," among others, for Gennett Records of Richmond, Indiana. Best known for its recordings of jazz greats Jelly Roll Morton, Bix Beiderbecke, Hoagy Carmichael, and King Oliver, the Gennett label benefited from its proximity to the performing and transportation centers of Cincinnati, Cleveland, and Indianapolis. Gennett began in 1915 as a subdivision of the local Starr Piano Company, but grew quickly, reaching a volume of 1,250 recording masters—two-thirds of Victor's production—in 1928 before falling victim to the Depression in the early 1930s. (Gennett also had the distinction of recording the most famous speech by the Midwest's most famous populist politician, "The Cross of Gold" by William Jennings Bryan [1860–1925], in 1923.) Cincinnati finally acquired an important blues label when King Records, begun in 1944 by Sydney Nathan (1904–1968) as a label for "hillbilly" recordings of white musicians from nearby Kentucky and West Virginia, added a second label for "race music." Under the leadership of Henry Glover (1921–1991), America's second African American record producer, King recorded such blues stars as Alonzo "Lonnie" Johnson (1899–1970), a sometime Cincinnatian (from 1949 to 1955) and virtuoso guitarist who also who accompanied himself on piano, violin, harmonium, and kazoo. King Records, which suffered tremendously for its unfortunate role in the payola scandals of the 1960s, deserves to be remembered for its production achievements and race-blind hiring policies.[23]

Chicago Blues

Bluesmen from the South gravitated to Chicago and Detroit in the 1920s. Early urban or classic blues singers performed and recorded with a pianist or a small combo of piano and trumpet, or trombone, and with or without drums. When used with plunger mutes, trumpet and trombone were capable of generating growls and other sounds that interpreted or commented on the lyrics, which often contained double entendres. Among the early Chicago performers was singer Big Bill Broonzy (William Lee Conley, 1893–1958), who arrived in Chicago from Arkansas in 1920 and won wide recognition for a poetic style that bridged the country and urban styles. Broonzy often performed with Tennessee-born harmonica player "Sonny Boy" Williamson I (John Lee Williamson, 1914–1948), who came in 1937. Williamson's "squeezed notes" and other unique harmonica effects brought a new approach to solo blues harmonica. (Working in the same style, harmonica player Willie "Rice" Miller [1899–1965] was consequently known as Sonny Boy Williamson II.) Williamson recorded with a drummer and created a heavily accented style called "jump blues." Native Chicagoan James Edwards "Jimmy" Yancey (1898–1951) began his career as a singer and tap dancer, but achieved fame as a blues pianist in the boogie-woogie style that influenced subsequent boogie-woogie pianists such as Meade "Lux" Lewis (1905–1964), most famously in "Honky Tonk Train Blues" (1927/1935). Lewis was particularly adept at cross-rhythms. The folk, small-group effects of these bluesmen were displaced, however, as urban blues came under the influence of the Depression and, in the late 1930s, the instrumental amplifier. The Depression produced hardship that drove more southern blacks to the North. With the amplifier, blues guitarists gave greater prominence to the single-string riff that characterized accompaniments and functioned in a call-and-response manner with the vocal line. In the process, the emotional charge and passionate vocal delivery were amplified as well.

Chicago thus electrified the blues literally and metaphorically. Louisiana-born Little Walter Jacobs (1930–1968), who reached Chicago in the late 1940s, built his style on Sonny Boy's but amplified the harmonica, and he was probably the first to do so. Jacobs also added a rhythm section, an important move in the evolution of rhythm and blues. By the late 1940s most blues bands were amplified. Arriving in 1952, Howlin' Wolf (Chester Burnett, 1910–1976), so named for the howls that pierced his otherwise growling vocals, added to the blues harmonica tradition while his forceful singing helped define the hard Chicago sound. But the undisputed "King of Chicago Blues" was Muddy Waters (McKinley Morganfield).

Born in Rolling Fork, Mississippi, Waters began as a harmonica player but soon switched to guitar, which he played in the "bottleneck" style, with its characteristic slurs, whines, and blue notes. Even before he reached Chicago in 1943, Waters was a sufficiently accomplished singer and guitar player that Alan Lomax recorded him in 1941 for the Library of Congress' folk song archives. Waters debuted on records in 1948 with "I Can't Be Satisfied" and "I Feel Like Going Home," which accompanied traditional laments with a driving modern beat and amplified power. Over the next thirty-five years Waters abandoned rural themes to produce numerous compositions in the new Chicago style, among them "I Got My Mojo Working" (1956), "Rolling Stone" (1950), and a title that earned him an additional nickname—"Hoochie Coochie Man" (1954). Waters claimed that his Chicago style was the same as his playing in the Delta. But it was a bigger, more compelling sound, amplified and influenced by B. B. King (Riley "Blues Boy" King, b. 1925), Broonzy, and Howlin' Wolf, and supported by sidemen who were distinctive bluesmen in their own right, among them James Cotton (b. 1935) and Little Walter (harmonica), Otis Spann (1930–1970; piano), Jimmy Rogers (1924–1997), Hubert Sumlin (b. 1931), Buddy Guy (b. 1936), Luther Allison (1939–1997), and Luther Johnson (b. 1937) (all guitarists). Central to Waters' success was Willie Dixon (1915–1992), a bass player who also wrote and arranged around 500 blues compositions for Waters and other artists recording for the Chess label, which grew up with Chicago blues.[24]

Polish immigrants Phil and Leonard Chess, seeing the recording business as an adjunct to the nightclub they owned on Chicago's South Side, bought into the Aristocat label in 1947. The success of Muddy Waters' first hit, "I Can't Be Satisfied" on Aristocat, persuaded the brothers to buy out the company, rename it Chess, and concentrate on blues. Soon its studios on South Michigan Avenue reverberated not only with the sounds of Waters, but also those of Howlin' Wolf, Chuck Berry, Elmore James (1918–1963), Buddy Guy, and their successors in the next generation, including Keith Richards and the Rolling Stones. The Chess brothers' commitment to African American culture was reflected in their programming for Chicago radio station WVON, known fondly as the "Wonderful Voice of the Negro," which they owned during the crucial civil rights years of 1963–1969.[25] Arnold Shaw concludes, "[T]he Chess brothers tapped the richest vein of the Delta Blues and, through Howlin' Wolf, Muddy Waters, and Bo Diddley, behemoth bluesmen, promoted the transformation of Urban Blues into the abrasive, electrified, ensemble Rhythm & Blues of Chicago."[26]

The significance of Chicago blues went beyond its increased sonority and rhythmic drive. Chicago bluesmen fused elements of jazz, pop, spirituals, and gospel with the Delta blues, creating a distinctive sound. By mid-century Chicago blues was influencing popular music in Europe, and in no small way precipitated developments in rock and roll, hip-hop, rap, and the innumerable fusions and substyles that surfaced in the United States and the United Kingdom in the last four decades of the twentieth century. Annual European tours of the American Blues Festival, organized by Memphis Slim (Peter Chatman, 1915–1988) and Willie Dixon, began in 1962 and profoundly influenced English musicians, among them the Rolling Stones (named for the Muddy Waters song), the Yardbirds, Georgie Fame, the Beatles, and Eric Clapton. Chicago blues thus ushered in the era of the guitarist as superhero of popular music everywhere. Heir to the Delta and electric traditions, Mississippi-born B. B. King has influenced rock musicians from Eric Clapton to Mick Jagger. King combined enormous singing talent with a winning persona to raise Chicago blues to a stature and popularity unimaginable a few decades ago. The Chicago Blues Festival, the nation's largest, attracts some 500,000 music lovers to the city each spring.

Although Chicago led the way in electrified blues, Detroit—the Motor City—also developed a related blues tradition in the 1940s, powered by guitarist-singer John Lee Hooker (1917–2001). Detroit blues reached a wide audience through the Sensation label of Bernard Besman, which gave Hooker his start with "Boogie Chillen" in 1948. Born in rural Mississippi as its black exodus was in full swing, Hooker followed the river to Memphis and Cincinnati before reaching Detroit in the late 1940s, when his performance at the Apex Bar on Russell Street led to a recording session with Besman of Sensation Records. Hooker's strong beat, emphasized on recordings via a microphone near his tapping foot, helped move blues toward its R&B incarnation as dance music. The free-verse structure, suspended rhythms, and whispered lyrics of "Black Snake" illustrate his style.[27]

In 1949 the term "rhythm 'n' blues" replaced "race records," a catchall term for African American popular secular music in use since the 1920s. Rhythm 'n' blues had evolved into a distinguishable style: music for vocal ensemble or solo, supported by guitar, bass, piano, drums, and supplemental winds—saxophones were common. The songs were generally in twelve-bar blues form and used blues harmonies. Meter was usually duple (4/4) with strong accents on the first and third beats, and the somewhat earthy lyrics were delivered in call-and-response fashion. As in blues, the first line of text was sometimes repeated.

Rhythm 'n' blues, along with hip-hop and rap, can be traced to "soul raps," spiritual sermons of urban black churches, notably those in Detroit and Chicago. Performers of R&B, soul, blues, and gospel, among them Johnnie Taylor, Lou Rawls (b. 1935, Chicago), Isaac Hayes, James Brown, Aretha Franklin ("the Queen of Soul"), Nina Simone ("the High Priestess of Soul"), and Laura Lee, were usually "gospel graduates," singers in the choirs or members of urban Baptist, Pentecostal, African Episcopal, and other black congregations. The direct and immediate communication of the soul sermon derived from three factors: an African dialogue tradition format that expected the listener to respond, not sit dumbly; the vivid metaphors and imagery of the sermon topic; and alternation of powerful oratory with singing and drumming.[28] Together these features provided the aesthetic for the secular black musical genres that emerged in the second half of the twentieth century.

Recordings issued by Vee Jay Records document the style well. Founded in Chicago in 1953 by James Bracken (1909–1972) and Vivian Carter Bracken (1920–1989), the company had an enormous hit in 1954 with "Goodnight, Well It's Time to Go" by the Spaniels. Other engaging R&B singers include Lou Rawls, whose career began with the Pilgrim Travellers, a Chicago gospel group. Rawls moved comfortably among the best jazz musicians, as illustrated by the album *Lou Rawls Sings, Les McCann Ltd. Plays Stormy Monday*, featuring sidemen Ron Jefferson, Leroy Vinnegar, and Les McCann (Capitol, 1962).

Other prominent R&B performers and groups in the region were William "Smokey" Robinson (b. Detroit, 1940), who formed the Miracles in the mid-1950s; Curtis Mayfield (b. Chicago, 1942), who formed the Roosters, which became the Impressions in 1956; and Martha Reeves (b. Detroit, 1941), who formed Martha and the Vandellas in 1963. Performers with roots in Motown and Chicago moved easily and convincingly among soul, gospel, R&B, blues, and blends of these. Generally, lyrics distinguish the styles more than the music, with R&B texts being about love and human relationships, and soul about social injustice, racial pride, and black militancy (e.g., James Brown's "Black Is Beautiful, Say It Loud: I'm Black and I'm Proud," 1968).

Distinctions became increasingly blurred, however, as new styles were generated by R&B. Rock and roll, soul, and other spin-offs arose in such rapid succession that *Billboard* abandoned its rhythm and blues best-seller charts for fifteen months from November 1963 to January 1965: "there were so many crossovers," historian Eileen Southern reports, "that the lists seemed superfluous."[29]

Motown

Detroit's most famous contribution to American music was named for the record label founded in 1960 by Berry Gordy, Jr. (b. 1929). Motown was a place, a recording company, and to some a style term synonymous with rhythm and blues. The Motown style grew from and alongside Chicago blues, but depended more than blues on writers, producers, engineers, and arrangers. Like the rock and roll to which it contributed, Motown was recorded for and distributed by radio for an audience of black and white youth.

Gordy, whose parents had come from Georgia to Detroit during the Great Migration, had modest success as a songwriter before he turned producer in 1957. Realizing that his ear for talent would support his own label, he founded Tamla in 1959, Motown in 1960, and Miracle in 1961. Almost immediately he struck gold: "Bye, Bye, Baby" by Mary Wells (d. 1992) in 1960, "Please, Mr. Postman" by the Marvelettes in 1961, "Fingertips, Part 2" by eleven-year-old Little Stevie Wonder (Stevland Morris, 1952–) in 1963, "Baby, I Need Your Loving" by the Four Tops in 1964. By 1972 these and other hits made Berry Gordy the richest black man in America.[30]

Motown ensembles like the Supremes, the Four Tops, and the Temptations combined sensuous choreography, vocal inflections reminiscent of gospel, and big band harmonies to produce a style that connected with black and white audiences. Early hits in the style include "Shop Around," by Smokey Robinson and the Miracles (1960); "Do You Love Me," by the Contours (1962); and "Where Did Our Love Go?" by the Supremes (1964). Gordy's successful formula was precisely that: he relied consistently on the same musicians, songwriters, and producers, who in turn gave Motown its distinctive sound.

Even a partial list of hit songs by the Supremes, who first auditioned for Gordy as the high-school Primettes, is impressive: "Where Did Our Love Go?" (1964), "Stop! In the Name of Love" (1965), "Baby Love" (1965), "You Can't Hurry Love"

(1966), "The Happening" (1967), "Love Child" (1968). The group's sweet sounds were particularly well suited to Motown's preferred upper register and plaintive lyrics. Lead singer Diana Ross (b. 1944) became a distinguished soloist after the group disbanded in 1969.

Motown's Jackson Five, formed in 1963 in Gary, Indiana, was the most popular of the numerous "boy bands" that dominated the scene during the 1970s and 1980s. Lead singer Michael Jackson (b. 1958) was eleven years old when they signed on with the Motown label in 1964, bringing out numerous hits, among them "The Love You Save," "I'll Be There," and "Mama's Pearl." Notable for his dance moves even as a youngster, as an adult Michael Jackson became internationally famous as a solo singer who blends rock rhythms, soul melodies, and funk playfulness. His 1982 album *Thriller* sold more than 40 million copies. Its success and Jackson's popularity owed much to the advent of the music video, which showcased his flair as a dancer.

THE RISE OF ROCK 'N' ROLL

The ultimate offshoot of the blues—rock 'n' roll—was promoted in Cleveland, where the Rock and Roll Hall of Fame now documents its rise. Central to the process was disc jockey Alan "Moondog" Freed (1921–1965), who popularized the term "rock and roll" on his late-night radio show over Cleveland's WJW-AM, "The Moondog Rock & Roll House Party." Freed began the show on July 11, 1951, at the suggestion of local record store owner Leo Mintz, who believed that rhythm and blues could attract a wide audience. The influence of rhythm and blues shows in an early example, "Sh-Boom," by the Chords, a male R&B group. The style of the Chords was sometimes called doo-wop, a smooth, usually all-vocal rhythm and blues sound, but the song defied classification when it debuted and was called pop when it made the Top Ten in 1954. But its novel sound, characterized by what rock historian Carl Belz called a "powerful incessant beat," "fragmentary or improvised lyrics," and notable instrumental accompaniment, immediately signaled a new musical direction.[31] What came to characterize rock 'n' roll was the fusion of country-western, pop, gospel, and rhythm and blues, and it reached its fullest synthesis in the recordings of Elvis Presley.

Like jazz and blues, rock 'n' roll began as music by and for blacks, but was quickly appropriated by whites. The style name had sexual connotations for blacks that were lost on most whites, and titles were sometimes sanitized when released as white covers (e.g., Etta James' "Roll with Me, Henry" became "Dance with Me, Henry" when covered by Georgia Gibbs). The rock 'n' roll era nevertheless was one in which black and white audiences listened to the same music at a time when segregation was beginning to weaken. Freed's "Moondog Coronation Ball," a dance at the Cleveland Arena in March 1952, attracted so many teens—20,000, more than twice the site's capacity, and most of them black—that it was cancelled on the spot; both the fire and police departments were called in to clear the building. The event marked the first link between rock 'n' roll and challenges to the status quo.

Well into the 1960s, whites and blacks lauded singers such as Chuck Berry (b. 1926) of St. Louis, who recorded "Maybellene" (1955) in Chicago after Muddy Waters introduced him to producers at Chess. Berry's "Roll Over Beethoven" (1956), later covered by the Beatles, and "Johnny B. Goode" (1958) remain rock 'n' roll classics. This new music, with its driving beat and sexually suggestive

The Rock and Roll Hall of Fame

Designed by the renowned architect I. M. Pei, the Rock and Roll Hall of Fame and Museum building is located at 1 Key Plaza (Northcoast Harbor), Cleveland, Ohio. The multilevel facility has 150,000 feet of display space and opened in 1999. It contains the Alan Freed Radio Studio and exhibits related to its members. Inductions to the Hall of Fame are made annually (the nineteenth annual induction ceremony was held March 15, 2004). Among its honorees are blues man Robert Johnson, country singer Jimmie Rodgers, piano man Billy Joel, and guitarist Eric Clapton.

lyrics—delivered in a more improvisatory and spontaneous manner by black performers—became the music of America's youth. It also attracted English musicians, an important development in the forthcoming transition from rock 'n' roll to rock.

AFTER ROCK 'N' ROLL

In the 1960s, rock 'n' roll became simply rock, a politically and socially charged music that expressed the indignation and hopelessness of a generation of youth worldwide. It soon became a music dominated by whites, in the United States and abroad, especially in England. Ongoing developments in sound amplification brought about and continue to influence the fusion of styles. A pioneer inventor-performer was Les Paul (originally Lester Polfus, b. 1915), a native of Waukesha, Wisconsin, who developed the prototype for the solid-body electric guitar in 1941 and was an early experimenter with multitrack recording. Rock groups in the Midwest included MC 5 (Motor City 5), a Detroit group formed in 1964 by Rob Tyner (Derminer, 1944–1991), Wayne Kramer, and Fred "Sonic" Smith (1949–1994). They became affiliated with the White Panther Party and subsequently were an acclaimed underground group. *Kick Out the Jams*, recorded for Elektra in 1969, documents the group at its peak. More conservative was Tracy Nelson (b. 1944) of Madison, Wisconson, who formed Mother Earth in 1966. The group mixed folk, rock, and pop. Similarly, Bob Seger (b. 1945) from Ann Arbor, Michigan, was influenced by Bob Dylan and Chuck Berry.

Iggy Pop (James Jewel Osterburg, b. 1947), from Ypsilanti, Michigan, is known as the "Godfather of Punk." He dropped out of the University of Michigan to study with Sam Ley, former drummer with Howlin' Wolf and the Paul Butterfield Blues Band in Chicago. When he returned to Detroit he had a new name—Iggy Stooge—and with Ron Asheton of the Chosen Few, organized the Psychedelic Stooges. *The Stooges Album* (1969) has typical punk titles: "I Wanna Be Your Dog" and "Funhouse." The Psychedelic Stooges were noted for their theatrics (e.g., jumping into the audience from the stage). They broke up soon after the release of their final album, *Metallic K.O.*, in 1976. But the influence of rock and its offshoots reached deep into American musical culture.

By the mid-1980s, country had severed its roots from folk music; sleek pop combined with mild rock 'n' roll was the prevailing sound. Many performers, finding country too smooth and sterile, were exploring a new direction. Alternative country (alt. country) aimed to fuse country roots with punk and rock. The premise was simple, but the lyrics presented a problem: it was difficult to create lyrics compatible with both traditional country and the more vigorous and primal music of punk and rock. Traditional country lyrics could be melancholy and drip with self-pity; punk and rock lyrics were explicitly sexual, bordering on obscene. There were mutually acceptable topics—problems facing women in middle age, for example—but most of the alternative lyrics ultimately evoked the spirits of bygone heroes, such as the Midwest's John Prine (b. 1946).

Prine was from Maywood, Illinois, and recorded for Atlantic, releasing his first album, *John Prine*, in 1972. It contained "Sam Stone," a song about a Vietnam War veteran and drug addiction, and it quickly made him a cult figure. Lyrics such as "There's a hole in daddy's arm where all the money goes, / And Jesus Christ died for nothing I suppose" made Prine the idol of punk, blue-collar folk, and country musicians. Prine's most ardent fans included two Belleville, Illinois, punk musicians, Jeff Tweedy and Jay Farrar (both born in 1968), the founders of Uncle Tupelo. Uncle Tupelo's influence was real and far-reaching, even though the original band broke up in 1994, before the alternative movement began. Their debut album, *No Depression* (1990), captured the melancholy of their idol, John Prine, and gave a name to their style.

Branson

Branson, Missouri, sometimes called the "Broadway of the Ozarks," today rivals Nashville as a musical performance center. Its location serves as a reminder that large numbers of white as well as black southerners populated the Midwest. African American rhythms are rare, and cutting-edge country music artists ordinarily do not compete with the venerable veterans of the Grand Ole Opry and the aging balladeers and vocalists who bring to Branson's stages music steeped in nostalgia, patriotism, and religion. Originally known for the Shepherd of the Hills pageant based on Harold Bell Wright's spiritual novel, Branson has been filled since the 1960s with theaters and theme parks that annually draw more than 6 million tourists. Nearly three dozen performers, including such stalwarts as Mel Tillis, Roy Clark, Moe Bandy, Tony Orlando, Glen Campbell, Andy Williams, and the Osmond Brothers, have established celebrity theaters named after themselves, usually headlining the nightly shows themselves. Mainstream artists such as Pat Boone, the Lennon Sisters, and the Radio City Rockettes routinely appear in extravaganzas.

The album included a 1930s gospel tune by the Carter Family entitled "Alternative Country," and the term came into general use after appearing in the fanzine *No Depression*, which was launched in 1995. The alternative style evolved over time. "It wasn't like we were ever intentionally trying to merge punk and country," Tweedy reflected. "That's just what came out."[32] After Uncle Tupelo disbanded, members formed spin-off groups that continued to advance the movement, among them Son Volt and Wilco.

The fusion of styles has resulted in nearly as many emphases as bands. For example, the Jayhawks of Minneapolis, formed in 1989 by Mark Olson, aligned themselves with alt. country. Souled American, a Chicago group headed by Joe Adducci and Chris Grigoroff, blend country, folk, rock, reggae, R&B, and Jazz. Eleventh Dream Day, another Chicago-based group with a female drummer (Janet Beveridge Bean), is finding new audiences for the alt. rock of *Prairie School Freakout* (1988; 2003). Perhaps most important, Hüsker Dü, a punk trio from Minneapolis, was formed in 1979 by Bob Mould, Grant Hart, and Greg Norton (the group's name is Norwegian for "Do you remember?"). Hüsker Dü's "Broken Home, Broken Heart" two-record album, *Zen Arcade* (SST Records, 1984), includes a song about a young boy's dream of leaving home. Their mix of hard core rock and melodic ballad had a profound impact on Nirvana, Green Day, and other stars of modern alternative music.

As these examples suggest, the "indie scene"—musicians and recording studios not affiliated with the major companies who record and distribute most of the music produced in the United States—exist in every state of the Midwest. Perhaps the most vibrant of the scenes is located in the Minneapolis–St. Paul area, which has fostered local bands since the 1970s. Cultural institutions in the Twin Cities, such as the Walker Art Center and the Weisman Art Center at the University of Minnesota, have nurtured hometown bands as deliberate promotions of rich regional identity, but just as important are the number of local music aficionados, the number of nearby bars and clubs and festivals (e.g., the annual August Midwest Music Summit, in Indianapolis) where bands can play, the number of small local commercial producers who record and sell the songs, and the number of Web sites that promote the results to a global audience. In the Twin Cities the music spectrum is wide, ranging from country, Christian, and ethnic music to pop, rock, and hip-hop. The band called 13 Hertz, for example, plays "metaphysical rock," but others, such as Align, Baby Monoxide, Bubblemath, Dan Israel and the Cultivators, Red Cloud, Snark, and Tow Truck Tom and the Roadside Wrecks, defy genres. Columnists in the local press, especially the *Minneapolis Star Tribune*, cover the music scene thoroughly and frequently.

Out of this milieu came the versatile Prince (Prince Rogers Nelson, b. 1960), who released his first album, *For You*, in 1978. *Prince*, a collection of romantic ballads, followed in 1979. A more earthy release, *Dirty Mind*, in disco style, was released in 1980. Prince's style at that point contained growls and moans, as in "Controversy" (1981). Perhaps his most successful recording was "When Doves Cry," from the 1984 film *Purple Rain*. Prince was awarded three Grammys in 1985.

Midwestern cities with large black communities—most notably St. Louis, Chicago, and Detroit—have nourished a hip-hop culture of dance and rap. Detroit star Eminem (Marshall Mathers III, b. 1974), a white rapper, was declared Wake Up Show Freestyle Performer of the Year by Los Angeles disc jockeys when his first solo album, *Infinite*, was released in 1997. *Slim Shady*, which won a Grammy for the best solo rap album of the year, gave him considerable notoriety. Some accused him of exploiting misery. Particularly offensive was "97 Bonnie and Clyde," a fantasy about the rapper killing his own mother as well as the mother of his daughter. Eminem's defenders maintain that such raps provide catharsis for teenagers growing up in today's suburbs. Meanwhile, Mathers has attracted critical attention in the world's leading newspapers and magazines, including the *New York Times*, *Time*, and *USA Today*. More recently, Mark (Tarboy) Williams (b. 1974) and Joe (Capo) Kent (b. 1973) have called attention to the St. Louis hip-hop scene. As the Trackboyz, Williams and Kent sell background music ("beats") to rappers on both coasts. Avoiding a signature sound in order to maintain a diverse group of clients, Williams and Kent got their start with a local rapper, Cornell "Nelly" Haynes, Jr. (b. 1978), whose "Country Grammar" (2000) and "Hot in Here" (2002) feature the distinctive midwestern inflections of his voice.

CLASSICAL MUSIC IN THE MIDWEST

Classical music, brought to the Midwest by its earliest European settlers, is nurtured in the region's conservatories, schools of music, libraries, and research centers. The University of Chicago and nearby Northwestern University offer degrees in performance, composition, theory, and musicology. Indiana University at Bloomington (founded 1820) has one of America's most distinguished schools of music, offering degree programs in opera, ballet, jazz, composition, and musicology. The University of Michigan, long recognized for its excellent academic programs and distinguished faculty, is especially noted for its band program and its summer music programs and camps for young artists. Washington University in St. Louis offers degrees in jazz and computer music as well as the Ph.D. in musicology and theory. Other midwestern schools of music include the Kansas City Conservatory of Music, founded in 1906 and now part of the University of Missouri, and the School of Music of the University of Iowa, Iowa City (founded 1919), known worldwide for the music aptitude testing system developed there by Carl E. Seashore.

The state of Ohio may have more schools of music, conservatories, opera companies, and orchestras per capita than any other state in the nation. Outstanding music schools in the state university system include Ohio University, Athens (founded 1804); Ohio State University, Columbus; and Kent State University, Kent. Among Ohio's conservatories are Oberlin, Cincinnati, and the Cleveland Institute. Baldwin-Wallace College at Berea, Ohio, is the home of the remarkable Riemenschneider Bach Institute which houses the Emile and Karl Riemenschneider Memorial Bach Library, a collection of manuscripts and early editions of Bach's works.

Orchestras and opera companies were formed across the Midwest as individual cities and towns were incorporated. Milwaukee (founded 1839; incorporated 1846), soon the most important musical center in the upper Midwest, was known as the "German Athens on Lake Michigan." Opera productions began in the 1850s, and the "Prelude" from Wagner's *Parsifal* was given in 1882. Early orchestral ensembles included Severence and William's Band (1850), Christopher Bach's Orchestra (1855), Zeitze's Orchestra (1857), John Kohler's Bay View Orchestra (1862), and Clauder's Orchestra (1878). The Music Hall, inaugurated in 1864 and renamed the Academy of Music in 1872, was long considered the finest concert hall in the Midwest. The now world-famous Milwaukee Symphony Orchestra dates from 1958.

Daniel W. Bantie formed a brass band in Kansas City (incorporated 1850) in 1858, and a string orchestra was formed in 1867. Coates Opera House opened in 1870, and an oratorio society was organized in 1897. Carl Busch arrived from Denmark in 1887 and organized the Kansas City Symphony Orchestra (KCSO) in 1911. He became a prominent teacher, counting among his students Kansas City native Robert Russell Bennett (1894–1981). The Kansas City Philharmonic, which succeeded the KCSO, was founded in 1934 by Karl Krueger (1894–1979), a native of Atchison, Kansas.

Chicago (incorporated 1833) has exhibited an unusual appreciation for opera. Among its early venues were Rice's Theater, McVicker's Theater, Tremont Music Hall, and Crosby's Opera House. The latter fell victim to the Great Fire of 1871 but was rebuilt by 1873. The Auditorium Theater opened in 1889 and the Civic Opera House in 1929. The Chicago Grand Opera Company was formed in 1910, the Lyric Opera Center for American Artists in 1973. Chicago has also been a significant production center for musicals; *Grease* was staged there before opening on Broadway in 1972.

By contrast, the early concert life of Indianapolis (founded 1821) centered on its churches. Choral organizations became numerous following heavy immigration of Germans in the 1830s and 1840s. Music festivals were organized in the 1870s and remained popular to the end of the century. A Mendelssohn choir was founded in 1916 and a Haydn festival choir in 1932. The Indianapolis Symphony Orchestra was founded in 1929.

Symphony and opera house orchestras of the Midwest were dominant forces in the world of music throughout the twentieth century. The Cincinnati, Cleveland, Minneapolis, Detroit, St. Louis, and Chicago orchestras, in particular, have long been recognized as major world-class ensembles. The finest conductors have served as their directors, among them Fritz Reiner (Cincinnati and Chicago), Georg Solti (Chicago), Antal Dorati (Detroit), Leopold Stokowski, Max Rudolf, Thor Johnson, Thomas Schippers (Cincinnati), Leonard Slatkin (St. Louis), Christoph von Dohnanyi (Cleveland), Eugene Ormandy, Dimitri Mitropoulos, Neville Marriner, and Pinchas Zuckerman (Minneapolis–St. Paul), among others.

Today when American composers seek to portray the "American spirit" in music they are often inspired by the Midwest, its land and lore, its people and their diverse ethnic and folk music, and their religious and moral values. Examples include Aaron Copland's *Fanfare for the Common Man*, first performed in Cincinnati in 1943, and *Lincoln Portrait*; Virgil Thomson's *The Plow that Broke the Plains*; and Roy Harris' *Symphony Number 3*.

Symphony orchestras and choral societies continue to thrive, even in communities of comparatively modest size, by expanding their mission to include free concerts, open rehearsals, preconcert lectures, and educational outreach programs for children. Most have Web sites providing current information.

Most larger urban centers in the region also maintain ballet companies. The Cincinnati Ballet was begun in 1970 and is housed in the city's Music Hall. The company offers an annual season of dance and also tours the Midwest. Dance is frequently programmed at the numerous midwestern summer festivals, among them the Ravinia Festival in Chicago and the May Festival in Cincinnati. The Chicago City Ballet was founded in 1979 and has had among its directors Maria Tallchief and Paul

Midwestern Music Industries

Instrument manufacturers, dealers, and music publishers have energized and supported the musical culture of the Midwest. The world's leading manufacturers of keyboard instruments include the Baldwin Piano Company of Cincinnati, the Hammond Organ Company of Chicago, the Wurlitzer Organ Company of Cincinnati, Chicago, and DeKalb, Illinois, and the prestigious Holtkamp Organ Company of Cleveland. The Wurlitzer Company specialized in theater organs that produced a wide range of instrumental and novelty sound effects.

Selmer of Elkhart, Indiana (founded 1927), specializes in wind instruments for the school market. Ludwig Music of Chicago, noted for its fine percussion instruments, merged for a time with Elkhart's C. G. Conn Company, maker of brass instruments, saxophones, and flutes and a popular electronic organ.

King Musical Instruments (founded in Cleveland, 1893), manufacturers of distinguished brass instruments, produced first a tenor trombone, improving the instrument's slide mechanism, bell taper, and bore size; then silver cornets, tubas, baritones, and trumpets. In 1966 King moved to Eastlake, Ohio, and in 1983 merged with Conn.

The Midwest has a large number of publishing companies that specialize in church music and music for schools. Prominent ones are the Lutheran publishing companies of Augsburg in Minneapolis, and Concordia in St. Louis. The World Library Company of Schiller Park, Illinois, publishes choral music and liturgical music for the Roman Catholic Church. Since 1991 it has emphasized music for Hispanic parishes. Nondenominational publishing houses include Hope, of Carol Stream, Illinois, and Lorenz Corporation of Dayton, Ohio. Sacred music publishing companies are usually family-owned (e.g., Lorenz), and some are multifaceted with sub-companies within and outside the United States. Hal Leonard Corporation of Milwaukee issues sacred and secular choral as well as instrumental music.

Mejia. Jeraldyne Blunden founded the Dayton Contemporary Dance Company, a pioneer of African American modern dance, in 1968.

CONCLUSION

The people of the Midwest have always made music. Since the time of European contact, each set of newcomers has added contexts, instruments, styles, and forms, creating a musical culture as diverse as the population. In its formative years, America had to overcome a cultural self-consciousness and the tendency to compare its music to European music. In the Midwest, a double complex had to be dispelled—a sense of inferiority not only to Europe, but also to the musical culture of the East Coast. However, the economic forces that made the Midwest a center of agriculture, commerce, transportation, and manufacturing inspired musical innovation as well as musical immigration. After blues traveled upriver from the South, midwestern entrepreneurs established record labels to distribute it. Rhythm and blues mutated into rock 'n' roll because midwestern disc jockeys and promoters saw economic opportunity in music that crossed racial boundaries. The region's history of amateur and professional bands fed the big bands of the swing era and today encourages performers and audiences of a rich "indie scene." Cities large and small, along with a wealth of universities and conservatories, sustain world music of the past and cutting-edge contemporary composition. The Midwest has never existed in cultural isolation, and just as American music comprises a plurality of styles found nowhere else in the world, so midwestern music will continue to enrich it.

RESOURCE GUIDE

Printed Sources

Benjaminson, Peter. *The Story of Motown*. New York: The New Press, 1979.

Blesh, Rudi. *Classic Piano Rags*. New York: Dover, 1973.

Blesh, Rudi, and Harriet Janis. *They All Played Ragtime*. Rev. ed. New York: Oak Publications, 1971.

Bokenkotter, Thomas. *A Concise History of the Catholic Church*. Expanded ed. New York: Doubleday, 1990.

Burton, Frederick R. *American Primitive Music*. New York: Moffat, Yard, 1909.

Connell, E. Jane. "Pioneers: Itinerant Painters and Early Portraiture." *Timeline* 20, no. 2–3 (March-June 2003): 4–23.

Davis, Elizabeth A. *Index to the New World Recorded Anthology of American Music: A User's Guide to the Initial One Hundred Records*. New York: Norton, 1981.

Dennison, Sam. *Scandalize My Name: Black Imagery in American Popular Music*. New York: Garland, 1982.

Densmore, Frances. *The American Indians and Their Music*. Rev. ed. New York: Womans [*sic*] Press, 1936.

———. *Chippewa Music*. 2 vols. Smithsonian Institution, Bureau of American Ethnology Bulletins 45, 53. Washington, DC: Government Printing Office, 1910–1913.

Dichter, Harry, and Elliott Shapiro. *Early American Sheet Music: Its Lure and Its Lore, 1768–1889*. New York: R. R. Bowker, 1941.

Hamm, Charles. "Patent Notes in Cincinnati." *Bulletin of the Historical and Philosophical Society of Ohio* 16 (1958): 293–310.

Hitchcock, H. Wiley. *Music in the United States: A Historical Introduction*. 3rd ed. Englewood Cliffs, NJ: Prentice Hall, 1988.

Hitchcock, H. Wiley, and Stanley Sadie, eds. *The New Grove Dictionary of American Music*. 4 vols. New York: Grove's Dictionaries of Music, 1986.

Hoover, Cynthia Adams. Liner notes to *19th Century American Ballroom Music: Waltzes, Marches, Polkas, and Other Dances, 1840–1860*. Smithsonian Social Orchestra & Quadrille Band, James Weaver, director. LP. Nonesuch H-71313.

Howe, Elias. *Howe's Complete Ball-Room Hand Book*. Boston: Oliver Ditson, 1858.

Jones, Rev. David. *A Journal of Two Visits Made to Some Nations of Indians on the West Side of the River Ohio, in the Years 1772–1773*. New York: J. Sabin, 1865. Reprint, Fairfield, WA: Ye Galleon Press, 1973.

Kurath, Gertrude P. *Iroquois Music and Dance: Ceremonial Arts of Two Seneca Longhouses*. Smithsonian Institution, Bureau of American Ethnology Bulletin 187. Washington: Government Printing Office, 1964.

Larkin, Colin, ed. *The Encyclopedia of Popular Music*. 8 vols. New York: Grove's Dictionaries of Music, 1998.

Loesser, Arthur. *Men, Women and Pianos: A Social History*. New York: Simon and Schuster, 1954.

Lowens, Irving, and Allen P. Britton. "A History and Bibliography of the First Shape Note Tune Books." *Journal of Research in Music Education* 1 (Spring 1953): 31–55.

Morgenstern, Dan. *Jazz People*. Englewood Cliffs, NJ: Prentice Hall, 1976.

Nathan, Hans. *Dan Emmett and the Rise of Early Negro Minstrelsy*. Norman: University of Oklahoma Press, 1962.

Nettl, Bruno. *Folk and Traditional Music of the Western Continents*. 2nd ed. Englewood Cliffs, NJ: Prentice Hall, 1973.

Nettl, Bruno, and Helen Myers. *An Introduction to Folk Music in the United States*. 3rd ed. Detroit: Wayne State University Press, 1976.

Norton, Wesley. *Religious Newspapers in the Old Northwest to 1861: A History, Bibliography and Record of Opinion*. Athens: Ohio University Press, 1977.

Russell, Ross. *Jazz Style in Kansas City and the Southwest*. Berkeley: University of California Press, 1973.

Schwartz, H. W. *Bands of America*. Garden City, NY: Doubleday, 1957.

Secular Music of the Nineteenth Century: Parlor Music, the Minstrel Show, Bands and Ragtime. Country Dance and Song [annual] 20 (1990).

Shaw, Arnold. *Honkers and Shouters: The Golden Years of Rhythm and Blues*. New York: Macmillan, 1978.

Southern, Eileen. *The Music of Black Americans: A History*. 3rd ed. New York: W. W. Norton, 1997.

Tirro, Frank. *Jazz: A History*. 2nd ed. New York: W. W. Norton, 1993.

Vitz, Robert C. *The Queen City and the Arts: Cultural Life in Nineteenth-Century Cincinnati*. Kent, OH: Kent State University Press, 1989.

Wetzel, Richard D. *Frontier Musicians on the Connoquenessing, Wabash, and Ohio: A History of the Music and Musicians of George Rapp's Harmony Society, 1805–1906*. Athens: Ohio University Press, 1976.

———. *"Oh! Sing No More That Gentle Song": The Musical Life and Times of William Cumming Peters, 1805–66*. Warren, MI: Harmonie Park Press, 2000.

———. "Some Notation Systems in Early American Hymn-tune Books." *Keystone Folklore Quarterly* 12, no. 4 (Winter 1967): 247–260.

Web Sites

Blackface Minstrelsy. Center for American Music, University of Pittsburgh.
http://www.pitt.edu/~amerimus/minstrel.htm

Ellertsen, Peter. "American Folk Hymnody in Illinois, 1800–1850."
http://www.sci.edu/classes/ellertsen/hymn102400.html

Hampson, Thomas. "I Hear America Singing: A *Great Performances* Special on the American Song." WNET-NY.
http://www.pbs.org/wnet/ihas/

Indie-music.com.
http://indie-music.com/
A national portal, with band listings by state.

Inductees. Rock 'n' Roll Hall of Fame.
http://www.rockhall.com/hof/currinductees.asp
Searchable database of career information on musicians inducted into the Hall of Fame.

Music Scene Minnesota.
http://musicscene.org
A portal emphasizing the Minneapolis "indie scene."

The Red Hot Jazz Archive.
http://www.redhotjazz.com
Site includes lists of bands and biographies of musicians.

Sacred Harp and Shape Note Singing.
http://www.fasola.org
Site includes links to performance groups in many states.

Sweet Home Chicago: Big City Blues, 1946–1966. Museum of Science and Industry.
http://www.msichicago.org/temp_exhibit/blues/index.html

Videos/Films

The EAV History of Jazz with Billy Taylor. 49 min. Produced and directed by Ruth Leon. Chicago: CLEARVUE/Educational Audio Visual, 1986. Videocassette and print guide.

Jazz. Produced and directed by Ken Burns. 10 videocassettes or videodiscs, approx. 19 hrs. Burbank, CA, and Washington, DC: PBS Home Video/Warner Home Video, 2000. Videocassette and DVD. Ten-part documentary series following the history of jazz from African American musicians in New Orleans through the 1990s. Includes archival footage, photographs, performances, and contemporary interviews and musical performances.

Martin Scorsese Presents the Blues: A Musical Journey. Directed by Wim Wenders et al. 7 videodiscs, 780 min. New York: Sony Music Entertainment/Columbia Music Video, 2003. DVD. Seven-part documentary series and twelve-page print guide tracing the evolution of the blues. Features archival performance footage of Muddy Waters, Howlin' Wolf, and Willie Dixon as well as performances of classic blues songs by contemporary musicians.

The Music Man. Music by Meredith Wilson. Produced and directed by Morton da Costa. 1961. 151 min. (videocassette); 181 min. (DVD). Burbank, CA: Warner Home Video, 1986, 1999. Film version of the musical drama focusing on the traditions of midwestern band and parlor music in early twentieth-century Iowa, with music by a native son.

St. Louis Blues. Starring Bessie Smith. Choral arrangements by W. C. Handy and Rosamond Johnson. Produced by Dick Currier and directed by Dudley Murphy. 16 mm, 16 min. Davenport, IA: Blackhawk Films, 1929. Streamed online at http://www.redhotjazz.com/stlouisblues.html. Bessie Smith's only film.

Sweet Home Chicago: The Story in Words and Music of Chicago Blues and Chess Records. Produced by Nina Rosenstein and directed by Alan Raymond and Susan Raymond. VHS and DVD, 64 min. Universal City, CA: MCA Music Video, 1993. Includes interviews with and historic footage of Muddy Waters, Buddy Guy, Otis Spann, Willie Dixon, Sonny Boy Williamson, Chuck Berry, Phil and Marshall Chess, James Cotton, John Lee Hooker, and Mick Jagger, among others.

Recordings

Big Band Jazz: From the Beginnings to the Fifties. Selected and annotated by Gunther Schuller and Martin Williams. Smithsonian Collection of Recordings. LP. RCA R03030 DMM 6-0610.

The Eighty-Six Years of Eubie Blake. LP. Columbia C2S 847.

The Gospel Ship: Baptist Hymns and White Spirituals from the Southern Mountains. Produced by Alan Lomax. LP. New World Recorded Anthology of American Music. NW 294.

The Louisville Orchestra. First Edition Records. Commissioning and Recording Project. LOU-5455 (ff). Series that includes, among many others, works by Gardner Read (b. 1913), Evanston, IL; Robert L. Sanders (b. 1906), Chicago, IL; Robert Ward (b. 1917), Cleveland, OH; Ernst Bacon (b. 1898), Chicago, IL; Leo Sowerby (b. 1895), Grand Rapids, MI; Ben Weber (b. 1913), St. Louis, MO; Everett Helm (b. 1913), Minneapolis, MN; David Van Vactor (b. 1906), Plymouth, IN; Herbert Elwell (b. 1898), Minneapolis, MN; Robert Kurka (b. 1921), Cicero, IL; Ross Lee Finney (b. 1906), Wells, MN; Hale Smith (b. 1925), Cleveland, OH.

Maple Leaf Rag: Ragtime in Rural America. Produced by Lawrence Cohn. LP. New World Recorded Anthology of American Music. NW 235.

Nineteenth Century American Ballroom Music. Waltzes, Marches, Polkas, and Other Dances, 1840–1860. Smithsonian Social Orchestra and Quadrille Band, James Weaver, director. LP. Nonesuch H-71313.

Piano Rags by Scott Joplin. Joshua Rifkin, piano. 3 vols. LP. Nonesuch HB-73026, H-71305.

Shake, Rattle and Roll: Rock 'n' Roll in the 1950s. LP. New World Recorded Anthology of American Music. NW 249.

Smithsonian Collection of Classic Jazz. Edited by Martin Williams. 5 CDs. RD 033 (Smithsonian A 19478, A 19482).

Steppin' on the Gas: Rags to Jazz (1913–1927). Notes by Lawrence Gushee. LP. New World Recorded Anthology of American Music. NW 269.

Festivals and Events

Blues Heritage Festival, St. Louis, MO (September), annual event at Laclede's Landing on the historic St. Louis riverfront.

Chicago Blues Festival, Chicago, IL (June), annual Thursday–Sunday event in Grant Park on the lakefront, featuring nonstop simultaneous performances by major performers. http://egov.cityofchicago.org/.

Chicago Jazz Festival, Chicago, IL (September), annual Thursday–Sunday event in Grant Park on the lakefront, featuring non-stop simultaneous performances by major performers. http://egov.cityofchicago.org/.

Midwest Composers' Symposium, location and date vary. http://www-camil.music.uiuc.edu: 16080/comptheory/Awards/Mwcs.html. Performance showcase of works by students in major midwestern composing programs.

Mississippi Valley Blues Festival, Davenport, IA (July 4th weekends), annual event. http://www.mvbs.org/fest.htm.

North Iowa Band Festival, Mason City, IA (June). http://www.masoncityia.com/bandfest/.

Sacred Harp/Shape Note Singing. Directory of local Sacred Harp (Shape Note) groups that meet to sing at least four times annually. http://www.mcsr.olemiss.edu/~mudws/regular.html.

Scott Joplin International Ragtime Foundation Festival, Sedalia, MO (June), annual ragtime festival. http://www.scottjoplin.org/festival.htm.

Organizations

Archives of Traditional Music
Indiana University
Morrison Hall 117 & 120
Bloomington, IN 47405-2501
(812) 855-4679
Fax: (812) 856-0193
E-mail: atmusic@indiana.edu

Largest university-based ethnographic sound archives in the United States: recordings of 350,000 songs from around the world and an extensive collection of recordings of music of North American Indians.

Sam DeVincent Collection of American Sheet Music
Lilly Library
1200 East Seventh Street
Indiana University
Bloomington, IN 47405-5500
(812) 855-2452
www.indiana.edu/~liblilly/devincent.shtml

One of many music collections in the Lilly Library, which also holds Hoagy Carmichael's manuscripts and correspondence. In addition, Indiana University's William and Gayle Cook Music Library, housed in the Bess Meshulam Simon Music Library and Recital Hall, holds more than 579,000 cataloged items.

Goldman Band Collection
Special Collections Dept.
Main Library
University of Iowa
Iowa City, IA 52242-1420
Phone: (319) 335-5921
Fax: (319) 335-5900
E-mail: lib-spec@uiowa.edu

Scott Joplin International Ragtime Foundation
321 S. Ohio
Sedalia, MO 65301
Phone: (660) 826-2271; toll free (866) 218-6258
www.scottjoplin.org

Scott Joplin House State Historic Site
2658A Delmar Boulevard

St. Louis, MO 63103
Phone: (314) 340-5790
www.mostateparks.com/scottjoplin/geninfo.htm

Sammy Kaye Collection
Robert E. and Jean R. Mahn Center for Archives and Special Collections
Alden Library
Ohio University
Athens, OH 45701
www.library.ohiou.edu/libinfo/depts/archives/index.htm

Ernst C. Krohn Collection of American Sheet Music
Gaylord Music Library
Gaylord Hall
6500 Forsyth Boulevard
Washington University
St. Louis, MO 63105
Phone: (314) 935-5563
Fax: (314) 935-4263
E-mail: music@wulib.wustl.edu

The 60,000-item collection is especially strong in regional composers and publishers.

Mississippi Valley Blues Society
102 South Harrison Street, Suite 300
Davenport, IA 52801-1811
Phone: (563) 322-5837 aka (563) 32BLUES
Fax: (563) 322-5832 aka (563) 32BLUE2
E-mail: mvbs@revealed.net
www.mvbs.org

Motown Historical Museum
2648 W. Grand Boulevard
Detroit, MI 48208
Phone: (313) 875-2264
Fax: (313) 875-2267
E-mail: info@motownmuseum.com
www.motownmuseum.com

Rock and Roll Hall of Fame
One Key Plaza
751 Erieside Avenue
Cleveland, OH 44114
Phone: (216) 781-ROCK
www.rockhall.com

RELIGION

Brian Wilson

The Midwest has long been stereotyped as the land of bland moderation and conformity, a judgment that seems to extend especially to midwestern religion. R.
Douglas Hurt, for example, in a chapter on "Midwestern Distinctiveness," writes
that "the statistical evidence indicates that midwesterners often are more moderate in their religious beliefs than people in other regions, usually falling between
the extremes of the southerners on the one hand and westerners and easterners on
the other." And yet, despite their supposed lukewarmness, midwesterners "have attended church on a typical Sunday more often than people in other regions," if
only out of habit, not conviction.[1] The picture that emerges from this statistical
snapshot is of a region where religion forms an indelible, but unobtrusive part of
the (largely static) cultural background; a region whose people are theologically
unreflective and spiritually complacent. Of course, the problem with such statistical analysis, as with all forms of stereotyping, is that it is designed ruthlessly to ignore both present difference and past history. If we look closer at the history and
pay attention to the differences where they have been and are influential, the picture of midwestern religiosity that emerges is far more rich, dynamic, and problematic than even those who live in the region might suspect.

AMERICAN INDIAN RELIGION IN THE PRECONTACT
AND FRONTIER MIDWEST

American Indian religious life in the precontact Midwest was complex, with each
tribe developing unique beliefs and practices. However, since most in this region
were of the Algonquian-Wakashan language family, contact between tribes occurred
often, and religious borrowing was frequent. Thus, within the welter of specific
tribal religions, one can highlight several beliefs and practices held in common.
Sacred stories celebrating the work of an omniscient Creator or "Master of Life"
were prominent, as were beliefs in a host of lesser spirits, some evil, such as the

"Desolator" or great horned serpent, others beneficent, such as the numerous animal spirits that served as spirit guides. Beliefs in the immortality of the soul and an abundant afterlife were also widespread. Indian ritual life centered around periodic festivals, either agricultural, funereal, or occasional (e.g., rituals to interpret dreams, prepare for war, cure epidemic disease, or identify the source of witchcraft). Typically, festivals were led by specially constituted "medicine" societies whose memberships were strictly controlled and whose political influence was considerable. In addition, individual ritual was widely practiced. It centered primarily on the shamanic treatment of disease or other personal distress, or on the transition of children to adulthood, as in, for example, the puberty fast and vision quest of the Menominee and Winnebago. Central to all these practices, however, was the Indian notion of spiritual power and the need for correct ritual to cultivate and keep it. Acquisition of spiritual power was necessary for success in almost all areas of Indian life.

American Indian religion was never static, but was constantly changing and adaptive; along with cultural borrowing, religious innovation occurred through the widespread practice of what whites came to call "prophecy" or visionary revelation. Such visions involved direct and sometimes terrifying encounters with the Great Spirit or other powerful supernatural beings. Visionary experiences often resulted in new spiritual knowledge or better rituals. As Anglo-Americans began to cross the Alleghenies in ever increasing numbers from the mid-eighteenth century on, prophecy became a powerful tool of Indian resistance to American expansion into the Midwest. Around such prophecy coalesced potent religiopolitical movements, which scholars now call "revitalization" movements. In the Upper Ohio Valley in the 1760s, for example, Neolin (c.1725–c.1775), soon to be known as the Delaware Prophet, had a series of visions in which the Master of Life warned that the Delaware's loss of spiritual power was due to their addiction to European trade goods, especially alcohol, and their neglect of ritual duties. Only by remedying these problems would the Delaware be able to resist the Anglo-Americans militarily and maintain their way of life. Neolin's message spread beyond his own tribe and formed the religious basis for Pontiac's uprising, which brought together just about every tribe in

Native American religious life in the precontact Midwest was complex, with each tribe developing unique beliefs and practices. Native American performing at traditional powwow on Harsens Island, Michigan. Courtesy Travel Michigan.

the Great Lakes region. Although the rebellion of Pontiac (c.1720–1769) was ultimately unsuccessful, new revitalization movements continued to arise in the Midwest, most notably that of Tecumseh (c.1768–1813) and his brother, Tenskwatawa (c.1768–1837), the Shawnee Prophet. After the 1832 Black Hawk War in Illinois, however, large-scale revitalization movements declined, probably due to the government's wholesale deportation of Indians beyond the Mississippi. Nevertheless, among many of those Indians who managed to remain in the region, indigenous beliefs and practices survived and the spirit of religious innovation lives on. This in part accounts for the renaissance of Indian spirituality in the Midwest during the latter half of the twentieth century.

French Roman Catholics had long conducted missionary work among the midwestern tribes, but Protestant missionaries, once they had the chance, were slower to cross the mountains in search of Native converts. David Zeisberger (1721–1808), a Moravian missionary, began work among the Delaware in Pennsylvania in 1765 and later helped found the Christian Indian villages of Schönbrunn, Gnadenhütten, Lichtenau, and Salem on the Tuscarawas in Ohio. Few followed up Zeisberger's work until after the turn of the century, and even then Protestant missionary efforts were sporadic. The Congregationalist Massachusetts and Connecticut Missionary societies did send a few missionaries to the Great Lakes region after 1811, and by 1823, the Methodists and Episcopalians had begun small Indian missions in northern Illinois and Wisconsin. Perhaps the outstanding example of successful missionary activity was that of Isaac McCoy (1784–1846), a Baptist who ran the Carey Mission in Niles, Michigan, between 1822 and 1826. By this time, however, American expansion into the Midwest had begun in earnest. With it, most Protestant clergy in the region turned their attention to ministering to their fellow Anglo-Protestants.

ANGLO-PROTESTANTISM ON THE MIDWESTERN FRONTIER

The Early National Period in the United States saw a profound shift in denominational loyalties among Anglo-Protestants, and this shift occurred primarily on the midwestern frontier. While Congregationalists, Presbyterians, and Anglicans (Episcopalians) predominated during the colonial period, these older confessions found themselves eclipsed by the Methodist and Baptist churches by the time of the Civil War. Reasons are not hard to find: the principles of religious freedom, newly enshrined in the Federal Constitution, encouraged a fierce competition for church members. Those denominations best able to satisfy the reigning needs of the majority were destined to win out in this religious "free market." Nowhere was this better illustrated than on the frontier. Here, relatively unlettered and unsophisticated settlers demanded a simple, comprehensible theology conveyed through unabashedly emotional worship. They found both supplied by the Methodist circuit rider and the Baptist "farmer preacher." In the end, all the Anglo-Protestant denominations found a place in the heartland, although from this early period on, the preponderance of Methodists and Baptists would become an enduring feature in much of the Midwest.

Methodists

Early Methodism was hierarchically organized into a series of annual and regional conferences. One of the principal duties of the regional conferences was to commission itinerant preachers or "circuit riders" to proselytize new settlements within specific geographical regions or "circuits." The first circuit riders in Ohio were sent by the Redstone conference of western Pennsylvania in 1787. Many more soon followed, commissioned primarily by new conferences in Kentucky and Tennessee. The circuit rider, now a figure of romantic lore, led a life of considerable toil and danger, rarely lasting more than a decade. Circuits could be several hundred miles in length, take several weeks to traverse, and include dozens of villages and isolated homesteads. James Finlay, an early Ohio circuit rider, took four weeks to complete the 475-mile Will's Creek Circuit on horse and on foot, and this only if the weather held. Housing was primitive or nonexistent, and not a few circuit riders succumbed to exposure and disease along the way. Once they arrived at a "preaching station," itinerants could hardly expect lavish church buildings. They preached wherever an audience could gather, be it a cabin, a barn, or an open field. Peru, Iowa, for example, heard its first Methodist sermon in a billiard parlor made ready for the occasion by a sheet thrown over "the offending furniture." If the audience was receptive, the circuit rider would gather a class and appoint a promising "lay exhorter" to continue weekly Bible study until his return. In time, the class would become a church, and, if prosperous enough, it would call a settled minister. The lay exhorter, too, could aspire to higher status, becoming a licensed preacher or perhaps a circuit rider himself. Educational requirements for this position were few: one had only to manifest a zealous spirituality and to be young, unmarried, and willing to endure the hardships of the wilderness for less than $100 a year. It is a testament to the attractiveness of the Methodist message that there was no shortage of takers. Several, like Illinois' Peter Cartwright (1785–1872), became leading citizens of their states. By the first decades of the nineteenth century, dozens of circuit riders were active in the Northwest Territory, which by this time had been organized into one vast Western Conference. Circuit riders reached as far west as St. Louis, Missouri, in 1818, and they entered the last of the midwestern states, Minnesota, by 1844. A scant decade later, thanks in large part to the work of circuit riders, Methodists controlled the Midwest, having more churches than any other denomination in Illinois, Indiana, Iowa, Michigan, Ohio, and Wisconsin.

Baptists

After the Methodists, the Baptists were destined to become the second largest American denomination in the nineteenth century. Again, huge gains were made on the frontier. Heirs to the Radical Reformation that insisted upon adult baptism, the Baptists formed a small but committed group during the colonial period. Unlike the Methodists, the Baptists rejected a rigid hierarchy: individual congregations would often form into regional associations for support, but these associations had no power to control the doctrine or polity of a congregation. Congregations called their own ministers, disciplined their own members, and joined or left associations as they saw fit. Scholars have pointed to the highly democratic ethos of

Revivalists from the Methodist, Baptist, and other Protestant churches celebrated their faith at camp meetings. Courtesy Billy Graham Center Museum.

the Baptist church as one of the reasons for its phenomenal success during the Early National Period. Important, too, was the denomination's method of recruiting clergy. Any man who felt the "call" to ministry could ask to be licensed to preach, and in due time, if popular, he might be ordained a minister by a congregation, occasionally one that he had gathered himself. Out of this new congregation might come others who sought to preach, and in this way, the Baptists advanced with the frontier. The first Baptist church in the Northwest Territory was organized in 1790 by the Reverend Stephen Gano (1762–1828) on the Little Miami River in Ohio. By 1812, there were approximately 2400 Baptists in the state, organized into five regional associations. Baptists were first to found Protestant churches in Indiana (1798), Illinois (1796), and Missouri (1804), and by 1826, these three states had a total of 250 Baptist ministers and licensed preachers. A scant generation later, Baptists could claim congregations in all the midwestern states except Minnesota.[2]

Presbyterians and Congregationalists

Presbyterians and Congregationalists were poised for major expansion into the frontier Midwest after the Revolution. Presbyterianism, primarily Scotch and Scotch Irish in origin, and Calvinist in theology, was rigidly hierarchical and centralized. This meant that, like the Methodists, the Presbyterians could engage in aggressive, well-funded, and highly coordinated missionary campaigns across the mountains. Presbyterians were early in Kentucky and Tennessee, and from these bases ministers moved across the Ohio into the Northwest Territory. The Reverend David Rice (1733–1816) founded the first Presbyterian church in Cincinnati in 1790, and by 1815 the Synod of Ohio was constituted. Presbyterianism spread fast: the Reverend Salmon Giddings (1782–1828) organized the first Presbyterian church west of the Mississippi in the Belleville Valley of Missouri in 1816, and as early as the 1840s, the denomination could be found in every midwestern state including Minnesota. On the other hand, the descendants of the Puritans, the Congregationalists, did far worse on the frontier. Scholars estimate that if sufficient attention had been paid to 800,000 or so New Englanders who migrated West by 1830, Congregationalism might have retained its position as a major denomination.[3] And yet the tradition's leaders were too focused on New England to care. Congregationalist missionary organizations were created in Connecticut, Massachusetts, and New Hampshire, but most of their efforts in this period were directed to Vermont and Maine, and only later to Ohio and beyond. Most Congregationalists on the frontier affiliated with Presbyterian churches since the Presbyterians' Calvinist theology closely resembled their own. In fact, in 1801, the Presbyterians and Congregationalists entered into a Plan of Union calling for the creation of mixed "Presbygational" congregations in which denominational identity was decided by majority vote. With the abrogation of the Plan in 1852, most "Presbygational" churches became Presbyterian, further swelling their numbers. Nonetheless, Presbyterianism remained a distant third on the frontier. The denomination's high educational requirements for the clergy, its nondemocratic institutional structure, its unyielding Calvinism, and its repudiation of the camp meeting revivalism embraced by Methodists and Baptists are several reasons why Presbyterianism did not do better in the early Midwest.

Quakers

Although barely contenders in the race for members on the frontier, Quakers and Episcopalians nevertheless became abiding presences in the Midwest. The Quakers, or Society of Friends as they are officially known, began migrating into the Old Northwest after 1787, mainly to what would become western Ohio and eastern Indiana (the "Quaker Trace"). By 1845, some 18,000 Quakers had settled in Ohio and 30,000 in Indiana, where they were organized into several regional Yearly Meetings. Five years later, Quakers established meetings in Michigan and Illinois, but only in the 1890s did they venture into other midwestern states. Most Quaker settlers came west because they were repulsed by slavery in their home states. Many became ardent abolitionists and "conductors" on the Underground Railroad. Legendary are Levi Coffin (1798–1877) and his wife Catherine White Coffin (?–1909) of Newport, Indiana. In addition to aiding some 2000 fugitive slaves gain freedom, they also extended the Railroad into the South, began a Quaker school for African Americans, and organized the Indiana Yearly Meeting of Anti-Slavery Friends.[4]

Episcopalians

The Episcopal Church, which once held a dominant position in the English Americas in its Anglican form, barely established a foothold on the frontier. That it did was owing to the extraordinary energy of Philander Chase (1775–1852), the first Episcopal bishop of the Midwest. A product of Dartmouth and a convert,

Chase did missionary work in upstate New York and New Orleans before turning his attention to the Old Northwest, arriving in Ohio in 1817. He organized the Diocese of Ohio the following year and, as was the custom, became bishop through election by his parishioners. Subsequently, Chase ministered to congregations in Michigan and Illinois, and in 1835 was elected bishop of Illinois. By the time of his death in 1852, the seeds of Episcopalianism in the Midwest had been sown. Besides Ohio, Michigan, and Illinois, Episcopal churches were to be found in Missouri as early as 1819, in Wisconsin by the 1820s, in Indiana and Iowa by the 1830s, and in Minnesota by the 1850s. Wherever it established itself, the Episcopal Church acquired a reputation as an elite church of the rich and privileged. Thus, midwestern Episcopalians, though few, came to wield a disproportionate share of power and influence in the region, especially in politics.

Other Protestant Religions

These six denominations were not the only Anglo-Protestant traditions to establish themselves in the Midwest. Among others, one could also mention the Unitarians and Universalists, the newly emerging Disciples of Christ or Campbellite "Christians," or even the experimental Shakers and Mormons. However, the important point here is the dominance of Anglo-Protestantism in

Swedenborgians and Spiritualists

One of the more interesting new religions in nineteenth-century America was Swedenborgianism, or the Church of the New Jerusalem, a faith based on the writings of Emmanuel Swedenborg (1688–1772), an eighteenth-century Swedish scientist and mystic, who, among other things, believed that living people could communicate with the dead. Unitarians were especially attracted to this new faith, and thus, wherever you found Unitarians in the Midwest, you were likely to find Swedenborgians. The most famous Swedenborgian in the Midwest, however, was not a trained minister. His name was John Chapman (1774–1845), and beginning in 1801 he roamed the Ohio and Indiana frontiers distributing religious tracts and planting apple orchards. "Johnny Appleseed," as he came to be known in folklore, died in Ft. Wayne, Indiana, where his grave can still be seen in the Johnny Appleseed Memorial Park. Given Swedenborgians' interest in spirit communication, it was not surprising that they were in turn attracted to Spiritualism, which arose in 1848 in the Burned Over District of Upstate New York when the Fox sisters claimed they could talk to the dead through an elaborate code. In time, Spiritualism became highly ritualized in the séance and would become one of the fastest growing religions in Antebellum America. Spiritualism was widely popular in the Midwest, especially among those of the Yankee Exodus. In 1849, for example, the largest Methodist congregation in Grand Rapids, Michigan, lost the bulk of its members to the newly organized Swedenborgian Church in that city, which in turn spun off an active Spiritualist congregation shortly after. Numerous Spiritualist camps were formed throughout the area (some of which still exist today), Spiritualist periodicals became popular, and in 1893, the National Spiritualist Association of Churches was founded in Chicago by two Unitarian ministers turned Spiritualists, Harrison D. Barrett (1863–1911) and James M. Peebles (1822–1922). It is the largest Spiritualist organization in the United States today.

the early Midwest, for it led to the formation of the durable cultural background of the region. Granted the Midwest was populated by three eastern streams—New Englander, mid-Atlantic, and Southerner—but it was the fact that the three shared a common Anglo-Protestant background that allowed them to meld into a new regional identity: the midwesterner. Indeed, the values and attitudes that came to define the stereotypical midwesterner, at least during the nineteenth century, were largely Anglo-Protestant in origin: individualism, egalitarianism, voluntaryism, a narrowly legalistic frame of mind, not to mention the Protestant ethic and the spirit of capitalism. Later immigration would come to modify this regional identity in important ways, but the cultural substrate would remain stubbornly Anglo-Protestant.

RELIGION AND NINETEENTH-CENTURY EUROPEAN IMMIGRATION TO THE MIDWEST

The antebellum period saw the United States' demographic and religious profile shift drastically. Beginning in the 1840s, large-scale European immigration began again. Some, like the Welsh and Cornish, came from Britain, but most did not. Many came from Scandinavia, although the two largest non-British groups were the Germans and the Irish, of whom several million had migrated by the turn of the century. Germans, mostly middle class and with some means, headed directly to the Midwest, looking for farmland or a city or town in which to ply their skilled trades. The Irish, on the other hand, largely unskilled and poor, worked their way west, primarily as labor on the Midwest's rapidly expanding system of canals. This new European immigration was religiously complex, but two traditions predominated: Lutheranism and Roman Catholicism. For both, ethnicity would long be a vexing issue.

Lutherans

American Lutherans have been the most fractious of peoples, and their history is bewilderingly complex. For the Midwest, however, we can simplify it by talking about two waves of Lutheran settlement. In the late eighteenth and early nineteenth centuries, German Lutherans began crossing the Appalachians from Pennsylvania, New York, Georgia, and the Carolinas. As second- or third-generation Americans, their churches were heavily Americanized, theologically liberal, and English speaking. They thus fit in well in the Midwest and were largely welcomed as neighbors by Anglo-Protestants. Rapidly, these frontier Lutherans set about gathering congregations, and soon these congregations affiliated into regional synods. The earliest across the mountains was the Ohio Synod, formed in 1818, followed by four more synods in Ohio, two in Indiana, two in Illinois, and one in Iowa. Most of the midwestern synods affiliated with the newly formed eastern-based General Synod of Lutherans, a loose umbrella organization that, among other things, helped to channel needed money and personnel to the western churches.

The second and heavier wave of Lutherans into the Midwest came with the renewed European immigration that began during the 1840s. This wave contained not only German Lutherans, but also Lutherans from Denmark and Scandinavia, and later, Slovakia and Iceland. Although these new immigrants fanned out into the Midwest, most were concentrated in the Mississippi River Valley. To this day, Missouri, Iowa, northern Illinois, southern Wisconsin, and Minnesota remain the heartland of American Lutheranism. The newcomers were markedly more conservative theologically and ethnically than were their native-born coreligionists. They demanded strict orthodoxy, insisted on the importance of confessional statements, and continued to use their native languages in worship. For this reason, the churches and synods that formed from this migration refused to associate with the General Synod, preferring instead to erect their own independent bodies. Among the Germans, synods (associations of like-minded congregations) tended to coalesce around the teachings of charismatic pastors from specific districts in Germany. The Missouri Synod was founded by the Saxon pastor C.F.W. Walther

Home and Foreign Missionary Society of the Evangelical Lutheran Church. Third Biennial Convention, Springfield, Ohio, 1883. Courtesy Evangelical Lutheran Church in America.

(1811–1887); the Iowa Synod by Bavarians G. M. Grossmann (1823–1897) and John Deindoerfer (1828–1907); and the Wisconsin Synod by Prussian John Muehlhaeuser (1804–1868). Among non-German Lutherans, synods tended to form according to language and ethnicity. The Norwegian Synod was formed in 1853; the Augustana (Swedish) Synod in 1860; the Danish Synod in 1872; the Icelandic Synod in 1885; the Suomi (Finnish) Synod in 1890; and the Slovakian Synod in 1902. There were exceptions to this generalization, of course: Norwegians, Swedes, and Germans banded together to form the Northern Illinois Synod in 1851. Predictably, however, this experiment was short-lived and split along ethnic lines.

For generations, midwestern Lutherans tenaciously maintained ethnic distinctiveness. Frequently, synods set up parochial schools and separate seminaries to preserve the language and culture of the Old Country. This was an uphill battle, and by the twentieth century, ethnic differences among midwestern Lutherans were beginning to fade. The pressure to assimilate into the larger Anglo-Protestant society was a major factor for all ethnic Lutherans, but the Germans also faced intense anti-German sentiment during World War I. The decline of ethnicity resulted in a remarkable series of mergers and reorganizations, which by 1987 had united almost all Lutherans within three large bodies: the Evangelical Lutheran Church, the Lutheran Church-Missouri Synod, and the Wisconsin Evangelical Lutheran Synod. Despite their state names, both the Wisconsin and the Missouri synods have expanded well beyond their initial geographical base, and all three synods are especially heavily represented in Minnesota. Today, 22 percent of Minnesota's population is Lutheran in one form or another, making it the most Lutheran state in the Union.[5]

Roman Catholics

An estimated 50,000 Roman Catholics lived in the United States in 1800; by 1900, through natural increase, but mainly through immigration, this number stood at 12 million.[6] Much of this growth occurred in the Midwest. Indeed, by 1850, large concentrations of Catholics could be found in and around Cincinnati, Chicago, and St. Louis, as well as in southern Indiana (especially Vincennes and Terre Haute), Michigan (especially Detroit and Upper Michigan), and in a scattering of Catholic settlements in Iowa. Less than two generations later, new concentrations would arise in Cleveland and Toledo, Gary (Indiana), and St. Paul (Minnesota). The Irish and Germans were first, joined after 1880 by Poles, Italians, Belgians, Czechs, and others. Catholic immigrants to the Midwest were attracted by the lure of jobs and cheap land, and most immigration was spontaneous and due to individual initiative. In some cases, however, immigrants were actively recruited by midwestern Catholic clergy. From the 1850s to the 1860s, Bishop Mathias Loras (1792–1858) of Dubuque, Iowa, promoted the relocation of Catholics from the large eastern cities to the Midwest. The results for Iowa were limited, but a generation later, Bishop John Ireland (1838–1918) of St. Paul revived the idea for Minnesota: between 1876 and 1881, he organized several colonization efforts to bring Catholics to the state, setting up recruitment offices on the East Coast and in Europe. Bishop Ireland worked closely with the railroads and promised prospective immigrants that each settlement would have a church and a resident priest who would also act as land agent. Ten Catholic agricultural communities were eventually founded in Minnesota.

Most Catholic immigration to the Midwest was unplanned and uncontrolled by the Church. The Irish settled just about everywhere, but the Germans settled mostly in what came to be called the German Triangle—the region between Milwaukee, Cincinnati, and St. Louis. In recognition of this fact, John Martin Henni (1805–1881), a German, was appointed bishop of Milwaukee in 1844. Henni, like many of his countrymen, was convinced that the loss of German language in America would lead to an erosion of German culture and, ultimately, a rejection of the Catholic faith. Bishop Henni therefore appointed only German-speaking priests to his German parishes and insisted that school instruction in these parishes be in German only. This alarmed many Irish in the hierarchy, fearing it would lead to a nativist backlash. Bishop Ireland, like many high-ranking Irish-American churchmen, spoke for limited assimilation and "Americanization." He recommended that English be the sole language of the American Church and even suggested that Catholics send their children to public instead of parochial schools to show that Roman Catholicism was not incompatible with American values. Others went further, arguing that "Americanization" was necessary not only to avoid public distrust, but also because it would lead to the democratization of the Church, a result that most members of the hierarchy, including Bishop Ireland, viewed with some trepidation.

During the 1880s, the issue of whether the Church was to "Americanize" or remain ethnically segregated came to a boil. Irish American priests in Wisconsin accused their bishop of actively "Germanizing" his diocese, while German American priests in St. Louis accused their "Americanizing" bishop, Peter Richard Kenrick (1806–1896), of reducing them to the status of second-class citizens. In 1886, the controversy over ethnicity in the American Church was brought to the attention of the Vatican by Peter Abbelen (1843–1917), vicar general of the archdiocese of Milwaukee. He formally accused men like Ireland and Kenrick of endangering the survival of the American Church by promoting assimilation. The controversy continued to rage throughout the 1890s until finally, fearing the democratizing extremists, the pope condemned "Americanism" as a heresy in 1899. The pope's intent was more to preserve the authority of the Catholic hierarchy than to preserve ethnic difference per se, but the practical result was the survival and expansion of ethnic parishes throughout the United States. Large midwestern dioceses would thus remain complex mosaics of ethnic parishes for decades. Turn-of-the-century Chicago, for example, already had seventy-two ethnic parishes, including St. Stanislaus, the largest Polish parish in the United States. A generation later, the diocese of Cleveland comprised fifty-four ethnic parishes in which one could hear the mother tongues of Slovakians, Hungarians, Ukrainians, Italians, Lithuanians, Czechs, Germans, Slovenians, Croatians, Syrians, and Lebanese.[7] Only after the 1924 National Origins Act restricted immigration did ethnic parishes begin to fade.

Anti-Catholic Nativism

Nativism, or hatred of foreigners, has always fixed on religious difference as an obvious point of attack. Beginning in Colonial times, American nativists focused on Roman Catholics as their chief antagonists, imagining vast papal conspiracies to overthrow American democracy. This proved to be a durable myth, for as Catholic immigration rose, new versions continued to surface in the popular press. The Midwest became a particular concern for nativists. The Mississippi Valley already had a significant French Catholic presence, and as it attracted new Catholic immigration, some Protestants feared that the pope, aided by the Jesuits, had targeted the region for political takeover. Such was the thesis of Cincinnati minister Lyman Beecher's *A Plea for the West* (1835). Beecher (1775–1863) called for more Protestant missionaries armed with Protestant King James Bibles to be sent to the Valley, and he exhorted Protestants to take the lead in public education there lest more children be lost to the Catholic menace.

Throughout the nineteenth century, midwestern nativism waxed and waned, reaching an apex with the formation of the rabidly anti-Catholic American Protective Association in Clinton, Iowa, in 1887. The following century, wide support emerged again for such anti-Catholic groups as the terroristic Black Legion and the Ku Klux Klan, which virtually controlled Indiana politics during the 1920s. Public education remained an especially potent nativist rallying point, as the case of Michigan illustrates. For many Protestants, the public schools were seen as the key transmitters of the values of American democracy, while for many Catholics, they promoted a veiled Protestantism, making parochial schools a necessity. Nativist attacks against the Catholic school system in Michigan heated up in the 1920s when a constitutional amendment making public school attendance mandatory was introduced several times in the state legislature. By allying themselves with other religious groups that maintained parochial schools (e.g., German Lutherans, Christian Reformed, Seventh-Day Adventists) and by flexing their own considerable political muscle, Michigan's Catholics defeated the amendment each time it appeared on the ballot. Such legislative maneuvers were tried in many states at this time, and not just in the Midwest. It was not until the precipitous decline of the public school system in the 1960s that attacks on parochial schools in Michigan and elsewhere finally receded. By this time, anti-Catholic nativism in general had reached an all-time low in the United States.

The Growth of Midwestern Judaism

Organized Judaism has been present in America since 1654. Several Sephardic (historically Ladino-speaking) congregations were established on the eastern seaboard before the Revolution. From here, Jewish merchants and peddlers ventured west, becoming some of the earliest settlers of the Midwest. Ezekiel Solomon (?–c.1805), a Sephardic Jew, was one of the first residents of Fort Michilimackinac, an important fur-trading post on the Great Lakes, now in Michigan. Solomon would not be the last Jew to enter the frontier fur trade. The famous Gratz brothers from Pennsylvania had a trading concern that reached deep into the Illinois country well before the Revolutionary War. It was not until the nineteenth century, however, that significant numbers of Jews would immigrate to the United States and settle in the Midwest. These were largely Ashkenazic (historically Yiddish-speaking) Jews from Germany. Occupationally, except for a few homesteaders, most engaged in peddling or dry-goods retail. By 1850, Jewish populations were visible in Cincinnati, Cleveland, and St. Louis, and in the following decades Chicago, Milwaukee, Detroit, and Columbus would join their ranks as important centers of midwestern Jewish life. Unlike the case on the East Coast, Jews settled not only in the large cities of the Midwest, but in most small market towns as well, at least until the Great Depression sent them to the cities in search of work. Minnesota, for example, recorded Jewish families in the majority of its counties at the end of the nineteenth century, but by the 1990s only a few thousand lived outside of the Twin Cities.[8] This pattern was repeated throughout the Midwest.

Reform Judaism found an especially congenial home in the Midwest. The Reform movement began in Germany in response to a Jewish emancipation movement that called for citizenship for Jews and their assimilation into German society. Thus, Reform Judaism championed the notion that the tradition was adaptable to the times, and to this end Reform leaders fought for major changes in Jewish ritual and law, as well as outright rejection of such traditions as messianism, dietary restrictions, and the inviolability of the Sabbath. The course of Reform in America can best be seen in the career of Isaac Meyer Wise (1819–1900), the great leader of the movement in the nineteenth century. In 1853, Wise became the rabbi of Congregation B'nai Yeshurun in Cincinnati. He immediately led the congregation away from traditional practices and in 1857 published the book of Reform service, the *Minhag America* (*American Ritual*), to codify these radical changes. Of even more lasting importance were the series of national Reform organizations spearheaded by Wise. At a conference of Reform congregations held in Cincinnati in 1873, the Union of American Hebrew Congregations was formed. At its first meeting in Cleveland the following year, the Union voted unanimously to establish the Hebrew Union College, which opened in Cincinnati in 1875 with Rabbi Wise as president. Finally, to cap off these organizations, Wise was also instrumental in the creation of the Central Conference of American Rabbis in Detroit in 1889. From their base in the Midwest, each of these organizations helped to strengthen the cause of Reform Judaism throughout the country such that by the 1880s, most American Jews who were religious were members of a Reform synagogue.

Reform's dominance would not go unchallenged for long, however. A second wave of Ashkenazic immigration began after 1880. This wave consisted of Russian and other Eastern European Jews who had little contact with the German Reform

Coming-of-age class, Temple Israel, Columbus, Ohio, 1888. Courtesy American Jewish Archives, Cincinnati, Ohio.

movement in their home countries and, initially, were little welcomed by German Jews in the United States. Thus, when these newcomers joined a synagogue in the United States (if they chose to join at all), they usually affiliated either with Orthodox (Traditional) congregations or with the Conservative congregations that sought less radical change than Reform. Most of the second wave settled in the eastern cities, but a significant portion came to the Midwest, facilitated by such organizations as the Industrial Removal Office, a private Jewish charity dedicated to the settlement of new immigrant Jews outside the congested "gateway districts" of New York, Boston, and Philadelphia. Large numbers of Russian and Eastern European Jews in the Midwest settled in Chicago, Cleveland, and Milwaukee. Today, reflecting the later spread of descendants of both waves of Ashkenazic immigration, synagogues of all three Jewish movements—Reform, Conservative, and Orthodox—can be found in most of the larger cities of the Midwest.

African American Religions to the Great Migration and Beyond

Although there were African Americans in the Midwest before the Civil War, small communities of free blacks and ex-slaves could be found throughout the region, especially in the larger cities. Organized church life was a priority for these communities. Typically, black congregations in the Midwest were independent Baptist churches, branches of the African Methodist Episcopal (AME) church, or affiliates of a white denomination (e.g., Methodists, Episcopalians, and Presbyterians). The Baptists were usually the first on the scene. As early as 1835, six black Baptist churches in Ohio formed the Providence Baptist Association, and by 1857, there were five black Baptist regional associations in Illinois, Indiana, and Ohio. The AME church followed closely, having adopted circuit riding as its mode of evangelization. It quickly formed three midwestern conferences before the Civil

War: Ohio (1840), Indiana (1855), and Missouri (1855).[9] The other two major black denominations, the African Methodist Episcopal Zion Church (AMEZion) and the Colored (later Christian) Methodist Church (CME) came much later to the Midwest, having no presence here until after the Civil War.

The Great Migration indelibly changed the religious landscape of the Midwest. Beginning in 1915 and reaching a torrent with the entry of the United States in World War I, thousands of blacks began leaving the rural South for northern cities. Alternately pushed by a lack of opportunities and oppressive social conditions in the South and pulled by the need for cheap labor in the North, African Americans saw the North as "the Promised Land," a place of economic and social justice. What they found fell far short of this ideal, of course, but still they came: in the decade between 1910 and 1920, the black population in Chicago exploded from 44,000 to 109,000, and in Detroit, from a mere 6,000 to 41,000.[10] Migration did not slacken until the onset of the Depression, only to begin again with World War II. By this time millions had made the move.

In the North, African Americans had a range of choices to fulfill their religious needs. Many joined white denominations, which either already had segregated congregations or created them to accommodate blacks. For example, after 1900, new all-black congregations of Catholics, Congregationalists, Presbyterians, and Northern Baptists arose in Detroit. Others joined the all-black denominations (Baptist, AME, AMEZion, or CME), swelling these churches' membership rolls and often leading to the creation of several new satellite congregations. In Chicago, the prestigious Olivet Baptist Church grew from 4,000 in 1915 to almost 9,000 five years later, becoming the largest Protestant congregation in the United States.[11] In turn, it spun off five new congregations by 1919, and many of these became prominent churches in their own right. Some older members of these established black churches feared the social effects of absorbing so many rural migrants, but most sought to ease their transition. Chicago's Olivet Baptist Church began a relief program for unemployed blacks in 1908, while Bethel AME of Detroit created separate social services, housing, and labor departments to reach out to the new migrants. Perhaps the most ambitious of such efforts was that spearheaded by the Reverend Reverdy C. Ransom (1861–1959), whose Institutional Church and Social Settlement of Chicago, founded in 1900, applied the methods of the Social Gospel to the problems of the black urban poor.

Despite attempts at outreach, not all migrants found the established churches welcoming: many were too large and too impersonal, worship was too formal, and there were few opportunities to participate in leadership. Many opted for the small house or "storefront" churches. These were usually small groups, led by preachers of little education but great charisma, operating on a shoestring and meeting in whatever structures they could afford: front parlors, empty store buildings, even tents. Most of these storefront churches remained independent of the established denominations and identified themselves as either Baptist, "Sanctified," or Spiritualist. Sanctified churches are those that blend elements of the Holiness tradition with then newly emerging Pentecostalism. Holiness people, who derive their doctrine from Methodism, believe in a second work of grace, or sanctification, after conversion. Pentecostals take this further and recognize a "third blessing" of the Holy Spirit, manifesting itself in spiritual healing, prophecy, and speaking in tongues (glossolalia). Pentecostalism, which dates from 1906 when the black Ho-

Derided by outsiders as "Holy Rollers," members of the Pentecostal Church revel in the highly emotional and expressive forms of worship found in their music. Courtesy Library of Congress.

liness preacher William J. Seymour (1870–1922) led the famous Azusa Street Revival in Los Angeles, quickly spread throughout both black and white Holiness communities in the United States. Derided by outsiders as "Holy Rollers," members of the Sanctified churches nevertheless reveled in the highly emotional and expressive forms of worship found in these bodies, especially their music. Indeed, Sanctified churches welcomed into the sanctuary a much wider array of musical instruments (e.g., guitars, pianos, drums, etc.) than usual, an important step in the development of twentieth-century gospel music. The largest Sanctified church in the nation, the Church of God in Christ, had congregations in most large midwestern cities by the 1920s and continued to grow rapidly thereafter. Of the legion of Sanctified churches founded in the Midwest, one can mention Detroit's Holiness Church of the Living God (1909), Chicago's The Church of All Nations (1916), and Cleveland's First Unity of God (1927), a successful schism from the Church of God in Christ. So popular were these alternatives to the "mainline" black churches that Sanctified churches represented 23 percent of all black churches in Chicago by 1938.[12] They continue to be popular to this day.

While most African Americans found grinding poverty and pervasive discrimination in the so-called Promised Land, northern cities nevertheless provided the freedom to experiment with Christianity (such as the Sanctified churches) or reject it altogether. The Midwest specifically was the birthplace of the most important example of such a rejection, the Nation of Islam. Founded in 1930 by Wallace D. Fard (?–c.1934), who drew on earlier traditions of black Islam, the Nation of Islam achieved national prominence under the leadership of Elijah (Poole) Muhammad (1897–1975), a former Georgia sharecropper who came to Detroit during the Great Migration to work in the auto industry. Com-

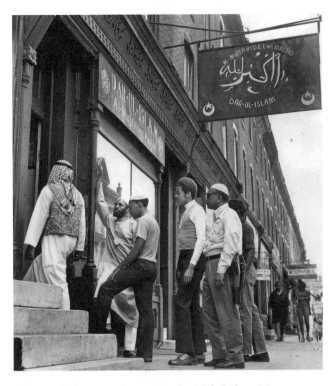

Nation of Islam members enter the Muhahideen Mosque.
Courtesy Temple University Archives.

bining Islam with black nationalism, and attracting such fiery figures as Malcolm X (1925–1965), the movement spread to most of the major cities of the Midwest and Northeast, experiencing its greatest growth in the 1950s and 1960s. After Elijah Muhammad's death in 1975, the Nation of Islam, now headquartered in Chicago, suffered a schism. The majority followed Muhammad's son, Wallace D. Muhammad (1933–   ), into the American Muslim Mission (later American Muslim Society), an orthodox Islamic group. A rump group, committed to the old black nationalist ideology, retained the name Nation of Islam and rallied around the charismatic and controversial Louis Farrakhan (1933–   ). The American Muslim Society now claims far more members, but the Nation of Islam under the leadership of Farrakhan still remains one of the most visible and vocal black non-Christian religions in America today.

MODERNISM VERSUS FUNDAMENTALISM IN THE HEARTLAND

In the late nineteenth century, fast moving theological developments led to the extreme polarization of American Protestantism into Modernist and Fundamentalist camps. Although the majority of American Protestants probably remained comfortably in the theological middle, the sheer vehemence of the Modernist-Fundamentalist debate captured the nation's attention and would become one of the defining aspects of the early twentieth century. And while many commonly associate this debate with the South, in reality it was nowhere more intense than in the Midwest.

Modernism was a term for an extreme form of theological liberalism that came to challenge traditional Protestant orthodoxy. Modernism's challenges came from two directions: Darwinian evolution and higher criticism of the Bible. The Darwinian mechanism behind evolution—natural selection or the survival of the fittest—was seen by many as an affront to Christian morality and inimical to "God's way of doing things." Moreover, the theory undercut the biblical account of creation, thus casting into doubt the truth of the Bible. Higher criticism (i.e., the historical deconstruction of the Bible) seemed to do the same thing: by demonstrating that the Bible was the work of many hands at many times, higher criticism called into question its divine inspiration. Higher critics also discerned in the Old Testament a clear religious evolution from polytheism to ethical monotheism, suggesting that religion did not simply transmit eternal verities, but evolved like any other human institution. Embracing these new ideas and their implications, Modernists stressed the immanence of God through normal human experience and gloried in a highly optimistic notion of humanity's progressive ethical improvement. In the Midwest, the Divinity School of the University of Chicago, which was founded in 1892 under Northern Baptist auspices, became the bastion of Modernism in the nation. Here, such theological giants as the Baptist Shailer Mathews (1863–1941), dean of the Divinity School for twenty-five years, and the Disciples of Christ minister and philosopher Edward Scribner Ames (1870–1958) trained generations of theology students in the tenets of theological Modernism.

Not all clergy embraced Modernism, and throughout the nation many fought tenaciously to uphold the standards of orthodoxy. In 1895, the Niagara Conference, an organization of conservative Protestant churchmen, enunciated what it considered were the five fundamentals of Christianity: the inerrancy of the Bible, the Virgin Birth, substitutionary atonement, the physical resurrection of Christ, and his imminent bodily return to Earth to inaugurate the millennium (premillennialism). These doctrines were widely disseminated in a series of pamphlets called *The Fundamentals*, a name that came to be applied to the wider pan-denominational movement. Fundamentalists could be found in all the "mainline" Anglo-Protestant denominations (i.e., Presbyterian, Congregationalist, Baptist, Disciples of Christ, Methodist, and Episcopalian). They also became prominent in most of the new Holiness and Pentecostal denominations then arising out of Methodism. In the South, where Modernism had not made much headway, the doctrines propounded by the Fundamentalists were simply seen as age-old orthodoxy, and little debate ensued. It was in regions such as the Midwest, where the forces of Modernism were roughly equal to the forces of Fundamentalism, that the battles were most hard fought and animosities were raised to a fever pitch.

A look at a local controversy within the Northern Baptist Convention will give a general idea of the results of this bitter conflict in the Midwest. In the first three decades of the twentieth century, tensions between conservatives and liberals within the Convention became acute. In 1909, the Grand Rapids, Michigan, Association of Baptist Churches was split over the question of whether to expel the archmodernist Fountain Street Church from its organization. The leader of the expulsion movement was the Fundamentalist pastor Oliver W. Van Osdel (1847–

African American Spiritualist Churches

A world apart from the mainline black and Sanctified churches are the Spiritualist churches. Spiritualist churches seem to have arisen independently in Chicago, Detroit, and New Orleans in the 1910s. They then spread throughout the Midwest and South in the following decades. Blending elements of Spiritualism, African American Protestantism, Roman Catholicism, and Voodoo, the Spiritualist churches offered members a this-worldly focus of financial success and health through emphasis on magic and esoteric knowledge. The most successful of these churches, the Metropolitan Spiritual Churches of Christ (MSCC), was founded in Kansas City, Missouri, in 1925 by a former CME minister, William F. Taylor, and Elder Leviticus L. Boswell, a former Holiness minister from the Church of God in Christ. By 1937, the MSCC boasted thirteen congregations in cities such as Chicago, Gary, Indiana, St. Louis, and East St. Louis (Illinois). Most Spiritualist churches never grew beyond a single congregation, although collectively they offered a viable alternative to mainline black churches: by 1938, 11 percent of all black churches in Chicago were Spiritualist churches.[13] Today, Spiritualist churches are less popular than the Sanctified or mainline black churches, yet they still attract a committed clientele eager for a more eclectic brand of Christianity.

1935). Ultimately, Van Osdel was unsuccessful, and more than half the churches followed him out of the Grand Rapids Association to form the Grand River Valley Association, which then began to associate with conservative Baptist congregations in Ohio, Indiana, and Illinois. These in turn formed the Independent Union of Regular Baptist Churches in 1927. Meanwhile, at the national level, Fundamentalists like Van Osdel, R.E. Neighbour (1872–1945) of Ohio, and W.B. Riley (1861–1947) of Minnesota attempted to exert control over the Chicago-based Northern Baptist Convention through the creation of the Fundamentalist Fellowship in 1920 and the even more militant Baptist Bible Union in 1922. Both of these organizations tried to steer the Convention into articulating more explicitly conservative stances, but were stymied by the loose structure of the Convention and the growing preponderance of modernists among the northern Baptists. Finally, in 1929, disgusted by the Convention's clear modernist drift, Van Osdel withdrew and helped to convert his regional organization into a new Baptist denomination, the General Association of Regular Baptists. Similar splits also occurred in other mainline denominations, such as the Presbyterians and Disciples of Christ. Fundamentalism even had an impact on midwestern denominations outside of the Anglo-American tradition (e.g., Dutch Reformed and Missouri Synod Lutherans). For the most part, the mainline denominations were glad to be rid of the Fundamentalists.

Having lost the battle for control of the mainline denominations, the Fundamentalist movement began to recede from public view in the 1920s. Broadcast live over WGN Chicago, the 1925 Scopes "Monkey" Trial, in which the rural Illinois-born William Jennings Bryan (1860–1925), attempting to defend biblical inerrancy, was made to look a fool by Chicago lawyer Clarence Darrow (1857–1938), further brought Fundamentalism into public disrepute. Indeed, the literati of the time seemed intent on a concerted campaign to discredit the movement. Witness Sinclair Lewis's (1885–1951) 1927 novel, *Elmer Gantry*, a biting satire about a hypocritical midwestern revivalist suspiciously like the famous Indiana-based evangelist Billy Sunday (1863–1935). Fundamentalism in the Midwest hardly disappeared, however. Rather, it retreated into what would become a highly resilient subculture of independent Bible churches or loosely organized denominations such as the General Association of Regular Baptists and the Orthodox Presbyterian Church. Moreover, much Fundamentalist activity came to be coordinated by a series of independent Bible institutes and colleges such as the Moody Bible Institute of Chicago or W.B. Riley's Minneapolis Northwestern Bible School which, for nearly four decades, trained Fundamentalist pastors for rural churches.

Whither Protestantism in the Midwest?

In 1924, two sociologists, Robert Lynd (1892–1970) and Helen Lynd (1896–1952), with a grant from the Rockefeller-funded Institute for Social and Religious Research, undertook an in-depth study of everyday life in Muncie, Indiana. The result of this research was the best-selling book *Middletown* (1929). Hailed by critics of the day as a meticulous portrait of a "typical" midwestern small town, *Middletown* by implication came to be seen as a window into American small-town life in general. Later scholars have come to doubt this wholesale extension, but nevertheless Muncie continues to attract sociologists who return periodically to gauge social change using the Lynds' study as a baseline. For our purposes, *Middletown* and its successors are important because of the attention paid to religion, especially Muncie's Protestant churches. For, while "Middletown" might not be completely typical of all American small towns, the career of Protestantism in Muncie during the twentieth century does point up some common aspects in the development of midwestern Protestantism in general.

What the Lynds found in 1920s Muncie was a town overwhelmingly white and Protestant. (Indeed, one of the least typical things about "Middletown" was the dearth of Catholics and blacks.) Of the old frontier denominations, the Methodists and Baptists still held sway with the largest number of members and churches. Muncie also played host to a large number of United Brethren, a German Methodist church that would eventually merge with the United Methodists. The other frontier churches (Presbyterian, Congregationalist, Episcopalian, Quakers, Disciples of Christ, Unitarians, and Lutherans) also remained comfortably established in town, although represented by single congregations only. All in all, Muncie was dominated by what would come to be called the Protestant mainline—churches that were moderate to liberal theologically and open to such ecumenical endeavors as the Federal (later National) Council of Churches. The Lynds noticed, however, that some interesting changes were afoot. After World War I, large numbers of white migrants from Appalachia began to arrive, drawn by the promise of factory jobs. They brought with them their allegiance to conservative evangelicalism as practiced in Fundamentalist, Holiness, and Pentecostal churches. Though largely despised by long-time residents and demeaned as "low class" and "backward," these "southern" churches thrived nonetheless. The 1931–1932 Muncie city directory shows that while there were nineteen Methodist and Baptist churches in Muncie, the conservative evangelical churches, taken as a group, were not far behind with seventeen.[14] Little did the people of Muncie know that this would be a long-term trend.

In 1976, more than fifty years after the original Middletown study, a new group of sociologists headed by Theodore Caplow returned to study Muncie's churches. The changes they found were startling. Methodists and Baptists still dominated with some sixty churches, but a major shift had occurred among the Baptists. Growth in this faith did not come in the liberal American (Northern) Baptist Convention, but in independent Fundamentalist Baptist churches or those associated with the very conservative Southern Baptist Convention (SBC). Moreover, among the Protestant mainline, most had declined in relative numbers, and some had lost members to more conservative branches (e.g., to the Fundamentalist Orthodox Presbyterian Church or the conservative Lutheran Church-Missouri Synod). Most strikingly, the Holiness, Pentecostal, and Fundamentalist churches had exploded into sixty-one congregations and now catered to over half of the church-going population of Muncie.[15] Several of these churches adopted the "megachurch" format in which congregations are recruited from beyond a single neighborhood and have memberships of a thousand or more. Caplow traced the recent growth of Muncie's conservative churches not only to renewed southern white migration during the 1950s, but also to a series of local revivals during the 1960s and the rise of Pentecostalism in the 1970s. Furthermore, Caplow's group found that class now played less of a part in the composition of these churches: one was just as likely to find middle-class people in the pews as working class. Caplow suggested that what divided Muncie's churches now was not class so much as a division between main-line and conservative, or perhaps better, between "northern" and "southern" religious styles.

How illustrative were the shifts in Muncie's religious scene of larger trends within midwestern Protestantism? Judging by the 2000 religious census for the Midwest, the answer is, very illustrative. Throughout the Midwest, the mainline Protestant churches still continue to have an important presence, although their numbers relative to all adherents continue to decline. Taken collectively, the main-line still forms a majority in Ohio, Indiana, Iowa, Michigan, Minnesota, and Wisconsin. Methodism still has the largest membership in Ohio and Indiana, whereas mainline Lutheranism has the largest in Minnesota, Wisconsin, and Iowa. However, conservative evangelical churches have made significant strides in all states, especially Ohio, Indiana, Illinois, and Missouri. In Missouri alone, the most southern of the midwestern states, the Southern Baptist Convention claimed a whopping 14.3 percent of the state's population in 2000—fully a quarter of all churchgoers in the state. Though not as spectacular as in Missouri, the SBC nevertheless has made large gains in Ohio, Indiana, and especially southern Illinois. Equally impressive has been the growth of the conservative Missouri Synod Lutherans who, in addition to strongholds in Minnesota, Wisconsin, and Iowa, now have significant populations in all midwestern states. And finally, the growth rate of Pentecostalism has been phenomenal. The Missouri-based Assemblies of God, the largest white Pentecostal denomination in the United States, now claims membership of over a half a million in the Midwest alone.[16] And since many of the smaller Pentecostal churches do not participate in censuses, the true number of Pentecostals in the Midwest is probably somewhat higher. If these trends continue, it appears that conservative "southern-style" Protestantism will soon reach a critical mass in the Midwest. Once it does, it will undoubtedly have a profound impact on the cultural and public life of the region.

Midwestern Catholicism and Judaism Reflect National Trends

In the 1950s, sociologist and theologian Will Herberg succinctly characterized the American religious landscape as "Protestant, Catholic, Jew." The aptness of this characterization signaled that Roman Catholicism and Judaism had by this time achieved a high degree of stability and influence in the United States, and that both traditions now enjoyed greater acceptance by larger numbers of Protestant Americans. Conversely, Herberg also meant by his famous phrase that Catholics and Jews were now under greater pressure than ever to accommodate their beliefs and practices to perceived "American" norms. Herberg's insights into the dynamics of American religious pluralism in the twentieth century are well illustrated by the stories of Roman Catholics and Jews in the Midwest.

The Roman Catholic Church Today

In the period from the 1920s to the 1960s, the Roman Catholic Church contended with several major issues. First, immigration of Catholics from Europe effectively ceased owing to the restrictive immigration legislation enacted by Congress after World War I. This in turn led to an acceleration of Catholic assimilation into the larger American culture, which consequently led to a greater sense of confidence with which to confront this culture, even in the face of renewed nativism in the 1920s. In response to these changes, the Church internally sought to centralize its operations and grow its institutions, as well as develop new strategies to keep present members within the fold. At the same time, the Church began to turn outward, aggressively seeking new converts and embarking on several activist programs designed to influence American culture through Catholic values. These forty years were years of unparalleled growth, not only in terms of "brick and mortar," but in membership too. The Catholic Church by now had the largest membership of any denomination in six out of the eight midwestern states: Illinois, Indiana, Iowa, Michigan, Ohio, and Wisconsin.[17] With the advent of the 1960s, however, Roman Catholics would confront a series of fresh challenges that would change the Church forever.

The defining event of the twentieth century for the Catholic Church was Vatican II. This Church council, held in Rome from 1961 to 1965, ushered in a period of unprecedented change. Its purpose was *aggiornamento* or "updating" in which Catholic belief and practice were to be brought in line with the modern world. Many of the Council's recommendations were controversial: greater lay participation, both in the Mass (now to be said in the vernacular) and in church governance; more relaxed lifestyles for clergy and religious; and a greater openness to people of other faiths. If we take Cincinnati as our "Middletown" for Catholicism, we can see in some detail how this and other challenges affected a "typical" midwestern archdiocese. Cincinnati's archbishop Karl Alter (1885–1977) was heavily involved in the business of the Council, serving on its Central Preparatory Commission (1961–1962) and, later, the influential Commission on Bishops and Government of Dioceses. As a result, upon Alter's return to Cincinnati, he quickly formed commissions on everything from liturgy to human rights, as well as initiating a major reorganization of the archdiocese's governing structures. Alter was a leader in the United States in implementing Council decrees, especially when it came to liturgical reform (despite resistance, the English Mass became standard in the archdiocese by 1969) and the appointment of laymen and women to positions of leadership in the archdiocese. Alter was also a proponent of freedom of conscience and ecumenicalism, both of which he championed at Vatican II. He subsequently spearheaded the formation of the Greater Cincinnati Interfaith Commission in 1966, as well as regularizing pulpit exchanges with Protestant and Jewish clergy. More concretely, for the first time he invited Protestants to march in the 1967 Holy Name Society parade, a major annual event for Cincinnati's Catholics. And, a year later, Alter would personally preside over Cincinnati's ecumenical prayer service in the wake of the assassination of Martin Luther King, Jr. (1929–1968).

The archdiocese of Cincinnati was not without its problems, however, and most of these were problems endemic to dioceses across the country. Under Alter's watch, the financial situation of the Cincinnati parochial school system worsened considerably even as enrollment rose. Costs had been held down by employing low-paid priests and religious as teachers, but as the number of vocations dropped during the 1950s and 1960s (partly in response to Vatican II), higher salaried secular teachers had to be hired. Moreover, brick-and-mortar projects slowed, with fewer churches being built between 1969 and 1996 than in any previous comparable period, and this in a time when more and more Catholics were moving to new suburbs and Hispanic immigration to the city was expanding. Increasing costs and declining numbers of clergy would continue to challenge Alter's successors, Paul Liebold (1914–1972), Joseph Bernardin (1928–1996), and Daniel Pilarczyk (1934–   ). All three instituted programs of church closings and consolidations throughout the archdiocese and engaged in strategic planning to confront the looming shortage of priests. From a high of 435 in 1968, the number of active priests in the archdiocese dropped to 215 by 2003, leaving thirty-five parishes without resident pastors and one parish closed. To deal with this problem, all three of the post–Vatican II archbishops of Cincinnati moved to involve the laity in active ministry. In 1974, Bernardin initiated a successful permanent deacons program (ordained deacons can fulfill many of the liturgical duties of a priest), while Pilarczyk's 1984 "For the Harvest" Program sought to make laymen and women more active in parish planning and staffing. Perhaps because of the increased involvement of the laity, declining rates of Mass attendance slowed in the late 1980s and 1990s and actually began to rebound beginning in 1998. By this year Cincinnati was second in the nation in Mass attendance, behind Milwaukee alone.[18]

Unfortunately, by this time, too, the burgeoning priest pedophilia scandals had begun to rock the American church. The Midwest was no exception. In response to accusations of priestly sexual misconduct in Cincinnati, regular attendance at Mass in the Archdiocese dropped 7 percent between 2001 and 2002, and regular giving seems to have dropped even more. Perhaps even more damaging, a newspaper poll in August 2003 reported that 56 percent of parishioners had lost confidence in church leadership owing to their handling of the scandals. It is impossible to say at this point what the long-term impact of the scandals will be on a church already reeling from priest shortages and financial shortfalls, but America's largest denomination still has plenty of resources and a long history to draw on. If Cincinnati is indeed a midwestern microcosm of the American church, then there is reason for optimism. Despite the myriad challenges facing the Church, 69 percent of respondents in the above poll also indicated that, despite it all, their allegiance to Catholicism was unchanged.[19]

Challenges to Judaism in the Midwest and the Nation

During the 1940s, American Judaism experienced a period of consolidation and seeming stability. Ethnic differences were beginning to fade, Jewish philanthropic organizations were enjoying unparalleled success, and as more and more Jews ascended the economic and educational ladder and moved to the suburbs, synagogue construction kept pace with this outmigration. The Holocaust and the establishment of the state of Israel in 1948 were major unifying foci for the American Jewish community, contributing in some ways to the revival of Jewish spirituality in the 1950s and 1960s that would temporarily swell synagogue ranks. In terms of the larger culture, major Jewish literary and academic figures rose to prominence, with the Midwest contributing its fair share (e.g., Chicagoans Saul Bellow [1915–   ], a Nobel Prize-winning novelist, and Mortimer Adler [1902–2001], one of the century's more engaging public intellectuals). Perhaps even more emblematic of Judaism's emergence on the national scene was the career of Hank Greenberg (1911–1986), first baseman for the Detroit Tigers from 1933 to 1947. Greenberg was celebrated by the Jewish community not only for being the first Jew to be elected to the Hall of Fame, but also for resisting anti-Semitism and for refusing to play on Yom Kippur. And yet, this "first Jewish superstar" was symbolic of twentieth-century American Judaism in other, more troubling ways. Greenberg, who went on to manage (but not to play for) the Cleveland Indians and become part-owner of the Chicago White Sox, was actually nonobservant for most of his life, did not give his children a religious education, and, after divorcing his first wife, married outside the faith. In this, he was not alone. By the 1980s and 1990s, assimilation had taken its toll on American Judaism. Less than 15 percent of all Jews in the United States now attend services on a regular basis, and the inter-marriage rate has reached well over 50 percent.[20] Coupled with a low birth rate and low rates of Jewish immigration, many fear for the long-term viability of the tradition in the United States. In addition to these problems, the Midwest suffers an added source of drain: since the 1980s, large numbers of Jews have fled the "Rustbelt" cities of Chicago, Cleveland, and Detroit for the better economy and environment of the Sunbelt.

American Judaism continues to face external as well as internal threats to its survival. In terms of nativism, anti-Semitism has been second only to anti-Catholicism in the Midwest. Since Jewish communities were small in the Midwest during the nineteenth century, anti-Semitism was relatively mild, though persistent. The charge that Jews were "Christ killers" was routinely taught in Sunday and public schools (for example, in McGuffey's *Eclectic Readers*), Jewish caricatures were staples in newspapers and popular novels, and occasionally midwestern politicians would openly voice anti-Semitic opinions (for example, Minnesota's Ignatius Donnelly [1831–1901], one of the founders of the Populist Party). In the twentieth century, however, anti-Semitism became much more pronounced, resulting in such proactive measures as formal restrictive housing covenants and restricted hotels and resorts, as well as informal quotas in education and the professions. Anti-Semitism also became a larger part of popular political discourse, especially after the dissemination of the conspiracy mythology of the forged *The Protocols of the Elders of Zion*. During the 1920s, the industrialist Henry Ford (1863–1947), for one, re-published *The Protocols* in his newspaper, *The Dearborn Independent*, and he followed this up with a series of articles denouncing supposed Jewish control of international finance and government. When these articles appeared in book form as *International Jewry*, none other than Adolf Hitler (1889–1945) cited them as an inspiration. More recently, anti-Semitism, long an undercurrent in the African American community, has found public expression. Chicago-based Jesse Jackson (1941–) made derogatory comments about Jews during the 1984 presidential campaign, and the sustained invective of Minister Louis Farrakhan, leader of the Nation of Islam, has been difficult to ignore. Reviving a theme heard from earlier Nation leaders such as Malcolm X, Farrakhan claims that Jews had a disproportionate share in the slave trade and still continue to victimize African Americans economically today. In recent years, this accusation has become depressingly widespread in the black community.

BEYOND "PROTESTANT, CATHOLIC, JEW" IN THE MIDWEST

Near the turn of the twentieth century, the Midwest was introduced to a number of unfamiliar religions with the meeting of the World's Parliament of Religions as part of the 1893 Chicago Columbian Exposition. According to one participant, the parliament was meant to promote "the nearness of man to man, the Fatherhood of God, and the brotherhood of the human race." To accomplish this, every religion in the world would be given the opportunity to present its case. Thus, in addition to representatives of Roman Catholicism, the major Protestant groups, and Judaism, also attending were representatives of Orthodox and Coptic Christianity, as well as Islam, Baha'i, Hinduism, Buddhism, Shinto, Taoism, Confucianism and many others. The parliament was a stunning and much remarked success, although few attending thought that any of the more "exotic" faiths would ever find a home in America, let alone the Midwest. And yet after a century of changing patterns of immigration, and especially after the easing of immigration restrictions in 1965, many of these traditions have indeed found a home in the American heartland.

South Asian Religions

South Asian religions such as Sikhism, Jainism, and Hinduism are now well established in the Midwest. Most of these Asian traditions date their arrival to the days of the World's Parliament of Religions. The colorful Swami Vivekananda (1863–1902), for example, introduced Americans to Vedanta, a highly philosophical variant of Hinduism that appealed to westerners. He went on to found several Vedanta centers around the country, including the Vivekananda Monastery and Retreat in the aptly named Ganges, Michigan. Later Hindu missionaries would follow, most visibly those promoting the Hare Krishna tradition so prominent in the 1960s and 1970s. With the large-scale influx of Asian Indians after 1965, however, missionary Hinduism was eclipsed by ethnic Hinduism, symbolized by the increasing numbers of architecturally correct temples that now dot the American landscape. In the Midwest alone, there are approximately forty Hindu temples.[21] Many, like the Hindu Temple of Greater Chicago and the Hindu Temple of St. Louis, have been exquisitely wrought in authentic Indian styles at great expense to their sponsoring communities. Temples function as both religious and cultural centers, just as the ethnic Christian churches did a century before. Here, religion, language, and culture are transmitted to the rising generation as a hedge against the corrosiveness of American culture. Some "Americanizing" accommodations have been made, of course: the Mississippi and the Ohio are now routinely used as substitutes for the sacred rivers of India in some Hindu rituals.

Buddhism

Another Asian tradition, Buddhism, also arrived in the nineteenth century; since then it has been present in both missionary and ethnic forms. The 1893 World's Parliament was perhaps the first time Americans had encountered Buddhist missionaries in the United States. Soyen Shaku (1859–1919), who represented Rinzai

Zen, a Japanese form of Mahayana Buddhism, and Anagarika Dharmapala (1864–1933), who lectured on Theravada Buddhism, had an immediate impact. One of the minor sensations of the parliament was the public conversion of Charles T. Strauss (Strauss, who happened to be Jewish, was the first in a long line of American Jews who would convert to Buddhism). More missionaries followed, including the famous D. T. Suzuki (1870–1966) who for years worked to promote Zen from his base at the Open Court Publishing Company in LaSalle, Illinois. Zen enjoyed a popular vogue in the United States after World War II. In the Midwest, the Chicago Buddhist Temple (now the Zen Buddhist Temple of Chicago) was founded in 1949 by Soto Zen master Soyu Matsuoka (1912–1997). In time, Matsuoka would entrust the temple to Richard Langlois (1935–1999), one of the first American Zen masters. Other forms of Buddhism also attracted Americans: the Japanese Soka Gakkai movement has appealed to African Americans and Hispanics, while Tibetan Buddhism has found favor among educated middle-class whites. Ethnic Buddhism arrived in the United States with the first Chinese and Japanese migrants, but the various restrictions on Asian immigration in the first half of the twentieth century inhibited its growth. Again, 1965 was the pivotal year: with renewed Asian immigration just about every Buddhist sect soon appeared in this country. Chicago, the midwestern center for Buddhism, now has dozens of temples and centers catering to Burmese, Cambodians, Japanese, Laotians, Koreans, Thais, Tibetans, and Vietnamese.[22] Unlike Hinduism, however, as ethnic Buddhism flourishes, so too does missionary Buddhism, frequently in tandem. For example, Chicago's Buddhadharma Meditation Center, a Thai Buddhist temple founded in 1986, has maintained its Thai congregation while actively seeking new American converts by offering regular services and meditation retreats in English. Other ethnic temples in Chicago have adopted a similar missionary strategy.

Islam

Of all the non-Christian traditions to be established in the United States during the twentieth century, by far the most successful has been Islam. Until now, America's religious landscape could be summarized as "Protestant, Catholic, Jew." Very soon, if demographers' predictions are correct, a better characterization will be "Protestant, Catholic, Muslim." The steadily growing number of Muslims in the United States is now estimated at around 5 million, roughly equal to that of the Jewish population. Islam has developed an especially visible presence in the Midwest. At last count in 2001, each of the midwestern states had numerous mosques: Minnesota (9), Iowa (14), Wisconsin (19), Missouri (21), Indiana (23), Illinois (57), Ohio (66), and Michigan (73). The greater Detroit area alone has more than forty mosques and Islamic Centers in operation, with several more planned for the near future. Conservative estimates put the number of practicing Muslims in the Detroit area at around 50,000.[23] This relatively new public presence, however, should not obscure the fact that Muslims migrated to the Midwest in substantial numbers throughout the last century, and while new Muslim immigrants continue to arrive, several Muslim communities in the United States are now three or four generations old.

Detroit's Islamic community is an excellent example of Muslims long established in the Midwest. Attracted by jobs in Ford's automobile plants, several Lebanese families began to settle in Highland Park in the 1900s and 1910s. By 1919, the community founded what was perhaps the first mosque in the country. It was an inclusive mosque in which members of Islam's two major divisions, Sunni and Shi'a, worshiped together. Plagued with financial difficulties, it closed within a few years. By this time, however, the Lebanese population had shifted to Dearborn's Southend neighborhood, closer to Ford's River Rouge plant. By this time, too, something occurred within the Lebanese Muslim community that is very common to many immigrant groups that achieve a certain size and critical mass: sectarian divisions reasserted themselves. The result was the creation of two Southend mosques, one predominantly Shi'ite and the other Sunni. In 1933, the Shi'ites, who are the majority in the Dearborn Muslim community, founded the Hashemite Club and in 1936 began worship in the Hashemite Hall under the leadership of Sheikh Kalil Bezzi. In response, the Sunnis founded the Moslem Mosque in 1939, employing the services of Sheikh Hussein Karoub, who had also led the Highland Park Mosque. Although relations between the groups remained cordial, the Sunni/Shi'a split became an enduring, if little discussed, aspect of Dearborn's Muslim community.

Even greater changes occurred within the Muslim community after 1965. Large numbers of Palestinians and Yemenis, and more recently, Iraqis, settled in Dearborn during this period. Religiously speaking, the impact of this new immigration on the older Lebanese community was like that experienced by German Jews in the face of Eastern European Jewish immigration. For years, the Sunni Moslem Mosque had been led by imams known for their Americanizing tendencies. In practice, Americanizing meant such things as worship services partially or completely in English, relaxed dress codes, Sunday services, and the use of the mosque as a social center as well as a place of worship. However, many of the newly arrived Palestinians and Yemenis wished to have a more conservative form of Islam, an Islam that reflected the stricter values of the Islamic renewal of the late 1970s and 1980s. Eventually, the conservatives wrested control of the Moslem Mosque from the Lebanese Sunnis, who responded by founding the American Moslem Bekaa Center. Similar tensions arose within the Lebanese Shi'ite community but with different results. In the 1960s, a group of Shi'ites broke away from the Hashemite Hall and formed the Joy Road Islamic Center, which quickly became the center for Shi'ite life in Dearborn. For decades, the Center was led by Imam Mohammed Jawad Chirri (1913–1994), a highly popular figure who also charted an Americanizing course. So influential was Chirri that despite the pressures of the conservative Shi'ite Muslims in the 1980s and 1990s, the Joy Road Islamic Center remained Americanizing in its outlook. The conservative Shi'ites broke away to found several new mosques, for example, the Islamic Institute and the Islamic Council of America.

Like any world religion that has been in America for any length of time, Islam is a tradition riven by internal divisions over sectarian differences, ethnicity, and assimilation. Similar divisions would be seen if one were to look at the development of other large midwestern Muslim communities, such as those of Toledo or Chicago. And yet, as with nineteenth-century attitudes toward Catholics, outsiders persist in seeing American Islam as a monolith, a fact that became painfully obvious after the tragic events of September 11, 2001. Since then, a third wave of nativism, this time anti-Islamic, has gripped the nation. Given its concentration of Muslims, the Midwest has been hit by this new nativism especially hard. In the immediate aftermath of the event, to be Muslim was to be a terrorist, and vandalism of mosques and Muslim-owned businesses was commonplace. Moreover, in the search for "sleeper cells," police investigations, aided by the expanded powers provided by the so-called Patriot Act, occasionally devolved into racial profiling and unwarranted detentions. Only now, some three years after 9/11, are Muslim Americans reemerging to assert their rights as citizens. Dearborn's Arab American Political Action Committee is aggressively registering Muslim voters, and local Muslim leaders now meet on a regular basis with the U.S. attorney for Eastern Michigan and the Immigration and Naturalization Service "to keep the lines of communication open." Others have sought proactively to educate Americans about Islam in an effort to forestall new outbreaks of anti-Islamic hate crimes. Recently, for example, the Indiana-based Islamic Society of North America teamed with the Catholic Church (which is more than familiar with nativism) to produce a series of videos entitled *Our Muslim Neighbors*. If past history is any indication, however, it will probably take several generations more before Muslims enjoy the level of acceptance in the Midwest and the rest of America that Catholics and Jews have struggled the better part of two centuries to acquire.

A MIDWESTERN RELIGIOSITY?

In the end, can we say anything about midwestern religiosity in general? As this chapter has shown, any attempt to do so is a shot at a moving target. Ever since the days of the American Indians, religion in the Midwest has been pluralistic and evolving. Anglo-Protestant traditions have predominated in the last two hundred years or so, and generalized Anglo-Protestant values have deeply informed midwestern culture. And yet, unlike Puritan New England or the Anglican South, the Midwest was an arena of fierce Protestant competition from the beginning of the European invasion. No one denomination or faction managed completely to stamp the region with its own particular attitudes and values, nor has one since. Moreover, the Anglo-Protestant Midwest was quickly overlaid with the ethnically plural Catholic and Lutheran Midwests, not to mention the later Jewish and black Protestant Midwests. If we tried to define some kind of generic "midwestern religiosity" that resulted from this interaction, we would somehow have to take into account all these religious Midwests. The problem becomes even more complicated as we move closer to our own times. As the resolutely Judeo-Christian Midwest gradually becomes a place where even Western world-views cannot be taken for granted, the calculus for determining "midwestern religiosity" becomes impossibly complex. Better perhaps to abandon such notions, as useful as they are for creating a mythical regional identity, and acknowledge the messier reality of a dynamic and religiously free society in the American heartland.

RESOURCE GUIDE

Printed Sources

Beecher, Lyman. *A Plea for the West*. 1835. New York: Arno Press, 1977.

Bonney, Charles Carroll. "Words of Welcome." In *The Dawn of Religious Pluralism: Voices from the World's Parliament of Religions, 1893*, edited by Richard Hughes Seager, 17–22. La Salle, IL: Open Court, 1993.

Cartwright, Peter. *The Autobiography of Peter Cartwright, the Backwards Preacher*. New York: Carlton and Porter, 1856.

Duchesne, Sister Rose Philippine. "Letter from Missouri." In Margory Erskine, *Mother Philippine Duchesne*. New York: Longmans, Green, 1926, 196–98.

Ireland, Bishop John. "Contract with the Winona and St. Peter Railroad for Lands in Lyon County, Minnesota." Reproduced in James P. Shannon, *Catholic Colonization on the Western Frontier*. New Haven: Yale University Press, 1957, 268–72.

Mathews, Shailer. Selections of *The Faith of Modernism*, reprinted in H. Shelton Smith, Robert T. Handy, and Lefferts A. Loetscher, eds., *American Christianity: An Historical Interpretation with Representative Documents, Volume II, 1820–1960*. New York: Charles Scribner's Sons, 1963, 238–45.

Muhammad, Elijah. *Message to the Blackman in America*. Atlanta, GA: Messenger Elijah Muhammad Propagation Society, 1997.

———. "The Muslim Program." Reprinted in Karl Evanzz, *The Messenger: The Rise and Fall of Elijah Muhammad*. New York: Vintage Books, 2001, 465–68.

Sunday, Billy. "Get on the Water Wagon" (sermon). Reprinted in Lyle W. Dorsett, *Billy Sunday and the Redemption of Urban America*. Grand Rapids, MI: Eerdmans, 1991, 181–207.

Wise, Isaac Meyer. "Establishment of the Union of American Hebrew Congregations." Reprinted in David Philipson and Louis Grossmann, eds., *Selected Writings of Isaac M. Wise*. New York: Arno Press, 1969, 381–83.

Secondary Sources

Bratt, James D., and Christopher H. Meehan. *Gathered at the River: Grand Rapids, Michigan, and Its People of Faith*. Grand Rapids, MI: Eerdmans, 1993.

Brown, Thomas Elton. "Patriotism or Religion: Compulsory Public Education and Michigan's Roman Catholic Church, 1920–1924." *Michigan History* 64, no. 4 (1980): 36–42.

Caplow, Theodore, et al. *All Faithful People: Change and Continuity in Middletown's Religion*. Minneapolis: University of Minnesota Press, 1983.

Dorsett, Lyle W. *Billy Sunday and the Redemption of Urban America*. Grand Rapids, MI: Eerdmans, 1991.

Dowd, Gregory Evans. *A Spirited Resistance: The North American Indian Struggle for Unity, 1745–1815*. Baltimore: Johns Hopkins University Press, 1992.

Fortin, Roger. *Faith and Action: A History of the Archdiocese of Cincinnati, 1821–1996*. Columbus: Ohio State University Press, 2002.

Gaustad, Edwin Scott, and Philip L. Barlow. *New Historical Atlas of Religion in America*. Oxford: Oxford University Press, 2001.

Holli, Melvin G., and Peter D'A. Jones, eds. *The Ethnic Frontier: Essays in the History of Group Survival in Chicago and the Midwest*. Grand Rapids, MI: Eerdmans, 1977.

Hurt, R. Douglas. "Midwestern Distinctiveness." In *The American Midwest: Essays on Regional History*, ed. Andrew R. L. Cayton and Susan E. Gray. Bloomington: Indiana University Press, 2001.

Lagerquist, L. DeAne. *The Lutherans*. Westport, CT: Praeger, 1999.

Lynd, Robert S., and Helen Merrell Lynd. *Middletown: A Study in Contemporary American Culture*. New York: Harcourt, Brace and World, 1929.

Nabeel, Abraham, and Andrew Shyrock, eds. *Arab Detroit: From Margin to Mainstream*. Detroit: Wayne State University Press, 2000.

Numrich, Paul David. *Old Wisdom in the New World: Americanization in Two Immigrant Theravada Buddhist Temples*. Knoxville: University of Tennessee Press, 1996.

Olson, James S. *Catholic Immigrants in America*. Chicago: Nelson-Hall, 1987.

Raphael, Marc Lee. *Jews and Judaism in a Midwestern Community: Columbus, Ohio, 1840–1975*. Columbus: Ohio Historical Society, 1979.

Schloff, Linda Mack. *And Prairie Dogs Weren't Kosher: Jewish Women in the Upper Midwest Since 1855*. St. Paul: Minnesota Historical Society, 1996.

Seager, Richard Hughes. *The World's Parliament of Religions: The East/West Encounter, Chicago 1893*. Bloomington: Indiana University Press, 1995.

Sernett, Milton C. *Bound for the Promised Land: African American Religion and the Great Migration*. Durham, NC: Duke University Press, 1997.

Shanabruch, Charles. *Chicago's Catholics: The Evolution of an American Identity*. Notre Dame, IN: University of Notre Dame Press, 1981.

Shannon, James P. *Catholic Colonization on the Western Frontier*. New Haven, CT: Yale University Press, 1957.

Sharfman, I. Harold. *Jews on the Frontier*. Chicago: Henry Regnery Company, 1977.

Shapiro, Edward S. *A Time for Healing: American Jewry Since World War II*. Baltimore: The Johns Hopkins University Press, 1992.

Sweet, William Warren. *Religion on the American Frontier*. 4 vols. New York: Cooper Square Press, 1964.

Trollinger, William Vance, Jr. *God's Empire: William Bell Riley and Midwestern Fundamentalism*. Madison: University of Wisconsin Press, 1990.

Van der Maas, Ruth F. "The Emergence of Baptist Fundamentalism in Grand Rapids, Michigan." *American Baptist Quarterly* (Spring 1994): 278–294.

Walbridge, Linda S. *Without Forgetting the Imam: Lebanese Shi'ism in an American Community*. Detroit: Wayne State University Press, 1997.

Wentz, Abdel Ross. *A Basic History of Lutheranism in America*. Philadelphia: Muhlenberg Press, 1955.

Web Sites

Archdiocese of Cincinnati
http://www.catholiccincinnati.org

Billy Graham Center Museum, Wheaton College, Illinois
http://www.wheaton.edu/bgc/museum/index.html
History of Evangelical Christianity in the United States and Midwest.

Conner Prairie Living History Museum
http://www.connerprairie.org/HistoryOnline/index.asp
Articles on the early religious history of Indiana.

Islamic Society of North America, Plainfield, Indiana
http://www.isna.net
Muslim life in America.

Midwest Buddhist Information Center
http://members.ync.net/jfred/
Information on Midwest Buddhism, including a listing of Chicago temples.

Pluralism Project
http://www.pluralism.org/resources/map/index.php
Interactive map of resources on religious diversity including the Midwest.

Videos/Films

Blue Collar and Buddha. National Asian American Telecommunications Association. 1987. Laotian Buddhists in Rockford, Illinois

Celebrating Faith the Hoosier Way. Pruitt's Studio. 1992.

Chicago's First Mexican Church. WTTW. 2002.

Chicago Sings. Tyscot, Inc. 1998. Gospel music in Chicago.

Churches and Synagogues. KETC9. 1996. Sacred architecture in St. Louis, Missouri.

City of Steeples. WMVS/WMVT. 1997. Sacred architecture in Milwaukee, Wisconsin.

Doorways to Diversity: 150 Years of Jewish Life in Cleveland. Electric Shadows Corp. 1991.

Emphasis Wisconsin: Music in American Religion. WMVS/WMVT. 1994. Sacred music of Wisconsin's denominations.

Fort Wayne: City of Churches. WFWA39. 1999.

German Catholic Country: West Central Ohio. WBGU. 1999.

Holy Cleveland: Cleveland's Sacred Landmarks. WVI-TV. 1997.

Keeping the Faith. PBS Home Video. 1987. African American churches in Chicago.

The Messenger: The Rise and Fall of Elijah Muhammad. C-SPAN. 2000. Discussion with Karl Evanzz, author of a biography of Elijah Muhammad.

Milwaukee's Polonia: The Second Homeland. McCullough Productions. 1989.

Of Mortar and Miracles: 150 Years of Chicago Catholicism. WGN. 1994.

Religion as a Window on Culture. Films for the Humanities, Inc. 1998. The religious traditions of Indianapolis, Indiana.

Schoenbrunn: A Meeting of Cultures. Ohio Historical Society. 1991.

The Shakers: Hands to Work, Hearts to God. PBS Home Video. 1996.

The Strangers Next Door: Welcoming Muslims. CBS News. 2002. Muslims in Detroit.

A Videoguide to Amish Country. Video Concepts. 1989.

The Voices of Trinity. WGTE-TV. 1992. History of Trinity Episcopal Church, Toledo, Ohio.

Under the Same Sky: German-Russian and Jewish Life from the Steppes of Russia to America's Midwest. The Chapter. 1996.

Festivals and Events

Hindu Festivals. For annual schedules, see Web sites of local Hindu temples (e.g., www.ramatemple.org/).

International Visakha Festival (Buddhist). Held every May in Evanston, Illinois. See Midwest Buddhist Information Center (members.ync.net/jfred) for details.

Native American powwows. For listings nationally and throughout the Midwest, see www.powwows.com.

Roman Catholic festivals. See local diocesan Web sites (e.g., www.archdiocese-hgo.org/).

Organizations, Museums, Special Collections, and Libraries

Basilica of Saint Louis
209 Walnut Street
Saint Louis, MO 63102
(314) 231-3250
www.catholic-forum.com/stlouisking

Oldest cathedral west of the Mississippi; also houses a museum focusing on history of Roman Catholics in Saint Louis.

Beecher House Museum
2950 Gilbert Avenue

Cincinnati, OH 45214
(513) 221-7900
www.ohiohistory.org/places/stowe

Home of Lyman Beecher, minister at the Presbyterian Lane Theological Seminary, author of *A Plea for the West*, and father of Harriet Beecher Stowe.

Billy Graham Center Museum
500 East College Avenue
Wheaton, IL 60187
(630) 752-5909
www.wheaton.edu/bgc/museum

Museum focusing on Protestant evangelization in the United States, especially the Midwest.

Billy Sunday Home
Winona Lake, IN 46590
(574) 268-9888
www.villageatwinona.com/BillySunday.asp

Home of the famous early twentieth-century midwestern revivalist.

Cahokia Mounds State Historic Site
One mile southwest of Collinsville, IL, off Route 55
(618) 346-5160
www.medicine.wustl.edu/~mckinney/cahokia/cahokia.html

Archaeological site of ancient Native American Mississippian people.

Conner Prairie Museum
13400 Allinsonville Road
Fishers, IN 46038
(317) 776-6000
www.connerprairie.org

Living-history museum focusing on life on the Indiana frontier, with exhibits on religion in nineteenth-century Indiana.

Du Sable Museum of African-American History
740 East 56th Place
Chicago, IL 60637
(773) 947-0600
www.dusablemuseum.org

Museum focusing on midwestern African American history, including religion.

Historic Adventist Village
411 Champion Street
Battle Creek, MI 49017
(269) 965-3000
www.adventistheritage.org/village.html

Reconstruction of nineteenth-century Battle Creek, headquarters of Seventh-Day Adventism.

Historic New Harmony
New Harmony, IN 47631
(800) 231-2168
www.newharmony.org

Nineteenth-century Rappite (German Lutheran) village. From Interstate 64, exit at Griffin (exit 4) and follow Indiana Highway 69.

Hopewell Culture National Historic Park
16062 Route 104
Chillicothe, OH 45601
(740) 774-1125
www.nps.gov/hocu

Archaeological site of ancient Native American Hopewell people.

Iowa Mennonite Museum and Archives
411 Ninth Street
Kalona, IA 52247
(319) 656-3271
www.kalonaiowa.org/village/index.html

Museum focusing on Iowa's Mennonite and Amish populations.

Kirtland Temple
9020 Chillicothe Road
Kirtland, OH 44094
(440) 256-3318
www.kirtlandtemple.org

First Mormon temple, built between 1833 and 1836, now open for public tours.

Levi Coffin House Museum
113 US 27 North
Fountain City, IN 47341
(765) 847-2432
www.in.gov/ism/HistoricSites/LeviCoffin/historic.asp

Home of famous Quaker abolitionist and conductor on the Underground Railroad.

Marquette Mission Park and Museum of Ojibwa Culture
500-566 North State
Saint Ignace, MI 49781
(906) 643-9161
www.stignace.com/index.html

Park and museum focusing on seventeenth-century interaction between Jesuit missionaries and the Native American Ojibwa.

Mennohoff Museum
510 S. Van Buren Street
Shipshewana, IN 46565
(260) 768-4117
www.mennohof.org

Museum focusing on Mennonite, Amish, and Hutterite history.

Morton B. Weiss Museum of Judaica
1100 East Hyde Park Boulevard
Chicago, IL 60615
(312) 924-1234

Small museum focusing on history of K.A.M. Isaiah Israel Temple, the oldest Jewish congregation in the Midwest.

Museum of Amana History
4310 220th Trail
Amana, IA 52203
(319) 622-3567
www.cr.nps.gov/nr/travel/amana/mah.htm

Museum focusing on the history of the Amana colonies, founded by the Inspirationists, a nineteenth-century German religious group.

Nauvoo Historic District
L.D.S. Visitor Center, Main and Young Streets
Nauvoo, IL 62345
(217) 453-2237

Joseph Smith Visitors Center
149 Water Street
Nauvoo, IL 62345
(217) 453-2246

The nineteenth-century Mormon city, site of the second Mormon temple.

Old World Wisconsin Outdoor Museum
S103 W37890 Highway 67
Eagle, WI 53119
(262) 594-6300
www.wisconsinhistory.org/oww

Living history museum focusing on ethnic and religious diversity on the Wisconsin frontier.

Plum Street Temple
726 Plum Street
Cincinnati, OH 45202
(513) 421-2556
www.wisetemple.org

The synagogue of Isaac Meyer Wise, founder of American Reform Judaism. Public tours available.

Polish Museum of America
984 North Milwaukee Avenue
Chicago, IL 60622
(773) 384-3352
http://pma.prcua.org/homeen.html

Museum focusing on the history of Chicago's large Polish population, with exhibits on its Roman Catholic heritage.

Schoenbrunn Village
Route 250, exit 81 off Route 77, 1 mile southeast of New Philadelphia
New Philadelphia, OH 44663
(800) 752-2711
www.ohiohistory.org/places/schoenbr

Eighteenth-century Native American Moravian village.

Shaker Historical Museum
16740 South Park Boulevard
Shaker Heights, OH 44120
(216) 921-1201
www.shakerworkshops.com/shm.htm

Museum focusing on Shakers in Ohio.

Spertus Jewish Museum
618 S. Michigan Avenue
Chicago, IL 60605
(312) 322-1747
www.spertus.edu/museum.html

The largest museum of Judaica in the Midwest.

Unity Temple
875 Lake Street
Oak Park, IL 60301
(708) 383-8873
www.unitytemple-utrf.org/

Landmark Unitarian-Universalist church designed by Frank Lloyd Wright. Public tours available.

William Jennings Bryan Museum
408 South Broadway
Salem, IL 62881
(618) 548-7791

Birthplace of the famous progressivist politician and fundamentalist.

Zoar Museum and Village
Route 212, 3 miles southeast of exit 93 off Route 77
Zoar, OH 44697
(800) 262-6195
www.ohiohistory.org/places/zoar

Reconstructed village of the Separatists, of Zoar, a nineteenth-century German religious group.

SPORTS AND RECREATION

Gerald R. Gems

The Midwest, with its forests, plains, and vast waterways, has always offered splendid opportunities for amusement. Taking pleasure in so diverse a landscape drew inhabitants out of doors, and recognizing the possibilities for bucolic recreation and cheerful sport kept them there. Over time, a consciousness of the progressive spirit associated with the heartland infused into organized play in the area a strong sense of shared values. Today that mixture of racial, ethnic, and religious cultures still manifests itself in the sports of the region.

AMERICAN INDIAN PASTIMES

Before the entry of European colonists into the midwestern region of North America, indigenous tribes engaged in a variety of pastimes, many of which involved gambling. Games of chance included dice and guessing games revealing hidden objects. Traditional songs and dances enlivened tribal activities, and youth practiced spearing objects. The spearing activity progressed to utilitarian sports, archery in particular, which served the functional needs of a hunting society. Anglo travelers into the region in the late eighteenth and early nineteenth centuries remarked that Indian boys began such archery practice at age four or five and spent much of their day engaged in the sport with remarkable skill. They shot at both fixed and moving objects, such as hoops, coins, or animals while on foot and, later, on horseback. They could hit a half-penny at 15 yards and a small bird at 50 yards.

Other utilitarian pastimes included fishing for sustenance and swimming, an activity enjoyed by both men and women. Both the Ojibwa and Menominee tribes of the upper Midwest constructed beautiful birch bark canoes to transport themselves along the numerous regional waterways. Among the Menominee and Ojibwa tribes storytelling proved not only an enjoyable pastime, but also a means to transmit tribal history and culture from one generation to another. Games served as yet another means to teach cultural values. Children and adults played a variety of ball games, with lacrosse being an almost universal pastime among North American tribes. Lacrosse, often played by large numbers at one time, involved the use of netted, long handled sticks to catch and throw a ball toward a vigorously defended goal of the opponents. The popular game resulted in a great deal of bodily contact and often produced serious injuries and even deaths. An Anglo report of a 1796 game among the Ojibwas detailed severe wounds and broken bones, yet the Indians felt that the game taught the important values of courage and fair play while it prepared men for inevitable wars. Though rare, on occasion women of the midwestern tribes played the game. More often they engaged in games of shinny, a game similar to modern field hockey. Both males and females competed in running races that developed speed and endurance, as Native American pastimes closely coordinated with the natural rhythms of their lives and the physical environment.

FRONTIER CULTURE

In the Great Lakes region French fur trappers intermingled harmoniously with the indigenous people, and a black man, Jean Baptiste du Sable (1745–1818), arrived with his Indian wife, the daughter of a Potawatomi chief, as the first permanent settlers of the Chicago area in the 1770s. The du Sables' trading post included a cabin, barns, bakery, dairy, smokehouse, and stables. In the late eighteenth century, a steady stream of white settlers immigrated to the western territories, displacing the indigenous population. The resultant rural, frontier culture that followed found its recreation in area taverns or way stations that served as regional gathering places. Mark Beaubien's (1800–1881) Sauganash Hotel in Chicago was typical of such watering holes. There Beaubien supplied more than lodging as he entertained transients with his fiddling, dancing, and storytelling. At such places, frontiersmen played cards and competed in contests of physical skill, such as shooting matches, foot races, or horseracing. An 1807 account of a shooting match in Missouri included both pistols and rifles; participants wagered on their ability to hit a mark. Such skills and prowess marked one's masculinity and ability to survive on the frontier. Settlers in more genteel villages sailed on the lakes in the summer months, while they traveled by sleighs and ice skates on frozen streams and rivers during the winter. An ice skating race held at Madison, Wisconsin, in 1854 drew a thousand spectators to watch competitors vie for the sizable prize of ten dollars. The winner of a half-mile race recorded a time of one minute and fifty-four seconds. In the growing riverfront town of Cincinnati, men found recreation and socialization in the formation of a fishing club in 1830. The Cincinnati Angling Club, as it was called, made excursions, to the Miami River, and elsewhere to try their hand at catching pike, salmon, and bass, with numbers and weights of each quantified. Members devised "inventions in angling apparatus" to improve their catch and ended their season with an annual banquet. Early tensions between the pace and tensions of urban life were reflected in men's contention that they sought refuge in their rural outings, which provided "recreation for the mind and calm and quiet contemplation. . . . in the soft music of the running stream and rural scenery . . . to escape the din and bustle of the city."[1]

In the outer reaches of the frontier, residents engaged in more bestial blood sports. Animal baiting usually involved a captured bear or, less frequently, a more valuable bull chained to a stake while wrestling to the death with a series of large hunting dogs. Spectators wagered on the expected winner or the number of dogs required to complete the task. When large game proved unavailable, spectators bet on vicious dog fights. In one celebrated match between a Boston dog and its Chicago opponent, the betting reached $30,000. On other occasions terriers were penned with a multitude of rats, and wagers were placed on the length of time it would take the dog to kill the vermin. The contentious and aggressive nature of frontier culture also included no holds barred wrestling among human participants. Matches continued until one man surrendered, with conquest often achieved by eye gouging or even abelarding, a means of castration. On the frontier a man's honor rested in his physical prowess, and stout riverboatmen extolled their exploits in storied yarns, songs, demonstrations of strength and endurance, or dancing exhibitions.

In the growing urban areas of the Midwest, a more genteel city culture evolved that adhered to middle-class standards of decorum, yet sport remained an important means for men to demonstrate their masculinity. Males gathered in taverns, adjacent bowling alleys and pool halls for drink and camaraderie. By the 1840s the Brunswick Company, a Cincinnati firm, began manufacturing ornate billiard tables and bowling equipment to meet the demand for such recreations. They soon expanded operations to Chicago as the wealthy ordered custom-made equipment for their private parlors. Tournaments and challenge matches established local and national stars, some of whom utilized their status to gain political office. In an early match, held in Detroit in 1859, Michael Phelan, the New York champion, traveled to meet John Seereiter, the local favorite, as 500 fans witnessed Phelan claim the $15,000 prize. By 1865, billiard tables were renting at a rate of $4,000 per day in Chicago, and legislators decided to issue licenses to the pool halls, bowling alleys, and shooting galleries to augment city revenues, despite the perceived evils of gambling.

MID-NINETEENTH-CENTURY RECREATION

During the nineteenth century, recreation evolved away from what was often merely roughhousing as the culture of the region became more decorous. Organized team sports displaced individual feats of prowess. In both rural and urban areas, women gradually became participants, especially in events with social emphasis.

Rural Areas

In rural areas, recreational practices were tied to agriculture, chores, seasonal rhythms, and communal gatherings. Farmers gathered together to assist each other in barn raisings and harvesting of crops. Catherine Beecher (1800–1878), an early advocate of women's rights, espoused sport and physical activity as a means to attain robust health for females. Beecher promoted gardening, horseback riding, calisthenics, and other outdoor pursuits as suitable for women. Indoors, activities such as quilting and spinning sometimes resulted in competitions. At county fairs women exhibited their crafts, culinary abilities, and baking skills for prizes. By the middle of the nineteenth century, women began pursuing more active forms of recreation, including baseball.

Rural men continued the utilitarian pastimes of hunting, fishing, boating, and horseback riding. By midcentury, steamboat racing on the Mississippi River provided a sometimes dangerous adventure for crew and passengers, when vessels challenged each other between New Orleans and midwestern ports such as St. Louis or St. Paul. As such cities grew throughout the nineteenth century, the United States faced a dilemma as competing urban–rural lifestyles posed differing cultural values. The communal and collective values of agrarian life that Thomas Jefferson had foreseen as best suiting the American character gave way to Alexander Hamilton's vision of an individualistic, commercialized, urban society. Sport, baseball in particular, provided one means of subordinating competition to a common interest. The game enjoyed widespread popularity in both cities and rural towns by midcentury. During the Civil War, soldiers played baseball during lulls in the action. The hostilities brought greater uniformity to the rules thereafter when New York's version became acceptable. Veterans returned to their Midwest homes with a more homogeneous "national" game.

Baseball espoused both rural and urban values in its communal teamwork in the field, while allowing individual achievements at bat. Both communities believed in the diligent work ethic, and in practice that produced success and bestowed communal pride and civic honor. An umpire assured adherence to middle-class standards of fair play, decorum, and deference to authority. The untimed nature of the game reflected preindustrial agricultural rhythms, while the green grass and open skies experienced in urban ballparks brought a measure of the countryside into the city. With the advent of fully professional baseball teams in Cincinnati in 1869 and Chicago in 1870, sport further assumed the mantle of an American meritocracy in which farmboys or immigrant youth might achieve greater socioeconomic status based solely on their abilities.

Urban Areas

Baseball gained great popularity, particularly among the bachelor subculture that proliferated in urban environments. Known as "cranks," ardent supporters followed their teams throughout the season with marching bands, patronage, and boisterous banquets that honored favored players. Albert Spalding (1850–1915) first earned fame as a teenage pitching sensation for the Rockford, Illinois, team. He soon graduated to professional ranks with the Boston and Chicago teams, assuming ownership of the latter. After founding a sporting goods business that made him a millionaire, he promoted America's national game throughout the world. The bachelor subculture, however, hardly adhered to the strict moral standards that made Spalding a success. With few young women in western communities, young males congregated in saloons, brothels, and pool halls. In such homosocial environments, bantering, physical prowess, and athletic challenges established one's status in the masculine hierarchy. In addition to baseball, billiards, and bowling, boxing offered a means of establishing one's dominance. In Chicago a good fighter could earn as much as $500 for a single fight in the 1850s, a sum equivalent to a laborer's annual wage. Gambling on athletic events proved central to bachelors' lifestyle and produced sports heroes who reached glorified heights. Countless saloons featured the visage of John L. Sullivan (1858–1918), the Boston Strong Boy who had established himself as the heavyweight champion by the 1880s.

Industrialization created social challenges because it robbed many men of their independence and self-esteem. Factories displaced previously independent craftsmen, who then had to work as "wage slaves" for employers who dictated their working hours, conditions, and pay. Some employers even tried to ensure that their employees spent their leisure time in wholesome activities. Workers who spent their leisure time in the saloon too often failed to report for work on "blue Mondays," or proved unproductive when they did so. Employers, nativists, and Protestant reformers all tried to curtail activities that they deemed injurious to moral and commercial health. Temperance societies, often led by women, decried the harmful effects of alcohol, but when Chicago's mayor attempted to enforce prohibition laws in 1855 German residents responded with the Lager Beer Riots that resulted in a death and several injuries before the imposition of martial law. A political referendum soon overturned the law as ethnic immigrants marshaled their political power in support of recreational practices. The Germans, in particular, drew a strong distinction between their beer halls, which provided musical and family entertainment, and the Irish saloons of the bachelor subculture.

The YMCA

Employers sought assistance from the Young Men's Christian Association, an evangelical Protestant organization founded in England in 1841. By the 1850s midwestern businessmen offered financial support for the organization in return for services for their employees. A YMCA survey of Chicago in the 1860s reported the annual consumption of twenty million gallons of liquor. The state of Illinois granted the YMCA a 1,000-year charter and tax-exempt status to curtail drunkenness, but the organization found little success and eventually began offering sports as a means to increase its membership. When the YMCA began constructing gymnasiums, employers hired the agency to inculcate in their employees the values of a "muscular Christianity": a sober mind, a temperate lifestyle, and a strong body to house one's soul.

After the national railroad strike of 1877, George Pullman (1831–1897), a Chicago manufacturer of railroad sleeping cars, determined to alleviate labor unrest by developing the first modern industrial recreation program in America. Pullman constructed a company town south of Chicago complete with a comprehensive athletic program and facilities for track and field, rowing, tennis, cricket, baseball, football, ice skating, billiards, bowling, and shooting. The town's lone bar, however, remained off limits to the workforce composed largely of ethnic and immigrant craftsmen, many of them bachelors. A local branch of the YMCA provided moral guidance. Newspapers covered field days, company teams, and the athletic spectacles that brought the town into national prominence and spawned similar communities. Despite such early promise, the Depression of 1893 alienated Pullman's workforce, which went out on a strike that garnered national headlines and required the use of federal troops to quell. Pullman's experiment in social control had proven a failure. His town was annexed by the city of Chicago; but the workers maintained their teams in the park districts, city leagues, and in intercity competitions.

Sports, Ethnicity, and Class

Although sport drew some into mainstream American culture, particular ethnic groups initially resisted such transformations. The Irish, Germans, Czechs, and Scandinavians were very active in the labor movements of the late nineteenth century, their socialist and radical tendencies alarming capitalist Anglo employers in midwestern cities. The Bohemian Sharpshooters even served as a workers' militia whose members maintained their shooting skills and joined workers' gatherings, picnics, and beer drinking in parks. The labor groups often met in the halls of the German turnvereins or the Czech sokols. Ostensibly nationalistic gymnastic societies, the German turnvereins, Czech sokol groups, and Polish falcon clubs, all of which were less politicized copies of gymnastic societies in their homelands, preserved European ethnic cultures and languages.

European immigrants brought their sporting pastimes with them to the Midwest. During the winter, both figure skaters and speed skaters practiced on the numerous frozen waterways of the region. John Johnson, a Minneapolis speed skater, won the North American championship from 1893 to 1895; another Minnesotan, John Nilsson, succeeded Johnson as the world champion. Wisconsin later became a national center for speed skating. Scandinavian immigrants brought skiing to North America; by the 1880s, clubs organized competitions in the Midwest. The United States Ski Club conducted its first tournament at Ishpeming, Michigan, in 1891. A year later the Aurora Ski Club of Red Wing, Minnesota, used the Michigan site to stage its ski jumping exhibition. Within two more years, clubs in Minnesota, Michigan, and Wisconsin competed for laurels in ski jumping and cross country skiing. Curling clubs had emerged in the Midwest around the same time, with at least fourteen in Wisconsin, Minnesota, and Illinois by the 1880s. An 1888 match at a rink in Portage, Wisconsin, drew 120 competitors from the home state and neighboring Illinois.

Among the European citizenry baseball retained the greatest popularity, but the game of croquet also gained wide acceptance during the 1860s. Victorian standards of decorum required proper introductions and chaperones for courting couples. Croquet allowed young men and women to gather informally on residential lawns or public greens in full view, thus limiting the necessity for a chaperone. Roller skating rinks soon appeared in urban locations and provided similar opportunities for socialization.

Cycling afforded even greater independence by the 1880s. Fascination with technology and speed fostered numerous cycling clubs. The relative expense of such vehicles could be offset by rentals, making the bicycle accessible to those of moderate means. The League of American Wheelmen, organized in 1880, campaigned for paved roads even before the advent of automobiles. Paved roads eased the travels of cyclists: while some engaged in "century runs" of 100 miles, "scorchers" raced at top speeds on high-wheeled mounts. Hitting a rock on dirt roads at high speeds inevitably produced "headers" that resulted in serious injuries. The speed at which young people traveled enabled them to elude their elderly chaperones as well, which might result in a stolen kiss.

Cycling challenged Victorian strictures in other ways. Female cyclists, unable to ride in the cumbersome dresses of the era, adopted bloomers and pants as a recourse. Outraged and threatened by the sight, clergymen denounced female cyclists as possessed by the devil, while town officials banned the wearing of pants by females while cycling. The women circumvented the law by inventing a clip that fastened their skirts near the waistline, thus achieving the same effect. Professional female cyclists by the 1880s challenged men in endurance races. Cycling's widespread popularity, persisting through the 1890s, led physicians to theorize that female riders achieved sexual gratification from a quivering seat or bar. By the 1890s Chicago alone had 500 cycling clubs, each with its own colors and uniforms. Cyclists banded together for formidable political clout; one club alone claimed 1800 voters. After a Chicago cycling show drew 100,000 fans in 1896, mayoral candidate Carter Harrison II (1860–1953) launched his political campaign with a century ride the following year. Such recreational pastimes thus enabled youth to challenge Victorian mores: cycling in particular allowed women to confront male hegemony and expanded feminine participation in the sporting culture.

Although some sports liberated diverse constituencies, others solidified class lines. Archery, which had sharpened the physical prowess of Native Americans, evolved within two generations into a more sedentary pastime. The National Archery Association held its first annual convention at Crawfordsville, Indiana, in 1879 with six of the eight clubs in attendance from the Midwest. The initial tournament, held in Chicago that year, allowed both male and female competitors. Although the membership encompassed a broader clientele over the next twenty-five years, midwesterners remained the core of the association and the majority of national tournaments took place at midwestern sites. Although the association provided for gender equality, its very nature restricted it to the emerging middle class, as the cost of equipment and travel prohibited working-class participants.

Sports and Recreation Clubs

Other sports organizations maintained deliberate isolationist policies. The burgeoning middle class formed clubs based on professional associations and leisure interests as a means of distinguishing and shielding themselves from the masses. Unable to engage in elite sporting activities such as yacht racing, polo, or horseracing, the middle class formed private tennis clubs with limited high-fee memberships that often required a sponsor. Acceptance into the clubs denoted prestige. Waiting lists were long, and the chosen few maintained membership in as many top clubs as financially possible. Such clubs sought athletic competitions only with peers, in imitation of the amateur ideology of the British aristocracy. Membership provided much more than recreation, as businessmen and entrepreneurs sought contacts to enhance social and pecuniary aspirations.

Race, religion, and ethnicity restricted recreational opportunities. African Americans might enter private sporting establishments only as servants or employees. Few Catholics could expect acceptance by Protestant clubs, leading them to promote their own outlets through Knights of Columbus organizations. Jews faced greater discrimination. Despite their accumulated wealth, by the 1890s successful German Jews in the United States were refused admission to exclusive clubs and responded by founding their own. Still, anti-Semitism persisted, and the Western

Golf Association continued to ban Jewish women from play, causing Jewish clubs to withdraw from the organization in 1921.

Country clubs by their very nature separated the wealthy from the urban masses as the wealthy sought refuge from the city's pollution, stench, and poverty. Country clubs offered tennis facilities and a private clubhouse for social affairs. The most desirable clubs offered golf as well. Equipment costs and the need for a large expanse of land restricted participation to social elites, although working-class youths might caddy for tips or wages. The Chicago Golf Club, organized in 1893, built the first eighteen-hole course in the United States in the suburb of Wheaton, socially and geographically isolating its members from perceived inferiors by restrictive membership covenants. To ensure male dominance, officers allowed wives and daughters of members to play on the course only when it was not being used by the men and usually only one day per week. Nonetheless, some women excelled. Margaret Abbott, a member of the Chicago Golf Club, became the first woman to claim a victory in the modern Olympic Games when she won the golf competition in Paris in 1900.

Despite its pretensions to elitism, golf spread rapidly to the middle class as technological advances made equipment affordable and as municipalities constructed public golf courses within city limits after the turn of the twentieth century. By that time, professional players had appeared on the links, diminishing the clubs' amateur ideals, while widespread gambling by wealthy golfers replaced wagers previously made on horse races, which many municipal authorities now banned. As golf bets increased, the game's idealized code of honor began to crumble. Open tournaments accepted both amateur and professional players, and the Midwest soon featured its first Western Open, the premier golfing event in the Midwest.

THE BEGINNINGS OF MODERN SPORTS

Amateur athletic participation reflected preferences in ethnicity, class, and gender. Towns and cities encouraged citizens to spend their weekends outside by setting aside playing fields and parks. Developing standards in popular sports manifested ideals of democracy and civic health, though with a capitalist bias.

Softball and Baseball

In Chicago, wealthy alumni of eastern colleges sat around a yacht club attending to the telegraphic report of a big football game in 1887. During a lull, one member picked up a stray boxing glove and threw it across the room at another, who grabbed a handy broomstick and swatted it back. The playful escapade evolved into the game of indoor baseball, later adopted for playground use as softball. Sporting goods firms soon manufactured a soft, oversized ball of restricted flight that permitted the adaptation of baseball to indoor arenas. Indoor leagues quickly proliferated throughout the city during winter months; the best players achieved semi-pro status, being paid for their efforts. As the game spread throughout the country, it became especially popular among women. While others played the game with baseball gloves and a 12-inch ball, Chicago-style softball evolved into a gloveless game played with a larger 16-inch ball known as a "clincher." Adopted by the working classes in playgrounds and park districts, the game spread as businesses, taverns, neighborhoods, and schools formed teams. By the 1930s, the American Softball Association boasted three million players. In Chicago the "Cripple-A League," sponsored by the Veterans of Foreign Wars for older players, claimed 2500 teams in that association alone.

Basketball for Boys and Girls

Other sports originally developed for middle-class players found widespread adoption among all social classes. The YMCA invented both basketball and volleyball at its Springfield, Massachusetts, training school in the 1890s. Luther Gulick, the school's physical education director, assigned James Naismith (1861–1939), a Canadian graduate student, to devise a game to keep the rowdy young men busy during the winter between football and baseball seasons. The first basketball game ensued on December 21, 1891, with nine men on each team, but rough play required modifications to the original rules. When the YMCA published the rules in its magazine, nearby women's colleges adopted the game by March 1892. The University of Chicago played a full schedule of seven games during the winter of 1894; the first recorded intercollegiate contest occurred in the Midwest between the Minnesota State School of Agriculture and Hamline on February 9, 1895.

Chicago high school girls formed a basketball league that same year, and Hull House sponsored a settlement team. By 1900, the *Chicago Tribune* proclaimed basketball the most popular indoor sport for young women. Although women took to the game enthusiastically, female physical educators grew concerned over the physicality of the game. They also feared that women might adopt the aggressive, competitive, and commercial forms of play favored by men. The rapid pace of the game brought dress reform as well when women began to forsake their long, cumbersome dresses for shorter skirts and bloomers that eventually evolved into gym suits. Consequently, new rules for women restricted players to only one of three designated zones on the court in order to limit their movement. Despite such changes, the game remained immensely popular, and companies throughout the country began

Hull House basketball in Chicago is a recreational league that is still in existence. Courtesy Jane Addams Memorial Collection, Special Collections Department, The University Library, University of Illinois at Chicago.

sponsoring women's teams to accommodate their working-class employees and to promote their products through sporting enterprises.

Public Parks

Employees' recreation and use of leisure time had long been issues as industrialization transformed midwestern cities. George Pullman provided a private model to address employers' concerns, but the problems of overcrowding, hygiene, pollution, juvenile delinquency, and education required the attention of civil authorities. In the latter half of the nineteenth century, midwestern city planners conceptualized urban parks to provide more healthful, open spaces. Class-based leisure practices, however, fostered civic debate over the nature and uses of such spaces. Upper-class patrons favored aesthetic parks based on European models, with passive forms of recreation such as flower gardens, topiary, fountains, statuary, and intellectual stimulants such as museums. The preponderant working classes wanted places for active play during the limited leisure that they enjoyed during the week. They sought ballfields and play spaces. Compromise led to the incorporation of both visions within the cities' parks. Neighborhood parks, however, catered largely to the interests of their constituents and to the intentions of Progressive Era reformers, who hoped that sports would enculturate particular value systems in the ethnic, immigrant masses.

Americanization through Sport and Recreation

Initial efforts to transform non-WASP groups began with the establishment of the Carlisle Indian School in Pennsylvania in 1879. Designed to assimilate American Indians into mainstream white culture, the school provided vocational training and a heavy regimen of sports, such as baseball, football, and track and field. Perhaps its most famous alumnus was Jim Thorpe (1888–1953), by some accounts the greatest of all male American athletes. The success of Carlisle resulted in numerous similar institutions throughout the United States, including government schools at Pipestone and Morris in Minnesota and Mount Pleasant in Michigan.

Government officials, educators, and specialists in the burgeoning field of sociology combined efforts to Americanize the European groups who flooded American shores after 1880. They did so systematically. After legislating to remove child workers from factories, they initiated education laws that compelled attendance at schools. Many students, however, did not speak English and failed to absorb their lessons in citizenship. G. Stanley Hall, one of the foremost psychologists of the era, theorized that humans progressed through several evolutionary stages on their way to a civilized state. He suggested that such stages could be traced through forms of play, with tag and chase games representative of more primitive hunting societies and the highly organized sports characteristic of the civilized nations. Despite Hall's ethnocentric biases, such beliefs found ready acceptance in educational circles; play, games, and sport became primary means of acculturation. Even students who could not speak English learned to compete through sports. Competition served as the basis for the capitalist economic system and could counteract the beliefs of the socialist and communist labor unions. Team sports, in particular, taught the virtues of self-sacrifice for the good of the whole, a valuable lesson in cooperation and democracy. Players learned time discipline, the rewards of a strong work ethic, and, most importantly for employers, deference to authority in the form of team captains, coaches, and referees. Baseball, America's "national game," even offered the opportunity for money and social status if one became a professional player—a true meritocracy based on physical prowess rather than wealth or social network.

Because employers valued such lessons, they supported schools and play spaces financially. Parks and playgrounds became extensions of the schools, with trained and uniformed male and female supervisors who instructed boys and girls in how to play. Adolescents, whose stage of development was newly identified by Hall, learned middle-class organizational standards by applying for play space permits and scheduling game times. The parks and playgrounds thus provided recreation, respite, and a more positive release of energy but did so in a manner prescribed to address delinquency and belief systems that threatened the capitalist system.

The parks also addressed hygienic concerns. In the teeming cities, working-class residents lacked proper sewage systems, living quarters, and bathing facilities. Open spaces offered escape from overcrowded conditions; some provided a swimming pool for bathing purposes. In midwestern cities located on lakes or waterways, working-class residents who lived within walking distance used the public beaches for bathing. Chicago opened the nation's largest civic beach in 1916, complete with floodlights for nighttime use. Users could rent a swimsuit, locker, and towel for 10 cents. More than a million users provided $30,000 in revenue to the city that year. Policemen patrolled to ensure decorum and proper attire. White or flesh-colored swimsuits were banned, and fines were administered for indecent exposure. Residents in the inner cities were relegated to private Turkish baths, a male sanctuary; they proved unaffordable for most.

Chicago assumed national leadership in the recreation movement in the early twentieth century, constructing large, brick fieldhouses in parks. Such buildings encompassed gymnasiums, separate locker rooms for males and females, play spaces, conference and crafts rooms, and even natatoriums (indoor pools). The fieldhouses and pools enabled park supervisors to attract residents the entire year. Cities throughout the United States soon adopted the Chicago model for their social and recreational needs.

Chicago solidified its stature with the creation of the Playground Association of America in 1907. Jane Addams (1860–1935), founder of the Hull House settlement, stated that the organization intended to "replace the theaters, dance halls, saloons, gambling, and vice with parks, playgrounds, recreation centers, and festivals to increase socialization, decrease class, ethnicity and age barriers."[2] Within three years 246 cities adopted Chicago's model for supervised playgrounds. By 1917, the number of cities had reached 504.

Interscholastic and Intercollegiate Sports

Within the schools adults took control of athletic teams that had previously been organized by the students. Illinois instituted a state high school athletic association in 1893, followed two years later by Wisconsin, in order to regulate the growing interscholastic competitions and to establish age, eligibility, and scholastic standards for participants. Such governing bodies preceded the National Collegiate Athletic Association, founded in 1905.

The Beginning of Football in the Midwest

By the late nineteenth century, football superseded baseball on high school and college campuses as a means to establish local and regional honor, uphold school pride, and recapture lost masculinity: without war to establish their courage and assuage aggressive tendencies, by the 1880s American middle-class males feared the feminization of culture. Raised by their mothers, then sent to school where they were taught by female teachers at the elementary levels, young men felt that they would lose the martial qualities deemed necessary to compete in the business world and to challenge world powers such as Great Britain for international supremacy. Football proved a ready antidote. It had evolved from soccer and rugby in the eastern colleges during the preceding decade, and midwestern high schools and colleges quickly adopted the game. Charles Adams, president of the University of Wisconsin, claimed that football developed "those characteristics that have made the Anglo-Saxon race preeminent."[3]

Football burnished a university's national reputation. When students at the University of Michigan challenged Cornell as early as 1873, Andrew White, Cornell's president, replied that he would not let his charges "travel 400 miles merely to agitate a bag of wind."[4] In 1881, Michigan traveled to the East to test itself against the dominant teams of Harvard, Princeton, and Yale, but the *Boston Herald* proclaimed the players to be "crude blacksmiths, miners, and backwoodsmen."[5] Throughout the 1890s, Michigan and the newly founded University of Chicago carried the midwestern banner against national foes to challenge eastern notions of cultural supremacy. The University of Chicago hired Amos Alonzo Stagg (1862–1965), a Yale All-American, as the first professional coach accorded faculty status at any American university. Stagg's salary surpassed that of the professors and initiated a national trend to recruit coaches and players to enhance a school's image and athletic status. Chicago's regional rival, the University of Michigan, soon hired Fielding Yost to direct its football fortunes. Yost produced "point a minute" offenses, overwhelming Stanford 49–0 in the first Rose Bowl in 1901. Michigan held its

Midwestern Style and Speed Against Eastern Mass Plays and Force

While eastern teams clung to mass plays and brute force to dominate opponents, midwestern teams played an "open" style that favored speed and featured end runs and deceptive reverses. A challenge match between Hyde Park High School of Chicago and Brooklyn's Polytechnic featured the contrasting styles of play. Both Stagg and Yost tutored the Chicago boys as the Brooklyn team traveled to the Midwest. Hyde Park devastated the New Yorkers 105-0, allowing their opponents only one first down. New York complained that the Brooklyn team was not its best and clamored for a rematch in the East the next year. Chicago sent its North Division High School to challenge the Brooklyn Boys' High School. Darkness forced an end to the game with the Chicagoans leading 75-0. The East reluctantly admitted to midwestern superiority at the interscholastic level, and coaches nationwide sought players from the Midwest. Within the region Chicago, Michigan, Wisconsin, and Northwestern vied in recruiting wars that offered ever increasing inducements to prized players. The intercity series promoted similar ventures on a national scale as interscholastic teams from the Midwest traveled to both coasts in search of games or hosted schools from other areas in contests for regional supremacy.

opponents scoreless that year while amassing 501 points, including a 128–0 rout of the University of Buffalo. The next year a Chicago high school squad established the ascendance of the Midwest.

The brutality of early football, however, begged for reform. Serious injuries and a mounting death toll resulted in bans at several colleges. At least a dozen deaths occurred in 1902. Two years later a survey recorded twenty-one deaths and more than 200 serious injuries. At least 18 deaths and 159 serious injuries occurred during the 1905 season; but only Northwestern University temporarily prohibited the game in the Midwest. By 1909, the figures had reached 30 killed and 216 injured. The National Collegiate Athletic Association, formed in 1905 to reform the game, allowed for some modification of the rules, easing prohibitions on the forward pass to open up the game. It remained for a midwestern team, St. Louis University, to demonstrate its ef-

Michigan–Ohio State Football Rivalry

The football rivalry between the University of Michigan and the Ohio State University began in 1897 and has lasted since 1900—so long that it has come to seem one of the greatest sports rivalries of the twentieth century. Since 1935, the antagonists have always met on the last Saturday of the regular season schedule. On such occasions the league championship has often been at stake, and victories by the underdog have regularly marred otherwise unbeaten seasons. In perhaps the most notable game ever played, both teams entered the 1973 fray undefeated. Ohio State was ranked #1 and Michigan #4. With a postseason Rose Bowl berth and chances for the national championship on the line, the teams played to a 10–10 tie. In a secret ballot vote by the athletic directors of the schools in the Big Ten Athletic Conference, Ohio State was picked to go to the Rose Bowl, where they beat USC 42–21. The raucous atmosphere of the competitions between Ohio State and Michigan is enhanced by the school bands, stirring halftime productions, and campus revelry. Huge, thunderous crowds always fill two of the biggest stadiums in America: both facilities seat more than 100,000. The mania of game day overflows the stadia as citizens of both states jockey for bragging rights. The result of the contest very often has national implications in the football wars.

fectiveness. St. Louis enjoyed an undefeated season in 1906 and led the nation in scoring. While teams in the West and South adopted the innovative style of the Midwest, eastern powerhouses remained mired in their mass plays. In 1913 Notre Dame, then a small Catholic school in Indiana, traveled to New York to face the West Point team, symbolic of eastern might. Knute Rockne (1888–1931), then a player on the Notre Dame squad, remarked that "We went out to play the Army . . . believing that we represented not only our school but the whole aspiring Middle West." Notre Dame employed the forward pass in a stunning 35–13 victory, firmly establishing the validity of the pass and a national reputation for Catholic football. The victory encouraged parochial schools to adopt the game and Notre Dame's style of play to defeat their Protestant foes. Such contests fostered greater inclusion of a previously insular and largely immigrant Catholic community in the mainstream secular culture.

The game particularly appealed to the working-class miners and steel workers of the Midwest. Professional football began in western Pennsylvania in 1892 when the Allegheny Athletic Association hired Pudge Heffelfinger, a former Yale All-American, to ensure its massive wagers with the Pittsburgh Athletic Club. Heffelfinger proved decisive, and professionalism soon spread to towns in eastern Ohio. Townspeople and civic boosters backed teams with significant wagers and sought advantages by hiring star players for a particular game, then eventually for the entire season. Athletes from numerous midwestern colleges found ready employment on Sundays on such teams in Ohio, Indiana, Illinois, and Wisconsin before the establishment of the National Football League in Canton, Ohio, in 1920.

Collegiate athletes also engaged in national and international ventures as baseball teams routinely barnstormed throughout the country. The University of Wisconsin went all the way to Japan for a series of games against Japanese schools in 1909. The University of Chicago followed in the next year and continued the series at five-year intervals thereafter. Japanese students attended midwestern colleges; one, Heita Okabe, even became a protégé of Coach Stagg at Chicago. He returned to become a coach of Japan's national teams, introducing his mentor's philosophy and methodologies to Asia.

Nineteenth-Century Commercialized Sport

Tours, sport spectacles, and gala events had already shaped midwestern recreational practices by the late nineteenth century. Chicago sporting goods entrepreneur Albert Spalding embarked on a worldwide tour with two professional baseball teams in 1888 to boost "America's game" and his own business interests. But Spalding's promotions failed to equal the social cachet of horseracing's American Derby, the midwestern equivalent of the Kentucky Derby, held at Chicago's Washington Park starting in 1884. Economist Thorstein Veblen characterized the meeting as an "ostentatious display" of wealth and social class: elite spectators sought to be seen, and newspapers obliged by reporting on the assembled plumage, high fashion, uniformed livery, and social recognition that established one's credentials in high society. Detailed descriptions of the crowd and its foremost socialites greatly surpassed reports of the race itself.

The less wealthy sought commercialized entertainment in public arenas that offered a variety of sports competitions. Indoor tracks provided for pedestrianism, long-distance walking races that tested endurance over a period of days. Individuals or partners alternated between bouts of activity and rest on trackside cots. Spectators might wander in to watch the races throughout the week or wait for the culminating race date. Pedestrianism soon developed into indoor track competitions and cycling races in which female participants even challenged male riders in feats of speed or endurance, although most females appeared as trick riders performing bicycle stunts in tights that attracted a large male audience. Roller skating at indoor sites provided less erotic thrills but enabled couples to court in public without formal chaperones.

By the late nineteenth century, bowling, often practiced in German saloons and turners' clubs, gained widespread acceptance in the mainstream middle class. Businessmen's leagues proliferated by the 1890s, and the American Bowling Congress (ABC) was established in 1895. Despite the ABC's New York origins, bowlers from the Midwest filled its administrative posts and remained a dominant influence in the organization for years. ABC standards for rules and equipment remained largely intact over the next century. Professional all-star teams barnstormed throughout the East and Midwest to promote the sport, sponsored by equipment manufacturers like the Brunswick Company. Brunswick moved beyond its Midwest clientele to become a nationally successful manufacturer for the saloon trade, specializing in elaborate bars, pool tables, and bowling equipment. Chicago and St. Louis were prominent in the ABC, and Chicago hosted the first national tournament in 1900, which included singles, doubles, and team championships. International tournaments included Canadian bowlers that same year. Intercity matches fueled regional and national rivalries and newspaper coverage. By 1905, Chicago claimed more than 30,000 bowlers. Female bowlers, who had labored under auxiliary status in the men's clubs, gained their own national tournament in 1907 and formed the Woman's [sic] International Bowling Congress in 1916.

Bowling offered numerous opportunities for gambling, an interest that crossed all class lines. When municipalities moved to ban horseracing because of the doping of horses and the influence of professional gambling interests, wealthy socialites turned to golf and their traditional aesthetic pastimes. Opera had long been an acquired taste of the educated who supported the construction of opera houses and theaters in the larger midwestern cities in the later nineteenth and early twentieth centuries. The Children's Educational Alliance, founded in New York in 1903, aimed to bring community theater to the masses, but the effort proved unsuccessful. The Drama League of America, established in 1910, managed to send theatrical productions to outlying areas. In 2003, Minneapolis offered the most theater seats of any city in the United States other than New York.

POPULAR CULTURE

Formal theater aside, staged performances included so-called freak shows and circuses. In the circuses, agents exhibited human oddities, such as bearded ladies, conjoined twins, or obese people to the fascinated gaze of onlookers. Freak shows might be included as part of traveling circuses that also displayed animal acts, acrobats, clowns, and assorted entertainers as well as games of chance.

Such entertainment attracted children as well as adults, but children found other pastimes as well. Manufacturers began producing toys in quantities after 1865. The earliest manufactured toys proved expensive, so most children improvised. Games of varying levels of organization often emphasized physical skills, mental abilities, or the reinforcement of adult roles. Typical games might include marbles, tag, hide and seek, or dramatic play with dolls. By the 1870s children adopted more active recreation like roller skating and winter sledding on manufactured apparatus. Technology assumed a recreational role during the twentieth century as photographic cameras, phonographs, and radios drew the attention of youths. Music and dancing attracted all genders, while boys gravitated toward electric trains, building blocks, and other construction materials. By the 1930s toy cars, miniature soldiers, radio programs, and comic books gained great popularity. A 1943 survey showed that 95 percent of all boys between the ages of six and eleven read comic books. By the 1950s, television began to take up significant amounts of children's time. Aggressive advertising promoted gender-specific toys, such as guns and G.I. Joes for boys and glamorous Barbie dolls for girls. Both television and movies marketed cowboys, military heroes, and other "action" figures throughout the remainder of the century. Electronic video games appeared in the 1970s to challenge toys as sedentary forms of recreation. Such games often promoted fantasies and drew criticism for their inherent violence.

Boys, in particular, continued to engage in the less controversial and long popular hobby of card collecting. Tobacco companies began producing baseball cards to accompany products as incentives for adult customers in the 1880s. By World War I, producers of gum and candy products offered cards to children. By the

1950s, baseball card collecting had become one of the top hobbies for American males. Football, basketball, and other popular sports also generated cardboard artifacts as the trading of cards mimicked larger capitalist markets. By the 1970s, adults held conventions to trade cards with speculative value, a kind of poor man's stock market.

Midwest Boys' and Girls' Organizations

Although clubs are generally associated with urban and suburban cultures, rural youth had their own. As increasing numbers departed the land for urban life after the turn of the twentieth century, concerned midwestern state administrators devised plans to retain rural residents. Illinois, Iowa, Indiana, and Ohio began offering cash prizes for the best corn. The success of such contests engendered similar trials for milk and other products of agricultural science. Such competitions fostered the formation of 4-H clubs in the Midwest, most often headed by female volunteer workers. Boys and girls maintained separate clubs until a merger in the 1960s. Girls' projects usually focused on arts and crafts or cooking, while boys produced crops and livestock for judgment at county and state fairs. The 4-H conducted an annual convention in Chicago and began exporting its programs to urban youth in that city in the 1960s. Representatives of 4-H delivered leadership, citizenship, health, and nutrition classes to public schools and residents of housing projects.

Another organization designed to build character and to bridge the urban and rural environments appeared in 1910 with the formation of the Boy Scouts of America. The Boy Scouts originated in Great Britain and favored a military approach through their uniforms, ranked status, camping, and the awarding of badges for outdoor skills and proficiencies. The YMCA soon allied with the movement and assumed control of its direction. Protestant churches and other religious groups who were attracted to its character-building tenets and inherent conservatism sponsored many troop units throughout the remainder of the century. Originally intended for boys ages from twelve to eighteen, the Boy Scouts formed a Cub Scouts program for younger boys in 1930. By the end of the century, membership in the Cub Scouts was double that of the Boy Scouts. The lack of female inclusion led to the formation of the Camp Fire Girls and the Girl Scouts. The preadolescent version of the Girl Scouts became known as the Brownies because of the distinctively colored uniforms. Girl Scouting also grew quickly. By the end of the century, the midwestern states of Michigan, Illinois, and Ohio had become leaders in the camping movement. Within urban locations many day care centers assumed the sobriquet of day camps that employed youthful instructors and supervisors to manage younger children while their parents worked.

Unsupervised children had long been a concern of urban administrators. During the Progressive Era, researchers recorded the pastimes of midwestern boys in cities such as Cleveland and Chicago. Many activities, like handball, stickball, and hopscotch, took place on city streets where children were often injured or caught up in delinquent behavior. Frederic Thrasher, a researcher in Chicago, counted more than 1300 gangs in that city by the early twentieth century. Many of the gangs had been organized under the guise of social-athletic clubs by politicians seeking support and offering patronage. "Basement clubs" engaged in card playing, gambling, and more nefarious entertainment without the guidance of adults. Children also flocked to the numerous storefront nickelodeons that proliferated in cities. In 1907, Chicago passed the first censorship law in the United States to combat pornography and images of nudity. While some children spent their time in ice cream parlors and soda fountains, many found refuge in neighborhood streets where myriad ethnic and racial groups contested for space.

Such youthful, territorial groups, often labeled gangs, posed particular challenges for urban administrators and law enforcement officials. The gangs attracted working-class boys and, increasingly, girls who had less social mobility than their middle-class counterparts. Gangs engaged in lucrative bootlegging during Prohibition, along with car theft and drug sales. Competition between rival gangs led to the spread of increasing levels of violence. Gang life adopted codes of distinctive clothing, colors, language, and hand signals assisted by glorification of gang culture in movies and music.

The Boys and Girls Clubs of America attempted to stem the growth of such groups by offering alternative activities in inner-city neighborhoods. Among the first such organizations, the National Newsboys' Association originated in Toledo, Ohio, as early as 1892 with the purpose of inculcating middle-class standards of decorum and capitalist enterprise. After World War II, the Boys and Girls' Clubs assumed a national presence but remained devoted to an inner city constituency, to whom it offered a variety of athletic programs and activities.

World's Fairs

The Midwest showcased American aspirations in a series of world's fairs beginning in 1893. At that time, the rapid growth and cultural ascendance of Chicago assured its place as the site for the Columbian Exposition over the protests of New York. The bluster of Chicago's supporters earned it the nickname of the "Windy City." Despite an economic depression, Chicago produced a magnificent fairgrounds designed by famed architect Daniel Burnham (1846–1912) and landscape architect Frederick Law Olmsted (1822–1903) that portrayed a grandeur and elegance in the "White City" that rivaled European imperial capitals and signaled a greater American role on the world stage. A Court of Honor surrounded a grand basin that extolled American achievements. The aesthetic expression of the fair organizers included cultural and technological exhibits as well as educational forums. Among the latter, Frederick Jackson Turner (1861–1932), then a professor at the University of Wisconsin, offered his treatise on the American frontier which claimed the exceptionalism of the American people.

The glamorous pretensions of high culture were balanced by American popular culture on the commercialized Midway. Sideshows and carnival barkers attracted the curious to Buffalo Bill's Wild West Show, the lascivious dancing of Little Egypt, and the great Ferris Wheel that transported forty people in each of the thirty-six giant cars above the fairgrounds.

The fantastic ride was disassembled and carted to St. Louis as that city hosted the World's Fair of 1904 to celebrate the centennial of the Louisiana Purchase. The St. Louis fair also hosted the Olympic Games, although few foreign competitors made the trek to challenge American athletes. The exposition gained a measure of notoriety for its inclusion of "Anthropology Days," an ongoing exhibit of American Indians, newly colonized Filipino tribes, and other international cultural groups—depicted as lower than white on the evolutionary scale.

The world's fair returned to Chicago in 1933 for that city's centennial, which it deemed "The Century of Progress." Befitting its title, Chicagoans emphasized science and technology, including the famous sky ride and modernistic architecture. Commercialized entertainment at such venues spawned a number of midwestern amusement parks that attracted millions over the course of the twentieth century. Riverview Park, located on the Chicago River, claimed to be the world's largest during its existence from 1904 to 1967. It featured attractions such as a parachute ride, seven roller coasters, sideshows, and a dark Tunnel of Love. The White City Park, also established in Chicago in 1906, offered jazz bands, two dance halls, rides, and a nighttime light show with a quarter million luminaries. It proclaimed itself the finest Beaux Arts Park in the entire nation. Chicago eventually transformed its Navy Pier into a similar entertainment complex that included a dance hall, a theater, restaurants, and an art gallery.

By the latter half of the twentieth century, amusement parks had followed the lead of California's Disneyland and transformed themselves into theme parks. The Great America park served both Chicago and Milwaukee, while Busch Gardens drew fans from St. Louis. Residents of Cleveland and the surrounding area traveled to Cedar Point in Sandusky, Ohio. Wisconsin Dells provided water parks for the summertime recreation of midwesterners. Valleyfair in Shakopee, Minnesota, is also typical of enterprises featuring rides, roller coasters, live entertainment, and fast-food services. The Mall of America in Bloomington, Minnesota, attracts a national patronage as the largest shopping and entertainment complex in the United States, with more than 500 stores, an indoor amusement park, nightclubs, and an aquarium. Each year the mall draws more visitors than the combined numbers at Disney World and the Grand Canyon.

MIDWEST SPORT IN THE TWENTIETH AND TWENTY-FIRST CENTURIES

Greater leisure led to demand for entertaining sports events that soon became highly professionalized and capitalized. Massive gate receipts in larger and larger stadia led to substantial profits. Newspapers routinely ran statistics, schedules, and reports on teams and athletes. Later, radio and television broadcast games and matches to regional and national audiences.

Sport as Spectacle

Large crowds have been attracted to sporting spectacles over the past century, many of them in the Midwest. The American League opened its baseball headquarters in Chicago in 1901. It offered a "moral alternative" to the National League brewery owners who used sport to peddle alcohol.

By the turn of the century boxing enjoyed similar prominence, fueled by Social Darwinian theories about race and ethnicity. Between 1908 and 1915, Jack Johnson (1878–1946), an African American, ruled the heavyweight boxing ranks and taunted white notions of superiority. In a reversal of acceptable roles, Johnson hired white servants and a white chauffeur. From his home in Chicago he flaunted

Fans at Jacobs Field, home of the Cleveland Indians. Courtesy Ohio Division of Travel and Tourism, www.DiscoverOhio.com.

his romantic associations with white women, fostering a search for the Great White Hope who might make amends. The former undefeated champion, Jim Jeffries, ended his retirement in 1910 in a bid to return the crown to white hands. State boxing bans forced the bout to be staged in the hot sun of Reno, Nevada, on the Fourth of July. More than 20,000 traveled to the desert, including more than 500 reporters, who recounted Johnson's convincing triumph in the first "fight of the century." Johnson, forced to flee the country for violating the Mann Act, which prohibited the transport of women across state lines for illegal purposes, finally lost his title to the giant Jess Willard in a mysterious bout in Havana, Cuba, in 1915.

By that time Chicago had produced a less controversial sports treasure. The Federal League surfaced as a third professional baseball league, and its Chicago entrant, the Whales, played at Weeghman Park The league soon failed, but the park remained, rechristened Wrigley Field for the owner of the new tenants, the Cubs. The Cubs introduced the Star Spangled Banner at the 1918 World Series, thirteen years before its adoption as the national anthem. The following year the crosstown White Sox engaged in baseball's greatest national scandal when players conspired with gamblers to purposely lose the World Series to their midwestern opponents, the Cincinnati Redlegs. As a consequence, many Chicagoans shifted their allegiance to the Cubs. The White Sox, though shadowed for years by the scandal, gradually reestablished themselves. Today Comiskey Park, their home for decades, is the U.S. Cingular Stadium, and die-hard White Sox fans, though hardly so passionate as the following earned by the Cubs, flock there in preference to the Cubs' Wrigley Field.

A year later Andrew "Rube" Foster, a Chicago resident, founded the Negro Na-

Chicago Cubs Fans

Fans of the Cubs have become a phenomenon unto themselves, despite—or perhaps because of—the woes of their favorite team over the last fifty years. The monumental collapse of the Cubs during the 1969 season fostered an ever-growing camaraderie among supporters, who hopefully exclaimed, "Wait 'til next year," and explained the foibles of their "lovable losers" as the machinations of the "Billy goat" curse—uttered by a disgruntled fan who was denied a ticket for his accompanying pet goat for a 1945 World Series game against the Detroit Tigers. He prophesied that the Cubs would never win another title. By the 1970s, ardent supporters known as the Bleacher Bums for their assigned meeting place gathered to heckle opponents, bask in sunshine and beer, and laud the ballpark and its players in a ritualized fashion. Opponents' home runs are immediately thrown back, even by the ballhawks who reside on the street outside the "friendly confines" of the stadium. Cub heroes receive a ceremonious bow of affection, matched by adoration for Wrigley Field itself, its aesthetic ivy-covered walls, and archaic, manually operated scoreboard. Fans revere the memory of the ebullient Hall of Famer Ernie Banks, whose love for the game initiated the cry "Let's play two" (games, as in a doubleheader). Harry Caray, the famed but flawed Cubs broadcaster, was enshrined in the pantheon of Cub heroes after he died in 1998. Steve Bartman, whose interference with a foul ball in the 2003 playoffs cost the Cubs a potential World Series appearance, conversely received death threats. While hopeful Cub fans take their team seriously and the most ardent forgo job and family responsibilities to attend games, frivolity reigns. Fans covet the rooftop seating of private homes outside the outfield walls, which serve as open-air beer parties. They have transformed the neighboring streets, known as Wrigleyville, into a succession of bars and summer festivals. The convivial atmosphere thus overshadows the plight of the team and results in sold-out games regardless of the quality of play.

tional League to provide opportunities for the African American baseball players banned from the segregated major leagues. The league showcased a number of outstanding midwestern teams, including the Chicago Giants, the Indianapolis ABCs, and the Kansas City Monarchs. Black baseball and basketball teams barnstormed throughout the country in the intervening years. The most famous basketball team began as the Savoy 5 in Chicago in 1927 but soon changed its name to the Harlem Globetrotters to reflect their pride in the renaissance of African American culture then taking place in that New York neighborhood. Another curious barnstorming team emanating from the Midwest revolved around a religious cult. The House of David settled in Benton Harbor, Michigan, and believed that it represented one of the lost tribes of Israel. Long-bearded, celibate vegetarians, the group promoted its views in an attempt to gain followers through its traveling athletic teams.

The Midwest did not lack athletic phenomena. In 1924 Harold "Red" Grange captivated football crowds at the University of Illinois. At the inaugural game in Champaign's Memorial Stadium he garnered four touchdowns in the first twelve minutes of the game against the University of Michigan. After the season, Grange turned professional by signing a contract with the Chicago Bears, thus initiating the still common practice of college athletes forgoing their education to accept commercial contracts. The Bears quickly capitalized on Grange's fame by embarking on a whirlwind national tour. In New York 70,000 showed up to witness Grange's abilities, giving instant credibility to the fledgling pro football circuit. Grange and his agent, C. C. Pyle, then formed their own short-lived American Football League. Grange's celebrity foreshadowed the creation of the modern athletic media star.

Although Grange personified individual greatness, the Notre Dame football team exemplified a more communal approach in its Four Horsemen during the 1924 season. Representing a small Catholic school from South Bend, Indiana, the team enjoyed an undefeated season under the guidance of a Norwegian immigrant, Coach Knute Rockne. The synchronized backfield won All-American honors, brought prestige to the institution, and gained an invitation to the Rose Bowl, where it defeated Stanford University. Ethnic Catholics adopted the team as their own.

Catholics found increasing involvement in the secular world through sport. Johnny Weissmuller, a Catholic swimming champion, found sponsorship with the Illinois Athletic Club in 1922. He soon became an Olympic champion and a star of *Tarzan* movies. Sybil Bauer, another member of the Illinois Athletic Club, surpassed the men's national backstroke record and gained Olympic gold. Annette Rogers, another Catholic athlete, competed on a women's club track team by the age of fourteen and won a gold medal at the 1932 Olympics. The gymnasts of the Czech sokol clubs won similar honors for the United States, and the recruitment of such working-class athletes produced heroes that bridged ethnic and class divisions as it enhanced the perception of sport as a meritocracy.

The 1920s, labeled the Golden Age of Sport, mounted one of its greatest spectacles in the Midwest when Jack Dempsey faced Gene Tunney for the heavyweight championship in Chicago in 1927. The 1920 census indicated that urban dwellers surpassed rural residents for the first time. The two fighters represented the dichotomy of social classes and the urban–rural divide. Dempsey, a brawling, rough-hewn miner from Colorado, had escaped service in World War I, while Tunney, a marine officer, educated gentleman, piano player, and familiar figure on the social scene, carried the banner of the urban middle-class. Tunney had won a 1926 bout with the working-class hero, yet 120,000 filled Chicago's Soldier Field for the much anticipated rematch. They were not disappointed: Tunney won one of the most controversial victories in boxing history when the referee failed to administer the count over the fallen Tunney until Dempsey returned to a neutral corner after the knockdown. The delay saved Tunney from defeat.

Depression Era Recreation

American lifestyles took a dramatic turn in the 1920s as the Jazz Age brought youthful rebellion following the horrors of World War I. Radio quickly became the most popular form of entertainment; many families had a set by the end of the decade. Despite the ban on alcohol, nightclubs and dance halls proliferated. In urban centers the so-called taxi dance halls offered males female companionship for a dime a dance. Moralists charged that such enterprises fostered vice. Others worried about the nature of the dances, which included the sexy shimmy and acrobatic moves. Chicago boasted the Trianon, constructed in 1922 at a cost of $1,500,000, as the most luxurious public dance hall in the United States. Great jazz musicians in the black and tan cabarets brought both white and black patrons to African American neighborhoods. Such interracial contact slowly dispelled the racial segregation of entertainment sectors. Chicago, Kansas City, and St. Louis offered local varieties of jazz and the blues as black southern migrants increasingly took up residence in northern cities.

In addition to music, better technology produced widespread interest in the movies. Silent films gave way to "talkies," and city residents as well as small-town dwellers flocked to movie theaters. In the roaring economy of the 1920s, urban movie theaters took on the appearance of palatial estates where ticket holders engaged their fantasies both on and off the screen.

With the onset of the Depression, recreation assumed some new and even eccentric forms, such as the dance marathon fad. Dance marathons, an import from New York, began in 1928 in the Midwest offering free meals and cash prizes to participants who stayed mobile for the longest period of time. Contests stretched into days, weeks, and months as newspapers covered weary dancers who struggled to outlast the other competitors. Six-day bicycle races followed a similar format, with coed teams circling an indoor track. Roller derbies followed along the same lines with coed teams striving for endurance records in indoor arenas. Roller derbies evolved into a team sport that featured fast skaters, physical contact, and occasional scuffles between opponents as players tried to pass each other on laps of the rink to score points for the team. Spectators paid to watch the struggling performers vie for prizes.

Others turned to more sedentary forms of leisure, such as card games or pinball machines which allowed participants to gamble with each other. Bingo became a staple at fairs, carnivals, and churches, which used them to raise funds. Bingo games were simple: players hoped to cover a preprinted card of various numbers that were randomly selected from a spinning hopper and called out by an announcer. Participants might buy and play multiple cards at one time, hoping to win prizes or cash.

Table tennis, or ping-pong, provided more active recreation as yet another 1930s fad. The game had originated in the 1880s as a miniature version of tennis played on a table, and it enjoyed bouts of recurring popularity thereafter as a parlor game. By 1931, the game assumed a more competitive nature with the formation of the American Ping-Pong Association, an organization founded by Parker Brothers, a manufacturer of board games. Millions of Americans bought such tables for their home amusement, and by 1938 the ping-pong organizers merged with a rival faction to create the U.S. Table Tennis Association to promote competition.

For less affluent boys boxing provided not only a means to test their courage and toughness, but also an opportunity for recognition and remuneration. City dwellers had long battled ethnic and racial rivals for control of neighborhood streets and parks before the *Chicago Tribune* successfully challenged the Illinois ban on boxing in 1924. Legalization of the sport enabled the *Tribune* to organize the 1928 Golden Gloves tournaments. Here fighters vied for local, regional, and national honors. The national competition involved challenge matches against counterparts from New York. The widespread popularity of boxing led to tournament sponsorship by local affiliates of religious organizations such as the Knights of Columbus, the Catholic Youth Organization (CYO), and the B'nai B'rith Youth Organization (BBYO). Thousands of youths competed in boxing tournaments each year for prizes and medals, which many pawned for cash in the hard economic times.

Arch Ward (1896–1955), the Catholic sports editor of the *Tribune*, worked closely with the Catholic Church to recruit fighters from the CYO program and to stage other athletic spectacles. National broadcasts and international boxing ventures against European teams brought stardom to previously unknown street kids and high school dropouts. Among the boxers who emerged from the Golden

Gloves tournaments was Joe Louis from Detroit who proceeded to international fame and the world championship.

In the CYO program even boxers who did not achieve such gloried status earned significant rewards. CYO champions won college scholarships, suits of clothes, and international trips. For those who decided to turn professional, the CYO offered management services to avoid the pitfalls of nefarious agents. The CYO athletic program, founded by Chicago Bishop Bernard J. Sheil (1888–1969), showcased boxing amid a comprehensive array of sports for both boys and girls. Its basketball league of 1931 claimed to be the largest in the world, with 415 teams. Swimming and track meets soon followed as Bishop Sheil extended his program beyond Chicago to the entire Midwest and eventually to the nation. It included both Catholics, largely from ethnic parishes, and non-Catholics, with close ties to the BBYO. Sport thus fostered the amalgamation of previously marginalized groups into the mainstream culture.

Under Ward's direction, the *Tribune* sponsored several other sporting spectacles that brought fame and profit to the newspaper during the Depression. In 1933, the *Tribune* initiated the first major league All Star baseball game at Comiskey Park, soon followed by the Negro Leagues All Star game in the same locale. The next year Soldier Field hosted the first College All Star Football Game, an annual classic in which collegians took on the reigning NFL champions. The *Tribune* also launched the Silver Skates Derby, a winter competition that boosted its readership. Other newspapers in Chicago and throughout the Midwest offered similar events, with ice skating competitions gaining particular favor in Wisconsin and Minnesota.

Other organizations offered regional and, eventually, national competition in a variety of sports. American Legion baseball, founded in 1925, fielded more than 5000 teams by 1999. Little League baseball followed in 1939 and reached international levels within a generation. The Pop Warner football program originated in 1929, and the Midwest subsequently produced a number of national championship teams.

At the intercollegiate level, basketball gained immense popularity, particularly for women. They began play at Smith College shortly after invention of the game at the YMCA training school in Springfield, Massachusetts in 1881. By 1893, women in Chicago and female students at Carleton College in Minnesota and at Iowa State College had taken up the game. By 1900, the women's game had spread throughout the state of Iowa, overshadowing the male version. Educators, concerned about the debilitating effects of running and jumping on female bodies, adapted modified rules for girls' play that limited exertion by dividing the court into two or three zones. Teams consisted of five to nine players who were restricted to operating within their own zones. Iowa eventually adopted a two-zone system with six players, three on each side of the

Shifting Collegiate Rivalries

Perhaps because girls' basketball overshadowed boys' basketball, Iowa boys turned to wrestling. The University of Iowa and Iowa State University produced numerous national championship teams throughout the twentieth century. Whereas the universities of Michigan and Chicago had carried midwestern laurels in football during the early part of the century, Minnesota assumed the regional honors during the 1930s. The award passed to Indiana as Notre Dame consistently gained the most national championships of the modern era.

court. Players became offensive or defensive specialists, and Iowa girls often led the nation in scoring.

The Beginnings of Sports for Girls and Women

A state basketball tournament for girls was set up in Iowa in 1920 with twenty-four initial entrants. Six years later, 159 schools fielded girls' teams, and by the 1950s, 70 percent of high school girls in the state competed on basketball teams. In 1985, the state provided the option of playing by boys' rules with five players on a full court, thus eliminating zone play. Tradition prevailed, however, as most schools opted for the divided court, necessitating separate state championships for the differing styles of play into the 1990s.

The enthusiasm for girls' basketball in Iowa historically superseded the interest in the boys' teams. During the World War II era, the girls attracted a million spectators to their games during the basketball season. Another 225,000 fans attended the championship tournament. Television coverage began in 1951, yet more than 15,000 showed up for a single game that year. By the start of the twenty-first century, every high school in Iowa fielded a girls' basketball team; attendance surpassed that for the state's collegiate teams.

While other states in the union minimized opportunities for girls and women throughout much of the century, Iowa held fast, even before Title IX legislation (1972) forced institutions to reapportion funding for women's athletics to reflect population ratios. Female Iowans continued to play basketball on college and industrial teams after their high school careers. Industrial teams offered employment and travel opportunities, as well as a sense of pride and public recognition not readily available to most women during the era. At least 20 percent of the Amateur Athletic Union first team All Americans between 1940 and 1960 came from Iowa. With the passage of Title IX increasing athletic opportunities for women students and the demise of corporate sport programs, athletic endeavors for women shifted to the collegiate level, for which Iowa players were sought out by coaches.

The Amateur Athletic Union began its national basketball tournament for women in 1926 in Wichita, Kansas. After 1939, St. Joseph, Missouri, hosted the competition. Most of the women's teams represented businesses in the Midwest and the South; the newspaper coverage of winners provided free publicity for the employers.

While many educators throughout the United States decried females' participation in athletics as physically and psychologically harmful, some midwestern women fought the dilution of women's programs. At Ohio State University, Gladys Palmer, a physical education teacher, formed a women's intercollegiate athletic association in 1941, and Ohio State sponsored the first women's intercollegiate golf tournament that year. Other competitive events for college women grew slowly thereafter.

Early African American Participation in Midwest Sports

Most other sports enjoyed extensive support throughout the region. Even small towns and villages fielded baseball teams. At the University of Chicago, famed coach Amos Alonzo Stagg instituted a national invitational basketball tournament for high school teams starting in 1918. The contest heralded the unofficial national champions but neglected to invite Catholic and African American teams. In response, Loyola University of Chicago offered its own National Catholic Interscholastic Tournament, which began in 1925. African American teams representing the segregated public schools began to break down racial barriers with their play in city and state tournaments in the Midwest. Some of the Chicago players graduated to positions on the famous Globetrotters teams in the 1930s, while the success of black teams in Indianapolis, a breeding ground for high school players, helped to erode Indiana racism, fomented by the state's anachronistic Ku Klux Klan.

Generally more liberal than the South, the Midwest usually provided a safer haven for African American players. For example, George Jewett starred for both Michigan and Northwestern in the 1890s, and Charles Follis played professionally for the Shelby, Ohio, team from 1904 to 1906. Branch Rickey (1881–1965), Follis' college roommate and later the general manager of the Brooklyn Dodgers, brought Jackie Robinson (1919–1972) from the Kansas City Monarchs baseball team to the National League in 1947, thus desegregating the national pastime. At Minnesota Bob Marshall won All American honors in 1905 and 1906 before embarking on a professional football career that lasted more than twenty years. Fritz Pollard (1894–1986), a native Chicagoan, became a national hero in the African American community as an All American at Brown University, the first black to appear in the Rose Bowl in 1916, the first of his race to play quarterback in the National Football League, and the first African American head coach (with the Akron Pros in 1919) in the professional ranks. Jack Trice, the first black athlete at Iowa State, did not fare as well. He died after suffering injuries in a 1923 game with Minnesota. Fred "Duke" Slater, however, enjoyed a stellar performance at the University of Iowa and an All Pro term with the Chicago Cardinals before advancing to a career as a judge in Chicago. Such sport opportunities in the Midwest provided entrees into other professional fields and slowly began to dismantle entrenched racist attitudes.

Some midwestern African American athletes became national heroes. Jesse Owens (1913–1980), a Cleveland resident, set four world records in the course of about an hour as a student at Ohio State. He then won four gold medals at the Berlin Olympics of 1936, destroying Hitler's myth of Aryan supremacy. Joe Louis (1914–1981), a Detroit boxer, seemed invincible in his quest for the heavyweight championship until knocked out by the German champ, Max Schmeling, in 1936. Louis avenged his loss by destroying Schmeling in the first round of their 1938 rematch. Louis held the world title until 1949; his character as well as his boxing skills won both black and white fans.

Religious and Class Divisions in Sports of the 1930s–1950s

Sport practices altered not only racial but also religious perspectives. Catholics, somewhat marginalized and isolated from mainstream American society in ethnic parishes often governed by Old World pastors, found greater inclusion in sport. In Chicago the Catholic League football champions challenged their presumably Protestant counterparts from the public league for the city championship in 1927. By 1936 the Catholics joined with the public schools to initiate an annual championship game. The 1937 championship game drew 120,000 fans to Soldier Field, the largest crowd ever to see a football game in the United States, a figure that surpassed later Super Bowl totals. Shortly thereafter, the religious adversaries merged in an all-star team, representing the Midwest in contests against West Coast opponents.

As the economic downturn of the Depression curtailed many industrial recreation programs, labor unions sought to use sport as a way to solidify their ranks. The Amalgamated Clothing and Textile Workers Union, with more than 16,000 members in Chicago alone, had its own gym, handball courts, exercise room, boxing and wrestling facilities, bowling alleys, and billiard tables. The Chicago Association of Street, Railway and Motor Coach Employees Union opened a $1 million building with recreational amenities for its workers as well. Many unions throughout the Midwest sponsored teams in bowling, basketball, volleyball, and softball for both men and women as the union halls became social centers.

Softball, in particular, provided practical alternatives to work in the 1930s. More than club or neighborhood pride would be at stake in tournaments or local clashes. Some competitions offered $1,500 in prize money, and even boys earned $10 or $20 each for victories in neighborhood leagues run by small-time gamblers and local taverns. Politicians and bar owners sponsored teams at no cost to the players, and the underground economy kept money circulating within the local community.

Bowling provided similar opportunities, with cash prizes and jewelry offered to tournament winners. The national women's tournament in 1935, held in Chicago, awarded more than $15,000 in prize money. The indoor nature of the sport held particular attraction for women, and more than 15,000 Chicagoans alone held membership in the Woman's International Bowling Congress (WIBC). By 1938, there were 900 bowling leagues, 9000 teams, and 500,000 bowlers in that city. Midwestern women dominated national bowling championships for nearly fifty years.

To help alleviate the effects of the Depression and unemployment, the government instituted programs to influence recreational practices. The Civilian Conservation Corps (CCC), established in 1933, provided employment, for more than 500,000 young men by 1935. Under the direction of the army, the men lived mostly in rural camps while they engaged in public works projects, many of them in the Midwest. The CCC built shelters, stocked rivers and lakes with fish, tended historic sites, cleaned up campgrounds and beaches, and planted trees to address erosion and losses from wildfires and lumbering. Midwesterners enjoyed the recreational benefits of their labors for generations afterward.

Midwestern communities found in sport the means to gain national recognition and commercial reward. Boys' tennis tournaments, traditionally held in the East since the late nineteenth century, accepted a Midwest venue in 1943. Kalamazoo College in Michigan hosted the national tournament for boys aged sixteen to eighteen and soon built a lighted stadium for that purpose. More than 3000 spectators often witnessed finals matches, and community support earned Kalamazoo permanent site status. Fans have seen many stars play there before moving to the professional circuit.

In Cincinnati, electric lighting was first used by the Cincinnati Reds for night baseball games in 1935 to improve attendance. Mindful of the success of this strategy, midwestern barnstorming teams started carrying portable lights that could be attached to cranes mounted on truck beds. Cincinnati was also the first team to televise a baseball game—a 1939 contest with the Brooklyn Dodgers.

Midwestern Sports and Television

By the 1940s, national media began to transform the nature of sporting events. Weekly televised boxing events, known as the "Friday night fights," brought pugilistic encounters to millions of Americans' homes and a national audience to razor-manufacturer Gillette, the sponsor. Other businesses soon realized the potential of sport as a sales mechanism. Boxers profited handsomely, earning about $4,000 per fight—a year's salary for many workers. On the negative side, profits drew unsavory promoters, and televised bouts undermined spectatorship at local arenas. Widespread corruption brought federal investigations by the 1950s. Boxing interest revived in the 1960s with the ascent of the charismatic Muhammad Ali (born Cassius Clay in Louisville), who looked brilliant on television.

Telecasts of major league baseball games doomed myriad minor league franchises in the 1950s. Of the fifty-one minor leagues operating in 1949, only twenty remained by 1970. College baseball teams now began to supplant the minor leagues as a source for major league talent. Television also directly affected the revenues of big league teams, and teams soon sought more lucrative markets, some in the Midwest. In 1953, the Boston Braves left the East for a new home in Milwaukee. A decade later they moved yet again—to rapidly growing Atlanta in 1964. The St. Louis Browns opted for Baltimore in 1954, and the Philadelphia Athletics arrived in Kansas City the next year. Minnesota eventually gained a franchise known as the Twins. Even so, large-market eastern teams generated more revenue, allowing them to buy more of the better players, and they generally dominated the weaker teams. Between 1950 and 1980, the New York Yankees won sixteen American League pennants, while the Brooklyn/Los Angeles Dodgers took eleven titles in the National League. The owners' unwillingness to share their revenues continued to hamper the game throughout the remainder of the twentieth century. As a result, professional football surpassed baseball in popularity.

Concerns over the stability of baseball produced an alternative phenomenon in the Midwest as early as the 1940s. As many players joined the military in World War II, the talent level of teams suffered. Fearing a loss of patronage and the possible cancellation of baseball during the war, Philip K. Wrigley (1894–1977), owner of the Chicago Cubs, concocted a scheme for a women's league. The All American Girls Baseball League opened play in 1943 and lasted until 1954 with teams in as many as ten midwestern cities in Illinois, Wisconsin, Indiana, Michigan, and Minnesota. Careful to promote a proper image, the league required chaperones for each team, and players had to attend etiquette and beauty classes. They competed in skirts that provided no protection to players sliding into a base. Despite the hardships, the women displayed exceptional skill and drew more than a million fans in 1948. Those pioneers starkly contrasted with the popular television images of women as happy homemakers.

The Midwest also took a leading role in the resurgence of professional basketball. A national professional league had operated from 1925 to 1931 with teams from Boston to Chicago, coming to an end with the Depression. By 1936, a midwest league was established featuring several industrial teams in Ohio and town teams elsewhere in the region. In 1937 the association reorganized as the National Basketball League (NBL) with squads in Ohio, Indiana, Illinois, Wisconsin, Pennsylvania, and New York. Although not a league member, the New York Rens, a famous African American unit, barnstormed through the Midwest to compete with NBL teams. In 1946 teams in Chicago, St. Louis, Cleveland, and Detroit joined eastern contingents in an urban-based Basketball Association of America (BAA). The NBL and the BAA merged in 1949 to form the National Basketball Association. The emergence of George Mikan, a 6' 10" center for the Minneapolis Lakers, and the hiring of star black players transformed basketball, producing a commercial bonanza by the end of the century.

OUTDOOR RECREATION IN THE MIDWEST

The geography of the Midwest lends itself to outdoor pursuits. Thousands of lakes, rivers, and streams allow swimming, fishing, and boating. Minnesota claims more than 12,000 lakes; the southeastern portion of the state provides 600 miles of trout streams alone, while the northern part offers fly-fishing. During the winter, ice fishing is an obsession throughout the region, with numerous practitioners in Michigan, Minnesota, Wisconsin, and Illinois. Peoria, Illinois, hosts a national bass fishing tournament.

In addition to fishing, the waterways supply ample opportunities for snorkeling, scuba diving, and boating. The annual yacht race from Chicago to Mackinac, Michigan, is a highlight of the summer season in the Midwest. The Boundary Waters

area of northern Minnesota is considered among the best canoeing spots in the United States, but all of the midwestern states offer navigable waterways and numerous paddling clubs for enthusiasts. Kayakers practice in both urban and rural locales, but the north shore of Lake Superior outlines a designated trail and Voyageurs National Park in Minnesota extends possibilities. Houseboats are easily accommodated on lakes and larger rivers, while the more adventurous can pursue whitewater rafting on the St. Louis River in Minnesota or in the Ozarks region of Missouri. Companies in Minneapolis-St. Paul, St. Louis, and Cincinnati all provide steamboat cruises on the Mississippi River. Sheboygan, Wisconsin, located on Lake Michigan, even offers a surfing venue in the Midwest.

In addition to aquatic activities, the Midwest furnishes excellent terrain for numerous other pastimes. In each state, hikers enjoy forest preserves, state parks, and nature trails. Regional favorites include the Indiana Dunes, Isle Royale (MI) National Park in Lake Superior, the Lake Superior Hiking Trail in Minnesota, Yellow River State Forest in northeast Iowa, the Missouri Ozarks, Lake Maria State Park near Minneapolis, the Ice Age Trail in Wisconsin, and Starved Rock State Park in Illinois, which boasts eighteen canyons. Hikers can backpack or camp in designated park camp sites.

Competitive hikers engage in the sport of orienteering, a race that requires navigational skill and problem-solving abil-

Mountain bikers enjoy the rugged trails in the Midwest. Courtesy Ohio Division of Travel and Tourism, www.DiscoverOhio.com.

ities. The Midwest has several orienteering clubs, some of which conduct their races on horseback, while others organize rogaines, extended events that may last a full twenty-four hours and involve teams of two to five people. Adventure races usually involve multiple sport skills over varied terrain, such as running, cycling, rappelling, canoeing, kayaking, or swimming. Races conducted year round may include cross-country skiing, snowshoeing, or other winter sports. Although usually set in remote areas of Wisconsin or the Ke-

Midwesterners Lead in Outdoor Recreation

A 1997 national Roper survey of outdoor recreation in the United States proclaimed the Midwest the leader among all regions in that respect, with 67 percent of its residents participating on a monthly basis. Among the most popular activities were walking, swimming, fishing, hiking, cycling, wildlife viewing, and golf. Iowa, Michigan, Minnesota, and Wisconsin were among the leading golf states based on per capita income, equipment purchases, and the number of high school teams.[6] Golf course design has become an increasing element of residential community development in the Midwest.

weenaw Peninsula in Michigan, orienteering for urbanites in Chicago and Indianapolis requires the climbing of buildings and the traversing of sewer systems.

Minnesota and Wisconsin locations attract rock climbers, and Minnesota has constructed 450 miles of scenic bike trails as well. Both the Superior and Chippewa National Forests accommodate mountain bikes. Missouri provides a unique opportunity for spelunking in more than 5,000 caves. Some caves are easily accessible by paved walkways, while most are still labeled wild in nature. Underground enticements are complemented by aerial diversions, as midwesterners take to the skies in airplanes, gliders, and hot air balloons. The more daring attempt skydiving and bungee jumping.

Winter Sports

The climate of the Midwest lends itself equally well to winter activities. The Upper Peninsula of Michigan gets 300 inches of snow per year, which is ideal for skiing, snowshoeing, snowmobiling, and dogsled racing. The Mackinaw Mush claims to be the largest dogsled race in North America, though the U.P. 200 is another well-known event. The area is also known for the Grand Prix on Ice, a snowmobile race across the Bay of Huron. Snowmobiles were invented in Minnesota, a state that supplies 15,000 miles of trails for their use. Michigan's Upper Peninsula offers another 500 miles of snowmobile trails. Avid snowmobilers can be found in any of the midwestern states throughout the winter months, however. Minnesotans

Midwesterners take to the skies in airplanes, gliders, and hot-air balloons. Courtesy Travel Michigan.

501

Many resorts in the Midwest featurer alpine skiing, snowboarding, and snow tubing, as well as action on mogul runs and cross-country trails. Courtesy Ohio Division of Travel and Tourism, www.DiscoverOhio.com.

also enjoy dogsled racing and skiing. Minnesota claims the highest and largest ski areas in the Midwest, although the Pine Mountain Ski Jump in Michigan is the site of World Cup competition. Built in 1938 by the WPA, Pine Mountain held its first event the following year. Expansion of the facility has increased the run to more than 1000 feet, allowing jumpers to achieve a speed of 55 miles per hour. Among more than a dozen locations that offer midwestern sites for ski jumping are Duluth, St. Paul, and the Coleraine Club of Minnesota; the Norge Club in Fox River Grove, Illinois; Eau Claire, Madison, and Minocqua, Wisconsin; and Ishpeming, Michigan. Many other resorts use snowmaking equipment to groom hills for alpine and mogul skiing, snowboarding, and snow tubing to supplement cross-country trails. Sledding and toboggan slides are found in selected state parks and forest preserve areas throughout the Midwest.

Among the oldest of winter sports, ice skating can be practiced on any winter pond or lake, though park districts flood selected areas or unused ballfields in the winter for the same purpose. Scandinavian immigrants fostered speed skating contests throughout the Midwest, and by the early twentieth century newspapers sponsored local tournaments. The Pettit National Olympic Training Center for elite speed skaters, located in Milwaukee, Wisconsin, attests to the popularity of the sport in the Midwest.

Ice hockey is nearly as old as skating and is widely practiced throughout the region. Minnesota and Michigan are particular spawning grounds for top players, and their universities are often strong contenders for national honors. Youth club teams proliferate throughout the Midwest, including more than eighty girls' teams in 2000. Other traditional winter sports, like curling, have adherents in the area with regular bonspiels (tournaments) in Minnesota and Wisconsin. Sleigh riding, too, can still be seen in some rural areas, particularly during the Christmas season.

Skating is available year-round at indoor rinks, but rollerblading can also be found on city streets and pathways. Municipalities have constructed skating parks for skateboarders, who engage in competitive events and acrobatic feats. Others, like the winter skaters, have transformed the activity into game forms, such as roller hockey or roller soccer played on community streets or in organized leagues in park districts.

Skateboarding, in particular, represents a sense of youthful rebelliousness in a subculture that incorporates clothing and hairstyles along with a distinct vocabulary borrowed from surfers of Southern California. Manufactured skateboards appeared by the late 1950s, and the sport grew quickly. In 1965, a televised national championship took place in California. Physicians' concerns over injuries and municipal bans on skateboarding only piqued the interests of recalcitrant youth. The "sidewalk surfers" soon began experimenting in pipelines and empty swimming pools, creating new tricks and aerial maneuvers. Skateboard parks opened in Florida and California in 1976, and eventually the phenomenon reached the Midwest. The movement has since been coopted by commercial sponsors, who televise events in international competitions and promote them in specialized magazines and products. Skatopia in Rutland, Ohio, serves as a skateboarding museum.

Auto Racing

Carl Fisher first proposed the Indianapolis Motor Speedway in 1906, and a corporation was formed for that purpose in 1909. A five-mile race occurred later that year but with disastrous results that cost six lives. The Indianapolis 500 Motor Race, first run in 1911, eventually became the highlight of the racing season. The Speedway Hall of Fame and Racing Museum opened in 1976. In 1994, the Brickyard 400 event initiated NASCAR racing at the speedway. Disputes between the racers led to the formation of an alternative association known as the Championship Auto Racing Team (CART) in 1978. By 1996, CART offered the U.S. 500 at the Michigan International Speedway as a Memorial Day option to the Indianapolis 500. In 2000 the Indianapolis locale began offering United States Grand Prix Formula One racing.

Hunting, Exploring, and Other Leisure Pursuits

Less mechanized, traditional frontier sports still retain their appeal in the Midwest. Avid hunters patrol prairies and woodlands in search of fowl and deer. The Missouri Ozarks offer a more varied terrain, whereas bow hunters especially favor Michigan. In Missouri, patrons flock to rodeos and an elk ranch. For the more aesthetically inclined, the Midwest harbors a wide range of species for birdwatchers. More than a hundred types of songbirds inhabit the territory during the summer months, and eagles, spending their winter along the Mississippi River, can be seen from viewing points in Missouri, Iowa, Illinois, Wisconsin, and Minnesota. The Superior National Forest in Minnesota shelters another 155 species. Loons are so plentiful that Minnesotans claim the species as their state bird. The Detroit Lakes region of the state counts another 250 varieties. Raptors such as hawks, as well as geese and swans, can be found throughout the Midwest. Blue herons nest in Missouri, and pelicans and cormorants migrate through that state. Among the most distinctive animals and among the most difficult to view in the wild are wolves. The International Wolf Center is located in Ely, Minnesota, a state with one of the largest populations of the predators. Near Peoria, Illinois, the Wildlife Prairie State Park allows visitors to see wolves, bison, elk, bears, and cougars.

Motor Sports

Other thrill-seekers pursue their recreation with motorized vehicles. On summer nights many towns schedule custom car shows that revel in nostalgia and music from a bygone era. Nearly all midwestern states provide facilities for motor sports, such as dirt tracks for motorcross racing, or drag racing for both cars and motorcycles. Sheboygan, Wisconsin, accommodates stock car racers, while motorcycle ice racing takes place in Michigan. The Motorcycle Hall of Fame is located in Pickerington, Ohio.

Photographers trek to such natural areas for exquisite shots of flora and fauna. Families with young children generally encounter such natural fascinations on trips to urban zoos and gardens. Many find relaxation in tending to their own gardens or in pursuing more sedentary pastimes such as reading, sewing, crafts, or other assorted hobbies. Weekly card parties provide socialization for many and gambling opportunities for others.

For gamblers, riverboat casinos have become weekend and, in some cases, nightly haunts. Imitating the flashy environment of Las Vegas, the casinos entice customers with meals, entertainment, slot machines, and a variety of card and dice games of chance.

A similar cornucopia of interests attracts children to arcades with pin ball machines, video games, and sports challenges. Some include baseball batting cages, miniature golf courses, and go kart tracks. Larger amusement centers have roller coasters or water parks. One center in Sheboygan, Wisconsin, reenacts the famous Buffalo Bill Wild West Show. Still one of the major interests, movie theaters continue to attract the young and the old to ever larger complexes that offer multiple screens and an arcade setting.

Theme Parks, Festivals, and Sports Museums

At least one-third of midwesterners supplement local recreation with travel on annual vacations. Among the locations of regional interest for families are the major amusement parks: Six Flags in St. Louis, Missouri, and Gurnee, Illinois; King's Island in Ohio; and Indiana Beach in Monticello, Indiana.[7]

Small towns and large urban areas attract visitors with festivals that honor ethnic heritage and particular historical events. Indians conduct state powwows that educate sightseers about indigenous culture, food, dance, customs, and crafts. The Amana colonies in Iowa, a national historic landmark, serve a similar function. Dyersville, Iowa, sports the Field of Dreams of movie fame. Hannibal, Missouri, capitalizes on the Mark Twain Museum, while across the state St. Joseph promotes the home of the outlaw Jesse James and the Pony Express Museum. Iowa, Illinois, Missouri, Indiana, and Ohio publicize their presidential centers, and sports-related institutions beckon a variety of enthusiasts. St. Louis

Among the locations of regional interest for families are the major amusement parks. Courtesy Ohio Division of Travel and Tourism, www.DiscoverOhio.com.

hosts the Bowling Hall of Fame, and Canton, Ohio, the Pro Football Hall of Fame. Its college counterpart as well as the Studebaker National Museum exists in South Bend, Indiana. The U.S. National Ski Hall of Fame and Museum is housed in Ishpeming, Michigan. Kansas City prides itself on its Negro Leagues Baseball Museum.

Missouri draws a variety of music lovers to the annual bluegrass festival in Branson, the blues and jazz festival in Kansas City, and the ragtime festival in Sedalia. Cleveland's Rock and Roll Hall of Fame is well known, as is the Kansas City American Jazz Museum.

Aficionados of the good life sample the products of the many midwestern wineries, but an increasingly sedentary lifestyle has contributed to an epidemic of obesity and cardiovascular disease. A movement aimed at correcting such maladies has generated a rash of fitness clubs and competitive events. Yoga, aerobics, and cardiovascular training draw paying customers for businesses and personal trainers, while weight lifting programs are designed to strengthen the bodies of school age children and adults, as well as combat osteoporosis in the elderly. Practitioners of racket sports like tennis, badminton, racquetball, and pickleball find ready exercise in local clubs. Thousands sign up for endurance races and triathlon competitions. Major marathons draw tens of thousands in the Midwest.

For the somewhat less vigorous, the Midwest is home to two teams in the Women's Professional Softball League. Seniors aged fifty to more than seventy can still compete in the six divisions of the Midwest Senior Softball Club. Local park district leagues travel to qualifying tournaments on weekends in quest of a national championship. This diversity of athletic recreational offerings is reflected in the midwestern commitment to the Special Olympics, where volunteers assist in the organization, administration, and production of athletic festivals comprising dozens of events for thousands of developmentally disabled participants.

CONCLUSION

The variety of recreational practices in the Midwest attests to its unique history and the role of sport in the construction of racial, class, gender, ethnic, religious, and regional identities. Midwesterners adhere to the frontier hunting, fishing, and recreational practices of their ancestors. The Indians, of course, introduced their own games. African American migrants and European immigrants introduced their activities, and both agricultural and urban lifestyles transformed the nature of sport and recreation. The Midwest became a national leader in the formation of professional baseball, football, and basketball leagues, as well as archery, golf, and bowling associations. By the end of the nineteenth century, sport became a means for the Midwest to challenge the hegemony of the eastern establishment. The World's Fair of 1893 and interscholastic football signaled a transition in American culture as the Midwest began to exert its own power. By the mid-twentieth century, the Big Ten Conference dominated intercollegiate gridirons, and Notre Dame assumed legendary status. Social reform centered in the parks, playgrounds, and settlement houses of midwestern cities. The accomplishments of midwestern women in baseball, basketball, golf, archery, bowling, softball, swimming, track and a host of industrial recreation activities nurtured the women's rights movement for more than a century. The industrial recreation program of the Pullman Company set the national standard for all others. Religious organizations like the

CYO assumed international significance and brought a greater degree of unity within the American polity to previously disparate groups.

RESOURCE GUIDE

Printed Sources

Primary Documents

Harmon, Daniel Williams. *A Journal of Voyages and Travels in the Interiour [sic] of North America, Between the 47th and 58th Degrees of North Latitude, Extending from Montreal Nearly to the Pacific Ocean.* Andover, VT: Flagg and Gould, 1820.

Louisiana Purchase Exposition Company. *The Greatest of Expositions.* St. Louis: Louisiana Purchase Exposition Company, 1904.

Quaife, Milo Milton, ed., *John Long's Voyages and Travels in the Years 1768–1788.* Chicago: Lakeside Press, 1922.

Roper Starch. *Outdoor Recreation in America 1997.* Washington, DC: Recreation Roundtable, 1997.

Schulz, Christian. *Travels on an Inland Voyage through the States of New York, Pennsylvania, Virginia, Ohio, Kentucky and Tennessee, and Through the Territories of Indiana, Louisiana, Mississippi, and New Orleans; Performed in the Years 1807 and 1808, Including a Tour of Nearly Six Thousand Miles.* New York: Isaac Riley, 1810.

Secondary Sources

Badger, Reid. *The Great American Fair.* Chicago: Nelson & Hall, 1979.

Bale, John. *Sports Geography.* London: Routledge, 2003.

Borish, Linda J. "The Robust Woman and the Muscular Christian: Catherine Beecher, Thomas Higginson, and Their Visions of American Society, Health, and Physical Activities." *International Journal of the History of Sport* 4, no. 2 (1987): 139–154.

Carroll, John M. *Fritz Pollard: Pioneer in Racial Advancement.* Urbana: University of Illinois, 1992.

Clement, Priscilla Ferguson, and Jacqueline S. Reiner, eds. *Boyhood in America.* Santa Barbara, CA: ABC–CLIO, 2001.

Duis, Perry. *The Saloon: Public Drinking in Chicago and Boston, 1880–1920.* Urbana: University of Illinois Press, 1983.

Gems, Gerald R. *For Pride, Profit, and Patriarchy: Football and the Incorporation of American Cultural Values.* Lanham, MD: Scarecrow Press, 2000.

———. *Windy City Wars: Labor, Leisure, and Sport in the Making of Chicago.* Lanham, MD: Scarecrow Press, 1997.

Hult, Joan S., and Marianna Trekell, eds. *A Century of Women's Basketball: From Frailty to Final Four.* Reston, VA: American Alliance for Health, Physical Education, Recreation, and Dance, 1991.

Nasaw, David. *Going Out: The Rise and Fall of Public Amusements.* New York: Basic Books, 1993.

Oxendine, Joseph B. *American Indian Sports Heritage.* Champaign, IL: Human Kinetics, 1988.

Powers, Madelon. *Faces Along the Bar: Lore and Order in the Workingman's Saloon, 1870–1920.* Chicago: University of Chicago Press, 1998.

Rader, Benjamin G. *American Sports: From the Age of Folk Games to the Age of Spectators.* Englewood Cliffs, NJ: Prentice-Hall, 1983.

Randle, Nancy. "Their Time at Bat." *Chicago Tribune Magazine*, July 5, 1992, 10–15.

Riess, Steven A. *City Games: The Evolution of American Urban Society and the Rise of Sports*. Urbana: University of Illinois Press, 1991.

Shortridge, James R. *The Middle West: Its Meaning in American Culture*. Lawrence: University Press of Kansas, 1989.

Web Sites

BigTenChallenge.org
www.bigtenchallenge.org

This Web site lists the Big Ten schools: Illinois, Indiana, Iowa, Michigan, Michigan State, Minnesota, Northwestern, Ohio State, Penn State, Purdue, and Wisconsin. Its goal is to create "a means by which participating Big Ten universities can compete to see who has the most loyal alumni."

Cruisin' Times Magazine
www.cruisintimes.org

Cruisin' Times provides information about car "cruising,'" including car shows, swap meets, parts and accessories, and "cruise-ins."

HeartLand Boating Magazine
www.heartlandboating.com

This news magazine lists information about boating in the rivers and lakes of the Midwest and Southeast, including where to stay, boat safety, calendar of events, boating stories, etc.

Midwest MTB
www.midwestmountainbiker.com

This site contains information about rides, bike trails, races, and "do-it-yourself" information for how to fix a mountain bike.

Midwest Sunbathing Association
www.midwestsun.com

The Midwest Sunbathing Association site lists links to American Association for Nude Recreation (AANR), The Naturist Society, and to the Yahoo!Groups for AANR Government Affairs sign up site. The Web site also features information by state for nudist clubs.

Silent Sports
www.silentsports.net

This is "a monthly magazine that provides solid, reliable and timely regional information on cross country skiing, bicycling, running, paddle sports, multisports (triathlons, biathlons and duathlons), snowshoeing and other related activities we loosely define as 'aerobic outdoor activities.'" It lists information for aerobic non-motorized outdoor activities.

Ski Jumping Central
www.skijumpingcentral.com

The mission of this site is to "promote the sport of ski jumping across a diverse audience: families, communities, spectators, competitors, clubs, sponsors, and media." It provides ski industry news and links to regional, national and international ski sites.

Organizations

American Association of Leisure and Recreation
1900 Association Drive
Reston, VA 20191-1599
Phone: (703)-476-3472
Fax: (703)-476-9527

Wisconsin Office
Christine Tipps, President Elect
University of WI—Oshkosh
103 Albee Hall
800 Algoma Boulvard
Oshkosh, WI 54901-8630
Phone: (920)-424-0368
E-mail: tipps@uwosh.edu
www.aalr.org/

American Camping Association
5000 State Road 67 North
Martinsville, IN 46151
Phone: (765) 342-8456
www.acacamps.org/

There are over 500 camps associated with the "Mid-America" region:
find.acacamps.org/cgi/search.cgi?philosophy=&agency=&health=&religion=&
independent=&fee=&location=reg_mid&session_length=&ages=&Submit3=Search.

American Hiking Society
1422 Fenwick Lane
Silver Spring, MD 20910
Phone: (301) 565-6704
Fax: (301) 565-6714
http://www.americanhiking.org/

See site for affiliated AHS clubs for each of the eight states.

American Trails
P.O. Box 491797
Redding, CA 96049-1797
Phone: (530) 547-2060
Fax: (530) 547-2035
E-mail: trailhead@americantrails.org
http://www.americantrails.org/

Directors based in the Midwest:
Christine Jourdain
American Council of Snowmobile Associations
271 Woodland Pass, #216
East Lansing, MI 48823
Phone: (517) 351-4362
Fax: (517) 351-1363
E-mail: Cajourdain@aol.com
www.snowmobileacsa.org

Mike Passo
Wilderness Inquiry
808 14th Avenue

Minneapolis, MN 55414
Phone: (612) 676-9400, ext. 416
Fax: (612) 676-9401
E-mail: mikepasso@wildernessinquiry.org
www.wildernessinquiry.org

Terry Whaley
Ozark Greenways
P.O. Box 50733
Springfield, MO 65805
Phone: (417) 864-2014
Fax: (417) 864-1497
E-mail: terry_Whaley@CI.Springfield.MO.US
www.ozarkgreenways.org

Affiliated organizations:
Hoosier Horsemen:
8181 West 100 South
Farmland, IN 47340
Contact: Yvette Anderson Rollins, President
E-mail: rollinsy@indiana.edu

Indiana DNR—Division of Outdoor Recreation:
Department of Natural Resources
402 West Washington Street
Indianapolis, IN 46204

Northwestern Ohio Rails-to-Trails Association, Inc. (NORTA, Inc.)
P.O. Box 234
Delta, OH 43515
Phone: (800) 951-4788 or (419) 822-4788

Wisconsin ATV Association, Inc.
5531B N Highway 42
Sheboygan, WI 53083
Phone: (920) 565-7531
Fax: (920) 565-7534
E-mail: info@watva.org

AMA (American Motorcyclist Association)
13515 Yarmouth Drive
Pickerington, OH 43147
Phone: (614) 856-1900
Fax: (614) 856-1920
General e-mail address: ama@ama-cycle.org

Midwest District of the American Alliance for Health, Physical Education, Recreation, and Dance
Illinois:
IAHPERD
1713 S. West Street
Jacksonville, IL 62650
Phone: (217) 245-6413
Fax: (217) 245-5261
E-mail: iahperd@iahperd.org

Indiana:
Indiana AHPERD
Nikki Assmann
School of Physical Education
Ball State University
Muncie, IN 47306
www.indiana-ahperd.org/about.htm

Michigan:
Phone: (517) 347-0485
E-mail: admin@mimahperd.org

Ohio:
OAHPERD
631 Wellesley Circle
Avon Lake, OH 44012
Phone: (800) 828-3468
Fax: (440) 930-7774

Annual Events

Air and Water Show, August, Chicago, Illinois
American Birkebeiner Ski Race, February, Hayward, Wisconsin
Bix Beiderbecke Jazz Festival, July, Davenport, Iowa
Bud Billiken Parade, August, Chicago, Illinois
Cleveland Grand Prix, July 3, Cleveland, Ohio
Indianapolis 500, Memorial Day, Indianapolis, Indiana
Indian Summer Festival, September, Milwaukee, Wisconsin
National Hot Air Balloon Championships, August, Champaign County, Illinois
National Hot Rod Association Nationals, Labor Day Weekend, Indianapolis, Indiana
Octoberfest, October, Milwaukee, Wisconsin
Road America CART Race, August 8, Elkhart, Wisconsin
Tulip Festival, May, Holland, Michigan
Western Open Golf Tournament, June–July, Chicago Suburbs
World Championship Snowmobile Derby, January, Eagle River, Wisconsin

TIMELINE

12,000 B.C.E.	Nomadic Paleo Indian spear-making groups hunt large game across the Midwest.
9000 B.C.E.	Archaic Period in which seminomadic Amerindians harvest fruit and hunt small game and fish near waterways.
3000–2500 B.C.E.	Inhabitants of the Late Archaic Period create conical or dome-shaped mounds.
1000–100 B.C.E.	Cultivation of maize spreads from Southeast to Midwest; early Woodland-Adena mound-building culture arises in Ohio and Mississippi River valleys.
100 B.C.E.–500 C.E.	Middle Woodland-Hopewell period.
400 C.E.–1300	"Effigy Mound People" flourish in southeastern Minnesota, northeastern Iowa, and southern Wisconsin.
800–1550	Mississippian culture of Algonquian peoples, Oneonta, is centered around Cahokia (Illinois); enjoys peak accomplishments, 1100 to 1300; petroglyphs of Sanilac Historic Site (Michigan) are created.
1070	Great Serpent Mound is built near present-day Peebles, Ohio.
1100–1400	Mississippian Towosahgy community flourishes in southeastern Missouri.
1630–1700	Iroquois and midwestern Algonquian groups contest each other for control of fur-bearing animals' habitats in "Beaver Wars."
1634	Jean Nicolet reaches Lake Michigan's western shore (today's Green Bay, Wisconsin) and mistakes the Win-

	nebago nation ("people of the sea") for a Pacific coast people.
1641	Jesuit priests Isaac Jogues and Charles Raymbault move from Huron mission to site of Sault Ste. Marie (Michigan).
1642	Iroquois, armed by Dutch from New Amsterdam and seeking to control Dutch access to fur trade with western Indians, attack Hurons.
1648	Iroquois destroy remaining Hurons and their French missionaries; push Algonquins west of Lake Michigan.
1650	Iroquois move into Ohio Valley, displaced by European settlers on the Atlantic coast and in search of new sources of fur.
1668	Sault Ste. Marie (Michigan) founded by French.
1669	René-Robert Cavelier, Sieur de La Salle (1643–1687), explores Ohio River Basin.
1673	Jacques Marquette and Louis Jolliet explore present-day Illinois; French establish fur-trading post at Prairie du Chien (Wisconsin).
1701	Antoine de la Mothe Cadillac builds Fort Pontchartrain, which becomes Detroit.
1725	Shawnee nation reunites in Ohio from their dispersal at the hands of the Iroquois.
1756	The Seven Years' War begins, pitting the French and Indians against the British until 1763.
1758	British capture French Fort Duquesne, renamed Fort Pitt.
1763	In the Treaty of Paris, France cedes to Britain the area west of the Allegheny Mountains and north of the Ohio River; a confederacy of Indian nations attacks forts from the Mississippi River to Lake Superior under the leadership of Ottowa chief Pontiac, who is defeated after laying siege to Detroit.
1764	Fur trapper Pierre Laclede establishes St. Louis as a trading post.
1769	Pontiac is murdered by a Peoria Indian in Cahokia, Illinois Territory.
1779	Fur trader Jean Baptiste du Sable ["the black"] establishes trading post at Eschecagou on Lake Michigan; he and his Indian wife, daughter of a Potawatomi chief, became first permanent settlers in what is now Chicago.
1785	Some Wyandots, Delawares, Ottawas, and Ojibwas cede lands between the Ohio and Maumee rivers in Treaty of Fort McIntosh; Northwest Ordinance of 1785 authorizes sale of lots in the Northwest Territory.

1786	Federal surveyors lay out seven ranges along the Ohio River; a confederacy of Iroquois, Hurons, Miamis, Delawares, Shawnees, Ottawas, Ojbiwas, and Potawatomies declares that only "the confederacy" of Indian nations can cede land.
1787	Congress passes second Northwest Ordinance, which included prohibition of slavery and set terms by which territories could enter the union as states; first Methodist circuit riders to reach Ohio are sent by the Redstone conference of western Pennsylvania.
1790	Indian Intercourse Act requires native lands to be ceded through treaty to the United States before any individual or state can buy them; Reverend Stephen Gano organizes the Northwest Territory's first Baptist church on the Little Miami River (Ohio); confederacy led by Little Turtle and Blue Jacket forces retreat of General Josiah Harmar's army from northeastern Indiana to the Ohio River.
1791	Little Turtle and Blue Jacket defeat General Arthur St. Clair's army in northwestern Ohio.
1793	*Centinel of the North-Western Territory* begins publication in Cincinnati; unenforceable amendment to the Indian Intercourse Act provides $1,000 penalty for acquiring native land not first formally ceded to the United States.
1794	General Anthony Wayne defeats Shawnees at the Battle of Fallen Timbers, Ohio Territory; Whiskey Rebellion in (western Pennsylvania) leads to William Findley's *History of the Insurrection* (1795), an early insider's description of "western" values.
1795	Indian leaders, except Little Turtle, cede lands by signing the Treaty of Greenville; Connecticut Land Company, headed by Moses Cleaveland, buys 3 million acres of the Western Reserve, holding the western portion (26 miles known as "Fire Sufferers' Lands," or "Firelands") for Connecticut victims of British raids during the Revolution.
1796	Moses Cleaveland surveys land around Lake Erie that becomes Cleveland.
1799	Mennonites have established themselves in Ohio.
1803	Ohio becomes seventeenth state, first area of Northwest Territory to achieve statehood; Fort Dearborn (Chicago) established; United States acquires French lands west of the Mississippi River for $15 million in Louisiana Purchase; Sauk cede territory around Rock Island, Illinois, contested by Black Hawk in 1832; Amish are established in Ohio.
1804	Meriwether Lewis and William Clark begin their journey to the Pacific Ocean outside St. Louis; Ohio University,

	first university in the Northwest Territory, is founded in Athens.
1808	*Missouri Gazette* begins publication in St. Louis.
1809	Illinois Territory separated from Indiana Territory.
1810	Tecumseh rises as leader of Shawnees and new confederacy of regional Indian nations.
1811	U.S. forces led by William Henry Harrison defeat Shawnees led by Tecumseh at the Battle of Tippecanoe; steamboats appear on the Ohio River.
1812	Regular steamboat service begins on Mississippi River. Indian-U.S. wars continue within the War of 1812, during which the United States cedes the Michigan Territory (Lower Peninsula) to Britain but regains it following Oliver Perry's success in the 1813 Battle of Lake Erie.
1813	Shawnee leader Tecumseh dies in battle outside Detroit.
1815	George Rapp founds New Harmony, Indiana, as a religious community, which becomes home of Indiana's first musical ensembles; all Indian nations east of the Mississippi—the Wyandots, Shawnees, Delawares, Miamis, Ojibwas, Potawatomies, Winnebagos, Sauks—have signed peace treaties with the United States.
1816	Indiana becomes nineteenth U.S. state.
1817	The first showboat appears on the Mississippi River; Philander Chase brings Episcopalian worship to the Midwest.
1818	Illinois becomes twenty-first U.S. state; Methodist circuit riders first reach St. Louis; Lutherans establish Ohio Synod, the region's first.
1819	Settlement of what is today Minneapolis begins at Fort Saint Anthony (later Fort Snelling); Cincinnati publishes its first city directory; regular steamboat runs begin on the Missouri River.
1820	Missouri Compromise permits Missouri's admission as a slave state to be offset by Maine's admission as a free state; boundaries of slavery pushed south of Iowa.
1821	Missouri becomes twenty-fourth U.S. state.
1822	Legendary keelboatman Mike Fink dies; Isaac McCoy begins the Baptist Carey Mission to Indians in Niles, Michigan, which runs until 1826; Ely Seth publishes *Sacred Music*, featuring patent (shape) notes, in Cincinnati.
1824	New Harmony (Indiana) promotes trousers as element of women's dress reform.
1825	New Harmony is sold to Robert Owen; Erie Canal opens, linking Lake Erie with the Hudson River.

1827	Red Bird leads attack on Prairie du Chien (Wisconsin) in response to encroachment by white lead miners on Winnebago land.
1828	New Harmony experiment of progressivism is abandoned.
1830	Congress passes, and President Andrew Jackson signs, Indian Removal Act, leading Sauk and Fox nations to sign treaty ceding lands in Illinois and Missouri; the National Road reaches Indianapolis from Maryland.
1831	Cyrus McCormick invents a mechanical reaper.
1832	Black Hawk War, battle between Sauk Indian leader Black Hawk (1767–1838) and U.S. forces over Sauk and Fox villages along the Rock River (Illinois), ends with Battle of Bad Axe; Indiana University establishes a brass band.
1833	Ojibwas, Ottawas, and Potawatomies sign "Treaty with the Chippewas" in Chicago, ceding land and agreeing to population removal; Oberlin College, the first coeducational institution of higher learning, is founded.
1835	Minister Lyman Beecher of Cincinnati publishes *A Plea for the West*, seeking Protestant missionaries for the region; six black Baptist churches in Ohio form the Providence Baptist Association.
1836	William Holmes McGuffey publishes his first *Eclectic Readers*.
1837	Michigan enters the United States as twenty-sixth state.
1838	Miamis of Indiana sign treaty ceding land (Forks of the Wabash, Indiana); John Deere of Moline, Illinois, devises steel plow to break up prairie sod.
1840	William Henry Harrison, running on the anti-Indian slogan "Tippecanoe and [John] Tyler Too," is elected ninth president of the United States; African Methodist Episcopal Church establishes Ohio conference.
1841	President Harrison catches cold at his inauguration and dies of pneumonia a month later; Benjamin Drake publishes his *Life of Tecumseh*; Pre-emption Act provides free land to settlers who develop it.
1843	Ohioan Daniel Decatur Emmett forms the Virginia Minstrels.
1844	Methodist circuit riders enter Minnesota.
1845	Legendary Johnny Appleseed (John Chapman) supposedly dies on the Indiana frontier.
1846	Iowa becomes twenty-ninth U.S. state; Wyandots sign treaty ceding last lands in Michigan and Ohio to United States.

1847	First theater is built in Chicago; first issue of the *Chicago Tribune* is published; Miamis of Indiana forced by arrival of U.S. troops to remove to Marais des Cygnes, Kansas; Cyrus McCormick begins large-scale manufacture of his mechanical reaper in Chicago.
1848	Illinois and Michigan Canal completed; Wisconsin becomes thirtieth state.
1849	Dan Emmett composes "In Dixie's Land," subsequently the Confederate anthem, as a minstrel finale.
1851	Installments of Harriet Beecher Stowe's novel *Uncle Tom's Cabin* begin appearing in an abolitionist weekly; treaty restricts Santee Dakotas to reservation in southwest Minnesota; Sojourner Truth speaks to women's rights convention in Akron, Ohio.
1852	Alice Cary publishes *Clovernook, or Recollections of Our Neighborhood in the West*; Marshall Field opens a dry-goods store in Chicago; Studebaker wagon works open in South Bend, Indiana.
1855	Michigan constructs Soo Canal to link Lakes Superior and Huron; African Methodist Episcopal Church establishes Indiana and Missouri conferences.
1856	Its 700 miles of track make the Illinois Central Railroad the world's longest.
1857	U.S. Supreme Court rules in *Scott v. Sandford* that the Missouri slave is property whose status does not change by residence in a free state; Rabbi Isaac Meyer Wise of Cincinnati publishes the first Reform Jewish prayerbook, *Minhag America [American Ritual]*; Meskwaki Indians return to Iowa from Kansas.
1858	Minnesota becomes the thirty-second U.S. state.
1859	Naperville (Illinois) Band is established with tax revenues to provide free public concerts.
1860	Two midwesterners, Abraham Lincoln and Stephen Douglas, both of Illinois, vie for the U.S. presidency.
1861	Abraham Lincoln is inaugurated sixteenth president of the United States.
1862	Dakota Conflict under leadership of Little Crow leads to deaths of 500 civilians, soldiers, and Indians in southern Minnesota and execution of thirty-eight Dakota following trial; Homestead Act encourages settlement of western lands by offering 160 acres in exchange for five years of continuous habitation; Morrill Act establishes land grant colleges; music teacher D. H. Baldwin opens music store in Cincinnati.

1863	John D. Rockefeller builds an oil refinery that is soon the largest in the area. With a few associates he incorporates the Standard Oil Company (Ohio) in 1870. He buys out competitors to control the oil-refinery business in Cleveland (1872) and in the United States (1882).
1864	Nine railroad companies purchase 320-acre site for a stockyard in southwestern Chicago.
1865	Illinois repeals black laws.
1866	In Liberty, Missouri, Jesse James commits his first armed robbery.
1867	Illinois Central Rail Road introduces refrigerated shipping in ice-cooled cars.
1868	Hungarian immigrant Joseph Pulitzer begins his journalism career as a reporter for the St. Louis German-language daily *Westliche Post*.
1868	Civil War general Ulysses S. Grant of Ohio is elected eighteenth president of the United States.
1869	Pillsbury flour mill established in Minneapolis.
1871	The Chicago fire; Edward Eggleston publishes *The Hoosier School-Master*.
1872	Montgomery Ward establishes catalog sales business in Chicago; clothing manufacturer Hart, Schaffner, and Marx is established in Chicago.
1873	Architect Louis Sullivan arrives in Chicago, begins tradition of building in which "form follows function"; Reform Jewish rabbis establish the Union of American Hebrew Congregations [now Union for Reform Judaism] in Cincinnati; John B. Singenberger of Milwaukee forms a Caecilian group, the first group in the United States to restore chant to the Catholic Mass.
1874	Women's Christian Temperance Union founded in Cleveland by Frances E. Willard, aesthetics professor and president of the Woman's College of Northwestern University; Ohioan Lewis Miller and a New York minister originate what becomes the Chautauqua movement; S. L. and Frederick Thorpe start the magazine *Home*, later, the highly successful *Women's Home Companion*, in Cleveland; Thomas Barlow Walker of Minneapolis opens his personal art collection to visitors; the American Free Dress League holds its inaugural meeting in Painesville, Ohio.
1876	Ohioan Rutherford B. Hayes is elected nineteenth U.S. president.
1879	St. Louis School and Museum of Fine Arts is established with Halsey Cooley Ives, later art curator for the 1893 and

1904 world's fairs, as director; Chicago Academy of Fine Arts is established with William M. R. French as director; National Archery Association holds its first annual convention at Crawfordsville, Indiana; James Ritty invents the cash register in Dayton, Ohio.

1880   Ohioan James Garfield is elected twentieth U.S. president.

1882   John D. Rockefeller establishes the first commercial trust company, the mechanism for modern corporate capitalism; Gustavus Franklin Swift begins shipping meat in custom-designed refrigerated railroad cars; Quaker Oats is established in Cedar Rapids, Iowa.

1883   Detroit Art Loan Exhibition displays nearly 3000 European and U.S. paintings, inspiring the 1885 founding of the Detroit Museum of Art, now Detroit Institute of Arts; James Whitcomb Riley popularizes regional vernacular in *The Old Swimmin' Hole*.

1884   Mark Twain publishes British edition of *Adventures of Huckleberry Finn* in December (American edition published in January 1885).

1885   Home Insurance Building of Chicago is the first skyscraper.

1886   Haymarket Riot results from Chicago workers' strike for an eight-hour workday; conflict over ethnic identities of regional Catholic churches prompts Milwaukee's vicar general to seek clarification from the pope about "Americanism"; Charles H. Kerr Company, a socialist publishing house, opens in Chicago.

1887   Idea for softball originates in Chicago as an indoor version of baseball; Richard Warren Sears of North Redwood, Minnesota hires watchman Alvah C. Roebuck of Indiana to help with the year-old watch business that he had relocated from Minneapolis to Chicago; Dawes Act provides for the gradual elimination of most tribal ownership.

1888   William S. Burroughs invents the adding machine; George Pullman builds company town for railroad workers, establishing recreational program for workers; Charles Waddell Chesnutt demonstrates narrative possibilities of African American lore in "The Goophered Grapevine"; Sears and Roebuck publish their first mail-order catalog; Benjamin Harrison of Ohio is elected twenty-third U.S. president.

1889   Jane Addams and Ellen Gates Starr found Hull House, model settlement house, in Chicago; E. W. Scripps expands ownership of *Detroit News*, *Cleveland Press*, and *Cincinnati Post* into the Scripps-McRae League of Newspapers, an early newspaper chain and proponent of Progressive politics; Central Conference of American Rabbis is established in Detroit.

1890	Waiters form unions in St. Louis, St. Paul, and Chicago; Indianapolis waiters follow the next year.
1891	R. W. Sears Watch Company becomes Sears, Roebuck and Company, and begins publishing regular catalogs; United States Ski Club conducts its first tournament at Ishpeming, Michigan; William Marion Reedy edits the *St. Louis Mirror*; music store owner D. H. Baldwin of Cincinnati manufactures his first pianos.
1892	National Newsboys' Association (Toledo, Ohio) organized to inculcate middle-class values in urban youth.
1893	Chicago hosts the Midwest's first World's Fair, the Columbian Exposition; the Fair's more than 10,000 artworks exceed the capacity of the Palace of Fine Arts, today the mammoth Museum of Science and Industry; Crackerjack debuts in Chicago; Illinois establishes the Illinois High School Athletic Association, forerunner of the National Collegiate Athletic Association (established in 1905); Paul Laurence Dunbar launches career as America's first full-time African American man of letters with publication of *Oak & Ivy*; Frederick Jackson Turner presents "The Significance of the Frontier in American History" to the American Historical Association.
1894	Railroad workers strike against the Pullman Palace Car Company; the term *Midwest* enters usage as an abridgment of "Middle West."
1895	Seven midwestern universities unite to regulate intercollegiate athletics, establishing the Big Ten Conference in 1896; first intercollegiate basketball competition occurs on February 9, between Minnesota State School of Agriculture and Hamline College; Wisconsin manufacturer OshKosh B'Gosh begins making overalls for fashion as well as function.
1896	Ohioan William McKinley is elected twenty-fifth U.S. president.
1897	Pianist Tom Turpin's "Harlem Rag" is published in St. Louis.
1898	Eugene V. Debs and others found the U.S. Socialist Party.
1899	Ransom E. Olds builds Michigan's first automobile factory; Scott Joplin's first ragtime composition, "Original Rags," is published in Kansas City; John Stark launches his ragtime publishing career and Scott Joplin's international fame by publishing "The Maple Leaf Rag" in Sedalia, Missouri.
1900	Eugene Debs makes the first of five consecutive runs (1900–1920) for U.S. president on the Socialist ticket; Grand

	Rapids (Michigan) Furniture Fair introduces Gustav Stickley's furniture in the new Arts & Crafts style; Theodore Dreiser publishes *Sister Carrie*.
1901	Baseball's American League establishes headquarters in Chicago; Zitkala-Sa (née Gertrude Simmons Bonnin) publishes *Old Indian Legends*.
1902	George Dayton opens Goodfellows department store, the antecedent of Target Corporation, in downtown Minneapolis.
1903	Chicago sculptor Lorado Taft compiles an early survey, *The History of American Sculpture*; William Dean Howells calls attention to "The Chicago School of Fiction" in an essay for the *North American Review*.
1904	St. Louis, America's fourth largest city, introduces Dr. Pepper and ice cream cones while hosting the Olympic Games and the World's Fair, called the Louisiana Purchase Exposition; Polish National Catholic Church splits off from American Catholic organization.
1905	Eugene Debs and others found the Industrial Workers of the World (IWW); unemployed black lawyer Robert Abbott begins publishing the Chicago *Defender*; Madame C. J. Walker sells her first hair-straightener for African Americans.
1906	Upton Sinclair publishes *The Jungle*, exposing abuses in the Chicago Stockyards, and Congress promptly passes the first Pure Food and Drug Act; Will Keith (W. K.) Kellogg founds the Battle Creek Toasted Corn Flake Company to produce corn flakes.
1907	Finnish immigrant miners in northern Minnesota lead the Mesabi Iron Range Strike.
1908	Ford begins production of the Model T; William Howard Taft of Ohio is elected twenty-seventh U.S. president.
1909	Planning begins for Indianapolis Motor Speedway, proposed by Carl Fisher in 1906; *The Progressive* begins publication as [Robert M.] *La Follette's Weekly* in Madison, Wisconsin; the Association of Baptist Churches (Grand Rapids, Michigan) begins two decades of splintering over conflict between modernist and conservative practice; Helen May Butler and her Ladies Brass Band perform at the Minnesota State Fair.
1910	Jessie Bonstelle establishes the Detroit Civic Theater; Hannah Shapiro's walkout at Hart, Schaffner, and Marx expands to become America's most successful labor action to date.
1911	First Indianapolis 500 Motor Race.
1912	Ellen Van Volkenburg and Maurice Browne open the Chicago Little Theatre; Harriet Monroe brings out first issue of *Poetry*.

1914   Upton Sinclair's novel *The Jungle* is made into a film; Wisconsin Players "Little Theater" group is established in Milwaukee; musician W. C. Handy publishes "St. Louis Blues."

1915   Edgar Lee Masters publishes *Spoon River Anthology*; Susan Glaspell publishes *Suppressed Desires*; Oberlin graduates Rowena and Russell Jelliffe establish Cleveland's Karamu House as a settlement, including what is now America's first black theater company; Gennett Records begins operations in Richmond, Indiana.

1916   Market Square, a community and shopping area planned around a parking lot, designed by Howard Van Doren Shaw, opens in Lake Forest, Illinois; silent film, *The Crisis*, set in St. Louis, dramatizes the region's divided sympathies during the Civil War; Cleveland Museum of Art opens.

1917   Dozens of African Americans die in East St. Louis, Illinois, when violence erupts between black and white workers; H. L. Mencken declares Chicago America's "most civilized city."

1918   Chicago Cubs, playing in the World Series, introduce "The Star Spangled Banner" thirteen years before its adoption as the national anthem; Jazz trumpet-player "King" Joe Oliver moves from New Orleans to Chicago, forms new band in 1920.

1919   Chicago "Black Sox" produce baseball's greatest scandal, purposely losing the World Series to the Cincinnati Reds; racial violence in Chicago leaves 38 dead and 500 wounded; Sherwood Anderson publishes *Winesburg, Ohio*.

1920   Cleveland hosts first Pulitzer Trophy race (succeeded by the Cleveland Air Show) to mark its innovations in air transport; Ku Klux Klan is active throughout Ohio, Indiana, Michigan, Illinois, Wisconsin, and Minnesota; National Football League is established in Canton, Ohio; Chicagoan Andrew "Rube" Foster founds the Negro National (baseball) League; Zona Gale wins Pulitzer Prize for *Miss Lulu Bett*; three black circus employees are lynched in Duluth, Minnesota; Sinclair Lewis publishes *Main Street*; Warren G. Harding of Ohio is elected twenty-ninth U.S. president; Mamie Smith of Cincinnati makes the first Blues vocal recording.

1922   Country Club Plaza, an early shopping mall, opens in Kansas City, Missouri; jazz cornet-trumpet player Louis Armstrong leaves New Orleans to join King Oliver's band in Chicago; OKeh Records begins capturing live Jazz and Blues performances across the Midwest.

1923   Dumas Drama Club at Karamu House renames itself Gilpin Players; Benny Moten of Kansas City makes his first Blues recordings for OKeh.

1924	Charlie Jackson records the first Country Blues for Paramount Records in Chicago; Ole Edvart Rolvaag publishes *Giants of the Earth*; Elliott Meredith of Des Moines gives his magazine *Fruit, Garden and Home* a new name, *Better Homes and Gardens*; Ku Klux Klan wins local and state elections in Indiana, Ohio, Illinois, Missouri, and Wisconsin.
1925	Frank Lloyd Wright establishes the Taliesin Fellowship near Spring Green, Wisconsin; F. Scott Fitzgerald publishes *The Great Gatsby*; WGN radio (Chicago) broadcasts the 1925 Scopes "Monkey" Trial, which pits rural Illinois-born William Jennings Bryan against Chicago lawyer Clarence Darrow.
1926	Sinclair Lewis wins America's first Nobel Prize for Literature.
1927	Harlem Globetrotters begin life as Chicago's "Savoy 5"; the stage review *Chicago* opens, satirizing the city's contemporary underworld of prostitution, drugs, organized crime, gangsters, and corruption in the justice system; Sinclair Lewis publishes *Elmer Gantry*, satirizing Indiana evangelist Billy Sunday; Walker Art Gallery opens as a museum; Paul Whiteman takes over the Goldkette bands; Carl Sandburg publishes *The American Songbag*.
1928	Herbert C. Hoover of Iowa is elected thirty-first U.S. president.
1929	Hoagy Carmichael composes *Star Dust*; pianist Bill Basie joins the Benny Moten (Kansas City Swing) Orchestra; sociologists Robert and Helen Lynd publish their study of everyday life in Muncie, Indiana, *Middletown*.
1930	Grant Wood paints *American Gothic*, winning instant fame on its exhibition in Chicago later that year; Hostess Twinkies debut in Chicago; Constance Rourke publishes *American Humor: A Study of the National Character*; Father Charles E. Coughlin of Detroit begins anti-Semitic radio broadcasts.
1931	Austrian American Irma S. Rombauer of Cincinnati publishes *The Joy of Cooking*; Jane Addams receives the Nobel Peace Prize.
1932	James T. Farrell publishes *Studs Lonigan*; Stith Thompson establishes folklore as a scholarly field with the first of his six-volume *Motif-Index to Folklore*.
1933	"The Century of Progress" World's Fair in Chicago celebrates the city's centennial; Shi'ite Muslims of Dearborn, Michigan, found Hashemite Club.
1934	Steak 'n' Shake begins operation in Normal, Illinois; Lebanese Muslims near Cedar Rapids, Iowa, build what is now America's oldest extant mosque.

1935	John L. Lewis and others form the Committee for Industrial Organization (CIO); Works Progress Administration (WPA) establishes the Federal Theater Project across midwestern states; Thomas Hart Benton begins his mural for the Missouri State House, *A Social History of the State of Missouri*, completed in 1936; the United Automobile Workers union is formed in Detroit.
1936	Cleveland's Jesse Owens, an African American, exposes the fallacy of Nazi racial theory by winning four gold medals at the Berlin Olympics; Elijah Muhammad of Detroit establishes headquarters of Nation of Islam in Chicago.
1937	"Sit-Down Strike" of United Automobile Workers succeeds in Flint, Michigan; the first issue of Iowan Gardner Cowles' *Look* magazine appears; Blues harmonica-player "Sonny Boy" Williamson I (John Lee Williamson, 1914–1948) moves to Chicago.
1938	Mies van der Rohe, fleeing Nazi Germany, becomes director of architecture at the Armour Institute (Chicago); New Glarus, Wisconsin, celebrates its Swiss heritage by staging its first annual performance of *Wilhelm Tell*; Dairy Queen opens with signature ice creams in Kankakee, Illinois.
1939	Cincinnati Reds play broadcast television's first baseball game (against the Brooklyn Dodgers); Sunni Muslims found Dearborn, Michigan's Moslem Mosque; WPA publishes state guides by notable authors; *The Wizard of Oz*, starring Minnesota-born Judy Garland, popularizes midwesterners' love of home.
1940	Richard Wright publishes *Native Son*; film *Knute Rockne, All-American* stars Pat O'Brien as the legendary coach of Notre Dame's "fighting Irish" and Ronald Reagan as "the Gipper" to whom the team dedicate their game; Henry Fonda stars in the film *Young Abe Lincoln*.
1940s	Columbus, Indiana, creates living museum of contemporary architecture by inviting prominent architects to design its buildings.
1941	Langston Hughes establishes the Skyloft Players theater company (Chicago).
1942	John H. Johnson begins publishing the *Negro Digest* in Chicago, the start of an African American publishing empire; Stith Thompson of Indiana University leads the first institute on folklore study; *bracero* program brings Mexican workers to midwestern farms; University of Chicago scientists generate the world's first self-sustaining nuclear reaction; *Wayfaring Stranger*, a radio show featuring folksinger Burl Ives, begins broadcasting on CBS.

1943	Blues singer and guitar-player Muddy Waters arrives in Chicago.
1944	Saul Bellow publishes *Dangling Man*; Harry S Truman of Missouri becomes thirty-third U.S. president on the death of Franklin D. Roosevelt; Sydney Nathan begins King Records in Cincinnati.
1945	First issue of Johnson's *Ebony* magazine appears.
1946	Richard Dorson's *Bloodstoppers and Bearwalkers* inaugurates ethnographic, regional orientation of folklore research with study of tales from Michigan's Upper Peninsula.
1947	Phil and Leonard Chess buy into the Aristocat record label.
1948	Muddy Waters debuts on records with "I Can't Be Satisfied" (Aristocat).
1949	Soto Zen master Soyu Matsuoka founds Chicago Buddhist Temple, now Zen Buddhist Temple of Chicago.
1951	Disc jockey Alan Freed hosts the first regular rock 'n' roll radio program, *The Moondog Rock & Roll House Party*, over WJW-AM, sponsored by Cleveland's Record Rendezvous.
1952	Wisconsin Senator Joseph R. McCarthy chairs hearings on suspected communists in government.
1953	Hugh Hefner publishes the first issue of *Playboy* in Chicago; Sheboygan, Wisconsin, celebrates its first Bratwurst Day; Vivian Carter Bracken, James Bracken, and Calvin Carter found Vee Jay Records in Gary, Indiana.
1954	Ernest Hemingway wins the Nobel Prize for Literature.
1955	Ray Kroc opens McDonald's first franchise restaurant in Des Plaines, Illinois.
1956	Detroit Tigers first baseman Hank Greenberg becomes first Jewish player elected to baseball's Hall of Fame.
1957	*The Music Man*, Meredith Wilson's musical about small-town life in early twentieth-century Iowa, opens on Broadway; Chicago's Old Town School of Folk Music opens with Win Stracke as director.
1959	Lorraine Hansberry's *A Raisin in the Sun* becomes the first Broadway play by an African American woman; Second City comedy club opens in Chicago; St. Lawrence Seaway completes series of links between Great Lakes and the Atlantic Ocean.
1960	Alfred Hitchcock transplants the crime depicted in *Psycho* from Wisconsin to the far west; Berry Gordy, Jr., founds Motown Records, whose first hit is "Bye, Bye, Baby" by Mary Wells.

1961	Film version of Lorraine Hansberry's play *A Raisin in the Sun* stars Sidney Poitier.
1962	Film of *The Music Man* opens, starring Robert Preston and Shirley Jones; Indiana University establishes the Folklore Institute for teaching and research; Memphis Slim and Willie Dixon begin annual European tours of the American Blues Festival; Bob Dylan releases his first album.
1963	Gary Comer founds Lands' End; eleven-year-old "Little Stevie Wonder" makes his first recording for Motown Records; Bob Dylan performs "Blowin' in the Wind."
1964	End of *bracero* program limits legal immigration by Mexican farm workers; The Supremes release "Where Did Our Love Go?"; The Jackson Five sign on with Motown Records; Bob Dylan writes "The Times They Are a-Changin'."
1965	Immigration and Nationality Amendments Act abandons quest for European ethnic majority in the United States, enabling increased immigration from Asia to the Midwest; popular audiences discover Bob Dylan through his recording of "Like a Rolling Stone"; Dylan's "Mr. Tambourine Man" is the first folk-rock hit single.
1966	Eero Saarinen's 630-foot Gateway Arch opens to commemorate the role of St. Louis in exploring and developing the West.
1967	Richard Brooks adapts Truman Capote's "nonfiction novel" *In Cold Blood* (1967) depicting the murders by two men from Missouri; Detroit suffers the worst race riot in U.S. history; Studs Terkel publishes *Division Street: America*.
1968	Democratic National Convention nominates Minnesotan Hubert Humphrey for president while Chicago police, across the street, battle demonstrators protesting the Vietnam War and advocating Black Power; protests lead to the arrest and 1969 trial of the "Chicago Eight."
1969	Industrial pollution causes the Cuyahoga River to catch fire, leading to the U.S. Clean Water Act; Compuserve introduces computer time-sharing; The Supremes disband; the Punk group Psychedelic Stooges release *The Stooges Album*.
1970	Film director Melvin Van Peebles imagines a white bigot who turns black in *Watermelon Man*; Dave Thomas opens the world's first "drive thru window" at a Wendy's Old Fashioned Hamburgers restaurant in Columbus, Ohio; Toni Morrison publishes *The Bluest Eye*; composer William Bolcum publishes "Seabiscuits Rag."

1971	David D. Anderson and others found the Society for the Study of Midwestern Literature.
1973	Marvin Hamlisch's sound track for *The Sting* revives wide interest in ragtime.
1975	David Mamet's first play, *American Buffalo*, opens at Chicago's Goodman Theatre.
1976	Indianapolis Motor Speedway Hall of Fame and Racing Museum opens; Saul Bellow wins the Nobel Prize for Literature; Harvey Pekar and Robert Crumb contribute to the development of underground comix with the first installment of *American Splendor*.
1978	Prince releases his first album, *For You*.
1979	*Talley's Folly* opens, the first play in Lanford Wilson's tetralogy set in Lebanon, Missouri; court in Ann Arbor, Michigan, orders teachers at Martin Luther King Elementary School to learn about African American English in order to improve students' acquisition of Standard English.
1980	Compuserve introduces real-time chat; Jane Smiley publishes *Barn Blind*; Ronald W. Reagan, born and educated in Illinois, is elected fortieth U.S. president.
1982	Former Cincinnati city councilman and mayor Jerry Springer begins his broadcasting career as a political commentator for WLTW-TV; W. P. Kinsella publishes *Shoeless Joe*, the basis for the 1989 film *Field of Dreams*; Michael Jackson releases *Thriller*.
1984	Oprah Winfrey arrives in Chicago to host *AM Chicago*, a talk-show on WLS-TV, which is renamed *The Oprah Winfrey Show* a year later; Minneapolis-based Lens Publishing founds the *Utne Reader*, continuing the midwestern tradition of progressivism; Sandra Cisneros publishes *The House on Mango Street*; David Mamet wins Pulitzer Prize and New York Drama Critics Circle Award for *Glengarry Glen Ross*.
1985	Garrison Keillor publishes *Lake Wobegon Days*; Prince wins three Grammy Awards.
1986	Chicago's *Oprah Winfrey Show* begins nationally syndicated broadcasts.
1989	Filmmaker Michael Moore's *Roger and Me* documents the closing of a Flint, Michigan, General Motors plant.
1990	Debut album of Uncle Tupelo, a Belleville, Illinois, group, pioneers a new musical style, "Alternative Country."
1992	Mall of America opens in Bloomington, Minnesota.
1993	Rita Dove is named U.S. Poet Laureate, the first African American appointed to the post.

1994	Brickyard 400 inaugurates NASCAR racing at the Indianapolis Speedway; *Hoop Dreams* chronicles the lives of two Chicago youths who dream of becoming basketball superstars; Winnebago Nation of Green Bay, Wisconsin, readopts its earlier name, Ho-Chunk (People of the Big Voice) Sovereign Nation; Uncle Tupelo disbands.
1995	Clint Eastwood's *The Bridges of Madison County* depicts hollowness in the Heartland.
1996	Chicago Poetry Center founder Lisel Mueller wins Pulitzer Prize for *Alive Together*.
1999	Rock and Roll Hall of Fame opens in Cleveland.
2001	Jonathan Franzen publishes *The Corrections*.
2002	Eminem stars in the film *8 Mile*, which explores racism, poverty, teen pregnancy, violence, and ambition in Detroit.
2003	The film version of Harvey Pekar's *American Splendor* deconstructs superheroes and other urban fantasies.

NOTES

Introduction

1. Garrison Keillor, *Lake Wobegon Days* (New York: Viking, 1985), 3. On the relation of escape to exile, see Judith Yaross Lee, "If I Forget Thee, O Lake Wobegon: Exiles and Defectors in *Leaving Home*," in *Garrison Keillor: A Voice of America* (Jackson: University Press of Mississippi), 148–179.

2. James R. Shortridge, *The Middle West: Its Meaning in American Culture* (Lawrence: University Press of Kansas, 1989), 143.

3. Gloria Anzaldúa, *Borderlands: The New Mestiza = la Frontera*, 2nd ed. (San Francisco: Aunt Lute Books, 1999), [19].

4. Jennifer M. Spear, "French Settlements in North America," in *Oxford Companion to United States History*, ed. Paul Boyer (New York: Oxford University Press, 2001), www.anb.org/articles/cush/e0577.html.

5. I am indebted to R. Douglas Hurt, *The Indian Frontier, 1763–1846* (Albuquerque: University of New Mexico Press, 2002), for this discussion of politics on the midwestern frontier and details of the major Indian battles. Quoted in ibid., 107.

6. Edward Watts, *An American Colony: Regionalism and the Roots of Midwestern Culture* (Athens: Ohio University Press, 2002); Andrew R.L. Cayton and Peter S. Onuf, *The Midwest and the Nation: Rethinking the History of an American Region* (Bloomington: Indiana University Press, 1990), 12.

7. "Holdings of University Research Libraries in the United States and Canada, 2001–02," *The Chronicle of Higher Education Almanac Issue* 50.1 (August 29, 2003): 28.

8. Kim M. Gruenwald, *River of Enterprise: The Commercial Origins of Regional Identity in the Ohio Valley, 1790–1850* (Bloomington: Indiana University Press, 2002); Saul Steinberg, cover ["The New Yorker's View of the World"], *New Yorker*, March 29, 1976.

9. Andrew R.L. Cayton, "The Anti-Region: Place and Identity in the History of the American Midwest," in *The American Midwest: Essays on Regional History*, ed. Andrew R.L. Cayton and Susan E. Gray (Bloomington: Indiana University Press, 2001), 159.

10. Frederick Jackson Turner, "The Significance of the Frontier in American History" (1893; rpt. in *The Frontier in American History*, New York: H. Holt, 1921), 1–38.

11. Bureau of the Census, Fig. 1.2, "Center of Population, 1970–2000," *2003 U.S. Statistical Abstract*, Population, 21, www.census.gov/prod/2004pubs/03statab/pop.pdf.

12. Stephen A. Vincent, *Southern Seed, Northern Soil: African-American Farm Communities in the Midwest, 1765–1900* (Bloomington: Indiana University Press, 1999), xii; R. Douglas Hurt, "Midwestern Distinctiveness," in Cayton and Gray, *American Midwest*, 169.

13. Cayton and Onuf, *Midwest and Nation*, 93.

14. Edward A. Ross, "The Middle West: Being Studies of Its People in Comparison with Those of the East," *Century Magazine* 83 (1912): 612.

15. Patricia M. Lengermann and Jill Niebrugge-Brantley, *The Women Founders: Sociology and Social Theory, 1830–1930: A Text/Reader* (Boston: McGraw-Hill, 1998), 235.

16. David M. Chalmers, *Hooded Americanism: The History of the Ku Klux Klan*, 2nd ed. (New York: New Viewpoints, 1981), 175–78.

17. Marilyn J. Atlas, "Midwestern Literature, 1860–Present," unpublished essay.

18. Anzaldúa, *Borderlands*, 25; Richard Rodriguez, *Brown: The Last Discovery of America* (New York: Viking, 2002).

19. Richard Mertens, "Where the Action Was," *University of Chicago Magazine* 96 (April 2004): 35.

20. Richard Manning, "The Oil We Eat: Following the Food Chain Back to Iraq," *Harper's* 308 (February 2004): 37–45; Michael Pollan, "The (Agri)Cultural Contradictions of Obesity," *New York Times Magazine*, October 12, 2003, 41ff.; Norimitsu Onishi, "On U.S. Fast Food, Okinawans Are Super-Sized," *New York Times*, March 30, 2004, A1, A4; Ron Powers, *Tom and Huck Don't Live Here Anymore: Childhood and Murder in the Heart of America* (New York: St. Martin's Press, 2001), 67.

21. Stephanie Simon, "Latinos Take Root in Midwest," *L. A. Times*, October 24, 2002, www.latimes.com/news/nationworld/nation/la-na-migrants24oct24.story.

22. "Converting Swine Manure to Oil: U of I Makes the Process Faster, Easier," web .aces.uiuc.edu/news/stories/news2702.html; Anzaldúa, *Borderlands*, 99.

Art

1. Frederick Jackson Turner, *The Significance of the Frontier in American History*, 1893, reprinted in *The Frontier in American History* (New York: Henry Holt, 1958).

2. Robert Stearns et al., eds., *Illusions of Eden: Visions of the American Heartland* (Minneapolis: Arts Midwest, 2000), 74.

3. William Gerdts, *Art Across America: Two Centuries of Regional Painting, 1710–1920*, vol. 2 (New York: Abbeville, 1990), 302.

4. Wayne Craven, *Sculpture in America*, rev. ed. (Newark: University of Delaware Press, 1984), 55.

5. Lorado Taft, *The History of American Sculpture*, rev. ed. (New York: Macmillan Co., 1917).

6. *Cosmopolitan*, September 15, 1893, www.boondocksnet.com/expos/wfe_1893_cosmo_besant.html.

7. *American Review of Reviews*, June 7, 1893, www.boondocksnet.com/expos/wfe_1893_amrr_art.html.

8. www.wuga.wustl.edu/history.html.

9. Ibid.

10. *American Review of Reviews* 29 (May 1904), www.boondocksnet.com/expos/wfe_1904_amrr_art.html.

11. Barbara Haskell, *The American Century: Art & Culture, 1900–1950* (New York: Whitney Museum, 1999), 36.

12. Ibid.

13. Ibid., 223.

14. Wanda Corn, *Grant Wood: The Regionalist Vision* (New Haven, CT: Yale University for Minneapolis Institute of Arts, 1983), 90.

15. An extensive study of the program and its workings is found in Karal Ann Marling's *Wall-to-Wall America: A Cultural History of Post Office Murals in the Great Depression* (Minneapolis: University of Minnesota, 1982).

16. Haskell, *The American Century*, 242.

17. John Franklin White, *Art in Action: American Art Centers and the New Deal* (Metuchen, NJ: Scarecrow Press, 1987), 10.

18. Ibid., 13.

19. Patricia McDonnel, "Charles Biederman: A Tribute to the Life of the Mind," in *Charles Biederman* (Minneapolis: University of Minnesota, 2003), 49.

20. "Julian Stanczak, Painter," www.clevelandartsprize.org/visart_1969.htm.

21. Many works by Tolson and other American folk artists can be found in the Julie and Michael Hall Collection of American Folk Art at the Milwaukee Art Museum.

22. Michael Martone, "The Flyover," in *Imagining Home: Writings from the Midwest*, ed. Mark Vinz and Thom Tammaro (Minneapolis: University of Minnesota, 1995), n.p.

23. James L. Riedy, *Chicago Sculpture* (Urbana: University of Illinois Press, 1981), 253.

24. In subsequent years, similar projects have appeared in Cincinnati—first pigs and then baseball bats were the themes—and in Columbus, Ohio—where ears of corn sprouted through sidewalks.

Ecology and Environment

1. John Fraser Hart, "The Middle West," in *Regions of the United States*, ed. John Fraser Hart (New York: Harper and Row, 1972), 258.

2. The Tiffin report was issued in a letter dated November 30, 1815, by Surveyor General Edward Tiffin to Joseph Meigs, Commissioner of the General Land Office. The letter, infamous in Michigan, popularized a view of the land as worthless. www.geo.msu/geo333/Tiffin.html.

3. Bill Novak, "State's Tally of Deer with CWD Increases to 44," (Madison, Wisconsin) *Capital Times*, December 7, 2002, 2.

4. John B. Jackson, "In Search of the Proto-landscape," in *Landscape in America*, ed. George F. Thompson (Austin: University of Texas Press, 1995), 50.

5. Wilbur Zelinsky, "Classical Town Names in the United States: The Historical Geography of an American Idea," *Geographical Review* 57 (1986): 463–495.

6. John C. Hudson, "North American Origins of Middlewestern Frontier Populations," *Annals of the Association of American Geographers* 78 (1988): 395–413.

7. Kathy Barks Hoffman, Lansing, Michigan, Associated Press State and Local Wire, March 2, 2004: "Michigan, meanwhile, has seen its unemployment rate average more than 7 percent for much of last year. The state has lost more than 300,000 jobs since mid-2000, including 170,000 in manufacturing."

8. Dale Dempsey, "State Set to Issue in March New Fish Eating Advisories," *Dayton Daily News*, December 19, 2003, 1.

9. William M. Denevan, "The Pristine Myth: The Landscape of the Americas in 1492," *Annals of the Association of American Geographers* 82 (1992): 369–385.

10. Kevin A. Brown, "The FermiLab Prairie: A Functioning Ecosystem," *FermiLab Report* (May/June 1988): 33-39; Frederick Turner, "A Field Guide to the Synthetic Landscape: Toward a New Environmental Ethic," *Harper's* 276 (April 1988): 49–55.

11. Aldo Leopold, *A Sand County Almanac, and Sketches Here and There* (New York: Oxford University Press, 1948), 129–132, 204.

12. Charles Bartsch, *Brownfield Policies in the Midwest* (Chicago: Federal Reserve Bank of Chicago, 1995).

13. L. King et al., "Optimal Transportation Patterns of Coal in the Great Lakes Region," *Economic Geography* 47 (1971): 401–413.

14. M. Hawthorne, "Cheshire—Death of a Village," *Columbus Dispatch*, November 10, 2002. Gavin ranked seventh in the nation among power plants for total emissions of carbon dioxide and eighteenth for nitrogen oxide. The plant ranked fourteenth for mercury emissions during 2000, the latest year for which figures on that pollutant are available.

Ethnicity

1. Chief Justice John Marshall, in *Cherokee Nation v. Georgia*, 1831, promulgated the concept of Indians as "domestic dependent nations" and thus without citizenship standing, but the U.S. government generally treated native peoples as colonial wards after the 1780s. See Francis Paul Prucha, *The Great Father: The United States Government and the American Indians* (Lincoln: University of Nebraska Press, 1986), 14–22, 75–76.

2. For a fuller treatment of this regional conflict, see Kenneth Carley, *The Sioux Uprising of 1862* (St. Paul: Minnesota State Historical Society, 1962), passim.

3. An important case study is Walter D. Kamphoefner, *The Westfalians: From Germany to Missouri* (Princeton, NJ: Princeton University Press, 1987). See also Frederick C. Luebke, *Germans in the New World: Essays in the History of Immigration* (Urbana: University of Illinois Press, 1990), and Kathleen Neils Conzen, *Immigrant Milwaukee, 1836–1860: Accommodation and Community in a Frontier City* (Cambridge, MA: Harvard University Press, 1976).

4. See, generally, Kerby A. Miller, *Emigrants and Exiles: Ireland and the Irish Exodus to North America* (New York: Oxford University Press, 1985).

5. Three helpful studies are John G. Rice, *Patterns of Ethnicity in a Minnesota County, 1880–1905* (Umeå, Sweden: Dept. of Geography, University of Umeå, 1973); Robert C. Ostergren, *A Community Transplanted: The Trans-Atlantic Experience of a Swedish Immigrant Settlement in the Upper Middle West, 1835–1915* (Madison: University of Wisconsin Press, 1988); and Jon Gjerde, *From Peasants to Farmers: The Migration from Balestrand, Norway, to the Upper Middle West* (Cambridge, MA: Harvard University Press, 1985).

6. Robert P. Swierenga, *Faith and Family: Dutch Immigration and Settlement in the United States, 1820–1920* (New York: Holmes & Meier, 2000), especially chapters 2, 3, 8, and 9.

7. On the issues of "birds of passage" and repatriation, see Walter Nugent, *Crossings: The Great TransAtlantic Migration, 1870–1914* (Bloomington: Indiana University Press, 1992), 35–37, 156–161. See also H. S. Neilli, *From Immigrants to Ethnics: The Italian Americans* (New York: Oxford University Press, 1983), and John W. Briggs, *An Italian Passage: Immigrants to Three American Cities, 1890–1930* (New Haven, CT: Yale University Press, 1978).

8. Eva Moraskwa, "Labor Migrations of Poles in the Atlantic World-Economy, 1880–1914," *Comparative Studies in Society and History* 31 (April 1989): 237–272. Two helpful studies are John J. Bukowczyk, ed., *Polish Americans and Their History: Community, Culture, and Politics* (Pittsburgh: University of Pittsburgh Press, 1996), and F. Mocha, *Poles in America: Bicentennial Essays* (Stevens Point, WI: Worzalla Publishing Company, 1978).

9. Simon Kuznets, "Immigration of Russian Jews to the United States: Background and Structure," *Perspectives in American History* 9 (1977): 35–124.

10. See, generally, C. C. Moskos, *Greek Americans: Struggle and Success* (Englewood, NJ: Prentice-Hall, 1980); A. Scourby, *The Greek Americans* (Boston: Twayne Publishers, 1984).

11. Karen Rignall, "Building an Arab-American Community in Dearborn," *The Journal of the International Institute*, www.umich.edu/~iinet/journal/vol15nol/rignall3. See also S. Y. Abraham and N. Abraham, eds., *Arabs in the New World: Studies on Arab-American Communities* (Detroit: Center for Urban Studies, Wayne State University Press, 1983).

12. Regionally specific is James R. Grossman, *Land of Hope: Chicago, Black Southerners, and the Great Migration* (Chicago: University of Chicago Press, 1989).

13. On the black megachurch, see www.easternstarchurch.org/ministries.

14. A. W. Carlson, "The Settling Process of Mexican Americans in Northwestern Ohio," *Journal of Mexican American History* 5 (1975): 24–38.

15. T. D. Boswell, "Puerto Ricans Living in the United States," in Jesse O. McKee, ed., *Ethnicity in Contemporary America: A Geographical Appraisal*, 2nd ed. (Lanham, MD: Rowman & Littlefield, 2000). See also C. E. Rodriguez, V. S. Korrol, and J. O. Alers, *The Puerto Rican Struggle: Essays on Survival in the United States* (New York: Puerto Rican Migration Research Consortium, 1980).

16. "Latinos Surge in Midwest," *Rural Migration News*, July 1996, migration.ucdavis.edu/rmn/Archive_RMN/jul_1998–01; Karen Brach-Brioso, "Hispanics in the St. Louis Area," March 7, 2001, www.stltoday.com/stltoday/news/special.

17. Joan M. Jensen, *Passage from India: Asian Indian Immigrants in North America* (New Haven, CT: Yale University Press, 1988); Roger Daniels, *Asian America: Chinese and Japanese in the United States since 1850* (Seattle: University of Washington Press, 1988); H. Brett Melendy, *Asians in America: Filipinos, Koreans, and East Indians* (Boston: Twayne Publishers, 1977); Ronald Takaki, *Strangers from a Different Shore: A History of Asian Americans* (New York: Penguin, 1989); "Korean Americans: History and Current Issues," www.msmc.la.edu/ccf/LAC.Korean; and Sam Chu Line, "Scattered but Strong: Korean Americans," *Asian Week*, January 10, 2003, www.asianweek.com/2003_01_10/feature_scattered.

18. N. M. Hung, "Vietnamese," in D. W. Haines, *Refugees in the United States: A Reference Handbook* (Westport, CT: Greenwood Press, 1985), 195–208; Mark E. Pfeifer, "Regional Trends in Vietnamese Residential Distribution," *Review of Vietnamese Studies*, 2001, site.yahoo.com/vstudies/marepfeifphd.

19. "Hmong Communities in the Twin Cities," www.cla.umn.edu/twocities/rprojs/hmong/hmong; Mark E. Pfeifer, "Settlement Patterns of Four Major Indochinese Groups," www.hmongstudies.org/growandsetpa; David Peterson, "More Hmong Find Home in Midwest," *Star Tribune*, August 15, 2001, health.csuohio.edu/healthculture/culture.

20. Lynda Gorov, "Living in Fear: Guatemalans Seek Refuge Community in Chicago," *Chicago Reporter*, www.chicagoreporter.com/1990/01–90/0190%20Living%20.

21. Lourdes Medrano Leslie, "Sights, Sounds of Africa Increasing in Minnesota," *Star Tribune*, www.startribune.com/stories/1507/2879199; Nahal Toosi, "Fear Tinges Hope for Somalis in U.S.," *JSOnline*, www.jsonline.com/news/metro/jan02/12510.asp; Kate Herman, "From Mogadisu to the Midwest," *New Democrat Online*, www.ndol.org/blueprint/2002_jan-feb?06b_communities_midwest; Zoltan Grossman, "Somali Immigrant Settlement in Small Minnesota and Wisconsin Communities," www.uwec.edu/grossmzc/somali.

Fashion

1. John McIntosh, *The Origin of the North American Indians: with a faithful description of their manners and customs . . . including various specimens of Indian eloquence as well as historical and biographical sketches of almost all the distinguished nations and celebrated warriors, statesmen and orators, among the Indians of North America* (New York: Nafis & Cornish, 1843), 26.

2. *The Cincinnati Directory* (Cincinnati, 1819), 22.

3. Daniel Boorstin, *The Americans: The Democratic Experience* (New York: Vintage, 1974), 98–99.

4. Charles Robbins, *Last of His Kind: An Informal Portrait of Harry S. Truman* (New York: William Morrow, 1979), 59.

5. *Godey's Lady's Book* 48 (May 1854): 467.

6. Claudia B. Kidwell, *Cutting a Fashionable Fit: Dressmakers' Drafting Systems in the United States* (Washington, DC: Smithsonian Institution Press, 1979), 2.

7. Daniel Edward Ryan, *Human Proportions in Growth* (New York: Griffith & Byrne, 1880).

8. Catherine Steiner, *Ornate & Simple Forms: Pomeroy Furniture & Fashion, 1840–1880* (Athens, OH: Ohio University Press, 1990).

9. Ibid., 16.

10. See "Ezekiel Solomon," Michigan Jewish History, www.michjewishhistory.org/pdfs/vol38.pdf; accessed April 25, 2004.

11. Daniel J. Boorstin, *Portraits from "The Americans: The Democratic Experience"* (New York: Random House, 1975), 55.

12. See Oliver Hazard Perry, *The Hunting Expeditions of Oliver Hazard Perry* (Cleveland, 1899; rpt. DeForest, WI: St. Hubert's Press, 1994); see also Bill Heavey, "The Toughest Deer Hunter Ever," *Field & Stream* 108 (April 2004): 78–79.

13. Ross Atkin, "Durable Baseball Caps," *Christian Science Monitor Online* search, casmonitor.com/durable/1999/o9/21/fp23s2-csm.shtml.

14. Gayle V. Fischer, *Pantaloons and Power: Nineteenth-Century Dress Reform in the United States* (Kent, OH: Kent State University Press, 2001), 31.

15. *New Harmony Gazette*, June 28, 1826.

16. Patricia Cunningham, *Reforming Women's Fashion, 1850–1920: Politics, Health, and Art* (Kent, OH: Kent State University Press, 2001), 58.

17. Ibid., 51.

18. Ibid., 53–54.

19. Ibid., 44.

20. Ibid., 64–65.

21. Ibid., 153.

22. See Joseph W. Slade, "A Brief History of American Pornography," in *Pornography and Sexual Representation: A Reference Guide*, 3 vols. (Westport, CT: Greenwood Press, 2001), 1: 43.

23. Ruth M. Reichmann, "Native Dress, Fashion or Costume," *Indiana German Heritage Society Newsletter* 12, no. 4 (Fall 1996): 27–28.

Film and Theater

1. Tom Gunning, "The Cinema of Attractions: Early Film, Its Spectator and the Avant-Garde," in *Early Film*, ed. Thomas Elsaesser and Adam Barker (London: British Film Institute, 1989).

2. American Film Institute, *The American Film Institute Catalog of Motion Pictures Produced in the United States: Film Beginnings, 1893–1910*, vol. A (Metuchen, NJ: Scarecrow Press, 1989). All plot descriptions, catalog quotations, and so on, in this section come from the AFI catalog.

3. David Bordwell, Janet Staiger, and Kristin Thompson, *The Classical Hollywood Cinema: Film Style and Mode of Production to 1960* (New York: Columbia University Press, 1986).

4. Although many films from the silent period have been restored and made available on video (thanks to companies such as Kino and Milestone in New York, together with film preservationists like David Shepard in California), the overwhelming majority of these films have vanished. Surprisingly, this is a problem for films made during the sound era as well, as some scholars estimate that roughly 50 percent of all films ever produced are now lost. Thus, this section relies to some extent on sketchy catalog descriptions, summaries written by movie buffs lucky enough to have seen rare prints of the films, and various online resources.

5. Internet Movie Database, www.imdb.com. Throughout this section, numerous plot synopses are taken from this invaluable online resource.

6. The 1962 version shifts the action from the Midwest to Texas.

7. "Happy Lies," user comments by RJC-4 for *Happy Land*, Internet Movie Database, www.imdb.com.

8. Gerald Bordman, *The Oxford Companion to American Theatre* (New York: Oxford University Press, 1984).

9. American Film Institute, *The American Film Institute Catalog of Motion Pictures Produced in the United States: Feature Films, 1911–1920* (Berkeley: University of California Press, 1989).

10. Curiously, the real-life Annie Oakley appeared as "herself" in an 1894 film shot in Thomas Edison's "Black Maria" studio in New Jersey.

11. Donald Lyons, *Independent Visions: A Critical Introduction to Recent Independent American Film* (New York: Ballantine, 1994).

12. James W. Merrick, "'Anatomy' Operation Before a Bar of Justice: Screen Version of Book Takes Shape in Authentic Courtroom Setting," *New York Times*, April 12, 1959.

13. Charles M. Berg, lecture on *Medium Cool* (American Popular Culture of the 1960s), University of Kansas, June 2003.

14. Roger Ebert, review of *Fargo*, *Chicago Sun-Times*, March 8, 1996.

15. Lyons, *Independent Visions*, 132.

16. Bordman, *The Oxford Companion*, 141.

17. Joseph Wesley Zeigler, *Regional Theatre: The Revolutionary Stage* (Minneapolis: University of Minnesota Press, 1973).

18. Anthony Slide, *The Encyclopedia of Vaudeville* (Westport, CT: Greenwood Press, 1994).

19. Ibid., 388–389.

20. Ibid., 280–284.

21. Ibid., 92–93.

22. Ibid., 464–465; Bordman, *The Oxford Companion*, 618–619.

23. Paul Sporn, *Against Itself: The Federal Theater and Writers' Projects in the Midwest* (Detroit: Wayne State University Press, 1995). The bulk of information regarding ethnic theater and the FTP is a redaction of Sporn's excellent account.

24. Mark Lowry, "Chitlin Circuit Continues to Tap into Need for a Theater of Our Own," July 24, 2003, www.blackvoices.com.

25. Zeigler, *Regional Theatre*, 9.

26. Ibid., 143–144.

27. Literally, "agitation-propaganda," a confrontational form of theater that more often than not espoused revolutionary ideals.

28. Zeigler, *Regional Theatre*, 56.

29. Quoted in ibid., 9.

30. Sporn, *Against Itself*.

31. Gerald M. Berkowitz, *New Broadways—Theatre Across America: Approaching a New Millennium*, rev. ed. (New York: Applause, 1997).

32. Ibid., 73.

33. Ibid., 75; Zeigler, *Regional Theatre*, 70.

34. Berkowitz, *New Broadways*, 94–95.

35. Ibid., 94.

Folklore

1. Robert H. Lavenda, *Corn Fests and Water Carnivals: Celebrating Community in Minnesota* (Washington, DC: Smithsonian Institution Press, 1997), ix.

2. Timothy Cochrane, "Commercial Fishermen and Isle Royale: A Folk Group's Unique Association with Place," in *Michigan Folklife Reader*, ed. C. Kurt Dewhurst and Yvonne Lockwood (East Lansing: Michigan State University Press, 1988), 89–105.

3. K. Bernice Stewart and Homer A. Watt, "Legends of Paul Bunyan, Lumberjack," in *Wisconsin Folklore*, ed. James P. Leary, 139–148 (Madison: University of Wisconsin Press, 1998).

4. Barbara Allen, "Regional Studies in American Folklore Scholarship," in *Sense of Place: American Regional Cultures*, ed. Barbara Allen and Thomas J. Schlereth (Lexington: University Press of Kentucky, 1990), 9.

5. Vance Randolph, *Pissing in the Snow and Other Dark Tales* (Urbana: University of Illinois Press, 1976), 76–77.

6. Recorded July 2, 1998, in Washington, D.C., during "Hunting Stories," a narrative session held as part of the Smithsonian Folklife Festival. Tape housed at the Wisconsin Arts Board.

Food

1. Barbara G. Shortridge, "Not Just Jello and Hot Dishes: Representative Foods of Minnesota," *Journal of Cultural Geography* 21, no. 1 (2003): 79.

2. Resources on Native American foods in the Midwest include Anne R. Kaplan, Marjorie A. Hoover, and Willard B. Moore, *The Minnesota Ethnic Food Book* (St. Paul: Minnesota Historical Society Press, 1986), 15–33, 263–270; Pamela Goyan Kittler and Kathryn Sucher, *Food and Culture in America* (New York: Van Nostrand Reinhold, 1989), 51–80; Thomas Vennum, Jr., *Wild Rice and the Ojibway People* (St. Paul: Minnesota Historical Society Press, 1988); E. Barrie Kavasch, *Enduring Harvests: Native American Foods and Festivals for Every Season* (Old Saybrook, CT: Globe Pequot Press, 1995).

3. Midwestern frontier foods are discussed in Marjorie Kreidberg, *Food on the Frontier: Minnesota Cooking* (St. Paul: Minnesota Historical Society Press, 1975); Estelle Woods Wilcox, ed., *Buckeye Cookery and Practical Housekeeping*, 1876 (reprint, St. Paul: Minnesota Historical Society Press, 1988); Jacqueline Williams, *Wagon Wheel Kitchens: Food on the Oregon Trail* (Lawrence: University Press of Kansas, 1993); Barbara M. Walker, *The Little House Cookbook: Frontier Foods from Laura Ingalls Wilder's Classic Stories* (New York: HarperCollins, 1979).

4. Shortridge, "Not Just Jello," 71–94.

5. James Hope and Susan Faylor, *Bountiful Ohio: Good Food and Stories from Where the Heartland Begins* (Bowling Green, OH: Gabriel's Horn, 1993), 186 (adapted from a restaurant in Waterville, Ohio).

6. The term *foodways* refers to the totality of activities surrounding food. It also includes beliefs and superstitions about food and eating, the aesthetics of food, and the cultural construction of taste. The foodways model was introduced by Don Yoder in the early 1970s and has been developed primarily by folklorists working in food studies. See Don Yoder, "Folk Cookery," in *Folklore and Folklife: An Introduction*, edited by Richard M. Dorson 325–350 (Chicago: University of Chicago Press, 1972).

7. Linda Civitello, *Cuisine and Culture: A History of Food and People* (Hoboken, NJ: John Wiley, 2004), 196.

8. General sources for British and Celtic traditions include Kittler and Sucher, *Food and Culture in America*, 81–112; Kaplan, Hoover, and Moore, *Minnesota Ethnic Food Book* 67–85, 296–308; unpublished fieldwork by Lucy Long and other scholars.

9. English food in the Midwest is included in general discussions of the British midwestern traditions. An essay on English tea rooms in Ohio is found in Jim Comer, "Some Remarks on Tea," *Digest: An Interdisciplinary Study of Food and Foodways* 17 (1997): 25–30.

10. A source for Welsh food in the Midwest is Jeff Smith's *The Frugal Gourmet on Our Immigrant Ancestors* (New York: William Morrow, 1990), 493–502.

11. Information on Cornish immigration to Michigan and their food is found in Yvonne R. Lockwood and William G. Lockwood, "Pasties in Michigan's Upper Peninsula: Foodways, Interethnic Relations, and Regionalism," in *The Taste of American Place*,

edited by Barbara G. Shortridge and James R. Shortridge (New York: Rowman and Lit-tlefield, 1998), 21–36.

12. A source for Scottish American food is Smith, *Frugal Gourmet*, 437–448.

13. Sources for Irish food include Smith, *Frugal Gourmet*, 207–220; and Lucy M. Long, "Soda Bread in Ireland," *Digest: An Interdisciplinary Study of Food and Foodways* 13 (1993): 2–8.

14. German midwestern foodways are discussed in Kittler and Sucher, *Food and Culture in America*, 131–155; Kaplan et al., *Minnesota Ethnic Food Book*, 86–101, 309–319; La Vern J. Rippley, *The German-Americans* (Boston: Twayne, 1976); Henriette Davidis, *Pickled Her-ring and Pumpkin Pie: A Nineteenth-Century Cookbook for German Immigrants to America* (Madison, WI: Max Kade Institute for German-American Studies, 2003).

15. Marica Adams, *Cooking from Quilt Country: Hearty Recipes from Amish and Mennon-ite Kitchens* (New York: Crown, 1989); Marcia Adams, *New Recipes from Quilt Country: More Folkways and Food from the Amish and Mennonites* (New York: Clarkson Potter Publishers, 1997) ; Henry and Amanda Mast, *Cooking with the Horse and Buggy People* (Sugarcreek, OH: Carlisle Press, 2001); Fred J. Wilson, Johnny Schock, and Larry Rogers, eds., *Wonderful Good Cooking from Amish Country Kitchens* (Scottdale, PA: Herald Press, 1974). A classic cookbook contributed to by Mennonites around the world, many of whom are based in Ohio, is Doris Janzen Longacre, *More-with-Less Cookbook*, 25th anniversary ed. (Scottdale, PA: Herald Press, 2000). Also see www.mennolink.org for more information about both groups.

16. Barbara G. Shortridge, "Ethnic Heritage Food in Lindsborg, Kansas, and New Glarus, Wisconsin," in *Culinary Tourism*, edited by Lucy Long, 268–296 (Lexington: Uni-versity Press of Kentucky, 2004).

17. See Kaplan et al., 34–47, 272–281; Kittler and Sucher, 171–199.

18. For an overview of Scandinavian foodways, see Kittler and Sucher, 156–170, and Ka-plan et al., 102–108.

19. Kaplan et al., 105.

20. For more on Norwegian foods, see Smith, *Frugal Gourmet*, 335–346; Kaplan et al., 109–120, 320–325.

21. Kaplan et al., 118.

22. See Kaplan et al., 131–143, 336–345; Smith, *Frugal Gourmet*, 459–470. A discussion of Swedish American food tourism is found in Barbara G. Shortridge, "Ethnic Heritage Food in Lindsborg, Kansas, and New Glarus, Wisconsin," in Long, *Culinary Tourism*, 268–296.

23. Ibid., 121.

24. Ibid., 144–162, 346–357; Lockwood, "Pasties in Michigan's Upper Peninsula," 21–36.

25. This recipe was adapted from Kaplan, Hoover, and Moore, *Minnesota Ethnic Food Book*, 302–303.

26. Ibid., 152.

27. A general overview of Eastern Europeans is found in and Sucher and Kittler, 131–155, although they are identified as Central Europeans.

28. "Elinor's Kitchen," www.e.schrabal.home.att.net/ (accessed March 1, 2004).

29. See Smith, *Frugal Gourmet*, 163–182. For a detailed study of one community, see Lynn Hamer, "Recipes and Ethnic Identity," in *Hungarian American Toledo*, edited by Thomas E. Barden and John Ahern, 175–199 (Toledo: University of Toledo Urban Affairs Center, 2002).

30. See Smith, *Frugal Gourmet*, 363–378, and unpublished research by Lucy Long.

31. Kaplan et al., 214–234, 402–419; Smith, *Frugal Gourmet*, 399–410, 503–514; Kittler and Sucher, 131–155.

32. Kaplan et al., 163–179, 358–373.

33. Timothy C. Lloyd, "The Cincinnati Chili Culinary Complex," in *Taste of American Place*, ed. Shortridge and Shortridge, 45–56.

34. For a discussion of an Italian American festival, see Sabina Magliocco, "Playing with Food: The Negotiation of Identity in the Ethnic Display Event by Italian Americans in Clinton, Indiana," in *Taste of American Place*, Shortridge and Shortridge, eds., 145–162. Italian foods in Utah are similar to the Midwest as in Richard Raspa, "Exotic Foods among Italian-Americans in Mormon Utah: Food as Nostalgic Enactment of Identity," in *Ethnic and Regional Foodways in the United States: The Performance of Group Identity*, edited by Linda Keller Brown and Kay Mussell, 185–194 (Knoxville: University of Tennessee Press, 1984). Also see Kaplan et al., 180–195, 374–385.

35. See Kaplan et al., 48–66, 282–296; Smith, *Frugal Gourmet*, 309–320; Kittler and Sucher, 201–225. For a study of tamales in Illinois, see Brett Williams, "Why Migrant Women Feed Their Husbands Tamales: Foodways as a Basis for a Revisionist View of Tejano Family Life," in *Ethnic and Regional Foodways*, Brown and Mussell, eds., 113–126. For the Americanization of Mexican food, see Amy Bentley, "From Culinary Other to Mainstream America: Meanings and Uses of Southwestern Cuisine," in Long, *Culinary Tourism*, 209–225; and Jeffrey M. Pilcher, "From 'Montezuma's Revenge' to 'Mexican Truffles,'" in Long, *Culinary Tourism*, 76–96.

36. For an overview of Chinese food in the United States in general, see Kittler and Sucher, 248–268.

37. See Smith, *Frugal Gourmet*, 259–274.

38. For an overview of Southeast Asian immigrant foods, see Kittler and Sucher, 285–311. An excellent discussion of Hmong traditions in the United States is Kaplan et al., 235–260, 420–428. See also Smith, *Frugal Gourmet*, 99–106 on Cambodian immigrant foods; 131–140 on Filipino; 471–482 on Thai; and 483–492 on Vietnamese.

39. For Japanese food traditions in the United States, see Kittler and Sucher, 269–284; Smith, *Frugal Gourmet*, 233–246.

40. See Smith, *Frugal Gourmet*, 285–298, 347–362, and 425–436. Also see publications by Yvonne Lockwood and William Lockwood.

41. See Kaplan et al., 196–213, 386–401; Smith, *Frugal Gourmet*, 247–258.

42. Vincent Delgado, *A Taste of Freedom: A Culinary Journey with America's Refugees* (Lansing, MI: Global Workshop, 2003).

Language

1. Ives Goddard, ed., *Handbook of North American Indians*, vol. 17, *Languages* (Washington, DC: Smithsonian Institution Press, 1996). Much of the information on Native American and immigrant languages reported in this chapter is abstracted from papers presented at the State Linguistic Profiles Conference held in Columbus, Ohio, in May 2001. A volume of these papers is forthcoming, to be edited by Dennis Preston and Brian Joseph (Bloomington: Indiana University Press). Brief citations to individual papers and articles referred to throughout this chapter will be made in the text; complete citations can be found in the Resource Guide.

2. Goddard, *Handbook of North American Indians*, vol. 17; John D. Nichols, "The Indigenous Languages of the Midwest" (paper presented at the State Linguistic Profiles Conference, Columbus, OH, May 2001).

3. See Beverly Olson Flanigan, "American Indian English and Error Analysis: The Case of Lakota English," *English World-Wide* 6 (1985): 217–236; and Colin Baker, *Foundations of Bilingual Education and Bilingualism*, 3rd ed. (Clevedon, England: Multilingual Matters, 2001).

4. For more information on the etymologies of anglicized place names, see, among others, Goddard, ed., *Handbook of North American Indians*, vol. 17; William Bright, "Native American Placenames in the Louisiana Purchase," *American Speech* 78 (2003): 353–362; and Donald M. Lance, "The Pronunciation of *Missouri*: Variation and Change in American English," *American Speech* 78 (2003): 255–284.

5. Steve Hartman Keiser, "Research Findings on Deitsch (Pennsylvania German) in Ohio" (paper presented at the State Linguistic Profiles Conference, Columbus, OH, May 2001).

6. See Charles A. Ferguson, "Diglossia," *Word* 15 (1959): 325–340.

7. See Einar Haugen, *Bilingualism in the Americas*, publication of the American Dialect Society 26 (University: University of Alabama Press, 1956); Joshua Fishman, *Handbook of Language and Ethnic Identity* (New York: Oxford University Press, 1999); and Calvin J. Veltman, *Language Shift in the United States* (New York: Mouton, 1983).

8. Jaap Van Marle, "On the Divergence and Maintenance of Immigrant Languages: Dutch in Michigan" (paper presented at the State Linguistic Profiles Conference, Columbus, OH, May 2001); and Peter Trudgill, *On Dialect: Social and Geographical Perspectives* (New York: New York University Press, 1983).

9. See Einar Haugen, *The Norwegian Language in America: A Study in Bilingual Behavior*, 2nd ed. (Bloomington: Indiana University Press, 1969).

10. Bartek Plichta, "Aspect in American Polish" (paper presented at the State Linguistic Profiles Conference, Columbus, OH, May 2001).

11. Robert J. Di Pietro, *Language Structures in Contrast*, rev. ed. (Rowley, MA: Newbury House, 1978).

12. See Linda Dégh, "Hungarians," in *Peopling Indiana: The Ethnic Experience*, edited by R. M. Taylor and C. A. McBirney, 224–242 (Indianapolis: Indiana Historical Society, 1996); Andrew Kerek, "Hunglish in Ohio," *The New Hungarian Quarterly* 33 (1992): 140–143; Miklós Kontra, "Hungarian(s) in the Midwest: Select Bibliography" (paper presented at the State Linguistic Profiles Conference, Columbus, OH, May 2001); and Pekka Hirvonen, "Finnish in the Upper Midwest" (paper presented at the State Linguistic Profiles Conference, Columbus, OH, May 2001).

13. Charlotte Schaengold, "Yiddish in Cincinnati"; Panayiotis A. Pappas, "Greek in Columbus"; and John A. C. Greppin, "Armenian in Cleveland," all papers presented at the State Linguistic Profiles Conference, Columbus, OH, May 2001.

14. Table 4 displays census data on the numbers of non-English-speaking residents in the eight states of the Midwest. Except for Spanish, individual languages are not listed. Note, however, that Illinois far outstrips the other states in the region in numbers of speakers of languages other than English. Almost one-fifth of the state's population speaks another language; half of those speak Spanish, but other European languages also have large numbers. Only Minnesota outranks Illinois in speakers of Asian and Pacific Island languages, largely because of its Hmong and Cambodian immigrants.

15. For more information on Hispanic Americans, see Terrell A. Morgan, "Field Report on Spanish in Ohio"; Michelle Ramos-Pellicia, "Spanish Phonology of Lorain, Ohio"; and Amy Shuman and Norma Mendoza-Denton, "On Language, Ethnicity, Heritage, and Identity," all papers presented at the State Linguistic Profiles Conference, Columbus, OH, May 2001. On the use of "mixed" varieties and code-switching by Hispanics, see Carmen Fought, *Chicano English in Context* (New York: Palgrave Macmillan, 2003).

16. Martha Ratcliff, "Southeast Asian Languages in the Midwest" (paper presented at the State Linguistic Profiles Conference, Columbus, OH, May 2001).

17. Heather Boyce, *Language Attitudes and Classroom Practices: In or Out with Arabic, English, and Somali?* (M.A. research paper, Ohio University, 2003); and Aleya Rouchdy, "Arabic in the Midwest" (paper presented at the State Linguistic Profiles Conference, Columbus, OH, May 2001).

18. For a brief history of the Linguistic Atlas project, see Hans Kurath, *Studies in Area Linguistics* (Bloomington: Indiana University Press, 1972).

19. Local terms are taken *passim* from Allan Metcalf, *How We Talk: American Regional English Today* (New York: Houghton Mifflin, 2000). For more detailed information on the provenance of dialect vocabulary, see the *Dictionary of American Regional English (DARE)*, ed. Frederic G. Cassidy and Joan Hall (Cambridge, MA: Belknap Press, 1985–).

20. On grammatical and other differences in our region, see Albert H. Marckwardt, "Principal and Subsidiary Dialect Areas in the North-Central States," *Publications of the American Dialect Society* 27 (1957): 3–15; and Raven I. McDavid and Virginia G. McDavid, "Grammatical Differences in the North Central States," *American Speech* 35 (1960): 5–19.

21. The principal work on pronunciation changes in the United States has been done by William Labov; a detailed delineation of the emerging dialect areas is "The Three Dialects of English," in *New Ways of Analyzing Sound Change*, ed. Penelope Eckert, 1–44 (New York: Academic Press, 1991).

22. For features of Hispanic and American Indian English, see Lizette Alvarez, "It's the Talk of Nueva York: The Hybrid Called Spanglish," in *Language: Readings in Language and Culture*, 6th ed., edited by V. Clark, P. Eschholz, and A. Rosa, 483–488 (New York: St. Martin's Press, 1998); and Flanigan, "American Indian English and Error Analysis."

23. On vocabulary in the Northwest Ordinance, and specifically the Ohio Valley, see Robert F. Dakin, "South Midland Speech in the Old Northwest," *Journal of English Linguistics* 5 (1971): 31–48; and Beverly Olson Flanigan, "Mapping the Ohio Valley: South Midland, Lower North, or Appalachian?" *American Speech* 75 (2000): 344–347. On the transmission of Appalachian English to the Ozarks, see Donna Christian, Walt Wolfram, and Nanjo Dube, *Variation and Change in Geographically Isolated Communities: Appalachian English and Ozark English* (Tuscaloosa: University of Alabama Press, 1988).

24. Beverly Olson Flanigan, "'I Might Could Be Polylectal': Report from the Mid-American Field," *Ohio University Working Papers in Linguistics and Language Teaching* 15 (1996): 103–121 (Athens: Department of Linguistics, Ohio University).

25. On the merger of *collar/caller/color*, see Clyde T. Hankey, "Notes on West Penn-Ohio Phonology," in *Studies in Linguistics in Honor of Raven I. McDavid, Jr.*, ed. Lawrence M. Davis, 49–61 (Tuscaloosa: University of Alabama Press, 1972). On vowel fronting in the Midwest, see Erik R. Thomas, "Vowel Changes in Columbus, Ohio," *Journal of English Linguistics* 22 (1993): 205–215. On the pronunciation of final vowels in place names, see Donald M. Lance, "The Pronunciation of *Missouri*: Variation and Change in American English," *American Speech* 78 (2003): 255–284.

26. On the movement northward of Southern English, see William Labov, "The Triumph of the Southern Shift" (paper presented at the Southeastern Conference on Linguistics, Norfolk, VA, April 1999).

27. See Beverly Olson Flanigan and Franklin Paul Norris, "Cross-Dialectal Comprehension as Evidence for Boundary Mapping: Perceptions of the Speech of Southeastern Ohio," *Language Variation and Change* 12 (2000): 175–201.

28. See Walt Wolfram and Natalie Schilling-Estes, *American English: Dialects and Variation* (London: Blackwell, 1998).

29. For detailed explications of Black English, see William Labov, *Language in the Inner City* (Philadelphia: University of Pennsylvania Press, 1972); and Wolfram and Schilling-Estes, *American English: Dialects and Variation.*

30. The Ann Arbor court case and its educational implications are discussed in Judge Charles W. Joiner, *The Ann Arbor Decision: Memorandum Opinion and Order and the Educational Plan* (Arlington, VA: Center for Applied Linguistics, 1980).

Literature

1. Ralph Leslie Rusk, *The Literature of the Middle Western Frontier*, 2nd ed., 2 vols. (New York: Ungar, 1926), 2:1.

2. See Hector St. John de Crevecoeur, *Letters from an American Farmer and Sketches of 18th-Century America* (New York: Penguin, 1981); Frederick Jackson Turner, *The Frontier in American History* (New York: Holt, 1920); R. W. B. Lewis, *The American Adam: Innocence,*

Tragedy, and Tradition in the Nineteenth Century (Chicago: University of Chicago Press, 1966).

3. Hamlin Garland, *Crumbling Idols: Twelve Essays on Art Dealing Chiefly with Literature, Painting and the Drama* (Cambridge, MA: Stone and Kimball, 1894).

4. William Davis Gallagher, "Sketches on the Literature of the West," in *The First West: Writing from the American Frontier, 1780–1860*, edited by Edward Watts and David Rachels (New York: Oxford University Press, 2002), 700–706.

5. Drake's essays on this subject are reprinted in Watts and Rachels, *The First West*, 341–367.

6. Cutler's tract "An Explanation of the Map of Federal Lands" (1787), is reprinted in *The First West*, 43–50.

7. See Scott Michaelsen's *The Limits of Multiculturalism: Interrogating the Origins of American Anthropology* (Minneapolis: University of Minnesota Press, 1999).

8. Mary Schriber's *Writing Home: American Women Abroad, 1830–1920* (Charlottesville: University Press of Virginia, 1997), Larzer Ziff's *Return Passages: Great American Travel Writing, 1780–1910* (New Haven, CT: Yale University Press, 2000), Terry Caesar's *Forgiving the Boundaries: Home as Abroad in American Travel Writing* (Athens: University of Georgia Press, 1995), and others have revived the popular genre of travel writing as an important site of cultural interaction and exchange.

9. See June Namias' *White Captives: Gender and Ethnicity on the American Frontier* (Chapel Hill: University of North Carolina Press, 1993), Michelle Burnham's *Captivity and Sentiment: Cultural Exchange in American Literature, 1682–1861* (Hanover: University Press of New England, 1997), and Christopher Castiglia's *Bound and Determined: Captivity, Cultural Crossing, and White Womanhood from Mary Rowlandson to Patty Hearst* (Chicago: University of Chicago Press, 1995). The classic work on captivity narratives is Richard Slotkin, *Regeneration through Violence: The Mythology of the American Frontier, 1600–1860* (Middletown, CT: Wesleyan University Press, 1973).

10. On captives' returns, see James Axtell's "The White Indians of Colonial America" in *American Encounters: Natives and Newcomers from European Contact to Indian Removal, 1500–1850*, edited by Peter C. Mancall and James H. Merrell (New York: Routledge, 2000), 324–350.

11. See William G. B. Carson's *The Theatre on the Frontier: The Early Years of the St. Louis Stage* (1932; reprint, New York: S. Blom, 1965) for more on this topic.

12. On the implicit feminism of "Republican motherhood," see Linda K. Kerber's *Women of the Republic: Intellect and Ideology in Revolutionary America* (New York: W. W. Norton, 1986).

13. William T. Coggeshall, ed., *The Poets and Poetry of the West* (Columbus, OH: Follet, Foster, 1860), 437.

14. William David Sloan, ed., *The Media in America: A History*, 5th ed. (Northport, AL: Vision Press, 2002), 179–180.

15. See Frank Luther Mott, *A History of American Magazines: 1741–1850*, 5 vols. (Cambridge, MA: Harvard University Press, 1957–1968), 1: 457; Margaret A. Blanchard, ed., *History of the Mass Media in the United States: An Encyclopedia* (Chicago: Fitzroy Dearborn, 1998), 3; and Sloan, *The Media in America*, 147.

16. Sloan, *The Media in America*, 205, 215.

17. W. A. Swanberg, *Pulitzer* (New York: Charles Scribner's Sons, 1967), 3–44, 47–51.

18. Michael Emery, Edwin Emery, and Nancy L. Roberts, *The Press and America: An Interpretive History of the Mass Media*, 8th ed. (Boston: Allyn and Bacon, 1996), 174.

19. Blanchard, *History of the Mass Media in the United States*, 434.

20. See ibid., 600; and Emery, Emery, and Roberts, *The Press and America*, 220–222.

21. Emery, Emery, and Roberts, *The Press and America*, 220–221.

22. See Blanchard, *History of the Mass Media in the United States*, 131; Emery, Emery, and

Roberts, *The Press and America*, 233–234; Lee Finkle, *Forum for Protest* (Cranbury, NJ: Associated University Presses, 1975), 39; and Lawrence D. Hogan, *A Black National News Service: The Associated Negro Press and Claude Barnett, 1919–1945* (Cranbury, NJ: Associated University Presses, 1984), 28.

23. For the most complete discussion of the *Chicago Defender*'s campaign to get blacks to come north, see Martin Terrell, "The *Chicago Defender*'s Great Northern Drive" (master's thesis, Ohio University, 1991).

24. Mott, *A History of American Magazines*, vol. 1, 205–207.

25. Ibid., vol. 2, 89.

26. Magazine statistical data included in this chapter derives from *SRDS Business Publication Advertising Source, Part 1*, July, 2000, and *SRDS Consumer Magazine Advertising Source*, July, 2000.

27. Mott, *A History of American Magazines*, vol. 3, 157–158.

28. Ibid., 3, 652–656.

29. Mott, *A History of American Magazines: 1905–1930*, vol. 5 (Cambridge, MA: Harvard University Press, 1968), 179–190.

30. Ibid., vol. 5, 293.

31. Ibid., vol. 4, 763–772; Theodore Peterson, *Magazines in the Twentieth Century*, 2nd ed. (Urbana, IL.: University of Illinois Press, 1964), 128–145; and Kathleen L. Endres, "Woman's Home Companion," in Kathleen L. Endres and Therese L. Lueck, eds., *Women's Periodicals in the United States: Consumer Magazines* (Westport, CT: Greenwood Press, 1995), 444–55.

32. See Mott, *A History of American Magazines*, vol. 5, 36–48; and R. Craig Endicott, "Top Magazines Gain 3% in 2002," *Advertising Age*, September 22, 2003, S-2.

33. See Peterson, *Magazines in the Twentieth Century*, 351–54; and Alan Nourie, "Look," in Alan Nourie and Barbara Nourie, eds., *American Mass-Market Magazines* (New York: Greenwood Press, 1990), 225–233.

34. Mott, *A History of American Magazines*, vol. 4, 374.

35. See "The History of *The Progressive Magazine*," http://www.progressive.org/history.html, accessed February 28, 2004; Bill Lueders, *An Enemy of the State: The Life of Erwin Knoll* (Monroe, ME: Common Courage Press, 1996), 119–200.

36. See Peterson, *Magazines in the Twentieth Century*, 65–7; and *SRDS Consumer Magazine Advertising Source*.

37. Endicott, "Top Magazines Gain 3% in 2002."

38. See Vicki L. Tate, "Playboy," in Nourie and Nourie, eds., *American Mass-Market Magazines*, 367–75; Peterson, *Magazines in the Twentieth Century*, 316–20; John Tebbel and Mary Ellen Zuckerman, *The Magazine in America, 1741–1990* (New York: Oxford University Press, 1991), 282–88; William H. Taft, *Magazines for the 1980s* (New York: Hastings House, 1982), 124–27; and Endicott, "Top Magazines Gain 3% in 2002."

39. Henry Nash Smith, *Virgin Land: The American West as Symbol and Myth* (New York: Random House, 1950).

40. Marilyn J. Atlas, "Midwestern Literature, 1860–present," unpublished essay.

41. See, for example, Jay Martin's discussion of Edward Eggleston's fiction in his study *Harvests of Change: American Literature 1865–1914* (Englewood Cliffs, NJ: Prentice-Hall, 1967), 111–116.

42. James Whitcomb Riley, "Dialect in Literature," *The Complete Works of James Whitcomb Riley*, vol. 10 (New York: Harper & Brothers, 1916), 2678.

43. Carl Sandburg, "Abraham Lincoln: The Soil and the Seed," *Literary History of the United States*, edited by Robert Spiller (New York: Macmillan, 1946), 779.

44. Quoted in Glen Johnson, "Abraham Lincoln," *Encyclopedia of American Literature*, edited by Stephen Serafin (New York: Continuum, 1999), 669.

45. See, for example, Henry Nash Smith, *Mark Twain: The Development of a Writer* (Cambridge, MA: Harvard University Press, 1962), 71–91.

46. *Old Times on the Mississippi, Mark Twain: Tales, Speeches, Essays, and Sketches*, edited by Tom Quirk (1875; reprint, New York: Penguin, 1994), 128.

47. See, for example, David Carkeet, "The Dialects in *Huckleberry Finn*," *American Literature* 51 (November 1979): 315–332.

48. Ernest Hemingway, *The Green Hills of Africa* (New York: Scribner's, 1935).

49. Victor A. Doyno, *Writing Huck Finn* (Philadelphia: University of Pennsylvania Press, 1991).

50. Joseph Blotner, *Faulkner: A Biography*, 2 vols. (New York Random House, 1974), 526.

51. "Big Two-Hearted River: Part I," *The Complete Short Stories of Ernest Hemingway: The Finca Vigía Edition* (New York: Macmillan, 1991), 164.

52. F. Scott Fitzgerald, *The Great Gatsby*, edited by Matthew Bruccoli (New York: Scribner's, 1995), 184.

53. See, respectively, Lee Clark Mitchell, "Naturalism and the Languages of Determinism," and Eric J. Sundquist, "Realism and Regionalism," *Columbia Literary History of the United States*, edited by Emory Elliott (New York: Columbia University Press, 1988), 543, 503.

54. Carl Sandburg, "Chicago," *Complete Poems* (New York: Harcourt Brace, 1950).

55. Cary Nelson, "The Diversity of American Poetry," *Columbia Literary History of the United States*, edited by Emory Elliott (New York: Columbia University Press, 1988), 915.

56. Susan Glaspell, *Trifles, Plays by Susan Glaspell*, edited by C.W.E. Bigsby (New York: Cambridge University Press, 1987).

57. Ekaterini Georgoudaki, "Rita Dove: Crossing Boundaries," *Callaloo* 14, no. 2 (Spring 1991): 419–433.

Music

1. Frances Densmore, *The American Indians and Their Music*, rev. ed. (New York: Womans [*sic*] Press, 1936), 79.

2. *The New Grove Dictionary of American Music*, s.v. "Crow Indians." See also Bruno Nettl, *Folk and Traditional Music of the Western Continents*, 2nd ed. (Englewood Cliffs, NJ: Prentice Hall, 1973), 163.

3. Rev. David Jones, *A Journal of Two Visits Made to Some Nations of Indians on the West Side of the River Ohio, in the Years 1772 and 1773* (New York: J. Sabin, 1865; reprint, Fairfield, WA: Ye Galleon Press, 1973), 78–79.

4. Gertrude P. Kurath, *Iroquois Music and Dance: Ceremonial Arts of Two Seneca Longhouses*, Smithsonian Institution, Bureau of American Ethnology Bulletin 187 (Washington D.C.: Government Printing Office, 1964), 66–67.

5. Densmore, *America Indians*, 64.

6. Examples are found in Frederick R. Burton, *American Primitive Music* (New York: Moffat, Yard, 1909).

7. *New Grove Dictionary*, s.v. "Indians, American."

8. Frances Densmore, *Chippewa Music*, 2 vols., Smithsonian Institution, Bureau of American Ethnology Bulletins 45, 53 (Washington, DC: Government Printing Office, 1910–1913), 1:5.

9. *New Grove Dictionary*, s.v. "Minstrelsy."

10. Ibid., s.v. "Rice, Thomas Dartmouth ('Daddy')."

11. Quoted in Hans Nathan, *Dan Emmett and the Rise of Early Negro Minstrelsy* (Norman: University of Oklahoma Press, 1962), 56.

12. See ibid., 87–88, 95.

13. Elias Howe, *Howe's Complete Ball-Room Hand Book* (Boston: Oliver Ditson, 1858), quoted in Richard Powers, "Guidelines for Performing Traditional Social Dance," *Country Dance and Song Society of America Annual* 20 (1990): 17.

14. *New Grove Dictionary*, s.v. "Bands."

15. Cited in H.W. Schwartz, *Bands of America* (Garden City, NY: Doubleday, 1957), 128–129.

16. Rudi Blesh, introduction to *Classic Piano Rags* (New York: Dover, 1973), v. Most of the titles mentioned in this section are found in this source. See also Rudi Blesh and Harriet Janis, *They All Played Ragtime*, rev. ed. (New York: Oak Publications, 1971).

17. Blesh and Janis, *They All Played*, 16, 17.

18. *New Grove Dictionary*, s.v. "Cincinnati."

19. Frank Tirro, *Jazz: A History*, 2nd ed. (New York: W.W. Norton, 1993), 202–203.

20. Dan Morgenstern, *Jazz People* (Englewood Cliffs, NJ: Prentice Hall, 1976), 45.

21. Ross Russell, *Jazz Style in Kansas City and the Southwest* (Berkeley: University of California Press, 1973), 122–123.

22. Ibid., 12–13.

23. Steven C. Tracy, *Going to Cincinnati: A History of the Blues in the Queen City* (Urbana: University of Illinois Press, 1993), 14, 114–153; Starr-Gennett Foundation, "The Starr Piano Company and Gennett Recording Studio" http://www.starrgennett.org/museum.

24. The Official Muddy Waters Website, http://www.muddywaters.com/bio.html.

25. D. Thomas Moon, "Strange Voodoo: Inside the Vaults of Chess Studios," http://www.bluesaccess.com.

26. Arnold Shaw, *Honkers and Shouters: The Golden Years of Rhythm and Blues* (New York: Macmillan, 1978), 273.

27. *Grove Music Online*, s.v. "Hooker, John Lee."

28. David Toop, *Rap Attack #3: African Rap to Global Hip Hop* (London: Serpent's Tail, 2000), 47.

29. Eileen Southern, *The Music of Black Americans: A History*, 3rd ed. (New York: W.W. Norton, 1997), 517.

30. Vivian M. Baulch, "The Golden Age of the Motown Sound," *Detroit News*, www.detnews.com/history/motown/motown.htm.

31. *The Encyclopedia of Cleveland History*, s.v. "Rock 'n' Roll"; Belz, quoted in Southern, *Music*, 519.

32. Quoted in Peter Doggett, *Are You Ready for the Country?* (New York: Penguin, 2001), 494.

Religion

1. R. Douglas Hurt, "Midwestern Distinctiveness," in *The American Midwest: Essays on Regional History*, edited by Andrew R.L. Cayton and Susan E. Gray (Bloomington: Indiana University Press, 2001), 170.

2. Clifton E. Olmstead, *History of Religion in the United States* (Englewood Cliffs, NJ: Prentice Hall, 1960), 250–251; Harry Thomas Stock, "Protestantism in Illinois Before 1835: The Baptists," *Journal of the Illinois State Historical Society* 12, no. 1 (April 1919): 3.

3. Olmstead, *History of Religion*, 242–243; see also Roger Finke and Rodney Stark, *The Churching of America 1776–1990: Winners and Losers in Our Religious Economy* (New Brunswick, NJ: Rutgers University Press, 1992), chap. 3.

4. Olmstead, *History of Religion*, 254; Suzanne Winckler, *The Smithsonian Guides to Historic America: The Great Lakes Region* (New York: Stewart, Tabori & Chang, 1998), 135.

5. Dale E. Jones et al., *Religious Congregations and Membership in the United States 2000* (Nashville, TN: Glenmary Research Center, 2002), 27.

6. Brett E. Carroll, *The Routledge Historical Atlas of Religion in America* (New York: Routledge, 2000), 90–91.

7. James S. Olson, *Catholic Immigrants in America* (Chicago: Nelson-Hall, 1987), 106–108.

8. Linda Mack Schloff, *And Prairie Dogs Weren't Kosher: Jewish Women in the Upper Midwest Since 1855* (St. Paul: Minnesota Historical Society, 1996), 57.

9. Mechal Sobel, *Trabelin' On: The Slave Journey to an Afro-Baptist Faith* (Princeton, NJ: Princeton University Press, 1988), 215–216.

10. Hans A. Baer and Merrill Singer, *African American Religion: Varieties of Protest and Accommodation*, 2nd ed. (Knoxville: University of Tennessee Press, 2002), 42.

11. Ibid., 48.

12. Ibid., 51.

13. Ibid., 51, 189.

14. Theodore Caplow et al., *All Faithful People: Change and Continuity in Middletown's Religion* (Minneapolis: University of Minnesota Press, 1983), 310.

15. Ibid.

16. Denominational statistics for midwestern states can be found in Jones, *Religious Congregations and Membership in the United States 2000*.

17. Statistics on midwestern Catholicism can be found in Jones, *Religious Congregations and Membership in the United States 2000*.

18. For the number of priests in 1968, see Roger Fortin, *Faith and Action: A History of the Archdiocese of Cincinnati 1821–1996* (Columbus: The Ohio State University Press, 2002), 375; for 2003, see the diocesan Web site, www.catholiccincinnati.org/; for mass attendance, see Robert Anglen, "Shaken, Catholics Shunning Church," *Cincinnati Enquirer* (August 30, 2003), and Stephen Huba, "Many Empty Church Pews: We Say We Attend More Than We Do," *The Cincinnati Post* (April 9, 1998).

19. Anglen, "Shaken, Catholics Shunning Church."

20. Stephen J. Whitfield, "Jews," *Encyclopedia of American Cultural and Intellectual History*, edited by Mary Kupiec Cayton and Peter W. Williams (New York: Charles Scribner's Sons, 2001), 2: 382.

21. Edwin Scott Gaustad and Philip L. Barlow, *New Historical Atlas of Religion in America* (Oxford: Oxford University Press, 2001), 271.

22. See Chicago listings in Don Morreale, ed., *The Complete Guide to Buddhist America*, edited by Don Morreale (Boston: Shambhala, 1998).

23. The exact size of the Muslim population in the United States is a contentious issue: see the discussion at www.Adherents.com. For the number of mosques in the Midwest, see www.usinfo.state.gov/products/pubs/muslimlife/musmap.htm/; for statistics on Detroit's Muslims, see *The Detroit Almanac: 300 Years of Life in the Motor City*, ed. Peter Gavrilovich and Bill McGraw (Detroit: Detroit Free Press, 2000), 599.

Sports and Recreation

1. "An Angler," "The Cincinnati Angling Club," in *The American Turf Register and Sporting Magazine* (March 1832), reprinted in *Sports in North America: A Documentary History*, ed. Larry K. Menna (Gulf Breeze, FL: Academic International Press, 1995), 2: 311.

2. Jane Addams, quoted in Gerald R. Gems, *Windy City Wars: Labor, Leisure, and Sport in the Making of Chicago* (Lanham, MD: Scarecrow Press, 1997).

3. Charles Adams, quoted in Steven A. Riess, *Sport in Industrial America, 1850–1920* (Whelling, IL: Harlan Davison, 1995), 128.

4. Andrew White, quoted in David M. Nelson, *Anatomy of a Game: Football, the Rules, and the Men Who Made the Game* (Newark: University of Delaware Press, 1994), 25.

5. *Boston Herald*, quoted in Alexander M. Weyland, *The Saga of American Football* (New York: Macmillan, 1995), 56.

6. Roper Starch, *Outdoor Recreation in America 1997* (Washington, DC: Recreation Roundtable, 1997), 7–8.

7. Ibid.

# BIBLIOGRAPHY

Adams, Rosemary K., ed. *A Wild Kind of Boldness: The Chicago History Reader*. Grand Rapids, MI: W.B. Eerdmans; Chicago: Chicago Historical Society, 1998.

Addams, Jane. *Twenty Years at Hull-House, with Autobiographical Notes*. New York: Macmillan, 1910. Rpt., edited by Victoria Brown, Bedford Series in History and Culture, Boston: Bedford/St. Martin's Press, 1999.

Allen, Barbara, and Thomas J. Schlereth, eds. *Sense of Place: American Regional Cultures*, ed. Lexington: University Press of Kentucky, 1990.

Allen, Hayward. *The Traveler's Guide to Native America*. Minocqua, WI: NorthWord Press, 1992.

Allen, Michael. *Western Rivermen, 1763–1861: Ohio and Mississippi Boatmen and the Myth of the Alligator Horse*. Baton Rouge: Louisiana State University Press, 1990.

Anderson, David D., ed. *Michigan, a State Anthology: Writings about the Great Lake State, 1641–1981, Selected from Diaries, Journals, Histories, Fiction, and Verse*. Literature of the States Series. Detroit, MI.: Gale Research Co., 1983.

Anderson, Sherwood. *Tar: A Midwest Childhood*. New York: Boni and Liveright, 1926.

Anderson, William M. *The Detroit Tigers: A Pictorial Celebration of the Greatest Players and Moments in Tigers' History*. Great Lakes Books. Detroit, MI: Wayne State University Press, 1999.

Aponte, Robert, and Marcelo Siles. *Winds of Change: Latinos in the Heartland and the Nation*. East Lansing: Julian Samora Research Institute, Michigan State University, 1997.

Apps, Jerold W. *Rural Wisdom: Time-Honored Values of the Midwest*. Amherst, WI: Amherst Press, 1997.

Arndt, Karl John Richard. *Economy on the Ohio, 1826–1834: The Harmony Society During the Period of Its Greatest Power and Influence and Its Messianic Crisis [Ökonomie Am Ohio, 1826–1834: Die Harmoniegesellschaft in der Zeit Ihres Höchsten Internationalen Ein Flusses und Ihrer Messias Krise]*. Edited by Karl John Richard and George Arndt. George Rapp's Third Harmony. Worcester, MA: Harmony Society Press, 1984.

Asher, Robert, Ronald Edsforth, and Stephen Merlino. *Autowork*. Albany: State University of New York Press, 1995.

Ashworth, William. *Great Lakes Journey: A New Look at America's Freshwater Coast.* Great Lakes Books. Detroit, MI: Wayne State University Press, 2000.

Atherton, Lewis Eldon. *The Frontier Merchant in Mid-America.* University of Missouri Studies. [Columbia, MO]: University of Missouri Press, 1971.

———. *Main Street on the Middle Border.* Bloomington: Indiana University Press, 1954. Rpt., Bloomington: Indiana University Press, 1984.

Ayers, Edward L. *All over the Map: Rethinking American Regions.* Baltimore, MD: Johns Hopkins University Press, 1996.

Baierlein, E. R. *In the Wilderness with the Red Indians: German Missionary to the Michigan Indians, 1847–1853.* Edited by Harold W. Moll. Translated by Anita Z. Boldt. Great Lakes Books. Detroit, MI: Wayne State University Press, 1996.

Bailey, Beth L. *Sex in the Heartland.* Cambridge, MA: Harvard University Press, 1999.

Baraga, Frederic. *A Short History of the North American Indians,* 1837. Reprint, translated and edited by Graham A. MacDonald. East Lansing: Michigan State University Press, 2004.

Barry, James P. *Old Forts of the Great Lakes: Sentinels in the Wilderness.* Lansing, MI: Thunder Bay Press, 1994.

Beecher, Catherine. *Miss Beecher's Domestic Receipt Book Designed as a Supplement to Her Treatise on Domestic Economy.* New York: Harper, 1846.

———. *A Treatise on Domestic Economy for the Use of Young Ladies at Home and at School.* New York: Harper, 1846.

Beecher, Catherine, and Harriet Beecher Stowe. *The American Woman's Home or, Principles of Domestic Science: Being a Guide to the Formation and Maintenance of Economical, Healthful, Beautiful and Christian Homes.* New York: J. B. Ford, 1869.

Bernard, Richard M., ed. *Snowbelt Cities: Metropolitan Politics in the Northeast and Midwest Since World War II.* Bloomington: Indiana University Press, 1990.

Berry, Chad. *Southern Migrants, Northern Exiles.* Urbana: University of Illinois Press, 2000.

Bigham, Darrel. *Southern Indiana.* Chicago: Arcadia Publishing, 2000.

Bigham, Darrel E., ed. *Indiana Territory, 1800–2000: A Bicentennial Perspective.* Indianapolis: Indiana Historical Society, 2001.

Birmingham, Robert A., and Leslie E. Eisenberg. *Indian Mounds of Wisconsin.* Madison: University of Wisconsin Press, 2000.

Blair, Emma Helen. *The Indian Tribes of the Upper Mississippi Valley and Region of the Great Lakes as Described by Nicolas Perrot, French Commandant in the Northwest; Bacqueville de la Potherie, French Royal Commissioner to Canada; Morrell Marston, American Army Officer; and Thomas Forsyth, United States Agent at Fort Armstrong.* 1911. Reprint, Lincoln: University of Nebraska Press, 1996.

Blatti, Jo. *Women's History in Minnesota: A Survey of Published Sources and Dissertations.* St. Paul: Minnesota Historical Society Press, 1993.

Blocker, Jack S. *American Temperance Movements: Cycles of Reform.* Social Movements Past and Present. Boston: Twayne Publishers, 1989.

———. *"Give to the Winds Thy Fears": The Women's Temperance Crusade, 1873–1874.* Contributions in Women's Studies. Westport, CT: Greenwood, 1985.

Blocksma, Mary. *Great Lakes Nature: An Outdoor Year.* Ann Arbor: University of Michigan Press, 2004.

Blum, Peter H. *Brewed in Detroit: Breweries and Beers Since 1830.* Great Lakes Books. Detroit, MI: Wayne State University Press, 1999.

Bogue, Allan G. *Frederick Jackson Turner: Strange Roads Going Down.* Norman: University of Oklahoma Press, 1998.

———. *From Prairie to Corn Belt: Farming on the Illinois and Iowa Prairies in the Nineteenth Century.* Chicago: University of Chicago Press, 1963. Reprint, Ames, IA: Iowa State University Press, 1994.

Boorstin, Daniel J. *The Americans: The Democratic Experience.* New York: Random House, 1973.

————. *The Americans: The National Experience*. New York: Random House, 1965.

Borchert, John R. *America's Northern Heartland*. Minneapolis: University of Minnesota Press, 1987.

Borrello, Joe. *Wineries of the Great Lakes: A Guidebook*. Lapeer, MI: Raptor Press, 1995.

Boryczka, Raymond. *"United in Purpose": A Chronological History of the Ohio AFL-CIO, 1958–1983*. Columbus: Ohio Historical Society, 1984.

Boryczka, Raymond, and Lorin Lee Cary. *No Strength Without Union: An Illustrated History of Ohio Workers, 1803–1980*. [Columbus]: Ohio Historical Society, 1982.

Boyer, Paul, ed. *Oxford Companion to United States History*. New York: Oxford University Press, 2001.

Brackman, Barbara, and Cathy Dwigans. *Backyard Visionaries: Grassroots Art in the Midwest*. Lawrence: University Press of Kansas, 1999.

Bradford, James C., ed. *Atlas of American Military History*. New York: Oxford University Press, 2003.

Brehm, Victoria. *"A Fully Accredited Ocean": Essays on the Great Lakes*. Ann Arbor: University of Michigan Press, 1998.

————, ed. *The Women's Great Lakes Reader*. Tustin, MI: Ladyslipper Press, 2000.

Brooks, H. Allen. *The Prairie School: Frank Lloyd Wright and His Midwest Contemporaries*. New York: W. W. Norton, 1976.

Brown, Jeffrey Paul, and Andrew R. L. Cayton. *The Pursuit of Public Power: Political Culture in Ohio, 1787–1861*. Kent, Ohio: Kent State University Press, 1994.

Brown, Paul. *Twelve Months in New-Harmony, Presenting a Faithful Account of the Principal Occurences Which Have Taken Place There Within That Period Interspersed with Remarks*. Cincinnati, OH: W. H. Woodward, 1827.

Brown, Victoria. *The Education of Jane Addams*. Politics and Culture in Modern America. Philadelphia: University of Pennsylvania Press, 2004.

Buechler, Steven M. *The Transformation of the Woman Suffrage Movement: The Case of Illinois, 1850–1920*. New Brunswick, NJ: Rutgers University Press, 1986.

Calder, J. Kent, and Susan Neville, eds. *Falling Toward Grace: Images of Religion and Culture from the Heartland*. Bloomington: Polis Center and Indiana University Press, 1998.

Caldwell, Erskine. *Afternoons in Mid-America: Observations and Impressions*. New York: Dodd, Mead, 1976.

Campbell, Thomas F. *Background for Progressivism: Machine Politics in the Administration of Robert E. McKisson, Mayor of Cleveland 1895–1899*. Cleveland: Western Reserve University, 1960.

Campbell, Thomas F., and Edward M. Miggins. *The Birth of Modern Cleveland, 1865–1930*. Cleveland: Western Reserve Historical Society and Associated University Presses, 1988.

Carpenter, Allan, ed. *The Encyclopedia of the Midwest*. New York: Facts on File, 1989.

Carver, Jonathan. *Three Years Travels Through the Interior Parts of North-America for More Than Five Thousand Miles*. Philadelphia: J. Crukshank, 1784.

Cary, Alice. *Clovernook, or, Recollections of Our Neighborhood in the West*. New York: Redfield, 1852.

Cayton, Andrew R. L. *Frontier Indiana*. Bloomington: Indiana University Press, 1996.

————. *The Frontier Republic: Ideology and Politics in the Ohio Country, 1780–1825*. Kent, OH: Kent State University Press, 1986.

————. *Ohio: The History of a People*. Columbus: Ohio State University Press, 2002.

————. *Pathways to the Old Northwest: An Observance of the Bicentennial of the Northwest Ordinance: Proceedings of a Conference Held at Franklin College of Indiana, July 10–11, 1987*. Indianapolis: Indiana Historical Society, 1988.

Cayton, Andrew R. L., and Susan E. Gray, eds. *The American Midwest: Essays on Regional History*. Bloomington: Indiana University Press, 2001.

Cayton, Andrew R. L., and Peter S. Onuf. *The Midwest and the Nation: Rethinking the History of an American Region*. Midwest History and Culture. Bloomington: Indiana University Press, 1990.

Cayton, Andrew R. L., and Fredrika J. Teute, eds. *Contact Points: American Frontiers from the Mohawk Valley to the Mississippi, 1750–1830*. Chapel Hill: University of North Carolina Press, 1998.

Cheek, William F., and Aimee Lee Cheek. *John Mercer Langston and the Fight for Black Freedom, 1829–65*. Blacks in the New World. Urbana: University of Illinois Press, 1989; rpt., 1996.

Clement, Priscilla Ferguson, and Jacqueline S. Reiner, eds. *Boyhood in America*. Santa Barbara, CA: ABC–CLIO, 2001.

Clifton, James A., and Frank W. Porter. *The Potawatomi*. New York: Chelsea House Publishers, 1987.

Colton, Calvin. *Tour of the American Lakes, and Among the Indians of the North-West Territory, in 1830: Disclosing the Character and Prospects of the Indian Race*. London: F. Westley and A. H. Davis, 1833.

Conzen, Kathleen Neils. *Immigrant Milwaukee, 1836–1860: Accommodation and Community in a Frontier City*. Harvard Studies in Urban History. Cambridge, MA: Harvard University Press, 1976.

Conzen, Kathleen Neils, Mack Walker, and Jörg Nagler. *Making Their Own America: Assimilation Theory and the German Peasant Pioneer*. Translated by Jörg Nagler. New York: Berg, 1990.

Conzen, Kathleen Neils, and Minnesota Historical Society. *Germans in Minnesota*. The People of Minnesota. St. Paul: Minnesota Historical Society Press, 2003.

Cowie, Jefferson R., and Joseph Heathcott. *Beyond the Ruins: The Meanings of Deindustrialization*. Ithaca, NY: ILR Press, 2003.

Crocker, Ruth. *Social Work and Social Order: The Settlement Movement in Two Industrial Cities, 1889–1930*. Urbana: University of Illinois Press, 1992.

Cronon, William. *Nature's Metropolis: Chicago and the Great West*. New York: W. W. Norton, 1991.

Davidson, Osha Gray. *Broken Heartland: The Rise of America's Rural Ghetto*. Iowa City: University of Iowa Press, 1996.

Davies, Richard O., Joseph A. Amato, and David R. Pichaske, eds. *A Place Called Home: Writings on the Midwestern Small Town*. St. Paul, MN: Borealis Books, 2003.

Delp, Michael, Conrad Hilberry, and Herbert Scott, eds. *Contemporary Michigan Poetry: Poems from the Third Coast*. Detroit, MI: Wayne State University Press, 1988.

Dempsey, Dave. *On the Brink: The Great Lakes in the 21st Century*. East Lansing: Michigan State University Press, 2004.

Detroit Institute of Arts and David Penney. *Art of the American Indian Frontier: A Portfolio*. New York: New Press, in conjunction with the Detroit Institute of Arts, 1995.

Devens, Carol. *Countering Colonization: Native American Women and Great Lakes Missions, 1630–1900*. Berkeley: University of California Press, 1992.

Disturnell, John. *The Western Traveller: Embracing the Canal and Railroad Routes, from Albany and Troy*. New York: J. Disturnell, 1844.

Doherty, Robert. *Disputed Waters: Native Americans and the Great Lakes Fishery*. Lexington: University Press of Kentucky, 1990.

Donald, David, ed. *Lincoln Reconsidered: Essays on the Civil War Era*. 2nd ed. New York: Vintage, 1989.

Drury, John. *Midwest Heritage, with Hundreds of Old Engravings*. New York: A. A. Wyn, 1948.

Duffey, Bernard I. *The Chicago Renaissance in American Letters: A Critical History*. 1954. Reprint, Westport, CT: Greenwood Press, 1972.

Duncan, Marvin R., and David M. Saxowsky, eds. *Industrialization of Heartland Agriculture: Conference Proceedings, 1995*. Fargo: North Dakota State University, 1995.

Dunn, Walter S. *Opening New Markets: The British Army and the Old Northwest*. Westport, CT: Praeger, 2002.

Dunnigan, Brian Leigh. *Frontier Metropolis: Picturing Early Detroit, 1701–1838*. Great Lakes Books. Detroit, MI: Wayne State University Press, 2001.

Edmunds, R. David. *The Shawnee Prophet*. Lincoln: University of Nebraska Press, 1983.

———. *Tecumseh and the Quest for Indian Leadership*. The Library of American Biography. Boston: Little, Brown, 1984.

Edmunds, R. David, and Joseph L. Peyser. *The Fox Wars: The Mesquakie Challenge to New France*. Civilization of the American Indian Series. Norman: University of Oklahoma Press, 1993.

Ekberg, Carl J. *French Roots in the Illinois Country: The Mississippi Frontier in Colonial Times*. Urbana: University of Illinois Press, 1998.

Elazar, Daniel Judah. *Cities of the Prairie: The Metropolitan Frontier and American Politics*. Studies in Federalism. New York: Basic Books, 1970.

———. *The Metropolitan Frontier and American Politics: Cities of the Prairie*. New Brunswick, NJ: Transaction, 2003.

Elazar, Daniel Judah, and Rozann Rothman. *Cities of the Prairie Revisited: The Closing of the Metropolitan Frontier*. Lincoln: University of Nebraska Press, 1986.

Emerson, Thomas E., and R. Barry Lewis, eds. *Cahokia and the Hinterlands: Middle Mississippian Cultures of the Midwest*. Urbana: University of Illinois Press, 1991.

Emerson, Thomas E., Dale L. McElrath, and Andrew C. Fortier, eds. *Late Woodland Societies: Tradition and Transformation Across the Midcontinent*. Lincoln: University of Nebraska Press, 2000.

Ervin, Jean, ed. *The Minnesota Experience: An Anthology*. Minneapolis, MN: Adams Press, 1979.

Etcheson, Nicole. *The Emerging Midwest: Upland Southerners and the Political Culture of the Old Northwest, 1787–1861*. Bloomington: Indiana University Press, 1996.

———. *The Southern Influence on Midwestern Political Culture: Ohio, Indiana, and Illinois from Frontier to Disunion*. Bloomington: Indiana University Press, 1991.

Faragher, John Mack. *Sugar Creek: Life on the Illinois Prairie*. New Haven, CT: Yale University Press, 1986.

Farnham, Eliza W. *Life in Prairie Land*. New York: Harper & Bros., 1846.

Faue, Elizabeth. *Community of Suffering & Struggle: Women, Men, and the Labor Movement in Minneapolis, 1915–1945*. Chapel Hill: University of North Carolina Press, 1991.

Federal Writers' Project. *Illinois: A Descriptive and Historical Guide*. Chicago: WPA Federal Art Project, 1936.

Fellows, Will, ed. *Farm Boys: Lives of Gay Men from the Rural Midwest*. Madison: University of Wisconsin Press, 1996.

Fine, Lisa M. *The Souls of the Skyscraper: Female Clerical Workers in Chicago, 1870–1930*. Philadelphia: Temple University Press, 1990.

———. *The Story of Reo Joe: Work, Kin, and Community in Autotown, U.S.A.* Philadelphia: Temple University Press, 2004.

Fink, Deborah. *Cutting into the Meatpacking Line: Workers and Change in the Rural Midwest*. Chapel Hill: University of North Carolina Press, 1998.

———. *Open Country, Iowa: Rural Women, Tradition and Change*. Albany: State University of New York Press, 1986.

Fink, Leon. *In Search of the Working Class: Essays in American Labor History and Political Culture*. The Working Class in American History. Urbana: University of Illinois Press, 1994.

———. *Workingmen's Democracy: The Knights of Labor and American Politics*. Urbana: University of Illinois Press, 1983.

Fink, Leon, Stephen T. Leonard, and Donald Reid, eds. *Intellectuals and Public Life: Between Radicalism and Reform*. Ithaca, NY: Cornell University Press, 1996.

Fixico, Donald Lee, ed. *An Anthology of Western Great Lakes Indian History*. Milwaukee: American Indian Studies, University of Wisconsin-Milwaukee, 1989.

Fliege, Stu. *Tales and Trails of Illinois*. Urbana: University of Illinois Press, 2003.

Folmar, John Kent, ed. *This State of Wonders: The Letters of an Iowa Frontier Family, 1858–1861*. Iowa City: University of Iowa Press, 1986.

Frazer, Timothy C., ed. *"Heartland" English: Variation and Transition in the American Midwest*. Tuscaloosa: University of Alabama Press, 1993.

Friedberger, Mark. *Shake-Out: Iowa Farm Families in the 1980s*. Lexington: University Press of Kentucky, 1989.

Frost, John. *Border Wars of the West*. Auburn, NY: Derby and Miller, 1853.

Fry, Katherine. *Constructing the Heartland: Television News and Natural Disaster*. Cresskill, NJ: Hampton Press, 2003.

Gabin, Nancy Felice. *Feminism in the Labor Movement: Women and the United Auto Workers, 1935–1975*. Ithaca, NY: Cornell University Press, 1990.

García, Juan Ramon. *Mexicans in the Midwest, 1900–1932*. Tucson: University of Arizona Press, 1996.

Garland, John H. *The North American Midwest: A Regional Geography*. New York: John Wiley, 1955.

Garner, John S., ed. *The Midwest in American Architecture*. Urbana: University of Illinois Press, 1991.

Garreau, Joel. *The Nine Nations of North America*. Boston: Houghton Mifflin, 1981.

Gibbon, Guy E., ed. *The Woodland Tradition in the Western Great Lakes: Papers Presented to Elden Johnson*. Minneapolis: University of Minnesota, 1990.

Gibbs, Wilma L., ed. *Indiana's African-American Heritage: Essays from "Black History News & Notes."* Indianapolis: Indiana Historical Society, 1993.

Ginzberg, Lori D. *Women and the Work of Benevolence: Morality, Politics, and Class in the Nineteenth-Century United States*. New Haven, CT: Yale University Press, 1990.

———. *Women in Antebellum Reform*. Wheeling, IL: Harlan Davidson, 2000.

Gjerde, Jon. *From Peasants to Farmers: The Migration from Balestrand, Norway to the Upper Middle West*. Interdisciplinary Perspectives on Modern History. Cambridge [England] and New York: Cambridge University Press, 1985.

———. *The Minds of the West: Ethnocultural Evolution in the Rural Middle West, 1830–1917*. Chapel Hill: University of North Carolina Press, 1997.

Gjerde, Jon, and Carlton C. Qualey. *Norwegians in Minnesota*. The People of Minnesota. St. Paul, MN: Minnesota Historical Society Press, 2002.

Gorn, Elliott J. *Mother Jones: The Most Dangerous Woman in America*. New York: Hill and Wang, 2001.

Graham, Margaret Ann Baker. *Victorian America: A Family Record from the Heartland*. Kirksville, MO: Truman State University Press, 2003.

Grant, H. Roger. *The Corn Belt Route: A History of the Chicago Great Western Railroad Company*. Dekalb: Northern Illinois University Press, 1996.

———. *Railroads in the Heartland: Steam and Traction in the Golden Age of Postcards*. Iowa City: University of Iowa Press, 1997.

Grant, H. Roger, Donovan L. Hofsommer, and Osmund Overby. *St. Louis Union Station: A Place for People, a Place for Trains*. St. Louis, MO: St. Louis Mercantile Library, 1994.

Gray, Susan E. *The Yankee West: Community Life on the Michigan Frontier*. Chapel Hill: University of North Carolina Press, 1996.

Grearson, Jessie Carroll, and Lauren B. Smith. *Love in a Global Village: A Celebration of Intercultural Families in the Midwest*. Iowa City: University of Iowa Press, 2001.

Greasley, Philip, et al., eds. *Dictionary of Midwestern Literature*. Vol. 1: Authors. Bloomington: Indiana University Press, 2001.

Great Lakes. Hawthorn, Victoria, and Oakland, CA: Lonely Planet Publications, 2000.

Green, Paul Michael, and Melvin G. Holli, eds. *Restoration 1989: Chicago Elects a New Daley*. Chicago, IL: Lyceum Books, 1991.

Greene, Lorenzo J., Gary R. Kremer, and Antonio Frederick Holland. *Missouri's Black Heritage*. 1980. Rev. ed., Columbia: University of Missouri Press, 1993.

Grossman, James R. *Land of Hope: Chicago, Black Southerners, and the Great Migration*. Chicago: University of Chicago Press, 1989.

Grossman, James R., Ann Durkin Keating, Janice L. Reiff, eds. *The Encyclopedia of Chicago*. Chicago: University of Chicago Press, 2004.

Gruenwald, Kim M. *River of Enterprise: The Commercial Origins of Regional Identity in the Ohio Valley, 1790–1850*. Bloomington: Indiana University Press, 2002.

Haeger, John D. *John Jacob Astor: Business and Finance in the Early Republic*. Detroit, MI: Wayne State University Press, 1991.

Hall, Michael D., and Pat Glascock. *Great Lakes Muse: American Scene Painting in the Upper Midwest, 1910–1960: The Inlander Collection in the Flint Institute of Arts*. Flint, MI: Flint Institute of Arts, 2003.

Harmon, Daniel Williams. *A Journal of Voyages and Travels in the Interiour (sic) of North America, Between the 47th and 58th Degrees of North Latitude, Extending from Montreal Nearly to the Pacific Ocean*. Andover, VT: Flagg and Gould, 1820.

Hartman, Sheryl. *Indian Clothing of the Great Lakes, 1740–1840*. Illustrated by Greg Hudson, Joe Lee, and Ralph Heath. Liberty, UT: Eagle's View Publishing. Co., 1988. Rev. ed., 2000.

Hatfield, Ken. *Heartland Heroes: Remembering World War II*. Columbia: University of Missouri Press, 2003.

Havighurst, Walter. *The Long Ships Passing: The Story of the Great Lakes*. Illustrated by John O'Hara Cosgrave. New York: Macmillan, 1942.

———. *The Midwest*. Grand Rapids, MI: Fideler Co., 1964.

Heidenreich, Conrad, et al. *The Early Fur Trades: A Study in Cultural Interaction*. Historical Patterns Series. Toronto: McClelland and Stewart, 1976.

Heinz, Thomas A. *Frank Lloyd Wright: Field Guide*. London: Academy Editions, 1996.

Hendricks, Wanda A. *Gender, Race, and Politics in the Midwest: Black Club Women in Illinois*. Bloomington: Indiana University Press, 1998.

Hennepin, Louis. *Nouvelle Decouverte d'un Tres Grand Pays Situé dans l'Amérique [A New Discovery of a Vast Country in America]*. Illustrated by Louis Joliet. Utrecht: G. Broedelet, 1697. Rpt., London: Henry Bonwicke, 1699.

Hinderaker, Eric. *Elusive Empires: Constructing Colonialism in the Ohio Valley, 1673–1800*. New York: Cambridge University Press, 1997.

Hinderaker, Eric, and Peter C. Mancall. *At the Edge of Empire: The Backcountry in British North America*. Baltimore, MD: Johns Hopkins University Press, 2003.

Hine, Darlene Clark. *When the Truth Is Told: A History of Black Women's Culture and Community in Indiana, 1875–1950*. [Indianapolis]: National Council of Negro Women, Indianapolis Section, 1981.

Hine, Darlene Clark, and Patrick Kay Bidelman. *The Black Women in the Middle West Project: A Comprehensive Resource Guide, Illinois and Indiana: Historical Essays, Oral Histories, Biographical Profiles, and Document Collections*. Indianapolis: Indiana Historical Bureau, 1986.

Holli, Melvin G. *Reform in Detroit: Hazen S. Pingree and Urban Politics*. Westport, CT: Greenwood Press, 1981.

Holli, Melvin G., and Paul M. Green. *A View from Chicago's City Hall: Mid-Century to Millennium*. Charleston, SC: Arcadia, 1999.

Holli, Melvin G., and Peter d'Alroy Jones, eds. *Ethnic Chicago: A Multicultural Portrait*. 4th ed. Grand Rapids, MI: W.B. Eerdmans, 1994.

———, eds. *The Ethnic Frontier: Essays in the History of Group Survival in Chicago and the Midwest*. Grand Rapids, MI: W.B. Eerdmans, 1977.

Holter, Darryl, ed. *Workers and Unions in Wisconsin: A Labor History Anthology*. Madison: State Historical Society of Wisconsin, 1999.

Howard, Robert P. *Illinois: A History of the Prairie State*. Grand Rapids, MI: W.B. Eerdmans, 1972.

Hudson, John C. *Crossing the Heartland: Chicago to Denver*. Touring North America. New Brunswick, NJ: Rutgers University Press, 1992.

———. *Making the Corn Belt: A Geographical History of Middle-Western Agriculture*. Bloomington: Indiana University Press, 1994.

Hurt, R. Douglas. *The Indian Frontier, 1763–1846*. Albuquerque: University of New Mexico Press, 2002.

Jackson, Deborah Davis. *Our Elders Lived It: American Indian Identity in the City*. DeKalb: Northern Illinois University Press, 2002.

Jensen, Joan M., and Sue Davidson, eds. *A Needle, a Bobbin, a Strike: Women Needleworkers in America*. Philadelphia: Temple University Press, 1984.

Jensen, Richard J. *Illinois: a History*. Urbana: University of Illinois Press, 2001.

———. *The Winning of the Midwest: Social and Political Conflict, 1888–1896*. Chicago: University of Chicago Press, 1971.

Jensen, Richard J., and Mark Friedberger. *Education and Social Structure: An Historical Study of Iowa, 1870–1930*. Chicago: Newberry Library, 1976.

Judson, Katharine Berry. *Myths and Legends of the Mississippi Valley and the Great Lakes*. Chicago: A.C. McClurg, 1914.

———. *Native American Legends of the Great Lakes and the Mississippi Valley*. DeKalb: Northern Illinois University Press, 2000.

Kennedy, Roger G. *Hidden Cities: The Discovery and Loss of Ancient North American Civilization*. New York: The Free Press, 1994.

Kent, Timothy J. *Ft. Pontchartrain at Detroit: A Guide to the Daily Lives of Fur Trade and Military Personnel, Settlers, and Missionaries at French Posts*. Ossineke, MI: Silver Fox Enterprises, 2001.

———. *Tahquamenon Tales: Experiences of an Early French Trader and His Native Family*. Ossineke, MI: Silver Fox Enterprises, 1998.

Kerr, K. Austin. *Organized for Prohibition: A New History of the Anti-Saloon League*. New Haven, CT: Yale University Press, 1985.

Kersten, Andrew Edmund. *Race, Jobs, and the War: The FEPC in the Midwest, 1941–46*. Urbana: University of Illinois Press, 2000.

Kirkland, Caroline M. *A New Home—Who'll Follow? or, Glimpses of Western Life*. New York: C.S. Francis: Boston, J.H. Francis, 1839. Reprint, edited by Sandra A. Zagarell. New Brunswick, NJ: Rutgers University Press, 1990.

Kleppner, Paul. *The Cross of Culture: A Social Analysis of Midwestern Politics, 1850–1900*. New York: The Free Press, 1970.

Kolmerten, Carol A. *Women in Utopia: The Ideology of Gender in the American Owenite Communities*. Bloomington: Indiana University Press, 1990.

Kolodny, Annette. *The Land Before Her: Fantasy and Experience of the American Frontiers, 1630–1860*. Chapel Hill: University of North Carolina Press, 1984.

Kramer, Dale. *Chicago Renaissance: The Literary Life in the Midwest, 1900–1930*. New York, Appleton-Century, 1966.

Kramer, Frank R. *Voices in the Valley: Mythmaking and Folk Belief in the Shaping of the Middle West*. Madison: University of Wisconsin Press, 1964.

Kremer, Gary R. *James Milton Turner and the Promise of America: The Public Life of a Post-Civil War Black Leader*. Columbia: University of Missouri Press, 1991.

Kubiak, William J. *Great Lakes Indians: A Pictorial Guide*. Grand Rapids, MI: Baker Books, 1999.

Landau, Diana. *Ohio: The Spirit of America*. New York: Abrams, 2001.

Lapham, Increase A. *The Antiquities of Wisconsin: As Surveyed and Described*. Washington, DC: Smithsonian Institution, 1855. Reprint available; or electronic edition at www.library.wisc.edu/etext/Antiquities/.

Lasley, Paul. *Beyond the Amber Waves of Grain: An Examination of Social and Economic Restructuring in the Heartland*. Boulder, CO: Westview Press, 1995.

Lavenda, Robert H. *Corn Fests and Water Carnivals: Celebrating Community in Minnesota*. Washington, DC: Smithsonian Institution Press, 1997.

Lawson, Ellen NicKenzie, and Marlene Merrill, comps. *The Three Sarahs: Documents of Antebellum Black College Women*. Studies in Women and Religion. New York: E. Mellen Press, 1984.

Leary, James P. *Midwestern Folk Humor*. Little Rock, AR: August House, 1991.

Lengermann, Patricia M., and Jill Niebrugge-Brantley. *The Women Founders: Sociology and Social Theory, 1830–1930: A Text/Reader*. Boston: McGraw-Hill, 1998.

Library of Congress. *The American Guide Series: State Territorial Guides Prepared by WPA Writers' Program*. Washington, DC, 1944.

Lloyd, Timothy C., and Patrick B. Mullen. *Lake Erie Fishermen: Work, Tradition, and Identity*. Urbana and Chicago: University of Illinois Press, 1990.

Loew, Patty. *Indian Nations of Wisconsin: Histories of Endurance and Renewal*. Madison: Wisconsin Historical Society Press, 2001.

Look [Magazine]. *The Midwest*. Boston: Houghton Mifflin, 1947.

Lorence, James J. *Organizing the Unemployed: Community and Union Activists in the Industrial Heartland*. Albany: State University of New York Press, 1996.

Lott, R. Allen. *From Paris to Peoria: How European Piano Virtuosos Brought Classical Music to the American Heartland*. New York: Oxford University Press, 2003.

Lukermann, Barbara, Miriam Goldfein, and Sandra De Montille. *Trade Centers of the Upper Midwest: Three Case Studies Examining Changes from 1960 to 1989*. Minneapolis, MN: Center for Urban and Regional Affairs, 1991.

Lurie, Nancy Oestreich. *Wisconsin Indians*. Madison: Wisconsin Historical Society Press, 2002.

Lynd, Robert Staughton, and Helen Merrell Lynd. *Middletown: A Study in Contemporary American Culture*. New York: Harcourt, Brace, 1929.

———. *Middletown in Transition: A Study in Cultural Conflicts*. New York: Harcourt, Brace and Company, 1937.

MacDowell, Marsha, ed. *African American Quiltmaking in Michigan*. East Lansing: Michigan State University Press in association with the Michigan State University Museum, 1997.

Madison, James H. *The Indiana Way: A State History*. Bloomington and Indianapolis: Indiana University Press and Indiana Historical Society, 1986.

———. *A Lynching in the Heartland: Race and Memory in America*. New York: Palgrave, 2001.

———, ed. *Heart Land: Comparative Histories of the Midwestern States*. Bloomington: Indiana University Press, 1988.

Mahoney, Timothy R. *Provincial Lives: Middle-Class Experience in the Antebellum Middle West*. New York: Cambridge University Press, 1999.

———. *River Towns in the Great West: The Structure of Provincial Urbanization in the American Midwest, 1820–1870*. New York: Cambridge University Press, 1990.

The Mapping of the Great Lakes in the Seventeenth Century: Twenty-Two Maps from the George S. & Nancy B. Parker Collection. Providence, RI: John Carter Brown Library, 1989.

Marshall, Howard W. *Barns of Missouri: Storehouses of History.* Virginia Beach, VA: Donning, 2003.

———. *Folk Architecture in Little Dixie: A Regional Culture in Missouri.* Columbia: University of Missouri Press, 1981.

———. *Vernacular Architecture in Rural and Small Town Missouri: An Introduction.* Columbia: University Extension, University of Missouri-Columbia, 1994.

Martin, John Bartlow. *Call It North Country: The Story of Upper Michigan.* Detroit, MI: Wayne State University Press, 1986.

Martin, Susan R. *Wonderful Power: The Story of Ancient Copper Working in the Lake Superior Basin.* Detroit, MI: Wayne State University Press, 1999.

Martone, Michael, ed. *A Place of Sense: Essays in Search of the Midwest.* Iowa City: University of Iowa Press, 1988.

Mason, Ronald J. *Great Lakes Archaeology.* Caldwell, NJ: Blackburn Press, 2002.

Matuz, Roger. *Albert Kahn: Builder of Detroit.* Great Lakes Books. Detroit, MI: Wayne State University Press, 2002.

Mayer, Harold M., and Richard C. Wade. *Chicago: Growth of a Metropolis.* Chicago: University of Chicago Press, 1969.

McAvoy, Thomas Timothy, et al. *The Midwest: Myth or Reality? A Symposium.* Notre Dame, IN: University of Notre Dame Press, 1961.

McGuffey, William Holmes. *The McGuffey Readers: Selections from the 1879 Edition.* Edited by Elliott J. Gorn. Bedford Series in History and Culture. Boston: Bedford Books, 1998.

McLellan, Marjorie L., and Kathleen Neils Conzen. *Six Generations Here: A Farm Family Remembers.* Madison: State Historical Society of Wisconsin, 1997.

Meyerowitz, Joanne J. *Women Adrift: Independent Wage Earners in Chicago, 1880–1930.* Chicago: University of Chicago Press, 1988.

The Midwest: A Collection from Harper's Magazine. New York: Gallery Books, 1991.

Midwest, Images of America. New York: Gallery Books Image Bank, 1986.

Missouri: The WPA Guide to the "Show Me" State. 1941. Reprint, St. Louis: Missouri Historical Society Press, 1998.

Motz, Marilyn Ferris. *True Sisterhood: Michigan Women and Their Kin, 1820–1920.* Albany: State University of New York Press, 1983.

Murphy, Lucy Eldersveld. *A Gathering of Rivers: Indians, Métis, and Mining in the Western Great Lakes, 1737–1832.* Lincoln: University of Nebraska Press, 2000.

Murphy, Lucy Eldersveld, and Wendy Hamand Venet, eds. *Midwestern Women: Work, Community, and Leadership at the Crossroads.* Bloomington: Indiana University Press, 1997.

Nelson, Daniel. *Farm and Factory: Workers in the Midwest, 1880–1990.* Bloomington: Indiana University Press, 1995.

Nemanic, Gerald. *A Bibliographical Guide to Midwestern Literature.* Iowa City: University of Iowa Press, 1981.

Nesper, Larry. *The Walleye War: The Struggle for Ojibwe Spearfishing and Treaty Rights.* Lincoln: University of Nebraska Press, 2002.

Newberry Library. *A Midwest Bibliography: Supplementary Number of the Newberry Library Bulletin, June, 1947.* Chicago: Newberry Library, 1947.

Nicholson, Meredith. *The Hoosiers.* New York: Macmillan, 1900.

———. *The Valley of Democracy.* New York: Scribner's, 1919.

Noble, Allen George, and Hubert G. H. Wilhelm, eds. *Barns of the Midwest.* Athens: Ohio University Press, 1995.

Noe, Marcia, ed. *Exploring the Midwestern Literary Imagination: Essays in Honor of David D. Anderson.* Troy, NY: Whitston, 1993.

Nye, Russel Blaine. *Midwestern Progressive Politics: A Historical Study of Its Origins and Development, 1870–1950.* East Lansing: Michigan State College Press, 1951.

Onuf, Peter S. *Statehood and Union: A History of the Northwest Ordinance*. Bloomington: Indiana University Press, 1987.

Osborne, Karen Lee, and William J. Spurlin, eds. *Reclaiming the Heartland: Lesbian and Gay Voices from the Midwest*. Minneapolis: University of Minnesota Press, 1996.

Ostergren, Robert Clifford, and Thomas R. Vale, eds. *Wisconsin Land and Life*. Madison: University of Wisconsin Press, 1997.

Oswalt, Wendell H. *This Land Was Theirs: A Study of North American Indians*. 7th ed. Mountain View, CA: Mayfield, 2001.

Ozanne, Robert W. *The Labor Movement in Wisconsin: A History*. Madison: State Historical Society of Wisconsin, 1984.

Pederson, Jane Marie. *Between Memory and Reality: Family and Community in Rural Wisconsin, 1870–1970*. Madison: University of Wisconsin Press, 1992.

Penney, David W., ed. *Great Lakes Indian Art*. Detroit, MI: Wayne State University Press, and the Detroit Institute of Arts, 1989.

Perkins, Elizabeth A. *Border Life: Experience and Memory in the Revolutionary Ohio Valley*. Chapel Hill: University of North Carolina Press, 1998.

Perrucci, Robert. *Japanese Auto Transplants in the Heartland: Corporatism and Community*. Social Institutions and Social Change. New York: Aldine de Gruyter, 1994.

Philliber, William W. *Appalachian Migrants in Urban America: Cultural Conflict or Ethnic Group Formation?* New York: Praeger, 1981.

Philliber, William W., and Clyde B. McCoy, eds., with Harry C. Dillingham. *The Invisible Minority, Urban Appalachians*. Lexington: University Press of Kentucky, 1981.

Pitzer, Donald E., ed. *America's Communal Utopias*. Chapel Hill: University of North Carolina Press, 1997.

Power, Richard Lyle. *Planting Corn Belt Culture: The Impress of the Upland Southerner and Yankee in the Old Northwest*. Indianapolis: Indiana Historical Society, 1953.

Powers, Elmer G. *Years of Struggle: The Farm Diary of Elmer G. Powers*. Edited by H. Roger Grant and L. Edward Purcell. DeKalb: Northern Illinois University Press, 1995.

Powers, Ron. *Tom and Huck Don't Live Here Anymore: Childhood and Murder in the Heart of America*. New York: St. Martin's Press, 2001.

Profiles of America. *Midwest Region: An Informational, Statistical, and Relocation Encyclopedia of All U.S. Cities, Towns, and Counties*. Milpitas, CA: Toucan Valley Publications, 1995.

Prosterman, Leslie. *Ordinary Life, Festival Days: Aesthetics in the Midwestern County Fair*. Washington, DC: Smithsonian Institution Press, 1995.

Quimby, George Irving. *Indian Life in the Upper Great Lakes 11,000 B.C. to A.D. 1800*. Chicago: University of Chicago Press, 1960.

Rasmussen, Charlie Otto. *Where the River Is Wide: Pahquahwong and the Chippewa Flowage*. Odanah, WI: Great Lakes Indian Fish & Wildlife Commission Press, 1998.

Recipes from Across Indiana: The Best of Heartland Cooking. Carmel: Guild Press of Indiana, 1998.

Reed, Earl C. *Midwest Aviation History in Pictures*. Kansas City, MO: N.p., 1960.

Ridder, Kathleen C. *Shaping My Feminist Life: A Memoir*. Midwest Reflections. St. Paul: Minnesota Historical Society Press, 1998.

Rikoon, J. Sanford. *Threshing in the Midwest, 1820–1940: A Study of Traditional Culture and Technological Change*. Bloomington: Indiana University Press, 1988.

Riley, Glenda. *Frontierswomen: The Iowa Experience*. Ames: Iowa State University Press, 1981.

Rohrbough, Malcolm J. *The Land Office Business: The Settlement and Administration of American Public Lands, 1789–1837*. New York: Oxford University Press, 1968.

———. *The Trans-Appalachian Frontier People, Societies, and Institutions, 1775–1850*. New York: Oxford University Press, 1978.

Ross, Edward A. "The Middle West: Being Studies of Its People in Comparison with Those of the East." *Century Magazine* 83 (1912): 609–615, 686–692, 874–880; 84 (1912): 142–148.

Rottenberg, Dan, ed. *Middletown Jews: The Tenuous Survival of an American Jewish Community*. Bloomington: Indiana University Press, 1997.

Rugh, Susan Sessions. *Our Common Country: Family Farming, Culture, and Community in the Nineteenth-Century Midwest*. Bloomington: Indiana University Press, 2001.

Rusk, Ralph L. *The Literature of the Middle Western Frontier*. Reprint. New York: F. Ungar Publishing Co., 1962.

Samora, Julian, and Richard A. Lamanna. *Mexican-Americans in a Midwest Metropolis: A Study of East Chicago*. [Los Angeles: n.p., 1967].

Schimel, Lawrence, and Martin Harry Greenberg. *Fields of Blood: Vampire Stories from the American Midwest*. Nashville, TN: Cumberland House, 1998.

Schneirov, Richard, Shelton Stromquist, and Nick Salvatore, eds. *The Pullman Strike and the Crisis of the 1890s: Essays on Labor and Politics*. Urbana: University of Illinois Press, 1999.

Schob, David E. *Hired Hands and Plowboys: Farm Labor in the Midwest, 1815–60*. Urbana: University of Illinois Press, 1975.

Schoolcraft, Henry Rowe. *Narrative Journal of Travels Through the Northwestern Regions of the United States . . . in the Year 1820*. Albany: E. & E. Hosford, 1821.

Schultz, Christian. *Travels on an Inland Voyage . . . in the Years 1807 and 1808*. New York: Isaac Riley, 1810.

Seelye, John. *Beautiful Machine: Rivers and the Republican Plan, 1755–1825*. New York: Oxford University Press, 1991.

Sernett, Milton C. *Bound for the Promised Land: African American Religion and the Great Migration*. Durham, NC: Duke University Press, 1997.

Shortridge, James R. *The Middle West: Its Meaning in American Culture*. Lawrence: University Press of Kansas, 1989.

Sisson, Richard, and Christian Zacher, eds. *Encyclopedia of the Midwest*. Bloomington: Indiana University Press, forthcoming in 2005. www.allmidwest.org/main_frame.html

Skaggs, David Curtis, and Larry L. Nelson, eds. *The Sixty Years' War for the Great Lakes, 1754–1814*. East Lansing: Michigan State University Press, 2001.

Sleeper-Smith, Susan. *Indian Women and French Men: Rethinking Cultural Encounter in the Western Great Lakes*. Amherst: University of Massachusetts Press, 2001.

Sporn, Paul. *Against Itself: The Federal Theater and Writers' Projects in the Midwest*. Detroit, MI: Wayne State University Press, 1995.

Stearns, Robert, et al. *Illusions of Eden: Visions of the American Heartland*. Minneapolis, MN, and Columbus, OH: Arts Midwest and the Ohio Arts Council, 2000.

Stromquist, Shelton, and Marvin Bergman, eds. *Unionizing the Jungles: Labor and Community in the Twentieth-Century Meatpacking Industry*. Iowa City: University of Iowa Press, 1997.

Suckow, Ruth. *The Folk Idea in American Life: A Forerunner to Miss Suckow's Monumental New Novel to Be Published in 1934: The Folks*. New York: Scribner's, 1930.

———. *Iowa Interiors*. New York: A. A. Knopf, 1926.

Suggs, Henry Lewis, ed. *The Black Press in the Middle West, 1865–1985*. Westport, CT: Greenwood Press, 1996.

Sugrue, Thomas J. *The Origins of the Urban Crisis: Race and Inequality in Postwar Detroit*. Princeton, NJ: Princeton University Press, 1996.

Tanner, Helen Hornbec, et al., eds. *Atlas of Great Lakes Indian History*. Cartography by Miklos Pinther. Norman: Published for the Newberry Library by the University of Oklahoma Press, 1987.

Tarkington, Booth. *The Gentleman from Indiana*. New York: Doubleday & McClure, 1899.

Taylor, Robert M., Jr., and Connie A. McBirney, eds. *Peopling Indiana: The Ethnic Experience*. Indianapolis: Indiana Historical Society, 1996.

Teaford, Jon C. *The Twentieth-Century American City*. Baltimore, MD: Johns Hopkins University Press, 1993.

Terkel, Studs. *Chicago*. New York: Pantheon Books, 1986.

———. *Division Street: America*. New York: Pantheon Books, 1967.

———. *Giants of Jazz*. 1957. Rev. ed., with Milly Hawk Daniel. New York: New Press, 2002.

Testa, William A., ed. *The Great Lakes Economy: Looking North and South*. Chicago: The Bank, 1991.

Thelen, David P. *The New Citizenship: Origins of Progressivism in Wisconsin, 1885–1900*. Columbia: University of Missouri Press, 1972.

———. *Paths of Resistance: Tradition and Dignity in Industrializing Missouri*. New York: Oxford University Press, 1986.

———. *Robert M. La Follette and the Insurgent Spirit*. 1976. Reprint, edited by Oscar Handlin. Madison: University of Wisconsin Press, 1985.

Thornbrough, Emma Lou. *Indiana Blacks in the Twentieth Century*. Edited by Lana Ruegamer. Bloomington: Indiana University Press, 2000.

———. *The Negro in Indiana Before 1900: A Study of a Minority*. Bloomington: Indiana University Press, 1993.

Tillson, Christiana Holmes. *Reminiscences of Early Life in Illinois*. N.p., n.d.

Trollope, Frances Milton. *Domestic Manners of the Americans*. London: Printed for Whittaker, Treacher & Co., 1832. Reprint, Mineola, NY: Dover, 2003.

Trotter, Joe William. *Black Milwaukee: The Making of an Industrial Proletariat, 1915–45*. Urbana: University of Illinois Press, 1985.

———. *River Jordan: African American Urban Life in the Ohio Valley*. Lexington: University Press of Kentucky, 1998.

———, ed. *The Great Migration in Historical Perspective: New Dimensions of Race, Class, and Gender*. Bloomington: Indiana University Press, 1991.

Turner, Frederick Jackson. *The Frontier in American History*. New York: H. Holt, 1921. Reprint, with commentary by John Mack Faragher. New Haven, CT: Yale University Press, 1998.

Van Tassel, David D., and John G. Grabowski, eds. *The Encyclopedia of Cleveland History*. 1987. 2nd ed. Bloomington: Indiana University Press in association with Case Western Reserve University and the Western Reserve Historical Society, 1996.

Vargas, Zaragosa. *Proletarians of the North: A History of Mexican Industrial Workers in Detroit and the Midwest, 1917–1933*. Berkeley: University of California Press, 1993; Reprint, NetLibrary, 1999.

Venable, William Henry. *Beginnings of Literary Culture in the Ohio Valley: Historical and Biographical Sketches*. Cincinnati, OH: R. Clarke & Co., 1891.

Vinz, Mark, and Thom Tammaro. *Imagining Home: Writing from the Midwest*. Minneapolis: University of Minnesota Press, 1995.

Vitz, Robert C. *The Queen City and the Arts: Cultural Life in Nineteenth-Century Cincinnati*. Kent, OH: Kent State University Press, 1989.

Voegeli, V. Jacque. *Free But Not Equal: The Midwest and the Negro during the Civil War*. Chicago: University of Chicago Press, 1967.

Wade, Richard C. *The Urban Frontier: The Rise of Western Cities, 1790–1830*. Urbana: University of Illinois Press, 1996.

Waitley, Douglas. *Portrait of the Midwest: From the Ice Age to the Industrial Era*. New York: Abelard-Schuman, 1963.

Wald, Elijah, and John Junkerman. *River of Song: A Musical Journey Down the Mississippi*. Photographs by Theo Pelletier. New York: Smithsonian Institution and Filmmakers Collaborative in association with St. Martin's Press, 1998.

Walker, Juliet E. K. *Free Frank: A Black Pioneer on the Antebellum Frontier*. Lexington: University Press of Kentucky, 1983.

———. *The History of Black Business in America: Capitalism, Race, Entrepreneurship*. New York: Macmillan Library Reference-Prentice Hall, 1998. Reprint, New York: Palgrave, 2002.

Walker, Kenneth R. *A History of the Middle West from the Beginning to 1970*. Little Rock, AR: Pioneer, 1972.

Walthall, John A., ed. *French Colonial Archaeology: The Illinois Country and the Western Great Lakes*. Urbana: University of Illinois Press, 1991.

Warren, Kenneth. *Big Steel: The First Century of the United States Steel Corporation, 1901–2001*. Pittsburgh: University of Pittsburgh Press, 2001.

Warren, Wilson J. *Struggling with "Iowa's Pride": Labor Relations, Unionism, and Politics in the Rural Midwest Since 1877*. Iowa City: University of Iowa Press, 2000.

Watts, Edward. *An American Colony: Regionalism and the Roots of Midwestern Culture*. Athens: Ohio University Press, 2002.

Way, Peter. *Common Labor Workers and the Digging of North American Canals, 1780–1860*. Baltimore, MD: Johns Hopkins University Press, 1997.

Weber, Ronald. *The Midwestern Ascendancy in American Writing*. Bloomington: Indiana University Press, 1992.

White, Richard. *The Middle Ground: Indians, Empires, and Republics in the Great Lakes Region, 1650–1815*. New York: Cambridge University Press, 1991.

Whites, LeeAnn, Mary Neth, and Gary R. Kremer, eds. *Women in Missouri History: In Search of Power and Influence*. Columbia: University of Missouri Press, 2004.

Willard, Frances Elizabeth. *Woman and Temperance or, The Work and Workers of the Woman's Christian Temperance Union*. New York: Arno Press, 1972.

Wisconsin Cartographers' Guild. *Wisconsin's Past and Present: A Historical Atlas*. Madison: University of Wisconsin Press, 1998.

Woolley, Lisa. *American Voices of the Chicago Renaissance*. DeKalb: Northern Illinois University Press, 2000.

INDEX

Illustrations are noted in italics.

ABOUT THE EDITORS AND CONTRIBUTORS

JUDITH YAROSS LEE, Professor of Communication Studies and Co-Director of the Central Region Humanities Center at Ohio University, is an authority on the history of American popular culture, especially literary humor. She is the author of *Garrison Keillor: A Voice of America* (1991), *Defining New Yorker Humor* (2000), and three dozen essays on American media and culture. Her editorial work includes *Beyond the Two Cultures: Essays on Science, Technology and Literature* (with Joseph W. Slade, 1990) and the journal *Explorations in Media Ecology*, founded with Lance Strate in 2002.

JOSEPH W. SLADE, Professor of Telecommunications and Co-Director of the Central Region Humanities Center at Ohio University, has written extensively on communication, culture, literature, and film. His books include *Thomas Pynchon* (1974 and 1990), *Beyond the Two Cultures: Essays on Science, Technology, and Literature* (edited with Judith Yaross Lee, 1990), *Pornography in America: A Reference Handbook* (2000), and *Pornography and Sexual Representation: A Reference Guide*, 3 vols. (Greenwood, 2001).

BRIAN W. BELTMAN is Adjunct Professor at the University of South Carolina, where he teaches the history of the American West. He is the author of a number of articles and book chapters on Dutch immigrant history as well as a book entitled *Dutch Farmer in the Missouri Valley: The Life and Letters of Ulbe Eringa, 1866–1950*. Dr. Beltman also works as a regulatory specialist for an electric and gas utility company in Columbia, South Carolina.

JOSEPH P. BERNT (journalism) is Professor of Journalism in the E.W. Scripps School of Journalism at Ohio University. He has contributed to *Newspaper Research Journal, Journalism and Mass Communication Quarterly, American Periodicals, Journalism History*, and a variety of multiauthor encyclopedias, guides, and directories.

The Big Chill: Investigative Reporting in the Current Media Environment, which he co-wrote and co-edited with his colleague Marilyn Greenwald, received the Sigma Delta Chi Award for Research in Journalism from the Society of Professional Journalists in 2001. He is currently working on a biography of Norman Anthony, editor of *Judge*, *Life*, and *Ballyhoo* humor magazines in the 1920s and 1930s.

SCHUYLER CONE is Assistant Professor of Human and Consumer Sciences at Ohio University.

JOSEPH CSICSILA (post–Civil War literature) is Assistant Professor of English Language and Literature at Eastern Michigan University. He is the author of *Canons by Consensus: Critical Trends and American Literary Anthologies* (2004) and essays on American literature in *American Literary Realism, 1870–1910*, *Studies in American Humor*, *The Faulkner Journal*, and *Critical Matrix*.

BEVERLY OLSON FLANIGAN is Associate Professor of Linguistics at Ohio University. Originally from Minnesota, she received an M.A. from St. Louis University in 1965 and her Ph.D. from Indiana University in 1981. She has published on second-language acquisition, linguistic stylistics, American Indian English dialects, and dialect variation in southeastern Ohio. She is a member of the Executive Council of the American Dialect Society. Current projects include developing a book on dialects in southern Ohio and computerizing the records of the Linguistic Atlas of the north-central states.

JOSEPH FREY (architecture of the historical period) was educated at the University of Illinois–Urbana, earning a B.A. in rhetoric and philosophy. He lives in Chicago, where he is a docent for the Chicago Architecture Foundation and architecture writer for *Dialogue* magazine.

GERALD R. GEMS is Professor of Health and Physical Education at North Central College in Naperville, Illinois, and current president of the North American Society for Sport History. Among his publications are *Windy City Wars: Labor, Leisure, and Sport in the Making of Chicago* (1997).

JOHN E. HANCOCK (prehistoric architecture), Professor of Architecture at the University of Cincinnati, is author of many national and international publications. He is a co-founder and project director of CERHAS (The Center for the Electronic Reconstruction of Historical and Archaeological Sites), which for the past four years has been developing *The Earth Works Project*, a multimedia, interactive-video production on the architecture of the ancient Ohio Valley. Hancock and *Earth Works* have won notable awards and contracts, including large grants from the Ohio Board of Regents, the National Endowment for the Humanities, and the National Park Service, as well as three awards at the Columbus International Film and Video Festival.

RODNEY HILL, a doctoral candidate in theater and film at the University of Kansas, is writing a dissertation on the films of Jacques Demy. He has also taught at the University of Paris XII and the University of Wisconsin–Madison. Hill is the co-author of *The Encyclopedia of Stanley Kubrick* (2002) and co-editor of *Francis Ford Coppola: Interviews*.

ARTIMUS KEIFFER is Assistant Professor of Geography at Wittenberg University in Springfield, Ohio. His primary interest is in the form, function, and social aspects of architecture as impacted by technology. He has received several awards for his environmental and ecological efforts in both Ohio and Indiana. He is the editor of *Material Culture: The Journal of the Pioneer America Society* and the chair of the Cultural Geography Specialty Group in the Association of American Geographers, and is at work on several texts, including *A Geography of the U.S. and Canada* and a revision of *The Geography of Ohio*.

LUCY M. LONG is Assistant Professor of Popular Culture at Bowling Green State University in Bowling Green, Ohio. A folklorist, enthnomusicologist, and anthropologist, Long is the editor of *Culinary Tourism* (2004).

CHRIS MAYDA is Associate Professor in the Department of Geography and Geology, Eastern Michigan University, Ypsilanti, Michigan. Her research interests include rural and agricultural geography and food systems.

RUTH OLSON is Associate Director of the Center for the Study of Upper Midwestern Cultures at the University of Wisconsin.

JENNIFER A. SCOTT is a Research Associate in the Central Region Humanities Center and a doctoral student in the School of Communication Studies at Ohio University, Athens, Ohio.

ROBERT STEARNS is Senior Program Director of Arts Midwest, a regional arts organization. He has served as director of The Kitchen, New York; The Contemporary Arts Center, Cincinnati; performing arts director, Walker Art Center, Minneapolis; and founding director of the Wexner Center for the Arts, The Ohio State University, Columbus.

PATRICK S. WASHBURN (journalism), Professor of Journalism in the E.W. Scripps School of Journalism at The Ohio University, is the author of *A Question of Sedition: The Federal Government's Investigation of the Black Press During World War II* (1986).

EDWARD S. WATTS (antebellum literature) is Professor of English at Michigan State University. His books include *An American Colony: Regionalism and the Roots of Midwestern Culture* (2002) and *Writing and Postcolonialism in the Early Republic* (1998). He co-edited *The First West: Writing from the American Frontier, 1780–1860* (2002) and *Messy Beginnings: Postcoloniality and Early American Studies* (2003).

RICHARD D. WETZEL, Professor of Music History and Literature at Ohio University, specializes in American music. His book *Frontier Musicians on the Connoquenessing, Wabash, and Ohio* is the definitive work on German American music of the eighteenth and nineteenth centuries. His essays have appeared in *American Music, Essays in American Music* (1994), *The New Grove Dictionary of American Music*, and elsewhere. He has just completed *William Cumming Peters (1805–1866)*, a monograph on the composer's life and works. Wetzel is also a composer and hymnologist, and his liturgical music is found in numerous denominational hymnals. He has received Ohio University's Outstanding University Professor Award and is currently Chair of Graduate Studies in the School of Music.

BRIAN WILSON is Professor and Chair of the Comparative Religion Department and Interim Chair of the Philosophy Department at Western Michigan University. He specializes in theory and method in the academic study of religion and American religious history, with an emphasis on religion in the Midwest. Among his recent publications are *The Pocket Idiot's Guide to Christianity* (2002) and *Religion as a Human Capacity* (2003), co-edited with Timothy Light. He is currently researching a book on Yankee religion in the Midwest and co-editing a volume on comparativism in the study of religion.

The Greenwood Encyclopedia of American Regional Cultures

The Great Plains Region, *edited by Amanda Rees*

The Mid-Atlantic Region, *edited by Robert P. Marzec*

The Midwest, *edited by Joseph W. Slade and Judith Yaross Lee*

New England, *edited by Michael Sletcher*

The Pacific Region, *edited by Jan Goggans with Aaron DiFranco*

The Rocky Mountain Region, *edited by Rick Newby*

The South, *edited by Rebecca Mark and Rob Vaughan*

The Southwest, *edited by Mark Busby*